The Prophet and the Age of the Caliphates

The Prophet and the Age of the Caliphates is an accessible history of the Near East from c.600 to 1050 AD, the period in which Islamic society was formed.

Beginning with the life of Muhammad and the birth of Islam, Hugh Kennedy goes on to explore the great Arab conquests of the seventh century and the golden age of the Umayyad and Abbasid caliphates when the world of Islam was politically and culturally far more developed than the West. The crisis of the tenth century put an end to the political unity of the Muslim world and saw the emergence of the Fatimid caliphate in Egypt and independent dynasties in the Eastern Islamic world. The book concludes with the advent of Seljuk Turkish rule in the mid-eleventh century. This new edition is fully updated to take into account recent research and there are two entirely new chapters covering the economic background during the period, and the north-east of Iran in the post-ʿAbbasid period. Based on extensive reading of the original Arabic sources, Kennedy breaks away from the Orientalist tradition of seeing early Islamic history as a series of ephemeral rulers and pointless battles by drawing attention to underlying long-term social and economic processes.

The Prophet and the Age of the Caliphates deals with issues of continuing and increasing relevance in the twenty-first century, when it is, perhaps, more important than ever to understand the early development of the Islamic world. Students and scholars of early Islamic history will find this book a clear, informative and readable introduction to the subject.

Hugh Kennedy is Professor of Arabic at SOAS, University of London. His previous publications include *The Armies of the Caliphs: Military and Society in the Early Islamic State* (2001), *The Great Arab Conquests: How the Spread of Islam Changed the World We Live In* (2007) and (as editor) *Warfare and Poetry in the Middle East* (2013).

A History of the Near East

The Prophet and the Age of the Caliphates
The Islamic Near East from the Sixth to the Eleventh Century
Hugh Kennedy

The Age of the Crusades
The Near East from the Eleventh Century to 1517
P. M. Holt

The Making of the Modern Near East 1792–1923
M. E. Yapp

The Near East since the First World War
M. E. Yapp

Medieval Persia 1040–1797
David Morgan

The Formation of Turkey
C. Cahen

The Arab Lands under Ottoman Rule, 1516–1800
J. Hathaway

https://www.routledge.com/A-History-of-the-Near-East/book-series/PEAHNE

The Prophet and the Age of the Caliphates

The Islamic Near East from the Sixth to the Eleventh Century

Fourth Edition

Hugh Kennedy

Routledge
Taylor & Francis Group
LONDON AND NEW YORK

Cover image: "A street in old Yazd, Iran." Photo: the author.

Fourth edition published 2023
by Routledge
4 Park Square, Milton Park, Abingdon, Oxon, OX14 4RN

and by Routledge
605 Third Avenue, New York, NY 10158

Routledge is an imprint of the Taylor & Francis Group, an informa business

First edition published by Pearson Education Limited 1986
Third edition published by Routledge 2016

British Library Cataloguing-in-Publication Data
A catalogue record for this book is available from the British Library

Library of Congress Cataloging-in-Publication Data
Names: Kennedy, Hugh (Hugh N.), author.
Title: The prophet and the age of the Caliphates: the Islamic Near East from the sixth to the eleventh century / Hugh Kennedy.
Other titles: Islamic Near East from the sixth to the eleventh century | History of the Near East.
Description: Fourth edition. | Abingdon, Oxon; New York, NY: Routledge, 2022. |
Series: A history of the Near East | Includes bibliographical references and index.
Identifiers: LCCN 2021057075 (print) | LCCN 2021057076 (ebook)
Subjects: LCSH: Islamic Empire—History—622–661. | Islamic Empire—History—661–750. | Islamic Empire—History—750–1258.
Classification: LCC DS38.5.K38 2022 (print) | LCC DS38.5 (ebook) | DDC 956/.013—dc23/eng/20211214
LC record available at https://lccn.loc.gov/2021057075
LC ebook record available at https://lccn.loc.gov/2021057076

ISBN: 978-0-367-36690-2 (hbk)
ISBN: 978-0-367-36689-6 (pbk)
ISBN: 978-0-429-34812-9 (ebk)

DOI: 10.4324/9780429348129

Typeset in Times New Roman
by codeMantra

In memory of my daughter, Susannah Louise,
who died far too young.
Loved and remembered every day, bright star.

Contents

Maps

Genealogical tables

Preface to the first edition

This work is intended as an introduction to the history of the Near East in the early Islamic period, from the time of the Prophet to the vast upheaval caused by the arrival of the Seljuk Turks in the mid-fifth to eleventh centuries. In it, I have attempted to strike a balance between a presentation of factual material, which may seem too dry, and speculative interpretation. Some will no doubt find this approach traditional and unadventurous, but I have tried to bear in mind the needs of the reader who is approaching the history of the Near East for the first time and requires a basic framework of chronological narrative. At the same time, I have tried to avoid the impression that Islamic history is full of ephemeral rulers and pointless battles and to devote space to long-term social and economic changes and to the positive aspects of Muslim government and the immense achievements of the period, which are too often neglected in Western writing. Whether I have reached the right balance is for the reader to judge. In writing this book, I am deeply conscious of the debt I owe to many scholars who have worked on the period. I have been especially helped by the works of W.M. Watt on Muhammad and F.M. Donner and M. Morony on the Islamic conquests. The articles of G.M. Hinds on the reign of ‘Uthma-n and the battle of S·iff ı ¯n are of fundamental importance. For later periods, I have been greatly helped by the work of J. Lassner and F. Omar on the ‘Abbasid caliphate, R.M. Adams on the economic and archaeological background to the breakup of the caliphate and the works of R. Bulliet and R. Mottahedeh. Although we may disagree on some interpretations, I owe much to the teaching of M.A. Shaban. I should also draw attention to the excellent and wide-ranging studies of W. Madelung and C.E. Bosworth, both of whom have contributed greatly to our understanding of the period. It is inevitably invidious to single out individual authors, and there are many others to whom I owe much. The list of secondary sources at the end of this volume gives details of works I have found useful. I must emphasize that all the errors in this work are my own. I owe particular debts of gratitude to Professor P.M. Holt, who has edited this volume with the greatest care and saved me from numerous mistakes. I would also like to thank friends and colleagues who have encouraged me, and especially Helen and Robert Irwin for friendship and hospitality in London.

H. Kennedy, St Andrews, February 1985

Preface and acknowledgements

This is the fourth edition of a book originally published more than 35 years ago. In this time, it has evolved in many ways and this new edition has further extended its scope. In the first place, the bibliography and discussion of the sources have been updated. It seems to me that we are now in a golden age of scholarship on the pre-modern history of the Muslim world and every month seem to see new innovative and original publications. It is both a labour and a delight to keep up with these. Of course, nobody believes that they live in a golden age until it passes and they look back with regret: let us hope the gold continues to shine and universities, scholars and students continue to recognise the fundamental importance of understanding the pre-modern history of the Muslim world.

It is almost 60 years since I first became interested in the history of what we might call, with some hesitation, the history of the medieval Middle East but I firmly believe that both the standards of scholarship and the breadth of imagination have revealed so many ways of explanation and analysis which were hardly dreamt of back in the 1960s. I was Arthur Arberry's last pupil. He and I would sit on opposite side of the hissing gas fire in his rooms in Pembroke College Cambridge while he explained to me, exactly as he had to generations of students before, the *ʿUyūn al-Akhbār* of Ibn Qutayba. He was not, it must be said, the most inspirational of teachers, indeed the other members of the small class had largely stopped coming. But I persisted, at least in part for fear of hurting the old man's feelings, and absorbed something of his lasting devotion to the close reading of classical Arabic sources. But it was a limited, philological, vision, even if cogent on its own terms. There was no discussion of the wider historical context certainly nothing about the evidence from archaeology and material culture. So many scholars have now been investigating the ideas and questions which were swimming around my 18-year-old head and revealing a richness and complexity to the history of this period which is both inspirational and exciting. The best, of course, is yet to come. I hope my discussion of the current scholarship and its potential will be timely and useful.

The scope of the book has been expanded in line with the recommendation of the anonymous reviewers approached by the publishers. This involves new chapters on the economic history and on the Islamic east. The Samanids and Ghaznevids now appear for the first time.

I thank my publishers, Routledge, and especially my editor Laura Pilsworth, for support and help.

I thank colleagues at the Invisible East project based in Oxford who have made helpful suggestions. I also thank Mike Athanson for preparing new maps which are a huge improvement on those in previous editions.

The field constantly evolves and I am already collecting ideas and material for the fifth edition. But for now, this is my updated account and I hope it will continue to be of use to students and researchers alike.

Hugh Kennedy, London, 16 March 2022

Notes on names, titles and dates

Names and titles

There was an elaborate system of nomenclature among the Arabic-speaking peoples in the early Islamic period. In full, each individual's name could consist of four elements:

1 The personal name (Arabic, *ism*). This was most commonly Arabic (e.g. Aḥmad Fāṭima) or Qur'ānic (e.g. Ibrāhīm, Mūsā). With the arrival of Turks in the service of the caliphate, Turkish names became common among the military (e.g. Utāmish, Alptakīn); the correct form of these names is often difficult to determine, and variant spellings may be encountered. The Buyid family often used Persian names, e.g. Bakhtiyār, and a particular problem attaches to the transliteration of Persian names ending in *ūya*; this can also be transliterated as -*wayh*, so Būya becomes Buwayh, Ḥasanūya becomes Ḥasanwayh, etc. In general, the -*ūya* usage is becoming more common, but readers should be aware of both forms.

2 The *kunya*, sometimes inaccurately called the patronymic, which takes the form Abū —— and Umm —— i.e. "Father of ——", "Mother of ——". In early Islamic times, this usually denoted actual parentage, e.g. the Prophet's *kunya* was Abū'l-Qāsim, from the name of his son al-Qāsim, who died in infancy. This was a more intimate way of addressing a ruler than a formal title, and some 'Abbasid caliphs with very common *isms* were generally known by their *kunyas*, e.g. al-Manṣūr, whose *ism* was 'Abd Allāh, was generally known as Abū Ja'far after his eldest son. Likewise, al-Mu'taṣim, whose *ism* was Muḥammad, was known as Abū Isḥeq.

3 The patronymic (*nasab*) indicating the individual's father or extended pedigree. This takes the form *ibn* —— or *bint* ——, i.e. "son of ——", "daughter of ——", abbreviated to *b.* The plural form *banū*, literally "sons of", indicates a tribe or clan.

4 The generic epithet (*nisba*) indicating a tribe or area to which an individual belonged, e.g. al-Sulamī meaning "from the tribe of Sulaym",

al-Khurāsānī meaning "from the province of Khurāsān". The *nisba* was an adjective ending in ī (masc.) or *iyya* (fem.) and several might be appended to a name.

A ruler, a member of a ruling group or a dignitary might have a title or honorific (*laqab*) prefixed to his name. The Rāshidūn and Umayyad caliphs were simply known by their *isms*, but both 'Abbasids and Fatimids adopted regnal titles indicating the fact that they were supported by Allah or that they were upholders of the Faith (*dīn*) and it is by these titles, or shortened versions of them, that caliphs are generally known, e.g. al-Manṣūr, al-Mu'izz. From the fourth/tenth centuries onwards, members of successor dynasties used titles of the form 'Imād *al-Dawla*, Rukn *al-Dawla* meaning "Support or Pillar of the ('Abbasid or Fatimid) State", and this nomenclature became widespread. For a full discussion of titles and their development, see the article *Laḳab* by C. E. Bosworth in the *Encyclopaedia of Islam* (Second edition).

The part of the name which is conventionally used by modern writers, including this one, is quite arbitrary and is more dependent on convention than logic.

Dates

The Muslim era opens with the *Hijra* (often spelt *Hegira*), i.e. the emigration of Muḥammad from Mecca to Medina in AD 622. Muslim years are therefore indicated by the abbreviation AH (*Anno Hegirae*). The Muslim year consists of twelve lunar months and is therefore approximately eleven days shorter than the solar year of the Western calendar. This also means that the months do not always occur in the same seasons of the year. There is no Muslim equivalent of BC dating. To find the AD equivalent to Muslim AH dates and vice versa, conversion tables are necessary. There are a number of easily accessible web-sites which will now do the conversion easily and accurately.

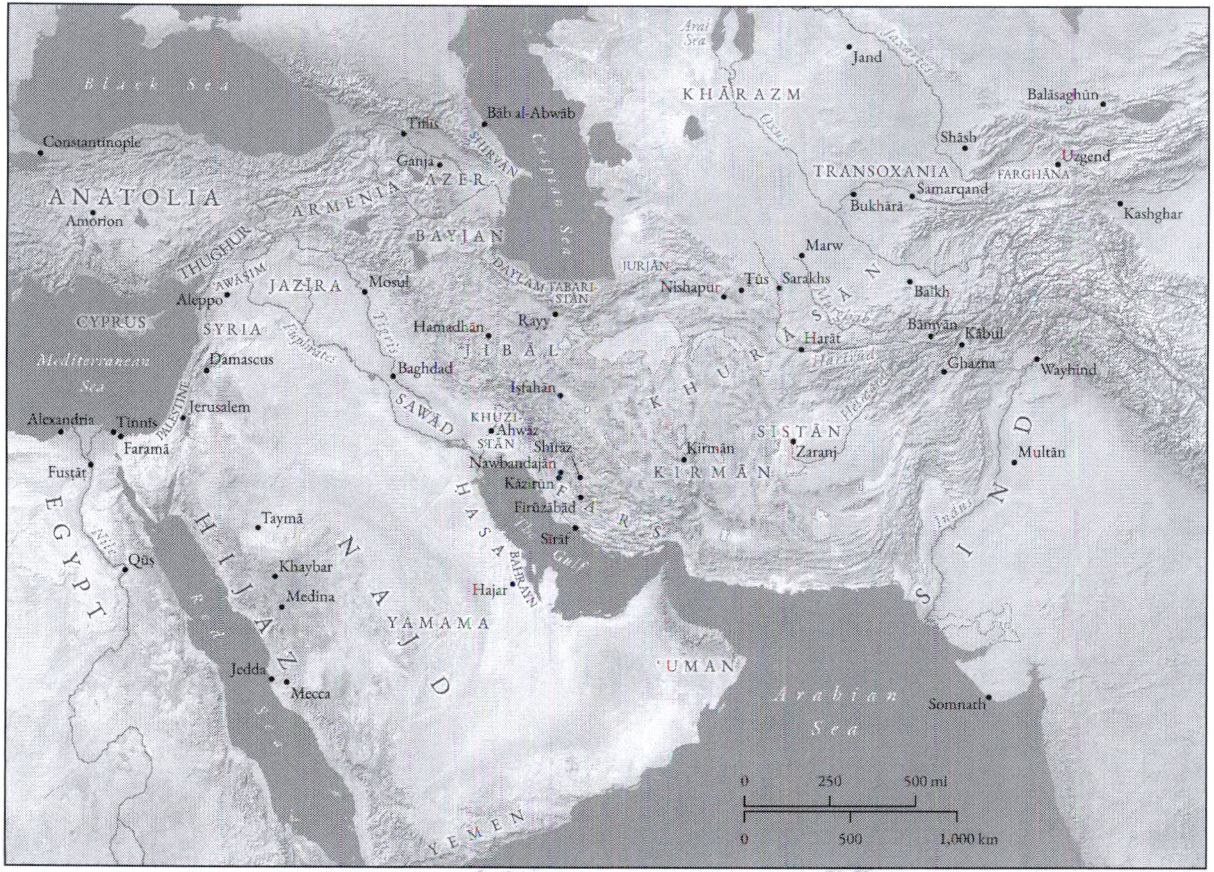

MAP 1 The Central Islamic Lands.

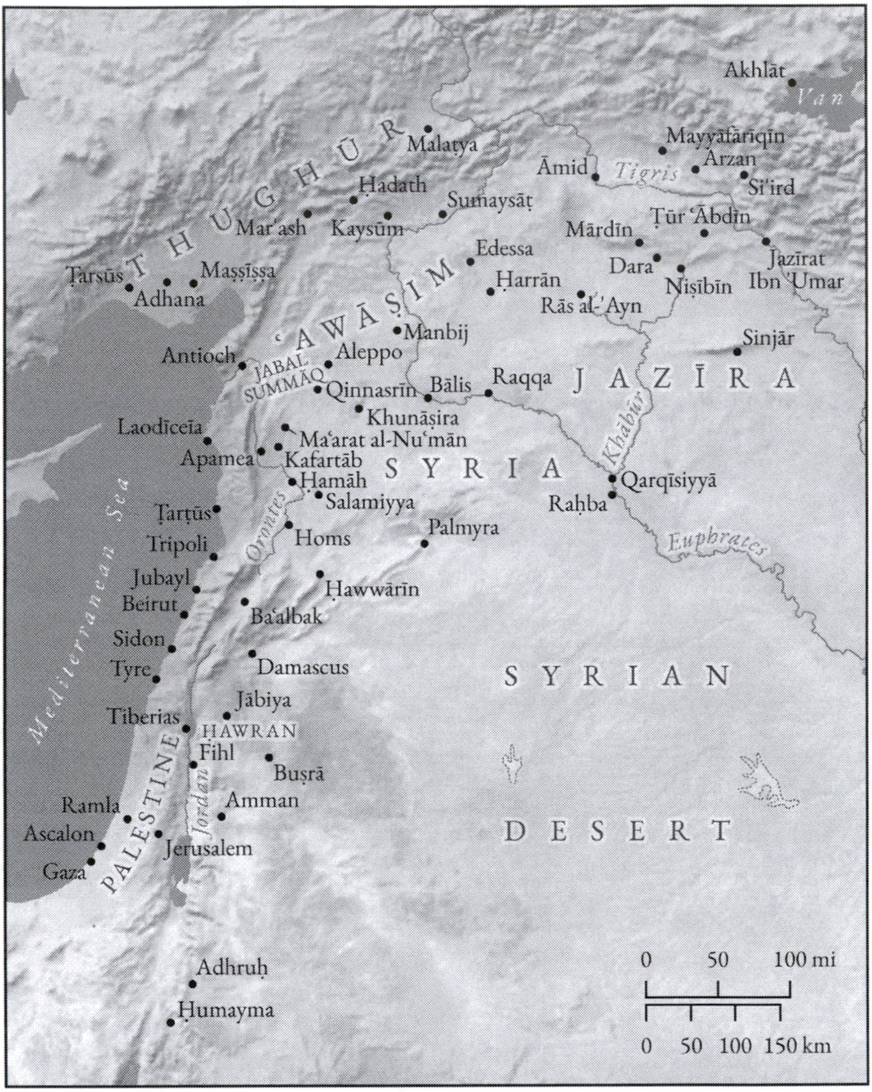

MAP 2 Syria and the Byzantine Frontier.

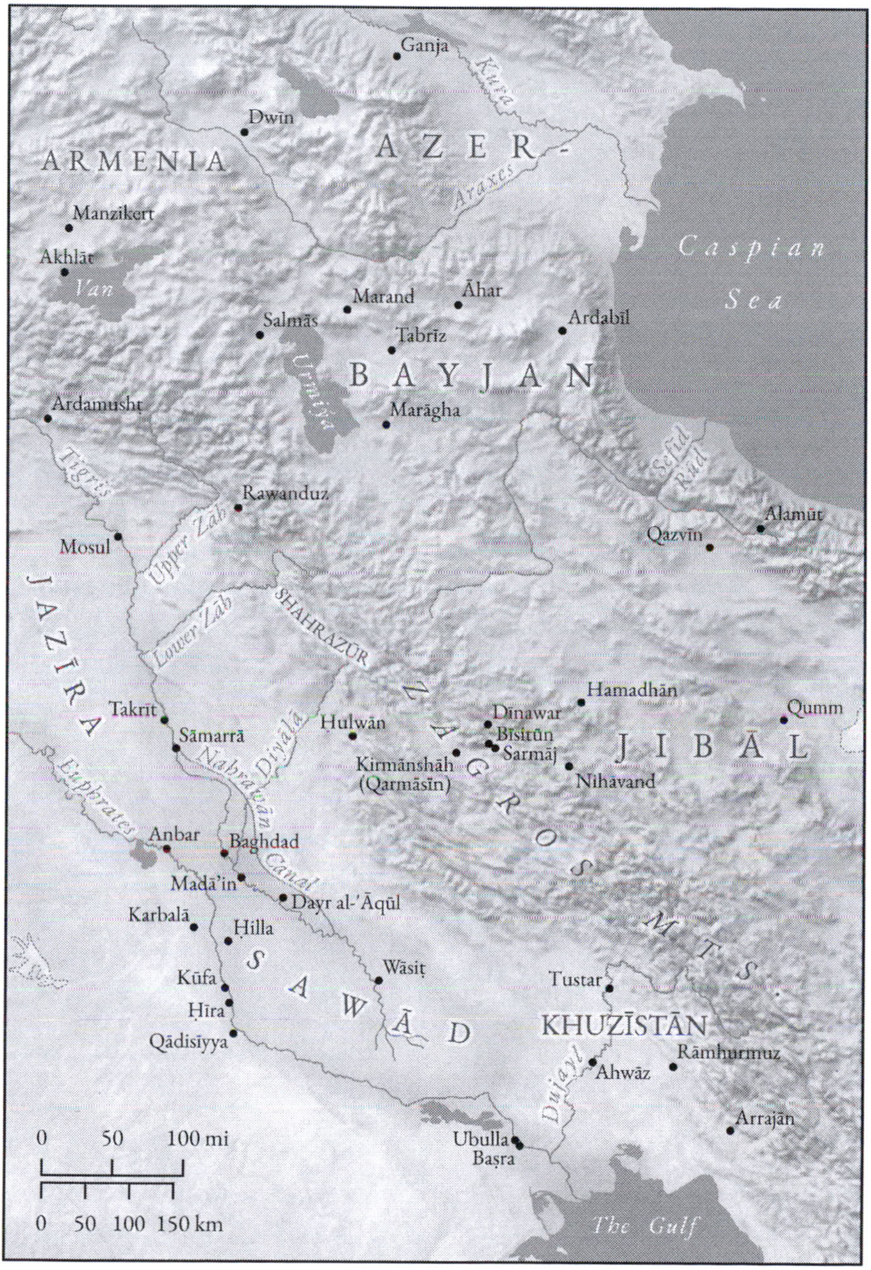

MAP 3 Iran and the Caucasus.

Table 1 Muḥammad and the Descent of the Caliphs

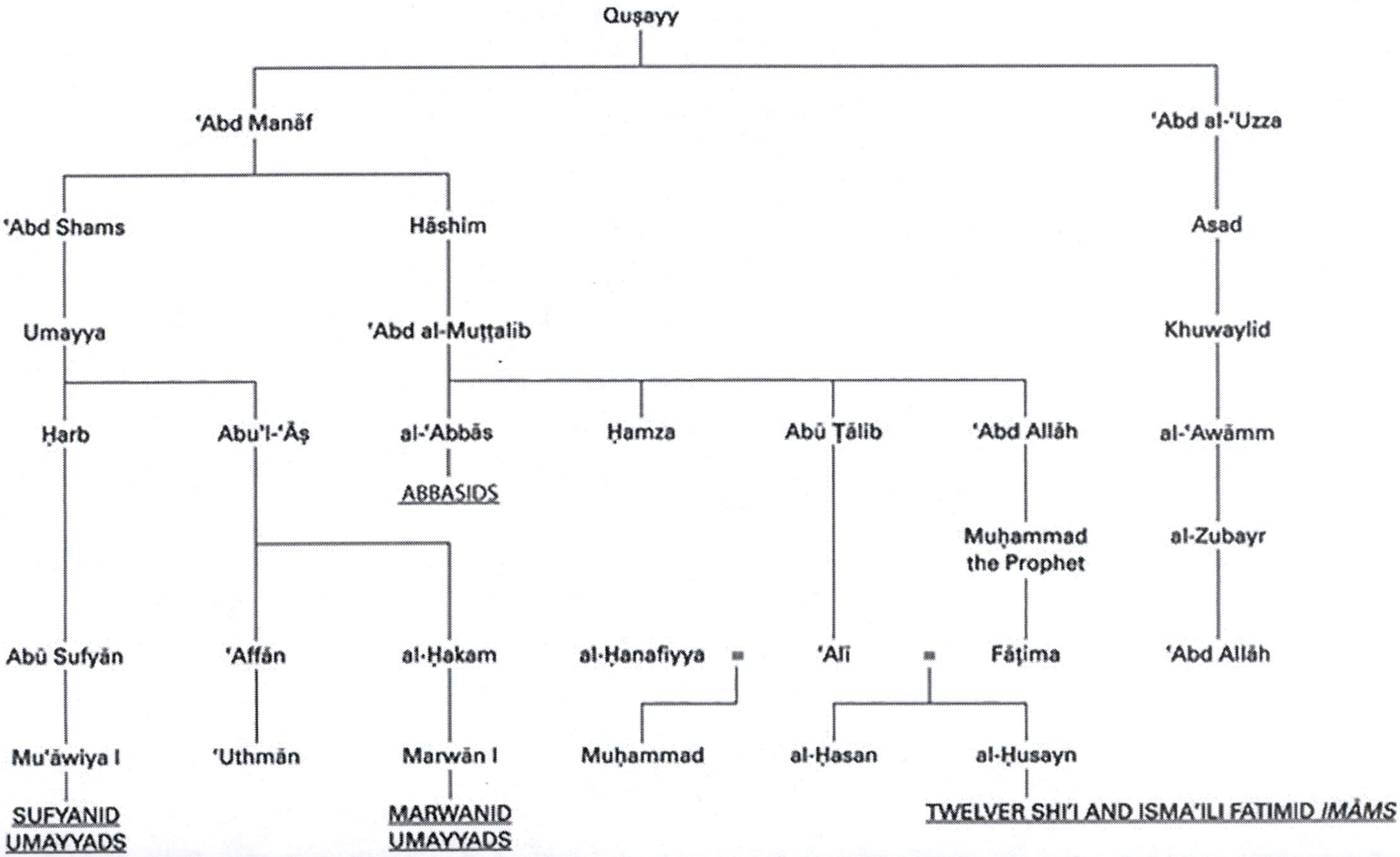

Table 2 The Umayyad Caliphs

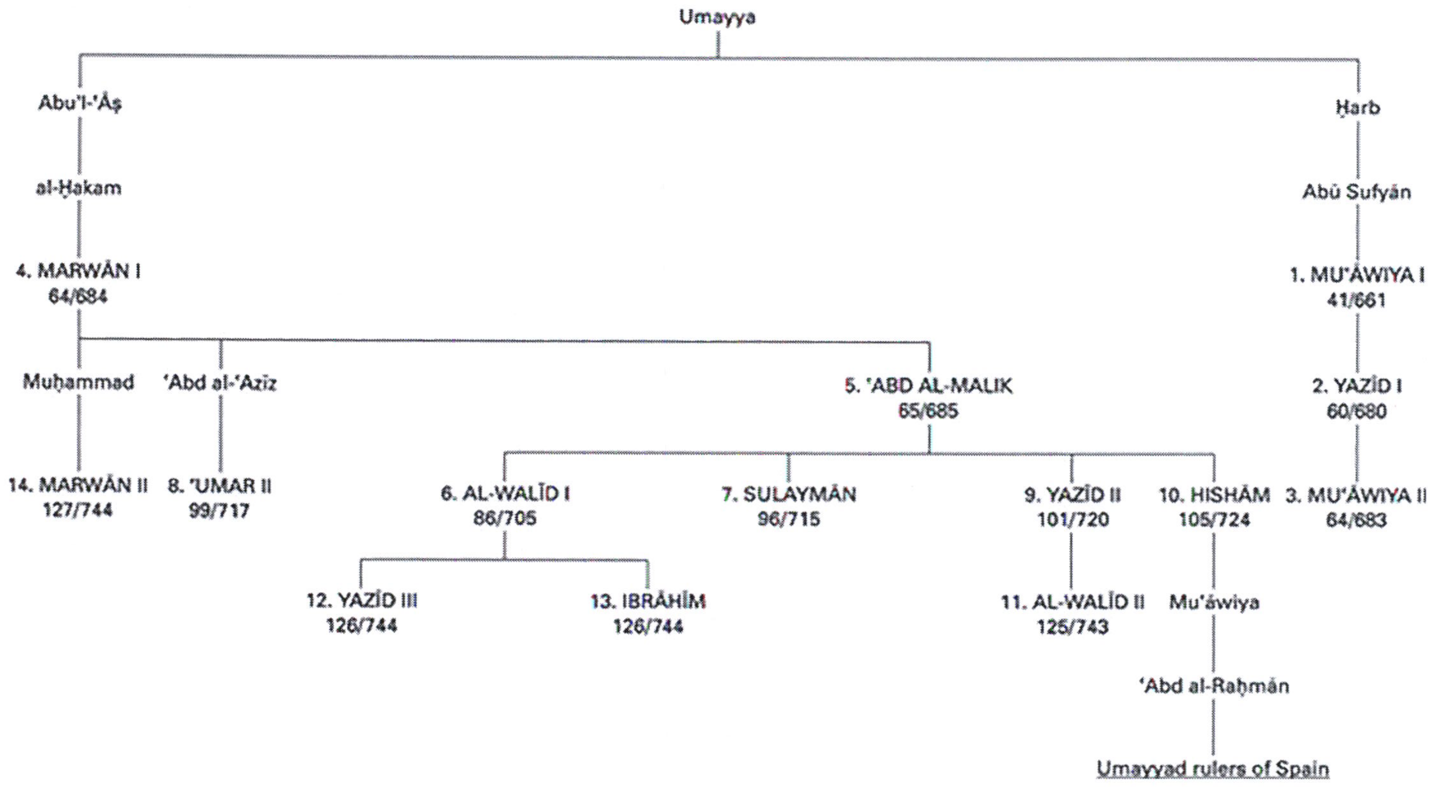

Table 3 The ʿAbbasid Caliphs

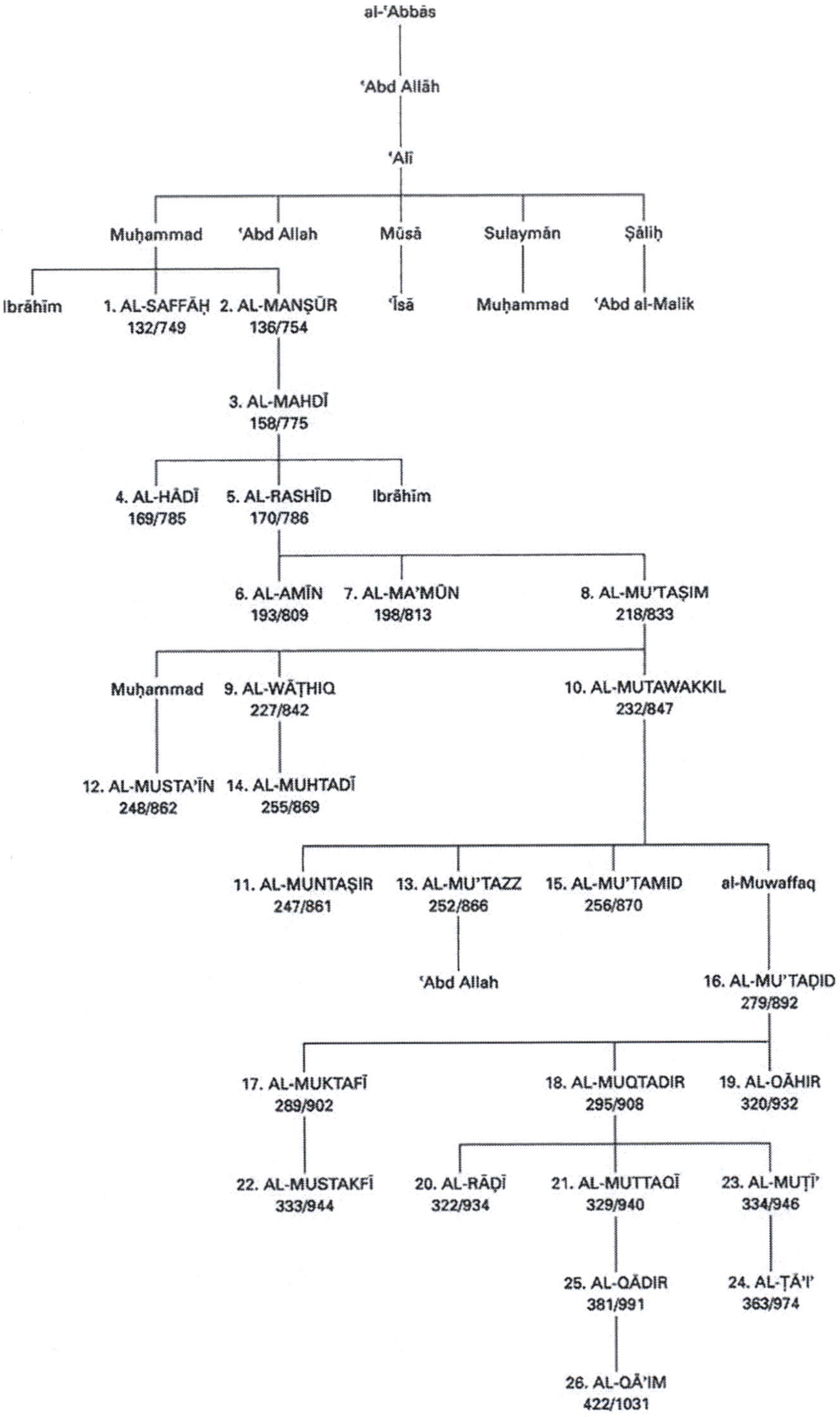

Table 4 The Principal Buyid Rulers

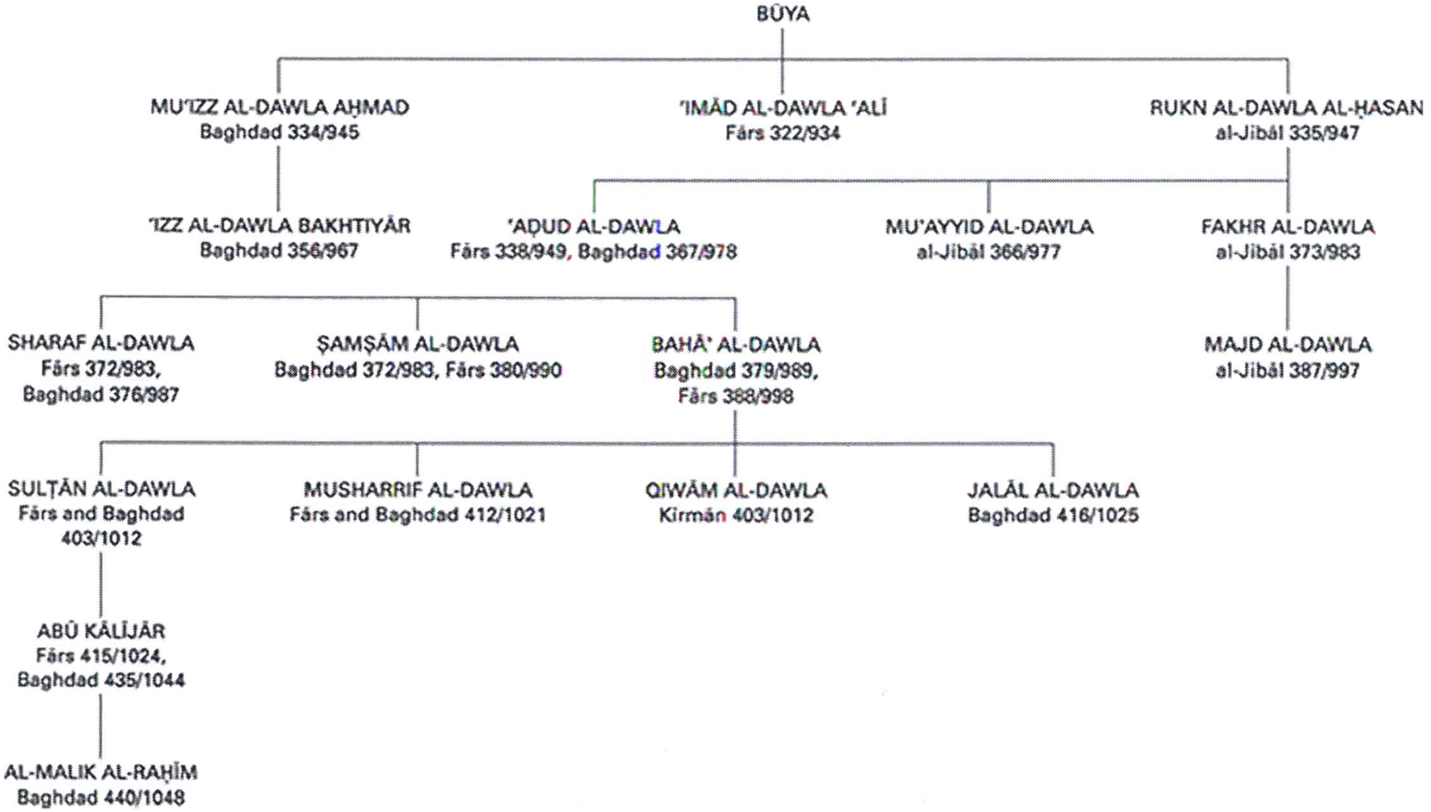

Table 5 The ‘Uqaylids of Mosul

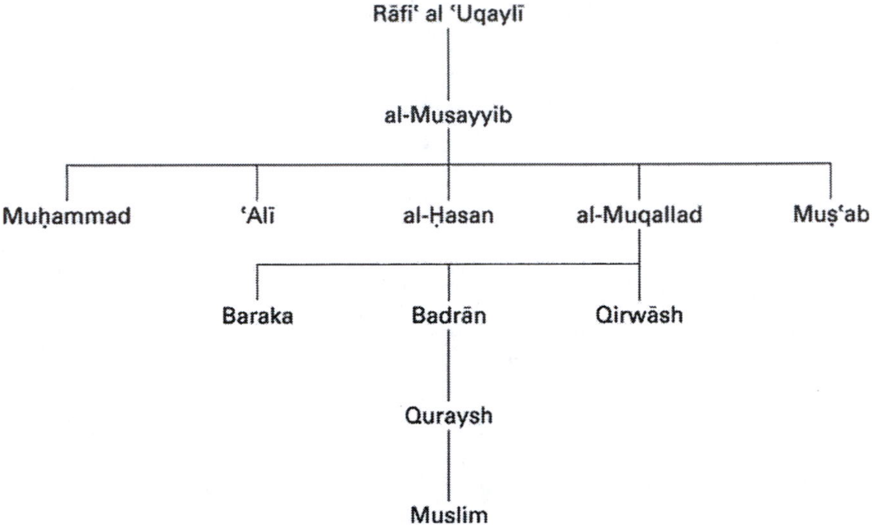

Table 6 The Hamdanids of Aleppo and Mosul

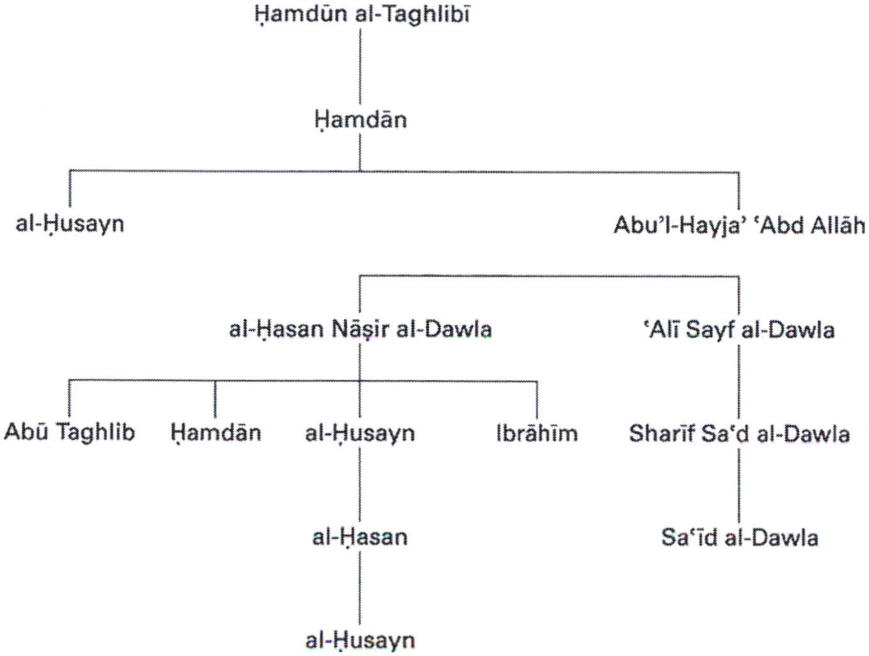

1 The matrix of the Muslim world

The Near East in the early seventh century

The Near East before the coming of Islam was dominated, as it had been for the previous half-millennium, by two great empires, the Roman–Byzantine to the west and the Persian to the east. The frontier between these two empires had fluctuated considerably during this time. In the late sixth century, the last period of stability before the upheavals of the seventh century, the frontier had run roughly from north to south, through the wild uplands of eastern Anatolia and bisecting the fertile and well-populated plains of the land between the middle Tigris and Euphrates rivers, the prairie and steppe country which the Byzantines called Mesopotamia and the Arabs were to know as al-Jazīra, "the Island" between the two great rivers. On the Byzantine side of the frontier lay the massively fortified towns of Amida (now Diyarbakır) and Dara, while the Persians held the ancient cultural centre of Nisibis (Niṣībīn). On the Euphrates, the frontier zone was marked by the sixth-century Byzantine fortress of Zenobia. It was in this zone of the frontier that campaigns between the armies of the two empires took place; the heavy, slow-moving forces could not hope to cross the waterless stretches of the Syrian Desert to the south.

South of the Euphrates, there was no firm frontier. During the second half of the sixth century, both Byzantines and Sasanians had reached arrangements with leading clans among the Arab bedouin tribes, the Ghassanids and the Lakhmids, respectively, who provided an element of administration in the frontier areas as well as defence against their opposite numbers on the other side of the desert. This reliance on pastoral peoples for the defence of the empires testifies to their growing importance along the desert margins and the inability of the settled people to provide their own defence.

In the year 600, the Byzantine Empire presented a superficial picture of ageless continuity. The emperor of the day, Maurice, bore the title of Augustus and claimed to be the successor of that first Augustus who had established his personal power in Rome over 600 years before. It is true that the capital had since moved to Constantinople and that Christianity had become the official religion of the empire, but the emperor still ruled with the assistance of the senate, consuls were still appointed, the laws of the empire were based on Justinian's great codification of classical practice and Latin

DOI: 10.4324/9780429348129-1

was still used as an official language, although it was increasingly being replaced by Greek for administrative purposes.

This impression of continuity, however, masked a large number of changes, and the Roman Empire was continually evolving in response to fluid circumstances. Many of the features which had seemed central to the classical empire were no longer in evidence. Until the fourth and fifth centuries, the eastern half of the empire had at least in theory boasted a large number of self-governing towns which managed their own affairs under their own councils and collected taxes from the surrounding countryside. This urban government had brought great prosperity to some cities and resulted in a burst of civic architectural activity which can have had few parallels and which created the great monumental baths, theatres and colonnaded streets whose ruins remain so impressive today. By the sixth century, this picture had substantially changed; the cities had lost their political and financial autonomy; their councils had been superseded by governors appointed by the imperial authorities and their civic revenues had been confiscated for the benefit of the imperial treasury. While churches and monastic buildings continued to be constructed, large-scale civic building effectively came to a halt.

The sixth century saw further blows to the urban culture of late antiquity. In 541, bubonic plague struck the eastern empire for the first but by no means the last time; it was to recur with a horrifying frequency throughout the sixth and early seventh centuries. Mortality is impossible to gauge with any accuracy, but using contemporary accounts and comparing them with the much better documented Black Death of 1348 onwards, it seems probable that at least a third of the population was lost. Furthermore, it is likely that the highest mortality was in densely populated urban areas, while the nomad populations were comparatively unaffected. There certainly seems no evidence that the plague spread into the Arabian Peninsula. This massive loss of population was compounded by a further series of disasters, both natural and man-made. The mid-sixth century saw a number of devastating earthquakes which effectively destroyed Beirut, until then a flourishing intellectual and legal centre, and other cities on the Lebanese coast. At the same time, the Persians launched a series of very destructive invasions of the Syrian provinces, including the sack of the great city of Antioch in 540 and of Apamea in 573. In 582, the major provincial capital of Bostra (now Buṣrā) in the Ḥawrān was sacked by the followers of the Ghassanids, protesting the arrest of their chief by the Byzantine authorities. These incursions were paralleled elsewhere; in Italy, most of the lands which Justinian had painstakingly retaken from the Visigoths were lost to the empire when the Lombards invaded from the north in the second half of the sixth century. Nearer the capital, the Balkan provinces were devastated by the attacks and settlements of Avars and Slavs.

These catastrophes had a fundamental effect on the Byzantine Empire. Most obviously, it was weakened militarily – the loss of population and the constant wars reduced the army greatly; the system of *limitanei*, frontier guards who performed military service in exchange for land, was largely abandoned, and it seems that by the early seventh century, imperial armies were increasingly composed of people from the fringes of the empire, Armenians and Arabs, rather than the settled inhabitants of the central areas. In addition, the empire was becoming a rural and agrarian society, not just in Italy and the Balkans, but also in the Near East, where urban life was slightly more resilient. There was still Mediterranean trade until the end of the sixth century, notably in grain from Egypt and in pottery, but the cities of the Syrian and Palestinian coasts seem to have lost much of their commercial vitality. In so far as trade was carried on, it was likely to be centred on fairs attached to pilgrimage centres rather than on large urban markets, and it is possible that monasteries and churches had replaced urban notables as the most important landowners. Nor were there any traces left of local self-government. For both administration and defence, the people of the Byzantine Near East were dependent on imperial armies and officials. By the end of the sixth century, the Byzantine Near East had effectively lost its classical aspect and was going through a series of profound economic and social changes not dissimilar to those which occurred in western Europe at the same time. It is against this background that the achievements of the Islamic conquest and Muslim state-building must be measured.

In addition to these general changes, Syria and Egypt had a number of problems which made them rather different from the rest of the empire. The first was one of language and ethnic identities. Both countries were essentially lands of two cultures, the one urban, Greek-speaking and influenced by classical cultural norms and lifestyles. This culture was at its strongest in the great urban centres like Antioch and Alexandria, but also thrived in many lesser coastal and inland towns. The other culture was vernacular, Coptic in Egypt, Aramaic or, increasingly, Arabic-speaking in Syria. This was the culture of the villages and the pastoral peoples, who had no access to the traditions of the classical world and little taste for the amenities of urban life. For almost a millennium, since the conquests of Alexander the Great, these two lifestyles had coexisted in mutual incomprehension. Now, with the relative decline of urban populations and prosperity, the vernacular world was in the ascendant.

These cultural differences were reflected in religious ones. During the sixth century, the bulk of the rural populations of Egypt and Syria (but not, it would seem, of Palestine) became attached to the Monophysite, also known as Miaphysite, faith, in distinction to the official, imperial, Diophysite view. The differences between these two views concerned the nature of Christ. The Diophysites maintained that He had two complete natures, one human, like our humanity, and one divine, miraculously fused in one person. The Monophysites refused to accept this, holding that Christ had one, divine, nature, that His humanity was not as ours, to them a blasphemous idea, but only an aspect of His divine nature. Superficially, the differences may seem to be trivial, but in fact they show a fundamentally different way of looking at the Incarnation, and they stem from different religious traditions: the Diophysite looks back to the Hellenistic tradition of humanizing the divine, whereas the Monophysite looks to aspects of the Jewish tradition with its deep distrust of any representations of divinity.

The differences of theological opinion would probably have remained talking points among theologians if they had not reflected the broader cultural distinctions. The Monophysite church used vernacular languages for liturgy, theological debate and general literature – Syriac (a literary form of the Aramaic dialect of Edessa) in Syria and Coptic in Egypt; both of these languages, incidentally, remain in use as liturgical languages to the present day. The Monophysite church, too, was essentially rural, at least in Syria, where its leaders, although they took the ancient title of patriarch of Antioch, always lived in monasteries far from the city itself. The differences were greatly exacerbated by the fact that the Byzantine authorities, in a struggle to enforce ideological uniformity, began the systematic and often brutal persecution of the Monophysite church, especially in Syria. The Monophysite church had, however, powerful lay supporters in Syria, notably the Ghassanids who controlled the desert frontier and provided both money and refuge for persecuted members of the sect when they were forced to flee from the centres of population. The significance of this for the longer-term history of the Near East was that it meant that a significant proportion of the population was alienated from the ruling class both culturally and because the church they were devoted to was regarded as heretical and subject to dire official sanctions. It is important, at the same time, not to overestimate the significance of this: there is no evidence that either the Copts or the Monophysites of Syria actually cooperated with the Islamic conquests. What can be said is that they felt little enthusiasm for the Byzantine cause. In some parts of Syria, the conquerors were actually welcomed; in no part was there significant and prolonged resistance from the local population, as there was, for example, in the Anatolian highlands, Armenia or the province of Fārs in southern Iran.

The long-term weaknesses of the Byzantine Empire in the Near East were revealed in the series of catastrophes which followed the death of the Emperor Maurice in 602. Maurice, a capable and energetic soldier, if a slightly ham-fisted politician, had devoted his reign to the maintenance of the frontiers of the empire. In doing so, he had been greatly aided by a long-term alliance with the Persian King Khusrau II Parvēz, whom he had previously helped to the throne. This breathing space in the east had allowed Maurice to devote his attentions to securing the frontiers of the state in the Balkans. In 602, he was murdered, along with all his family, by a brutal and incompetent usurper called Phocas. Not only did Phocas prove totally unable to continue his predecessor's work in the Balkans, but his action gave Khusrau II the pretext to launch a major invasion of the Byzantine Empire to avenge his dead benefactor. The effect was catastrophic: the

Persians penetrated much farther than ever before; not only were Antioch (613) and Jerusalem (614) taken, and with them all the provinces of Syria and Palestine, but so was Egypt, and much of the Anatolian uplands were devastated by raids; recently discovered archaeological evidence testifies to the extent of destruction of Anatolian cities at this time. Meanwhile, in 610, Phocas was himself deposed, by a soldier from the Byzantine territories in north Africa, Heraclius. Heraclius was altogether more effective than his predecessor. In 622, the same year that Muḥammad made his *Hijra* from Mecca to Medina, he set off from the beleaguered capital at Constantinople and led an expedition through the Black Sea to take the Persians from the rear. In a series of brilliant campaigns, he destroyed the Persian army and marched into the heartlands of the Sasanian Empire in Iraq. Khusrau was deposed, and in 628 (the year Muḥammad reached agreement with the people of Mecca), Heraclius entered the Sasanian capital at Ctesiphon. The Persian conquests in Syria and Egypt were restored to Byzantine control and the relic of the True Cross, taken by Khusrau, was restored to Jerusalem.

The appearance of a return to normality was deceptive. The long years of warfare had accelerated and confirmed the tendencies of the previous century towards demographic and urban decline. Many previously settled areas on the fringes of the Syrian Desert were now deserted, their inhabitants being dead, in exile or converted to pastoral lifestyles more easy to sustain in the chaotic conditions. Furthermore, a whole generation had grown up which had no memory or experience of Byzantine rule: those who were adults at the time of Heraclius' triumphs had been children when the wars began, and they can have had little residual loyalty to the Byzantine state. Heraclius was faced with a multitude of problems, none of which he had time to solve. The military and administrative organization of the recovered provinces had been hardly developed and, apart from Arab tribesmen, taken on as allies, there was no chance to develop the sort of local defence unit, the *theme*, which was to prove so effective in Anatolia. City walls and fortifications were probably in drastic need of repair. The emperor also failed to resolve the religious issue. In Syria, he attempted to reach a compromise between Diophysite and Monophysite views, putting forward a formula known as Monotheletism. This was to form the intellectual basis of Maronite Christianity, and as such still survives to this day, but at the time it served to please no one, least of all the wild and truculent monks who led the Monophysite party. In Egypt, he was unwise enough to appoint, as both patriarch and governor of Alexandria, a militant Diophysite, Cyrus, bishop of Phasis, in the Caucasus (hence his Arabic name, al-Muqawqis). Cyrus proved to be both incompetent and intolerant, and the restoration of Byzantine rule in Egypt was marked not by the restoration of Christian unity but by the systematic alienation of the majority of the population from the government. If Heraclius and his successors had been able to enjoy the fruits of their triumph for a few decades, it is possible that a new structure would have emerged in the Byzantine Near East. But this was not to be; the Islamic armies arrived when Byzantine rule was recent, shaky and widely resented. The Islamic conquest of Syria and Egypt was as much a product of the decline of Byzantine civilization in the area as the blow which destroyed it.

The Sasanian Empire of Persia of the late sixth century was, like the Roman–Byzantine Empire, heir to an ancient imperial tradition. The great Achaemenid Empire of Cyrus, Darius and Xerxes had flourished when Rome was a village, and the Sasanian family were well aware of the fact that the Persian Empire had existed since remotest antiquity. The ruling family had come to power over 300 years before; the first member of the dynasty, Ardashīr Pāpagān, was the sub-king of Fārs, the area of southern Iran which had been the cradle and centre of the Achaemenid dynasty. Even though Achaemenid power had vanished 600 years previously when Alexander the Great took and burned Persepolis, Ardashīr chose to have his achievements commemorated among the great monuments of that vanished supremacy.

Unlike the Byzantine Empire, power in the Sasanian Empire was essentially dynastic. In Byzantium, it was possible for a family, like that of Constantine in the fourth century, to establish control of the empire for several generations, but a dynastic ideology never developed. In Iran, however, by the sixth century, the Sasanian house was held to have a divinely given right to the throne, and when, from the late sixth century, generals of non-dynastic origins challenged and usurped this right, they could not command the necessary prestige to hold the empire together. In Byzantium, a successful usurper like Heraclius could be, and was, accepted as legitimate sovereign. In the Sasanian Empire, rebels like Bahrām Chōbīn (590–591) and Shahrbarāz in 628, although both were of aristocratic descent and proven military ability, failed to win general acceptance because they were not of the ruling dynasty. In the crisis conditions which prevailed in the empire after the deposition and death of Khusrau II Parvēz in 628, this weakness made it difficult for an effective sovereign to emerge; in the years 628–632, there were at least ten different kings or would-be kings, and by the time that Yazdgard III, a scion of the Sasanian house who had been discovered hiding in the ancient capital of Iṣṭakhr in Fārs, had been established on the throne, the Muslim armies were already attacking the empire.

There were other ways in which the Sasanian imperial style differed from the Byzantine. Both claimed to rule by divine pleasure, and the Sasanian sovereigns claimed the support of Ahurā Mazdā, the Good God. But they also claimed divinity for themselves, and the ancient Near Eastern idea of the God-King remained very much part of the imperial ideology. With it went a vastly elaborate court ceremonial, a hierarchy of offices at least as formal as anything devised in Constantinople and a concern to distance the sovereign from even the greatest of his subjects. There was also a different imperial iconography: the Byzantine emperor, like Justinian in the Ravenna mosaics, tends to appear as a formal, distant, immobile figure, almost always in civilian dress. Khusrau II Parvēz, in the rock reliefs he caused to be carved at Ṭāq-i Bustān, had himself portrayed as a mighty hunter, on horseback in pursuit of game; it was an imperial image which dated back to the Assyrian monarchy of the first half of the first millennium BC. In a real sense, the Sasanian was the last of the great monarchies of the ancient Near East.

At the end of the sixth century, the Persian Empire controlled virtually the whole of the Iranian plateau and all of modern Iraq. On the west, its frontiers coincided with the edge of the settled lands, and the Sasanian clients and allies, the Banū Lakhm of Ḥīra, extended this influence over a confederation of bedouin tribes. To the north, the Persians held Nisibis (Niṣībīn) and their influence was preponderant in Armenia. Under Khusrau I Anūshirvān (531–579), the northern frontier had been established in the Araxes valley, at Tblisi in Georgia and at Darband, the great fortress on the Caspian coast which controlled the eastern flanks of the Caucasus; in this area, the Muslims inherited Sasanian political geography, manning the same frontier fortresses and settling in the same cities as their Persian predecessors. The northeastern frontier was always disturbed and far from the heartlands of Iranian power. The lands of the Oxus valley and beyond had been invaded from the fourth century by Hunnic people known as the Hepthalites. In around 560, Khusrau I, in alliance with the Turkish nomads who also inhabited the region, defeated the Hepthalites and their kingdom was broken up. From this time, the Sasanian frontier was established at Marv, where a frontier official called the *marzbān* was established. Recent archaeological research has revealed remains of the great Gurgan Wall, a well-planned military installation with regular forts along it, which demonstrates the power and efficiency of the Sasanian military machine and rivals any of the systems of fortifications constructed by the Romans. Beyond that, various independent principalities were ruled by Hepthalites or Soghdians, largely settled people of Iranian origin. The steppe lands and deserts of this area were the province of the Turks, pagan, horse-based nomads whose domain stretched as far as the borders of China and who were destined to play an immensely important part in Islamic history. In the southeastern direction, the frontiers of the empire seem to have coincided roughly with those of the eastern frontiers of modern Iran, including Sīstān, where there was a *marzbān* at the capital Zaranj when the Arabs arrived, and Kirmān.

In the sixth century, Sasanian influence was not confined to Iran and Iraq. Some areas of the Arabian Peninsula, notably Baḥrayn and al-Yamāma and from 572 Yemen in the southwest, were also controlled by the Sasanians or their allies and they encouraged a trade in the Gulf which was to continue after the Muslim conquest.

Despite the impression of great antiquity and the appeals to a great imperial past, the Sasanian Empire, like the Byzantine, was by no means static; during the sixth century, it had gone through remarkable and deep-rooted changes. The history of the Sasanian monarchy can be interpreted as one of constant tensions between the attempts of the dynasty to establish a centralized authority and the determination of the higher aristocracy and local kinglets to maintain their rights and independence. The Parthian monarchy, which had preceded the Sasanians, had been little more than a confederation of minor kingdoms. The early Sasanian monarchs tried to create a more centralized regime, but during the fifth century, this process was largely reversed and there was something of an aristocratic reaction. This, in turn, provoked the Mazdakite uprisings of the late fifth and early sixth centuries. Mazdakism seems to have been a religious movement with strong social overtones. Its enemies, whose accounts are the only ones we have, portray the Mazdakites as campaigning for the abolition of private property and class distinctions and for the holding of women in common; the last is probably in part a malicious slander, but may also reflect opposition to the conventional Iranian aristocratic view of marriage as vital for the transfer of property and the production of heirs. At first perhaps surprisingly, the movement had the backing of the then king, Kavād I (488–531), who saw it as a way of reestablishing royal control over the fractious aristocracy. However, he was temporarily deposed and on his return to power, with the help of the Hepthalites he began to distance himself from these revolutionaries.

During the last part of his reign, he came increasingly under the influence of his son and heir, Khusrau, who persuaded him to take serious measures against the Mazdakites, who were outlawed and many of them massacred. The movement is of great interest, however, partly because of its avowedly egalitarian ideology but also because it gives an all too rare insight into the social discontents of Iran. It is worth, perhaps, noting in this context that the Western Roman Empire had been disturbed by a series of peasant revolts during the fifth century but that these do not seem to have had any counterparts in Syria, Anatolia or Egypt. The Mazdakite movement also left an ideological legacy. In Umayyad and early 'Abbasid times, there were a number of revolts – the most famous of which was led by Bābak in Āzarbayjān at the beginning of the third/ninth century – which are usually referred to by the name of Khurramiyya or Khurramdīniyya and which seem to have been influenced by radical Mazdakite ideas.

Khusrau I Anūshirvān (The Immortal Soul), who came to the throne in his own right on the death of his father in 531, was essentially the architect of the Sasanian state as it existed in the second half of the sixth century. He was determined to crush the Mazdakites without allowing the aristocracy to take over again. In order to do this, he introduced a series of administrative reforms which seem to have been, ultimately, dependent on the reforms Diocletian had introduced into the Roman Empire in the late third century and which were reflected in contemporary Byzantine practice. Basically, this consisted in a systematization of the land tax, which had probably existed before. This was now collected, not as a proportion of the harvest, but at a fixed rate depending on the area. With the money, he began to institute a paid army of horsemen and foot in place of the unreliable feudal levies which had existed before. The details of the reforms are vague, but it seems clear that the system of taxation paying for a regular army now became a central feature of Sasanian administration and as such was to have a profound effect on early Islamic practice.

Much of the land, especially in Iraq, however, was state land on which the cultivators paid up to a third of their produce, since this was both rent and taxes, a forerunner of the *ṣawāfī* of the early Islamic state. In addition, Khusrau organized the payment of a poll tax which was to be levied on all members of society according to their wealth, except the aristocracy and the priests of the official religion. In this way, paying the poll tax acquired a social stigma which seems to have remained after the Muslim conquest, when the basis for paying the poll tax became religious (that is to say that only non-Muslims paid) rather than social.

At the same time, he regularized the system of provincial administration. The whole empire was divided into four quarters – north, east, west and south – under supreme military commanders. These quarters disappeared at the time of the Muslim conquest, with the exception of the eastern quarter, known as Khurāsān, which remained virtually intact under early Islamic rule and was consequently larger and more powerful than the other provinces of Iran. Below the quarters were some thirty-seven provinces, known as *ōstāns* or, in Iraq, *kūras*, and these units tended to survive the Muslim conquest, with modifications, and became the basis of the new Muslim provincial organization. He also extended the system of appointing *marzbāns* along the frontiers and of settling populations of marginal people as peasant soldiers in vulnerable areas, again a reflection of Byzantine practice.

Urban life and institutions probably played a smaller part in the life of the Sasanian Empire than of the Byzantine. Before the coming of the Sasanians, some towns had had some administrative autonomy, inherited from Seleucid days when Greek urban institutions had been spread in the Macedonian colonies of Asia. By the sixth century, however, such institutions had long since vanished. In the Sasanian Empire, as in Byzantium, the cities were centres of local government and sometimes of upper-class social life, but they had no self-governing institutions. In contrast to the Byzantine Empire, the main religious institutions, including the great fire temple at Shiz (Takhti Sulayman), where the Sasanian kings were inaugurated, were situated in mountainous areas, well away from the main urban centres. It is perhaps necessary to stress this because it is often suggested that Islam is somehow hostile to the development of local councils and urban autonomy, but before accepting such assertions, it is worth noticing that no such institutions existed in the cities the Muslims conquered. Khusrau I took pains to develop towns, notably the Iraqi capital at Ctesiphon (Ar. al-Madā'in), which became the effective capital of the empire, a fact still witnessed by the surviving ruins of the great palace at the Ṭāq-i Kisrā. He did this at least in part by settling prisoners taken from the Byzantine Empire when he conquered Antioch in 540, and it would seem that they brought not just increased population and no doubt industrial skills, but also ideas of urban life, including public bath-houses, which had not until then been widely known in the

Persian Empire but were, of course, an important part of urban life in both the Roman and Muslim worlds. By and large, Sasanian cities seem to have been small country towns rather than great metropolises, and it is indicative that for nearly a quarter of a century, Khusrau II Parvēz did not live in his capital but at a rural palace at Dastagird in the Zagros Mountains; it would have been unthinkable for a Byzantine emperor to leave the city of Constantinople in that way. As far as we can tell, the aristocracy was based in their rural estates, and the main fire temples were on hills in the country or remote mountain sites rather than in the heart of cities like the cathedrals of the Byzantine towns of Syria.

If the towns were not especially important, the aristocracy was. The Sasanian aristocracy was divided into many different classes, but apart from the royal family it can be divided into two distinct groups. The first was the upper aristocracy, composed of a few great families, some of whom claimed that they were descended from the Parthian kings and could claim the title of sub-kings. Among these were the Suren family based in Sīstān, the Kāren family of Media and the Mihrān family from the Rayy area. It was against these families that the sixth-century rulers had to be on their guard, and it was one of them, Bahrām Chōbīn from the Mihrān family, who temporarily deposed Khusrau II at the start of his reign. This suspicion of the great magnates may account for Khusrau's subsequent, and very ill-advised, decision in 602 to abolish the Lakhmid buffer kingdom of Ḥīra which guarded the desert frontier of Iraq. The second group were the lesser aristocracy of *dihqāns*, a word which can almost be translated as gentry. Some of these were urban, absentee landlords, but many others lived in villages and formed a link between them and the government. Unlike the higher aristocracy, some of them, especially in Iraq, were not Persian at all but Aramaean or even Arab. They seem to have provided a counterweight to the higher aristocracy, and it was they who formed the foundation of Sasanian power. It was also the *dihqāns* who were the main mediators of Persian culture and administrative systems to the Arabs, since, unlike the higher aristocracy and the royal family, they retained much of their power after the Islamic conquest. Many administrators as late as the third/ninth century were drawn from *dihqān* families of Iraq.

Like the Byzantine Empire, the Sasanian had a state religion, Zoroastrianism, which was administered by a caste of priests called Magi, from which the followers of the religion are sometimes called Magians. Worship and ritual concentrated on the fire temples, fire being a pure and sacred element, and were much concerned with ritual purity and formal practice. The Magi themselves administered vast estates which were attached to the fire temples and on which they were responsible for justice in these areas as well as the collection of rents and revenues. The Magian religion was attached to a number of practices, especially the exposure of the dead to be picked clean by birds and beasts, and the encouragement of incestuous marriages, which were deeply repugnant to members of other faiths. The religion seems to have had only limited popular support; somewhat like the paganism of imperial Rome, it was more concerned with the proper performance of ceremony and the administration of its properties than it was with the more personal needs of the worshippers. Hence, again like the religion of Rome, it was increasingly challenged by other faiths, notably Christianity, and it would seem likely that, in Iraq at least, practising Magians were in a minority by the sixth century.

Of the religions which challenged the Magian state organization, the most widespread was the Church of the East (sometimes referred to, misleadingly, as the Nestorian Church), especially strong in Iraq but also active as far east as Sīstān and the eastern frontiers of the empire. By the sixth century, the Church of the East had developed an organized hierarchy of bishoprics and a network of monasteries and religious schools. In the main, the Sasanian rulers tolerated the Church of the East, and while none of them were themselves converted, they married Christian wives. Christian bishops were in some ways incorporated into the Sasanian administrative hierarchy, being entrusted with tax-collecting and other aspects of the governance of their followers. Evidence suggests that by the end of the sixth century, Christianity was making converts from Zoroastrianism in Iraq even from those, the Persian upper class, who might have been expected to remain loyal to the imperial faith. These conversions, along with the fear that the followers of the Church of the East were secret sympathizers of the Byzantines (unlikely in reality, for "Nestorianism" was a heresy even more severely proscribed than Monophysitism in Byzantium), led to intermittent outbreaks of persecution and martyrdom which culminated in a more general attack during the long struggle with Byzantium between 602 and 628. The Church of the East was also challenged, at least in northern Iraq, by the rival Monophysite church, which began making numerous converts during the sixth century but does not seem to have spread widely elsewhere in the empire.

Along with the Christians, there was a well-established Jewish community which seems to have been in existence since the time of the exile and which produced the great commentary on Jewish law known as the Babylonian Talmud. It would seem that Jews formed a majority of the population around the ancient city of Babylon, in the lands later known as the Sawād of Kūfa. Like the Christians, their relations with the Sasanian authorities in the sixth century were not always easy. There had been intermittent persecutions in the fifth century, which were renewed from 581 onwards by Hormizd IV. This led Jewish leaders to join the revolt of Bahrām Chōbīn in 590–591, and when this failed, they were subject to more violent attacks from the triumphant Khusrau II.

Other religious communities consisted of pagans and Manichaeans who had survived the persecutions of their dualist faith. Christianity had almost entirely eliminated paganism in the Byzantine Empire by the sixth century, but it is likely that ancient beliefs lingered on in Iraq and many areas of upland Iran. In their great struggle with the Muslims after the loss of Syria and

Egypt, the Byzantines were sustained by the possession of a common faith; no such shared beliefs inspired the Sasanian resistance.

This mixture of religious beliefs was paralleled by an ethnic and linguistic diversity more widespread than anything in the Byzantine world. The Persians formed the ruling class but they were almost certainly a minority in the empire. Even today, there are large numbers of non-Persian-speaking people within the borders of Iran and there can be no doubt that this was the case under the Sasanians; we know that there were Kurds in the Zagros Mountains and Daylamites in the north of Iran, and no doubt there were Lurs and Baluchis as well as other ethnic minorities in rural areas. In Iraq, the position is much better documented. Here, most of the settled population were Aramaic-speaking, including most of those who were Jewish and Christian. There were also considerable numbers of Arabs, in the Lakhmid-controlled kingdom of Ḥīra and in the pastoral lands of al-Jazīra. In Iraq, the Persians seem to have been confined to the cities and to certain frontier areas like Niṣībīn in northern Iraq, where they were settled as garrisons against the Byzantines.

For most of the people in Iraq, and for many of those in Iran, the Sasanian Empire with its attendant religion was alien and often oppressive and hostile. Many, if not most, of the people shared neither language nor religion nor custom with their political masters. It is unsurprising therefore that few of them, except in areas like Fārs where the Persian element was dominant, were prepared to struggle to preserve the old order once the imperial armies had been defeated.

As in Byzantium, these long-term weaknesses had been exacerbated by short-term problems, notably the violent and unpredictable policies of Khusrau II Parvēz and the struggle for his succession. Khusrau II Parvēz, unlike his great namesake Khusrau Anūshirvān, was not a great administrator or politician. His attempts to assert the power of the central monarchy led to the alienation of much of the upper class; even after the suppression of the rebellion of Bahrām Chōbīn at the outset of his reign, he faced a ten-year rebellion in Khurāsān and later executed the governor of Nimruz (Nēmrōz), the southern quarter of the empire, so making an enemy of his family. Most damaging of all, his determination to assert his authority led to the arrest and eventual execution of al-Nu‘mān, the last of the Lakhmid kings of Ḥīra, and his replacement by a Persian governor. It was perhaps to deflect attention from these internal problems that Khusrau in 602 began the great war with the Byzantines, which was to prove so catastrophic for both empires. The initial stages of the war saw the extension of Persian power to Syria, Palestine and Egypt, but after 622 the tide began to turn. In 627–628, Heraclius advanced through Iraq. Unlike his great rival, Khusrau was not himself a distinguished general and he failed to lead any effective resistance to the enemy, who took the capital at Ctesiphon. There were other problems too, such as extensive floods in the irrigated area of southern Iraq, and it is possible that the resistance of the empire had been weakened by the plague which caused so much devastation in Byzantium. As if flood, plague and foreign invasion were not enough, a murderous rivalry for succession began between the ailing king's sons. The details are obscure, but it seems that Khusrau's failings as a military commander eventually led to his deposition and the proclamation of the ten different kings already mentioned. Ten years previously, the Persian Empire had seemed stronger than at any time since the Achaemenids 1,000 years before, now it was ruined and bitterly divided. In the circumstances, it is perhaps surprising not that the Persian armies were defeated but that they fought as well as they did.

In the territories it inherited from the Sasanians, as in those it took over from Byzantium, Islam came into contact with a rapidly changing society. Despite the superficial continuity of empire and monarchy, both Byzantine and Sasanian states had undergone far-reaching and fundamental changes in the century before the coming of the Muslims. Many of the social, economic and structural developments, like the increased importance of pastoral peoples and the absence of civic autonomy, which are usually associated with the development of Islamic society, were in fact already under way in the sixth century if not before. The idea that the Muslim conquest broke up an age-old, changeless, deeply conservative world order is far from the truth; it would be more accurate to say that it entered an already changing world and shaped and accelerated some of the existing trends. The dynamic development of the Islamic world can only be understood against this background.

2 The birth of the Islamic state

The Islamic state was created by Arabic-speaking peoples during the course of the seventh century AD, and its political organization and the dissensions which troubled it had their origins in the Arabian background. According to the widely accepted historical narrative, the Arabs were ancient people who suddenly irrupted onto the world stage in the late sixth and early seventh centuries establishing an Arab-ruling elite and expressing themselves through the ancient Arabic language, now recorded in a newly developed Arabic script. The Islamic conquests, in fact, were given force by an existing Arab identity. Recently, this has been challenged by Peter Webb, *Imagining the Arabs*, in which he argues that there are few if any references to the Arabs as a group at this time and that an Arab ethnic identity was essentially constructed in Umayyad and early ʿAbbasid times. In this argument, Arab identity was a product of, rather than a cause of, the great Arab conquests. In the account which follows, the term Arab will refer to Arabic speakers.

Arabia in the sixth century

At the beginning of the seventh century, Arabic speakers inhabited the Arabian Peninsula and its northward extension, the Syrian Desert. Apart from some areas of south Arabia, where pre-Arabic languages were still spoken, Arabic was the language of the pastoral peoples throughout the Arabian Peninsula and as far north as the Euphrates. There was also some limited Persian settlement in Yemen and on the eastern, Gulf shore of Arabia. In the north, the frontier of the Arabic-speaking peoples coincided roughly with the borders between the steppe lands and the areas of settled agriculture. In southern Iraq, Arabs lived in the deserts along the lower Euphrates and colonized a few towns, like Ḥīra along the fringes of the alluvial plains. Further north, Arab nomads were found in the area between the Tigris and the Euphrates known as the Jazīra or "Island", a vast expanse of sparse grazing which could support a considerable population of pastoralists. On the western, Syrian edge of the desert, the picture is complicated by the fact that many Arabs had become more or less integrated into the Byzantine state and mingled with non-Arabic-speaking groups. In the century before the

DOI: 10.4324/9780429348129-2

Islamic conquest, Arab nomad tribes had penetrated into previously settled areas in northern Syria around Aleppo (Beroea) and Qinnasrīn (Chalcis), in the lands to the east of the Jordan and the southern borders of Palestine. In addition, much of the population of cities such as Damascus and Homs on the edge of the desert was of Arab origin. The divisions between Arab and non-Arab in these areas were blurred, and while we can probably assume that most of the nomadic pastoralists in the area were Arabic speakers, so too were the inhabitants of some of the settled areas. Some regions by contrast seem to have been almost completely unaffected by Arab immigration before the coming of Islam. These include the alluvial plains of southern Iraq, known as the Sawād, the mountain and coastal areas of Palestine and Syria and, in the north, the mountains of southeastern Anatolia. Neither Egypt nor Iran was in any sense an Arab country at this time.

These Arabic-speaking populations were united by a common language and the idea of a common kinship. There must have been widely differing dialects of Arabic over so vast an area, although little evidence of them has survived in the literary sources, but during the sixth century, there had developed, partly at the court of the Arab kings of Ḥīra, a common poetic language, generally understood throughout the Arabic-speaking lands. The possession of this common language was of vital importance for the development of the Islamic state. It meant that the fundamental teachings of Islam, as enshrined in the Qur'ān, were comprehensible to many different tribes and that communication was possible among groups from many different areas. If the Arab tribes had not enjoyed this common language, the achievements of the conquests and the Muslim empire would have been impossible. The Arabs also seem to have shared the idea that they came from one, or perhaps two, common ancestors, the second being introduced to account for the widespread cultural and later political differences between the northern (Qays/Muḍar) and southern (Yaman) Arabs. Later genealogists worked out elaborate structures to explain the kinship between different groups and, though these were in part later rationalizations, they could only have been developed if there was already an idea of common kinship.

Despite this linguistic and ethnic unity, the Arabs had no central political organization or administration. In previous centuries, there had been Arab kingdoms with some form of government, but these had usually been on the fringes of the Arab lands and under the patronage or protection of outside powers. The most famous of these were the Nabatean kingdom of Petra, taken over by the Romans in AD 106, and the third-century kingdom of Palmyra (Tadmur), both of which derived much of their wealth from the control of caravan routes and were heavily influenced by Greek and Roman cultures. In the extreme south of the peninsula, there were other kingdoms, based on the settled lands of south Arabia and Yemen but, like their northern counterparts, deriving much of their wealth from the organization of trade. In the fifth century AD, with the support of the Himyaritic rulers of south Arabia, the kings of Kinda established control over the tribes and commerce of much of central Arabia. By the second half of the sixth century, however, the kingdom of south Arabia had disintegrated and been taken over by Ethiopian and Persian invaders, while the tribes of central Arabia lacked any form of political authority. On the frontiers of the great empires, Arab client states had been established in the sixth century – the Ghassanids in Syria and the Lakhmids on the frontiers of Iraq. The Ghassanids, who organized much of the Syrian steppe for the Byzantines, were the leaders of a confederation of Arab tribes who lived a pastoral, nomadic existence along the borders of the settled lands. The Lakhmids had a fixed capital at Ḥīra; their kings enjoyed close relations with the Sasanian rulers of Iran and they managed the trade routes of much of eastern and central Arabia. By the beginning of the seventh century, however, these systems had been swept away because of changes of policy by both the Byzantines and the Sasanians and by the long, gruelling war between the two great powers from AD 602 to 628. The nascent Islamic state was faced by no rival power among the Arabs, and indeed it arose in part to fill the recently created political vacuum.

Such organized kingdoms were always, however, marginal to the lives of most nomad Arabs, for whom the tribe was the largest grouping to which they owed allegiance. In theory, the tribe was considered to be the descendants of a remote common ancestor from whom its members took their names. Thus, the descendants of a, probably mythical, Tamīm were referred to as the Banū Tamīm, or sons of Tamīm, and individuals would take the tribal designation al-Tamīmī as the last element in their names. Anthropological research suggests that in practice, tribal connections and genealogical links are developed to explain existing alliances and that if two groups wish to establish close links for pastoral, commercial or political reasons, they will tend to do so by "discovering" a common ancestor.

Not all tribes were equal in numbers, status or internal organization. Some tribes, notably those with a settled focus or nucleus, like the Quraysh of Mecca and the Banū Ḥanīfa of Yamāma in eastern Arabia, seem to have had a considerable degree of group solidarity. Others, like the Tamīm in northeastern Arabia and the Ghaṭafān in the Ḥijāz, for example, lacked any common unity of leadership or purpose. Some tribes seem to have been in the process of disintegration; the Bakr b. Wā'il, again in northeastern Arabia, never acted as a unit, and the most important groups were subdivisions like the Shaybān, whose leaders played a dynamic role in the conquest of Iraq. In the circumstances of pre-Islamic Arabia, most tribes never acted together, either for defence or for seeking pasture, nor was there any meeting place for the entire group. Instead, for most purposes, the bedouin of the seventh century, like the bedouin of the present day, identified with the much smaller lineage or clan which claims a common descent, often for five generations, and may share the ownership of wells vital for survival through the rainless summer, or with the tenting group who may or may not be related but who camp together and defend their members against attack. Early Islamic history is often described in terms of tribal rivalries, as if tribes had a common purpose and ambition. In fact, both detailed study of the early sources and the experience of modern anthropologists make it plain that tribes have no such unity and that, while tribal loyalties may help to cement an alliance, lineages and tenting groups make decisions according to their own perceived interest, rather than out of blind allegiance to a tribal leadership. Converts to Islam, for example, usually came as individuals or small groups, almost never as entire tribes. However, the ideological justification for alliances is often given in terms of kinship and a genealogical explanation produced. Thus, early Muslim writers may present in genealogical terms – that is, in terms of tribal solidarity and rivalry – conflicts that were in reality more concerned with down-to-earth matters like grazing and access to political power.

This kinship system, the identification of each individual with a group which would protect him against a rival group, is a logical response to the condition of ungovernment. In pre-Islamic Arabia, there was no law enforcement agency to protect persons and property, and safety was provided not by the state but by the kin and the principle of retaliation; if a man was robbed or murdered, then his kin were obliged to seek revenge or compensation. In this way, a measure of security for life and property was obtained without any formal structure of government, but it meant that the obligations of kinship were very important, since no one could survive without being a member of, or protected by, an effective kin. This system applied not only to the bedouin but also to the settled populations of towns such as Mecca and Yathrib (Medina) as well. One result of this method of maintaining order was that Arab society was a society geared to warfare; among full members of the tribe (as opposed to slaves and others of low status), there were no "civilians". All adult males, and sometimes females, could be mobilized to defend the camp or participate in raids. At the time of the Islamic conquests, most Arab men would have had military training and experience, in contrast to the peoples of much of the Byzantine and Sasanian Empires, where the peasant and urban populations took little part in military activities.

Power within the tribe was invested in the hands of chiefs. Leadership in traditional Arab society was both hereditary and elective. Leaders were chosen from ruling kin or a lineage within the tribe, but among the members of the lineage, power was exercised by the most able and effective, rather than by the eldest son of the previous holder of power. Chieftainship might be held jointly among several members of the same clan, while a large tribe might have a number of different leaders, as the Tamīm seem to have had in Muḥammad's time, and no paramount chiefs at all. In other cases, there were rival lineages which contested the chieftainship of the tribe, as in the Shaybān, where the different leaders sought alliance with either Muḥammad or the Persian authorities to strengthen their positions. The powers of the chief were very limited and were dependent on his abilities for their maintenance. His functions were to arbitrate in disputes, to find adequate grazing for his followers and to defend their wells and beasts against the depredations of rivals. He was also expected to be generous and to entertain visitors and his followers, and to this end he was sometimes allowed to collect contributions from the tribe. A reputation for generous hospitality had an important function, encouraging visitors who would provide information about grazing, the movement of other groups and other news vital for making effective choices of action. In general, there was not, in purely pastoral societies, an overwhelming difference in wealth between chiefs and others, since vast flocks and large sums of money were difficult to safeguard and provided no great advantage. A reputation for wisdom and generosity brought more power and influence than the accumulation of treasure or animals. The tribal chief had no coercive power. He could, if called on, give judgement in a case involving two parties within his own tribe, but there was no mechanism for enforcing it except insofar as public opinion sustained his verdict and put pressure on the parties concerned, since a man who consistently defied the opinion of his kinsmen would find himself friendless and exposed in time of danger. This lack of effective power has led to desert society being described as democratic and egalitarian, and there is some truth in this. Each family head had his own means of subsistence, his flocks, and could make his own decisions about where he camped and with whom he arranged marriage alliances. At the same time, there was a significant difference between the chief who was able to entertain guests to feasts and his poorer followers who could only scrape a meagre and insecure subsistence.

The pattern of tribal life was drastically changed by the Islamic conquests and the settlement often in large urban communities which followed. In some ways, tribal solidarity was enhanced because of the government policy of settling members of the same tribe in the same quarters of cities. Thus, Tamīmīs who were settled in the Tamīm quarter of Kūfa might find themselves next door to fellow tribesmen they had never met before but with whom they now had, for the first time, interests in common. As time passed, however, and the Umayyad government became more effective, tribal solidarity became less important, and men could pursue their own economic interests protected not by their kinsmen but by agents of the government.

The other important change caused by the post-Islamic settlement was to increase the distance between the ordinary tribesmen and the chiefs, the men the early Muslim writers refer to as the *ashrāf* (sing. *sharīf*). From the fourth/tenth century, if not before, this term is used for members of the Alid family, and tribal leaders are referred to as *mashāyikh* (sing. *shaykh*). The *ashrāf* were able to take advantage of the opportunities presented by the newly won lands and wealth and above all from their position as intermediaries between the government and their followers. It was they who arranged for the distribution of salaries and assignment of land while they acted as channels through which their followers could bring their complaints and petitions to the governor or caliph. They also had opportunities for acquiring great wealth from government office and military campaigns and investing it in land, much more secure and easier to safeguard than flocks. In some cases, tribal chiefs seem to have bartered tribal lands in Arabia for estates in Iraq which became their own property. All this led to the development of social tensions within the tribe which had seldom existed in the circumstances of pastoral life. Especially in Iraq, hostility to the newly acquired power and wealth of the *ashrāf* was a constant source of violent discontent.

In inner Arabia, most of the Arabs were pagans. Their paganism took different forms and seems to have been fairly basic – the worship of local idols and the practice of various techniques of divination. As far as the bedouin were concerned, attachment to the honour of both individual and kin and to the ideals of generosity and military prowess, a set of ideals sometimes referred to as "tribal humanism", was probably more important than attachment to any deity. The pagan deities seem to have been very localized and to have demanded favours and gifts more than worship and commitment. In Mecca itself, ideas of monotheism were not unknown before the coming of Muḥammad, but the worship of the idols of the Ka'ba was too important to the prosperity of the community to be challenged seriously. Elsewhere, Christianity was by far the most important religion among the Arabs. The tribes of the Syrian steppe and those of the Jazīra seem to have been almost entirely Christian, mostly of the Monophysite creed – indeed, the Ghassanids had been among the most important patrons of Monophysite Christianity when it had been under attack from the Byzantine authorities in the sixth century. There were both Christians and Jews in the Ḥijāz as well, the Christians settled mostly in the south at Najrān on the Yemeni borders, while the Jews were concentrated in Yathrib and the nearby oases.

Most of the Arab population in pre-Islamic times depended on pastoralism, the rearing of camels or sheep and goats for their subsistence. The camel nomads were mostly found in the heartlands of Arabia, and the literature of the period makes very clear the importance of camels for both transport and subsistence. We hear much less about sheep-rearing tribes but it would seem likely that many bedouin, then as now, depended on flocks for their living. This is especially true in the semi-desert bordering the settled areas of Syria and Iraq, partly because the sheep are better adapted to the more moderate climate and partly because sheep products need a nearby market. Many members of the shepherd tribes, like the Tanūkh and Taghlib along the Euphrates, probably lived in villages for at least part of the year, and the distinction between the nomad and the sedentary was often blurred. But although sheep and camels alike could provide milk, meat and wool, the pastoral life was not self-sufficient, and even the camel nomads of inner Arabia needed to be able to acquire dates, weapons and other goods from outside their own circle. This meant that the tribesmen needed a source of wealth apart from their own herds. This wealth could be acquired in a number of ways. They could exchange the products of pastoralism – wool, meat, cheese and hides – at market towns. While those who lived near markets could probably provide for themselves in this way, it was much more difficult for the inhabitants of remoter areas. They could raid other tribes. These raids, called *ghazw*, were exciting and served to confirm the unity of the kin group and give its members military experience; they could also be profitable, but often resulted in a pattern of mutual raids which left no one much better off.

Another way of improving the standard of subsistence was by extracting taxes from the settled people, either by raiding and pillaging or by establishing protection and receiving payment in exchange; thus in the century before the advent of Islam, the Ghassanids in Syria had established themselves as protectors of the settled population, and their leaders had become wealthy and distinguished chiefs, patrons of poetry and builders of palaces. On a smaller scale, many tribes must have collected dues from the peoples of the small oases, but opportunities of this sort were limited and settled communities comparatively few. The last option was the taxation of traders. The relationship between traders and nomads was a very close one. Often, the merchants were themselves of nomad stock, like the Quraysh merchants of Mecca, but they also needed the protection of the nomads through whose areas they passed. A trade route could only be successful if the organizers could rely on a network of agreements with local tribes to secure the safe passage of goods in exchange for a subsidy. Such arrangements were still in operation as late as the nineteenth century when the subsidies paid by the Ottoman government to secure the safe passage of the *ḥajj* (pilgrimage) were an important source of income for Ḥijāzī tribes.

The nomad pastoral society was inherently unstable for economic reasons. Any government which sought to pacify the tribes, establish peace in Arabia and abolish the *ghazw* had to find a substitute; if the tribesmen were not to attack each other, then they had to attack someone else.

It would be wrong, however, to imagine that all the inhabitants of the Arabian Peninsula were nomads, and that livestock were the only means of subsistence or tribal leadership the only basis of authority. There were areas like Yemen and parts of ʻUmān where the rainfall in the mountains was sufficient to allow settled village agriculture, and even away from the mountains and the water-bearing monsoons of the south coast, there were oases where date palms grew in abundance or crops could be cultivated. Such were settlements like Taymā and Khaybar in the northern Ḥijāz – or Yathrib, later known as Medina, further south, with its date palms and barley fields cultivated by settled folk living in permanent houses. In the hills just to the east of Mecca lay the town of Ṭā'if, where the upland climate allowed wheat and vines to be grown. In eastern Arabia too, there were areas of settled habitation, notably in Yamāma, where the Banū Ḥanīfa grew wheat and dates and had a permanent settlement at Ḥajar, both a shrine and a trading centre, as their capital. Despite their settled way of life, the people of these oases did not produce centralized states of the sort that were common in other settled areas in the Near East; they were too small and scattered. They maintained close contacts with the neighbouring nomads and a pattern of society divided into tribes and lineages – indeed, some tribes, like the Banū Ḥanīfa of Yamāma, for example, had both a nomad and a settled division. On the whole, the agriculturalists were looked down on by their nomad neighbours and were not regarded as truly noble. Thus in the early Islamic period, the people of Medina, despite their great contribution to the success of Islam, were never able to produce an important political leader from their own ranks.

However, it was neither a nomad community nor an agricultural community which produced the Prophet Muḥammad. Probably since the beginning of the first millennium BC, Arabia had been an important highway for commerce, and this commerce had profoundly affected the history and society of the people of the area. In classical times, the commerce was of two main kinds. The first was transit trade in goods imported by the Roman Empire from the Indian Ocean basin. This meant above all spices but also other sorts of perfumes and high-value luxury products. The routes by which these goods reached the shores of the Mediterranean varied according to political circumstances. The easiest and most logical was by ship to the head of the Gulf and thence by the Euphrates route and entrepôts like Palmyra and Edessa to the cities of Syria and the Mediterranean ports. But this route lay through the heart of the Persian Empire; it was frequently interrupted by war, and even in times of peace, the Persians extracted considerable tolls. It was this which made the harder, western routes more attractive. The Red Sea could be used for shipping, but navigation was very hazardous and much of the commerce passed overland from south Arabia, through the Ḥijāz to the Syrian markets, Petra during the early Roman Empire, but later Gaza and Bostra (or Buṣrā, on the edge of the desert, about 80 miles south of Damascus).

The other kind of trade was in the products of south Arabia, called Arabia Felix by classical writers on account of its great prosperity. This meant above all frankincense and myrrh, which were in vast demand in the Roman Empire for ritual and funerary purposes. These precious perfumes were gathered from the trees of the south Arabian hills, and there is no doubt that their cultivation contributed greatly to the prosperity of the inhabitants of the area and those who controlled the camel caravans which transported these products from there to the markets in the north.

This traditional trade in high-value luxury products seems to have declined by the end of the sixth century. The economic problems of the Byzantine Empire in the second half of the sixth century coupled with the almost complete collapse of the Italian and western European urban economies can have left little money for importing incense, cloves and pepper, and even where such commerce did survive it was on a much reduced scale. The sources for the late sixth and early seventh centuries give few details about the nature of the trade, but it seems to have been essentially the exchange of locally produced goods. Hāshim, Muḥammad's great-grandfather, is said to have received permission to bring skins and textiles (probably from

Yemen) to Syria, and the Prophet himself is said to have traded in skins. In exchange, the merchants brought back grain and wine from Syria. In Iraq too, we are told that the tribes along the borders of the settled lands bought supplies from the kings of Ḥīra, presumably in exchange for animal products. In fact, the trade of Muḥammad's time seems to have been more the exchange of the products of pastoralists and agriculturalists than the large-scale international trade of previous centuries. It seems likely, however, that trade was vital to the livelihood of the people of Mecca among whom the Prophet grew up and that he himself went on trading expeditions to Syria.

Recent research suggests that there may have been another factor at work. Historical and geographical sources mention a number of gold and silver mines in the Arabian Peninsula, mostly, but not entirely, in the Ḥijāz area. Archaeological work has confirmed the existence of extensive mining operations which flourished from the fifth century AD to the early 'Abbasid period. More research is needed to substantiate the evidence, but it appears as if the development of precious-metal mining was a fundamental part of the emergence of Mecca as a commercial centre: the Arab population of the area now had money to spend on importing agricultural products and other luxuries. This supply of gold and silver certainly would account for the frequent mentions of large cash sums which we find in the traditional Arab accounts of the early history of Islam.

The control of these trade routes and the enjoyment of the profits they produced were perhaps the most important factor in the pre-Islamic politics of the Arabian Peninsula. The main problem faced by anyone attempting to organize the caravan traffic was to ensure the passage of valuable goods through the lands occupied by nomad tribes. Because of the vast distances and the difficulty of finding supplies, sending a large armed escort with each party was not a practical proposition. The alternative was to reach some sort of agreement with the tribes whereby the caravans would be allowed to pass in exchange for favours, support or protection.

At the beginning of the sixth century, the south Arabian kingdom was strong enough to be able to organize the caravan trade. To do this, a client tribal kingdom of Kinda was supported in central Arabia and seems to have arranged for the passage of caravans. During the first half of the sixth century, however, this system broke down. This was partly because Ghassanid–Lakhmid rivalry in the Fertile Crescent made trade unsafe, but it may also have reflected the impoverishment of the Mediterranean market, which resulted in reduced profits. The kingdom of Kinda disappeared leaving central Arabia in chaos, while in south Arabia itself the indigenous Himyaritic kingdom was taken over by the rulers of Ethiopia, probably acting in alliance with the Byzantines to forestall an attack by the Persians or their Lakhmid protégés. The period of Ethiopian rule, from about 530 to 575, saw attempts by various parties to reconstitute the system. The Lakhmid rulers of Ḥīra attempted to maintain a series of agreements with neighbouring tribes, notably the Tamīm and Bakr b. Wā'il in their own immediate vicinity but also with the Sulaym, who could ensure the passage of Lakhmid caravans to the Ḥijāz and the markets of western Arabia. The Lakhmid system was based on treaties, subsidies and diplomacy backed up by occasional raids, but despite Persian military support, the kings of Ḥīra could never enforce their authority much beyond the boundaries of the settled lands.

In Yemen, the Ethiopian viceroy, Abraha, attempted to revive a system based on the old Sabaean kingdom. Abraha was essentially independent of the ruler at Axum, and despite his attack on Mecca, he receives a good reputation in the Muslim sources. He repaired the great dams at Mārib in an attempt to revive the agricultural economy and his attack on Mecca was a clear indication of his intent to bring eastern Arabian trade under his control. In the 570s, however, his successors were removed by a rebellion of the local people aided by a Persian fleet under one Vahrīz, who eventually stayed on as Persian viceroy until after 628. Persian rule does not, however, seem to have been as strong as Ethiopian, and an attempt to control Arabian trade on a Ḥīra–Yemen axis and so bring it all under the indirect control of the Sasanian Empire was frustrated by the feebleness of Ḥīra and the Persian rulers of Yemen, as well as the rising power of a new trading centre, Mecca.

The site of the sanctuary at Mecca is without doubt an ancient one. The role of the sanctuary, known in Arabic as the *ḥaram*, was very important in pre-Islamic Arabia, and similar institutions, under the name of *ḥawṭa*, still exist in many areas of south Arabia today. In the conditions of tension and hostility which often existed between neighbouring tribes, it was essential to have some neutral area where members of different groups could meet to exchange goods and settle disputes: the *ḥaram* or *ḥawṭa* fulfilled this role. The *ḥaram* was originally founded (often on the borders between tribal territories or at the junction of several *wādīs*) by a holy man who declared it neutral ground. This inviolability extended not just to the shrine itself, usually a very simple structure, but also to the immediately surrounding area, often demarcated by stone posts. Within this area, no violence or killing was permitted and enemies could meet together confident of their security. The holy man (*manṣab* is the modern term) could also be resorted to for arbitration and accepted as a judge. Naturally, markets grew up in the *ḥaram*, where the property of the various merchants would be safe. Those who used the *ḥaram* and were attached to it were obliged to pay the holy man dues for his services, and in exchange the holy man would feed and entertain the tribesmen. In a country without a centralized law enforcement system, the *ḥaram* played a vital role in the social and economic life of the people, and the holy man could become a figure of great political power and influence. After his death, the authority usually passed to his family, who became thereby a "holy lineage". They took over the duties of guarding the *ḥaram*, ensuring its inviolability and entertaining visitors and pilgrims. The foundation of the *ḥaram* at Mecca is ascribed by the Muslims to Abraham, but though the original founder had long since passed away, the *ḥaram* was held and administered by a series of lineages which became holy families for several generations before being replaced by new lineages who felt that they had a better right to the position. This happened probably in the first half of the sixth century when the existing guardians of the *ḥaram* at Mecca were replaced by one Quṣayy, who installed himself and his tribe, the Quraysh, as guardians and whose descendants became the new holy family. Among his direct descendants was Muḥammad b. ʿAbd Allāh, the Prophet of God, and it is impossible to understand his background or success without remembering his position with regard to the *ḥaram*.

Although the *ḥaram* at Mecca was very ancient, the commercial network of which it was the centre by the early seventh century was comparatively recent. It does not seem that there was any city to speak of when Quṣayy and the Quraysh took over the *ḥaram*, and the urban development of Mecca must be seen as a phenomenon of the second half of the sixth and early seventh centuries. The foundation of the trading network probably belongs to the generation of Quṣayy's grandsons. Under the protection of the *ḥaram*, fairs were held at ʿUkāẓ a few miles east of Mecca, where goods, as well as poetry and ideas, could be exchanged between groups who would normally be at war. The traditional Muslim account, which probably has at least a symbolic accuracy, shows the four brothers all establishing commercial relations with different areas; ʿAbd Shams in Abyssinia, Hāshim in Syria, al-Muṭṭalib in Yemen and Nawfal in Iraq, and all the brothers except ʿAbd Shams are said to have died in the countries they made contact with, Hāshim in Gaza. Until this point, the *ḥaram* at Mecca had been simply one of a number serving the surrounding tribes; even in the immediate vicinity, there were others like it managed by the Thaqīf at Ṭa'if and oneat Nakhla between Mecca and Medina, where the holy family came from the tribe of Sulaym. The commercial expertise of the Quraysh, both the direct descendants of Quṣayy and other clans, most notably the Makhzūm, transformed this position. They made the city the centre of what has been described as the "Meccan commonwealth", a commercial and diplomatic network which enabled caravans organized in Mecca under Quraysh patronage to travel to Syria, Iraq and Yemen in comparative security. This was done by a variety of means. There were tribes which recognized the religious status of the *ḥaram* and the sanctity of the holy months, when violence was not supposed to be practised; these included not just the Quraysh but probably also the Khuzāʿa, Thaqīf and Kināna, who controlled the route south to Yemen, although the lists given in the sources are somewhat contradictory. Among those tribes who were not attached to the Kaʿba in this way, the Quraysh entered into partnership. The alliance with other tribes who considered themselves part of the Muḍar group, like the Asad and especially the Tamīm, with whom the Quraysh established close links and who frequently acted as judges in the fair at ʿUkāẓ, helped in this process. With them and other tribes – the Ṭayy, for example – they entered into profit-sharing agreements, called *īlāf*, with the chiefs, who were guaranteed payment in exchange for securing the passage of the caravans. The commonwealth was held together by the prestige of the sanctuary at Mecca and of its holy family, along with diplomacy, tact, payment and self-interest. The Quraysh had no army with which to enforce their rule, although they did occasionally go to war to defend their interests, as, for example, in the case of the war of Fijār, which occurred when the Prophet was a young man, the object of which was to ensure that caravans from Yemen to Iraq came under the patronage of the Quraysh.

External circumstances seem to have increased the importance of the Meccan commonwealth in the early seventh century. In 602 with the assassination of the Emperor Maurice, there began a generation of savage warfare between the Byzantines and the Sasanians, which meant that direct trading links across the frontier between the two empires must have become impossible. In 602 as well, the Persians executed al-Nu'mān III, the last of their client kings of Ḥīra, and Ḥīra ceased to be an important independent political force in the northeast of Arabia. Tribes like the Tamīm, which had had close contacts with Ḥīra, now began to look to Mecca and the Quraysh for trading partners and even for arbitration in their quarrels. The victory of the Arab tribes over the Persian armies at Dhū Qār in 611 meant the final end of any pretensions of the Persians to exert authority over northeast Arabia and left the way open for the expansion of Quraysh influence. So during the lifetime of the Prophet, the Quraysh network, based on the *ḥaram* at Mecca, had become the leading commercial organization in northern and western Arabia but it must be remembered that its success was ultimately based on the prestige of the *ḥaram* and the popularity of the fairs that took place under its protection at 'Ukāẓ. If the position of the *ḥaram* were to be challenged in any way, then the whole position of the city would be put in jeopardy.

Trade was no luxury for the people of Mecca. The site of the city is barren and rocky and no agriculture was possible except with great expense and difficulty. The water supply was dependent on wells, notably the sacred well of Zamzam, the maintenance of which played a large part in city life. This meant that virtually all food had to be imported. In the early days of Quraysh domination, no doubt much of the population remained nomadic pastoralists living from the produce of their herds, and the agriculture of the neighbouring towns of Ṭā'if and Yathrib probably sufficed for their needs. In about 570, for example, the Prophet's grandfather possessed a herd of 200 camels as well as commercial interests in Mecca. But during the life of Muḥammad, there is no doubt that much of the population consisted of sedentary townspeople and merchants who produced no food themselves. The population was probably increasing with the prosperity of the city and in addition there was the burden of feeding the visitors and pilgrims whose visits were so vital to the prosperity of the town. These factors meant that Mecca was dependent on imported foodstuffs, not just from the surrounding area but from as far afield as Yamāma in the east and Syria and even Egypt to the north. Keeping the trade routes open was vital to the survival of the people of Mecca.

The inhabitants of Mecca were not, of course, a homogeneous group. There were many slaves and others who were not members of the Quraysh and therefore did not share in the wealth and prestige of the tribe. Among the Quraysh, there were lineages with greater or lesser prestige and wealth, and there can be no doubt that by Muḥammad's time, there were very sharp divisions between the richer and poorer members of the tribe. Despite their urban and sedentary ways of life, the Quraysh still retained their tribal organization. There was no system of public justice, no police and no courts; safety and security of goods and person depended, as it did in the desert, on the lineage, and a man from a weak lineage or one who lost the support of his close relations was in a very vulnerable position. Among the clans or lineages of the Quraysh, the descendants of Quṣayy held pride of place, and it was they who had inherited responsibilities in the *ḥaram* though there were other clans, notably the Makhzūm, whose commercial success had put them among the leaders of Meccan society. Quṣayy had left the guardianship of the *ḥaram* to his son 'Abd al-Dār, but 'Abd al-Dār and his descendants had failed to sustain their position against the claims of the more dynamic clan of 'Abd Manāf, and by the time of the Prophet, they had largely fallen out of the leading group. As always in Arabia, leadership was both hereditary and elective. No one who was not of the Quraysh and the clan of Quṣayy could claim to lead the holy family, but among that group, leadership lay with the strong and the shrewd, not necessarily with the eldest or with the father's choice. 'Abd Manāf, in turn, had four sons whom tradition credits with establishing the fortunes of the Quraysh: 'Abd Shams, Nawfal, Hāshim and al-Muṭṭalib. These four shared out among themselves the various offices connected with the *ḥaram* and the pilgrimage. As might be expected, there developed a rivalry between the clan of Hāshim (supported by the weaker descendants of al-Muṭṭalib) and the clan of 'Abd Shams (later called after his son Umayya, usually but not always supported by the Nawfal and Makhzūm) for power and influence in Mecca which was to have profound and far-reaching effects on the early Islamic state.

The early life of Muḥammad[1]

Muḥammad belonged to the clan of Hāshim. The status of the clan in the years immediately before the emergence of Islam is not entirely clear and Western historians have suggested, perhaps wrongly, that the early Islamic sources exaggerated its importance in an attempt to magnify the social position of the Prophet. Hāshim was certainly a man of great importance among the Quraysh; besides being connected with the opening up of the Syrian trade route, he is also said to have been responsible for the feeding and watering of the pilgrims and people of Mecca, a man of wealth and generosity, in contrast to his brother 'Abd Shams, who was constantly away on trading expeditions and was said to have been a poor man with a large family. After Hāshim's death, however, the status of the clan seems to have declined. In contrast to the increasing commercial success of 'Abd Shams, the clan of Hāshim suffered a number of disappointments. His son 'Abd al-Muṭṭalib was clearly a person of some consequence, however; at the time of Abraha's expedition against Mecca – known to the Muslims as the Day of the Elephant (probably around 570) – he appears as the spokesman for the Quraysh in negotiations with Abraha. He was also responsible for the reopening of the well Zamzam, again emphasizing the close connections of the clan with the *ḥaram*. 'Abd al-Muṭṭalib had four sons, 'Abd Allāh, who died young, and al-Zubayr, Abū Ṭālib and Abū Lahab, who succeeded each other as the head of the clan. It was shortly after 'Abd al-Muṭṭalib's death (in the late 570s?) that the clan became one of the leading members of the *ḥilf al-fuḍūl* or "Confederation of the Virtuous". This was probably an association of the less successful clans to ensure fair trading and prevent the establishment of trading monopolies by 'Abd Shams and other dominant clans. This suggests that despite their close association with the *ḥaram*, the Banū Hāshim were no longer among the wealthiest or most politically powerful of the Meccan clans and that considerable social tensions were developing in the city between the richest clans and their poorer kinsmen.

It was into this family, direct descendants of Quṣayy, members of the holy family of Mecca and closely connected with the *ḥaram*, that Muḥammad b. 'Abd Allāh b. 'Abd al-Muṭṭalib b. Hāshim was born probably around the year 570 when Abraha the Abyssinian made his ill-fated attack on Mecca. Despite his illustrious family background, his immediate circumstances were not especially prosperous. His father had died before he was born, on a trading expedition to Syria, and his mother Amīna and his grandfather 'Abd al-Muṭṭalib supervised his early childhood. In accordance with Quraysh customs, he was found to be a wet-nurse, Ḥalīma, from the Hawāzin bedouin tribe and spent his early years with them in the desert; the Muslim sources relate how reluctant the bedouin women were to take on an orphan with no economic prospects. His early life was further clouded by the deaths of his mother when he was six and of his famous grandfather, 'Abd al-Muṭṭalib, when he was eight, but the clan looked after him, and his uncle Abū Ṭālib, now its head, saw to his upbringing. We have few details of his early life. He lived through a period of growing Meccan prosperity and influence; he is said to have taken part in the war of Fijār to secure the Quraysh hold over the trade route of western Arabia and is pictured on a caravan expedition to the Syrian city of Bostra, where his future greatness was recognized by the Christian monk Baḥīra. It was also a period of increasing social tensions, and as a child he was said to have been present at the foundation of the *ḥilf al-fuḍūl*.

It was natural that the young man sought to make a career for himself in commerce. Because of his honesty and trustworthiness, he was taken on, when in his twenties, as a business manager for a wealthy Qurashī widow, Khadīja, whom he married shortly afterwards. His marriage to Khadīja brought him material security and children, including Fāṭima, whose descendants were to prove so important in later Islamic history. It also seems to have been a genuinely companionate marriage, Khadīja bringing him comfort and moral support in times of difficulty.

Thus far, Muḥammad's career had been quietly successful and he was clearly one of the leading young men of the Quraysh. We cannot be certain of the exact chronology of events, but it was probably in about 610, when he was around forty years old, that Muḥammad began to receive the Revelation of the Qur'ān. The circumstances are recorded by a number of early sources; the Prophet had retired from Mecca, probably for a period of meditation and reflection, to the neighbouring mountain of Ḥirā' and it was here that the command came to him to recite the first *sūra* or "verse" (almost certainly 96: 1–5).

> *Recite: In the name of thy Lord who createth,*
> *Createth man from a clot.*
> *Recite: And thy Lord is the Most Bounteous,*
> *Who teacheth by the pen,*
> *Teacheth man that which he knew not.*

The dating of the Revelation of the Qur'ān is problematic but it is generally accepted that the earliest *sūras* are those which come towards the end of the received text of the Qur'ān. Short and simple but very powerful, they stress the glory and majesty of Allah, his mercy and generosity, the importance of doing good, particularly the obligations of the rich to the poorer members of society, and the inevitability of the day of judgement.

In the year which followed the Revelation, Muḥammad began his public preaching, calling on people to acknowledge the glory of Allāh and pray to him. His first convert was his wife, followed by people closely related to him, his cousin 'Alī b. Abī Ṭālib and his freedman Zayd b. Ḥāritha. But the message soon spread beyond his immediate household, and Abū Bakr, certainly one of the first Muslims, was a prosperous merchant from the Quraysh clan of Taym. Most of the early converts came, as might be expected, from his own clan of Hāshim, and others, like Sa'd b. Abī Waqqāṣ and 'Abd al-Raḥmān b. 'Awf from his mother's clan of Zuhra. Most of them were young men and they seem to have come from clans of some standing in Mecca who had missed out on the great commercial successes of the recent years. It has been described as a movement of the "nearly hads" rather than of the "have nots" and there were few representatives of the wealthy clans of 'Abd Shams (Umayya) or Makhzūm. It is interesting to note as well that they were all converted as individuals, not as clans. Even within Hāshim itself, there were important figures, Abū Tālib, the head of the clan, and his brother Abū Lahab, for example, who did not accept the Revelation, while, however, there was no clan of standing which did not provide at least one recruit for the new movement.

At first, there is no evidence that the preaching aroused any opposition among those who did not accept it, but as the Revelation became more specific and more widely accepted, conservative elements in Mecca began to see it as a threat to their position. A challenge to the *ḥaram* and its idols could be seen as a challenge to the religious and hence commercial standing of Mecca, and to acknowledge Muḥammad as the Prophet of God meant to accept that he had a status within the community superior to that of rich merchants like Abū Jahl of the Makhzūm and Abū Sufyān of the Umayya who were the leading figures in Mecca at the time. In addition, Muḥammad's insistence that those who did not recognize Allāh were consigned to hell meant that many feared for the souls of their ancestors. At one stage, Muḥammad was persuaded to introduce the "Satanic verses" into the Revelation, which gave some status to the goddesses of neighbouring sanctuaries, and this may represent an attempt to come to terms with the Meccan leaders. If so, Muḥammad soon realized that he had been led astray and repudiated the verses, thus confirming that Allāh was the only God and that idols could have no place in the religion of Islam.

This seems to have marked the end of the period when Muḥammad's activities had been tolerated, and his followers now found themselves under increasing pressure. This mostly took the form of ostracism, verbal attacks, commercial sanctions and, in the case of lower-class Muslims without influential protectors, actual physical violence. Against this background, a number of Muslims left Mecca to settle in Ethiopia, probably in 615, where they enjoyed the protection of the Christian ruler. There does not seem to have been any intention of removing the entire Muslim group from Mecca, however, and Muḥammad himself and the most prominent of the early converts remained in Mecca. That they were able to do so was because of the solidity of the clan system; Muḥammad himself was protected by the clan of Hāshim and its leader Abū Ṭālib. Even though Abū Ṭālib was not himself a Muslim, he felt it part of his duty to support a member of the clan who was under threat despite the fact that prominent Meccans urged him to disown the troublemaker. People became Muslims as individuals but they did not at this stage become a separate community, and when persecuted Muslims needed protection they still turned to their non-Muslim blood relatives rather than to their fellow Muslims. All that was to change when the community moved to Medina. The next stage of the opposition was to try to isolate the whole clan of Hāshim and to boycott them both commercially and socially. This attempt does not seem to have lasted very long and began to disintegrate when members of other clans who were related by marriage and other ties to Hāshim began to resume contacts.

The collapse of the boycott was not, however, the end of the Prophet's troubles. In 619, his beloved wife Khadīja and his uncle Abū Ṭālib both died. It had been Abū Ṭālib who had united Hāshim in their support of Muḥammad, but he was succeeded as the head of the clan by his brother Abū Lahab, who had different ideas. Abū Lahab was not prepared to protect his nephew in the same way, and Muḥammad's position in Mecca soon became increasingly difficult. In response to this pressure, Muḥammad began to look outside his native city for support. The first and most obvious area was the neighbouring city of Ṭā'if, where many of the Quraysh had property and contacts. However, Ṭā'if was no more welcoming than Mecca had been. The Prophet then tried to approach some of the neighbouring bedouin tribes with the intention of preaching to them, but once again he was rebuffed. The period from 619 to the *Hijra* in 622 was really the crisis of Muḥammad's ministry and the biggest test he faced since he had begun to preach his message.

At this crucial point, however, Muḥammad was approached by the inhabitants of the settlement of Yathrib (known after 622 as Medina, meaning "the city"). The people of this community made their living from agriculture in their oasis. Despite their sedentary life, they, like the Quraysh, had maintained their tribal distinctions and their systems of clan security. The Arabs of this oasis were divided into two main tribes, the Aws and the Khazraj, who were said to have migrated from south Arabia to settle the area in the mid-sixth century. In addition to these two main groups, there were three small tribes of Jews or Judaized Arabs, the Banū Qurayz-a, the Banū'l-Naḍīr and the Banū Qaynuqā'. The Aws and Khazraj had been feuding for many years but in the years before the *Hijra* these feuds had become more serious and general, culminating in the battle of Bu'āth in about 617, which had resulted in a peace of exhaustion. Clearly, it was a community in need of a leader and arbitrator to put an end to this murderous internecine strife. Clearly too, this leader would have to be an outsider, since no local person would be acceptable to the entire population.

It was in these circumstances that a group of Medinese first approached Muḥammad, probably in 620. They went home to Medina and returned the next year for the pilgrimage. In 622, about seventy people from Medina, all converts to Islam, met the Prophet by night at 'Aqaba outside the city; Muḥammad was careful to ensure that they swore to obey him and fight for him and to ensure that he was invited by men of both Aws and Khazraj and so would not be the candidate of only one party. He also insisted that twelve *naqībs* be appointed to represent his interests in Yathrib. Muḥammad then was careful to safeguard his position in advance and be sure that his position would be accepted by a considerable proportion of the population. The Muslims then began to move in small groups, careful not to attract attention to themselves, while the Prophet remained behind until he and Abū Bakr made their way by obscure paths to Medina, which they reached on the 24 September 622. A new era had begun.

Muḥammad in Medina

The *Hijra*, or migration of the Prophet from Mecca to Medina during the summer of 622, marked a major turning point in the history of the Islamic movement. His followers in Mecca, later known as the *Muhājirūn* or Emigrants, some seventy in number, had left in small groups through July,

August and September. The *Hijra* meant that the Muslims were now free of the hostility of the leaders of the Quraysh and the restricting atmosphere of Mecca and were now settled among people who had invited them and at least some of whom were Muslims; Muḥammad could preach and they worship with an openness which had been impossible before. But the emigration from Mecca also meant that the *Muhājirūn* had abandoned the traditional clan links which had guaranteed their security and clearly they could no longer rely for protection on relatives they had left behind. The traditional system may not have been perfect and in the case of the Prophet himself, it had become increasingly ineffective, but it had provided a framework in which they could live. The early converts had become Muslims as individuals, not in clans, and even after they had adopted Islam, the clan remained the basic social link. Now with the move to Medina, a new form of social organization was required.

To begin with, the Emigrants were quartered in the houses of those among the people of Medina who had invited them, now known as the *Anṣār* or Helpers of the Prophet, but if this arrangement had continued, they might have become little more than hangers-on, constantly needing help and protection. To avoid this, a series of agreements were drawn up in the first two or three years after the *Hijra*, agreements which are known collectively as the "Constitution of Medina". This takes the form of agreements between the *Muhājirūn* and the people of Yathrib. All the believers are described as *umma*, a community apart from the surrounding pagan society, and they are to make war as one. The bond between members of the *umma* transcends any bonds or agreements between them and the pagans, and they are all to seek revenge if any Muslim is killed fighting "in the way of God". If, however, one Muslim kills another, then the normal rules of retaliation continue to operate, with the proviso that the *Muhājirūn*, who had no close relatives in the city, were to be considered as a clan like any of the native clans of Medina. There are also clauses dealing with relations with the Jews, who are partners in the affairs of Medina and bear their share of the expenses of warfare as long as there is no treachery between them and the Muslims, although both Muslims and Jews would keep their own religion. Muḥammad is mentioned only twice, both times to emphasize that the arbitration of any disputes belongs to God and Muḥammad; no other arbitrators are mentioned. The documents, then, tried to solve the problems of justice within the city and relations with outsiders, but they do not suggest that the power of Muḥammad was absolute or lay any emphasis on religious affairs. Medina was to be a *ḥaram* as Mecca was, for its people, and Muḥammad was to be its founding holy man.

Clearly, the Constitution of Medina only illustrates some aspects of Muḥammad's authority in the early years after the *Hijra*. In the eight momentous years which followed, his energies and those of his followers were devoted to establishing his unquestioned authority within Medina, conducting an effective struggle against Mecca, attracting the alliance of as many of the surrounding nomad tribes as would cooperate and working out the rules and role of the Muslim community. All these processes went hand in hand and the struggle against the Meccans was instrumental in the establishment of power within Medina, while the support of outside tribes contributed materially to his eventual success.

The stages by which Muḥammad established his power in Medina are difficult to distinguish, and both traditional accounts and modern commentators have tended to lay more emphasis on the external conflicts, since here the issues and chronology are clearer. Muḥammad seems to have begun the struggle against the Meccans almost as soon as he arrived at Medina; he must have realized that successful aggressive warfare was one of the best ways of providing for his supporters and of attracting new recruits, but he also knew that until the Quraysh, with their great prestige and widespread contacts, were subdued and won over, Islam would never be more than a local cult in Medina; the struggle against Mecca was essential for the success of the new religion. Attacking the city of Mecca was impractical, and so it was to the trade caravans to Syria which were forced to pass fairly close to Medina that Muḥammad and his followers turned their attentions. This would not only destroy the commerce on which the prosperity of the enemy depended but would also eventually starve the city into surrender, since it relied on imported food.

Preliminary raids by small numbers of Muslims took place during the first eighteen months of the *Hijra* but the first real trial of strength came in the spring of 2/624 when a large caravan with some 50,000 *dīnārs* worth of goods set out from Gaza to Mecca. It was led by one of the most important figures in Meccan politics at the time, Abū Sufyān, of the clan of Umayya and father of the future Caliph Mu'āwiya, who had with him an escort of about 70 men. Even by the standards of Meccan commerce, this was a very valuable convoy indeed, and its safe passage was vital to the continuing prosperity of the city. Alarmed by the prospect that Muḥammad might intercept it, the Meccans gathered a large force of 950 men under the leadership of Abū Jahl to come and protect it on the last, difficult stages. The caravan passed along the coast road and as a result of Abū Sufyān's quick thinking escaped to Meccan territory without injury. The relief force, however, continued to advance, determined to put an end to the menace of Muḥammad for good and all. Muḥammad, with a much smaller force of 86 *Mubājirūn* and 230 *Anṣār*, was waiting for them by the wells at Badr and, as a result of their possession of the water source and the Prophet's leadership, they were able to score a major victory. Abū Jahl himself was killed and numerous valuable prisoners and animals were taken.

Badr was a total triumph and for later Muslims marked a decisive turning point; participation in the battle of Badr was a sure sign of early commitment to Islam, and the names of those who had been prepared to risk their lives for Allāh and his Prophet were immortalized in tradition. The victory solved many of the Prophet's immediate problems; the profits of the ransoms and booty provided for the needs of both Emigrants and Helpers, and a fifth of all the spoils, which was the Prophet's share, was used to provide for the needs of those Muslims who were in distress. The victory did not dispose of the Meccan threat; the caravan had got through and the number of dead had not been crippling, but it must have destroyed much of the prestige on which the reputation and trade of the Quraysh rested; bedouin tribes would no longer look on Meccan leaders with the same respect. But the most important result of the victory was the consolidation of Muḥammad's position within Medina. In the aftermath of the *Hijra*, the attitudes of the population towards their new leader were varied. Some, like the important leader Sa'd b. Mu'ādh, became enthusiastic adherents of the new religion, but there were others who were less convinced. Some no doubt remained pagans, though they do not seem to have been a very significant group, but many more remained sceptical or half-committed. Among these was 'Abd Allāh b. Ubayy, an important figure in the town before the arrival of Muḥammad and a man who might have aspired to the role of arbiter and leader himself. He had adopted Islam, no doubt hoping that it would benefit his position, but he resented the authority of the newcomer, and his allegiance was doubtful. Such doubters, *Munāfiqūn* or Hypocrites the Muslim sources call them, were temporarily silenced by the Prophet's success; many of them were no doubt permanently won over to Islam and even those who remained sceptical were silenced for the time being. The success at Badr also allowed Muḥammad to move against the Jews. The Jewish clans of Medina had been invited to accept Islam but few had responded. Unlike the pagans, they provided a real ideological challenge to Muḥammad and in the years which followed Badr, acceptance of his political authority became impossible without also accepting his claims to Prophethood. It was impossible for Muḥammad to allow Jews to coexist with Muslims in Medina without putting his whole achievement and position in jeopardy.

The first of the Jewish groups to be attacked in the aftermath of Badr were the Banū Qaynuqā', the silversmiths who controlled much of the commerce of the town. There were good reasons why they should be singled out; there were Muslims, like 'Abd al-Raḥmān b. 'Awf, who had earlier shown an interest in commerce, which offered a livelihood to Emigrants who had no agricultural land. In addition, they were allies of 'Abd Allāh b. Ubayy, the one man in the oasis whom Muḥammad could still fear as a rival. A trivial quarrel in the market, a dead Jew and a dead Muslim, was the occasion for Muḥammad to demonstrate his power. He ordered the execution of the entire clan and 'Abd Allāh b. Ubayy was able to secure no more for his allies than the commutation of the sentence to banishment and confiscation of property.

The Meccans meanwhile could not afford to sit back and do nothing. Their prestige had been severely damaged and the trade route cut. An attempt to find an alternative route through Iraq proved disastrous when the caravan was captured by Muḥammad's forces after the defenders had fled.

Besides, the dead of Badr had to be avenged and it was unthinkable that retribution should not be sought. Accordingly, the next spring when there was ample grazing for the Meccan cavalry and the crops of Medina would be especially vulnerable, a large-scale expedition was organized in Mecca, led by Abū Sufyān, who had taken over Abū Jahl's role as a leader of the city. The army also had with it some volunteers from the Thaqīf, the leading tribe of Ṭā'if, a sign that the conflict was beginning to take on a wider dimension. The army of about 3,000 camped on the outskirts of Medina, near the hill of Uḥud, where they could raid the crops of the townspeople but would not become involved in fighting among the palm groves or attacking the fortresses of the oasis where their superiority in cavalry would be useless; probably, their objective was to destroy Muḥammad's prestige and his offensive power rather than to conquer the city; if they defeated him in battle, the Medinese might no longer accept him as their leader. The arrival of the Meccans put Muḥammad in a quandary; if he failed to take action against them, they would destroy the crops, and the townspeople could well accuse him of failing to protect them. If, however, he went out to meet them, he was risking battle against a superior enemy on terrain of their choosing. In the end, he decided to do battle but many people in the oasis, including 'Abd Allāh b. Ubayy and a number of his followers, doubted the wisdom of the strategy and did not join in. In addition, the two main Jewish clans who remained stayed neutral; the strain of the Meccan attack showed how deep the rifts within the city still were and how Muḥammad was far from being accepted as the unquestioned leader. The fight (Shawwāl 3/March 625) was bitter and hard but the Meccan cavalry, under Khālid b. al-Walīd, later famous for his role in the Islamic conquests, drove the Medinese from the plain and forced them to take refuge among the lava flows, where the horses and camels were unable to penetrate. The Prophet himself was cut off with a small band of followers on the hill of Uḥud and was forced to defend himself vigorously, sustaining slight injuries; his uncle Ḥamza, one of the heroes of early Islamic tradition, was killed. At nightfall, the Meccans retired from the scene and made their way back to their home town, unwilling to press their victory. The scattered remains of the Muslim army made their way back to the oasis while a party set out as if in pursuit of the Meccans, although they were careful to keep their distance.

The indecisive result of the battle made the Prophet's position less secure than it had been at any time since Badr, and his enemies in Medina, especially 'Abd Allāh b. Ubayy and the Jews, were anxious to take advantage of this setback. However, the Meccans had failed to dislodge Muḥammad or secure the caravan route to the north, and both sides realized that there was more fighting to be done. Within Medina, the Prophet realized that he had to reassert his authority in a decisive manner; not to do so could see his position gradually eroded. Muḥammad felt that the main obstacle to his overall control lay in the Jews, who could not accept the religious message which was the basis of his position. As long as they remained, he could never be totally secure in Medina. The Qur'ān laid increasing stress on the differences between Muslim and Jew and accused the Jews of spurning their prophets and falsifying the Revelation. It was probably shortly after Uḥud that he decided to take positive action against the Banū'l-Naḍr, the most wealthy among the surviving Jewish clans. Claiming that they were plotting treachery against him, Muḥammad and his followers besieged the clan in its fortresses, while the allies they had relied on, Ibn Ubayy and the bedouin Ghaṭafān tribe, failed to make any move to help them. After a short time, terms were arranged, the Jews were to leave Medina with all they could carry except their arms, and 600 camels laden with goods set out for the oasis of Khaybar to the north, where there was a large Jewish population. The vacant lands were divided up, mostly among the *Muhājirūn*, many of whom, like Muḥammad himself, became landowners in the oasis for the first time. This show of strength also humiliated Ibn Ubayy, who had been unable to save his allies, and his attempt to exploit the setback at Uḥud to restore his position had failed.

Apart from Muḥammad's assertion of authority within Medina, the two years between the battle of Uḥud in March 625 and the siege of Medina in Dhū'l-Qa'da 5/March 627 were spent by both sides trying to win over the hearts and minds of the bedouin of the surrounding areas. Uḥud had shown that neither side was strong enough to eliminate the other entirely and that only with overwhelming nomad support could either side be victorious. The spring raiding season of 4/626 was spent by both sides in a show of strength at the annual fair held by the wells at Badr; armies from both sides put in an appearance, no doubt to convince the bedouin that they were still powerful, but they seem to have been careful not to come into conflict. Apart from this, both Muḥammad in Medina and Abū Sufyān in Mecca attempted, by alliances, raids and bribery, to find allies among the Ḥijāzī tribes. The dispute was no longer confined to the two cities and the settled populations but now embraced most of the nomads of western Arabia as well.

The results of these manoeuvres became apparent in the spring of 5/627. Abū Sufyān had by this time gathered an impressive coalition of some 10,000 men, from Quraysh itself and from the Sulaym and Ghaṭafān. As at Uḥud two years before, the attackers tried to assault the city from the north, the only side on which it was not protected by lava flows, those choppy seas of almost impenetrable black stone which are so common from Syria south to the Ḥijāz. This time, however, the battle was different; the coalition had arrived at Medina slightly later, the barley crop was already in and Muḥammad was not under pressure to risk taking the offensive. With only about 3,000 men under his command, he could not afford an open conflict, so he caused a trench, or *khandaq*, to be dug (the Persian word was used, perhaps suggesting that this was an un-Arab technique of warfare). The besiegers had no equipment or supplies for a siege; they had come for battle and for booty, not for a war of attrition. Insults were exchanged for about three weeks and there were some sporadic skirmishes, but there was no serious attempt to breach the trench which protected the city. The Meccans may well have hoped that dissident elements in Medina, notably the remaining Jewish tribe of Qurayz-a and perhaps Ibn Ubayy as well, would give them aid from within the city and attack the Muslims from behind. But nothing happened, and the vast force, unable to supply itself for long and unwilling to continue what was clearly a profitless campaign, simply melted away.

The failure of the Meccans at the *khandaq* was the last episode in the struggle that established Medina as an equal rival power to Mecca; neither side could win absolute victory, but both could make life intolerable for the other. But the *khandaq* marked an important stage in Muḥammad's battle for undisputed authority within the city as well. He had obviously been anxious at the prospect that the Jews would in fact cooperate with his external enemies and he was determined that such a weakness should not be allowed to continue. Besides, their continuing presence in the city where Muḥammad was regarded not just as a secular leader but also as a Prophet and the chosen spokesman of God was a continuing irritation. After the threat from outside had disappeared, the Muslims attacked the Jews, eventually forcing them into unconditional surrender. Muḥammad appointed a member of the Aws, the tribe to which they were traditionally allied, to be their judge, but the man he chose, Sa'd b. Mu'ādh, one of the earliest and most influential converts to Islam in the oasis, was no friend of theirs. He was already dying from wounds received at the *khandaq* but he ordered that all the male Jews should be executed, while the women and children were sold into slavery. When the sentence had been carried out, Muḥammad could consider himself undisputed master of Medina. Apart from a few individuals, the Jews had been expelled or killed. 'Abd Allāh b. Ubayy, the one man in the city who had by his personal status and charisma been a serious rival to the Prophet, was now powerless and ageing, and was finally reconciled a couple of years later. From now on, Muḥammad could negotiate with the Quraysh, confident that Medina and the Muslim *umma* there were entirely behind him.

The events of the *khandaq* had shown that neither the Muslims nor the Meccans were in a position to overcome their opponents by military force and that Muḥammad would not be removed by internal dissension in Medina. Furthermore, both sides had good reason to seek some sort of compromise. The Meccans were suffering serious trading losses; caravans were unable to get through and were having difficulty securing food supplies. Although Muḥammad was in a strong position, he realized that he too needed to reach an agreement. He was always far-sighted in practical matters and knew that the Islamic community would never reach its full potential without the energy and expertise of the Meccans. Without the talents of the Quraysh, Islam might be no more than a local Medinese cult. But despite these incentives, one major stumbling block remained: Muḥammad's claim that Allāh was the one and only God and that he, Muḥammad, was his Prophet; for many in Mecca, attached to the cults of their ancestors and remembering the modest beginnings of Islam and the contempt in which Muḥammad had been held by the Meccans, this was very difficult to swallow, while for Muḥammad this was the cornerstone of his position, an item of faith on which no compromise whatever was possible. These considerations meant that two more years of hostility, struggle and diplomacy were necessary before Muḥammad could again be accepted in his native city.

In the immediate aftermath of the *khandaq*, Muḥammad, free of the dangers of internal subversion and Meccan attack, began to spread his interests further afield. The main object of his policy was to bring the trade route to Syria under Medinese control, perhaps with the object of developing Medina as the centre of western Arabian trade. Muḥammad sent a messenger to arrange terms with a Byzantine official, probably the governor of Bostra, the normal market for Arabian goods in the north, and began to reach agreements with some of the tribes, mostly Christian, who controlled the southeastern marches of Syria. Some of the Judhām, a tribe which was to play an important role in southern Palestine for several centuries to come, were converted to Islam while ʿAbd al-Raḥmān b. ʿAwf, the Muslim merchant *par excellence*, led an expedition to the desert market centre of Dūmat al-Jandal, where the Christian ruler, from the tribe of Kalb, was prepared to make a treaty and marriage alliance. There is no evidence that at this stage Muḥammad was doing more than trying to reconstruct the Meccan trading commonwealth using Medina as a centre, but there were important differences; the Meccan commonwealth had worked on partnership and diplomacy, while Muḥammad's men were summoning the tribes not just to alliance but to Islam, which meant submission to the will of Allāh and, more immediately, the authority of his Prophet. While Muḥammad was engaged in these northern expeditions, he also took care to win over or at least secure the neutrality of the local Ḥijāzī tribes, especially those who had joined the Meccan alliance at the *khandaq*, but there was no attempt at this stage to launch an attack on the enemy city itself; Muḥammad was more keen to win over Mecca than to destroy it in bitterness and violence.

The next spring (6/628) Muḥammad decided to take the initiative and lead an expedition to Mecca. This was not to be a military attack but a peaceful pilgrimage to the Kaʿba. The Muslims had originally prayed in the direction of Jerusalem but during the break with the Jews, the direction of prayer (*qibla*) had been changed to Mecca. Furthermore, the status of the Kaʿba was assured in the Qurʾān, which explained how the shrine had been founded by Abraham and his son Ismāʿīl, the ancestor of the Arabs. True, it had been profaned in more recent times by the worship of idols, but it still remained the dwelling place of the "friend of God" Abraham and deserved the reverence of true believers. This being so, Muḥammad requested permission for himself and his followers to come and pay their respects, and a large party of about 1,500 set out, reached the outskirts of the Meccan *ḥaram* area and camped by the well at Ḥudaybiyya. Their arrival put the Meccans in a difficult position, and it seems to have exacerbated existing tensions within the city. To accede to Muḥammad's request would be an admission of weakness and an acceptance of his status, but to oppose him by force was probably beyond their military power. So a truce was worked out; there was to be peace between Muḥammad and the Meccans for the next ten years. The Muslims were not to enter Mecca that year for the pilgrimage, but the next year the Meccans were to abandon their city for three days, while the Muslims were permitted to visit the Ka'ba. No doubt, there were people in Mecca who felt that too much had been given away, and there were certainly Muslims who had hoped for an outright victory, the humiliation of the Quraysh and booty for all. But the Prophet's political instinct was sounder than theirs and he was well aware how valuable the Quraysh could be to him as supporters, not enemies.

In the aftermath of Ḥudaybiyya, Muḥammad continued his previous policies, continuing to make converts and allies among the local tribes but also continuing the northward expansion. The trade blockade against Mecca may have lifted and there is evidence that the Quraysh of Mecca tried to resume their commercial activities as before. Muḥammad, however, continued his policy of securing the routes to the north with vigour and determination. In order to secure the acquiescence of the Arab tribes, settled along the southeastern marches of the Byzantine Empire, he sent a large expedition of some 3,000 men in the autumn of 8/629 commanded by his adopted son Zayd b. Ḥāritha. According to the Muslim sources, they found that the Emperor Heraclius himself was campaigning in the area but most of the fighting seems to have been with the tribesmen of Judhām, Lakhm and Balī. The Muslims met the opposition near the village of Mu'ta on the edge of the cultivated lands east of the Dead Sea and were severely defeated. Zayd himself and the second in command, Ja'far b. Abī Ṭālib, brother of 'Alī, were both killed and it was left to Khālid b. al-Walīd, a recent defector from the Meccan camp, to lead the remains of the army back to Medina.

Despite this reverse, the pressure on the Meccans was growing and divisions began to appear in their ranks. When in the spring of 8/629 the Muslims performed the pilgrimage agreed on at Ḥudaybiyya, the Meccans abandoned their city for three days but refused his proffered reconciliation. Clearly, this was a position which could not last. Some leading citizens, like Abū Sufyān, favoured a compromise, attempting to enter into secret negotiations with the Prophet, while others, like the brilliant military leader Khālid b. al-Walīd and 'Amr b. al-'Āṣ, were actually converted to Islam and moved to Medina. There remained, however, a diehard party, mostly from the clan of Makhzūm, led by ṣafwān b. Umayya and Abū Jahl's son 'Ikrima, who were opposed to any concessions. But they could only postpone the inevitable; the next January (Ramaḍān 8), Muḥammad set out from Medina with 10,000 men, including allies from some of the local tribes. The Meccans do not seem to have known of the expedition until it was almost upon them and there were few who refused to accept his offers of security of life and property. The Muslim army divided and it entered the city from several different directions; only Khālid b. al-Walīd, commanding a group of bedouin allies, encountered any resistance, but this was crushed and the diehard leaders, Ṣafwān b. Umayya and ʿIkrima fled. The Prophet's attitude was conciliatory; the *ḥaram* was cleansed of idols but the Kaʿba remained, as it is today, the focus of Muslim worship and the Prophet demonstrated openly how important the Meccan shrine was to be. There were few killings and those in the Muslim army, like Saʿd b. ʿUbāda, the leading figure among the *Anṣār* after the death of Saʿd b. Muʿādh, who wanted a bloody war of conquest and pillage, were restrained. There were a small number of executions, not of leaders of the Quraysh but of men who had apostatized from Islam or singers who had mocked the Prophet. Even Ṣafwān and ʿIkrima soon returned from exile to be reconciled. It was a great triumph for Muḥammad; the Quraysh had been won over and even the most sceptical of them were to use their talents in the service of the new movement.

The importance of this was demonstrated very shortly afterwards. Muslim Mecca was threatened barely three weeks later by a great confederation of bedouin tribes called the Hawāzin, led by the Thaqīf, the ruling tribe of the nearby city of Ṭāʾif. The concentration of power in the hands of Muḥammad seriously threatened the position of Ṭāʾif, which had frequently been a rival to Mecca in the past. But Muḥammad and his followers were equal to the task, and the vast nomad army, said to have numbered 20,000, was decisively defeated at Ḥunayn. This victory was almost as important as the capture of Mecca. Not only did it confirm Muḥammad's prestige among a large group of tribesmen, among whom he had not hitherto had many contacts, but it also cemented his alliance with the Quraysh. Meccan leaders like Abū Sufyān could see how the new movement had enabled them to humiliate a traditional enemy whom their own forces had been unable to crush, and the Prophet went out of his way to be more than generous to the Meccan leadership when dividing the spoils.

The fall of Ṭāʾif followed soon after Ḥunayn. The idols of the town were destroyed and it lost its religious status. However, members of the ruling clans of the Thaqīf were incorporated into the *umma*. Here, they made use of their new opportunities, and the Thaqīf were to play a major role in the conquest and administration of Iraq. Once again, Muḥammad had secured the allegiance and services of an able and experienced group.

In this triumph, there was one group of Muslims who had some reason to feel uneasy about the way things had gone; these were the *Anṣār* of Medina. We have already seen how one of their leaders, Saʿd b. ʿUbāda, had wished to destroy Mecca. Was this new-found closeness between Muḥammad and his fellow-citizens and relatives to leave the Medinese out in the cold after all they had done for Islam? After the victory at Ḥunayn, Muḥammad had given most of the spoils to the Quraysh and the Meccans, and the *Anṣār*, led by Saʿd b. ʿUbāda, held a protest meeting, complaining that the Prophet was neglecting them, but they were mollified when he announced that he would continue to live in Medina and, but for the accident of birth, he would have considered himself a true Medinese in every way.

The last two years of his life, from the victory at Ḥunayn in Shawwāl 8/January 630 to his death in 11/632, Muḥammad devoted his energies to expanding his influence among the Arabs.

While Muḥammad devoted most of his military efforts to securing the control of the road to Syria, the Islamic community began to find friends and allies in other areas of the Arabian Peninsula. This was accomplished more by diplomatic means than by military expeditions, and often it was the other tribes which took the initiative, anxious to enter into friendly relations with so powerful an organization as the new *umma*. In the year 9/630, numerous tribes sent delegations (*wufūd*) to make terms with the Prophet. They came to acknowledge Muḥammad as the Prophet of Allāh and, in many but by no means all cases, agreed to pay the *ṣadaqa* or alms to Medina. In many cases, like the Tamīm in northeast Arabia, for example, these were tribes which had long enjoyed good relations with the Quraysh, some of whose members now saw the necessity of regularizing their position with Muḥammad. The collapse of Persian influence in the area also helped attract men to ally with the rising power in the Ḥijāz. Among the ʻAbd al-Qays in Baḥrayn, for example, it seems to have been the pro-Persian party which now appealed to Muḥammad for an alliance, while the Bakr b. Wā'il and Taghlib, along the frontiers of settled Iraq, negotiated a treaty, probably so that they and the Muslims could launch joint raids on the Persian territory. In Yamāma, the major tribe, the Banū Ḥanīfa, seems to have been split between the larger, settled group who supported Musaylima, the "local" prophet of the area, and a smaller nomad faction who joined the Muslims. Even in faraway ʻUmān, there was a faction in the leadership which was prepared to accept Islam and a Muslim finance officer, ʻAmr b. al-ʻĀṣ, in order to secure Muḥammad's alliance against their rivals.

Among the more settled peoples of south Arabia, the Muslim cause was spread by letters and messengers and, as in the east, tribal leaders and others came on delegations to the Prophet. In many cases, this was a result of struggles for leadership within a tribe, or the attempt of one tribe to gain advantage over another. Farwa b. Musayk al-Murādī, for example, came to visit the Prophet as his own tribe had recently been worsted in a tribal encounter. In return for his conversion, he was made the Prophet's governor over the neighbouring tribes of Zubayd and Madhḥij as well as his own Murād. Like the Azd of ʻUmān, he was assigned a Qurashī Muslim finance officer, Khālid b. Saʻīd b. al-ʻĀṣ, to manage the *ṣadaqa*. Also from south Arabia was a delegation of Kinda, led by al-Ashʻath b. Qays, with their makeup and their silken clothes, who were obliged to put away their finery on accepting Islam. In Yemen proper, the position was very complex, with the disintegration of Persian rule allowing native Arab leaders to assert themselves once more. Here, it seems that many of the local Persian *abnā'* (i.e. sons), that is, the descendants of the Persian settlers of the late sixth century, turned to

Islam to find support against the local Arab rebels, and their leader, Fayrūz al-Daylamī, was to play an important role on the Muslim side in the *Ridda* wars which followed the Prophet's death.

By the end of his life, the Prophet had secured a measure of acknowledgement in most of the Arabian Peninsula. Propaganda and diplomacy had played a much bigger part in this process than warfare, and Muḥammad had certainly used the diplomatic talents and experience of the Quraysh to good effect. But this does not mean that all Arabia was under the control of Muḥammad or that all its people had become Muslims. To begin with, Muḥammad had spread his influence in many cases by supporting one faction in a local dispute, and this inevitably made their opponents into enemies of Islam as well. Nor is it entirely clear how far the people of these areas acknowledged Muḥammad as the Prophet of Allāh. In the case of the Bakr b. Wā'il and Taghlib on the Persian frontier, for example, the tribes seem to have made an alliance with Medina while retaining their own, mostly Christian faith. In the early campaigns to Syria as well, it had been possible for tribes to remain Christian and yet be full allies of Muḥammad. Towards the end of his life, however, this became less possible, and Christians, like those of Najrān on the northern border of Yemen, were obliged to pay the *jizya* (in the earliest Islamic usage, *jizya* seems to have meant tribute in a general sense; by the third/ninth century, it referred specifically to the poll tax paid by non-Muslims) and so adopt an inferior but secure role in the new order of things. Paganism, however, was fiercely opposed. Jarīr b. 'Abd Allāh al-Bajalī, for example, came to the Prophet and accepted Islam and was sent off to destroy the idol, Dhu'l-Khalaṣa, which was worshipped by his own and neighbouring tribes; and there are other stories to show that Muḥammad deliberately tried to break down pagan taboos – about food, for example. Despite the efforts of messengers and letters, however, there must have been a vast number of people in eastern and southern Arabia whose knowledge of Islam was effectively nonexistent and whose commitment to the Muslim alliance was very tenuous – both of these were problems which became apparent as soon as Muḥammad died.

The last two years of the Prophet's life were spent in his adopted home of Medina. In the spring of 632, he announced his intention of making the pilgrimage to Mecca once again. This time, however, it would not be the *'umra*, the lesser pilgrimage which he had made the year after the agreement with the Quraysh at Ḥudaybiyya, but the great pilgrimage, or *ḥajj*. His behaviour on this *ḥajj*, known as the Farewell Pilgrimage, was to define the correct procedure for this important ritual. On his return to Medina, he set about preparations for another great Syrian expedition, led this time by Usāma, the young son of Zayd b. Hāritha, who had been killed by the Byzantines at Mu'ta. It was shortly before this expedition set out that Muḥammad became seriously ill, and he was soon too weak to lead the community in prayers, a responsibility he entrusted to Abū Bakr. On 13 Rabī' I/8 June 632, he died in the house of 'Ā'isha, Abū Bakr's daughter and perhaps his favourite wife. He was about sixty years old.

The Muslim community at the time of his death was an impressive and very personal achievement. In some ways, his career had been similar to the guardians who had established and built up *ḥarams* in other areas of Arabia. He himself came from the holy family of the *ḥaram* in Mecca and had established another *ḥaram*, at first in competition, later in alliance, at Medina and moved on to attract tribes which would attach themselves to the *ḥaram* and its ruling group. Muḥammad had also competed with and eventually incorporated the alliances which had formed part of the Meccan commercial commonwealth; especially after the taking of Mecca, many of the tribes which had had links with the Quraysh in pre-Islamic times shifted those ties to the newly emergent Muslim community and Muḥammad inherited and took over a network of contacts throughout Arabia and beyond. Equally, the Muslim *umma* had some of the features of a traditional tribe and has indeed been described as a "super-tribe"; it defended its members against outside attack, organized raids to supplement their incomes and provided a framework for the solving of internal disputes. The seeking of retaliation or blood money remained the responsibility of the individual, not of the state, but there was a strong emphasis on settling disputes within the community peacefully, accepting arbitration and compensation rather than demanding blood.

Having acknowledged the debt that Muḥammad owed to traditional forms, it must be said that the *umma* by the time of his death was a community which had no parallels in traditional Arabian society. The most important difference, of course, was Muḥammad's uncompromising monotheism and his own status as the Apostle of God. Previous temples and their holy families had had an authority limited to their own areas and accepted as natural that there should be others in different places. For Allāh and his Prophet, however, the whole world was their area and other deities had no place in it. It was this factor above all others which distinguished Muḥammad from other "prophets" who appeared in his wake, notably Musaylima among the Banū Ḥanīfa of Yamāma; for them, a fair division of influence was only reasonable; for Muḥammad, it was totally unacceptable. Pagans could not be treated as equals, since anyone who refused to accept the Revelation of Islam was thereby damned, but, however, no one was excluded for reasons of social status or tribal origin from joining the *umma* and they could do this as individuals. This universality of Islam marked a radical break with the pagan cults which had preceded it and accounts for much of the dynamism of the emerging community.

The question of whether Islam can be said to have been a distinct religion at this stage is very uncertain. The Muslim tradition is clear: this was indeed a new religion. You either accept the role of the Prophet as the Messenger of God and the Qur'an as God's word or you did not. This historical reality seems to have been more complex. To the outside world, the new movement was recognized as a heresy or a new variant within a monotheistic spectrum. In his book, *Muhammad and the Believers* (2010), Fred Donner made a powerful argument that Muhammad's movement attracts followers from across the monotheistic spectrum and it was only later that the "Muslims" established a distinct confessional identity.

In the same way, Muḥammad's authority within the *umma* was vastly greater than a traditional tribal leader's among his followers. Muḥammad was the one and only Prophet of Allāh; to disagree with him was to challenge God Himself. This is not to say that Muḥammad acted in a dictatorial or high-handed way. When he first arrived in Medina, he had needed all of his skills and diplomacy, and considerable determination, to establish his position as the undisputed secular leader as well as religious sage. The Muslims were careful to distinguish between the Revelation of the Qur'ān, which could not be questioned, and decisions on day-to-day matters on which the Apostle often consulted his closest followers and took their advice. But behind all his pronouncements was the knowledge that Muḥammad was the chosen of Allāh and that there would be divine punishment, horrible and unrelenting, for those who disobeyed his command, while those who followed his ways could be sure of everlasting bliss. His practices and decisions, known as the *Sunna*, were to be the future guidelines in the Muslim community. These considerations made Muḥammad as superior to a traditional tribal leader as the *umma* was to a traditional tribe.

The emergence of the *umma* meant the emergence of a new kind of élite. The traditional tribal criteria for choosing chiefs – membership in the ruling clan; skill at warfare, counsel and mediation; bravery and generosity – were only partly applicable to the *umma*. The Qur'ān (49: 13) says, "The noblest of you in the sight of Allāh is the best in conduct"; that is that religious excellence rather than wealth or breeding was going to decide membership in the new ruling class. In practice, since excellence of conduct is impossible for any man to judge, this meant that priority in Islam (*sābiqa*) and closeness to the Prophet were the most important signs of distinction. It was above all the *Muhājirūn*, who had endured the persecutions of the Meccans with the Prophet and then left home, clan and security to follow him, who had the highest status. With them were the first of the *Anṣār*, especially those who had fought at Badr when the *umma* was in its infancy. But few of the leaders of the *Anṣār* – Sa'd b. Mu'ādh perhaps, and his successor Sa'd b. Ubāda – attained the intimacy with the Prophet which was enjoyed by *Muhājir* leaders like Abū Bakr, 'Umar b. al-Khaṭṭāb, 'Uthmān b. 'Affān and 'Abd al-Raḥmān b. 'Awf, and none of the Prophet's wives, was chosen from among the women of his adopted hometown.

The takeover of Mecca added a new and very important element to the new élite, the Meccan leaders. The incorporation into the Muslim *umma* of the Quraysh and their rivals the Thaqīf of Ṭā'if meant that they brought all their expertise, experience and contacts to the service of the community, and these talents were to prove vital for the expansion and administration of the

Muslim territories. At the same time, their incorporation introduced new tensions, since noble families of Mecca – the Umayyads led by Abū Sufyān and his sons Yazīd and Muʿāwiya, for example – felt that they had natural rights to positions of leadership, while these claims were naturally resented by many among the *Anṣār* and *Muhājirūn* who had endured so much for Islam. The new leadership was also overwhelmingly urban in origin, and nomad tribal leaders enjoyed little prestige. Muḥammad and his advisers viewed the bedouin lifestyle with considerable suspicion; those who became Muslims were enjoined to abandon not only their old religion but also their nomad ways and to settle down in urban communities.

Despite the role played by the Meccans, it would be wrong to suggest that Muḥammad had simply restored the old Meccan trading commonwealth under new management. The old system had been a series of agreements among equals, whereas the expansion of Islam was to mean the imposition of the authority of the Muslim élite by force if necessary. The *umma* could not stand still, it had to expand or disintegrate. So long as there were Arabs who did not accept the authority of Muḥammad, the ideological position of Islam would be challenged. If raiding within the community was to be abolished, another outlet had to be found for the martial energies of the tribesmen and another source of revenue for the impoverished nomads. Muḥammad had understood this well, and his expeditions in the direction of Syria pointed the way. But Islam was to be the religion of all humanity, not just the Arabs, and there was no reason why the authority of the *umma* in Medina should be confined to the Arabic-speaking peoples; the Islamic conquests were a natural continuation of the Prophet's work.

Note

1 This history of the life of Muḥammad is essentially based on that offered by the Muslim sources. While these sources contain many confusions and contradictions, the broad outlines of the account they offer seem to me the most convincing description of the emergence of Islam. Despite this, details of names and dates should be treated as indicative rather than certain. Readers should be aware that some scholars take a much more sceptical view of these sources, seeing them as much later attempts to account for developments whose real nature had long since been forgotten or to provide exegesis of texts whose contexts were no longer known. For these views, see especially M. Cook and P. Crone, *Hagarism* and P. Crone, *Meccan Trade*. See also the discussion of the sources on pp. 298–304 of this volume.

3 Conquest and division in the time of the Rāshidūn caliphs

Abū Bakr and the *Ridda* wars: 11–13/632–634

The death of the Prophet on 13 Rabīʿ I, 11/8 June 632 meant that the Muslim community was faced with a number of problems which had not arisen during his lifetime. He had left no generally acknowledged successor and had made it clear that he was "the seal of the Prophets", the last and greatest, and there could be no question of anyone inheriting his role. The first question which confronted the Muslims, therefore, was one of leadership: Who should lead the *umma* and what status and power should such a leader have? Was he to be the first among equals, like a tribal chief, arbitrating and solving disputes, or was he to have a more real and effective power, even a measure of divine sanction for his decisions? Was he to be chosen by the community or to take power by some process of hereditary succession within the Prophet's clan? If the question of leadership was in doubt, so too was the question of deciding who were to form the élite in the new community, whether to choose those who demonstrated their piety and zeal for Islam from an early stage or those who had political experience and status before the coming of Islam. These questions were to become the major concerns of the Muslims in the years which followed Muḥammad's death, and the problems they caused, compounded and complicated by the conquests and settlements of the surrounding areas, were to prove extremely intractable. It was a very unusual situation in the history of human societies, since there were no precedents and no established and generally accepted ideas of authority and social structure which the community could use as reference points. The political and constitutional issues were entirely new and required new solutions. The experimental nature of early Islamic politics goes a long way to explaining the confusions and difficulties which occurred.

During the Prophet's lifetime, the tensions within the *umma* resulting from the incorporation of the Meccan oligarchy and had been kept under control, and the efforts to subdue and win over the rest of Arabia must have absorbed the energies of the whole community. After his death, however, the divisions came to the surface once more.

DOI: 10.4324/9780429348129-3

The *Anṣār* were concerned lest the *Muhājirūn* make common cause with their relatives from the Quraysh of Mecca and use their joint strength to control the *umma* and the city of Medina itself, leaving only a subservient role to the *Anṣār*. There was a clear injustice in this, since the *Anṣār* had welcomed both Muḥammad and his supporters at a time when his own people had rejected him; they had stayed with him through the days of adversity, and to be thrust aside in this time of prosperity was wholly wrong. In order to counter this threat, the *Anṣār* gathered as soon as Muḥammad's death became known, intent on electing one of their own members, if not as the sole leader of the *umma*, at least as an equal partner with a leader from the Quraysh. The *Anṣār* held a meeting in a hall in Medina, the *saqīfa* of the Banū Sā'ida, to decide on their course of action, but old divisions between the different clans meant that they had not reached a decision when events were taken out of their hands by the prompt action of the leaders of the *Muhājirūn*.

Within the Quraysh group of Meccans and *Muhājirūn*, there were also important differences, and once again the main problem was the integration of the Meccan leaders into the Islamic élite. Some members of the *Muhājirūn*, among whom 'Umar b. al-Khaṭṭāb was the most important, remained suspicious and hostile towards these new converts, while others, like Abū Bakr, were more prepared to accept them and put their talents to good use. In addition, there was the Prophet's cousin and son-in-law, 'Alī b. Abī Ṭālib, who had married Muḥammad's daughter Fāṭima. He was perhaps too young at this time to be generally accepted as a candidate for leadership, but he had known Muḥammad very well and had been brought up in his household. His two sons al-Ḥasan and al-Ḥusayn had been very dear to their grandfather. In the confusion immediately following the Prophet's death, 'Alī was occupied in washing the body and preparing it for burial and so played no part in the discussions, but he was soon to emerge as an important focus for political loyalties, especially among the *Anṣār*.

When Muḥammad's death became known, the Muslims were, in the words of a contemporary, "like sheep on a rainy night". While the *Anṣār* debated in the *saqīfa* of the Banū Sā'ida, 'Umar seized the initiative by swearing allegiance to Abū Bakr as a leader. Then, the triumvirate of *Muhājirūn* leaders, Abū Bakr, 'Umar and 'Abū 'Ubayda b. al-Jarrāḥ, went to the meeting place of the *Anṣār* and put an end to their deliberations, obliging them to acquiesce in their own choice. The next day, Abū Bakr was formally acknowledged as a leader, in the mosque before the whole community.[1] In the Muslim tradition, Abū Bakr was acknowledged as both Commander of the Faithful (*Amīr al-Mu'minīn*) and Caliph (*khalīfa*). Commander of the Faithful was the term by which the ruler was usually addressed and the term used in decrees and correspondence. It stresses the secular role of the ruler as a leader of the faithful (Muslim) people in warfare and administration. The term *khalifa* appears first in poetry in the writings of Ḥassān b Thābit (d 54/674.) and on a few coins. Even then, the exact significance of term is problematic. Crone and Hinds (*God's Caliph*) have shown that the title, which is first securely attested in the time of 'Uthmān, was *khalīfat Allāh*, the implication being that the early caliphs and their Umayyad successors were the deputies of God on earth and claimed some sort of divine sanction for their rule. By the third/tenth centuries, the title was usually taken to be *khalīfat rasūl Allah* the Successor the Messenger of God), pointing to a secular role with no divine approbation. Abū Bakr could not be a Prophet but at the same time it was unthinkable that he should take a secular title like king, which would deny the unique nature of the *umma* and imply a degree of power which he did not have. The title *khalīfa*, however, left many questions open and left scope for the office to develop. He was acknowledged by the taking of the *bay'a*, that is, an oath of allegiance by the members of the community, and the taking of the *bay'a*, not a coronation ceremony, was to formalize the accession of all succeeding caliphs. Abū Bakr was the first of the four caliphs (his successors being 'Umar, 'Uthmān and 'Alī) who led the community from 11 to 40 (632–661) and are often known as the Rāshidūn or "rightly guided" caliphs, to distinguish them from the Umayyads who followed them. During this period, the great Islamic conquests were begun and the outlines of the Muslim state were decided.

Abū Bakr was in many ways an ideal choice. Now an old man, he had been one of the first converts to Islam; it was with Abū Bakr as his sole companion that Muḥammad had made the perilous journey from Mecca to Medina at the time of the *Hijra*, and it had been Abū Bakr who led the prayers during the Prophet's last illness. He was also related to Muḥammad by marriage, since his daughter 'Ā'isha had married Muḥammad and become his most influential wife. It was not just his close connections with the founder of the *umma* which made Abū Bakr acceptable, however; he showed qualities which were to prove invaluable to the community in the difficult early years and were to have a profound effect on its development. He was gracious and diplomatic, with a vast knowledge of the tribes and tribal politics of the Arabian Peninsula, all perhaps a heritage of his Quraysh origin. But, like Muḥammad, he also had a very clear sense of what was really important; he might be polite in his dealings but he never compromised on essentials. It has been said of him that he became caliph because he was everybody's second choice; he was the most acceptable of the *Muhājirūn* to the *Anṣār* of Medina. 'Umar seems to have tried to secure the appointment of Abū 'Ubayda, a man whose views were closer to his own, but soon realized that he would not command sufficient support and turned to Abū Bakr. The Meccans also accepted his authority more readily than they would have 'Umar or one of the *Anṣār*. Nonetheless, hostility did remain and the *Anṣār* still felt that they had been cheated of their rightful status, while 'Alī was very reluctant to accept a coup d'état in which he had played no part.

Abū Bakr soon made it clear that he would continue in Muḥammad's tradition. He showed this immediately in the case of Usāma's expedition to Syria. Before his death, Muḥammad had arranged an expedition to Syria which was to be led by Usāma, son of his adopted son Zayd b. Ḥāritha, who had been killed by Byzantine troops in the area three years before. This expedition aroused some misgivings in Medina, especially among the *Anṣār*, because they felt that Usāma was not a fit person to lead it simply because he was his father's son, and perhaps because they did not wholeheartedly support the aim of invading Syria. Abū Bakr was determined that the expedition should go, partly because the Prophet had ordered it and to cancel it would lay him open to the charge of betraying Muḥammad's wishes, but partly too to stress his commitment to the same policy, the expansion of the Muslim state towards Syria. In the event, the raid was not a great success, but the whole episode had shown the new caliph's determination and sense of purpose.

His determination was certainly needed. The years preceding Muḥammad's death had seen the extension of some sort of Muslim authority over much of the Arabian Peninsula. The nature of this authority had varied greatly from one area to another. The Ḥijāz and its cities were firmly incorporated in the Muslim state, accepting Islam and paying the *ṣadaqa* tax. In the Najd and the areas of northeast Arabia, some tribes, like the Ghaṭafān, Asad and Ṭayy, had mostly agreed to pay the tax and accept Islam, while others, farther from Medina, like parts of Tamīm, paid taxes but were not converted to Islam. The Banū Ḥanīfa of Yamāma had allied with Medina but had never paid taxes or acknowledged the religious nature of Muḥammad's office; with his death, they united in opposition to Medinese control around their own Prophet, known to history as Musaylima. In Baḥrayn and 'Umān, the position was different again. Here, some local leaders had formed alliances with Muḥammad in order to secure their own position against their local enemies. In Baḥrayn, al-Mundhir b. Sāwā, the local king who had previously been the Persian agent in the area, now turned to the Muslims, and he may have agreed to send the taxes to Medina instead. In 'Umān, the sons of the Persian agent Julanda sought Muslim support against their local rivals and seem to have agreed that the *ṣadaqa* should be paid and distributed to the local poor. In south Arabia and Yemen, the situation was more complicated, some tribal leaders making alliances with the Muslims and others remaining hostile. In Yemen, it was the *abnā'*, the descendants of the Persian garrison, who sought support against their enemies.

The response to the Prophet's death depended on the local circumstances. The tribes of Najd tried to arrange a compromise whereby they remained Muslims but no longer had to pay the tax to Medina. The Tamīm were as divided as always, some supporting the prophetess Sajāh., while others continued to look to Medina. Musaylima and the Banū Ḥanīfa could simply feel relieved that their most powerful rival in the peninsula was no more. In Baḥrayn and 'Umān, the local supporters of the Medina alliance found their position seriously weakened; al-Mundhir b. Sāwā in Baḥrayn was killed, while the sons of Julanda in 'Umān were forced to flee to the hills by their rivals. Throughout south Arabia, those who had opposed the Muslim alliance took advantage of the situation, while those who had relied on it were temporarily forced onto the defensive – some, like al-Ash'ath b. Qays al-Kindī, even rejected their allegiance to Islam and joined the opposition. Except in the Ḥijāz and the cities of Mecca, Medina and Ṭā'if, the system of alliances and conversions which had been developed during the Prophet's last years disintegrated.

Attitudes in Medina to those developments seem to have been confused. It seems that the *Anṣār* and perhaps 'Umar and those among the *Muhājirūn* who shared his attitudes were unsure as to how far force should be used to restore the position. Abū Bakr, however, showed no such hesitation. The Prophet had punished those who broke their alliances with him and had forced them to surrender to his authority, and his successor was going to follow in the same tradition. In this view, he was supported by some *Muhājirūn* and by a number of Meccans. Perhaps to show their zeal for their new-found faith, or because of their wish to restore the Meccan trading commonwealth, new converts, especially from the influential clan of Makhzūm, provided much of Abū Bakr's support in the campaigns which followed. Among the Makhzūmīs were 'Ikrima b. Abī Jahl, son of that Abū Jahl who had led the opposition to Muḥammad in Mecca and who had died at the battle of Badr, and the man who was to prove the greatest of the early Islamic generals, Khālid b. al-Walīd.

Traditionally, these various upheavals were known as the *Ridda*. This word is usually translated as "apostasy" and implies that those who were involved had previously been Muslims but had rejected their new faith. As we have seen, this was not the case in many areas, and each part of Arabia had rather different problems and attitudes.

Abū Bakr faced these challenges with energy and determination. Almost as soon as Muḥammad was dead, the Najd tribes sent representatives to ask that, while remaining Muslims, they should not be obliged to pay taxes to Medina. While many among the *Anṣār* and the *Muhājirūn* were prepared to accept such terms, Abū Bakr was not and he at once collected an army and marched out to defeat a small section of the Ghaṭafān at Dhū'l-Qaṣṣa, the last time a caliph was to lead an army in person until the disturbances after the death of 'Uthmān, thirty years later. After this small victory, Abū Bakr entrusted the command of the Muslim army to Khālid b. al-Walīd, the Makhzūmī who had commanded the Meccan cavalry at the battle of Uḥud. While the nucleus of his forces was recruited in Medina, many Muslims distrusted Khālid; he faced continuous criticism from the *Anṣār* and, it would seem, from 'Umar. Nevertheless, Abū Bakr continued to support him and he won a series of brilliant victories. He turned his attention first to the Najd tribes. Here, after the breakdown of negotiations with Medina over the taxation issue, Ṭalḥa b. Khuwaylid al-Asadī, an experienced tribal chief, had put together a coalition of tribesmen from the Ṭayy, Ghaṭafān and Asad. Khālid succeeded in detaching some of the tribes of Ṭayy from the alliance and defeating the rest at Buzākha. Thereafter, his progress in northeast Arabia encountered little serious opposition, and it seems that he was able to recruit reinforcements for his small army among the Tamīm and other tribes of the area.

With this augmented force, Khālid moved on to attack the most serious problem the Muslims faced, the Banū Ḥanīfa, led by their Prophet Musaylima. Yamāma, where the tribe lived, was a settled agricultural area of palm trees and grain growing, an area which sometimes exported grain to the Ḥijāz. Until 630, it had been ruled by a Christian "king", Hawdha b. 'Alī, who had worked in alliance with the Persians. On his death, his place was taken by Musaylima, who proclaimed himself a Prophet for the Yamāma and Ḥanīfa as Muḥammad had for the Ḥijāz and its people. Unlike Muḥammad, however, Musaylima does not seem to have aspired to more than local power and was able to suggest that the peninsula be divided into two different spheres of influence. In the face of Khālid's advance, the Ḥanīfa were, in the main, united and determined to fight, both for their Prophet and for their local independence. In a hard-fought battle at 'Aqrabā' (11–12), Khālid defeated the Ḥanafīs with a great slaughter; while Musaylima was killed in the fighting, the survivors of the defeated army agreed to accept the control of Medina.

Compared with the battles fought by Khālid, the campaigns in the rest of Arabia were on a smaller scale. In Baḥrayn, al-'Alā' b. al-Ḥaḍramī, who had been Muḥammad's agent in the area, was able to reestablish the Medina alliance after some hard fighting. In other areas, the Muslim armies were independent of Khālid's. 'Ikrima b. Abī Jahl had been Muḥammad's agent with the Hawāzin tribes, traditionally closely attached to Mecca. When 'Ikrima was instructed to reassert the Muslim presence in 'Umān, he did so with an army largely raised from among the Hawāzin themselves. In the same way, the army which Muhā-jir b. Abī Umayya led to Yemen was recruited, not in Medina but in Mecca and among the Bajīla tribes and the people of Najrān en route. Muslim authority was soon reestablished among the divided peoples of Yemen, and the tribes of the area were encouraged to participate in the campaigns being launched from Medina towards Syria. In south Arabia, taxation seems to have been the main source of discontent, and a rebellion among the Kinda was rejoined, against his better judgement, by al-Ash'ath b. Qays. After the defeat of this rebellion by Muhājir b. Abī Umayya, al-Ash'ath was sent to Medina, where, in honour of his status as a great chief, he married Abū Bakr's sister and, despite his role as an "apostate", was integrated into the Muslim élite.

The Muslim success in Arabia can be ascribed to a number of factors. The most important of these was the continuing loyalty of the people of the Ḥijāz, city-dwellers and nomads alike, to the *umma*. While some may have disagreed with the policies of Abū Bakr and Khālid, there was no significant *Ridda*. The *Ridda* wars were in fact the conquest of Arabia by the urban people of the Ḥijāz, the Quraysh and the Thaqīf, and their allies. While the Ḥijāzīs were united, their opponents were not. Tribal divisions and feuds meant that in every area, even among the Ḥanīfa of Yamāma, there were factions who were eager to make alliances with the Muslims to secure their local position. Not only did the Muslims have powerful forces, they also had the powerful ideological backing of the new religion. Of their opponents, only the Ḥanīfa seem to have had a religious objection to the acceptance of Islam; elsewhere, the objections were based on attachment to old traditions, local independence and, above all, the reluctance to pay taxes to Medina. There were substantial Christian populations, not only among the settled folk of Najrān but among the nomad Tamīm and in Baḥrayn and other coastal areas in the east, but the Christians never made any effort to unite against Islam at this stage. Also important were the consequences of the breakdown of the Persian Empire; in Baḥrayn, 'Umān and Yemen, Muslim power was based on those who had previously looked to the Persian kings and their Lakhmid vassals for leadership and support. With the collapse of the Persian Empire under the assaults of Heraclius, these groups looked for new allies and naturally found them in the expanding and dynamic *umma*. In addition to all these factors, many men joined the Muslim community because of the opportunities it was seen to provide. The *Ridda* wars were the first stage of the Arab conquests, and the expeditions to Syria took place at the same time as the campaigns in the Arabian Peninsula. They provided an opportunity for those who wished to abandon the old bedouin life and seek new and exciting destinies within the Islamic community, and many left their tribal homelands to join up.

'Umar and the early Islamic conquests: 13–23/634–644

On 22 Jumādā II 3/23 August 634, Abū Bakr died. His reign had been short but his achievement was enormous. He had maintained the traditions of the Prophet and had set the Muslim community on the road to expansion; he had seen the conquest of Arabia almost completed and the conquest of Syria begun. Despite the differences between them, he had maintained 'Umar as one of his closest advisers, and there seems to have been little complaint when he designated 'Umar as his successor. 'Umar appears in Muslim tradition as the epitome of the stern, uncompromising, incorruptible ruler. He is famous for his personal austerity and the high standards he expected from those entrusted with office. But, like Abū Bakr before him, he was a man of very considerable practical ability. Not only did he direct the Islamic conquests, but he also developed the system of settlement and in particular the *dīwān* system with its arrangements for paying pensions to the conquerors rather than distributing lands among them, a system which was to have far-reaching results for the political future of the Islamic world. But the most famous achievement of his reign was, of course, the great conquests in Iraq, Iran, Syria and Egypt which transformed the ancient world.

In terms of the internal politics of the Muslim community, 'Umar showed a marked preference for appointing long-established members of the

Muhājirūn to the most important posts; his colleague Abū 'Ubayda, for example, was sent to take over command in Syria, while another early Meccan Muslim, Sa'd b. Abī Waqqāṣ, was sent to perform the same task in Iraq, and al-Zubayr b. al-'Awwām was sent to help the recently converted 'Amr b. al-'Āṣ in Egypt. The *Anṣār* were given few important posts, while among the newly converted Meccans, 'Umar favoured the Umayyad family, Yazīd and Mu'āwiya, sons of Abū Sufyān. The Makhzūmīs whom Abū Bakr had promoted, Khālid b. al-Walīd and 'Ikrima b. Abī Jahl, were by contrast reduced in power and status.

'Umar's domestic policy meant that great prestige was accorded to those with *sābiqa* (precedence in Islam), that is to say that the highest posts were to be entrusted to those who had become Muslims the earliest. This did not mean that people who showed great valour or commitment could not rise above their allotted position on occasion, but in general, long devotion to the cause was regarded as the main qualification for membership in the élite. By contrast, tribal origin and membership of *ashrāf* families was not to be considered important. One result of this was that the early Islamic leadership was drawn almost entirely from the settled people of the Ḥijāz and above all from the Quraysh of Mecca and the Thaqīf of Ṭā'if, with the *Anṣār* a poor third. It also meant that some people who had enjoyed great power and influence before the coming of Islam, such as al-Ash'ath b. Qays al-Kindī and Ṭalḥa b. Khuwaylid al-Asadī, found their position much reduced and their ancient glory considerably diminished. Not surprisingly, they bitterly resented this change of fortune, and in this they were joined by many of their fellow tribesmen, who preferred to look for leadership from their traditional chiefs than from the new Muslim élite, with whom they had little in common. They were not only resentful, but powerful – a combination which was to prove dangerous in the long run.

Muḥammad had made Syria his most important objective, and it was natural that the early caliphs should consider expanding the Muslim world in that direction. There was no break with the Prophet's policy or with the *Ridda* campaigns and no sharp dividing line between Syria and Arabia. The object of the *Ridda* campaigns was to ensure that all Arab tribesmen accepted the authority of Medina and the Muslim leadership and this applied as much to the bedouin of the Syrian Desert and the lands along the Euphrates as it did to those in 'Umān or Baḥrayn.

The expeditions against Syria were organized in Medina. It is sometimes imagined that the Arab conquests of these areas were an unplanned migration of vast numbers of ill-disciplined tribesmen. Examination of the sources, however, reveals a very different picture. The armies were assembled and the leaders appointed – always from leading groups in the Ḥijāz – by the caliph, who decided who should be despatched to which front. Men tended to join not in tribes, but in fairly small groups or as individuals, and the different armies always contained men from different tribes. Nor were the numbers vast; there were probably only about 24,000 men involved in the conquest of Syria and considerably fewer in Iraq, and there is no evidence that they took their families or their herds with them. These first expeditions were not migrations of barbarian tribes driven by pressure of population or moved by religious enthusiasm to invade neighbouring territories; they were organized military expeditions led by an élite anxious to enforce and maintain its authority over the bedouin. After the success of the conquests, there were further waves of immigration, and it was then that families and dependents would have arrived.

There is also a widespread view among non-Muslims that "Islam was spread by the sword", the implication being that it was violence or the treat of violence that ensured the success of the new religion. However, it is important to bear in mind the difference between conquest and conversion. The early Muslim conquests were certainly achieved by violence – armies were defeated and many men were killed. This conquest was essentially a political act which established Muslim rule over non-Muslims. It was also, in historical terms, a very swift process, most of the central Middle East, including Egypt and Iran, being conquered less than twenty years after the Prophet's death. Conversion of the majority of the subject populations to Islam, however, was a much slower process: although figures are very speculative, it was probably four centuries before a bare majority of the population of the area were converted to the new religion. It was also a largely peaceful and attractive change because people, whether for religious or social and economic reasons or both, elected to adopt Islam, and Muslim political hegemony certainly produced a favourable environment for this. So perhaps we can conclude that Islam was not spread by the sword, but without the sword, Islam would not have spread, or at least not in the way it did.

Apart from the Prophet's example, the reasons for the conquests are fairly clear. It was intolerable that there should be Arab tribes which did not accept the authority of Medina; from there, it was easy to argue that the same applied to the Arab inhabitants of settled centres such as Ḥīra and Damascus. At the same time, such conquests were vital for maintaining the hold of the leadership over the bedouin. As has already been pointed out, raiding and warfare were essential for the economic survival of the tribesmen. The establishment of a *pax Islamica* in Arabia meant that such opportunities were no longer available; one Muslim tribe should not raid another. Only by directing the energies of the tribesmen against an outside enemy could the unity of the Muslim state be preserved. The *ghazw* had been an essential part of Arab life in the *Jāhiliyya* (the times before Islam) – now, under Islam, all the Muslims were to cooperate in launching raids against their opponents. In addition, the launching of the conquests gave the Muslim leadership great powers of patronage; only those who were Muslims could participate in the conquests and share the rewards, which were to be determined by the Medina government. Many a tribesman must have felt that joining the armies of Islam was a way to an earthly, as well as a heavenly, paradise. The conquests were, in short, a necessary consequence of the unification of Arabia under Muḥammad and Abū Bakr; without this external opportunity, the hold of Medina over the Arab tribes would inevitably have disintegrated; "expand and survive" was the political philosophy.

The Arab conquests in Syria and Iraq pose the historian an unusual problem. The Arab literary sources which describe them are very full, with a great deal of anecdotal and circumstantial details about battles and the heroes who participated in them. They are, however, hopelessly confused about the chronology and order of the main events. What has come down to us are several apparently authoritative accounts which seem to be incompatible with each other; no amount of comparison and emendation can persuade them to agree on more than a general outline. It would not be helpful, however, to accept one outline, for arbitrary reasons, and claim that all the others were false. No annals were written in the years immediately after the events; details were preserved by oral tradition, just as details of the *ayyām* (lit: "days", i.e. battles) of the Arabs had been preserved in pre-Islamic tradition. By then, they had not been preserved as a year-by-year historical narrative but rather as unconnected vignettes, short stories to illustrate the heroic deeds of an ancestor or fellow-tribesman in the great days. When Muslim annalists, like Ibn Isḥāq and al-Wāqidī, came to use this material more than a century later in the early 'Abbasid period, they, like the modern historian, wanted to put these details into a logical order. They knew the names of the battles and sieges, and the names of many individual participants with records of their doings and they tried to construct a framework which would provide an outline chronology. Like modern historians too, they reached a number of different conclusions. The inevitable result is that none of the outlines can be accepted without hesitation; the details might be more reliable than the general picture.

The conquest of Syria seems to have taken place in three distinct phases. Before the *Ridda* campaigns had ended, Abū Bakr had despatched four armies, each with its own leader. Abū 'Ubayda, Yazīd b. Abī Sufyān and Shuraḥbīl b. Ḥasana all went to the area east of the Jordan, while 'Amr b. al-'Āṣ, who had traded with Gaza before the coming of Islam, was sent to the southern borders of Palestine. Each of these armies was probably fairly small, about 7,000, but smaller still in the case of 'Amr's, and composed mostly of the settled people of the Ḥijāz but also of Najdīs and Yamanīs as they became available. The object at this stage seems to have been to subdue the Arab tribes of the Syrian borderlands like the Judhām and Lakhm rather than to conquer the entire province. These preliminary campaigns occurred during Abū Bakr's reign, and before his death the caliph ordered that Khālid b. al-Walīd should join the forces in Syria. After the defeat of Musaylima, Khālid had gone to the lower Euphrates area, where he offered support to local tribal leaders against the Persian garrisons of the riverain cities. Abū Bakr, however, clearly saw Syria as the more important front, and Khālid, with a fairly small force, crossed the desert, perhaps in spring 13/634, to join the armies in Syria. This great march, which has excited the admiration of many subsequent writers, was made either through the oasis of Dūmat al-Jandal in the south or via Palmyra in the north and it is typical of the sources that we have fairly detailed accounts which completely contradict each other. We can, however, be certain that Khālid was transferred from one front to the other, and this illustrates again how firm a hold the caliph kept on the conduct of operations.

The arrival of Khālid must have coincided more or less with the death of Abū Bakr, and Khālid was replaced as the commander-in-chief by 'Umar's ally Abū 'Ubayda. Between 13 and 16 (634–637), there occurred three battles of which we have fairly detailed descriptions: Ajnādayn, probably in southern Palestine, Fiḥl (Pella) in the Jordan valley and the greatest of them on the Yarmūk river to the south of Damascus. There were also a number of sieges of towns, although it would seem that Damascus, Caesarea and Tripoli were the only centres to put up prolonged resistance. What order these events happened in is not at all clear, but it seems that the battle on the Yarmūk was the last decisive confrontation. What we can be sure of is that by the year 16/637, the power of the Byzantine army in Syria was broken and the country lay open to the Muslim armies. In the nature of the sources, we also have a good deal of information about the numbers and composition of the armies, especially on the Yarmūk. The Byzantine force was probably larger than that of the Arabs and besides a contingent of Armenians, it also contained a large number of Arabs from the tribes of the Syrian borderlands, the Lakhm, Ghassān and Judhām, which had been traditionally allied to the Byzantines; it is possible that there were as many Arabs fighting for the Byzantines as there were fighting for Islam. The Muslim army consisted of large numbers of Qurashīs, volunteers from Yamāma tribes who had been sent up after the end of the *Ridda* in their homeland, and some members of tribes from the northern Ḥijāz who had presumably joined up en route. Conspicuous by their absence were the *Anṣār* of Medina and members of the Najdī and eastern Arabian tribes. The makeup of the conquering army was to have lasting effects on the political life of the country.

After the defeat on the Yarmūk and the final fall of Damascus, which must have occurred by 16/637, the Byzantines put no more armies into the field. Abū 'Ubayda as the supreme commander moved north to Homs, from where he sent out Khālid to reduce Qinnasrīn, Antioch and Aleppo, all of which fell without difficulty. Meanwhile, 'Amr seems to have finished operations in southern Palestine. It was at this stage too that the Emperor Heraclius, who had directed campaigns without being present in person at any of the battles, finally abandoned Syria, laid waste the frontier lands of Cilicia and retreated to the fastnesses of Anatolia. A few coastal cities, notably Caesarea in the south and Tripoli farther north, resisted for a few more years with the aid of naval support from Byzantium.

The fall of Jerusalem was probably the immediate cause of 'Umar's visit in about 17/638, since it was said that the Patriarch Sophronius would surrender to only the caliph. It was the only time he left Medina to visit the scene of the conquests he had done so much to organize, and his ragged and austere appearance made a great impression. Jerusalem was much revered by the Muslims and it was only appropriate that the caliph should come in person to take possession, but there were other, more worldly matters which demanded his attention as well. At about this time, the plague, which had been endemic in Syria since the middle of the sixth century, struck at the nomad conquerors, and many perished, including the leading Muslim generals Yazīd b. Abī Sufyān and Shuraḥbīl b. Ḥasana. A new governor was found in the person of Yazīd's brother, Mu'āwiya b. Abī Sufyān. His family had owned estates in the Balqā' in Transjordan in pre-Islamic times, and he now supervised the settlement and organization of the province. 'Umar attempted to establish a Muslim garrison town at Jābiya, the old Ghassanid centre south of Damascus, where the Muslims were to live separate from the local population, as they did in Kūfa and Baṣra in Iraq. In Syria, however, this scheme soon broke down, perhaps because many of the existing inhabitants of the area were Arabic-speaking, and Damascus, rather than Jābiya, became the Muslim capital. The rest of the province was divided into *junds* in which divisions of the conquering army were settled. These were Homs, where most of the settlers were Yamanīs under the leadership of al-Simt. b. al-Aswad al-Kindī, Damascus, Urdunn (or Jordan) based on Tiberias, and Palestine. Arabs, both native Syrians and conquerors, were settled in the coastal and frontier areas to defend them against Byzantine attack. This dispersal of the Muslims, under the control of Mu'āwiya, avoided many of the tensions which emerged in the Iraqi cities of Kūfa and Baṣra. The settlers in Syria were a fairly close-knit group from the élite in Islamic society, and Mu'āwiya was in a position to control any further immigration into the province. Some problems still remained, notably the tensions between old-established Arab tribes like the Judhām and Kalb and newly arrived settlers – but in general, under the presiding genius of Mu'āwiya, Syria remained calm and organized throughout the period of the first four caliphs.

To the north and east of Syria, across the Euphrates river, lay the Jazīra, the "island" between the Tigris and Euphrates rivers. It was natural that Abū 'Ubayda turned his attention in this direction when the conquest of Syria had been completed. He appointed a Qurashī, 'Iyād. b. Ghanm, a member of his own clan of Fihr, as the leader of the expedition. 'Iyād. had been involved in the conquests from the beginning when he had accompanied Khālid b. al-Walīd on his early Iraqi campaigns – he had fought at the battle of the Yarmūk, and there are reports that Abū 'Ubayda wished 'Iyād. to succeed him as the governor of Syria but that he was overruled by 'Umar, who chose Yazīd b. Abī Sufyān and his brother Mu'āwiya instead. As might be expected, there was an important Qurashī element in the small (5,000 men) force, and the rest of the troops seem to have been drawn from the *Anṣār* or from Ḥijāzī tribes like the 'Abs and Sulaym, whose members were to be influential in Armenia for centuries to come. The campaign involved no important battles and no long sieges, as the defenders seemed to feel that there was no possibility of support from Byzantium. ʿIyāḍ's force crossed the Euphrates in Shaʿbān 18/August 639 and made a show of force outside Raqqa (Callinicum), which soon surrendered. He then went on to the capital, Edessa, once Heraclius' headquarters, where the bishop negotiated terms after a short resistance. With the fall of Edessa, most of the other towns soon surrendered, and ʿIyād. even went as far as the territory of Akhlāṭ, north of Lake Van, before returning to the plains. His subordinates fanned out across the Jazīra, subduing the other towns until he joined up with Muslim forces operating from Iraq. Sinjār and Niṣībīn were conquered from the Jazīra, while Mosul remained in the Iraqi sphere of influence. By 20/641, he was back in Homs, of which he had been appointed the governor and where he died later in the same year. In the Jazīra, he was eventually succeeded by ʿUmayr b. Saʿd, one of the very few *Anṣār* to achieve high office, and in 25/645–646 ʿUthmān incorporated the province into Muʿāwiya's Syrian domains.

The settlement of the province was different from Syria, Iraq or Egypt in that there was no attempt to establish Muslim garrison towns like Kūfa, Jābiya or Fusṭāṭ. Although the details are very uncertain, it seems as if ʿIyād. had made a series of treaties with the leaders of the urban communities which guaranteed their property and freedom of worship in exchange for a tax called *jizya* (which later meant poll tax but probably referred to general taxes on property and individuals at this early stage), while payments in kind for the support of the Muslims were taken from rural areas. In a few districts where there was more prolonged resistance – Sumaysāṭ, for example – ʿIyād. left an agent with a few men, but in the main tax collection was left to the local people. A peculiar problem was caused by the Banū Taghlib, Christian Arabs who inhabited the middle Euphrates area. They stubbornly refused to accept Islam but demanded to be taxed as bedouin, that is, to pay the *ṣadaqa* demanded of other tribes but not the demeaning poll tax. ʿUmayr b. Saʿd, who was the governor by this time, consulted ʿUmar, who was in favour of strong measures until it was pointed out that they might defect to the Byzantines, and in the end a compromise was reached with the Taghlib paying the *ṣadaqa* but at double the rate demanded of Muslim tribes. When ʿUthmān entrusted the area to Muʿāwiya, he ordered him to settle more tribesmen in the Jazīra to relieve pressure in the towns of Kūfa and Baṣra, and quite large numbers of Tamīm, Asad, Qays and other tribes from the northeast of Arabia were moved and were to form the nucleus of the Qays party in the area in Umayyad times. In the end, the province was divided into districts named after the tribal groups who had dominated it: Diyār (country of) Muḍar, Rabīʿa and Bakr. In contrast to Iraq, this moving of tribes did not involve their abandonment of the nomad way of life, and they were assigned areas of unused land away from existing urban and agricultural communities. The Arab immigration does not seem to have swamped the local culture (as it came to do in Iraq), and Syriac Christianity, to say nothing of the paganism of the Sabaeans of Ḥarrān, continued to flourish throughout the early Islamic period. Mu'āwiya also stabilized the northern frontier, establishing garrisons on the upper Euphrates, notably at Malaṭya (Melitene), which became an important Muslim base in the wars against the Byzantines.

Contemporary with the conquest of the Jazīra was the extension of the Arab conquests to the west, to Egypt. The sources for the conquest of Egypt are more helpful than those for Syria or Iraq; we have an early and full Arab account in the work of Ibn 'Abd al-Ḥakam and an almost contemporary Coptic account in the work of John, bishop of Nikiou. The conquest of Egypt was also unusual in that it was to a large extent the achievement of one commander, 'Amr b. al-'Āṣ. Arabs from the Ḥijāz had traded with Egypt before the coming of Islam; there are reports that 'Amr b. al-'Āṣ was among them, and his military campaigns certainly show a degree of familiarity with the country. When 'Umar came to Jābiya to settle the affairs of Syria, 'Amr asked him for permission to lead an invasion of Egypt. 'Umar seems to have given only grudging and reluctant consent, and the army which accompanied 'Amr was only some 4,000 in number, recruited among the tribe of 'Akk from the southern Ḥijāz. No leading companions or important Meccans chose to accompany him.

In Egypt as in Syria, the Persian invasions had severely shaken the Byzantine hold on the country, and the invaders had been in control for about ten years when they were finally forced to withdraw to defend their homelands in 627, when Muḥammad was already well established at Medina. In 631, Heraclius entrusted the administration of Egypt, both civil and religious, to one Cyrus, bishop of Phasis in the Caucasus. Cyrus, now a patriarch of Alexandria, was determined to enforce the Orthodox faith among the native population of Egypt, who were almost entirely Monophysites of the Coptic Church. For ten years, he persecuted dissenters with great savagery, and there can be no doubt that he alienated much of the local population from Roman rule. To some extent, this had happened in Syria, where there were substantial Monophysite communities, but there the persecution was sporadic and the Monophysites were balanced by substantial Melkite (i.e. Orthodox) populations, especially in Palestine. In Egypt, almost the entire rural population was Monophysite in sympathy, with its own alternative hierarchy, and the persecution was more determined and sustained.

How far 'Amr was aware of these factors is impossible to gauge. There is no evidence that the Copts invited the Arabs to invade or that they gave them active help. However, they offered the imperial armies no support or local levies, and this passive attitude of the local people may explain something of the ease of the conquests.

'Amr's small troop probably entered Egypt in the late autumn of 18/639 and soon took Faramā (Pelusium), the first port on the Nile delta, before moving on to attack the great fortress known as Babylon, just to the south of the site where Cairo was later constructed. 'Amr was clearly anxious not to advance straight across the waterways of the delta to the capital at

Alexandria and reckoned rightly that if he could destroy the bulk of the Byzantine army before entering the delta, his task would be much easier. During this time, 'Amr's small forces were joined by a larger number, perhaps 12,000, under al-Zubayr b. al-'Awwām and other senior companions of the Prophet; it is noteworthy, however, that 'Amr retained command. With these new troops, he was able to defeat the Byzantine forces at Heliopolis, to the north of modern Cairo, in Rajab 19/June 640 and in September began the siege of Babylon. The siege lasted some seven months, while Cyrus, probably in Alexandria, made futile attempts to negotiate with the invaders. The news of the death of Heraclius, in February 641, finally persuaded the defenders to surrender on terms, which they finally did in Rabī' II 20/April 641. The Arab forces then advanced on Alexandria, defeating the Byzantines again at Nikiou en route. Alexandria, well fortified and easily supplied from the sea, should have been able to hold out for many months but in the event, confusion amounting almost to civil war in Byzantium and in the local garrison paralysed the resistance, and Cyrus made terms for the surrender of the city. After an eleven-month period of grace, it was finally surrendered in Shawwāl 21/September 642 and the Arabs were in control of the whole country. Despite a Greek counterattack three years later in 25/645, the Muslim hold on Egypt was never seriously threatened again until the time of the Crusades.

Settlement followed conquest. A new town was established for the Muslims at Fusṭāṭ, by Babylon, and this, rather than Alexandria, became the new capital; as usual, the Arabs chose a site on the edge of the settled lands in easy communication with Arabia. Outside Fusṭāṭ, Arab settlement was very limited; there was a small garrison in Alexandria and some other towns, but no large-scale immigration followed the conquest. The administration of the Byzantines was taken over and streamlined, but many of the old methods and officials continued to be used at a local level, while Arabic language documents were issued by the governors from the first year after the conquest. The Coptic hierarchy, relieved from persecution, was allowed the same rights as the Melkites. The Arabs remained a small minority, the spread of Islam and the Arabic language was slow and the province played a very limited role in the politics of the early Islamic state.

The conquest of Iraq, an area which was to play a vital and central role in the formation of the Islamic state, began as a sideshow, almost by accident. As with the conquest of Syria, exact chronology is difficult to ascertain but here at least, the general outline of events is clear. Iraq had always had a secondary place in the calculations of the Quraysh, and the Prophet had sent no expeditions there. The Sawād of Iraq was certainly wealthy but its canals and agricultural landscape were much less attractive for nomads than Syria or the Jazīra, with their rich grazing grounds. The first attacks on Iraq were a natural follow-up to the *Ridda* campaigns, and it was partly as a result of this that the participants in the conquest were in marked contrast to those in Syria. The Quraysh were hardly represented at all, whereas there was a considerable number of *Anṣār* from Medina and Thaqafīs from Ṭā'if. In addition to these settled people, there were many tribesmen from the neighbouring areas of northeast Arabia, Tamīmīs and members of the Bakr b. Wā'il confederation, especially the Shaybān, and there were also some from the southern Ḥijāz, Azdīs and Bajalīs under the command of their tribal leader, Jarīr b. 'Abd Allāh. In the course of the conquest, reinforcements were needed and it was in these campaigns that tribesmen who had joined the *Ridda* against the Muslim community after Muḥammad's death were allowed to participate and establish their position in the Islamic system. The conquest of Iraq, in short, was largely carried out by those who were already second-class citizens in the new regime, while the élite turned their attention to Syria.

The Arab incursions in Iraq had begun before the arrival of any Muslim army. From the dissolution of the Lakhmid kingdom of Ḥīra by the Persian authorities in 602, the nomads had been taking an increasingly aggressive stance towards the settled people. This process was hastened by the catastrophes which affected the Persian Empire, Heraclius' invasion of Iraq, the death of Khusrau II in 628 and the consequent civil war. Raids which might otherwise have led to reprisals were now allowed to go unpunished. Among the Arab leaders was Muthannā b. Ḥāritha from the Shaybān tribe, who enlisted the help of Khālid b. al-Walīd, who had just finished his campaigns against the *Ridda* in northeast Arabia, to give him support in his raids.

In this way, Muslim armies first came into conflict with the Persians. Khālid helped Muthannā to capture some districts along the edge of the desert, notably the largely Arab city of Ḥīra, but Syria remained the priority and Khālid was ordered west, leaving the local tribes to continue their forays on their own. On his accession in 13/634, 'Umar sent a Thaqafī, Abū 'Ubayd, to take control of this activity with a small army of about 5,000, mostly *Anṣār* of Medina with some recruits picked up from the desert tribes on the way. This army was decisively defeated by the Persians at the Battle of the Bridge and Abū 'Ubayd himself was killed. 'Umar could not allow such a defeat to go unavenged, but for a year or two, the shortage of manpower meant that there was little he could do about it. As contingents became available, he sent them to the front, notably the 1,500 Bajalīs under Jarīr b. 'Abd Allāh, but eventually he was forced to relax the principle that men who had joined the *Ridda* could not share in the conquests and for the first time men like Ṭalḥa b. Khuwaylid al-Asadī from the Najd and al-Ash'ath b. Qays al-Kindī from south Arabia, both tribal chiefs who only two or three years before had been in arms against the Muslims, were allowed to participate. These reinforcements were put under the command of a Qurashī of impeccable Muslim credentials, Sa'd b. Abī Waqqāṣ, who had been with the Prophet at Badr and who proved an acceptable leader for this disparate army. Even compared with the forces which conquered Syria, the army Sa'd led was small, probably no more than 12,000 men. Against him, the Persians assembled a much larger number under the veteran general Rustam. The battle which followed at Qādisiyya was decisive, the Persian host was totally defeated and very shortly afterwards the Persian capital at Madā'in (Ctesiphon) was occupied by Sa'd and his victorious army (probably 16/637). A further victory at Jalūlā' a few months later, forced the Persian king Yazdgird III to withdraw to the Iṣfahān area and secured the position of the Muslims, small groups of whom now moved to take control of the towns and villages of Iraq as far north as Mosul.

Southern Iraq and the neighbouring province of Khūzistān were taken in a separate campaign by a separate army. The Muslim force seems to have been small, about 4,000, and there was some fierce fighting around the port of Ubulla and the town of Sūq al-Ahwāz, but there was no single decisive battle like Qādisiyya. On this front, the core of the army seems to have been recruited among the Thaqīf of Ṭā'if. The first commander sent by 'Umar, 'Utba b. Ghazwān, had married into the Thaqīf, while his successor, al-Mughīra b. Shu'ba, was the first of many Thaqafī governors who were to be influential in Iraq. After al-Mughīra was dismissed by 'Umar in 17/638 for alleged adultery, he was replaced by Abū Mūsā al-Ash'arī, a companion of the Prophet who was to prove an important moderating influence in the politics of Iraq.

By the year 17/638, the Muslim armies had taken control of almost all of the plains of the Tigris and Euphrates valleys. The Persian king, his court and much of the ruling class had fled to the Iranian plateau, but many of the peasants and the small landowners and administrators known as *dihqāns* had remained on the land. At first, Sa'd's men stayed in the Persian capital at Madā'in and some of them seem to have been given land. The Caliph 'Umar, however, soon reversed this policy and ordered Sa'd and al-Mughīra b. Shu'ba in the south to found garrison towns where the Muslims could be settled, just as he had ordered 'Amr not to settle in Alexandria but to develop a new town at Fusṭāṭ. Two settlements were founded, both on the edge of the desert. The veterans of the central Iraq campaign were established at Kūfa, near the old centre of Ḥīra, while those of the southern campaign were settled at Baṣra. A mosque and governor's palace were established in each town to act as a focus, and the troops were settled in tribal groups so that they could be more easily administered and controlled through their leaders. 'Umar's decision was partly made on military grounds; if the Muslims were dispersed throughout the area of the Sawād, they would be vulnerable to outside attack, whereas kept together they would be in a much stronger position to defend their gains. The threat of a Persian counterattack was very real. Isolation in Muslim communities would help to prevent the newly converted Muslims from being affected by local beliefs. Settlement in cities was also intended to solve the problem of governing the nomad tribesmen. If they were left to their traditional way of life, the fragile unity which had been encouraged by Islam and enforced by the campaigns against the *Ridda* would soon be lost and the desert would become as ungovernable as it had been in pre-Islamic times. Only if the tribesmen were settled and involved in further campaigns of conquest could they be controlled.

If the Muslims were not to remain nomads, they were not to become farmers either. The land was to remain in the hands of the previous owners, if they had not fled at the time of the conquest, and they were to pay taxes to the Muslims as they had previously paid to the Sasanian government, basically a land tax (*kharāj*) based on the area and type of crops cultivated and, for non-Muslims, a poll tax (*jizya*) on each adult male, although the terminology used to describe these taxes remained fluid until the ʿAbbasid period. Lands which had been abandoned by the Sasanian royal family, the upper aristocracy and the Zoroastrian priesthood were to become the common property of the Muslim community, but the administration of the lands, known in Arabic as the *ṣawāfī*, was to be a subject of controversy for years to come. The government would then distribute this money to the Muslim settlers in the form of salaries known as *ʿaṭā*'. ʿUmar laid down the principles according to which *ʿaṭā* was to be distributed in a system known as the *dīwān*. The *dīwān* recorded the names of all those entitled to salaries and the rates at which they were to be paid, for not all Muslims were to enjoy the same pay. The different scales were paid according to the individual's *sābiqa*, that is to say his precedence in Islam. We can see this process most clearly in Iraq, where the earliest participants in the war against the Persians were to be paid at the rate of 3,000 silver *dirhams* per month, while those who arrived later would be paid proportionally less, down to those who had only migrated to Baṣra or Kūfa after the conquests, who could not expect more than 200 *dirhams*. This naturally resulted in social tensions and anomalies; a new privileged class was created among those who enjoyed the highest salaries, and it was quite possible for one man to be getting ten times the amount given to his neighbour, even if they came from the same tribe and background, simply because he had joined the armies of Islam five years before. This could be particularly galling if the late arrival belonged to a family which, in the tribal scale of values, had enjoyed high prestige, and it was no wonder that ʿUmar's system was defended with enthusiasm by those who had come early but caused strong resentment among many latecomers.

The rule of the various provinces was entrusted to leaders called *amīrs*, a term which can be loosely translated as governors. In ʿUmar's reign, these were almost always those who had led the original conquest and had naturally stayed on to organize administration and settlement; Saʿd b. Abī Waqqāṣ remained the governor of Kūfa; Abū Mūsā al-Ashʿarī, who had completed the conquest of southern Iraq, stayed in Baṣra. In Syria, the position was complicated by the deaths of both Abū ʿUbayda and Yazīd b. Abī Sufyān in the plague, but succession passed naturally to Yazīd's brother Muʿāwiya, while in Egypt ʿAmr b. al-ʿĀṣ retained control of the land he had so recently won. These *amīrs* tended to be fairly independent of the government in Medina and responsive to the needs of the men they had led to victory. In particular, despite some pressure from ʿUmar, they seem to have retained most of the revenues of their provinces for the benefit of the Muslims who had settled there, rather than sending any surplus to Medina, and this fiscal autonomy was to prove a source of conflict later.

'Uthmān and the beginnings of internal strife: 23–35/644–656

In 23/644, 'Umar was assassinated by a Persian slave in Medina; there seems to have been no political motivation behind this deed. His ten years as caliph had seen the expansion of the Muslim conquests throughout Egypt and the Fertile Crescent and the beginning of the attacks into Iran. Just as significant, it had seen the development of many important Muslim institutions, the system of taxation, the *dīwān*, the urban settlements and the development of a privileged group of those who received the highest *'aṭā'*. Though he gave orders and guidance to his *amīrs*, there was little in the way of central government or direct control from Medina, where the caliph lived in pious simplicity, avoiding both the power and the pomp of Byzantine emperor or Sasanian king.

On his deathbed, 'Umar had appointed a *shūrā*, or committee, to choose a successor. This had six members, all of them *Muhājirūn* from the Quraysh, and neither the *Anṣār* of Medina nor more recent converts were represented. Two possible candidates emerged, 'Alī b. Abī Ṭālib, the Prophet's cousin and son-in-law, and 'Uthmān b. 'Affān, who came from the Meccan clan of Umayya but had supported the Prophet from the very beginning of his mission. The election was a question of both personalities and policies. It seems that 'Alī was offered the leadership if he would guarantee to continue the policies of his predecessors, by which was meant the continued predominance of the Quraysh in the leadership of the Muslim community. He refused, perhaps because he realized that the continued grip of the Meccan aristocracy was dividing the *umma* and he wished to have the power to open the leadership to other groups as well, especially the *Anṣār*, with whom he had forged close links. For 'Uthmān, however, the conditions posed no problems; despite his early adherence to Islam, 'Uthmān had retained his links with his clan and benefited from the experience in practical affairs which his upbringing as a Meccan merchant had given him. He became caliph with a definite political programme, to ensure that the Muslim empire, for such it now was, remained under the control of the Quraysh, a policy the origins of which went back to the practice of the Prophet himself. In some ways, he reacted against 'Umar's attempts to build a new Islamic élite based on *sābiqa*, and turned back to the well-tried methods of clan government. He believed in the centralization of power; governors were to be chosen and dismissed by the caliph and both political and the all-important financial affairs of the provinces were to be decided not by local leaders, but in Medina. He also set about producing a single, definitive version of the Qur'ān. Muslim society was to be ordered according to the provisions of the Holy Book, and it was essential, therefore, that the text be generally agreed upon and that variant readings did not develop in different areas. In practice, the differences do not seem to have been very significant, but the fact that the caliph decided that he should organize this process was an important sign of his authority over the whole community. His programme was a bold attempt to create a viable administrative system for the new empire, but it naturally aroused opposition from many who regarded it as a breach with 'Umar's policies and a betrayal of the principles of Islam. The opposition crystallized around two issues: the declining status of the Islamic élite of early converts, especially in Kūfa, and the question of whether or not surplus revenue from the provinces (that is, the residue after the local *'aṭā'* had been paid) should be forwarded to Medina – and it was a combination of these two grievances which led to the disasters of the end of the reign.

He also saw that the expansion of the Muslim state had to continue if the needs of all the members of the *umma* were to be satisfied. In the west, there were expeditions to Nubia and North Africa as well as the development of Muslim naval power in the Mediterranean under the control of the governors of Syria and Egypt. Cyprus was forced to pay tribute, and in 34/655 the Muslims won a decisive naval victory over the Byzantines at the Battle of the Masts off the Lycian coast. In the east, 'Uthmān's reign saw the effective conquest of the Iranian plateau. This movement had begun under 'Umar in 21/642 when the Iranians had tried to mount a counterattack on the Arabs to regain Iraq. This counterattack was met and defeated at the battle of Nihāvand in the Zagros Mountains. This battle meant the destruction of a large part of the Iranian army and laid much of western Iran open to Arab raids; during the next two years, troops from Kūfa took Iṣfahān, Hamadhān, Qazvīn and Rayy and even ventured as far as distant Ardabīl in Āzarbayjān, but permanent settlement was only gradually undertaken. It is interesting to note that some latecomers to Iraq participated in these conquests and were able to improve their status, and we find tribal chiefs like Jarīr b. 'Abd Allāh al-Bajalī and al-Ash'ath b. Qays al-Kindī powerful in the newly won territories; neither of these developments was likely to please the earlycomers in Kūfa. As before, separate expeditions were mounted from Baṣra under the leadership of Abū Mūsā al-Ash'arī and from 24/645 these forces were engaged in a long, hard struggle to take Fārs, the heartland of the Sasanian monarchy. The area was defended by many castles and fortified towns, and it took five years to subdue it; nowhere else did the Arabs encounter such sustained popular resistance by the local inhabitants.

In the year 30/650, the Arabs began a new series of expeditions in Iran. From Kūfa, the governor, Sa'īd b. al-'Āṣ, led his men along the north of the Iranian plateau, where they attempted to conquer the mountain peoples of that area, but the expedition achieved little before it returned to base, thus aggravating the increasing tensions within the city. The Baṣran forces, however, marched along the southern fringes of the Iranian desert, pursuing the Sasanian king Yazdgird III as he fled eastwards trying to rally support.

Detachments were left to make terms for the submission of Kirmān and Sīstān, while, in 31/651 'Abd Allāh, b. 'ūmir, the newly appointed governor, reached Nīshāpūr, capital of the rich, northeastern Iranian province of Khurāsān. Here, he and his men spent the winter and secured the submission of most of the local princes, who agreed to pay tribute. The Muslims then returned to Baṣra leaving a small detachment at Marv. This was not a conquest in the sense that the taking of Syria or Iraq was; it was rather a raiding expedition which secured the payment of large annual tributes. The army of Baṣra was to collect this money, but it was not to settle in the area nor was it to set up a new administrative system. The local princes and magnates were to collect the taxes in the way that they had always done and were content to accept a Muslim rule that was certainly no more onerous than that of the Persian kings and which could provide protection for the settled people of the area against the marauding Turks to the northeast.

In much of Khurāsān, and in the mountains to the south of the Caspian in the areas known to the Arabs as Ṭabaristān and Daylam, the indigenous aristocracy retained its power and influence by treaties with the Arabs. This was in marked contrast to western Iran, to Fārs especially, where the prolonged fighting and the defeat of subsequent rebellions led to the virtual extermination of the ancient aristocracy. It is worth noting too that the Arab conquests mostly affected urban areas and the plains. Arab armies avoided the mountainous areas where traditional rulers, social structures, religions and languages survived almost unchallenged. This contrast was to have profound effects on both the political history of the area and the cultural life, since it was precisely in those areas where the local aristocracy remained that Persian culture survived most vigorously. For the moment, however, it is enough to note that before 'Uthmān's death, all Sasanian Iran was subdued, either by conquest or by treaty, but that Arab settlement in the areas was very limited indeed. Nor was the conquest totally secure; in western Iran, there were rebellions after the death of both 'Uthmān and 'Alī, while in Khurāsān the presence of the Turks along the eastern frontier meant that conditions were often unsettled.

Arab tradition divides 'Uthmān's reign into six good years at the beginning and six bad, the traditional turning-point being his loss of the Prophet's signet ring. In about the year 30/650–651, the problems began to increase; 'Uthmān tried to deal with them intelligently but he totally underestimated the strength of feeling and his attempts to cope with the discontent simply made the position worse. By the year 35/656, the position was so bad that rebellions in the provinces and disturbances in Medina itself led to the caliph's murder under dramatic circumstances. He was killed in his own house, defenceless and unarmed as he sat reading the Qur'ān. The assassination was one of the most traumatic incidents in early Islamic history and its effects were to have a profound bearing on the future development of the Islamic state. It is important, therefore, to examine the causes of this tragedy in detail and to ask the question, who killed 'Uthmān and why?

There were three main regions of discontent, Kūfa, Egypt and Medina. Because of the way the sources were compiled, we know more about the Kūfan events than those elsewhere, and it is there that we must start. In ʿUmar's time, Kūfa had been dominated by the earlycomers, those who had participated in the first campaigns. In many cases, these were not men who came from powerful tribes, and they had arrived as individuals or in small groups – but as a reward for their commitment to the Muslim cause, they had acquired wealth and status. This wealth was based partly on their entitlement to the highest salaries but also their control over the *ṣawāfī*, the state lands of the Sasanian kings, now ownerless and exploited by these earlycomers for their own benefit. The loose financial administration of ʿUmar's reign did not impinge significantly on this comfortable arrangement, and there is no evidence that any of the revenues of this vastly rich area found their way to Medina. Under ʿUthmān, this status began to be challenged from two directions. The first was from Medina. ʿUthmān's reign saw the appointment of a succession of Qurashī governors to Kūfa, culminating in Saʿīd b. al-ʿĀṣ, who were profoundly unsympathetic to the efforts of these people to maintain their privileged position. On instructions from the caliph, he began to demand that surplus revenue from the province be sent to Medina and to claim that the *ṣawāfī* belonged to the government, which could exploit them directly or give them to its supporters. The treasurer of the Sawād, ʿAbd Allāh b. Masʿūd, an earlycomer, resigned in protest at this appropriation of the revenues by the caliph but the policy went ahead nonetheless. The caliph added insult to injury by his brutal treatment of those who protested – Ibn Masʿūd, for example, was beaten up in the mosque at Medina despite his status as a respected companion of the Prophet.

The threat from Medina was reinforced by one from much nearer home. Immigration from the Arabian Peninsula into the settlements at Kūfa and Baṣra continued for some years after the initial foundation of the towns. Many of the later arrivals and their tribal leaders resented the privileged position the earlycomers had acquired and began to put pressure on the governors to abolish the distinctions. Tribal leaders were given key governorates in the newly conquered lands east of the Zagros, including the *Ridda* leader al-Ashʿath b. Qays in Āzarbayjān, and the latecomers looked to them for leadership. ʿUthmān also decided to allow al-Ashʿath, among others, to exchange lands in distant south Arabia for territories in the Sawād. As a result, the earlycomers began to organize in opposition to government policy. They took the name of *qurrāʾ*, which probably means 'Qur'ān readers', drew attention to their Islamic status and found a leader and spokesman in the person of Mālik al-Ashtar. The crisis came to a head in 34/655, when the *qurrāʾ*, about 3,000-strong, refused to allow the governor, Saʿīd b. al-ʿĀṣ, to return to the province after he had been conferring with ʿUthmān in Medina and chose instead Abū Mūsā al-Ashʿarī. Abū Mūsā had been one of the administrators the Prophet himself had sent to Yemen twenty-five years previously, who had played an important part in the conquest and settlement of Iraq. His Islamic credentials were impeccable and while not himself a member of the *qurrā'*, he was sympathetic to their plight. Having replaced the hated governor, the militants, led by Mālik, then marched to confront the caliph in his capital.

The other province where discontent led to rebellion was Egypt. Here, the sources are not so abundant, but as far as we can tell, the problems seem to have been similar. Egypt had been settled by two waves of colonists, those who had formed part of the original, small expeditionary force under 'Amr in 19/640 and larger numbers of later arrivals. As in Kūfa, many of the first wave of colonists arrived in small splinter groups and had little status in the old tribal system but did lay claim to Islamic status. In 'Umar's reign, the governorate of Egypt was held by the conqueror 'Amr. It seems that he looked after the interests of his original followers, but it is not at all clear that he forwarded any of the revenues of Egypt to Medina. 'Uthmān deposed 'Amr almost immediately after his accession, and his new man, Ibn Abī Sarḥ, was determined to reduce the privileges of the early arrivals and secure the surplus for Medina. Once again, there were local tribal leaders who were prepared to cooperate with the caliph, notably the south Arabian Mu'āwiya b. Ḥudayj al-Kindī, whose family were to be prominent in Egypt for the next two centuries and who played a role very similar to that of al-Ash'ath in Kūfa. As in Kūfa, then, there was a small but determined minority who felt their position under attack from the policies of the government. It was these "Egyptians", probably no more than 400–600, who began the violence. They marched to Medina, where they presented their grievances; 'Uthmān persuaded them to go home with fair words but sent a message to Ibn Abī Sarh. ordering that they be harshly treated. Inevitably, the message was discovered and, full of righteous indignation, they returned to Medina, accusing the caliph of betraying the Qur'ān and Sunna, of despising those who had been among the Prophet's companions and those with *sābiqa* in favour of his own family, and of tyrannical government. It was in this highly charged atmosphere that the violent siege of 'Uthmān's house began.

The old man could count on little support in Medina itself. Many of the Islamic élite there had become increasingly critical of his policies, alienated by his methods and reliance not on the Quraysh as a whole but on the Umayyad clan. Before his death in 32/652–653, 'Abd al-Raḥmān b. 'Awf, a prominent companion of the Prophet and one of the *shūrā* who had chosen 'Uthmān, began to attack him. Ṭalḥa b. 'Ubayd Allāh and al-Zubayr b. al-'Awwām, both important Qurashīs, were hostile, while others, like Sa'd b. Abī Waqqāṣ, the conqueror of Iraq, and 'Umar's son 'Abd Allāh remained neutral. Nor were the *Anṣār* any more helpful. 'Uthmān had come to rely increasingly on the talents of two of his Umayyad cousins, the brothers al-Ḥārith and Marwān b. al-Ḥakam, the latter subsequently to be caliph himself, and when he appointed Ḥārith to take charge of the market, the *Anṣār* felt that they had lost control, not just in the empire as a whole, but even in their own town. Such frustrations and bitterness meant that few in Medina were prepared to take any action to help the caliph in his time of need. 'Uthmān was killed because he was determined to assert the control of the traditional Quraysh élite over the Islamic state, even if this meant trampling on the rights and privileges of many early Muslims. He saw the need for central control, he saw that the Umayyad clan had the experience and ability to undertake it but he failed to make allowances for the interests of others who had different but equally strong claims to enjoy the fruits of the conquests.

The caliphate of 'Alī: 35–40/656–661

In the aftermath of 'Uthmān's death, 'Alī b. Abī Ṭālib was acknowledged as caliph in Medina without significant opposition, but the inheritance was poisoned by the memory of his predecessor's death, although he himself had taken no part in 'Uthmān's murder. From the moment of his accession, 'Alī had to face opposition from within the Muslim community from many different areas and shades of opinion. He had no honeymoon period, no breathing space in which to establish himself, and the problems came thick and fast.

The first challenge to 'Alī's authority came from within the Quraysh itself. His close identification with the *Anṣār* and his reluctance to accept the nomination of Abū Bakr had alienated him from many of the Quraysh, who now felt that they had to challenge him to preserve the position their tribe had won. The movement centred around al-Zubayr b. al-'Awwām, Ṭalḥa b. 'Ubayd Allāh and the Prophet's widow 'Ā'isha. Al-Zubayr was a Muslim of unimpeachable standing; he had been among those who took refuge in Ethiopia before the *Hijra* and he and 'Alī had been sent out as scouts before the battle of Badr. Now, a quarter of a century after the Prophet's death, there were few men left alive who had been so closely involved in the origins of Islam. In addition, he had married a daughter of Abū Bakr, which gave him a close kinship with 'Ā'isha, herself a daughter of the first caliph. Ṭalḥa was also an early Qurashī convert, although not as prominent as al-Zubayr. Both had been members of the *shūrā* which had chosen 'Uthmān. While they had not supported 'Uthmān's policies of concentrating power in the hands of the Umayyad clan, they did not wish to see power pass from the Quraysh as a whole and were determined to take action. They left the Ḥijāz to seek support in Baṣra, perhaps hoping that the Thaqīf interest which was prominent there would rally to their old allies in the Quraysh. 'Alī was compelled to follow them to Iraq; to have remained in Medina would have been courting the same fate as 'Uthmān, and he sought support in Kūfa. Al-Zubayr and his party seem to have misjudged the situation badly; they attracted only a modest following from Baṣra, while 'Alī was able to attract much larger numbers of Kūfans to his cause. The two armies met near Baṣra in a confrontation known to tradition as the Battle of the Camel, Jumādā II 36/December 656. The battle was easily won by 'Alī's more numerous army, al-Zubayr and Ṭalḥa were killed and 'Ā'isha forced into retirement. But for the first time there had been civil war among the Muslims, the gate of *fitna*, a strife, had been opened and, like Pandora's box, once opened it was impossible to close.

In order to defend his position against al-Zubayr and Ṭalḥa, 'Alī had sought support in Kūfa, whose people had no wish to see a Qurashī regime of the sort that al-Zubayr had stood for. He now set to work to remove 'Uthmān's appointees from positions of power to reward his supporters for their services.

His authority was accepted in Baṣra and his governor of Egypt, who was Qays, son of that Sa'd b. 'Ubāda who had emerged as the leader of the *Anṣār* in the last year of the Prophet's life, was able to establish himself. In Syria, however, the story was different. The governor, Mu'āwiya, was a member of the Umayyad clan and unlike 'Uthmān's other governors, who had been removed without great difficulty, he had a strong local power base in the country he had ruled without interruption almost since the conquest. He had built up a military following among the Arab population to defend the country against the real possibility of Byzantine attack, and he was not a man to be dismissed with ease or to stand by and see 'Uthmān's work undone. Furthermore, he had a moral claim against the murderers of the caliph; as the nearest surviving relative of the dead man, he had a right, even a duty, to seek vengeance for the wrong done to his clan. Historians have tended to treat this claim as a feeble pretext for his actions, but this does not perhaps do justice to Mu'āwiya's position – not to have taken revenge would have proclaimed the impotence of the Umayyad clan for all to see, and when 'Uthmān's widow sent him the dead man's bloodstained shirt, he could not afford not to take action. The heart of the problem was that in Kūfa, 'Alī was dependent for support on men who had been closely implicated in 'Uthmān's death, especially Mālik al-Ashtar, who, although he had not personally attacked the old man, had led the Kūfan delegation to Medina. Mu'āwiya absolutely refused to acknowledge 'Alī as caliph until he had punished his predecessor's murderers.

'Alī's move from Medina to Iraq had been forced upon him by the need to oppose al-Zubayr. Medina was not a place from which to conduct a military campaign; not only was it remote from the main centres of Arab population in Iraq and Syria, it was also dependent on grain shipments from Egypt, which made it particularly vulnerable. So 'Alī moved to Kūfa and became embroiled in its tortuous politics. As far as we know, he had never visited Iraq before, nor had the Iraqis particularly looked to him for leadership in 'Uthmān's reign. He may have reached an understanding with Mālik al-Ashtar at the time of 'Uthmān's death, but Mālik was representative of only a small part of Kūfan opinion. From the beginning of his stay in the city, 'Alī was forced to try to assemble a coalition strong enough to coerce Mu'āwiya into accepting his authority. The problem was to persuade the Kūfans that it was in their interests to march on Syria.

Kūfan politics had become polarized between the early Islamic élite of the *qurrā'* and the tribal leaders (*ashrāf*) supported by their followers, many of them late, and therefore underprivileged, convert to Islam. 'Alī's policy was a bold attempt to cut across these problems by stressing the importance of the equality of believers and the importance of the religious role of the caliph or *imām* (spiritual leader); the ruler was not to be a tyrannical tax gatherer and guardian of existing vested interests but a charismatic figure who would inspire and guide the believers in the formation of a truly Islamic community. This concern for Islamic government and for the problems of underprivileged Muslims was to be the hallmark of the appeal of 'Alī and his descendants throughout the early Islamic period. The immediate response was varied. 'Alī was joined by about 10,000 men, many of them early settlers who looked to him to right the injustices which had been done to them. 'Alī was probably helped in establishing his control in that the most prominent tribal leaders, al-Ash'ath b. Qays and Jarīr b. 'Abd Allāh, were serving in Iran at that time and did not return to Kūfa until after he had been generally acknowledged. Mālik al-Ashtar was the most determined and militant of 'Alī's followers and probably persuaded many of the *qurrā* to throw in their lot with him. He was also vigorously opposed to Mu'āwiya, who had expelled him from Syria a few years previously as a troublemaker.

In the year 37 (spring and summer 657), 'Alī led his forces, now swollen by the arrival of al-Ash'ath b. Qays and other tribal leaders, up the Euphrates, where they came into confrontation with Mu'āwiya's Syrian followers at Ṣiffīn, near Raqqa. There was a marked reluctance to do battle, and for three months the armies confronted each other with little more than occasional skirmishes. It was not at this stage a struggle for the caliphate, since Mu'āwiya had made no claims to this office; he wanted the punishment of the murderers of 'Uthmān and the acceptance of his right to continue as the governor of Syria. 'Alī for his part wanted his opponent to acknowledge his authority by taking the *bay'a* or oath of allegiance, while he was quite unable to punish all those implicated in the murder of 'Uthmān, since these included Mālik al-Ashtar, now his right-hand man in Kūfa, and others of his supporters. There also developed a strong regional aspect to the conflict. The Arabic sources often describe it as a conflict between the *ahl* ('people', but in this case the Arab fighters) of Iraq and the *ahl* of Syria, and tribes were often divided, with members of the Syrian branch fighting their Iraqi fellow-tribesmen. In Ṣafar 37/July–August 657, a real battle developed but was rapidly brought to a halt when the Syrians held up leaves from the Qur'ān and appealed for arbitration. Despite al-Ashtar's determination to continue to fight, there was a strong feeling on the Iraqi side against shedding Muslim blood and the battle was halted. There were many reasons for the Iraqis to offer peace, despite what seems to have been a military advantage. Al-Ash'ath b. Qays warned that the enemies of Islam would take advantage of the dispute; Mu'āwiya had not as yet secured a truce with the Byzantines, while al-Ash'ath, having been until recently in Iran himself, knew that the country was far from pacified. He also had no wish to see ʿAlī's power increased, since the caliph relied so heavily on the *qurrā* and the rivalry was given a personal edge when ʿAlī patronized a rival leader, Ḥujr b. ʿAdī, within al-Ashʿath's own tribe of Kinda. If the tribal leaders were reluctant to go all the way with ʿAlī, so were many of the *qurrā*'; after all, the Syrians were simply fighting for the sort of political and financial autonomy that the Iraqis had struggled for during the reign of ʿUthmān, and they too might have wanted a compromise which left the caliph with very restricted powers of interference.

In this way, ʿAlī was obliged to agree to arbitration, not about who should be caliph, but rather over the issues which divided him and Muʿāwiya. However, the arbitration agreement, of which the text survives, did not acknowledge his title of *amīr al-mu'minīn*, simply giving his personal name, as it gave Muʿāwiya's. Two arbitrators were then named; Muʿāwiya chose ʿAmr, the conqueror of Egypt, who was his chief adviser at this time, while the Iraqis chose Abū Mūsā al-Ashʿarī. This was another blow to ʿAlī's position, since Abū Mūsā was not especially attached to his cause but was rather the spokesman for Kūfan and other Iraqi interests. And so it was agreed that the arbitrators should meet in a year's time, probably on neutral ground at Adhruh. on the borders between Syria and the Ḥijāz.

The arbitration agreement fatally weakened Alī's position. He had been forced to deal with Muʿāwiya on equal terms and abandoned his unchallenged right to lead the community. With this advantage gone, many began to have doubts about his leadership, and the hastily assembled coalition began to disintegrate. Tribal leaders listened with interest to Muʿāwiya, who offered to guarantee their status in return for support, which many of them secretly gave him.

At the other side of the political spectrum, ʿAlī was rejected by some elements of the *qurrā*', who felt that he had forfeited his rights to their support by agreeing to the arbitration. On his return to Iraq, they split off from his army and went to Nahrawān in the heart of the Sawād. ʿAlī was able to persuade some of them to return, and the rest were attacked and defeated, but the survivors fled to continue the struggle elsewhere. Probably because they had gone out (Arabic *kharaja*) from ʿAlī's army, they were known as Khawārij (sing. Khārijī) and their influence on Islamic thought and politics was out of all proportion to their small numbers. In the beginning, they objected to ʿAlī because he had agreed to arbitration, while they held that God was the only true arbitrator and that ʿAlī and those who thought like him were not just wrong, they were unbelievers and not true Muslims; hence, the Khawārij should have no dealings with them. In the next half-century, the Khawārij established a whole series of little Islamic republics in the area of the Gulf, from which they terrorized the surrounding unbelievers. These groups rejected the urban life of Kūfa and returned to the bedouin ways they had so recently left, in the areas of eastern and northeastern Arabia, from which most of them had originally come. The movement must be seen as a fierce protest by small groups who believed that they were the only true Muslims in a world where Islam had become too easy and had become exploited by vested interests who had no understanding of true religion. They were opposed, as all the *qurrā* were, to the traditional tribal leaders but also to the Quraysh, whose claims to leadership they totally rejected. When a group chose a leader for themselves, they might call him *amīr al-mu'minīn*, but his powers were limited and descent was no qualification for office. Thus, their ideas reflect the rejection of traditional tribal society and, at the same time, the urban life the Ḥijāzī élite had forced on the Muslims by settling them in Kūfa and Baṣra and paying them pensions. They sought a third way of establishing Islamic society: pious, egalitarian, nomad and independent. Not all Khawārij, however, were violent, nor did all embrace the desert life. In Umayyad times, Baṣra became a centre of Khārijī thought and debate, as well as of missionary activity in 'Umān and north Africa. But in the Jazīra, the old tradition of Khārijī brigandage lingered on until the fourth/tenth century.

The secession of the Khawārij and the coolness of the tribal leaders meant that 'Alī's strength melted away slowly but steadily. Exactly what happened at the arbitration is not clear, since there are many different accounts. It is certain, however, that by the time the arbitrators met, the question of who was to be caliph was a very open one. Mu'āwiya, while not claiming the office for himself, suggested the appointment of a *shūrā*, and compromise candidates like 'Umar's son 'Abd Allāh tried but failed to win general approval. The meeting broke up without agreement but its deliberations were becoming irrelevant. Egypt was the next bone of contention; 'Alī attempted to secure this rich prize more firmly for himself by despatching Mālik al-Ashtar as the governor, but he was forestalled. There can be no doubt that 'Amr had supported Mu'āwiya's cause in exchange for the governorate of Egypt, the land he had conquered but been deprived of by both 'Uthmān and 'Alī. In the year after Ṣiffīn, he returned in triumph and remained in control until his death five years later.

The loss of Egypt to 'Alī's cause was accompanied by a more serious disintegration of his authority in Kūfa, and his coalition, divided by its own internal contradictions and demoralized by the apparent irresolution of its leader, soon dissolved; only the *Anṣār* and some elements of the *qurrā'*, who like Mālik al-Ashtar had remained loyal, continued to support his case. Meanwhile, after the arbitration, Mu'āwiya openly asserted his claims to the caliphate and reached agreement with many of the tribal leaders. The end came with unexpected swiftness in 40/661 when 'Alī was assassinated in the mosque of Kūfa, not by one of his rival's agents, but by a member of the Khawārij. His son al-Ḥasan was soon persuaded to abandon any claim to the succession, and Mu'āwiya, aided and supported by the *ashrāf* of Iraq, was able to occupy the country without serious resistance. It was not just a victory of Mu'āwiya over 'Alī but it was also a victory of the Quraysh and their Syrian followers over the Iraqis and, within Iraq itself, of the *ashrāf* over the *qurrā'*, but the conflicts were by no means over and in different forms they were to plague the Umayyad regime for the next century, and bring about its eventual downfall.

The death of 'Alī brings to an end the era of the *Rāshidūn*, the four "orthodox" caliphs of Islamic tradition, sometimes also known as the "patriarchal" caliphs. It had been a period of very great achievement. The vast Muslim conquests were by no means complete, northeastern Iran and Sind in the east and northern Africa and Spain in the west were not occupied until the Umayyad period, but a huge area was already under Muslim government; one vast empire had been destroyed, another severely weakened. But Muslim rule was not imposed by brute force alone: the armies were fairly small, and in areas like Egypt, the Jazīra and the Iranian plateau, the number of Muslim settlers was insignificant compared with the local population; and yet only in Iran there is an indication of widespread popular resistance. The Muslims may have had serious differences among themselves, but the local populations were either unwilling or unable to take advantage of this. Another remarkable achievement was the maintenance of the unity of the Muslim community in the face of regionalist tendencies. Despite their differences, almost all Muslims believed that they should be governed by a single caliph, and despite the vast geographical dispersal, they kept a common religion and a common culture.

Not everything had been easy or smooth, however, and problems had developed which divided the community both at this time and in the centuries to come. Essentially, they were those which had already been apparent after the Prophet's death, and the questions the community had faced at that time – who should be caliph and what powers he was to have and who should constitute the élite of the Islamic state – were no nearer a generally acceptable answer twenty-five years, four caliphs and one civil war later. It was resolution of these questions which was to take all the power and skill of the Umayyad caliphs and their servants.

Note

1 Crone and Hinds (God's Caliph) have shown that the title, which is first securely attested in the time of 'Uthmān, was khalīfat Allāh, not, as has been argued, khalīfat rasūl Allāh, that is successor to the Prophet. The implication of this is that the early caliphs and their Umayyad successors claimed divine sanction for their rule.

4 The Umayyad caliphate

The Sufyanid caliphs: Muʿāwiya and his family: 41–64/661–684

The assassination of ʿAlī b. Abī Ṭālib in 40/661 left his rival Muʿāwiya b. Abī Sufyān as the undoubted strongman of the Muslim community. Muʿāwiya was by this time in his fifties, having been born in the first decade of the seventh century. His father, Abū Sufyān, had emerged as a leader of the Meccans in the years that followed the battle of Badr and had conducted the negotiations which brought the city to acknowledge the authority of the Prophet. His young son received a political education in the best traditions of the Quraysh. Like his father, he became a Muslim at the time of the conquest of Mecca, that is, later than many over whom he was subsequently to rule, but his education meant that he became one of Muhammad's secretaries and part of the new Muslim élite. After Muḥammad's death, he and his elder brother Yazīd went on the expeditions to Syria, where the family had owned property before the coming of Islam. Yazīd's premature death from plague meant that Muʿāwiya came to be the leader of the family and governor of Syria after the death of Abū ʿUbayda. He remained the governor without interruption or challenge for the next twenty years, thus obtaining an unrivalled opportunity to build up and strengthen his power base in the province.

While his place in the affections of the Syrians was secure, even his enemies attested that the problems he faced in the rest of the Islamic world were formidable. He had to assert not only his personal power but also the credibility of the caliphate and the unity of the Muslim community, which had been so badly damaged in the preceding years, and he faced opposition not just from people who resented his assumption of power, but from people who resented the whole idea of a strong and effective government. Perhaps his greatest achievement was to ensure that despite the stresses his policy inevitably caused, the Muslim world remained united enough to resist the attacks of its enemies and to expand its own borders.

Muʿāwiya's character and policies emerge with some clarity from the sources, and even hostile commentators paid tribute to his abilities.

DOI: 10.4324/9780429348129-4

His virtues were those of the successful politician, not of the brilliant general or the religious leader; of these virtues, the most important was the quality the Arab sources describe as *ḥilm* – the shrewdness, moderation and self-control that the situation demanded. Money was as important a weapon as the support of the Syrian army; he knew that most people have a price and he was prepared to pay it to avoid conflict. The loyalty of the Syrians was assured and their army was the most effective in the Muslim world, but he did not use this military power as an instrument to keep control over other provinces; he used it to attack the Byzantines on land and sea. It was there as a reserve, but a reserve that was never needed after the death of his rival ʿAlī. He ruled rather by making agreements with those who held power in the provinces, by building up the power of those who were prepared to cooperate with him and by attaching as many important and influential figures to his cause as possible. It was not an absolute government in which governors were appointed and dismissed by a central authority but almost a confederation of different leaderships acknowledging one overall authority. From his provincial governors, the caliph demanded acceptance of his authority, that they keep order and that, in some cases, they forward revenues to the central government: it is recorded, for example, that of 60 million *dirhams* collected in the province of Baṣra, only 4 million was sent to Damascus, all the rest being spent in the province, mostly on paying the local military. Beyond that, governors were allowed to establish their own power bases and ensure the fortunes of their families and friends. Unlike his own relative and predecessor, ʿUthmān, however, he did not attempt to assert his authority through his own family. The Umayyads were an extensive family and contained a number of figures, notably Marwān b. al-Ḥakam, of great ability and political experience, but few of them were given important roles in the government, either as advisers at the court in Damascus or as provincial governors. They were mostly settled, in luxury, in Medina and the Ḥijāz, far from the real centres of power. Muʿāwiya's father had been a leading figure in the Meccan commonwealth, that system of trading agreements and alliances which had brought such prosperity to the city, and his son seems to have used this, rather than the absolutist models of the Byzantine Empire or the religious claims of ʿAlī b. Abī Ṭālib, as the inspiration for his statecraft.

The most serious difficulties he faced were in Iraq. The death of ʿAlī had not solved any of the deep-rooted problems which the conquest and the vast flood of immigrants had caused. The Iraqis were resentful of Syrian dominance, but this feeling did not lead to any sense of unity. There remained the social divisions between the *ashrāf* and the early Muslim élite, now itself divided between the *qurrāʾ* and their descendants who clung to the memory of ʿAlī, and the Khawārij who rejected any but their own rigorist interpretation of Islam. There were regional differences as well; the problems of Kūfa were not those of Baṣra, and the two cities were more rivals than allies. These tensions and divisions made violence almost inevitable and that it did not break out until after the death of the caliph was a tribute to his own talents and those of the men he chose.

In social terms, Muʿāwiya's triumph was the triumph of the *ashrāf* in Kūfa and the surrounding area. The fortunes of tribal leaders like al-Ashʿath al-Kindī and his son Muḥammad and Jarīr al-Bajalī prospered, while those who had challenged their status, like Mālik al-Ashtar and his son Ibrāhīm and Ḥujr b. ʿAdī al-Kindī, felt betrayed and resentful. As the governor of this most difficult city, the caliph chose a man of ability and experience if of somewhat disreputable morals. Al-Mughīra b. Shuʿba al-Thaqafī came from the holy family of Ṭāʾif, just as Muʿāwiya did from that of Mecca. Before the conquest of his city by the Muslims, he had fled to Medina and embraced the new religion in the year 8/629–630 to escape the consequences of a particularly outrageous murder. Islam, as Muḥammad said, cancelled all that had gone before, and al-Mughīra, like Muʿāwiya, became one of the Prophet's secretaries. When Ṭāʾif fell to the Muslims, al-Mughīra, helped by Abū Sufyān, was the man who destroyed the idol of the town and pillaged the temple treasury. Like many Thaqafīs, he joined in the conquest of Iraq, and his knowledge of Persian marked him out for administrative office. He became the governor of Baṣra under ʿUmar and was removed after allegations of adultery but reappointed as governor of Kūfa at the end of ʿUmar's reign. In the conflict between ʿAlī and Muʿāwiya, he had played a moderating role, advising ʿAlī to recognize Muʿāwiya in Syria. Nobody had more experience of the Iraqis and their problems, and Muʿāwiya appointed him the governor, a post he held for nearly ten years, from 41 to his death in 50 (661–670). He adopted a policy of keeping the peace and turning a blind eye to misdemeanours which did not threaten his authority. The Kūfans were allowed to keep for their own needs the revenues of the district known as Māh al-Kūfa in the Zagros Mountains, and the regular payment of salaries, something ʿAlī had never been able to achieve, must have done much to induce cooperation.

In Baṣra, Muʿāwiya turned at first to the obvious candidate, the Umayyad ʿAbd Allāh b. ʿĀmir b. Kurayz, who had already held the office under ʿUthmān and had begun the conquests of Khurāsān and Sīstān. Now reappointed, he again opened campaigns in the east, notably in Sīstān, and Arab armies even entered distant Kābul. While his fighting qualities were not in doubt, however, ʿAbd Allāh seems to have been either unable or unwilling to undertake the maintenance of law and order in Baṣra and there may have been some resentment against these distant campaigns. He was dismissed in 44/664 and replaced by the most remarkable of Muʿāwiya's subordinates, Ziyād b. Abīhi, otherwise known as Ziyād b. Abī Sufyān. Like al-Mughīra, he came from Ṭāʾif, from a Thaqafī background, although his exact parentage was obscure, as his name implies (Ziyād son of his father). He joined the Thaqīf in southern Iraq in the earliest stages; because of his education, he was put in charge of the division of the booty and then became the secretary to successive governors, including al-Mughīra, who became the patron of this bright young man. He was one of 'Alī's most consistent supporters, refusing to be reconciled to Mu'āwiya even after 'Alī's death and remaining in Fārs until 42/662–663, when, with al-Mughīra acting as intermediary, he was reconciled to the new caliph. Mu'āwiya recognized that he had both the abilities and the all-important local connections to be his right-hand man in Baṣra and he was duly appointed. Ziyād had a very positive view of the governor's responsibilities and his conception of the office was deeply influential in the later development of ideas of government. In a widely reported speech, he made to the people of Baṣra on his appointment, he is said to have offered both a carrot and a stick. The good news was that the '*aṭā*' was to be paid regularly and that they would not be forced on long campaigns in distant regions – he also promised to be accessible at all times to his subjects (he himself never led armies to the east). However, he promised draconian measures to enforce law and order within the city; there was to be a curfew; tribal and clan solidarities were no longer to be used to protect the guilty; and the *shurṭa*, or police force, was to ensure the maintenance of peace. He ended with the celebrated warning, as he surveyed the people gathered before him, that he saw heads tottering on shoulders and they were to make sure that their own stayed in place. The policies seem to have worked, and Ziyād enjoyed the favour and confidence of the caliph to the extent that he was acknowledged as Mu'āwiya's half-brother and was officially known as Ziyād b. Abī Sufyān as a result.

In 50/670 on al-Mughīra's death, he replaced his former patron as the governor of Kūfa as well as of Baṣra and hence became a virtual viceroy in the east.

In Kūfa, his firmness contrasted with al-Mughīra's more easygoing ways, but the reliability of his financial administration went far to compensate for this. He reorganized the city into four quarters, each with a chief appointed by and responsible to him in order to control the population. As the governor of Iraq, he also controlled appointments in Iran. Here, it is clear that he encouraged further conquests as a way of relieving the pressure on resources in Iraq. From 47/667 onwards, he sent a series of armies to Khurāsān. Hitherto the Arabs had maintained a small garrison in Marv but otherwise left the administration in the hands of the local princes. Ziyād decided to change this position in a way which was to have extremely important consequences for Islamic history. In 51/671, he sent to the provinces a large contingent of 50,000 troops from both Baṣra and Kūfa, not as a garrison but as settlers, and they established themselves in the Marv oasis. This meant that Khurāsān had a larger number of Muslim settlers than any other area outside the Fertile Crescent, more than Egypt and certainly more than any area in western Iran. For the moment, this emigration solved some of the problems of Iraq, but it was the descendants of these settlers who were, in the end, to destroy the Umayyad caliphate itself.

Iraq and the east then were managed by Mu'āwiya through what some must have seen as a Thaqafī mafia. Thaqafīs were experienced in the affairs of Iraq before the coming of Islam, were well educated (it is worth noting how important the education of both al-Mughīra and Ziyād was in ensuring their success) and had close connections with the Quraysh and the Umayyads from before Muḥammad's time. In addition, the Thaqīf had played a major role in the conquest of Iraq; nobody could say they were outsiders, creatures of a distant and unresponsive government. All these factors made for a system which worked for Mu'āwiya's reign; when the great Ziyād died in 53/673, he was succeeded a few years later in all his offices by his son 'Ubayd Allāh, more hasty and given to the use of force than his father, but a man whose devotion to the Umayyad cause could not have been doubted.

Mu'āwiya's power base was in Syria but, compared with Iraq, we are fairly badly informed about the position in the province. The Islamic historical tradition was developed in Iraq under 'Abbasid rule, and the sources tend to be indifferent to the Umayyads and much more concerned with Iraqi and Khurāsānī affairs. It is clear, however, that Mu'āwiya drew support from a wide cross section of Syrian tribes, both from those who had arrived at the time of the conquest and those who had been settled in Byzantine times. As yet the feud between the Qays and Yaman which was to plague Syria for so many centuries was not a major problem. He gathered around himself what might be described as a cabinet of Syrian leaders who were his right-hand men; some of these were Qurashīs, including 'Abd al-Raḥmān, the son of the great general Khālid b. al-Walīd, who was powerful in the Homs area, but none of them were Umayyads and they tended to come from the less important clans of the Quraysh, notably from the Fihrīs, like al-Ḍaḥḥāk b. Qays, who had played an important role in the conquest of the Jazīra. The others were mostly from Yamanī tribes, including Shuraḥbīl b. al-Simt. al-Kindī, whose power base was in Homs, and Ḥassān b. Mālik b. Baḥdal, chief of the powerful Kalb tribe. This inner circle assured the loyalty of different groups in Syria and the Jazīra and was occasionally used on difficult missions outside that area. While they were sometimes made governors of the districts within Syria, they were never appointed to Iraq or the east and the Syrian army was kept busy attacking the Byzantines. Rhodes was taken in 52/672 and Crete in 54/674, while during the last seven years of Mu'āwiya's reign, the caliph's son Yazīd led continuous attacks on Constantinople itself (54–60/674–680). These expeditions were mostly raids, and even areas such as the Mediterranean islands that were captured and held were used as sources of tribute but not for colonization. The Arabs of the Jazīra led similar expeditions into Armenia but again there was no extensive settlement of new areas such as the Iraqis were accomplishing in Khurāsān. This suggests that the motives for the warfare were to provide the Syrians with military experience and financial rewards rather than to cope with the problem of overpopulation. Mu'āwiya managed the Syrians with consummate skill and their loyalty to him was famous; it was only after his death that serious divisions began to appear.

Egypt was controlled almost as an appendage of Syria. Arab settlement here was very limited, being confined almost entirely to the cities of Fusṭāt. and Alexandria. In the struggle with 'Alī, Mu'āwiya had received the loyal backing of 'Amr b. al-'Āṣ, anxious to regain control of the province he had conquered for Islam, and 'Amr ruled Egypt almost as a partner until his death in 43/663. For most of the rest of the reign, 47–62/667–682, Egypt was governed loyally by Maslama b. Mukhallad, the only member of the *Anṣār* to achieve a high rank in Mu'āwiya's government.

If Mu'āwiya's caliphate was decentralized politically, it was decentralized administratively as well. No attempt was made to introduce a general, Arabic-speaking administrative system for the whole Muslim world. On the contrary, each province continued the local traditions of the previous rulers. In Syria, financial administration wasṭalmost entirely in the hands of local Christians, including Sarjūn, son of Manṣūr, who had held the same office for Heraclius at the time of the Muslim conquest. In Egypt, as we know from the evidence of the papyri, the Byzantine system continued with significant changes but with local headmen continuing to be responsible for tax collecting and administration at a local village level. It used to be thought that the Arab conquerors had little understanding of administration and simply carried on existing practices, but recent research has shown Arabic documents being issued from the year after the first conquest, 22/643, and an Arabic-writing administration ensuring that taxes were paid and brought to the capital at Fusṭāṭ. We have already seen that the local magnates in Khurāsān continued to manage their own affairs, only paying tribute to the Arabs. Even in Iraq, the area most affected by the Arab expansion, the native landowners continued to play a role in local administration. This local autonomy was typified by the coinage; there was no Islamic coinage as such, rather each province used and supplemented where necessary the existing money supply, the gold *dīnār* of the Byzantine areas and the silver *dirham* of the Sasanian countries. Taxation systems differed as a consequence and there was no uniformity in the dues paid by the native inhabitants of different areas, these being determined by local tradition and the circumstances of the conquest rather than by government policy. Mu'āwiya supplemented the limited income derived from provincial taxation in two ways; the first was by frontier warfare, and there can be no doubt that at this stage, booty and tribute helped to secure the loyalty of the Syrians. The second way was by extensive agricultural developments. We know most about this in the Ḥijāz around Medina, since his activities provoked considerable opposition, but no doubt other likely areas were developed as well. This large-scale farming, using the labour of *mawālī* (freedmen, sing. *mawlā*) or slaves meant a substantial income for the treasury. In Iraq, the extensive *ṣawāfī* lands which had caused so much anger during the reign of 'Uthmān were taken over as government property, or rather they ceased to be the *māl al-muslimīn* (wealth of the Muslims), controlled by the Muslims, but became rather the *māl Allāh*, controlled by the caliph. The Kūfans were paid their '*aṭā*', regularly and honestly, but they no longer had direct control over the lands which produced it.

The one serious problem which disturbed the later years of Mu'āwiya's reign was the ordering of the succession. Mu'āwiya was determined that his son Yazīd should succeed him and that he should be formally acknowledged by the Muslim community in his father's lifetime. Many were scandalized by the idea. No caliph had been so succeeded by his son, and those who opposed the plan were quick to call for a *shūra* or some more open form of decision and accused Mu'āwiya of attempting to set up a hereditary monarchy. Everyone understood that the acceptance of Yazīd would mean the maintenance of the sort of Syriā-based regime which his father had set up, and the idea was therefore bitterly opposed, not just by the Iraqis but also by those Umayyads and other Qurashīs in the Ḥijāz who had been effectively excluded from power by Mu'āwiya. In the end, the opposition was silenced by threats or payments, but when Mu'āwiya died in Rajab 60/April 680, his son, although able, well liked and of proven military ability, faced a whole series of challenges.

The Kūfans had not lost their enthusiasm for the house of 'Alī during the long years of Mu'āwiya's reign, since they believed that only the coming to power of the Family of the Prophet would restore Kūfa and the Kūfans to their rightful position. 'Alī's elder son al-Ḥasan had abandoned his claims to leadership, but his younger brother al-Ḥusayn was prepared to take up the cause. On the death of Mu'āwiya, al-Ḥusayn left his place of retirement in Medina and travelled across the desert towards Kūfa to seek his supporters, accompanied by only a small band of family and friends. The governor of Iraq, Ziyād's son 'Ubayd Allāh, was waiting for him; he prevented the small party from reaching the settled lands and, after some days of confrontation when al-Ḥusayn and his followers suffered increasingly from thirst, there was a short battle at a place called Karbalā', and al-Ḥusayn and most of his party were killed. The Kūfans had made no effort to support him. It was 10 Muḥarram 61/10 October 680. At the time, the attempt to raise the 'Alid banner in Iraq was a pathetic failure, but the events of the massacre at Karbalā' made a deep impression on the Muslim community. Many felt that the grandson of the Prophet, a man whom Muḥammad loved and had played with on his knee, had been brutally done to death by the forces of godless oppression. Al-Ḥusayn might be dead but his memory lived on; the accounts of his sufferings at the hands of Umayyad troops were elaborated in Kūfa to discredit the regime, and al-Ḥusayn became the symbol for the sufferings of all the weak and defenceless. To talk of Shi'ites in Iraq at this stage is misleading; the development of a Shi'ite "sect" was a much later development, but the death of al-Ḥusayn played an important part in the attachment of people's hopes and political aspirations to the family of 'Alī.

The death of al-Ḥusayn meant the effective end of trouble in Iraq; much more intractable were the problems of the Ḥijāz. Yazīd was well aware of the strength of feeling against him in the Holy Cities, and he made great efforts to be conciliatory, but some refused to take the oath of allegiance, notably ʿAbd Allāh, the son of that al-Zubayr who had died at the Battle of the Camel. An austere and determined figure, he held that the caliphate should not be the plaything of the Sufyanids but that the ruler should be chosen from all the Quraysh. Ibn al-Zubayr established himself in Mecca where he became a rallying point for all those who opposed Yazīd's claims, asserting that there should be a new *shūra*. The Medinese, for their part, were motivated by other considerations as well; it is clear that Muʿāwiya's agricultural activities in Medina had aroused widespread opposition, especially from the *Anṣār*, who felt that their city was being taken over by an absentee landlord, and they rallied to the anti-Umayyad party. There were some two years of negotiation and manoeuvre, while Yazīd and a series of governors attempted to defuse the situation. Finally, it came to open hostilities; the Umayyads in the city, led by Marwān b. al-Ḥakam, were driven out to Syria, while a Syrian expeditionary force marched on the Prophet's city. The Medinese attempted to defend themselves, just as the Prophet had done, by digging a trench around the town, but the Syrians were an easy match for them, and at the battle of the Ḥarra (Dhu'l-Ḥijja 63/August 683), they were defeated and the city sacked. It only remained now for the Syrians to march on Mecca and eject Ibn al-Zubayr, and it was while they were engaged in the unsavoury task of attacking the Kaʿba itself that news came of Yazīd's death and once more the whole situation was changed.

The disasters of Karbalā' and the Ḥarra cast a cloud over Yazīd's brief reign. Yet, it was not devoid of achievement. Compared with Muʿāwiya's ambitious raids, he tried to stabilize the frontiers between Syria and Byzantium; outposts on the Sea of Marmara were abandoned, while in the north of Syria itself, he carved up the overly large *jund* of Homs to make a new frontier province based on Qinnasrīn which was to include both Antioch and Manbij. Had he lived longer, his reputation might have recovered from the shocks of the early part of his reign; as it was, he died in his desert encampment at Ḥawwārīn in Rabīʿ I 64/November 683, when he was only about forty years of age.

Yazīd was succeeded immediately by his young son Muʿāwiya. His accession was due to the influence of his cousin, Ḥassān b. Mālik b. Baḥdal of Kalb, and the prince himself proved sickly. Muʿāwiya II, the last of the Sufyanids, died after only a few weeks.

The foundation of the Marwanid caliphate and the achievement of ʿAbd al-Malik: 64–86/684–705

The death of Muʿāwiya II led to a deep crisis in the Umayyad regime; Yazīd's other sons were too young to be generally acceptable and the major provinces of the empire were slipping rapidly from the control of the Syrians. ʿUbayd Allāh b. Ziyād was forced to flee Baṣra, despite a speech in which he not only recalled his own Baṣran connections but promised to retain the wealth of the province for its people. These concessions were not enough, and almost alone he fled along the direct desert road to the Ḥawrān in Syria. On his arrival in Syria, he found the Syrians in total disarray. Al-Ḍaḥḥāk b. Qays al-Fihrī, one of the last surviving members of Muʿāwiya's inner circle, held power in Damascus but wavered between acknowledging Ibn al-Zubayr and finding a suitable Syrian candidate. Many other Syrians were willing to acknowledge Ibn al-Zubayr as well, notably the Qaysī tribesmen of the northern part of the country, and even leading members of the Umayyad family were preparing to go to the Ḥijāz to offer their allegiance to him. Not all Syrians, however, were prepared to surrender their privileged position. The Kalbī chief Ibn Baḥdal was related by marriage to the ruling house and now put his power and that of his tribe firmly behind the continuation of the Umayyad house. ʿUbayd Allāh b. Ziyād had been taught by his experience in Baṣra how closely his own fortunes were linked to those of the dynasty and on his arrival in Syria he too set about organizing the resistance.

The most serious problem faced by Ibn Ziyād and the Kalbī chief was that of finding a suitable Umayyad candidate. Ibn Baḥdal favoured Muʿāwiya II's young half-brothers, but ʿUbayd Allāh turned to Marwān b. al-Ḥakam. Marwān was by this time an old man. He had served his uncle ʿUthmān as his right-hand man in Medina and after the caliph's assassination had remained to become the leader of the Umayyads in the Ḥijāz. He had never moved to Syria and had remained very much in the background during Muʿāwiya's reign, but the troubles which led to the battle of the Ḥarra had forced him to leave along with the rest of the Umayyads in Medina and make their way north as refugees. Marwān seems to have been resigned to accepting Ibn al-Zubayr when he was met by ʿUbayd Allāh, newly arrived from Iraq, who persuaded him to change his mind. Ibn Baḥdal then summoned a meeting of Syrian *ashrāf*, not in Damascus where al-Ḍaḥḥāk b. Qays remained in control, but in his own territory at the old Ghassanid centre of Jābiya. Here, he presided over a sort of extended *shūra* at which Marwān was finally acknowledged as the candidate of the Umayyad party, in exchange for financial promises. Marwān had no experience or contacts in Syria; he would be entirely dependent on the *ashrāf* from the Yamanī tribes who had elected him.

Not everyone in Syria could accept this, especially the leaders of the Qaysī party, who more and more turned to al-Ḍaḥḥāk b. Qays. They persuaded him not to go to the Jābiya meeting but rather to prepare for battle. The Yamanīs marched to meet them, Damascus was brought over to their side by the prompt action of a scion of the old Ghassanid ruling family and, in Muḥarram 65/July 684, just nine months after Yazīd's death, the two sides met in a terrible battle at Marj Rāhiṭ, on the road from Damascus to the north. The Yamanī tribesmen were victorious and the Qaysīs, although much more numerous than their opponents, were driven from the field with a dreadful slaughter, al-Ḍaḥḥāk himself being killed. While the remnants of the Qaysīs, led by Zufar b. Ḥārith al-Kilābī, fled to Qarqīsiyyā' on the Euphrates, Marwān was acknowledged as caliph in Damascus.

The war had been won, but the bloody victory at Marj Rāhit. had long-term consequences which were to be fatal for Syria and the Umayyads alike because it divided the Arabs of the province into two separate parties, Qays/Muḍar on the one side and Yaman on the other. The basic distinction between northern (Qays) and southern (Yaman) Arabs was an ancient but hitherto fairly harmless one. In theory, the allegiance of each tribe was decided according to complicated genealogies, but in practice there was considerable confusion and some tribes were claimed by both sides. In Umayyad times, the division was in part geographical, the Qaysī tribes being mostly settled in the northern parts of the province, in the newly created *jund* of Qinnasrīn, and in the Jazīra, including the Byzantine frontier areas as far east as Armenia. Yamanī tribes occupied the steppes around Homs, the Palmyrena, Palestine and the areas to the east of the Jordan valley. It was also a division arising from the Islamic conquests. Some Yamanī tribes like the Kalb, Tanūkh, Judhām and Taghlib had been in Syria before the coming of Islam, while the majority of Qaysīs like the Sulaym, Kilāb and 'Uqayl were newly arrived from the Arabian Peninsula, many of them brought to the Jazīra by Mu'āwiya in 'Uthmān's reign. Some newly arrived tribes from south Arabia, like the Kindīs and Haḍramīs settled in Homs, joined the Yaman group. Much of the hostility must have been the result of disputes over grazing rights. Many of the Yamanīs came from tribes that were still in part Christian, like the ruling house of Kalb where Ibn Baḥdal's grandfather had remained Christian until his death during 'Ali's caliphate. They had also in many cases been allies of the Byzantines, and in some ways the battle of Marj Rāhit. was the battle of the Yarmūk refought, with the victory this time going to the old-established Syrian tribes. The confused succession to Mu'āwiya II had led to the emergence of two coalitions, Qaysīs supporting al-Daḥḥāk b. Qays and Yamanīs supporting Ibn Baḥdal and Marwān – but the battle meant that the split continued beyond the immediate crisis. Qays had many dead to avenge and the feud was to continue for generations. As late as the nineteenth century, battles were still being fought in Palestine between groups calling themselves Qays and Yaman.

The newly established caliph had a mass of problems to contend with, but he and his supporters, 'Ubyad Allāh and Ibn Baḥdal, set about tackling them with energy and determination. Marwān's son Muḥammad was sent to contain the Qaysīs on the middle Euphrates, while 'Ubayd Allāh prepared for the reconquest of Iraq. An expedition to the Ḥijāz ended in failure, but the caliph, accompanied by Ibn Baḥdal and another of his sons, 'Abd al-'Azīz, had a signal triumph when, with the help of the *ashrāf* of Fusṭāṭ, they seized Egypt from the representative of Ibn al-Zubayr. Already the characteristics of the new regime were becoming apparent. Marwān looked back for his political guidance not to Mu'āwiya but to the uncle he had served so long and well, the Caliph 'Uthmān. Like 'Uthmān, he made the family the basis of his power, just as Mu'āwiya had neglected it; his sons Muḥammad and 'Abd al-'Azīz had been given military commands almost from the beginning, while his eldest son, 'Abd al-Malik, was soon acknowledged as heir to the caliphate. It was a shaky beginning, but a new regime had been born.

Marwān died, an old man by the standard of the day, in Ramaḍān 65/April 685 and he was succeeded immediately by 'Abd al-Malik, his son and designated heir, the accession being smoothlykk managed by the Yamanīs. The new caliph had been born in his father's house in Medina about 26/646–647, near the beginning of 'Uthmān's reign, and he was a boy when the old caliph was killed. Like most members of his family, his relations with Mu'āwiya were not close and he grew up a pious and serious young man in Medina, where he worked as his father's assistant in the administration. He came to Syria with his father after the expulsion of the Umayyads from the Ḥijāz and was one of his father's closest advisers during the few months of his caliphate. His political experience may not have been very extensive when, now, in his early forties, he found himself caliph, but he was methodical, careful and determined to make his power effective.

The obstacles the new caliph faced were formidable. The Syrians were far from united and he was heavily dependent on the Yamanī leaders, Ibn Baḥdal and Rawh. b. Zinbā' al-Judhāmī, and the support of members of his own family. Egypt was now firmly under Umayyad control again, but while it was an important source of income, the smallness of the Arab population meant that it provided little in the way of military support. Ibn al-Zubayr had consolidated his power in the Ḥijāz, while his brother Muṣ'ab had moved to Baṣra and was working to win over the whole of Iraq to his side. In Kūfa, on the other hand, Mukhtār b. Abī 'Ubayd was trying to turn local discontents to his own advantage and was seeking an 'Alid candidate for the throne. Finally, the Qaysīs of northern Syria and the Jazīra – defeated, bitter but by no means powerless – had established themselves under the leadership of Zufar b. al-Ḥārith al-Kilābī at Qarqīsiyyā' on the Euphrates and continued to acknowledge Ibn al-Zubayr as their caliph.

'Abd al-Malik's forces began to take the initiative immediately after his succession. 'Ubayd Allāh b. Ziyād, whose arrival in Syria had done so much to ensure the throne for the Marwanids, was now determined to return to Iraq and reestablish control. His progress was delayed by the activities of the Qaysīs in the Jazīra, and by the time he approached Iraq from the north, via Mosul, Mukhtār had consolidated his position in Kūfa. Against 'Ubayd Allāh, he sent the son of 'Alī's old champion, Ibrāhīm b. Mālik al-Ashtar, who was to prove his most effective military commander. After some setbacks, the Kūfans defeated the army and killed 'Ubayd Allāh himself at a battle on the river Khāzir, near Mosul (Muḥarram 67/August 686). With 'Ubayd Allāh gone, 'Abd al-Malik took no further initiatives to retake Iraq for the next five years. He contented himself with consolidating his power in Syria and waited while his opponents destroyed each other.

In Iraq, the social tensions which had led to the murder of 'Uthmān and the problems which confronted 'Alī broke out again with renewed virulence. Umayyad rule had tended to favour the interests of the *ashrāf*, and there had emerged a new landowning aristocracy in the neighbourhood of Kūfa, where families like those of al-Ash'ath b. Qays al-Kindī had become important property owners. Farther to the south, much land had been reclaimed in the marshes of southern Iraq, by Ziyād and Mu'āwiya's *mawlā*, 'Abd Allāh b. Darrāj, but the beneficiaries of this reclamation had not been the people of Iraq as a whole but the supporters of Ziyād and the Umayyad government. As in Medina, Mu'āwiya's large-scale agricultural developments had proved a major source of discontent. Along with these old disputes about landownership and social status among the Arabs, a new problem had emerged in the generation since 'Alī had died. Many of the local people, especially in the Kūfa area, had been converted to Islam. While this was no doubt welcome in many ways, it did pose serious problems to the rulers. The real question was how far these new converts, usually referred to as *mawālī* (clients or freedmen) of the Arab tribes, should be treated as first-class Muslims. While in theory all should be equal, objections were raised on two fronts. The non-Muslims paid a higher rate of tax on their landed property, the *kharāj* and a poll tax on top of that, while the Arab Muslims simply paid the *ṣadaqa*. This meant that conversion would result in a substantial loss of income for the government. Naturally, converts tended to be denied the fiscal benefits of their conversion and, equally naturally, they resented it. But the idea of raising the status of the *mawālī* was also opposed by the *ashrāf*, who feared that this flood of new converts would escape their power and undermine their privileges. In this way, a whole new set of destructive social antagonisms came into being.

As usual, it was in the turbulent city of Kūfa that these tensions became most apparent. The weakening of the Umayyad grip had led immediately to unrest. After Mu'āwiya's death, the Kūfans had looked to 'Alī's son al-Ḥusayn to provide leadership, and al-Ḥusayn's death had reinforced, rather than diminished, the loyalty of the Kūfans to the 'Alid family, now represented by al-Ḥusayn's son 'Alī and his half-brother, Muḥammad b. al-Ḥanafiyya, both in the Ḥijāz and both reluctant to become actively involved in politics in Iraq. The lack of any forceful 'Alid leader in Kūfa at this moment led to a certain jockeying for position among old associates of 'Alī until the leadership was gradually taken over by the enigmatic personality of Mukhtār b. Abī 'Ubayd, who by Rabī' I 66/October 685 had driven out the governors sent by Ibn al-Zubayr and made himself master of the city. Mukhtār was by this time an elderly man; he had been born in Ṭā'if around the time of the *Hijra* but seems to have gone to Iraq when 'Umar sent his father Abū 'Ubayd b. Mas'ūd to command the armies there. Abū 'Ubayd had been killed at the Battle of the Bridge, but the family remained in the area and acquired property, and Mukhtār himself held minor office during 'Alī's caliphate. Although a Thaqafī, he does not seem to have formed part of the

Thaqīf group enriched by Ziyād and his son and remained a representative of the old Islamic élite of Kūfa, anxious to regain its prestige. By the time he assumed control in the city, he was very experienced, and few could have had as good an understanding of the city and its problems.

At first Mukhtār seems to have tried to enter into partnership with Ibn al-Zubayr, but the latter distrusted him and negotiations came to nothing. He then espoused the cause of the ʿAlid family, but it was more difficult to find a candidate who would accept the doubtful honour; both ʿAlī b. al-Ḥusayn and Muḥammad b. al-Ḥanafiyya were in the Ḥijāz, under the eye of Ibn al-Zubayr, and neither of them were keen to share the fate of al-Ḥusayn; while ʿAlī refused absolutely, Ibn al-Ḥanafiyya's replies were ambiguous but allowed Mukhtār to claim that he enjoyed his support. He proclaimed Ibn al-Ḥanafiyya not just caliph but *mahdī*. This implied that he was a divinely guided saviour, a messiah, who would, with God's support, establish justice for all Muslims. This seems to have been a novel concept in Islam, but the idea of the *mahdī* was widely accepted and was to provide the ideological inspiration for many subsequent movements and rebellions. Ibn al-Ḥanafiyya's candidature marked a new departure in other ways. Al-Ḥasan and al-Ḥusayn were both sons of Fāṭima and hence direct descendants of the Prophet as well as of ʿAlī, but Ibn al-Ḥanafiyya was not; it was only his descent from ʿAlī that gave him a claim to belong to the holy family, and his acceptance is a sign of the increasing importance of the memory of ʿAlī among many in Iraq.

Mukhtār's supporters came from many different, largely irreconcilable groups. He took power with the support of Arabs from all the different tribes represented in the population and some *mawālī*, about 500 in number. While it was not originally a movement of *mawālī*, their numbers and influence seem to have grown as a result of Mukhtār's success, and one of their leaders, Abū ʿAmra Kaysān, was appointed the chief of police. Mukhtār's propaganda explicitly claimed that he was acting in the interests of the "weak" and of the *mawālī*. At the same time, he tried to win over the *ashrāf* and so create a united Kūfan militia, but the nobles were increasingly alarmed by the radical nature of Mukhtār's movement and their support was at best half-hearted.

The threat of ʿUbayd Allāh b. Ziyād attacking Kūfa from the north and the need to raise an effective army against the menace brought the tensions between Mukhtār and the *ashrāf* into the open. The latter complained that he had given the *mawālī* horses, paid them the *ʿaṭā'* and generally favoured them unreasonably, and this led to fighting in Kūfa itself, at which the *ashrāf* were worsted. At the same time, Mukhtār's relations with Muṣʿab b. al-Zubayr also became increasingly problematic, and after Mukhtār refused to accept a Qurashī governor from the Ḥijāz, Muṣʿab and he became rivals in Iraq. The defeated *ashrāf* of Kūfa took advantage of this and, under the leadership of Muḥammad b. al-Ashʿath, they and their followers, 10,000 strong, left Kūfa and joined Muṣʿab in Baṣra. With the Zubayrid forces, they then returned to Kūfa, defeated Mukhtār's supporters and finally killed him after besieging him in the governor's palace in 67/April 687.

Mukhtār's revolt had lasted less than two years and his control had never extended beyond Kūfa and its countryside. Nonetheless, it is of great importance in illustrating the problems of early Islamic society, showing clearly the antagonism between the *ashrāf* and other Arabs and the *mawālī*, who, for the first time, played a significant role in the politics of the community. The idea of the *mahdī* too was to have a lasting importance, and many of the ideas which had been developed in Kūfa during Mukhtār's brief, revolutionary rule survived among small, closely knit groups of Iraqi Muslims and were to provide the inspiration for future rebels. At the time, however, his failure was complete and Muṣ'ab and his forces extracted bloody reprisals on his supporters in Kūfa. He had tried to put together a coalition of all the groups in Kūfa, a united front which would once again restore the city to a position of influence in the Islamic community. Despite his attempts at compromise, he had been defeated by the internal divisions. He had also been let down by the 'Alid family, and even Ibn al-Ḥanafiyya's endorsements were ambiguous. Many supporters of the family were dubious about Mukhtār's claims to represent them.

The collapse of Mukhtār's rebellion meant that Ibn al-Zubayr and 'Abd al-Malik were now the major rivals for power. 'Abd Allāh b. al-Zubayr had asserted his claim to leadership on Mu'āwiya's death and had fled to Mecca rather than acknowledge Yazīd. He represented and was supported by those Qurashīs who resented the way in which the Umayyad family had monopolized power which they felt should have been more generally distributed among the Quraysh, especially members of his own clan of Makhzūm, rivals of the Umayyads since the days of Abū Jahl and Abū Sufyān. He himself was an austere, some said a miserly, figure, who directed operations from Mecca, gaining a certain prestige from his guardianship of the Holy Places but thereby distancing himself from events in the more populous parts of the Muslim world. In Iraq, he was represented by his more dynamic and worldly brother Muṣ'ab, who attempted to control Iraq. Muṣ'ab faced two main problems. In Kūfa, there was Mukhtār and in southern Iraq and the areas around the Gulf there were the Khawārij.

The Khawārij, who had deserted 'Alī, had remained largely quiescent under Mu'āwiya, but his death seems to have sparked new disturbances. Acting in small, fast-moving guerrilla groups, they were a constant threat to the government of the settled areas. The two principal groups which threatened Zubayrid control were the Najdiyya and the Azāriqa. The former were based in Yamāma, on the eastern side of the Arabian Peninsula and recruited almost entirely from the Ḥanīfa tribe, who had supported Musaylima the false prophet at the time of the *Ridda*. They tried, with some success, to assert their control over 'Umān and even Yemen, and for a period in 68/687 they had more power in the Arabian Peninsula than either Ibn al-Zubayr or the Umayyads. After 72/691, however, internal differences led to a breakup of their power and they were eventually subdued. Even more threatening were the Azāriqa of Ahwāz and Fārs, against whom the Zubayrids were compelled to wage a long and exhausting struggle. Fortunately for Muṣ'ab, he found a new and important ally to help him in this unrewarding task. Many Azdīs from 'Umān had moved to Baṣra towards the end of the reign of Mu'āwiya and their chief, al-Muhallab b. Abī Ṣufra, established himself as one of the most powerful men in the area and a very successful soldier. He is said to have introduced metal stirrups into Muslim armies. It was he and his men who provided the backbone of the Zubayrid army against the Khawārij and against Mukhtār. Despite his efforts, however, the Azāriqa remained a threat until after the family of al-Zubayr had been defeated.

Throughout this period of confusion and bloodshed in Iraq, 'Abd al-Malik had consolidated his position in Syria. In 71 (691), he reached an agreement with Zufar b. al-Ḥārith al Kilābī and his Qaysī followers in the Jazīra who agreed to abandon Ibn al-Zubayr in exchange for a privileged position at court and in the Umayyad army. After this, 'Abd al-Malik was able to turn his attention to Iraq without any fear of disturbances along his lines of communication. The end, when it came, was swift. Muṣ'ab was beset by troubles and resented by many Kūfans for the bloody way in which Mukhtār's rebellion had been suppressed while al-Muhallab was entirely occupied fighting the Khawārij in the south. The caliph in person led the army which defeated Muṣ'ab at Dayr al-Jāthalīq (72/691) and entered Kūfa to receive the homage of the people. In the south, al-Muhallab was reconciled without much trouble to the new regime. The final act was the despatch of a small force under al-Ḥajjāj b. Yūsuf to Mecca, where, after the bombardment of the city and the Ka'ba itself, Ibn al-Zubayr was finally killed in Jumādā I 73/October 692. The unity of the community had been restored. Once again, the dissensions in Iraq had allowed the Umayyads and their Syrian supporters to dominate the richer and more populous areas to the east. It now remained for 'Abd al-Malik to consolidate his gains and make his rule effective.

With the elimination of active opposition, 'Abd al-Malik could pursue his policy of consolidating his authority. It seems that the events of the early part of the reign and the crisis which had affected the Umayyad caliphate since Mu'āwiya's death had convinced him that the decentralized system that Mu'āwiya had introduced was not practical; under the control of a highly skilled manipulator like Mu'āwiya, it could be effective but it was not a solid foundation for building a state. He began a policy of administrative and political centralization which was to provide a model for many later Muslim governments. This involved the development of a standard Arabic coinage. Up to this time, the coinage had been essentially regional: in Iraq and the east, the Muslims had begun to issue silver *dirhams* based on Sasanian models with a simple Muslim overstrike from a very early period. As the governor of Iraq under Mu'āwiya, Ziyād b. Abī Sufyān had minted *dirhams* bearing his own name. This reflects the early development of the *dīwān* system of paying the military, which required large quantities of cash.

In Syria, by contrast, there is no evidence that gold or silver was minted before the reign of ʿAbd al-Malik. There is some suggestion that copper coins (*fulūs*) were minted locally but even that remains uncertain. This probably reflects the slower development of systems of military pay in Syria and the absence of any centralized *dīwān*.

After ʿAbd al-Malik's reforms, the old distinction between the silver (*dirham*) areas of the Sasanian Empire and the gold (*dīnār*) areas of Syria, Palestine and Egypt was maintained but from now on, after a few experiments with figurative designs, including a "standing caliph" portrait, all Arabic coinage was to be of a standard weight and design, bearing inscriptions but no images. The new gold *dīnārs* were introduced in 77/696–697 and the silver *dirhams* in 79/698–699. The gold *dīnārs*, which were probably produced in Damascus, carried pious phrases and the date but neither the place of minting nor the name of the ruler. The *dirhams* produced in a number of mints in Iraq and the east gave the name of the mints but not that of the caliph or governor. From the reign of the caliph Hishām, *dirham* production was centralized in Wāsiṭ, where the Syrian troops were stationed.

Along with this standardization of the coinage went an Arabization of the administration. From now on, all the administration in any part of the empire was to be conducted in Arabic, once again eliminating local differences and forcing those Persian and Greek officials who wished to continue to work for the government to learn the new ways. Nor was there any doubt that surplus taxation was to be forwarded to the treasury in Damascus; the Iraqis had lost the battle to retain the revenues of the Sawād in their own hands. All these activities served to introduce a unity and degree of control which had hitherto been lacking.

This administrative centralization reflected a broader political change. ʿAbd al-Malik's authority was based on his own family and on the Syrian army. His own family had been employed from Marwān's reign to govern different areas. His brother ʿAbd al-Azīz was the ruler of Egypt for almost the entire reign, from the time of its conquest from Ibn al-Zubayr in 65/685 to the year before the caliph's death, keeping the province loyal and peaceful. Other experiments were not as successful; his brother Bishr b. Marwān does not seem to have been able to control Iraq, and as we shall see, family rule was not continued there. Another brother, Muḥammad b. Marwān, however, was the governor of the Jazīra from its first subjection in 73/692–693 until 91/709–710, some years after the caliph's death. Here again, a key province was held by a member of the Marwanid family who secured its loyalty to the regime. One result of this was that the family itself tended to become divided and to represent different interests within the Syrian ruling group; Muḥammad b. Marwān, for example, became closely associated with the Qaysīs of the northern Jazīra and the Byzantine frontier region, while the caliph's son Sulaymān, living at Ramla in Palestine, became identified with the Yamanī interest. These associations were later to lead to differences and divisions within the ruling house itself.

The Umayyad élite and their allies benefited from the revenues of landed estates known as *qaṭā'i'* (sing. *qaṭī'a*), not to be confused with the *iqṭā'* or fief which became common in the Islamic world from the fourth/tenth century onwards. The settlement of the Arab conquerors in the time of 'Umar b. al-Khaṭṭāb and his successors had envisaged that all the resources of the conquered lands should be helped in common as the *fay'* of the Muslims, but from the earliest times members of the élite had sought to carve out private estates of their own. They were enabled to do this by means of a legal device, probably borrowed from Roman or earlier Mesopotamian land law. This allowed men who developed waste land and brought it under cultivation to claim it as their own property. It was heritable (they could pass it to their children), alienable (they could sell it) and defensible at law. Furthermore, these estates would pay only a tithe or *'ushr* rather than the much higher *kharāj* to which other lands were subject. This encouraged members of the élite to invest in irrigation and drainage systems, especially in the desert margins of the Fertile Crescent. So we see the early Muslim élite of Basra investing in canals to bring the barren lands around the city under cultivation, the sons of the caliph 'Abd al-Malik creating new agricultural settlements along the Middle Euphrates valley and various members of the élite, including the Caliph Hishām and the future Caliph al-Walīd b. Yazīḍ, constructing farms and palaces along the fringes of the Syrian desert from Qasr al-Hayr al-Sharqī in the north to the plains of the Balqā east of Amman in the south. The desert *quṣūr*, such a characteristic feature of the Umayyad period, were at least in part a product of this favourable fiscal regime. After the coming of 'Abbasid rule, new *qaṭā'i'* were rarely established in rural areas: by the third/ninth century, they had largely disappeared and with them the large-scale land reclamation which had been part of them.

The Syrian army also contained different groups. The Marwanids had been brought to power by the Yaman tribes under the leadership of the Kalbīs, who for the first seven years of the reign remained the mainstay of the forces. The agreements of 71/691 between the caliph and the Qaysī leader, Zufar b. al-Ḥārith at Qarqīsiyyā', however, broke this monopoly of power. From this point onwards, 'Abd al-Malik tried to balance the interests of these two groups, both at court and in the army. It was not an easy task. The feud between the Yamanī groups and the Qaysīs which had emerged after Yazīd I's death was exacerbated by raids and counterraids, at first in the Jazīra and Palmyrena but later as far away as the Ḥijāz and Iraq. Tribes which were not previously involved, and whose genealogical affiliations were obscure, were drawn into this conflict whether they liked it or not. The Taghlib, for example, were a tribe which had lived for many years on the middle Euphrates, but in the aftermath of the conquest, they found their position threatened by newcomers from Arabia, the Banū Sulaym. The Sulaym were attached to the Qaysī group at Marj Rāhiṭ, and so the Taghlib, to defend themselves, were forced to look for protection from Kalbī leaders and became attached to the Yamanī cause. In this way, the pernicious feud which had previously been confined to Syria alone was spread through much of the Islamic world. The violence, raiding and counterraiding were almost impossible to stop; the best that the caliph could do was to keep it under control by threats and to pay the blood money demanded to prevent further retaliation. Like the activities of the Khawārij, the Qays–Yaman feud illustrated the problems of transition from a nomad to a settled society and policy.

Iraq of course remained the major problem, and it was here that ʻAbd al-Malik employed his greatest and most celebrated helper, al-Ḥajjāj b. Yūsuf al-Thaqafī. He was born in Tā'if in 41/661 and was thus some twenty years younger than the caliph and still a young man when he was called to high office. He worked his way up through the military police, the *shurṭa*, and came to the caliph's attention during the preparations for the Iraq campaign of 71–72/690–691. After the fall of Kūfa, al-Ḥajjāj was sent to fulfil the unpopular task of reducing Ibn al-Zubayr in Mecca, and his efficiency and loyalty were shown to their fullest. ʻAbd al-Malik's experiments with family rule in Iraq had not been a success, so in 75/694, he turned to al-Ḥajjāj and put him in charge of both Baṣra and Kūfa, as Ziyād b. Abīhi had been before. In 78/697–698, Khurāsān and Sīstān were added to his responsibilities, making him an effective overlord of all the eastern half of the caliphate. He did not administer Khurāsān directly but appointed the Azdī leader al-Muhallab, who had fought the Khawārij so well and now became a major force in the Umayyad east. As soon as he was appointed to Iraq, al-Ḥajjāj demonstrated his fierce determination to rule effectively. In this, he was helped by his Thaqafī connections, and while his origins are usually described as obscure, his mother was actually the divorced wife of al-Mughīra b. Shuʻba al-Thaqafī, governor of Kūfa for Muʻāwiya.

From the beginning, he seems almost to have goaded the Iraqis into rebellion, as if looking for an excuse to break them. Under pain of death, he forced the armies of Kūfa and Baṣra into the field, to that most unrewarding of tasks, combating the Khawārij. Furthermore, in an effort at economy, he reduced their *ʻaṭā'*, so that they were actually paid less than the Syrians. There was bound to be an explosion, and five years after his appointment it came. The issue was an old bone of contention, the reluctance of the armies of Kūfa and Baṣra to go on long campaigns, and in the year 80/699, al-Ḥajjāj obliged ʻAbd al-Raḥmān b. Muḥammad b. al-Ashʻath to lead an expedition to Sīstān. Ibn al-Ashʻath was the greatest of the *ashrāf* of Iraq and a symbol of their pride and independence. His family had done much to undermine the positions of both ʻAlī and Mukhtār. To his army were attached a number of other *ashrāf*, so much so that it was called the Peacock Army, from the wealth and display of its leaders. The campaign was hard, but more difficult for the leaders to bear were the constant rebukes and instructions from al-Ḥajjāj, and this overbearing attitude finally drove Ibn al-Ashʻath to rebellion. He led his army west from Sīstān, through Fārs, and defeated al-Ḥajjāj's forces at Tustar, 81/701, before sweeping on to establish himself in his hometown of Kūfa. Al-Ḥajjāj maintained himself in Baṣra with Thaqafī support and a Syrian garrison, but without massive Syrian aid, he was powerless to take the initiative.

In Kūfa, Ibn al-Ash'ath was welcomed by all sections of the population, but there must have been many in the city who remembered how he and his family had betrayed the cause of Mukhtār, and the rifts soon began to show again. The caliph was seriously alarmed at the turn of events and, to al-Ḥajjāj's disgust, offered terms. These included the dismissal of al-Ḥajjāj, the appointment of Ibn al-Ash'ath to high office and the raising of the *'aṭā'* of Iraqi troops to the Syrian level. Ibn al-Ash'ath wanted to accept these terms but his more determined followers among the *qurrā'* rejected them and he was forced to continue the fight. With the breakdown of negotiations, al-Ḥajjāj and the Syrians took the initiative again, defeating Ibn al-Ash'ath in a series of battles, notably at Dayr al-Jamājim (Rabī' I 82/April 701), and dividing his supporters by generous offers of amnesty to all those who would lay down their arms. Ibn al-Ash'ath himself was forced to leave Iraq and fled to the east, where he eventually tried to take refuge with the Rutbīl, the prince of Zābulistān in southern Afghanistan, and the man he had originally been sent by al-Ḥajjāj to fight, but his followers were dispersed and he himself died soon after. Once again, the divisions among the Kūfans and the determined use of Syrian military power by 'Abd al-Malik and al-Ḥajjāj had frustrated the attempts of the Iraqis to recover their former status.

The aftermath of Ibn al-Ash'ath's rebellion saw the introduction of a new and more rigorous system of government in Iraq. The next year, al-Ḥajjāj established a permanent garrison of Syrian troops at a new military centre, Wāsiṭ, between Baṣra and Kūfa. Syrian troops seem to have developed effective military tactics: when faced by an enemy charge, they would get down on the ground and use their spears to present a bristling wall to the enemy. It required discipline, nerve and willingness to obey orders, but it proved effective against less well-organized opponents. Henceforth, these Syrian troops were to be the real ruling class in the area, and the Iraqis, whether *ashrāf*, *qurrā'* or *mawālī*, were reduced to subject status. The revolt had been an attempt by the local leadership to assert its control and now that it had been defeated, al-Ḥajjāj seemed determined to break it for ever.

There was also a fundamental change in the fiscal system of the state, at least as it operated in Iraq. Originally, the *'aṭā'* had been paid according to the role which the recipient, or his ancestors, had played in the Muslim conquests. It was, in fact, a reward for past service, and many in Iraq believed that it was their unalienable right. Al-Ḥajjāj was determined to change this. He saw clearly that this system meant that the caliph and his governor had very little executive authority and few rewards to offer their loyal supporters. He decided that the *'aṭā'* should be a salary, a payment for serving in the army, rather than a reward for what one's ancestors had done. People who did not fight would not be paid. Furthermore, this army was now largely made up of Syrian soldiers. This aroused the passionate hostility of many in Iraq, who claimed that the provisions laid down by ʿUmar and supported by ʿAlī were being destroyed by the impious Umayyads, but in the end al-Ḥajjāj's vision triumphed: by his death, the *ʿaṭā'* had become a salary paid for service, not a reward received by ancient right. Thus, the Muslim state developed a professional army and paid in cash salaries from the proceeds of public taxation, a structure familiar from the ancient world but virtually unknown in contemporary western Europe.

Al-Ḥajjāj and members of the Umayyad family, notably the caliph's son Maslama, began a policy of large-scale land reclamations and development in central Iraq, digging new canals and bringing areas under cultivation, but the fruits of this policy went to the Umayyad family and their supporters and the profits were spent in Syria. Investment tended to be concentrated around the new centre of Wāsiṭ, while the lands of the *ashrāf* and the *dihqāns* around Kūfa were neglected by the government. Thus, both politically and economically, al-Ḥajjāj destroyed the power of the Kūfan élite; the family of Ibn al-Ashʿath and others like them continued to enjoy a modest prosperity from the area but their political power was broken for ever. The people of Kūfa, which in the time of ʿUmar had been the greatest Muslim city of all, were now leaderless and cowed; only a radical and total revolution could reverse this unhappy state of affairs.

The partnership of ʿAbd al-Malik and al-Ḥajjāj lasted until the caliph's death. Al-Ḥajjāj was not just the ruler of Iraq, but he effectively controlled Khurāsān and all the east, appointing governors from among his protégés. He had made this control absolute when in 84/704 he had secured the dismissal from Khurāsān of Yazīd b. al-Muhallab, who had succeeded his father as the governor in 82/701–702. Despite his affinity with the *ashrāf*, al-Muhallab had resisted all attempts of Ibn al-Ashʿath to involve him in his rebellion and held the province for al-Ḥajjāj. Although they had proved their loyalty, however, the Muhallabīs were suspected because of their independent power base among the Azdī tribesmen and their great prestige. By 84/704, there seem to have been growing differences between them and al-Ḥajjāj, differences which the absolutist nature of al-Ḥajjāj's power could not tolerate.

ʿAbd al-Malik died in Damascus in Shawwāl 86/October 705 at the age of sixty. His reign had been a period of hard-won successes; he had established, in place of the decentralized Sufyanid system, a centralized, bureaucratic empire, dependent in the last resort on the power of the Syrian army. The Islamic community was sharply divided between the rulers and the ruled, where the ruled were no longer the conquered people and *mawālī* alone but included many Arabs, especially in Iraq and Khurāsān, who felt that the regime no longer represented their wishes or needs. It was in many ways an impressive achievement but was to prove something of a difficult inheritance for the later Umayyads. But ʿAbd al-Malik also left one legacy which we can still delight in today: the Dome of the Rock, the earliest great monument of Islamic architecture, constructed in Jerusalem on his orders and at his expense.

The sons of 'Abd al-Malik and 'Umar II – consolidation and division in the Marwanid caliphate: 86–125/705–743

'Abd al-Malik was succeeded by his son al-Walīd, already acknowledged as heir since the death of his uncle, 'Abd al-'Azīz b. Marwān, the longtime governor of Egypt, in the previous year. Al-Walīd's reign was in many ways a continuation of his father's and a period of prosperity and peace in many parts of the empire. He instituted a system of poor relief and public charity in Syria and began many building projects, notable the great Umayyad mosque in the centre of Damascus. He also attempted to keep the balance, as his father had done, among the different groups in the Syrian élite. The rivalry for power between the Qaysī and Yamanī leaders was as intense as ever, and it is at least possible that the caliph kept it on the boil so that one faction should not acquire a monopoly of power. He himself had a Qaysī mother, Wallāda, and seems to have allowed the Qaysīs certain privileges, but other members of the Marwanid family attached themselves to the rival party; his brother and heir Sulaymān was the governor of Palestine and firmly allied to the Yamanī interest, while his cousin 'Umar, son of 'Abd al-'Azīz b. Marwān, maintained the Yamanī contacts his father had built up in Egypt, and al-Walīd allowed him the prestigious position of governor of the Ḥijāz, which he used to afford a refuge to those who wished to escape al-Ḥajjāj's power in Iraq.

The reign of al-Walīd (86–96/705–715) also saw the farthest extension of the geographical frontiers of the Umayyad state. In the west, Spain was invaded in 92/711 and was almost entirely taken by 97/716, while parties of raiding Arabs turned their attentions to southern France. In the east, the expansion was under the aegis of al-Ḥajjāj, who appointed governors whose most important function was to extend the frontiers. In Khurāsān, Qutayba b. Muslim launched in 86–96/705–715 from his base in Marv a series of attacks on the area beyond the Oxus, which the Muslims had hardly reached before. Thus, he secured the submission of Bukhārā in 87–90/706–709, Khwārazm and Samarqand in 91–93/711–712 and distant Farghānā in 94/713. This raiding did not, however, result in massive settlements of Muslims in the newly conquered areas; Qutayba made treaties with the existing rulers or, if necessary, replaced them by other local candidates but he did not enforce direct government. The effect of this was to draw into the Umayyad network a number of local kings who, while retaining their own power, paid tribute to and worked in harmony with the Arab governor in Marv. In Sind too, al-Ḥajjāj's policy of expansion was pursued and he appointed a fellow Thaqafī, Muḥammad b. Yūsuf, to lead the Arab advance in the area. This policy of expansion had, since the time of the Prophet, served to absorb the energies of the Arabs and so preserve internal peace and provide an income and opportunities to those who might otherwise feel deprived. It was not, however, popular among all the participants. Conciliatory governors in Iraq from Ziyād's time on had promised that the armies of the area would not be sent on distant campaigns against their will, and the revolt of Ibn al-Ash'ath was at least in part a protest against the policy of expansion. Qutayba led his troops to many victories in the east, but when he tried to persuade them to support him in a revolt after the death of al-Walīd, they demonstrated clearly that these military activities had not won their loyalty and devotion.

Al-Ḥajjāj died in Ramaḍān 95/June 714 aged only fifty-five and the Caliph al-Walīd the next year, 96/715, setting the stage for a reaction against these policies. 'Abd al-Malik had settled the succession such that al-Walīd would be succeeded by his brother Sulaymān, and despite some efforts to alter this arrangement, Sulaymān, a generous and easygoing prince, now duly became caliph. As has already been noted, Sulaymān had been the governor of Palestine, where he had come in close contact with the local Yamanī leaders, and his tutor and chief adviser was Rajā' b. Ḥaywa al-Kindī, a religious figure attached to the Yamanī group who had served 'Abd al-Malik as, among other things, the manager of the construction of the Dome of the Rock. Sulaymān had used his position to make allies among those who opposed al-Ḥajjāj and his policies, including the deposed governor of Khurāsān, Yazīd b. al-Muhallab, who sought refuge with him in his capital at Ramla. Sulaymān's accession marks the return to power of the Yamanī group and the dismissal of many of al-Ḥajjāj's nominees, including Qutayba b. Muslim in Khurāsān.

There has been much controversy about exactly what the Yaman Qays–Muḍar parties stood for at this time. They certainly represented rival groups within the Syrian élite and army which claimed a common descent. The Arab sources tend to portray the conflict as essentially a tribal rivalry, *'asabiyya*. It is not convincing to argue that they were really different political parties, the Qaysīs supporting expansion of the empire and an Arab monopoly on political power, while the Yamanīs were less imperialist and concerned to make links with non-Arab Muslims. In reality, the conflict was between two factions based on tribal loyalties, which sought to control access to military power and the privileges that went with it. The prizes were the favour of the ruling caliph and the lucrative governorships in the provinces. What may have begun as a struggle in Syria soon spread elsewhere: in Iraq, the Azd tribe was drawn into the Yamanī group, while their great rivals, the Tamīm, became the centre of the Qays–Muḍar group in the province. These rivalries were, in turn, transported to Khurāsān, where the participation of the Arabs in military forces meant that the rivalries were especially fierce and violent. By the reign of Hishām, if not before, it was virtually impossible for any political or military leader to avoid relying on one faction or the other.

Sulaymān's reign was only two years (96–99/715–717). He had a reputation for luxurious living and certainly did not cultivate a pious image. His government appointments reflected his Yamanī leanings. Rajā' b. Ḥaywa al-Kindī remained his chief adviser, while Yazīd b. al-Muhallab was appointed to Iraq, Khurāsān and all the east. He himself continued to live in Ramla in Palestine, a clear sign of his continuing commitment to the Yamanī party. The main business of the caliph was the conduct of the Holy War. Maslama b. 'Abd al-Malik led the great expedition against Constantinople in 98–99/716–717, and Sulaymān himself died while on his way to lead an expedition against the Syrian frontier of the Byzantine Empire.

Sulaymān's unexpected death meant a crisis for his supporters, since they felt that 'Abd al-Malik's other prominent sons, Yazīd and Hishām, were committed to their opponents. In this crisis, the succession was managed by the caliph's adviser, Rajā' b. Ḥaywa, who persuaded him, just before his death, to nominate his cousin 'Umar b. 'Abd al-'Azīz instead.

It was thanks to Sulaymān's testament and Rajā's organization that 'Umar II became caliph. He is the most puzzling character among the Marwanid rulers. The Islamic tradition is unanimous in seeing him as a complete contrast to the other rulers of his family; where they are godless usurpers, tyrants and playboys, he alone is represented as pious and ruling like a true Muslim. Recent scholarship has confirmed the view that his reign marks an important break, although from a rather different point of view.

'Umar seems to have been determined to reintegrate the Muslim community, to try to break down the barriers between the Arab rulers and their non-Muslim subjects and between different groups of Arabs. Shaban has characterized this as an extreme Yamanī point of view, but this is not wholly borne out by the evidence. 'Umar seems to have tried to get away from this sort of party involvement and appeal to a broader cross section of the community.

In appointing governors, always a good indication of a ruler's policies, he made radical changes. In the east, he broke up the vast eastern governorate which had been developed by al-Ḥajjāj into different units, each responsible to him. Ibn al-Muhallab was deposed and arrested and in his place there were a variety of nominees; Kūfa was ruled by a member of the family of 'Umar I, for example. Few of these people could be described as Yamanīs, and indeed 'Umar II was responsible for appointing to the Jazīra a man who was to typify the hardline Qaysī attitude in years to come, 'Umar b. Hubayra al-Fazārī. Rather than favouring one party, he seems to have chosen governors over whom he had control and whom he believed to be competent. His activities suggested that he intended to keep a close eye on provincial administration. He saw that a major cause of friction between the *mawālī* and the government, especially in Iraq, was the system of taxation, which, under al-Ḥajjāj's iron grip, had meant that converts to Islam continued to be taxed as if they were unbelievers. This bred resentment, and it was to counter this that 'Umar produced his famous fiscal rescript, an attempt to reform the financial administration. The most revolutionary aspect of this was that the *mawālī* were to be taxed as if they were Muslims, that is to say they were to pay only the *ṣadaqa*, or alms. However, they were not allowed to sell their land to Muslims, and on conversion their land became the property of their villages, that is to say that their lands remained *kharāj* lands, paying the full rate of land tax. In this way, the anomaly could be removed without doing great damage to the treasury. It was an ingenious scheme and it is not entirely clear how successful it could have been; the reaction which followed his death certainly meant that it was allowed to lapse. It did establish, however, the fundamental point of Muslim taxation: that *kharāj* land remained *kharāj* land no matter who owned it. Unbelievers were required to pay the *jizya*, or poll tax, now clearly separated from the *kharāj*, and this lapsed on conversion, but the payment of *kharāj* was unaffected by this.

In this way, 'Umar attempted to resolve the tensions which threatened the community. He also forbade any further foreign wars and adventures. His character is difficult to assess. When he was in the Ḥijāz, he seems to have had a reputation for luxurious living, but on becoming caliph he adopted something of the austerity traditionally ascribed to his namesake 'Umar I. This piety may well have been genuine, but it was the mark of a skilled and determined politician trying to find new solutions to long-standing problems.

This programme of reform was brought to an untimely end by his early death in 101/720. His policies had threatened too many interests and the Qaysīs were determined to reestablish the old order. His successor, Yazīd II, was a caliph in the old tradition, more interested in amusement than the day-to-day business of government and prepared to let the governors of the provinces have their own way. He was content to be ruled by Qaysī advisers, but not everyone in the empire was prepared to accept the change gracefully. Yazīd b. al-Muhallab was allowed to escape from prison and immediately raised the standard of revolt in Iraq, pledging a Holy War against the Syrian rule. Ibn al-Muhallab was perhaps the only indigenous Iraqi leader to have survived al-Ḥajjāj's rule, and he immediately attracted a large following in Baṣra, where his own tribe was based and the provinces dependent on it. Then, he took the Syrian garrison town of Wāsit. and advanced on Kūfa, attracting some support from that city too. But not all Kūfans rushed to the standard, and there is no evidence that he received any support from the Yamanī party in Syria. He was opposed by one of the greatest soldiers of the age, Maslama b. 'Abd al-Malik, a hero of the Qays and of numerous wars against the Byzantines. In Ṣafar 102/August 720, Yazīd b. al-Muhallab was defeated and killed on the field of battle, the last of the old-style Iraqi champions. For the final time, the divisions among the Iraqis had allowed the Syrians to triumph and to assert their control, once more, over the east.

Maslama remained only a short time as the governor, apparently because he had failed to send surplus revenue from the province to Damascus. His replacement was the Qaysī thug 'Umar b. Hubayra, whom 'Umar II had promoted to be the governor of the Jazīra and who proved violent and brutal in his pursuit of the Muhallabīs and the Yamanī leaders.

Perhaps fortunately for the stability of the Umayyad caliphate, Yazīd himself died in 105/724 after a reign as caliph of only four years, and he was replaced by his much more able, austere and conscientious brother Hishām. Hishām had been born in Damascus in 72/691 and was in his thirties when he became caliph. Little is known of his early career beyond his outspoken opposition to the accession of 'Umar II, but his reign showed him to be shrewd, cautious and on the whole conciliatory. Like all the wiser and more successful rulers of his family, he attempted to stay above the Qays–Yaman feud and to avoid confrontation if possible. It is a measure of his success that the nineteen years of his reign were among the most peaceful of the entire Umayyad century, at least as far as internal opposition was concerned. In the all-important governorate of Iraq and the east, which now again took in Khurāsān and Iran as it had under Ziyād and al-Ḥajjāj, Hishām appointed a new man from the neutral tribe of Bajīla, Khālid b. 'Abd Allāh al-Qasrī. Khālid does not have the reputation of his great predecessors for statesmanship or ferocity, but he was thoroughly competent and totally loyal, conscious that he owed his whole career to the Umayyads and considering that his interests were totally bound up with theirs. For fifteen years, he ruled Iraq and it was a period without any serious disturbances.

Hishām's main problems were external invasion and the finances of the government. During his rule, the Islamic empire suffered three major challenges. The first of these threats was from the Caucasus area, where the Arabs' control of the passes to the west of the Caspian was seriously threatened by the attacks of the Khazars, Turks from the steppes of southern Russia. To combat these threats, the Qaysīs of the Jazīra were mobilized, as well as local Armenian troops. Command was given first to the veteran general Maslama b. 'Abd al-Malik and then from 114/732 onwards to another member of the ruling family, Marwān b. Muḥammad b. Marwān, a grandson of the Caliph Marwān. This command gave Marwān a unique opportunity to build up support among the Qaysīs and others in Armenia and the Jazīra and he became almost the only member of the ruling family with an independent military command. Armenia at this time was somewhat similar to parts of Khurāsān, in that the Arabs ruled through the native princes, or *nakharars;* who collected tribute and some of whose men were recruited for the army against the Khazars. Marwān took great care to remain on good terms with these local nobles, and ensured that their men received the pay owed to them. He also ensured the accession to leadership of the *nakharars* of his own protégé, Ashot the Bagratid, the ancestor of a long and famous line of Armenian kings, by expelling his enemies, the Mamikonian family. The campaign was difficult but in the end triumphant – the Khazars were driven back from the Muslim lands and in 120/738 Marwān raided as far as the Khazar capital on the lower Volga. After 121/739, he, with the help of his loyal Qaysī assistant, Isḥāq b. Muslim al-'Uqaylī, concentrated on consolidating his power and influence in the area.

The second threat came from the Berbers in North Africa. The conquest of the Berbers had been very superficial, and while Arab garrisons had been established in some centres of what is now Tunisia, like Qayrawān, there was very little organized government. The Muslim presence was essentially predatory, slaves and booty being the main concern of Arab-raiding parties. As with the *mawālī* in Iraq, it seems that the beginnings of conversion to Islam made the Berbers' grievances more acute, and this was brought home to them by missionaries from the Khawārij of Iraq who pointed out how the Umayyad government was exploitative and tyrannical. In 123/740–741, there was a massive rebellion which effectively drove the Arabs out. An expedition sent to retrieve the situation was heavily defeated and it was only with difficulty that the remnants of what had been a large Syrian army fought their way through to Spain, where they settled. In 124/742, another force, under a Kalbī leader, Ḥanẓala b. Ṣafwān, succeeded in restoring the position to some extent, and the rebellion ceased to be a danger. However, this disturbance did considerable damage to the state; Spain was now effectively cut off and the Umayyads maintained no military presence west of Qayrawān. What was more, a large number of Syrian troops had been lost and a further strain put on the Syrian military machine.

The third area of threat was Khurāsān. Here, as in the Caucasus area, the threat came from Turkish nomads, this time a confederation known to Western writers as the Turgesh, who were active in the areas beyond the Oxus and increasingly threatening not just the Arabs but the native people of the settled areas around Bukhārā and Samarqand as well. As the governor of the east, Khālid al-Qasrī first sent his brother Asad to attempt to do what Marwān later achieved in Armenia: to persuade the local people to fight alongside the Arabs against their joint enemies. The problem was more difficult here because the Arabs were reluctant to share any of their privileges with the native population, and in the end the government had to turn to more traditional means to restore the position. In 113/732, another 20,000 men from Iraq were sent, and in the end Asad was able to lead a combined force of Arabs and Iranians who defeated the Turgesh decisively in 119/737. The threat of invasion was lifted, but the immigration of more Iraqis and the mobilization of the local Iranian population were to lead to problems later.

The external threats were defeated but at considerable cost in money and manpower. Expansion had effectively ceased, except in France, where Arab-raiding parties from Spain continued to expand their range. On the Byzantine frontier, the regular summer raids continued but on a limited scale, and no more sieges of Constantinople were undertaken.

Apart from defence, Hishām's other major concern was money. The financial administration of the Umayyad caliphate is very obscure. The sources tell us a good deal, not always clearly or comprehensibly, about who paid what taxes on what land. It is much less certain how far this money was used to finance central government. There remained a widespread body of opinion, especially in Iraq, which held that the revenue from taxation and the *ṣawāfī*, the government lands, was the property of all the Muslims and should be spent in the province where it was raised – the sending of taxes to Damascus was a very contentious issue. Governors who were in a weak position or anxious to curry favour with the local people, as had ʿUbayd Allāh b. Ziyād at the death of Yazīd I in 64/683, always promised that this would not be done. As far as we can tell, even when it was done, only a very small proportion of the money collected was forwarded. ʿUmar II had agreed that the revenues of Khurāsān were to be spent in the province, while Maslama had been sacked from his position as the governor of Iraq for not forwarding any revenue. There seems to have been no elaborate central accounting organization of the sort that developed under the ʿAbbasids; the *dīwāns* or offices in Damascus dealt only with the collection of Syrian revenues. The caliphs were partly peripatetic, spending little time in Damascus itself. ʿAbd al-Malik and his entourage usually wintered at his palace of Ṣinnabra at the south end of the Sea of Galilee. In spring, he would go to Jābiya on the Golan Heights, then to Dayr Murrān on the western outskirts of Damascus. High summer would be spent in Ba'albak before he returned to Damascus and Ṣinnabra for the winter.

To supplement this meagre income, the Umayyad rulers continued large-scale irrigation and development projects on the *sawāfī*, and Hishām was one of the foremost organizers of this in both Syria and Iraq. Anecdotes in the sources portray him as having a real enthusiasm for horticulture, and a keen interest in the profits it could bring. In the city of Mosul, Hishām ordered that vast sums be spent on canal digging and erecting eighteen water mills. In southern Iraq, the development was undertaken by both Khālid al-Qasrī, who is said to have made 20 million *dirhams* out of his agricultural lands, and Maslama b. ʿAbd al-Malik, whose schemes were on an equally vast scale. The remains of numerous Umayyad palaces and castles in Syria show the extent of their developments in rural areas. As always, these activities benefited the government and the élite but were not always appreciated by the local people. A Syrian Christian commentator, Agapius of Manbij, reckoned that Hishām's profits from his landed estates exceeded the profits from taxation of the empire.

The last years of the caliphate were clouded by concern over the succession and saw a slight but important shift of policy. By previous sworn agreement, the succession was to pass to Yazīd II's son al-Walīd on Hishām's death rather than to his own children. Hishām resented this, not just because he favoured his own line but because he had sons who were competent, sober and hard-working like their father. This al-Walīd was not; the playboy of the Umayyads par excellence, he was a talented poet, an enthusiast for architecture (palaces, not mosques) and a heavy drinker. Hishām's attempts to change the arrangement were widely opposed within the Umayyad establishment, even by his closest political friend, Khālid al-Qasrī, and they came to nothing. It was perhaps in order to ensure stability after his death that Hishām seems to have come to rely more on the Qaysīs. Khālid al-Qasrī was deposed from Iraq in favour of Yūsuf b. 'Umar, a protégé of al-Ḥajjāj's and a member of the Thaqafī tribe, which had played such a large part in Iraqi politics. Khālid al-Qasrī may have had Yamanī sympathies; certainly, he was later claimed as a Yamanī. Yūsuf, however, was a determined and outspoken Qaysī. The change in Iraq was followed by one in Khurāsān, where again a committed Qaysī, the veteran military leader Naṣr b. Sayyār, was appointed (both changes in 120/738). Yūsuf made many enemies – at least in part because of his vindictive attitude towards Khālid and his family – and his brief spell as the governor saw the only real disturbance in Iraq during this period. In 122/740, there was an armed revolt in Kūfa led by Zayd b. 'Alī, a grandson of al-Ḥusayn who had arrived in the city from the Ḥijāz. The Kūfans promised large-scale support and Zayd agreed to put right all the old grievances, the Qur'ān and Sunna would be respected, the *'aṭā'* would be paid to all, the *fay'* (i.e. the revenues of the Sawād) would be distributed to the local Muslims, the weak protected and there would be no more distant campaigns. And of course there would be a caliph from the house of the Prophet with his rule based in Kūfa. Despite this popular appeal, the revolt came to nothing; the Kūfans deserted Zayd and he was easily killed by the Umayyad forces, but the revolt shows how all the old grievances were still alive.

The collapse of the Umayyad caliphate: 125–132/743–750

Hishām died in Rabī' II 125/February 743. He left a caliphate prosperous and secure. It is true that the differences between Qays and Yaman were not healed and that the majority of the people in Iraq and points east, both Arabs and *mawālī*, remained unenthusiastic about the regime. It is true too that the recent wars in the West had put an additional strain on the Syrian army. It should not be thought that collapse was inevitable or that another Hishām could not have sustained the empire. Such, however, was not to be the case. Al-Walīd II fulfilled Hishām's worse fears. His conduct was increasingly irresponsible; he seldom went to Damascus and paid little heed to normal administrative affairs, while squandering vast sums on ambitious if seldom finished palace projects. He left the administration the Qaysī advisers Hishām had bequeathed to him, and they took the opportunity to assert their position. Besides the caliph's generally negligent conduct, as offensive to many Muslims as Hishām's had been pleasing, two major affairs brought resentment to a head.

The first of these was the question of the succession. Spurred on perhaps by the evil genius of Yūsuf b. 'Umar, he was at once determined to seek the *bay'a* for his two young sons, al-Ḥakam and 'Uthmān. There was immediate opposition in Syria, and al-Walīd took the most drastic action against members of the Marwanid family; some were executed, while Hishām's son Sulaymān was flogged and exiled to 'Umān. Khālid al-Qasrī, now in retirement in Damascus, refused to swear allegiance to the children and for this he was handed over to his enemy Yūsuf b. 'Umar, who tortured him to death.

According to the historian al-Ṭabarī, al-Walīd arrested his cousins and turned the Yamanīs against him and so was responsible for his own downfall. Certainly a bare year after his accession, he had made himself so unpopular that there was a serious discussion of removing him by force. It must be emphasized that this was very unusual in the Umayyad family. Despite their differences, the princes usually displayed considerable family solidarity, and Hishām's respect for his brother Yazīd's testament is simply one example of this. The initiative was taken by a son of al-Walīd I called Yazīd. He developed the radical line, normally taken by Khārijīs, that al-Walīd's sins were so great that he was no longer fit to be caliph. He was joined by some members of Yamanī tribes anxious to regain their lost position, notably Manṣūr b. Jumhūr al-Kalbī, described as an uncouth bedouin. Many more Umayyads and others were extremely reluctant to support him, however great al-Walīd's crimes. The caliph's negligence and the drunkenness of the chief of police allowed the rebels to take Damascus, but it was only with difficulty and considerable expenditure that they were able to persuade an army to search out al-Walīd. True to form, he was in a desert castle at Bakhrā', about 20 kilometres south of Palmyra, almost defenceless. It was there that he was killed by the rebels in Jumādā II 126/April 744 – murdered, like the Caliph 'Uthmān, as he sat reading the Qur'ān.

Just as the murder of 'Uthmān led to the destruction of the Medinese regime of the Rāshidūn caliphs, so the death of al-Walīd led directly to the breakup of the Umayyad caliphate. It re-opened, in a much more vicious form than ever before, the feud between Qays and Yaman, which successive caliphs from 'Abd al-Malik on had tried to control. It would be wrong to imagine that all members of these two groups were implacably hostile; it would seem that the violence was begun by extremists like Yūsuf b. 'Umar for the Qaysīs and Manṣūr b. Jumhūr for the Yamanīs, but once it had begun, it was very difficult to stop and came to involve the whole Syrian army and political élite. It was this fatal division, more than anything else, which destroyed Umayyad government.

On his accession, Yazīd III made a number of commitments to redress grievances, almost identical to those that Zayd b. 'Alī had made in Kūfa, but including the provision that he was to be deposed if he did not fulfil his promises. He also recalled Sulaymān b. Hishām from exile and appointed the Kalbī leader Manṣūr b. Jumhūr as his governor in the east, but he soon replaced him with 'Abd Allāh, son of 'Umar II. It is difficult to know whether Yazīd III was a genuine reformer in the spirit of 'Umar II or simply an adventurer trying to win popularity. In Iraq, 'Abd Allāh b. 'Umar seems to have tried to win over powerful Kūfans by promising them salaries and a position in the army in exchange for their support. Yazīd III died after a reign of only six months, and his reforming ideals, if such they were, hardly had time to mature. His place was briefly taken by his unconvincing brother, Ibrāhīm, but he was unable to withstand the new strongman of the Qays, Marwān b. Muḥammad. Marwān had remained the governor of Armenia and Āzarbayjān, grudgingly accepting the changing rulers but keeping his power base intact. He now proclaimed himself the avenger of al-Walīd II and came south with his seasoned troops; the attempts to resist him by Ibrāhīm and Sulaymān b. Hishām, who seems to have recruited a private army of his own from among the *mawālī*, were futile, and in Ṣafar 127/December 744, he was proclaimed caliph in the mosque in Damascus.

In many ways, he was an excellent choice. Known as al-Ḥimār (the Ass) for his strength and perseverance, he was a tough military veteran, who might have been able to restore the position, but there were too many factors against success. He was not a member of the ruling branch of the Marwanids and furthermore his mother had been a Kurdish slave, not a freeborn Arab. Whether this was really important is difficult to say, but it gave his enemies a reason to attack him. On top of this, he had come to power with the support of only a small part of the Syrian élite, the Qays of the Jazīra and the Byzantine frontier. He had seized the capital by force and driven the Yamanī leaders out of Syria. That there would be no place for them in the new regime was confirmed when he moved himself, the court and the treasure north to Ḥarrān in the Jazīra, to his own territory. At first, he was conciliatory in Syria, allowing the *junds* to choose their own leaders, but after a series of rebellions, especially in the Yamanī centre of Homs, he resorted to bloody repression. The Kalbīs were finally humbled and by the end of 129/746, he had established a kind of peace.

In Iraq, the situation was extremely confusing and the details do not immediately concern us. In general, two main opposition movements appeared, both of them familiar in many ways from the earlier days. In the Jazīra, there was a rebellion of Khārijīs led by the Shaybānī leader al-Ḍaḥḥāk b. Qays, while in Kūfa, there was a rising in favour of a member of the ʿAlid family, ʿAbd Allāh b. Muʿāwiya. What distinguished these movements from similar ones in the past was not that they were more powerful or threatening but rather that the Umayyad response was confused and divided. ʿAbd Allāh b. ʿUmar had tried to forge an alliance of Yamanī groups from Syria and the Yamanīs of Iraq and Kūfa, and this group was bitterly opposed to Marwān and all he stood for. So hostile were they that their leaders were prepared to abandon the Umayyad cause altogether and side with their enemies. Sulaymān b. Hishām joined the Khārijīs, while Manṣūr b. Jumhūr and ʿAbd Allāh b. ʿUmar ended up with Ibn Muʿāwiya. Nothing could illustrate more graphically the breakup of the Syrian élite.

Marwān was determined to press ahead with his conquest of Iraq, despite troubles in Armenia, where his protégé Ashot the Bagratid had been deposed by his rivals. Armenia was held by his devoted lieutenant, the Qaysī leader Isḥāq b. Muslim al-ʿUqaylī, while Marwān sent another leading Qaysī, Yazīd b. ʿUmar b. Hubayra, son of Yazīd II's governor of Iraq, to attack Kūfa. Marwān's campaign showed the effectiveness of his troops and his own military skills. In a final last-ditch resistance, all the elements opposed to his rule – Ibn Muʿāwiya, the Khawārij, Syrian and Iraqī Yamanīs and even 'Abbasid supporters – came together for a combined stand. But Marwān's general Ibn Ḍubāra was too strong for them and they were scattered. By the spring of 130/748, peace was restored and Marwān II was caliph, while Yazīd b. 'Umar b. Hubayra in Wāsit. was his governor of the east, but it was the peace of exhaustion, the peace of the desert. Plague and famine and a terrible earthquake followed in Syria in the wake of the wars. It was a devastated country. Power now lay in the hands of men from the Jazīra and the mountains of Armenia. Recovery might have been possible even yet, but there was a cloud on the horizon in the shape of a rebellion in distant Khurāsān, led in the name of the Family of the Prophet by an obscure *mawlā* called Abū Muslim. By Jumādā II 130/February 748, Abū Muslim had established himself in the Khurāsānī capital at Marv, having driven out the Umayyad governor, Naṣr b. Sayyār, and was sending his armies to the west to challenge the Umayyads. Marwān was loyally supported by his Qaysī army. From his base in Wāsiṭ, Ibn Hubayra despatched armies under Nubāta b. Hanẓala al-Kilābī and 'Amir b. Dubāra al-Murrī to check the advance of the rebels on the Iranian plateau, but both were defeated by the opposing general, Qaḥṭabā b. Shabīb. In Iraq itself, the resentment against the Qaysī government of Marwān once more made itself felt; in Baṣra, a member of the famous Muhallabī clan, Sufyān b. Mu'āwiya, made an unsuccessful attempt to take the city, while Kūfa was held for the rebels by Khālid al-Qasrī's son Muḥammad. Alienated members of the Umayyad élite played a significant role in the triumph of the rebels in Iraq. By Rabī' I 132/October 749, the rebel army had occupied Kūfa, and a rival caliph, the 'Abbasid Abu' al-'Abbās al-Saffāḥ, had been proclaimed. Only in Wāsit. did Ibn Hubayra continue to hold out.

Faced with this new crisis, Marwān summoned his most loyal Qaysī supporters to march in Iraq but the 'Abbasid armies were ready to meet him. It seems that the 'Abbasids were heavily outnumbered but they still defeated Marwān at a battle on the river Zāb in Jumādā II 132/February 750, a battle which effectively broke Umayyad power forever. Marwān fled west, but the Syrians refused to rally to a man who had inflicted so much damage on their land. In Damascus, in fact, the Yamanī party opened the gates to the pursuing 'Abbasid forces. Marwān fled on to Egypt, perhaps hoping to reach north Africa, but at the end of Dhu'l-Ḥijja 132 (August 750), just six months after the defeat on the Zāb, he and his followers were surprised in the village of Būṣir, south of Fuṣṭāt, and the last Umayyad caliph was killed as he had lived, fighting.

The fall of the Umayyads can be explained in many ways. On an ideological level, they failed because they could not offer the sort of leadership which many Muslims wanted. It used to be accepted that the Umayyads claimed only secular authority, but Crone and Hinds in their book *God's Caliph* have demonstrated that the Umayyad caliphs did claim a religious authority; the ruler was God's Caliph (*khalīfat Allāh*) and had the authority to make decisions about Islamic law and practice. However, there were many Muslims, especially in Iraq, who felt that charismatic, truly Islamic leadership was necessary to establish the rule of the Qur'ān and Sunna. By the end of the Umayyad period, it had become an article of faith among such people that only the Family of the Prophet could supply this authority.

There were also regional problems. From 'Abd al-Malik's reign onwards, Umayyad government had increasingly meant Syrian government. Despite attempts by 'Umar II and others to broaden the base of the regime, the Muslims of Iraq were entirely excluded. This narrowness of support became even more pronounced with the Qaysī triumph under Marwān II; at the end, even Syria and Palestine were conquered territories and Damascus had been replaced by Ḥarrān in the Jazīra as the Umayyad capital. This restricted nature of support for the regime was made more serious because neither Syria nor the Jazīra was as rich or had such large Muslim populations as Iraq. In the second half of the eighth century, the revenues from the alluvial areas of southern Iraq amounted to four times those from Egypt and almost five times the revenues from the whole of Syria and Palestine. Constant warfare had certainly drained the resources of manpower in Syria. The wars of Hishām's reign against the Berbers and the internecine disputes which followed his death must have placed a considerable strain on the manpower of the Qaysī tribes who supported the last Umayyad. In addition, Marwān's policies had spread disaffection, not just among elements traditionally hostile to the regime but among people who had previously been loyal servants, like the family of Khālid al-Qasrī and even members of the Umayyad house itself, like Hishām's own son Sulaymān. In these circumstances, it is hardly surprising that the Umayyad state was swept away.

In the final judgement, however, it would be wrong to imagine that the fall of the dynasty was inevitable. The Umayyad regime had never been as strong as it had been under Hishām only a decade before the final collapse. It was only the failure of leadership and murderous conflicts which followed his death which led to disaster, and even at the end Marwān's Qaysī supporters could raise very formidable armies to oppose the 'Abbasids.

Julius Wellhausen, in the title of a famous book, described the Umayyad regime as *Das arabische Reich*, the Arab empire, and held that its passing marked the moment when the Arabs lost control of the movement they had created and the leadership of the *umma* passed to a new élite, some of Arab origin, many others of Iranian or, slightly later, of Turkish descent. Despite the challenges to this picture, it remains basically intact; no one who could not claim Arab descent played a leading role in Umayyad politics or court life, although the talents of non-Arabs in financial or agricultural administration were certainly used. But it was an Arab kingdom in another important sense as well; it was the period when the Arabic language came to dominate the Near East, not in the sense that the majority of the population became Arabic-speaking but in the sense that it became the language of bureaucracy, high court culture and, above all, the religion of the ruling class. The dominance of Arabic was bound up with the dominance of Islam, which retained its identity and separateness in a society where there were numerous ancient and highly developed religious traditions. To see how important this achievement was, we have only to compare the fate of the Arabs and their civilization with that of the Germanic conquerors who came to rule most of the Western Roman Empire from the fifth century onwards.

This linguistic and religious ascendancy was not achieved by mass conversion. Even at the end of the Umayyad period, Muslims still formed a very small proportion of the population of the Near East, and it was probably only in parts of Iraq and Khurāsān that conversion to the new religion had made significant progress. Nor was it achieved by forcible repression. One of the most striking features of the history of the period is the almost total absence of anti-Muslim rebellions. Christians, Jews and Zoroastrians seem to have accepted their role as subject peoples with comparative equanimity, and it was not until the pace of conversion began to increase in the early 'Abbasid period that violent protests developed in parts of Egypt and Iran. Much of this passivity can be put down to the role of these communities before the coming of Islam. The Monophysite Christians of Syria and Egypt, as well as all the Christians of the old Sasanian Empire and the Jews everywhere, had been a demilitarized subject population under the old dispensation. Much of the previous ruling class, the natural leaders of any opposition, had disappeared. At the conquest, many of the Byzantine officials had emigrated to Constantinople or further west to Sicily and Italy, while others had either become converted to Islam, e.g. the scions of the Ghassanid clan, or reached important administrative positions in the government, e.g. the family of St John of Damascus. The disappearance of the élite of Sasanian Persia is more puzzling, since, apart from the mountainous areas of northern Iran and Khurāsān – remote and uninviting districts – they had nowhere to flee to. Many may have lost their lives in the battles of the conquests, many more lost their castles, their lands and their lives in the long struggle to subdue the province of Fārs, the native territory of the Sasanian regime. Others must have been assimilated and become Muslim, perhaps making careers in the bureaucracy, even while remaining conscious of their descent from the Iranian aristocracy. In the fourth/tenth century, under the Buyids, it once again became a sign of status to claim descent from great Iranian families, and when we find in the same period a Fārsī bureaucrat with the Sasanian name of Sābūr (Shāpūr) b. Ardashīr, it is hard to believe that he was not of aristocratic or even royal lineage.

In some ways, the Arabs were in a similar position to the Germanic ruling minorities in western Europe, who equally dominated much larger populations whom they allowed to maintain their own customs and beliefs as long as they paid the required taxes. Perhaps we can see in St John of Damascus a parallel with those Roman officials (like the philosopher Boethius) who made it their business to serve the Ostrogothic kings of Italy, providing a link between the old regime and the new. In Iraq, the *dihqāns*, who had administered much of the country for the Sasanians, now did so at a local level for the Muslims, and once again bureaucratic practice passed from one empire to another; princes and generals might come and go, but those who understood the financial administration could always find employment. Visual evidence of this continuity and adaptation can be seen in early Muslim architecture. The Dome of the Rock in Jerusalem and the Great Mosque in Damascus build on and develop Byzantine architectural techniques, and the Umayyad palace at Khirbat al-Mafjar in the Jordan valley looks back to the Roman villa, just as Theodoric's work at Ravenna develops the styles employed when the city was a Roman capital.

This said, however, the Umayyad state was vastly different in many ways. The most important feature of this was a strong cultural self-confidence, born of the possession of Islam and the Arabic language in which God had communicated the Qu'rān. The Germanic rulers of early medieval Europe craved *Romanitas*, sought to integrate themselves in the culture, language and beliefs of the empire they had entered; Franks, Ostrogoths and Lombards alike abandoned their traditional beliefs and languages to acculturate to the Roman norm. It is strong evidence for the early maturity of the Arab-Islamic tradition that the Muslim conquerors felt no need to do this. The Germanic conquerors of the west abandoned their pagan or Arian beliefs in the face of the opposition of the subject peoples. Despite the vitality of Monophysite Christianity in Syria, Egypt and northern Iraq, the Muslims felt no need to accommodate themselves to the beliefs of the majority – indeed all the traffic was the other way, and it would seem that the more dynamic and ambitious elements in the Christian population soon began to be converted. Nor was there any linguistic imitation; the Arabic the Muslims used was a high-culture written language, the language of the Qur'ān, of a classical poetic tradition and very soon the language of administration and prose narrative. No one wrote Ostrogothic; when Paul the Deacon wrote a history of the Lombards or Gregory of Tours a history of the Franks, they naturally did it in Latin; when Ibn Isḥāq or Abū Mikhnaf wrote a history of the Prophet and of the caliphs in late Umayyad times, they would have not considered doing it in any other language than Arabic. Arabic could never have supplanted the indigenous high-culture and bureaucratic languages unless it had a highly developed written and literary tradition of its own. Where the language of government and culture led, the vernacular soon followed; Greek, Aramaic, Coptic soon ceased to be spoken languages and only in Iran did the language of the conquered, greatly altered in script, grammar and vocabulary, survive to reemerge in the tenth century as a written tongue.

This cultural and linguistic self-confidence was perhaps aided by the fact that the Muslims were heirs to not one but two cultural traditions, the Byzantine and the Sasanian, to say nothing of the Syriac tradition of Monophysite Christianity and the highly developed intellectual and cultural life of Babylonian Jewry. For the invaders of the Western Roman Empire, there could be only one language of learning and writing, and one religious tradition, Catholic Christianity, and it was very difficult to escape from the spell of this all-pervasive culture. For the Muslims in the Near East, however, there was no such universal norm; indeed, the multiplicity of languages and cultures meant that Arabic, far from being overwhelmed, actually became essential; like English in India, it was the only common language in which the peoples of a vast empire could communicate with each other.

The establishment of this culture and civilization owes everything to the Umayyad caliphs. If the Islamic world had broken up, as seemed possible after the death of ʿUthmān, it would have lost not just its political unity but also its cultural and perhaps even its religious identity as small, isolated groups of Muslims became absorbed into the societies of those they had conquered. The Umayyads seized the high ground. They made Islam the religion of a cultured court and an imperial administration. They made Arabic the language of literature and commerce. After the reforms of ʿAbd al-Malik, the Copt, Aramaean, Kurd or Iranian only had to look at the coins in his purse to see the proclamation of the religion and language of the élite. Many Muslims, at the time and later, have criticized the Umayyads for betraying true Islam. To an outside observer, it seems equally clear that Arab-Islamic civilization could never have developed without the achievements of great politicians like Muʿāwiya, ʿAbd al-Malik and Hishām in holding the Muslim world together during the crucial formative century.

It is difficult to discern any clear lines in Umayyad relations with the world beyond the Muslim frontiers or to talk with any confidence of a "foreign policy". Early Muslims divided the world into two zones, the *Dār al-Islām* (House of Islam) and the *Dār al-Ḥarb* (House of War), which the Muslims should attack whenever possible. Rather than peace interrupted by occasional conflict, the normal pattern was seen to be conflict interrupted by the occasional, temporary truce (*hudna*). True peace (*ṣulk.*) could only come when the enemy surrendered and accepted Islam or tributary status. This vision of the world was not in conflict with observable reality. Apart from the distant world of Tang China, the Muslims did not come into contact with any powers which were their equals in terms of wealth or military power and, like the Romans, they could afford to regard all others as barbarians. It was only towards the end of Umayyad rule that the Byzantines were able to face the Muslims on anything approaching an equal basis. There was therefore little incentive for sending diplomatic missions to establish a *modus vivendi* with other powers or to try to establish permanent relations with peoples who were soon to be defeated and incorporated within the *Dār al-Islām*.

The Umayyad period was a bleak time for the Byzantine Empire, when the iconoclast emperors concentrated all their energies on ensuring the survival of the state. The frontier provinces, devastated by war, were lands of ruined cities and deserted villages where a scattered population looked to rocky castles or impenetrable mountains rather than the armies of the empire to provide a minimum of security. The position was very similar at sea, where the Mediterranean was almost entirely a war zone rather than a commercial highway. There are some small signs of cultural and commercial interchanges – the mosaic workers from Byzantium who came to decorate the Great Mosque in Damascus for the Caliph al-Walīd, for example. But by and large, fruitful diplomatic and commercial exchanges were limited before the more settled conditions of the ʿAbbasid period.

With the contemporary Christian powers of Europe – the Lombard kingdom of Italy and the late Merovingian and early Carolingian rulers of France – the Umayyads had no communication at all. It is true that Muslim raiders attacked the Mediterranean shores of both these areas and that Arab expeditions from Spain, which was largely conquered by the Muslims from 92/711 to 97/716, penetrated deep into France, where they were finally defeated by the Carolingian Charles Martel at the battle of Poitiers in 114/732. Muslim raiders maintained themselves in their strongholds in the south of France for two centuries after this. But these were essentially unofficial raids; they led to no government or commercial contacts and the two societies existed in almost total ignorance of each other. Only the occasional pilgrim narrative, like those of Arculf in the first/seventh century and St Willibald at the beginning of the second/eighth would give any indication of the existence of the early caliphate to western Europe, and the writers were more concerned with the Christian Holy Places than with the political condition of the country through which they passed.

More positive were the relations between the Muslims and the Christian people of Nubia, to the south of Egypt. At first, the Muslims had attempted to conquer this area, but resistance proved very fierce and in 31/651–652 they concluded a treaty which allowed the Nubians to live at peace with their Muslim neighbours and obtain food from them on several conditions, notably that they paid a tribute of slaves. This treaty seems to have remained in force throughout the early Islamic period and proved something of a puzzle to Muslim jurists, since Nubia was clearly part of the *Dār al-Ḥarb* and yet the Muslims had signed a permanent and lasting peace treaty with its people, a situation unknown elsewhere on the frontiers.

In contrast to the Mediterranean, the Indian Ocean saw the extensive development of commercial links in the Umayyad period. In Sasanian times, ships had certainly sailed from the Gulf to India and probably to China, but under the Umayyads this traffic seems to have expanded greatly and ports like Ubulla and Baṣra in southern Iraq grew rich on the products of the trade. This, in turn, led to Muslim commercial settlements overseas, first in Sind (southern Pakistan), which was incorporated as a province of the Umayyad and early ʿAbbasid caliphates, then later in east Africa and even as far as distant China, where in 141–142/758, clashes between Muslims and the local people in Canton resulted in the destruction of much of the city. Not only did these Indian Ocean voyages introduce the Islamic world to new products, such as spices and aromatics from Indonesia and Zanzibar and porcelain from China, but they also provided a setting for imaginative adventure, from which the Sinbad the Sailor stories were to grow.

The northeastern frontiers of the caliphate were essentially a war zone. In antiquity, the overland "silk route" had been the main means of communication between the West and China, but in early Islamic times, it seems that this trade had largely dried up. This was partly because silk was now produced in the Near East – and transporting porcelain thousands of miles on the backs of pack animals was hardly a practical proposition – and partly because the area was now disturbed by Turkish nomads raiding the settled areas. It was just after the close of the Umayyad period that central Asia saw the first and only clash between Muslim forces and the army of the Chinese empire under the strong and expansionist rule of the Tang dynasty. In 133/751, Muslim and Chinese armies met at Talas beyond the Jaxartes river (Syr Darya) and the farthest reaches of Muslim settlement. The Muslim armies were victorious but did not pursue their enemies into the fearsome wastes of central Asia. Like the battle of Poitiers twenty years before, the battle at Talas has symbolic importance, marking the end of Arab Muslim expansion in the northeast of the Iranian world. As in the west, the military encounter was not followed up by any diplomatic interchange, and Muslim caliph and Tang emperor remained entirely ignorant of each other.

In a real sense, the Umayyad caliphate, like the Roman Empire, was a self-contained social, cultural and economic unit. The distances within it were so vast and there was such diversity within its frontiers that Muslims did not have the opportunity or the incentive to concern themselves with matters beyond those frontiers. There in the twilight zone of the *Dār al-Ḥarb* were numerous obscure and barbarous peoples like the Franks and Anglo-Saxons, but their lands were too poor, their merchants too few and their armies too weak to attract the attention of the rulers of Islam. This self-sufficiency sometimes makes early Islamic history seem rather remote to outsiders, as if all the events were somehow happening on a different planet, and this impression of separateness is probably correct. Nor was it confined to the Umayyad age. Under the 'Abbasids, closer relations were developed with Byzantium, but it was not until the Fatimids opened up the Mediterranean for shipping from the end of the fourth/tenth century that the affairs of western Europe and the Near East began to interact once again. It was the custom of the Arab Christian annalist of Alexandria, Sa'īd b. al-Biṭrīq to mention the names of all the patriarchs of the great ancient sees of Christendom, Alexandria, Jerusalem, Antioch, Constantinople and Rome. The popes of Rome were duly recorded up to the time of Agatho (678–681), when information was no longer available, and it was not until the early fifth/eleventh century that Sa'īd's continuator, Yaḥyā b. Sa'īd, was once again able to give an up-to-date pope's name. In antiquity, and again in the High Middle Ages, the voyage from Italy to Alexandria was a commonplace; in early Islamic times, the two countries were so remote that even the most basic information was unknown, and if the affairs of Rome were entirely obscure to the patriarch of Alexandria, they were much more so to the caliphs of Damascus. The early Islamic world was essentially self-contained and it was against this background of cultural self-sufficiency that Islamic civilization developed.

5 The early ‘Abbasid caliphate

The coming of the ‘Abbasid caliphate: 132–145/750–763

The Umayyad caliphate was overthrown by a movement in favour of rule by the Family of the Prophet, *Āl Muḥammad*. In the nine decades since the death of ‘Alī, it had become accepted by many discontented Muslims that the problems of the community would never be solved until the lead was taken by a member of the Holy Family. An *imām* or *mahdī* from the Family would be able to interpret the Qur'ān and Sunna and would have the necessary divine guidance to put right the injustices of Umayyad rule and end the violent disputes between Muslims. A more detailed plan of reform was not necessary; the accession of the just ruler and government according to the Qur'ān and Sunna would solve all problems.

During this period, however, it was not entirely clear who was included within the Family of the Prophet or how the leader would be chosen from among the many men who could claim this relationship. In later centuries, the Family of the Prophet was taken to be the descendants of ‘Alī and Fāṭima, and both Twelver and Isma‘īlī Shī‘īs alike accepted that the progeny of al-Ḥusayn b. ‘Alī were the true *imāms*. In Umayyad times, however, this was much less clear-cut and the boundaries of the Family more vague. At the time of Muhktār's revolt, the *imām* from the Family of the Prophet was to be Muḥammad b. al-Ḥanafiyya, a son of ‘Alī but not of Fāṭima, showing that direct descent from the Prophet was not considered essential. In the last decade of Umayyad rule, there was a large-scale rebellion, supported by many different opposition groups in Iraq and western Iran, in the name of ‘Abd Allāh b. Mu‘āwiya, a descendant of ‘Alī's brother Ja‘far. It was therefore with some justice that the ‘Abbasid family, descendants of the Prophet's paternal uncle al-‘Abbās, could claim to be members of the Family. They cultivated the idea that the Family consisted of the descendants of Hāshim, thus including the ‘Alids and ‘Abbasids but excluding the Umayyads. Later, Shī‘ī writers would restrict the Family to the descendants of ‘Alī, so condemning the ‘Abbasids as frauds and usurpers, but at the time of the ‘Abbasid revolution their claims seem to have met with a wide measure of acceptance.

DOI: 10.4324/9780429348129-5

The second problem was the choice of leader within this extended Family. There were three possible criteria. The first, the one which was later adopted by many of the Shīʿa, was that of hereditary succession in the line of al-Ḥusayn, but this idea was not universally accepted in Umayyad times. The second idea was the concept of *naṣṣ*, that is, designation by the previous *imām*. The person thus chosen would have to be a member of the Family but not necessarily the eldest son of the previous *imām*. The third was the Zaydī view that the imamate properly belonged to any member of the Family who was prepared to take up arms. Zayd b. ʿAlī had rebelled in Kūfa in 122/740. He claimed the leadership of the Family because he alone had the courage to lead them against the Umayyads. The rebellion was a dismal failure, but among some sections of opinion in Iraq, the idea persisted that the rightful *imām* was the one who took action against the oppressors.

The claim of the ʿAbbasid family was based on a combination of these elements. They were descendants of Hāshim and so could, in the climate of the Umayyad period, claim to be members of the Family. Al-ʿAbbās himself fought against the Muslims at Badr and only converted to Islam at the time of Muḥammad's conquest of Makka in 8/630. His son ʿAbd Allāh (d. 68/687–688) was an eminent Traditionist (that is to say one who passed on Traditions of the sayings and actions of the Prophet) but seems to have had no political ambitions, and it was not until the time of his grandson Muḥammad b. ʿAlī that the family began to make claims to political leadership. In 98/716–717, Abū Hāshim, the son of Muḥammad b. al-Ḥanafiyya, the *mahdī* to whom Mukhtār had pledged his allegiance, died. He had inherited a claim to the imamate from his father but he left no children to pass it on to. Various parties claimed that they had been designated as his successors, including Muḥammad b. ʿAlī al-ʿAbbāsī. This claim may have brought Muḥammad into contact with small groups of revolutionary activists in Iraq, and perhaps Khurāsān, who treasured the memory of Mukhtār, but it did not win general acceptance in the community. After their accession to power, the ʿAbbasids stressed that their claim was based more on Zaydī grounds, that they alone of the Hashimites had been able to overthrow the godless Umayyads and avenge al-Ḥusayn's martyrdom and that this gave them the right to lead the Family. Later, Shīʿī apologists were concerned to portray the ʿAbbasids as usurpers with no real claim to the throne, but by the standards of their time, their claim was in fact quite good. They were members of the Family, they could claim that Muḥammad b. ʿAlī had been designated by Abū Hāshim and it was clear that they had been able to translate the claims of the Family into reality.

The ʿAbbasids were able to do this because they secured the support of most of the Muslims of Khurāsān, the vast province on the northeastern frontiers of the Muslim world and the only one of the four quarters of the late Sasanian Empire to retain its identity after the Muslim conquest. As has already been explained, more Arabs settled in this area than in any other part of Iran during Umayyad times, and the settlement of large numbers of Muslims seems to have encouraged conversion among the local people. The integration of Arabs with local converts was aided by their participation in the long wars against Turkish raiders which led up to the final defeat of the Turgesh in Hishām's reign. The frontier nature of the province also meant that a high proportion of the Muslims of Khurāsān were experienced soldiers, compared with, for example, the Muslims of Kūfa, and their military skill is clearly demonstrated by the series of victories they won over the veteran troops of Marwān II. The Muslims of Khurāsān had many of the same grievances against the Umayyad government as their contemporaries in Iraq: rule by alien governors sent from Damascus and attempts to secure financial contributions from the province. The Qays–Yaman disputes which had originated in Syria had now spread as far as Khurāsān, producing unrest and uncertainty, and there was a genuine longing to put an end to the *fitna*, the civil strife, which had become so damaging in the years since Hishām's death. In Khurāsān, there was considerable integration between Arab and non-Arab. Many of the leaders of the 'Abbasid movement were of Arab origin but spoke Persian and had intermarried with the local people. The efforts of Marwān's Qaysī supporters to preserve their monopoly of power were not popular in these circumstances.

It was natural then that the Muslims of Khurāsān, like their contemporaries farther to the west, should look to the Family of the Prophet for leadership. How and when the 'Abbasid connection with the area developed is uncertain; the traditional Arabic accounts in al-Ṭabarī and elsewhere suggest that the 'Abbasid *ḍā'wa*, or mission, began in the year 100/718–719 when the 'Abbasids, based in Ḥumayma in southern Jordan, appointed twelve *naqībs* to represent their interests in Khurāsān, just as the Prophet a century before had appointed twelve to represent him in Medina before he arrived in person. Recent research has cast some doubt on this. There had probably been a movement in favour of the Family of the Prophet in Khurāsān for some years, but it was not until the failure and death of Zayd b. 'Alī in 122/740 that the people of the area began to turn to the 'Abbasid branch through the intermediary of a Kūfan supporter of the *Āl Muḥammad* called Bukayr b. Māhān, who won over leaders of the movement in Khurāsān, including Qaḥṭaba b. Shabīb al-Ṭayyī. In 127/745, Qaḥṭaba came west for the *ḥajj* and pledged his allegiance in person to Ibrāhīm, who had succeeded his father Muḥammad as the leader of the 'Abbasid clan. On his return, he took with him a freedman of the family known as Abū Muslim, who was to represent the 'Abbasids in Khurāsān. Thus, the movement had three centres: Ḥumayma, where the 'Abbasids lived; Kūfa, where Bukayr b. Māhān was replaced on his death by Abū Salama; and Khurāsān, where Abū Muslim coordinated the activities of Qaḥṭaba and other local supporters.

At this time, however, the propaganda simply called for a *riḍā min Āl Muḥammad*, a chosen one from the Family of Muḥammad, without specifying which branch he was to come from; probably, very few of the inner circle knew the true identity of the *imām*. The 'Abbasid cause was also aided in

Khurāsān in that the 'Alids had not really established contacts in the province. In Kūfa, the legacy and memory of 'Alī and al-Ḥusayn were too strong to be replaced, but in Khurāsān, there was no such attachment to a single branch of the Family. The 'Abbasid message, like the message of many rebels from Mukhtār's time onwards, seems to have emphasized the equality of all Muslims regardless of race and ancestry; the appointment of a freedman of obscure origins, Abū Muslim, to lead it is an indication of this aspect and it certainly attracted support in Khurāsān and elsewhere. The 'Abbasid revolution was not a coup d'état led by one faction in the ruling élite against another; it was rather an attempt to reconstruct the Islamic polity, to reintegrate rulers and the ruled in the *umma* under the leadership of the Family of the Prophet, and the movement brought together many different strands in early Islamic thought.

The eastern frontiersmen of Khurāsān defeated the men from the Byzantine frontier who supported Marwān, but this did not automatically mean the triumph of the 'Abbasid dynasty. The armies were directed by Abū Muslim and led by Khurāsānīs who had in many cases no direct contact with the 'Abbasid family at all; none of the 'Abbasids had participated in the long march across Iran and the fierce battles against the Umayyad armies of Nubāta b. Ḥanz-ala and 'Āmir b. Ḍubāra. Their position was made even more marginal when the designated *imām*, Ibrāhīm, was arrested and executed by the Umayyads and their chief contact among the Khurāsānīs, Qaḥṭaba b. Shabīb, was killed during the crossing of the Euphrates shortly before the 'Abbasid armies took Kūfa. The problem that faced the 'Abbasids was to have their authority accepted first by the Khurāsānīs and then by the wider Muslim world. Abū Salama, who had coordinated the movement in Kūfa, seized the opportunity to establish himself as a kingmaker and opened negotiations with various members of the 'Alid family with a view to offering them the caliphate, but he had not counted on the loyalty and efficiency of the 'Abbasids' man in Khurāsān, Abū Muslim. Abū Muslim had nothing to gain from seeing power pass to the 'Alids and Abū Salama, and he had clearly instructed his agents in the army to ensure that this did not happen. While Abū Salama negotiated, a small group of Abū Muslim's men made contact with the 'Abbasids, now in hiding in Kūfa, and selected a member of the family, Abu'l-'Abbās, a brother of the *imām* Ibrāhīm, and brought him to the mosque at Kūfa, where, in Rabī' I 132/October 749 he was publicly acknowledged as the first 'Abbasid caliph with the title of al-Saffāḥ. Confronted by the *fait accompli*, Abū Salama hastened to make his submissio

The proclamation of al-Saffāh. as caliph and his acceptance by the Khurāsānīs and the Kūfans only marked the beginning of the establishment of the 'Abbasids. A number of questions remained to be decided, notably whether the 'Abbasids were to be powerful sovereigns in the way that the Umayyads had been or simply symbolic rulers who would give legitimacy to Khurāsānī military rule, and the nature of the relationship between the

Khurāsānī army and other elements in the Muslim community – in other words, would the military dictatorship of the Qaysīs simply be replaced by that of the Khurāsānīs? When al-Saffāḥ. was acknowledged as caliph, the answers to these questions were very uncertain and it would be hard to exaggerate the precariousness of the position of the new dynasty. That 'Abbasid rule was established and accepted by most of the Muslim community was the achievement of the remarkable group of men who formed al-Saffāḥ's immediate family and particularly of his own brother Abū Ja'far, later the Caliph al-Manṣūr. Al-Saffāḥ. himself reigned for only four years (132–136/749–754), but this period saw the establishment of 'Abbasid power as it was to remain until after the death of Hārūn al-Rashīd. The caliph himself is sometimes portrayed as a rather nondescript character, even a weakling, and Shaban has argued that he was chosen by the Khurāsānīs precisely because he was not likely to assert himself. But the historical record suggests a man who was at once cautious and determined and the establishment of the 'Abbasids owed much to his low-key leadership in the early years.

The key to 'Abbasid success was to leave eastern Iran in the hands of the Khurāsāniyya (the men from Khurāsān who had made up the 'Abbasid army) and Abū Muslim while establishing members of the 'Abbasid family as commanders of armies and governors of provinces in Iraq, Syria, Egypt and the Arabian Peninsula. As soon as al-Saffāḥ. became caliph, he sent his uncle 'Abd Allāh b. 'Alī to lead the armies opposing Marwān on the river Zāb, while his brother Abū Ja'far went to take command of the army besieging the last Umayyad governor of Iraq, Yazīd b. 'Umar b. Hubayra in Wāsiṭ. Both 'Abd Allāh and Abū Ja'far thus acquired a following among the Khurāsāniyya in the armies who came to associate their interests with those of their 'Abbasid leaders. But both men also realized that to rely exclusively on the Khurāsāniyya was a recipe for disaster; it would mean that they were little more than puppets in the hands of the military leaders and that they would incur the lasting hostility of all the other groups in the western half of the Islamic world. It would be, in fact, a denial of all the objectives of the revolution. Among the other groups, they turned to of course the Arabs of the Yamanī party, who had opposed Marwān II. The most famous of these were the Muhallabī family, whose influence had survived the fall of Yazīd b. al-Muhallab from political power and who had attempted to take their hometown of Baṣra for the 'Abbasids at the time of the revolution. The family was now rewarded by governorships, in Baṣra itself and other areas, notably Ifrīqiya, and they enjoyed a new golden age of prosperity. Also rewarded was the family of another leading figure of the Yamāmī opposition, Hishām's long-serving governor of the east, Khālid b. 'Abd Allāh al-Qasrī, whose son Muḥammad had brought over the town of Kūfa to the 'Abbasid cause and was now rewarded with government appointments, although his family never achieved the eminence of the Muhallabīs.

More striking were the efforts the early 'Abbasids made to win over the leaders of the Qays. Abū Ja'far seems to have attempted a compromise with the arch-Qaysī Yazīd b. 'Umar b. Hubayra, but was thwarted by Abū Muslim, who instructed al-Saffāḥ. to have Yazīd executed. Both 'Abd Allāh and Abū Ja'far did, however, win over many of the Qaysīs of the Byzantine and Armenian frontier lands, notably Marwān's right-hand man in the area, Isḥāq b. Muslim al-'Uqaylī, who was to become part of al-Manṣūr's inner circle of advisers. Another Qaysī family which survived to enjoy honour and power were the descendants of Qutayba b. Muslim, the conqueror of Bukhārā and Samarqand, whose associations with the Umayyad cause did not prevent them from being recruited to the 'Abbasids. One group alone was excluded from this general reconciliation: the members of the Umayyad family itself. All the prominent Umayyads were hunted down and many of them executed by 'Abd Allāh b. 'Alī when he took over Syria – only one, 'Abd al-Raḥmān b. Mu'āwiya, a grandson of the Caliph Hishām, escaped to join supporters in Muslim Spain, where he founded a long-lived and successful branch of the dynasty at the western end of the Islamic world.

The reign of al-Saffāḥ. was not without strains and stresses; there were Qaysīs in Syria who refused to accept the new regime and went into open rebellion. And there were those among the Khurāsāniyya who were reluctant to acknowledge the growing authority of the dynasty or to share power with other groups, but in the main the policy was extremely successful. Compared with the Umayyad period, the early 'Abbasid period is free from major internal dissensions; even the Syrians seem to have come to terms with the new government, and much of the credit for this must rest with the members of the ruling family.

Al-Saffāḥ died in Dhu'l-Ḥijja 136/June 754 at a time of growing crisis. This crisis concerned the relationship between the three most powerful men in the state after the caliph himself: Abū Ja'far, 'Abd Allāh b. 'Alī and Abū Muslim; all three were determined and able, all three could call on numerous committed supporters, and a struggle for power was inevitable. Ominous signs were appearing in the months before the caliph's death that all was not well in the relationship between Abū Muslim and the 'Abbasids; Abū Ja'far had been sent on a mission to Khurāsān to see Abū Muslim and was dismayed to find him behaving very much as an independent potentate, and a cruel and violent one at that. Abū Muslim also felt that he should visit the west, perhaps to reestablish his influence among the Khurāsāniyya who had settled there, and announced his intention of making the *ḥajj*. Shortly before al-Saffāḥ. died, he and Abū Ja'far set off from Kūfa, the temporary capital, to Mecca. It was at this crucial juncture that the caliph died, nominating Abū Ja'far as his heir, to be succeeded, on his death, by his nephew 'Īsā b. Mūsā. As soon as he heard the news, Abū Ja'far hurried back to secure his position. He had no time to lose; his uncle 'Abd Allāh b. 'Alī was preparing a major campaign on the Byzantine frontier when the news reached him and he immediately decided to make a bid for the title of caliph. He could count on the support of many of the Khurāsānī army commanders he had with him and of many Qaysī tribal leaders from Syria, where he had been the governor for the previous four years. He based his claims on the fact that it had been he who had led the 'Abbasid troops which finally defeated Marwān, and this gave him a superior right to his nephew, Abū Ja'far.

Faced with this formidable threat, more dangerous because it divided 'Abbasid supporters, the new caliph turned to the one man whom most of the Khurāsāniyya would accept as a leader, Abū Muslim. It was here that the caliph's political skill began to show; Abū Muslim was persuaded to lead the army against 'Abd Allāh. In a confrontation near Niṣībīn in Jumādā II 137/November 754, Abū Muslim worsted 'Abd Allāh, who was forced to flee to Baṣra, where he was sheltered by a brother of his, Sulaymān b. 'Alī. The presence of Abū Muslim had led many among the Khurāsāniyya to abandon 'Abd Allāh's cause, while many Syrians could feel little confidence in a man who had defeated them at the battle of the river Zāb only four years before. 'Abd Allāh suspected treachery all around and fled before the battle really developed. The incident showed the continuing power of the Qays, and after the victory, al-Manṣūr was careful once again to conciliate them and make peace, a very different and much more successful approach than Marwān's brutal suppression of the Yamanīs when he had been caliph.

'Abd Allāh had been defeated and was later to die in captivity, but al-Manṣūr knew he had to strike against Abū Muslim. After the victory over 'Abd Allāh, relations between Abū Muslim and the caliph became increasingly strained. Abū Muslim was determined to return to Khurāsān, where he would be safe and could count on loyal support, but the caliph knew that if he missed this chance to dispose of his rival, he might never get another one. By a mixture of threats and persuasion, Abū Muslim, against his own better judgement and the advice of his counsellors, allowed himself to be lured to the caliph's camp, where he was quickly murdered. It is easy to condemn al-Manṣūr for ingratitude after all that Abū Muslim had done for the 'Abbasids, but Abū Muslim had made his own position impossible; the caliph was determined to secure the unity of the Muslim world under 'Abbasid rule and could not tolerate a virtually independent Khurāsān under Abū Muslim, nor could he allow Abū Muslim to remain as a rival focus of loyalty among the Khurāsāniyya. Once the deed was done, al-Manṣūr took immediate steps to reconcile Abū Muslim's leading supporters; the governorate of Khurāsān and the tax revenues remained in the hands of the Khurāsāniyya and most of the leaders who had supported the dead man are later found in the caliph's service. After the death of Abū Muslim, the Khurāsāniyya looked to the caliph and, increasingly, to his son Muḥammad, later the Caliph al-Mahdī, for leadership.

Al-Manṣūr's rule faced a third and more difficult threat. The 'Abbasids had come to power as representatives of the House of the Prophet, and both al-Saffāh. and al-Manṣūr had made attempts to win over the 'Alid branch of the family. To a considerable extent, they had succeeded, and 'Alids were now honoured guests at court with high pensions, a marked improvement in their status under the Umayyad caliphs. There were, however, some members of the 'Alid family who saw the 'Abbasids as usurpers, refused to give up their claims and preferred to go into hiding instead. From this position, they attracted the allegiance of those who were dissatisfied with 'Abbasid rule. The most active of these was Muḥammad b. 'Abd Allāh from the Hasanid branch of the 'Alid family, and his brother Ibrāhīm. Al-Manṣūr was well aware that these two were plotting a revolt but it was impossible for him to know where or when. The traditional centre of 'Alid support in Kūfa was kept under very careful watch and the brothers were unable to establish themselves there – but in the end they decided on a two-pronged revolt, with Muḥammad in Medina and Ibrāhīm in Baṣra, rather improbably, since that city had no record of devotion to the 'Alid cause. The caliph put pressure on other members of the 'Alid family and in the end forced Muḥammad to come out in open rebellion, in Rajab 145/September 762, before his brother was ready. Muḥammad was known as the Pure Soul, and despite his courage was a somewhat unworldly, even romantic, individual. He attracted considerable support in Medina, both from the *Anṣār* and from members of old *Muhājirūn* families who now lived there in virtual obscurity, but he refused to leave the city and seek support elsewhere as his practical advisers urged, preferring, like his distinguished ancestor, to endure a siege in Medina itself. The caliph was relieved that Muḥammad had declared himself in such a vulnerable place; he was able to cut off the grain supplies from Egypt on which the city depended and to despatch an army under the command of his nephew 'Īsā b. Mūsā. In Ramaḍān 145/November 762, the 'Abbasid army arrived outside Medina, and Muḥammad, with about 300 supporters, was killed, fighting bravely.

Only about two weeks before his brother's death, Ibrāhīm finally declared himself in Baṣra. Despite the unfortunate timing, this revolt proved much more threatening than the one in Medina, and attracted widespread support. Why so many should have come out for Ibrāhīm in this traditionally anti-'Alid centre is not at all clear, but it would seem that the motives were connected more with local grievances than with commitment to the 'Alid cause. At first, the rebellion was a great success; Ahwāz, Fārs and Wāsiṭ were taken and Ibrāhīm established a *dīwān* in Baṣra which was said to have had 100,000 names on it, but disagreements soon began to emerge. A body of committed 'Alid activists had slipped away from Kūfa, which remained under government control throughout, and now urged the Basrans to march on their hometown. Many in Baṣra, however, seem to have wanted to stay put and make terms. The delay enabled al-Manṣūr to summon troops from Syria and Iran, while the dissension lost Ibrāhīm much support. When the 'Abbasid and 'Alid armies finally met at Bākhamrā, on the road from Baṣra to Kūfa in Dhu'l-Qa'ada 145/February 763, Ibrāhīm's force had dwindled to some 15,000. His defeat and death mark the end of large-scale 'Alid rebellions for the next half-century.

The 'Alids failed to make good their claim essentially because they failed to attract the support of any powerful military groups; Khurāsāniyya,

Qaysīs and Yamāmīs were alike identified with the 'Abbasid cause as a result of al-Manṣūr's policies. Furthermore, the 'Alids were divided among themselves. Muḥammad b. 'Abd Allāh's claims to leadership were rejected by many, including the main Husaynid contender, the sixth *imām*, Ja'far al-Ṣādiq, who refused to swear allegiance not because he felt that his branch of the Family had the only true right to lead, but because Muḥammad was so young. Under Ja'far's guidance, it became possible to accept the spiritual role of the Husaynid *imāms* without committing oneself to open and violent opposition to the government. The old 'Alid constituency of discontented Iraqis, especially Kūfans, was now hopelessly divided by al-Manṣūr's claims to lead the Family of the Prophet, by the establishment of Iraq as the centre of government, and by differing views among the 'Alids themselves about their role in the community. Not until 'Abbasid power began to disintegrate for other reasons were the 'Alids able to make another serious attempt to mobilize popular support in their favour.

The golden age of the 'Abbasid caliphate: 145–193/763–809

After the disturbances of the early years, the period from 145/763 until the caliph's death in 158/775 was a time of comparative peace and calm. The political foundations which al-Manṣūr had laid proved durable and strong. The early 'Abbasid state owed much to the Umayyad example, and al-Manṣūr himself is said to have acknowledged the debt he owed to the examples of 'Abd al-Malik and Hishām. The 'Abbasid family played a part in government very similar to that of the Marwanids. In some cases, branches of the family established themselves as property owners and political leaders in the provinces, like Ṣālih. b. 'Alī and his family, who took over many of the Umayyad estates in Syria. At times too, they were appointed as governors of Syria, but the post was not hereditary and they could be, and were, deposed by the caliph. The acceptance of 'Abbasid rule in the area was in part the consequence of there being a resident branch of the ruling dynasty with whose interests the Syrians could identify themselves. The caliph and his advisers also chose provincial governors from other groups, like the Khurāsāniyya and the Muhallabīs. Although these might be appointed to areas where they had influence, the caliphs were powerful enough to appoint and dismiss governors at will.

In some ways, the early 'Abbasid state seems to have been more centralized than the Umayyad, especially in the fiscal administration, and this was a development which gathered pace under the Barmakid rule during the reign of Hārūn al-Rashīd. It is clear that there was an attempt to ensure that the provinces made substantial contributions to the finance of central government. We are particularly well informed about this in the case of Egypt, where determined efforts were made to extract surplus revenue. The large sums of money left by al-Manṣūr and Hārūn al-Rashīd would suggest that the government had some success in this. Nonetheless, the revenues of Iraq, the home province, so to speak, of the ʿAbbasid government, remained of crucial importance. Approximate figures suggest that Iraq and the adjacent irrigated lands of Khuzistan supplied four times as much revenue to the Baghdad government as the next most productive province, Egypt, and five times as much as all the districts of Syria and Palestine combined. Caliphs from al-Manṣūr to Hārūn also spent money on developing and extending the *ṣawāfī*, the state lands, and these probably continued to be an important source of revenue. Another aspect of government control was the appointment of *qāḍīs* (Muslim judges), a function which was now taken over by the central government. In Egypt under the Umayyads, for example, the *qāḍīs* had been appointed by the local governors, but this power was taken out of their hands under the early ʿAbbasids. From al-Mahdī's reign onwards, *qaḍīs* were appointed from Baghdad.

While the ʿAbbasid state was in many ways a development of the Umayyad, there were important differences. The most obvious of these was the fact that the centre of government moved from Syria to Iraq. The ʿAbbasids seem to have had no hesitation in choosing Iraq as their base. Khurāsān was on the fringes of the Islamic world and was, in any case, quite unfamiliar to them, while Syria, with its Umayyad connections, was hardly appropriate. Iraq had had a long tradition of attachment to the Family of the Prophet. There were also sound economic reasons for the shift. Iraq was by far the largest contributor to the revenues of the caliphate, and the revenue from Iraq was now made all the more valuable by the fact that the area was close to the centre of administration and so the revenue was easier to collect. Iraq was the breadbasket of the caliphate.

The shift of the centre of political activity also represented a change in the nature of the political élite. The Umayyad caliphate had essentially been run by Arabs for Arabs. In a time when most Muslims were Arabs, this was justifiable, but as conversion to Islam began to gather pace, the Arabness of the regime was less reasonable. The ʿAbbasid revolution was in part an attempt to break down these barriers. The early ʿAbbasid ruling class was much more varied in composition. There were still Arab tribal leaders, like Yazīd b. Mazyad al-Shaybānī, who would have seemed quite at home in the Umayyad court, but there were many others as well. The most important of these were the Khurāsāniyya who had come west at the time of the revolution and later. While many of their leaders seem to have been of Arab descent, and no doubt spoke Arabic, a large proportion of the rank and file were Iranian Muslims and Persian was widely spoken.

These Khurāsāniyya certainly appeared foreign to local Christian observers in Syria, and they were established in garrison towns like Baghdad and Raqqa and on the Byzantine frontier. These troops and their descendants also became known as *abnāʾ al-dawla*, sons of the (ʿAbbasid) dynasty or state, or more simply as *abnāʾ*, a designation which harkened back to the *abnāʾ* of Yaman, the Persian settlers who were converted to Islam during the Prophet's lifetime and supported the Muslims at the time of the *Ridda* wars. In the administration, clerks of Christian origin from Syria continued to play an important role, but they were joined by Iranians like the Barmakids and, increasingly, by *dihqāns*, small landowners of non-Arab extraction from the Sawād of Iraq whose expertise and local knowledge made them indispensable to the regime. ʿAbbasid government is sometimes said to be Persian in character and personnel, in contrast to the Arab rule of the Umayyads. There is some truth in this, and it is clear that people of Iranian origin became more important in both army and administration. One of the most obvious signs of this Iranian influence was the adoption of the tall conical *qalansuwa* as court headdress. The *qalansuwa* had been worn by the late Sasanian élite but not, apparently, at the Umayyad court. Under the early ʿAbbasids, it became an essential part of the black court dress of the time and seems to have remained so until the collapse of the caliphate in the fourth/tenth century. Nonetheless, Arabs still held very high positions, and Arabic remained the language of administration and all court culture. The early ʿAbbasid state was essentially a Muslim state, rather than a purely Arab or Persian one.

In the early days after the revolution, the caliphs had been based in Kūfa or in temporary settlements nearby, each known as Hāshimiyya. In 145/762, however, al-Manṣūr began the construction of a purpose-built capital at Baghdad to which he gave the official title of Madīnat al-Salām, or City of Peace. The location was at the northern end of the Sawād, but unlike Kūfa, it also lay on the great road from Iraq to Khurāsān, now such a strategic highway. This meant, among other things, that pilgrims from the eastern provinces of the caliphate would pass through Baghdad on their way to the *ḥajj*, and admire the splendours of the caliph's capital and seek the company of its scholars. It also had very good river communications with Baṣra to the south, and along the Tigris and the Euphrates with Mosul, Raqqa and the rich grain-growing areas of the Jazīra. Not only did these communications encourage trade, they also allowed Baghdad to import large amounts of food. The city rapidly expanded beyond the size which could be supplied from the immediate hinterland, and the grain of the Jazīra and the dates of Baṣra were vital for its inhabitants, a fact which gave rise to acute crises of supply when civil war or political unrest interfered with communications. The site was ideally chosen, and the subsequent prosperity of the city bears witness to the acumen of its founder. The city rapidly grew way beyond its official centre in the Round City. By the mid-third/ninth century, estimates suggest that it had a population of between 300,000 and 500,000 (at a time when London probably had less that 10,000 and Paris less than 20,000). Even the temporary movement of the administrative capital to Sāmarrā does not seem to have affected the vitality of the city as a commercial and cultural centre.

There were also political reasons for the establishment of Baghdad. It was founded to provide a base for the Khurāsāniyya, far from their homeland. They needed houses, obviously, but they also needed economic opportunities. The Khurāsāniyya were paid salaries and were supposed to be available for military service, but commerce and property owning also contributed to their prosperity. Leaders of the Khurāsāniyya were given plots of land to distribute to their followers and to rent out to merchants. Since the court was established in the city, the economic opportunities were very considerable, and the caliph was able to reward his followers handsomely. There was also the need for security, which had been graphically demonstrated some four years previously when the caliph had almost been murdered during a riot by some of his troops. To this end, he built a round, administrative city, sheltering a palace, a mosque and a garrison of picked troops and defended by a high wall. This was the nucleus of the city, but most people lived beyond the walls of the Round City, in the rapidly proliferating suburbs and the new quarters developed across the Tigris on the east bank by the caliph's son al-Mahdī. Baghdad became the prototype for numerous Islamic "new towns" (of which Sāmarrā and Cairo are the best known) founded by rulers to house their followers and to generate income, and al-Manṣūr's work had a lasting influence on urban development in the Near East.

Another factor which distinguished the early 'Abbasid state from its Umayyad predecessor was the changed position of Khurāsān. Under the Umayyads, Khurāsān had been a remote frontier province, usually ruled by governors despatched by the Umayyad viceroys in Wāsiṭ. The role that the Khurāsāniyya played in the establishment of the dynasty, and even more, the role they continued to play in the armies of the caliphate, made the province much more important. After the departure of Abū Muslim, it was integrated into the 'Abbasid state, but the governors were always chosen from among people of local origin, a privilege given to no other area. In 141/758–759, the caliph appointed his son Muḥammad to be the governor of Khurāsān, but he supervised the affairs of the province from Rayy on the western borders, prudently allowing local men to exercise authority on the spot. This period was important, however, because it meant that Muḥammad established close links with the Khurāsāniyya, many of whom accompanied him back to Baghdad when he returned ten years later. The support of the Khurāsāniyya was to be of crucial significance in the struggle for the succession. Khurāsān was not peaceful in the early 'Abbasid period. There were many rebellions, notably those of Ustādhsīs in the Badhghīs area north of Harāt in 150/767 and of al-Muqanna' in the mountains between the Oxus and Zarafshān valleys in 159–163/775–780. The accounts of these movements are frequently very confused, and it is difficult to explain them all. It seems, however, that most of them were anti-Islamic, usually in the name of a "false prophet", and that they originated in, and were largely confined to, mountainous areas on the edges of Muslim control. We should probably see them as attempts by the local people to maintain religious, political and cultural autonomy in the face of pressure from the Muslims of the plains, rather than as movements designed to overthrow the 'Abbasid government.

Nevertheless, it meant that the province was frequently disturbed and that the Khurāsāniyya often had to defend their homeland.

The question of the succession to al-Manṣūr was a complex one. When al-Saffāh. had made him heir apparent, he had stipulated that 'Īsā b. Mūsā should succeed him. This was probably a precaution in case al-Manṣūr, at that time on the *ḥajj* with Abū Muslim, should be murdered or die suddenly before he could assume control. 'Īsā b. Mūsā remained heir apparent, however, even after the crisis was passed. He was a friend of Abū Muslim and rendered valuable service to the 'Abbasid state; he was for many years the governor of Kūfa and led the army which suppressed the rebellion of Muḥammad the Pure Soul in Medina. In spite of this, he seems to have been very unpopular with many elements in the Khurāsāniyya, and the caliph was determined to replace him with his own son Muḥammad. After threatening demonstrations by the military, 'Īsā was forced to resign his claim in 147/764 in return for vast compensation and the right to succeed Muḥammad. He then retired from politics to the vast and imposing palace he had built at Ukhayḍir in the desert to the west of Kūfa.

This meant that when the caliph, now in his mid-sixties, died in Dhu'l-Ḥijja 158/October 775 he was succeeded by his son – who took the name of al-Mahdī – without any overt opposition. In many ways, al-Mahdī's reign was a continuation of his father's and he relied on the same supporters, notably the Khurāsāniyya, but there were significant changes of policy. The most obvious of these was the attempt to heal the rift between 'Abbasids and 'Alids and restore the unity of the Family of the Prophet. His own regnal title of al-Mahdī was, of course, one that had often been adopted by members of the Family. He sought to win over the 'Alids by kindness and gifts, by granting them estates and positions at court. He also attempted to win over the supporters of the 'Alids in the Ḥijāz, and 500 of the *Anṣār* of Medina were recruited as a special guard for the caliph. The caliph also demonstrated his care for Islam by the building of mosques, notably the mosque at Mecca and the Aqṣā mosque in Jerusalem. The concern for religion and the well-being of the Prophet's Family was an integral part of the attempt to gain general approval for 'Abbasid rule. The move was largely successful. Only a small group of 'Alid supporters, led by 'Īsā b. Zayd – son of that Zayd b. 'Alī who had attempted to rouse the Kufans against the Umayyads in 122/-740 – formed a clandestine group to keep the flame of resistance alive, and were thus constantly harassed by government agents.

The caliph's main intermediary in his efforts to win over the 'Alids and their supporters was his secretary, Ya'qūb b. Dāwūd, who had originally been imprisoned as an 'Alid supporter and now placed his contacts at the disposal of the caliph. For six years, 160–166 (777–782/3), he remained the caliph's chief adviser, using his position to secure control over many other aspects of the administration. Never before had a member of the bureaucracy established such control over policymaking. In the end, his power made him vulnerable. His ambitions made him many enemies, he failed to discover and reconcile 'Īsā b. Zayd and his control of the administration was increasingly resented, until finally he was trapped by his enemies, dismissed and brutally punished.

The influence Ya'qūb achieved points to the growing importance of two elements in the 'Abbasid élite, the secretaries and the *mawālī* (freedmen in this context) of the caliph. All rulers and governors had had secretaries to write their letters since the time of the Prophet. In early 'Abbasid times, however, these men began to grow in importance. The increasingly centralized nature of the administration and the complexities of revenue collection in the Sawād meant that the number of bureaucrats or *kuttāb* (plural of *kātib* = a secretary) increased until they became an important pressure group, under the leadership of the Barmakid family, whose name has passed into English as the Barmecides. The Barmakids, originally guardians of a great Buddhist shrine near Balkh in modern Afghanistan, had converted to Islam in the Umayyad period and had come west with the armies of the 'Abbasid revolution, soon establishing themselves in the administration. Yaḥyā b. Khālid the Barmakid became a close friend and adviser of al-Mahdī in the days when he had been acting as the governor in Rayy, and he became the tutor to al-Mahdī's young son Hārūn, to whom he was virtually a father. The Barmakids provided political leadership for the *kuttāb*, and it was largely through this that the bureaucrats became an important force in the 'Abbasid state. Long after the fall of the Barmakids, the *kuttāb* played a vital role in both the politics and the culture of the period, and in their writings they kept the memory of the family green.

The other group who emerged into prominence at this time were the palace servants, led by the ex-slave al-Rabī' b. Yūnus, who had been the *ḥājib* (chamberlain) and close confidant of al-Manṣūr and continued to advise his son. The fact that the 'Abbasid caliphs were frequently settled in one place, often in vast labyrinthine palaces like the surviving examples at Ukhayāir and Sāmarrā, meant that large numbers of servants were recruited to run the establishments and prepare the increasingly complex ceremonial. The *ḥājib* became a very powerful figure, since he could control access to the caliph and prevent his opponents from being able to put their cases, as al-Rabī' b. Yūnus did. Palace servants were of little importance at the simple peripatetic courts of the Umayyads; in the increasingly settled and complex world of the 'Abbasid palace, they became powerful and influential, although they seldom produced either statesmen or writers, as the *kuttāb* did. In the crisis years of the early fourth/tenth century, the 'Abbasid caliphs were virtually dominated by the *kuttāb* and the palace servants, and these developments can be traced back to the days of the early 'Abbasid rulers.

A sinister development was the growing tension between the newly emerging civil élite of secretaries and palace servants and the military leaders of the Khurāsāniyya. The dispute was basically about power and control of the administration. The civil party sought to centralize the administration as much as possible, since it was above all in the capital that their power lay. The military leaders tended to be more powerful as governors in the provinces, especially those like Khurāsān and Armenia where the situation meant that large numbers of troops were required. Since the civil administration collected the taxes which paid the soldiers' salaries, there was ample cause for disagreement. Increasingly the parties were sharply differentiated; the growing intricacy of the administration meant that most military men were effectively excluded from it, while it was rare for those trained as *kuttāb* (let alone as palace servants) to be given military commands or governorates. This tension between civilian administrators and the military was to be an increasingly important feature of the politics of the 'Abbasid caliphate until the final triumph of the military with the introduction of the office of *amīr al-umarā'* and the development of the *iqṭā'* system in the first half of the fourth/tenth century. It is noteworthy that such tensions are not apparent in Umayyad times but are found in the more sophisticated bureaucratic state of eleventh-century Byzantium.

As so often in early Islamic history, the divisions within the ruling class were reflected in the arrangements for the succession. Two sons of al-Mahdī had emerged as heirs to the throne. The elder was Mūsā, later the Caliph al-Hādī. He had acted as his father's deputy in Baghdad on several occasions and seems to have developed close links with military leaders in the city, which were certainly strengthened when in 167/783–784 he was given command of a large army sent to pacify the province of Jurjān at the southeastern corner of the Caspian Sea. The other candidate was his brother Hārūn, later to become the Caliph al-Rashīd. His education was entrusted to Yaḥyā the Barmakid, and while he was given military training in wars on the Byzantine frontier and overall supervision of the western provinces of the caliphate, his ties remained very much with the court party, with Yaḥyā his mentor and with al-Rabī' b. Yūnus the *ḥājib* and head of the palace *mawālī*. He also had another admirer in the person of al-Khayzurān. She was mother to both Mūsā and Hārūn but, for reasons that are not clear, seems to have favoured Hārūn above his elder brother. The original succession agreement was that Mūsā should be caliph until his death, when he would be succeeded by his brother, but there were rumours that al-Mahdī was intending to change these provisions and make Hārūn his immediate heir. Whether this was true can never be known, for in Muḥarram 169/August 785, the caliph was killed, apparently in a hunting accident, in the foothills of the Zagros Mountains to the east of Baghdad.

Mūsā was still in Jurjān when news came of his father's death, but his brother, who was on the spot, made no attempt to usurp the throne, and Mūsā succeeded, as the Caliph al-Hādī, without any overt opposition. When he was safely installed, the new caliph showed that he intended to follow different policies from those of his father. The military leaders were naturally to be his closest advisers, while Yaḥyā the Barmakid was arrested and al-Rabī' b. Yūnus only escaped a similar fate by his death from natural causes. Along with this reliance on the military party went a much harder line towards the 'Alids. They were deprived of many of their allowances and ceased to enjoy the privileged status at court they had had during his father's reign. In response to this, one 'Alid leader, al-Ḥusayn b. 'Alī, organized a rebellion in Medina in Dhu'l-Qa'da 169/May 786. In some ways, he was following in the steps of Muḥammad the Pure Soul a quarter of a century before, but his revolt was much smaller and much less well planned. He found supporters only in Medina, and even there many of those groups who had supported Muḥammad – the *Anṣār* and the old *Muhājirūn* families, for example – were now loyal to the 'Abbasids. In the end, al-Ḥusayn could recruit only about 300 followers to oppose the 'Abbasid army, which arrived shortly afterwards with the *ḥajj*, and his cause, as so often with the 'Alids, was doomed to failure. Al-Ḥusayn was killed as he fled towards Mecca. It would seem that al-Mahdī's policies had, to some extent, succeeded in drawing the sting of the 'Alid threat. The failure did, however, have the effect of dispersing the 'Alid family. One of the participants, Idrīs b. 'Abd Allāh, fled to Morocco, where he founded an 'Alid dynasty, while his brother Yaḥyā fled to the mountains of Daylam at the southern end of the Caspian Sea, where he established a connection between the local people and the 'Alids which was to last until Buyid times. The spread of 'Alid loyalties to outlying regions of the Muslim world, a development with lasting and important consequences, was essentially the result of the policies of the early 'Abbasid caliphs and the failure of the 'Alids to mobilize widespread popular support in the central Islamic lands.

It is difficult to assess al-Hādī's policies fairly because he died, in mysterious circumstances, after a reign of only thirteen months. He is said to have been ill for some time before his death but circumstantial evidence suggests that he was the victim of a plot. Once again, the question of the succession dominated political life. Under the terms of the arrangements made by al-Mahdī, Hārūn was to succeed his brother. This was clearly repugnant to al-Hādī's military supporters, who realized that the accession of Hārūn would be a victory for Yaḥyā the Barmakid and his supporters in the civil administration. It was not difficult to persuade al-Hādī that Hārūn should be removed from the position of heir apparent and replaced by his own son Ja'far, and the proposal was made more tempting because Hārūūn himself seems to have been prepared to renounce his rights. But the caliph and his advisers had not counted on the influence of his mother. It seems that relations between al-Khayzurān and her elder son had deteriorated sharply. Towards the end of al-Mahdī's life, she had been an influential figure in the counsels of the caliphate, but al-Hādī made it clear, in public, that he would not tolerate any interference. It may have been al-Khayzurān, therefore, who arranged that the caliph should be smothered in his sleep by one of the slave-girls of the palace. Whatever the truth of the matter, al-Hādī died in his bed in Rabī' I 170/September 786 and Hārūn's supporters were able to take rapid action. Yaḥyā the Barmakid was released from prison, al-Hādī's son Ja'far arrested and Hārūn proclaimed as caliph. The coup was swift and efficient, and al-Hādī's followers were unable to organize any serious resistance.

Hārūn al-Rashīd, the most famous of the ʿAbbasid caliphs, came to power as a result of an effective coup d'état mounted by his supporters, most prominent of them being the Barmakid family. It was inevitable, then, that they should have a powerful voice in the new administration, and the first ten years of his rule (170–80/786–96) can fairly be described as the decade of the Barmakids. Yaḥyā, his brother Muḥammad and his two sons al-Faḍl and Jaʿfar effectively monopolized the central administration. Their policy was to concentrate power at the centre in Baghdad. In political terms, this meant that provincial governors became much less important. Under al-Manṣūr's rule, the governors of Baṣra, Kūfa and Egypt had enjoyed long terms of office and had been among the most important figures in the state; under Hārūn, the governors were changed so frequently that the chronicles often fail to record their names, and real power now lay at court. This political centralization was paralleled by fiscal centralization; we can see this most clearly in the case of Egypt, where special investigators were sent from Baghdad to root out abuses in the tax collection, and the governor was on two occasions obliged to bring the revenues and the accounts in person to Baghdad to have them checked.

The weakness of the Barmakid policy lay in the lack of reliable military support. Many of the leading figures in the army of al-Hādī had retired or been disgraced with the accession of Hārūn and they could not easily be replaced. Barmakid fiscal measures aroused considerable discontent, which sometimes expressed itself in violent rebellion. The family made an effort to recruit more men, notably when al-Faḍl b. Yaḥyā was sent as the governor to Khurāsān and recruited 50,000 new men, of whom 20,000 were sent to the west and used to pacify north Africa. Matters came to a head in 178/794 with the rebellion of Walīd b. Ṭarīf, al-Khārijī who was able to dominate much of the Jazīra area and prevent the government from collecting any revenues. The success of his movement was partly due to the mobility of his followers, who could seek refuge in the mountains of eastern Anatolia if the need arose, but partly too because government taxation policies assured him a wide measure of sympathy from the local population, and the Barmakids had no military force capable of taking on so formidable an opponent. In the end, Harun was forced to call on the services of one of al-Hādī's closest collaborators, the bedouin chief Yazīd b. Mazyad al-Shaybānī, who with the support of his tribesmen defeated and killed the rebel. There could not have been a clearer indication of the weaknesses of Barmakid rule, and it was after this that their monopoly of power began to be broken, with Yazīd and other military leaders being returned to favour.

There was another field in which Barmakid policy attracted adverse comment and that was in its attitude to the ʿAlids. Although Hārūn had rejected many of his brother's attitudes, he continued the policy of hostility to members of the ʿAlid family. The Barmakids, however, advocated a more generous line, similar to that which had pertained in al-Mahdī's time. This did not mean that they were Shiʿites or sought to replace the ʿAbbasid by ʿAlids but rather that they wished to reconcile all the members of the Family of the Prophet. It is not entirely clear why they should have taken this line. The literary assemblies the Barmakids held were notable for the freedom with which unusual opinions were voiced, but it may be that there was a political dimension to this as well, that the Barmakids believed that the dynasty should aspire to a more absolute religious authority of the sort that supporters of the 'Alids advocated. In these ways, the views of the Barmakids anticipate those developed by the Mu'tazilī party at court in the next century. At the time, however, these views seem to have incurred the hostility of the caliph, as when al-Faḍl b. Yaḥyā gave a binding safe conduct to Yaḥyā b. 'Abd Allāh to persuade him to leave his mountain refuge in Daylam, a safe conduct which the caliph soon breached by having the unfortunate 'Alid executed.

In 180/796–797, the power of the family began to decline, although Ja'far b. Yaḥyā remained a close friend of the caliph, and when the end came with the famous fall of the Barmakids in 187/803, it was more the last phase of this decline than a radical change. The reasons for the fall of the Barmakids, the imprisonment of Yaḥyā b. Khālid and his son al-Faḍl and the dramatic murder of his other son Ja'far, Hārūn's closest friend, were a mystery to contemporaries and have remained so ever since. Part of the explanation lies in Hārūn's increasing political independence and his reluctance to be dominated by any particular group in the state. Since about 180/796, he had been attempting to balance Barmakid influence by favouring military leaders like Yazīd b. Mazyad and promoting the son of the old *ḥājib*, al-Faḍl b. al-Rabī' b. Yūnus, as a rival power in the central government. He now seems to have wished to remove their influence entirely, feeling that they were still overmighty subjects.

The immediate cause of the disgrace of the Barmakids was probably tension over the arrangements for the succession. Hārūn, like his father before him, decided that the caliphate should pass to several of his sons in succession, but he was determined that conflict should be avoided by specifying publicly and in great detail the rights which each was to enjoy. To this end, he, and most of the leading figures in the 'Abbasid regime, went to Mecca for the pilgrimage of 186/802, where formal and binding agreements were drawn up. The two most important contenders for the throne were his two sons Muḥammad, later al-Amīn, and 'Abd Allāh, later al-Ma'mūn, although some reports say that a third son was subsequently introduced as well. Muḥammad was the elder of the two, although both were born in the same year, 170/786, and he had originally been nominated as heir as early as 175/791–792. Although his first tutor was al-Faḍl b. Yaḥyā the Barmakid, he had subsequently become closely identified with the *abnā'*, the Khurāsānī soldiers settled in Baghdad, and had been left in the city as deputy during his father's frequent absences. 'Abd Allāh, however, had been nominated in 182/798–799 and remained under the influence of his Barmakid tutor, Ja'far b. Yaḥyā and his associates. The agreement stipulated that Muḥammad should succeed his father as caliph but that 'Abd Allāh should have during Muḥammad's lifetime an enlarged Khurāsān as an almost independent principality into which the caliph's agents were not allowed to penetrate.

This was the most elaborate of similar arrangements for dividing the caliphate between the sons of the ruler made by 'Abbasids from al-Mahdī through to al-Rāḍī. The object was probably to secure the succession should the heir apparent die suddenly, to administer the vast empire more efficiently and to contain the growing polarization within the ruling class, Muḥammad being effectively the leader of the *abnā'*, while 'Abd Allāh became the leader of the Barmakid party. The agreement was doomed to failure precisely because these tensions had become so marked and because there were small groups of men on each side who were determined to destroy the other party entirely, but it was not necessarily an unintelligent approach to the problems faced by the caliphate. The continuing power of the Barmakids could only be an obstacle to the peaceful working of these arrangements; if Muḥammad was to have any chance of establishing himself as caliph, they had to be removed, and the fall of the Barmakids took place as soon as the court returned to Iraq from Mecca.

The fall of the Barmakids caught the imagination of contemporaries and later historians. The suddenness and completeness with which the greatest family in the Muslim state had been brought low typified the uncertainties of political fortune and the unreliability of rulers. But this should not obscure the importance of the contribution they made to the 'Abbasid caliphate. They were the architects of the centralized administration that was developed to its full extent under al-Mu'taṣim and al-Wāthiq in the next century. They may have perished, but their influence lived on in the work of Ja'far's pupil 'Abd Allāh, later the caliph al-Ma'mūn, and bureaucrats such as al-Faḍl b. Sahl and al-Faḍl b. Marwān who were their protégés.

The years after the fall of the Barmakids were marked by Hārūn's campaigns against the Byzantine Empire and by his attempts to solve the problems of Khurāsān. Under the Umayyads, the Muslims had undertaken major expeditions by land and sea with the object of taking Constantinople and destroying the Byzantine Empire. In late Umayyad times, from the reign of Hishām onwards, there was a change in policy. The frontier was stabilized, with the Muslims establishing garrison cities in the Cilician plain at Adana, Maṣṣīṣa and Tarsus and in the mountains farther to the east in Mar'ash, Ḥadath and Malaṭya. Settlement was encouraged and the inhabitants of these military outposts received generous tax concessions to persuade them to stay. During his father's lifetime, Hārūn had made two major expeditions against the Byzantines, and when he became caliph, he took a more direct interest than any previous member of his family in the Holy War, establishing himself in Raqqa much of the time, to be close to the frontier zones. He also established a separate province called al-'Awāṣim behind the actual frontier zone (the Thughūr), the resources of which were to be devoted to warfare against the Greeks. In 190/806 and again the next year, he led the largest expeditions against the Byzantine Empire ever launched by the 'Abbasids. The results were not spectacular; frontier districts were raided but no permanent gains were made. The real purpose of the effort was, perhaps, to emphasize the caliph's role as the leader of the Muslims against the traditional enemy. Campaigns against the Byzantine Empire were the only military activities 'Abbasid caliphs undertook in person and should probably be compared to the leading of the *ḥajj* as a symbolic affirmation of the caliph's importance in the life of the Islamic community.

The other problem with which the caliph was forced to come to grips was the government of Khurāsān. From the time of the 'Abbasid revolution, the province had been ruled by representatives of the Khurāsāniyya military, the *abnā'*, who had originated in the province but were now mostly based in Baghdad and Raqqa. This policy resulted in growing unrest in the province, led by the local landowners and semi-independent princes of the frontier and mountain areas. This resentment may have been in part social – the *abnā'* were thought to be inferior to the established local ruling families – but a more fundamental issue was also raised: the spending of the tax revenues of the province. Since the time of the Caliph 'Uthmān, there had been tension between those who believed that the revenues should be spent for the benefit of the Muslims in the province where they were collected, and those who thought that the caliph should control the collection and distribution of revenue. In the early 'Abbasid period, the *abnā'* demanded that the revenues of Khurāsān be brought west to Baghdad to supply their salaries and pensions, but many notables in eastern Iran objected to this, arguing that the bulk of the money should be kept in the province and spent locally, as had happened during the brief governorate of al-Faḍl b. Yaḥyā the Barmakid. This was totally unacceptable to the *abnā'* of Baghdad, since they would lose control of the sources of their own livelihood, and they were determined to preserve their domination of Khurāsān, by force if necessary.

The grievances recorded in the Arabic sources certainly seem to be connected with taxation rather than class antagonisms. Under the Barmakids, this pattern was changed when in 177/793–794 al-Faḍl b. Yaḥyā was appointed the governor of the province. The Barmakids themselves came from an important eastern Iranian family, and al-Faḍl's rule was popular among the local notables; he spent money on building projects and military expeditions on the frontiers. This interlude did not last long, however, perhaps because of the opposition it aroused among the *abnā'* of Baghdad. In 180/796, Hārūn acceded to this pressure by appointing as the governor of Khurāsān one of the leading figures among the *abnā'*, 'Alī b. 'Īsā b. Māhān. Although the sources are hostile to him and must be treated with caution, it seems that 'Alī tried to exploit the resources of the provinces more ruthlessly than any of his predecessors. Inevitably, this aroused new opposition. There were Kharijite rebellions on a scale previously unknown in the province and a growing volume of complaints from the notables of the area. For some time, Hārūn remained deaf to their pleas, partly because 'Alī gave him a generous share of his gains, but in 190/805–806, a serious rebellion broke out in Samarqand led by Rāfiʿ b. Layth, the grandson of Naṣr b. Sayyār, the last Umayyad governor of the province. ʿAlī was quite unable to reestablish control, and this rebellion, coupled with the growing Kharijite menace, obliged Hārūn to dismiss him. Even in this, he was compelled to act by stealth, sending his right-hand military man, Harthama b. Aʿyan, ostensibly to support the governor, but in fact to depose him. In spite of this, the unrest remained, and in 192/808 Hārūn decided to go east to investigate the affairs of the province. Perhaps surprisingly, considering the important part it played in ʿAbbasid history, Hārūn was the only reigning caliph of the dynasty ever to visit Khurāsān in person. It was while he was on this expedition, in 193/809, that he died near the Khurāsānī city of Ṭūs.

The reign of Hārūn al-Rashīd has gone down in popular memory as the "golden prime" of the ʿAbbasid caliphate. Reading the contemporary annals, it is at first difficult to see why this should have been so. The caliph himself appears as a curiously nondescript character. Al-Manṣūr had been famous for his miserliness and cunning; al-Mahdī for his openness and generosity, but Hārūn seems to have had no clear characteristics of that sort. Nor, again unlike his grandfather and father, does he seem to have had any clear and consistent policies; during the first years of his reign, he was content to allow the Barmakid family to exercise power in his name, and even later on he seems to have taken little interest in the day-to-day business of government. Furthermore, his caliphate was constantly challenged by rebellions which the government often had difficulty suppressing, even when, like the revolt of Walīd b. Ṭarīf, they were in Iraq itself.

To understand Hārūn's later reputation, it is important to see it against the background of the disturbances and disasters which followed his death: the catastrophic civil war between his sons and the later domination of the caliphate by Turkish soldiers, while the economy of Iraq inexorably declined and provinces slipped out of the control of Baghdad. Hārūn's reign was the last period when all the central Islamic lands from Ifrīqiya in the west to Sind in the east were under the control of the caliph. It was also a period when the caliphate was still extremely wealthy. Hārūn left a vast surplus in the treasury – it seems that the civil war which followed his death saw the beginning of the economic problems which were to plague the ʿAbbasid caliphs in the next century. Under his rule, there were no mutinies by irate troops demanding their pay; a magnificent and cultured court was maintained; and golden *dīnārs* were showered on successful poets. Baghdad was an expanding and prosperous city and the caliph in person led the united armies of Islam against the Byzantine foe. He was also a great patron of the *ḥajj*. He went on the pilgrimage to Makka no less than eight times during the course of his rule: he was also the last reigning ʿAbbasid caliph ever to do so. His caliphate also saw the fullest development of the Darb Zubayda. This route (*darb* means path or road), named after his mother Zubayda, who contributed much of the costs from her private fortune, was the largest civil engineering project of the early Islamic period. As well as the clearing of the road itself, there were cisterns, guardposts and wells to enable the faithful to make the difficult journey from Iraq, across the Arabian Desert to the Holy Cities. It was clear testimony to the wealth and organizational capacity of the caliphate at this time. It is not surprising that the court and capital of Hārūn al-Rashīd became the setting for the earliest Arabic contributions to the "Thousand and One Nights". It was also the period when the *kuttāb* under the leadership of the Barmakids established themselves as a major political and cultural force in the caliphate, and since many of the historians on whom we depend for information about Hārūn were themselves *kuttāb* or had links with the bureaucracy, it was natural that they would stress their wealth, magnificence and political wisdom. All these factors combined to shed a sort of golden glow over Hārūn's caliphate, and for later writers – working against a background of continuous political and financial crisis, when Baghdad was degenerating into a collection of hostile villages and the great Round City of al-Manṣūr was a decrepit ruin – this was a period to look back on with deep nostalgia; it was easy to ignore the more prosaic reality.

Hārūn's reputation was also known to a wider world. Diplomatic relations between Byzantium and the 'Abbasids were conducted on a more regular basis than they had been with the Umayyads and were sometimes cordial. In the reign of al-Manṣūr, it was a visiting Byzantine ambassador who advised the caliph to move the markets outside the new Round City he had constructed, and in the time of al-Mahdī, a visiting Greek dignitary was provided with money by the caliph to build some water mills in Baghdad and the profits from these were even forwarded to him when he returned to Constantinople. Hārūn's relations with the Byzantines were less friendly, especially when he began raiding deep into Byzantine territory towards the end of his life, but the existence of embassies is a sign that the 'Abbasids accepted that the Byzantine Empire was a power with which they had to deal on equal terms.

More tantalizing is our fragmentary evidence of ambassadors sent to Hārūn by his great contemporary, the Frankish Emperor Charlemagne. These are not recorded in any Arabic source but Latin annals mention that Charlemagne sent envoys in 180–181/797 and 190/807 and that Hārūn returned the compliment on both occasions, including the sending of an elephant as a gift in 185/801. What the purpose of these missions was is difficult to tell – indeed, some writers have suggested that they never occurred at all. It does seem, however, that Charlemagne was interested in the Holy Places in Jerusalem, where he founded a hostel and library for pilgrims, and his missions to Baghdad may have been connected with that. The disintegration of the Carolingian Empire after his death in 198/814 meant that these initiatives were not followed up.

The great 'Abbasid civil war: 193–218/809–833

Soon after Hārūn died, the problems he had tried to avert in the succession arrangements began to appear once more. At first, all went according to plan. Muḥammad, who had remained in Baghdad while his father went east, immediately became caliph with the title of al-Amīn, and his popularity in the city ensured that there was no opposition. 'Abd Allāh, however, had already established himself in the administrative centre of Khurāsān at Marv, where he was planning to campaign against the rebels. Trouble began to develop over the status of the province of Khurāsān. The succession agreements made at Mecca in 186/802 had envisaged that Khurāsān, under al-Ma'mūn, should be effectively self-governing, but it is clear that this was totally unacceptable to an important group in the *abnā'*, led by 'Alī b. 'Īsā b. Māhān, who had been in prison in Baghdad when Hārūn died but was immediately released. They began to put pressure on al-Amīn to reestablish the control of Baghdad over the province, even if it meant deposing his brother and breaking his sworn agreements. 'Alī was joined in his determination by the *ḥājib* al-Faḍl b. al-Rabī', who had become the most powerful figure in the civil administration in Baghdad after the fall of the Barmakids. Many others, senior figures in the army and members of the 'Abbasid family, were very reluctant to break their oaths or to provoke a civil war, but they lacked a leader and were unable to prevent the onset of war.

For two years, attempts were made to find a negotiated settlement. Al-Amīn made a number of requests of his brother: that the western areas of Khurāsān should be transferred to him, that he should be allowed to keep agents in al-Ma'mūn's areas and, most important, that the revenue from the province should be sent to Baghdad. Al-Ma'mūn was very ill-equipped to withstand this kind of pressure. His military forces were small and their loyalty doubtful and he would probably have accepted his brother's demands had it not been for the advice of his *wazīr*, al-Faḍl b. Sahl. Al-Faḍl came from a Persian family, small landowners in the Sawād of Iraq. He had risen to importance through the patronage of the Barmakids and after their fall had been attached to the court of the young al-Ma'mūn. He is credited with strong Persian sympathies in some sources and does not seem to have become a Muslim until the very end of Hārūn's reign. He was determined to preserve the traditions of the Barmakids and it was this resourceful politician who showed the vacillating al-Ma'mūn the way out of his difficulties. He persuaded the young prince to make an alliance with those groups in Khurāsān, notably the princes and magnates of the peripheral areas, who had opposed the rule of 'Alī b. 'Īsā b. Māhān, since both they and al-Ma'mūn had a common interest in opposing control from Baghdad. While his brother continued his attempts to browbeat him into submission, al-Ma'mūn had himself proclaimed not caliph (that would come later), but *imām*. It was the first time a member of the 'Abbasid family had adopted this title (although all future caliphs were to use it) and it is probable that it was intentionally ambiguous, demonstrating his independent status without being openly provocative. The title was, of course, essentially a religious one, used of members of the 'Alid family, and al-Ma'mūn was certainly following in the footsteps of al-Mahdī and the Barmakids in emphasizing the religious nature of his rule, a development which would become more important as his reign progressed.

Fortified by his new alliance with the magnates of Khurāsān, al-Ma'mūn was able to turn a deaf ear to his brother's proposals. In Baghdad, 'Alī b. 'Īsā and al-Faḍl b. al-Rabī' began to organize a massive military expedition which would once again bring Khurāsān under the control of the *abnā'*. Meanwhile, the breach had become final when in ṣafar 195/November 810, al-Amīn had his own son Mūsā acknowledged as heir apparent, thus removing al-Ma'mūn from his place in the succession. Two months later (Rabī' II 195/January 811), 'Alī b. 'Īsā was appointed the governor of Khurāsān and an army assembled from the *abnā'*; it was reputed to number 40,000 and people in Baghdad said that it was the biggest army they had ever seen. Equipped with silver chains to secure the person of al-Ma'mūn, this mighty force then moved across Iran towards Rayy, the western frontier town of Khurāsān.

The arrival of this vast host threw al-Ma'mūn and his supporters into something of a panic and he himself considered fleeing. Against 'Alī's army, he sent Ṭāhir b. al-Ḥusayn to Rayy. Ṭāhir came from a family of Arab origin which had been settled in Khurāsān since Umayyad times and had become the governing family of the little town of Būshang, near Herāt. The force he commanded was small, probably under 5,000, and many at al-Ma'mūn's court, including Ṭāhir's own father, considered the mission doomed to failure, but when in Sha'bān 195/May 811 the two armies met outside the city walls of Rayy, Ṭāhir won a decisive victory, 'Alī b. 'Īsā was killed and his army fled west in disorder.

The battle at Rayy was a turning point; the policy of al-Faḍl b. Sahl was totally vindicated, and al-Ma'mūn's position in Khurāsān was now secure, so much so that he was proclaimed caliph. For the *abnā'*, it was an unqualified disaster – their prestige and power were damaged beyond repair and their most experienced and dynamic leader was dead. From this point, they were struggling for survival. Ṭāhir lost no time in following up his victory, defeating another, smaller army of *abnā'* at Hamadhān and establishing himself, before winter set in, in Ḥulwān on the edge of the Iraqi plains, only a few days' journey from Baghdad itself. In Baghdad, al-Amīn attempted to raise new armies to supplement the now depleted *abnā'*; he looked first to Arab tribal leaders like the Shaybānīs, whom his father had employed to put down the rebellion of al-Walīd b. Ṭarīf the Kharijite, and then to the Qaysīs of northern Syria, but in both cases the *abnā'* proved unwilling to cooperate with their supposed allies, while the Arabs were reluctant to fight for al-Amīn without substantial political concessions and payments. All attempts to organize a coalition foundered on the rock of *abnā'* intransigence.

The next year (196/812) saw a swift deterioration in al-Amīn's military position. In the spring, Ṭāhir was joined by a large army under the command of Harthama b. A'yan and was able to capture the cities of southern Iraq without any real difficulty. In Mosul, Egypt and the Ḥijāz, there were coups in favour of al-Ma'mūn, while Syria was taken over by different groups of

Qaysī or Yamanī Arabs. Only in Baghdad and the immediately surrounding area did al-Amīn exercise any authority, and even there he faced challenges. The pressures of defeat led to an increasing rift between the caliph and the *abnā'*, some of whom felt that he was betraying their interests by trying to raise support among the Arabs. By the summer, the forces of Ṭāhir and Harthama were preparing to attack Baghdad itself and al-Amīn felt that his position was increasingly desperate. In this extremity, he turned for support to the people of Baghdad – not the military *abnā'*, but the ordinary civilian population, to whom he now gave arms and gifts. The *abnā'* now felt that he had finally abandoned them and turned to Ṭāhir. By the time the siege of Baghdad closed in Dhu'l-Ḥijja 196/August 812, most of the *abnā'* leaders had joined Ṭāhir's army, and the Ḥarbiyya quarter, where many of them lived, became his base of operations. This alliance between Ṭāhir and his family and the *abnā'* was to continue long after the civil war had ended.

The siege of Baghdad, which lasted slightly over a year, was an episode almost without parallel in the history of early Islamic society. Al-Amīn had taken the decisive step of arming the people of the city and the Arab sources give us a clear picture of the social classes to which these people belonged. Contemptuously referred to as *'ayyārūn* (vagabonds), they were clearly the urban proletariat, not large property owners or the more substantial merchants, but rather people who sold trifles on the streets. They have left their own record in some remarkable poems in which they glory in the fact that they do not come from any noble family, that their "armour" was made of wool and their helmets of palm leaves, and they lament the barbarity of their attackers and the destruction of the city. There is also a strongly anti-military, even anti-war, strand in this poetry which is both striking and unusual. They fought for al-Amīn and for Baghdad but they do not seem to have had any particular religious viewpoint. We should probably see them as people from the country who had flocked to Baghdad in the previous two generations and had been unable to establish themselves as merchants or property owners; many of them are described as sleeping in the mosques and baths. The movement was a genuinely popular uprising and was perhaps the nearest that early Islamic history came to an attempt at social revolution.

In the end, military experience, as well as blockade and famine, began to tell. There was much hard hand-to-hand fighting and bombardment of the city by siege engines. In the end, it was diplomacy rather than military force which enabled the attackers to triumph. At the beginning of 198/September 813, Ṭāhir persuaded a number of the richer and more established citizens, increasingly apprehensive about the revolutionary situation in Baghdad, to cut the pontoon bridges which crossed the Tigris and provided the besieged with a vital means of communication between east and west Baghdad. This done, the eastern side of the city was easily occupied by Harthama and his men, while Ṭāhir launched a new attack on the west. Al-Amīn now attempted to surrender to his father's old friend Harthama, who sent a boat across the river to fetch him – but Ṭāhir was suspicious of any private deals which excluded him, the boat was overturned and the caliph captured and executed. Most of his misfortunes had been of his own making, but his death saddened many supporters of the dynasty, even his own brother, and it is arguable that the prestige of the ʿAbbasid family never fully recovered from the murder of the caliph in this way. And like the murders of ʿUthmān and al-Walīd II, the murder of al-Amīn solved no problems and was simply the prelude to new conflict within the Muslim community.

The years between the death of al-Amīn in 198/813 and the arrival of al-Ma'mūn in Baghdad in 204/819 saw prolonged and destructive fighting throughout the Near East but especially in Baghdad and the surrounding countryside. The local struggles for power seemed to generate their own momentum, and all over the area groups which had coexisted in peaceful rivalry for the previous half-century now took to arms. The fighting once begun was increasingly difficult to stop, and *bāb al-fitna*, the gate of civil strife, once opened, proved very difficult to close. Only a few areas remained immune, like Khurāsān under al-Ma'mūn and, perhaps ironically, the Byzantine frontier areas around Tarsus, described as a haven of peace.

The fundamental cause of the conflict lay in the policy of al-Faḍl b. Sahl and the influence he exercised over al-Ma'mūn. Al-Faḍl had forged the alliance between al-Ma'mūn and the leading Khurāsānīs which had ensured success in the struggle with al-Amīn. He was now determined not to lose the fruits of victory and, above all, that al-Ma'mūn should remain in Khurāsān and that Marv should be the capital of the caliphate. This was not just a question of geography; it meant that policy and government would be conducted by al-Ma'mūn's supporters; there would be no place in the new order for groups like the *abnā'* or the Qaysī Arabs, and Baghdad would become no more than a provincial town. It is hardly surprising that these policies aroused strong and active resistance. If al-Ma'mūn had come to Baghdad after his brother's death, he would probably have taken over the caliphate without any serious opposition, but attempts to govern from Marv proved, in the end, wholly impractical. In the attainment of his objective, al-Faḍl b. Sahl showed himself deeply distrustful of others who had contributed to al-Ma'mūn's victory. This included Ṭāhir, who was sent into virtual exile in Raqqa, where he remained in retirement until the fall of al-Faḍl, and Harthama b. Aʿyan, who was eventually recalled from Iraq and executed, on the *wazīr*'s orders, for treachery. This meant that the supporters of al-Ma'mūn were deprived of their two most experienced soldiers and the two men who could command the allegiance of substantial forces in the west. Furthermore, as time went on and disturbances still raged in Iraq, al-Faḍl b. Sahl was forced to deceive the caliph himself, by assuring him that all was under control. It was not until 202/817 that the caliph was convinced that these policies were leading to disaster. He had al-Faḍl murdered and began the move back to Iraq.

The civil wars in Iraq were confused and prolonged. They were essentially fought by different groups of ex-soldiers trying to establish their rights to government salaries. The main protagonists were the *abnā'* of Baghdad. They demanded that they should be paid regular salaries and that the capital should be returned to Baghdad. In this, they were supported by other inhabitants of the area and by many members of the 'Abbasid family. At first, they recognized al-Ma'mūn, while demanding that he should change both his advisers and his policies. From 201/817 onwards, however, they gave allegiance to a rival caliph, Ibrāhīm, son of al-Mahdī, but he proved more successful as a poet than a politician and his caliphate never gained general acceptance. When al-Ma'mūn approached Baghdad, Ibrāhīm was forced into hiding.

Faced with the intransigence of the people of Iraq, al-Faḍl b. Sahl was forced to look for expedients. He tried to govern Iraq through his brother al-Ḥasan. The attempt was not a success, partly because al-Ḥasan seems to have been very inept, with little understanding of local politics, and partly because the Baghdadis would not accept an agreement which denied them political influence. The fundamental problem was that al-Ma'mūn's faction had no firm base of support in the area and it was probably in an effort to remedy this that al-Ma'mūn adopted an 'Alid as his heir apparent. To understand this measure, it is important to note that popular enthusiasm for the 'Alid cause was by no means dead in Iraq and it is likely that the hardships of the war and resentment against the government in Marv encouraged people to look for leadership from that quarter. In Jumādā II 199/January 815, a rebellion broke out in Kūfa, led by an ex-soldier, Abu'l-Sarāyā, in the name of an 'Alid, Muḥammad b. Ibrāhīm, known as Ibn Ṭabāṭabā. The rebellion was initially very successful, attracting widespread support. The rebels came to control most of southern Iraq and almost reached Baghdad. Al-Ḥasan b. Sahl was forced to turn to his rival, Harthama b. A'-yan (shortly to be executed for his help), and the rebellion was crushed. It showed, however, that an 'Alid candidate to the throne could command a considerable militant following, which was exactly what al-Ma'mūn's cause lacked.

In Ramaḍān 201/March 817 in Marv, al-Ma'mūn proclaimed as his heir 'Alī b. Mūsā the 'Alid, called al-Riḍā, "the Chosen One". At first, this might seem to have been a handing over of the state to the 'Alids and their supporters, but this was not quite the case. It has already been pointed out that reconciling the 'Alids and unifying the Family of the Prophet had been an important objective of the policies of al-Mahdī and al-Faḍl b. Sahl's mentors, the Barmakids. According to the propaganda put out by the caliph's advisers, 'Alī was adopted as heir not because he was a direct descendant of 'Alī and al-Ḥusayn (which he was) but because al-Ma'mūn had considered all the available members of the house of the Prophet ('Alids and 'Abbasids) and found him the most suitable. Faced with the opposition of almost all the members of the 'Abbasid family to his policies, this was hardly surprising. Another factor suggesting that a radical break was not intended was that 'Alī was actually some twenty years older than the man whose heir he was supposed to be; thus while it was not impossible, it was unlikely that he would ever inherit.

In practical terms, the move was a disaster. News of it arrived in Iraq at a time when peace between the Baghdadis and al-Ḥasan b. Sahl seemed possible, and it provoked an immediate reaction, a new rebellion in the city led by members of the 'Abbasid family. Nor did it generate much popular enthusiasm among 'Alid supporters, since it promised no change in the unpopular policy of rule from Khurāsān. It also proved the undoing of al-Faḍl b. Sahl. 'Alī b. Mūsā, who had had first-hand experience of the position in Iraq, managed to persuade al-Ma'mūn that he had, essentially, been deceived by the Sahl brothers as to the scope and severity of the opposition and that only if he came to Baghdad in person could his government be accepted. In Jumādā II 202/December 817, he decided to leave Khurāsān. This meant a break with al-Faḍl, who was murdered, almost certainly on the caliph's orders. It also proved the undoing of the unfortunate 'Alī b. Mūsā, who was poisoned, his burial place at Mashhad in Khurāsān becoming one of the great Shi'ite pilgrimage centres.

Al-Ma'mūn's progress to Baghdad took over a year and a half, but when he arrived, in ṣafar 204/August 819, the opposition melted away and the rival caliph, Ibrāhīm b. al-Mahdī, went into hiding. Almost a decade of warfare came to an end and a start could be made at reconstructing the state.

Al-Ma'mūn's coming to Baghdad was in itself a gesture of compromise, and he proceeded to reconcile as many groups as he could. The 'Alid succession was abandoned. 'Alid green was replaced by 'Abbasid black as the official colour of the court. The unpopular al-Ḥasan b. Sahl, who was probably ill already, was retired, while Ṭāhir was received back into favour and he and his family given important positions at court. Despite the peaceful takeover of Baghdad, formidable problems faced the new administration. Many areas, including all of Syria, Palestine and Egypt, remained outside the control of the government. The loss of these provinces and the destruction caused by the fighting in Iraq must have meant that government revenues were severely depleted. Al-Ma'mūn also faced the problem that he did not command a large, loyal army. There was no equivalent of the Khurāsāniyya who supported the early 'Abbasids. He had had to compromise to be accepted in Baghdad, and he had to negotiate for military support.

To aid him in the work, al-Ma'mūn turned to Ṭāhir and his family. Ṭāhir had refused to help al-Ḥasan b. Sahl in his attempts to exercise power in Iraq and had probably watched his discomfiture with quiet satisfaction from his retreat at Raqqa. The contacts which he had made among the *abnā'* during the siege of Baghdad now proved very useful and he was able to secure their acceptance of al-Ma'mūn while he was allowed to choose the administrators of the city. This connection between the Ṭāhirids and the Baghdadis was to last for the next half-century and secured the peace of the city even when the court moved to Sāmarrā. Ṭāhir himself was appointed to Khurāsān as the governor in Rabī' II 206/September 821 but remained there for only just over a year before his death in Jumādā II 207/October 822. His return to his native province seems to have brought problems, and he found it difficult to reconcile his duties to the caliph with his obligations to old colleagues. At the time of his death, he is said to have omitted the caliph's name from the Friday prayers, a sign of rebellion. He was succeeded by his son Ṭalḥa. This did not in any sense mark the independence of Khurāsān, which remained an integral part of the 'Abbasid state, or at least as much an integral part as it had been since the 'Abbasid revolution, and the Tahirids remained as much concerned with affairs in Baghdad as in the east.

The lead in restoring the power of the caliphate in the west came from another member of the Tahirid family, 'Abd Allāh b. Ṭāhir. The first objective was northern Syria, which was in the hands of the Qaysī tribesmen who had dominated the area since Umayyad times, led by Naṣr b. Shabath al-'Uqaylī. Naṣr was prepared to accept al-Ma'mūn as caliph but demanded concessions for his Qaysī followers and the end to rule by the *'ajam* (a contemptuous term for Persians or other foreigners). In the end, it took a show of force outside his base at Kaysūm, in 209/824–825, to induce him to accept terms. Even then it was a peace of reconciliation rather than subjection. 'Abd Allāh moved on from Syria to Egypt. The long civil war had seen Egypt slide into virtual anarchy. There were prolonged and bitter disputes between the garrison of Fusṭāṭ, led by 'Ubayd Allāh b. al-Sarrī b. al-Ḥakam, and the Qaysī Arabs settled in the delta area, led by 'Alī al-Jarawī. To add to the confusion, Alexandria had been seized by refugees from Muslim Spain who maintained their independence. These rivalries meant that 'Abd Allāh's task was much easier. 'Alī al-Jarawī hastened to join him and offered his services as a naval commander, while 'Ubayd Allāh was forced to ask for terms and was exiled to Baghdad. After this, the refugees were forced to abandon Alexandria and remove themselves to Crete, and Egypt was once more effectively under the control of the 'Abbasid caliphate. 'Abd Allāh returned to Baghdad in triumph in late 211 or early 212 (827). Despite his slender military resources, his political and diplomatic skill had succeeded in regaining control of these areas with very little fighting or loss of life. The next year, 213/828, he replaced his brother Ṭalḥa as the governor of Khurāsān, while his role in the west was taken over by Abū Isḥāq, the caliph's brother, whose small but efficient private army of Turks was making him one of the most powerful men in the state.

If al-Ma'mūn's reign had its successes, it also had its failures. The province of Ifrīqiya was never regained after the civil war and remained in the hands of the Aghlabid family. Closer to home, Āzarbayjān was troubled by the anti-Muslim resistance movement led by Bābak among the indigenous mountain people of the area. Significantly, al-Ma'mūn lacked the military resources to suppress the rebellion directly. He relied instead on a series of commanders who offered to raise and pay armies at their own expense in exchange for the revenues of the province when it should be captured. Despite their ambitions, none of these entrepreneurs was able to make much headway in the difficult terrain, and it was not until al-Mu'taṣim turned his much more effective military machine in that direction that Bābak was finally crushed.

The reign of al-Ma'mūn marks the divide between the early and middle phases of the 'Abbasid caliphate. Many of the groups who had sustained the caliphate during the early years now disappeared from the scene. The most important of these were the *abnā'* of Baghdad, the descendants of the Khurāsāniyya who had made the 'Abbasid revolution and who had continued to form the military backbone of the old regime. They continued to have some influence in Tahirid Baghdad but no longer formed an important element in the armies of the caliphate and gradually lost both their military function and their group identity. The 'Abbasid family had been very important under the early caliphs, but again they played little part in the new state. Members of the family were no longer given important governorates or the command of armies, and only the caliph and his heir or heirs seem to have had any important political function. Equally, many of the old Arab families like the Muhallabīs and the chiefs of Shaybān disappear from the caliphal court.

During the course of al-Ma'mūn's reign, these groups were replaced by new men with a new ideology and new methods of government. The most important and powerful of these was the caliph's brother Abū Isḥāq, who succeeded in 218/833 as the Caliph al-Mu'taṣim and began a new era in 'Abbasid history.

6 The middle ‘Abbasid caliphate

The rise of the Turkish army and the caliphate of Sāmarrā: 218–247/833–861

The rise to power of Abū Isḥāq al-Mu‘taṣim, during the reign of his brother al-Ma’mūn, was to herald a change in the government of the Islamic state as profound as anything which had resulted from the ‘Abbasid revolution. But it was a change of a very different sort. The ‘Abbasid revolution was a broadly based popular movement which aimed to overthrow the established order and to replace it with a society which would more truly reflect the ideals of Islam and its founder. Al-Mu‘taṣim’s revolution, however, was conducted by a fairly small group enjoying virtually no mass support and concerned to preserve ‘Abbasid rule rather than to overturn it. To achieve this, the caliph felt that he had to use new men and new methods, to be guided by a new ideology and to found a new capital.

Al-Mu‘taṣim was in many ways a new man himself; one of Hārūn’s younger sons, he had been given no place in the elaborate succession arrangements his father had worked out and he was only fifteen years old at the outbreak of the civil war. He remained in Baghdad, and in the final stages of the war supported Ibrāhīm b. al-Mahdī in his opposition to al-Ma’mūn and the Banū Sahl. In 199/814–815, he began to buy slaves in Baghdad from their previous owners and to train them for military service, and both Itākh, a Khazar who had been a cook for his previous owner, and Ashinās were in his service before 202/817–818. He also entered into an arrangement with the Samanid family, who controlled much of the Samarqand area and sent him slaves directly from Turkestan. The private army he built up probably numbered only 3,000–4,000 by the end of al-Ma’mūn’s reign, but they were well trained and disciplined and formed a formidable fighting force. His leadership of this army meant that al-Mu‘taṣim, alone of all the members of the ‘Abbasid family, had military support on which he could call and al-Ma’mūn was increasingly obliged to turn to him for help. When in 213/828 ‘Abd Allāh b. Ṭāhir was appointed the governor of Khurāsān on the death of his brother Ṭalḥa, al-Mu‘taṣim took over all his responsibilities in Syria and Egypt, thus becoming one of the most powerful men in the caliphate. It

DOI: 10.4324/9780429348129-6

was this military power, coupled with al-Mu'taṣim's own forceful and determined personality, which induced al-Ma'mūn to set aside the claims of his own son al-'Abbās and to adopt al-Mu'taṣim as his heir. When al-Ma'mūn died in 218/833 during a campaign against the Byzantines, his brother was accepted as caliph, not without some murmurings of dissent from those who saw clearly what the new regime would bring.

The new order was based firmly on the army al-Mu'taṣim had built up. Few questions in the history of the period have caused as much controversy as this introduction of "slave soldiers" into the Muslim world, and scholars have seen this as an essentially Islamic phenomenon which was to culminate in the rule of Egypt and Syria by the Mamluk, or "Slave Dynasty", in the later Middle Ages. Two major interpretations have been offered in recent years of the emergence of slave soldiers; both Crone and Pipes see this as a major turning point and for Crone, at least, it represents the bankruptcy of the Islamic polity, the failure of the community itself to produce an acceptable ruling élite. For Shaban and, more recently, De la Vaissière, however, the problem has been misunderstood; they point out, rightly, that many of those who are lumped together as Turkish slaves were neither slaves nor Turks – al-Afshīn, for example, one of al-Mu'taṣim's foremost military commanders in the early years of his reign, was of Iranian extraction and the ruler of an independent principality in Transoxania. Al-Afshīn is a local royal title rather than a personal name. Neither of these views is wholly adequate. The evidence for the recruitment of slaves cannot be dismissed; al-Afshīn may have been a prince but the servile origins of the three most powerful military leaders to emerge during this period, Ītākh, Ashinās and Waṣīf, are beyond doubt. Gordon, in another recent discussion of the issue, makes the point that many of these soldiers were certainly of servile origin but that the links with the later "mamlūk paradigm" are far from clear. The word *mamlūk* is very rarely used to describe these men, and soldiers of slave origin are usually referred to as *ghilmān* (sing. *ghulām*), an Arabic word originally simply meaning boy. They are also described as Turks, an ethnic denominator, or as *mawālī*, which means, among other things, freedmen or ex-slaves. It is clear that these men came from the margins of the Muslim world but recruitment of marginal peoples to form a military élite was rather a process common to many cultures. In the contemporary Byzantine Empire, marginal peoples played a major role in the army, even producing emperors like Leo the Isaurian in 717 and Basil the Macedonian in 876. While neither Leo nor Basil were technically slaves, they were from remote frontier areas and as firmly outside the established élite of the empire as Ashinās or Ītākh were in the Islamic world. Certainly, there were soldiers who had been slaves, some of whom became very powerful, but at the same time there were many soldiers who were not slaves and there seems to have been no effective distinction between them. The real change was not that the community was ruled by slaves but rather that the army became the preserve of different minority groups: Turks, Armenians, Berbers, recruited from the fringes of empire, rather than from the towns and cities of Iraq and Syria or the bedouin tribes of the Arabian Desert. This meant that the military caste became separate from the rest of society. Generals did not have brothers who were merchants or teachers in the mosque. Ashinās, for example, though he ruled over half the caliphate, never learned to speak Arabic properly. This divorce of the military élite from the rest of society, by origin, language and custom, was to be a distinctive feature of many Islamic societies.

It seems that these new soldiers brought with them new military technologies. The Turks were well known for their skill as mounted archers. They were famous for their hardiness and their horsemanship, having been brought up to ride from a very early age. It was this ability that enabled them to use their short powerful bows from the back of fast moving horses to devastating effect. The mounted archers were the most formidable fighters of the day and comparatively small forces of mounted archers came to replace the larger armies of foot soldiers who dominated early Islamic warfare. As always, total numbers are very difficult to estimate, but the largest number of Turks mentioned in contemporary sources was 10,000 when they all united to depose the unfortunate caliph al-Muhtadī in 256/870. More typically, Turkish armies of the period numbered between 2,000 and 5,000. This compares with the 40,000–50,000 *abnā* that 'Alī b. 'Īsā b. Māhān had led out of Baghdad to attack al-Ma'mūn in 195/811 or the 135,000 soldiers Hārūn is alleged to have led against the Byzantines in 190/806. Like the mounted knights of western Europe, they were few in number but very expensive to maintain and support, and providing for them placed a massive strain on state resources.

Many groups which had been influential now lost this status. This can be clearly seen in the case of Egypt. The Egyptian chronicler al-Kindī says that when al-Mu'taṣim came to the throne, he dropped the names of the Arabs from the *dīwān*, meaning that they were no longer to be paid the *'aṭā'* (salary) as of right. Members of the old established Arab families, mostly in Fusṭāṭ, had drawn salaries from the revenues of Egypt by virtue of their descent from the conquerors, but this was now stopped and the locally recruited *jund* (army) disbanded. Most of the taxes of Egypt were to be sent to Sāmarrā and only the Turkish soldiers employed by the local governors were to receive salaries. This brought to an end the system of payments originated by 'Umar in the *dīwān*, and a link with the days of early Islam was severed forever.

It also marked the end of another long-running controversy over the extent to which the central government could collect taxes from the provinces. From the time of 'Uthmān, caliphs had tried to do this, but a strong body of opinion had held that revenues collected in, for example, Khurāsān should be distributed there. The Umayyads seem to have had only limited success in extracting revenues – the early 'Abbasids had probably done better, but under al-Mu'taṣim, the triumph of the central government was complete.

Even Khurāsān, always the most recalcitrant province, sent substantial sums to Iraq.

The new army was the basis of al-Muʿtaṣim's strength, and its leaders came to hold important provincial governorates. Ashinās was the governor of Egypt and Syria from 219/834 until his death in 230/844, and the Caliph al-Wāthiq put him in charge of all the lands from Sāmarrā to the far west. Ītākh's career blossomed more slowly but in 225/839–840 he was appointed to Yemen, and when Ashinās died, it was Ītākh who took over his powers in the west. These vast governorates did not, however, form independent power bases. Ashinās seldom visited the provinces he was in charge of, but appointed deputies, while he himself remained in Sāmarrā. This arrangement may simply have meant that he had charge of the revenues from these areas which he distributed to his military following. It represented a further centralizing of power, for the under-governors of the provinces seldom appeared at court and played little part in the making of political decisions.

The Tahirid family retained their power and influence under al-Muʿtaṣim and his successors. 'Abd Allāh b. Ṭāhir ruled Khurāsān until his death in 230/845, when he was succeeded by his son Ṭāhir; and the family remained firmly in control of the province until the disturbances which followed the death of the Caliph al-Mutawakkil in 247/861. They ruled a "greater Khurāsān" which stretched from Rayy in the west to the northeastern frontiers of the Islamic world and also included Sīstān to the south. This was the Khurāsān quarter of the old Sasanian Empire, the same area which Abū Muslim had ruled after the 'Abbasid revolution and which had been assigned to al-Ma'mūn under Hārūn's succession agreement. The capital was moved west to Nīshāpūr, and the Tahirids ruled in alliance with those local magnates, like the Samanid family in the Samarqand area, who had supported al-Ma'mūn in the civil war. Because of their great power and the fact that succession to the governorate ran in the family, the Tahirids are sometimes considered as the first independent Iranian dynasty, but such a view is misleading. The arrangement was effectively a partnership between the 'Abbasids and the Tahirids. Under Tahirid rule, Khurāsān contributed large sums in taxation to the central government, perhaps more than had ever been collected before, and we are also told of the caliphs providing money for irrigation projects in the province. Far from being the beginning of independence, Tahirid rule was the most successful solution the 'Abbasids ever devised for integrating the province into the caliphate.

It is important to remember, too, that the Tahirids were as powerful in Baghdad as in Khurāsān itself, and it is probable that the revenues of Khurāsān were used to maintain the family's influence in that city. When 'Abd Allāh b. Ṭāhir had left to take up his position in Khurāsān in 213/828, he was succeeded in Baghdad by his cousin Isḥāq b. Ibrāhīm, who remained an effective ruler of the city until his death over twenty years later in 235/850, after which he was followed by other members of the family. It was this Tahirid control which secured the loyalty of the Baghdadis to the caliphate, especially after al-Muʿtaṣim had moved the capital to Sāmarrā, and it was the Tahirids who suppressed the only real disturbance in the city during these years, the conspiracy of Aḥmad b. Naṣr al-Khuzāʿī in 231/846. One of the main reasons for the civil war had been the desire of the *abnā*ʾ under ʿAlī b. ʿĪsā to have access to the tax revenues of Khurāsān; now, under Tahirid patronage, their children had just that. Baghdad could prove useful to the caliphs as a rival source of power to Sāmarrā with its Turkish population; when al-Mutawakkil wished to dispose of the Turk Ītākh in 235/849, he arranged that the execution be carried out by the Tahirids in Baghdad, safely away from Ītākh's followers in Sāmarrā.

While the Turks and the Tahirids supplied the military force behind the new government, the administration was carried on by a new generation of bureaucrats in the Barmakid and Sahlid traditions. The government was dependent on the revenues of Iraq, and sometimes of neighbouring areas like Ahwāz and Fārs, and there can be no doubt that these areas had been severely damaged by the fighting in the civil war. It also seems that the tax registers had been largely destroyed by fire in Baghdad. In consequence, the caliphs needed men who knew and understood the collection of taxes in Iraq. To supply this need, a new class of administrators emerged. Like the Sahlids, these were drawn almost entirely from the landowners and merchants of the small towns of the Sawād, and they were almost without exception men of Persian or Nabatī (local Aramaean) extraction. Most of them were Muslims, often newly converted, but Christians played a minor role all through the period. While these men had no soldiers or military power of their own, even the most successful and ruthless Turkish soldiers were dependent on their cooperation, or at least the cooperation of one faction among them. When al-Muʿtaṣim became caliph, he kept on his old secretary, the cautious and frugal al-Faḍl b. Marwān, but he was soon replaced as the head of the administration by a rich merchant whose father had made a fortune supplying oil in Baghdad, Muḥammad b. al-Zayyāt. Muḥammad became *wazīr* in 221/836, retained the office all through the reigns of al-Muʿtaṣim and al-Wāthiq and was dismissed only after the accession of al-Mutawakkil. He was a competent financial expert but a callous and brutal man who made many enemies, not just among taxpayers but among his fellow *kuttāb* as well. As *wazīr*, he was not the major force in the formation of government policy as both the Barmakids and Sahlids had been at the height of their power, but he was in undisputed control of financial business.

The new regime used new personnel and adopted a new ideology. Throughout the early ʿAbbasid period, attempts had been made to reconcile to ʿAbbasid rule the partisans of the family of ʿAlī and all those who wanted a religious leadership. Al-Maʾmūn had gone furthest in this with the adoption of the ʿAlid heir and the abandonment of ʿAbbasid black for ʿAlid green as the colour of court robes. In the event, this total switch generated so much resentment among the Baghdadis and the members of the ʿAbbasid family that it had proved impossible to put into effect. Nonetheless, al-Maʾmūn and his successors remained committed to finding a halfway house between the secular monarchy of the Umayyads and the theocratic state espoused by many 'Alid supporters. The title of *imām*, originally assumed by al-Ma'mūn, continued to be used by the caliphs, announcing their claims to religious leadership as well as the secular authority embodied in their other title of *amīr al-mu'minīn*. Al-Ma'mūn also came to adopt a theological position known as Mu'tazilism. Mu'tazilism was essentially concerned with the nature of authority in the community, the question at issue being the relationship between the powers of the caliph and the authority of Revelation and Tradition. For some, the caliph was no more than an executive who was obliged to rule within the limits laid down by the Qur'ān and Sunna, while others allowed the *imām* to interpret and expand on Revelation to accommodate the changing needs of the community. Mu'tazilism stood somewhere between these two positions and defined itself by declaring that the Qur'ān was *created*, as distinct from the belief that it was eternal with God. If it was created in time, then it could be modified to suit different times, and the judgement of a God-guided *imām* might supersede it. This position also defined itself in historical terms in the discussion of the conflicts between 'Alī and his enemies; the Mu'tazilīs favoured neither one side nor the other and withdrew from the conflict (the name Mu'tazila derives from the Arabic word for withdrawal), although 'Alī, the archetype of the God-guided *imām*, was held in high esteem. It was, in short, a position which could hope to attract support from most shades of the theological and political spectrum and enhance the power of the caliph by giving his word theocratic force.

Mu'tazilism as a system of thought had existed before the reign of al-Ma'mūn and continued to exist after the reign of al-Mutawakkil, but it was only in the first half of the third/ninth century that the issue came to the centre of the political stage, generating all the fervour and passion of a Byzantine theological controversy. The reason for this was the close relationship between Mu'tazilī ideas and the ruling group which surrounded the caliph. It became in effect the philosophy of the Sāmarrā élite; if one opposed the Sāmarrā élite, one opposed Mu'tazilism. The man responsible for the close links between religious belief and political controversy seems to have been the chief *qāḍī*, Aḥmad b. Abī Du'ād, perhaps the most influential of all the caliph's counsellors at this time and a man whose influence continued unabated from the end of al-Ma'mūn's reign to the beginning of al-Mutawakkil's. Al-Ma'mūn and his advisers did not content themselves with proclaiming their own adherence to the doctrine – they also demanded that all other government functionaries do so too. The *imām*-caliph had given his view, and to question it was to oppose his authority; so belief in the createdness of the Qur'ān became the touchstone of political loyalty. In order to ensure conformity on this issue, al-Ma'mūn took the unprecedented step of setting up an "inquisition", the *miḥna*, to examine the views of his subjects. Never before had a caliph claimed the right to decide such matters of doctrine, and entrenched positions were taken up on both sides.

The Mu'tazilī position was accepted by many, not just those in Sāmarrā; the adherents of the house of 'Alī might appreciate the deference Mu'tazilīs paid to the memory of the fourth caliph, and Christians and Jews seem to have enjoyed the benefits of tolerance. But the doctrine aroused great opposition, notably in Baghdad. Here, a group of Traditionists, notably Aḥmad b. Ḥanbal, asserted the absolute inviolability of the Qur'ān and Sunna, arguing that no *imām* of the present day should presume to tamper with the reported utterances of the Prophet, and acceptance of the Sunna in its entirety was the *sine qua non* of true Islam. The resistance to Mu'tazilism was the sign of resentment against the Sāmarrā élite; it is significant that the one serious attempt to challenge the domination of that élite in Iraq was made in opposition to the doctrine of the createdness of the Qur'ān, in Baghdad under the leadership of a scion of one of the most important of the *abnā'* families, Aḥmad b. Naṣr al-Khuzā'ī in 231/846.

To house his new élite, al-Mu'taṣim decided to found a new city and to leave Baghdad permanently. There were many reasons for this; the most immediate was the deteriorating relationship between the newly important Turkish troops and remnants of the old *abnā'*, who resented their loss of status. But the foundation of a new capital demonstrated the establishment of the new regime. Here, the new army could be given land and economic opportunities which were totally impossible in Baghdad with its established landowners and merchants. Besides, in Sāmarrā, land was virtually free and the caliph could reward his chosen élite generously at virtually no cost to the exchequer; indeed, judging by some of the figures given, the government could hope to derive a substantial income from the development of shops and other commercial premises. In fact, the move was a sensible and realistic one. At one level, it allowed the caliphs to establish their followers, free from the constraints, even the contamination, of the existing city; on the other, it was a sort of gigantic property speculation in which both government and its followers could expect to benefit.

The site of the new city had to be in Iraq, since it was from Iraq that the revenues on which the government depended were drawn. After some debate, a site was selected at Sāmarrā about 80 miles north of Baghdad on the Tigris. Unfortunately, the planners showed none of the genius of al-Manṣūr which had ensured the success of Baghdad. The site was on a gravelly plain above the Tigris with no naturally flowing water supply and poor river communications. That such a site prospered at all was entirely due to the determination of the caliphs. The plan of the city can still be seen in aerial photographs today – the long straight streets bordered rectangular compounds where different military leaders could be established with their followers. The most important structures were the mosques and palaces of the favoured members of the 'Abbasid family and of grandees of the new order like Ashinās, the walls of whose palace are still visible. The building materials were those of the Mesopotamian plain, mud-brick buildings, often faced with stucco and roofed with wooden beams. Time has not on the whole dealt kindly with the ruins and they have little of the charm of the Umayyad palaces of the Syrian Desert, but the sheer size and obvious planning of the site remain impressive. The new town was always something of an anomaly; in Baghdad, al-Manṣūr had simply set the wheels in motion, and natural economic forces had ensured the survival and growth of the city. In Sāmarrā, massive investment by three successive caliphs failed to produce a thriving metropolis, and when the government abandoned the site, the city dwindled and shrank. But for the half-century of its glory, it was the capital of the caliphate and, just as Baghdad had been the city of the *abnā'*, so Sāmarrā was the city of the new army of al-Muʿtaṣim and his followers.

The years between the death of al-Ma'mūn in 218/833 and the assassination of al-Mutawakkil in 247/861 were on the whole years of prosperity and peace, at least in the heart of the empire. Al-Muʿtaṣim did not let his new army remain idle, and he acquired the reputation of being one of the warrior-caliphs of Islam. His most celebrated campaigns, and, as with his predecessors, the only ones in which he himself participated, were the attacks on the Byzantine Empire, especially the famous sack of Amorion in 223/838. The strength of the new army and the caliph's devotion to the cause of Islam could be demonstrated for all to see. The victories were certainly notable, even if Amorion was not the most impressive of Byzantine cities, but ʿAbbasid propaganda played them up to the full, and the lengthy accounts of the details of the campaigns in the chronicle of al-Ṭabarī and the poetry of Abū Tammām and others reflect the public relations side of the enterprise. Captives were certainly taken, and the frontiers of the Muslim world safeguarded, but no new territory was annexed.

The other campaigns for which the reign is famous are usually described as the suppression of rebellions, but this gives the impression that the caliphate was being weakened by internal dissent. In reality, these were operations of internal expansion; there were many areas within the boundaries of the caliphate where Muslim rule was very ineffective and where the local people and their chiefs retained almost complete independence. One such area was in northwestern Iran, in the mountains of Āzarbayjān. This wild and inaccessible area had been little visited by the early Muslims, who had contented themselves with establishing posts in lowland cities like Ardabīl and Zanjān and had left the mountain peoples largely undisturbed. Towards the end of the second century, however, this situation began to change. Arabs began to move into the region, mostly from the Mosul area, attracted by the rich mineral resources of the country. Here, they began to settle in cities such as Tabrīz and Marāgha. This influx of colonists disturbed the status quo and led the indigenous mountain people to defy the Muslims. This they did under the leadership of one Bābak, a man of obscure origins who by his determination and ability assumed the leadership. The rebellion had begun during the civil war in 201/816–817, and al-Ma'mūn's government had largely left the local Arabs to fend for themselves. Various expeditions were led by soldiers of fortune, hoping to reap the benefits of subduing the country, but Bābak had worsted them all. Al-Mu'taṣim, after his accession, decided that the government should take action against the insurgents and despatched one of his leading generals, al-Afshīn, to conduct the campaign. That Bābak was not a Muslim gave added justification for the action and attracted volunteers to fight alongside the caliphal army. Al-Afshīn was a cautious and determined commander: the caliph supported him with men and money and he gradually succeeded in subduing the country. Finally in 222/837, after three years of campaigning, Bābak's centre at Budhdh was occupied by al-Afshīn's troops and he himself was forced to surrender.

The second major campaign was against Māzyār b. Qārin, the ruler of Ṭabaristān at the southern end of the Caspian. Here again was a mountainous region which had never been wholly integrated into the empire. While there were Muslim cities like Āmul and Sāriyya on the plains along the shore of the Caspian, the mountains had remained in the hands of local dynasties who paid some tribute to the Muslims. Māzyār b. Qārin was ambitious and determined to extend his control in the area. He also strongly resented the Tahirids, being content to acknowledge the overlordship of the caliph but not that of a rival princely family. Māzyār was encouraged to defy the government by al-Afshīn, who, it is reported, hoped to use him to discredit the Tahirids and secure the governorate of Khurāsān for himself. Violence began in 224/838–839, when Māzyār's men began to attack the Muslim settlers in āmul and Sāriyya and destroyed their cities and executed many of the men. The Tahirids responded to appeals from the settlers, and Tahirid forces from Baghdad and Khurāsān, supported by the caliph, succeeded in defeating the rebel, who was taken to Sāmarrā and flogged to death. Solidarity between al-Mu'taṣim and the Tahirids had once again proved effective, but it is worth noting that the autonomy of the mountainous area of Ṭabaristān was not destroyed. Māzyār was replaced by a member of his own family who was prepared to cooperate with the Tahirids.

While the wars were the most important events of al-Mu'taṣim's reign, the caliph faced internal opposition from various quarters. Al-'Abbās b. al-Ma'mūn, passed over for the caliphate, was naturally a focus for discontent, and in 223/838, on the return from the Amorion campaign, a conspiracy came to light in which al-'Abbās and a number of eastern Iranian officers, some of them from very prominent families, were involved. Many of these were men who had fought for al-Ma'mūn and enjoyed high status but now found themselves supplanted by Ashinās and Ītākh, who, along with the caliph, were the main targets of their anger. The conspiracy was unmasked and the main participants put to death by subtle and ingenious tortures. The other major conspiracy was alleged to have been undertaken by al-Afshīn. The victor in the war against Bābak enjoyed great favour for a year or two after his triumph, but he was an odd man out among the élite. The ruler of the principality of Ushrūsana, he resented Ītākh and Ashinās but was also a deadly rival of the Tahirids, hoping to challenge their control of Khurāsān. His indiscreet correspondence with the rebel Māzyār came to light – his enemies were quick to strike, and a show trial was arranged in 225/840 (brilliantly reported by al-Ṭabarī). He was accused of apostasy, of being a false Muslim and of treasonous relations with Māzyār. Witnesses were called from Transoxania who testified to the divine status he enjoyed among his own people and his disregard for the ways of Islam; he and the other kings of Sughd (Soghdia), it was revealed, actually prevented people from becoming Muslims and flogged would-be missionaries. The discredited leader, who behaved with great dignity throughout, was led away to die in prison.

Al-Muʿtaṣim died in 227/842, after a reign of eight years, aged about forty-six. In many ways, his reign had been a success; he had destroyed all the opposition to his rule, and the army he had created gave the government an effective authority which it had not known since the days of Hārūn. But it was a highly centralized system. Power lay in the hands of a small number of senior army officers and civilian administrators. As long as the loyalty of these men was assured and their differences did not become open, all was well. Al-Muʿtaṣim was succeeded by his son Hārūn al-Wāthiq, who reigned from 227/842 to 232/847. No other caliph of the period has left so little trace of the history of his times, and it is impossible to form any clear impression of his personality. The government remained almost unchanged. Ibn al-Zayyāt continued as *wazīr* and Ibn Abī Du'ād as chief *qāḍī* and counsellor. Death removed a few of the old élite, notably Ashinās and ʿAbd Allāh b. Ṭāhir, both in 230/844–845, but their places were taken by new leaders: Waṣīf and the two Bughās (the Elder and the Younger) among the Turks and ʿAbd Allāh's son Ṭāhir, with the result that the ruling group remained effectively unchanged. The caliph died after a reign of some five years at the age of thirty-six.

He left no designated successor. There was then a sort of *shūra* held by the most prominent men in Sāmarrā to choose a new candidate from among the available princes of the ʿAbbasid house. Ibn al-Zayyāt and Ibn Abī Du'ād were naturally there, along with the two leading Turkish officers, Ītākh and Waṣīf, and two less important bureaucrats. What followed is something of a mystery; Ibn al-Zayyāt hoped to continue the status quo by appointing an infant son of al-Wāthiq, but Ibn Abī Du'ād, always a more scrupulous counsellor, objected to the appointment of a child, and so they eventually settled on a brother of the dead caliph, Jaʿfar, who took the title of al-Mutawakkil.

If the members of the *shūra* imagined that they had chosen a pliable candidate who would go along with their wishes, they were soon to find that they had made a serious mistake. The new caliph was determined to assert his own authority and to break with the policies and personnel who had dominated the government of his father and brother. He moved cautiously, attacking individuals, in turn. Ibn al-Zayyāt was the first victim; he had insulted the caliph before his accession, he belonged to no powerful party and was widely disliked because of his cruelty, and so when, in 233/847 he died in a torture apparatus of his own design, the caliph had won an easy victory.

In 235/849, just over a year later, al-Mutawakkil arranged with the Tahirids that Ītākh should be assassinated in Baghdad. It was a bold move not without risks, since Ītākh, after the death of Ashinās, was the most powerful of the Turkish officers, but there was no general rising of the Turks, many of whom may have hoped to gain from his disappearance.

In the same year, the caliph made arrangements for the succession. He appointed three of his sons to succeed each other, in turn; in the meantime, they were to take over the supervision of groups of provinces which had previously been entrusted to Ashinās and Ītākh. Al-Muntaṣir, the eldest, was in charge of Egypt and the west as well as the Jazīra and the property rents in Sāmarrā; al-Mu'tazz was to supervise the Tahirid areas in the east, while al-Mu'ayyad was given most of Syria and Palestine. There is no evidence that any of the young princes ever visited the areas over which they exercised control, but the object was probably to give them the experience of administration and the use of tax revenue to build support. In this way, the leading members of the élite in the next generation would be members of the 'Abbasid family rather than Turkish officers.

Al-Mutawakkil systematically pursued his policy of dismantling the old structure. In 237/851–852, he dismissed Ibn Abī Du'ād, the most influential of all the advisers of the Sāmarrā period and a man who had been largely responsible for his own accession. Along with this went a change in official ideology, a break with Mu'tazilism. 'Alī was cursed from the pulpits and the tombs of his descendants destroyed; legislation was introduced to humble Christians and Jews; and the caliph made an attempt to reconcile Baghdad opinion and the Traditionists – the body of the rebel Aḥmad b. Naṣr was allowed a fitting funeral.

In place of the old élite, the caliph employed new advisers: 'Ubayd Allāh b. Yaḥyā b. Khāqān was appointed *wazīr* in place of Ibn al-Zayyāt, while al-Fath. b. Khāqān (no relation, apparently) became the caliph's closest personal friend and counsellor. At the same time, new groups were encouraged to join the army to counterbalance Turkish influence. After al-Mutawakkil's death, we find 'Ubayd Allāh b. Yaḥyā seeking support against the Turks from, among others, Arabs, the *abnā'* of Baghdad, the Qaysīs of northern Syria and the Armenians. This last group seems to have been increasing in importance in the Islamic state at this time, and the campaign which Bughā the Younger conducted in the area may have served to encourage recruitment. These anti-Turkish groups could raise 20,000 horses and 13,000 feet in Sāmarrā itself at the time of al-Mutawakkil's death in 247/861, showing how far the Turkish monopoly of military power had been challenged.

With the change in policy came a change in capital. For much the same reasons as al-Mu'taṣim had left Baghdad, al-Mutawakkil was determined to leave Sāmarrā. In 244/858, he went to Damascus with the intention of moving the capital there, but the project was abandoned, ostensibly because of the plagues but probably because of violent Turkish protest in Sāmarrā. In the end, he compromised and built a new city, complete with palaces and mosques, some miles to the north of Sāmarrā, thus giving him a new site with all the advantages it accrued while he placated the opposition.

The reign was one of comparative peace. At no time perhaps had the caliph and his government exercised such real and effective control over the provinces. The east remained quiet under Tahirid rule, while the Turkish army was used to subdue such unruly groups as the bedouin of the ḥijāz and the people of the Caucasus areas. And yet, the very strength and centralization of the caliphate and the crucial role of the élite army corps in maintaining this unity was to prove a source of weakness. A crisis at the centre would result in the complete collapse of the government structure in the provinces.

The crisis which ended the reign of al-Mutawakkil was largely a product of growing Turkish discontent. The caliph was murdered not because the Turks were so strong that they could dispose of the ruler with impunity but because they felt their position being threatened. They were totally dependent on government salaries and support; without these, their influence and even their livelihood would disappear. Their coup against the 'Abbasid caliph was more a product of desperation than a sign of triumph. The immediate cause of the plot was that the caliph confiscated the estates of the senior-surviving Turkish leader Waṣīf and handed them over to his favourite, al-Fath. b. Khāqān. It was also said that al-Fath. and the caliph were plotting to murder Waṣīf and other leaders, and they must all have been mindful of the fate of Ītākh. All the killers who burst in on the caliph on the night of 4 Shawwāl 247/9–10 December 861 and slaughtered him and al-Fath. as they sat drinking were Turks.

The conspiracy might well have failed, however, if the Turks had not found an ally whose position was also slipping and in need of restoration: the heir apparent, al-Muntaṣir. In 235/849–850, he had been appointed heir, but by 247/861, it had become clear that his father was considering removing him from this position. 'Ubayd Allāh b. Yaḥyā and al-Fath. b. Khāqān seem to have been behind this, and determined that the second son, al-Mu'tazz, should take his place. Al-Muntaṣir was publicly humiliated by not being allowed to lead the prayers at the end of Ramaḍān and more privately when al-Mutawakkil ordered al-Fath. to slap his face as a punishment for his stupidity. Whether the connection between the prince and the Turks was long established is not clear, but we can be certain that they came together in a common cause and determined on a coup which would restore all their positions.

The anarchy at Sāmarrā: 247–256/861–870

The assassination of al-Mutawakkil ushered in the long, nine-year night of the "anarchy" in Sāmarrā. It was a period when caliphs succeeded one another with bewildering speed, four different rulers being proclaimed and accepted as caliphs, of whom at least three were subsequently killed by assassination or rebellion. To both contemporaries and later historians, it has seemed a time when the office of Commander of the Faithful was no more than a plaything in the hands of rival military factions and when the paralysis of the central government allowed disaffection and separatism to flourish unchecked in the provinces.

To understand the reasons for these confusing events, it is necessary to examine the motives of the main participants, the Turkish military leaders. Almost without exception, these were, as far as we can tell, men of obscure origins, slaves or sons of slaves who had risen to power as military commanders. Their fortunes and the livelihoods of their followers were entirely dependent on the favour of the caliph. Furthermore, they were mostly aliens in a strange land, cut off from the local people and without experience at trade or agriculture. These leaders needed a ruler who was going to rely on them, to the exclusion of other groups, for his support, and would, in turn, repay them with estates and gifts for the leaders and salaries for the rank and file. Bitterness and immediacy were added to the conflict because it seems to have taken place against a background of diminishing resources. Al-Mutawakkil had bequeathed a modest treasure to his successor, but this had soon been dissipated, and the confusion soon led to a steep decline in tax yields from the provinces as local governors kept the taxes for their own use. Evidence suggests that both caliphs and military leaders alike were frequently embarrassed for ready money. The military leaders were caught between a government which was either unable or unwilling to pay the necessary sums and their own men who would soon replace a leader who was unable to secure their salaries. The cutthroat competition for diminishing resources led to conflict between the Turks and other groups and, inevitably, among the Turks themselves. The apparently mindless violence bears the hallmark of the action of desperate and often frightened men.

The obstacles the Turks faced included many of the other groups in the state. First, there were the caliphs themselves. Without exception, the four caliphs of the period took measures to restrict their power and influence. None of them were puppet rulers, and at least two of them, al-Mu'tazz and al-Muhtadī, showed courage and determination in their efforts to restore the power of the caliphate. But their room for manoeuvre was limited; almost isolated at Sāmarrā, they found it difficult to raise support outside and even if they did, financial difficulties meant that they had no immediate rewards to offer. The Turks also faced the hostility of most of the *kuttāb* class. There were always secretaries prepared to work for Turkish leaders, but the most able and energetic of them, like al-Mu'tazz's *wazīr*, Aḥmad b. Isrā'īl, were determined to prevent the military exercising any direct control over the financial affairs of the caliphates and to restore the wazirate to the position it had enjoyed under Ibn al-Zayyāt and Ibn Khāqān. Then, there were other rival groups of soldiers (north African *Maghāriba* are the most frequently mentioned) who were sometimes grouped together under the name of *Shākiriyya*. They seem to have lacked the fierce *esprit de corps* and determined leadership of the Turks, but the Turks had to come to terms with them or remove them from influence. Finally and most deadly among the enemies of every Turkish leader were his rivals from his own kind. The triumph of one syndicate of leaders meant exile, disgrace, poverty and even death for another. The Turks showed some unity and common purpose in their action against al-Mutawakkil but almost immediately after that, divisions began to appear and much of the violence of the period occurred between rival Turkish leaders.

The assassination of al-Mutawakkil left his son al-Muntaṣir the unchallenged ruler of the caliphate. The new administration, under Aḥmad b. al-Khaṣīb the *wazīr*, stressed continuity with the old; it was given out that the caliph had been murdered by al-Fath. b. Khāqān, his favourite, who had subsequently been executed by the guard. Nonetheless, changes soon became apparent. The Turkish leaders claimed the reward of their support and became much more vocal in the making of policy; under pressure from Waṣīf and Bughā the Younger, al-Muntaṣir's brothers were obliged to resign their positions in the succession, while the Turks looked for a more amenable heir. Waṣīf was sent to the Byzantine front for four years with an army, largely drawn from the *Shākiriyya*, a connection he was later to make use of. Al-Muntaṣir restored the position of the Turks and also seems to have restored to favour the ʿAlid family, who were to enjoy the status which they had had in the years of Muʿtazilite government under al-Muʿtaṣim and al-Wāthiq but of which al-Mutawakkil had deprived them. How successful this government might have been is hard to tell, but in Rabīʿ II 248/June 862, the caliph died after a reign of six months, possibly of natural causes.

The Turks balked at the prospect of choosing one of his minor sons and felt that they could not trust his deposed brothers, so they turned to another branch of the family and chose a grandson of al-Muʿtaṣim, who was duly installed with the title of al-Mustaʿīn. From the beginning of the reign, the Turkish leaders tightened their grip on the government; Ibn al-Khaṣīb was sent to Crete in exile, while the wazirate passed, for the first time ever, to a Turkish leader, Utāmish. Unusually for a Turk, Utāmish busied himself with the financial administration, aided by his secretary, Shujāʿ b. al-Qāsim. The purpose of this arrangement was probably to ensure that the revenues were used for the benefit of the military without the interference of civilian advisers, but the experiment was not a success and many Turks believed that the *wazīr*, and his agent in the palace, along with the caliph's mother, was embezzling money rightfully due to them. In Rabīʿ II 249/June 863, Utāmish was murdered by troops incited by his rivals Waṣīf and Bughā the Younger. After a short period of civilian administration, Waṣīf assumed the position of *wazīr*, but he seems to have aroused the same hostility as Utāmish had done before him. Feeling his position in Sāmarrā under attack, he turned to the *Shākiriyya* connections he had forged on the Byzantine front (Waṣīf was the only Turkish leader who seems to have tried to seek military support from non-Turkish groups). He and Bughā the Younger left Sāmarrā for Baghdad, where they were followed by the Caliph al-Mustaʿīn in the beginning of

251/865. The Turks remaining in Sāmarrā were well aware that an alliance of the caliph, Waṣīf, Bughā the Younger, the Tahirids and *Shākiriyya* of Baghdad was a formidable threat to their position and they decided on war. They chose a new caliph for themselves, none other than al-Muntaṣir's brother al-Mu'tazz, and embarked on the siege of Baghdad.

The second siege of Baghdad echoed many of the features of the first during the reign of al-Amīn. Once again, it was long and hard-fought and once again the *'ayyārūn* (a word which originally meant vagabonds but seems to have lost its pejorative overtones and might be translated as irregulars) played an important role. Once again too, it was divisions among the defenders which led to the fall of the city. Waṣīf and Bughā the Younger did not wish to destroy the army of Sāmarrā, from which they themselves had sprung, and hand over power to others. Furthermore, the Tahirid leader became disillusioned with the rebels and so resistance collapsed – the unfortunate al-Musta'īn was exiled to Wāsiṭ but was murdered en route, and once again there was a caliph ruling in Sāmarrā with the support of the Turkish military (252/866).

The new caliph was able and determined. He appointed Aḥmad b. Isrā'īl as his *wazīr*, and civil and military administrations were once again divided in the old way. He ordered that the names of Waṣīf and Bughā be removed from the *dīwāns*; in 253/867, Waṣīf was murdered by his Turkish rivals; Bughā the Younger died the next year in prison; and Bughā the Elder's able son, Mūsā, was exiled to Hamadhān. But this operation did not proceed without opposition; predictably, many Turks opposed it, but so too did the caliph's own brother, Abū Aḥmad, later known as al-Muwaffaq, who had led the armies of Sāmarrā against Baghdad and established close links with many Turkish leaders, notably Mūsā b. Bughā. The caliph's position was further weakened by the decline of Tahirid power in Baghdad in the aftermath of the siege and especially after the accession of Sulaymān b. 'Abd Allāh b. Ṭahir in 255/869. This meant that the caliph was unable to look for support from that quarter.

In 255/869, the lead was taken by a partnership of Turkish military leaders: Wasīf's son, Ṣāliḥ, and Bāyikbāk. Their first target was the *wazīr* Aḥmad b. Isrā'īl. They began to assume governorships of provinces in their own name, sending deputies to administer them – Bāyikbāk sending Aḥmad b. Ṭūlūn to Egypt, for example. The object of this was again to avoid civilian control of the revenues, and the *wazīr* fought a determined but losing battle to keep the military out of the financial administration. In Jumādā II 255/June 870, Ṣālih. launched his attack and forced the removal of Ibn Isrā'īl. Al-Mu'tazz attempted to raise support from other troops, notably the *Maghāriba* but was fatally short of money. Unable to find 50,000 *dīnārs* (the sort of sum Hārūn had given to successful poets) to pay his supporters, he saw them defect to his enemies and a month after the removal of the faithful *wazīr*, he fell a victim to the Turks.

In his place, the military appointed Muḥammad, son of al-Wāthiq, who took the title of al-Muhtadī. Once again, they found themselves confronted by a caliph determined to take up the fight, against all odds, to restore the dignity of his office. He introduced a new style into caliphal behaviour; he was austere and puritanical, sat in court to listen to grievances in person and established a rapport with the common people of Sāmarrā which none of his predecessors seem to have enjoyed. For the first six months, the government was run by Ṣāliḥ. b. Waṣīf, but he was no more successful in providing adequate revenues than his father and Utāmish before him had been. Despite the execution of Aḥmad b. Isrā'īl and violent extortion from other *kuttāb*, his position continued to weaken until he was supplanted by Mūsā b. Bughā who came from his base in Hamadhān. Friction between the new man and the caliph continued to increase and, after eleven months of his reign in Rajab 256/summer 870, led to armed conflict. The caliph appealed to the religious status of his office and the affection of the people, but for the last time for half a century, the military were able to crush an obstreperous 'Abbasid and he died fighting bravely.

The revival of the 'Abbasid caliphate: 256–295/870–908

The anarchy came to an end with al-Muhtadī's death. This was partly because the feuds among the Turkish leaders had almost played themselves out, leaving Mūsā b. Bughā and his men in unchallenged control. It did not come to an end because an 'Abbasid caliph defeated and humiliated the Turks (the events of the previous nine years had shown that there was no real substitute for Turkish military power), but because they were assured of a place in the new regime and integrated once more into the structure of the state. This compromise came about as a result of the unusual personality and career of Abū Aḥmad al-Muwaffaq.

Unlike the other members of his family, it seems that from an early stage, al-Muwaffaq had embarked on a military career. During the recent civil war, he had been in command of the Sāmarrā forces of al-Mu'tazz against al-Musta'īn and the Baghdadis. Later, he had shown his identification with the Turkish cause by refusing to support al-Mu'tazz's move to curb the military and going into exile instead. He maintained especially close relations with another exiled member of the military, Mūsā, son of Bughā the Elder, who had been sent to Hamadhān, and when Mūsā returned to Sāmarrā during al-Muhtadī's reign to take over from Ṣāliḥ. b. Waṣīf, Abū Aḥmad was in a very strong position. After al-Muhtadī's death, however, he did not arrange for his own succession but allowed the appointment of his brother Aḥmad with the title of al-Mu'tamid. Al-Mu'tamid is often seen as a rather feeble personality, manipulated by his brother, but this is probably unfair. His brother, like al-Mu'taṣim in the reign of al-Ma'mūn, had put himself in an unchallengeable position because he alone of all the 'Abbasids could call on a reliable military force to support his political ambitions. Until his death in 264/877, Mūsā b. Bughā was al-Muwaffaq's right-hand military man, and after this date he continued to rely on Turkish leaders like Kayghalagh and

Isḥāq b. Kundājīq, who had been associated with Mūsā, thus building up a new and reliable army loyal to the 'Abbasid cause. For the Turkish leaders, the solution worked because al-Muwaffaq assured their status and their position as the army of the caliphate and al-Muwaffaq's role in the civil administration meant that they received their pay. At first, Abū Aḥmad was simply the governor of Iraq and Arabia, but in 261/875, he was given a place in the succession after al-Mu'tamid's son and responsibility for the eastern provinces as well.

The caliph, based in Sāmarrā, tried to maintain the independence of his position by seeking the alliance of the powerful governor of Egypt, Aḥmad b. Ṭūlūn, as a counterbalance to his brother. In 269/882, he tried to escape from his tutelage and join up with Ibn Ṭūlūn in Raqqa but was prevented by the governor of Mosul acting for al-Muwaffaq, and he was then brought south to Wāsiṭ. where he could be kept under closer watch. The struggle for power between the two brothers was reflected in the struggle to control the civil administration. At the beginning of his reign, al-Mu'tamid enjoyed the services of an experienced and able *wazīr*, 'Ubayd Allāh b. Yaḥyā b. Khāqān, who had been al-Mutawakkil's last *wazīr* and responsible for many of that ruler's moves against the Turks. He remained *wazīr* until his death in 263/877 and ensured his master some freedom of action. After 'Ubayd Allāh's death, however, al-Mu'tamid was forced to accept the services of his brother's secretary, Sulaymān b. Wahb, who was closely connected to the Turkish interests. Shortly afterwards, Sulaymān was himself disgraced and the caliph was again allowed his own *wazīr*, an Iranian by the name of Ismā'īl b. Bulbul, but most of the real power lay with al-Muwaffaq's secretary Ṣā'id b. Makhlad, who was his personal assistant from 265/878 onwards, helping in civil affairs and acting as a link between his master and the Turkish leaders, with whom his relations were close. In 272/885, his career was terminated and it was the turn of Ibn Bulbul to become *wazīr* to both brothers, with wide powers of appointment and command of a group of Berber troops in Baghdad.

These manoeuvres were the product of a continuing financial stringency, and the real questions at issue were first the rivalry between the caliph and al-Muwaffaq, and second whether the civil administration should be independently responsible to the caliph or controlled by men appointed by al-Muwaffaq and the military party. In these circumstances, two parties grew up among the *kuttāb*; Ismā'īl b. Bulbul, faced with the acute financial difficulties, had recruited two immensely able merchants to attempt to increase the revenues from the Sawād: Aḥmad and 'Alī b. al-Furāt, and they and their followers came to form one party in the administration. Opposed to them were a group of secretarial families, all originating from the countryside of the Sawād and many of them of Nestorian Christian origins. Sulaymān b. Wahb was one of these, but the most important and successful were the family of the Banu'l-Jarrāḥ, who became the most important rivals of the Banu'l-Furāt. The financial problems of the time meant that these men enjoyed great power, since even the most successful military leader was impotent unless he could enlist the cooperation and expertise of one of the dynasties of *wazīrs*.

The anarchy in Sāmarrā paralysed the central government and allowed provincial dissent to come into the open. The damage that the fabric of the caliphate sustained in those few years was never entirely repaired. In Iran, the control of the 'Abbasid–Tahirid partnership was challenged and destroyed by the Saffarids of Sīstān. Sīstān had always been on the fringes of the Islamic world, a natural place of refuge for rebels. Since Umayyad times, the rural areas away from the towns of Zaranj and Bust had been overrun by Khārijī rebels. Originally, these had been refugees from Umayyad government, but by the third/ninth century, Sīstānī Kharijism was a homegrown phenomenon. In order to combat these rural disturbances, the governors and the local people had set up vigilante groups, sometimes known as *'ayyārūn*. These groups became increasingly independent, and in 239/854 the governor of the Tahirids had been driven from Bust by the leader of one group. In 247/861, the year of al-Mutawakkil's assassination, the provincial capital at Zaranj was seized by another *'ayyār* leader, Ya'qūb b. Layth, who had been a coppersmith (Arabic *ṣaffār*) from a village in the area. By 251/865, Ya'qūb al-Ṣaffār had established his authority over all Sīstān, defeating both the Khārijīs and rival *'ayyār* leaders. There can be no doubt, however, that he incorporated many of their followers into his own armies, and the armies of the Saffarids were drawn from all sections of the population of Sīstān.

Once he had established himself in his home province, Ya'qūb turned his attentions to the surrounding areas. It was in pursuit of fleeing Khārijīs that he first invaded Tahirid Khurāsān, but by 253/867 he had defeated the Tahirid army and taken Harāt, and in 259/873 fifty years of Tahirid rule was brought to an end when the Saffarids took Nīshāpūr. At the same time, he led his men against the pagans to the east; in 256/870, he attacked Ghazna, Kābul and Bamyān. But from the point of view of the 'Abbasids, his most dangerous moves were when he began to turn his attention westwards. In an effort to deflect Ya'qūb's energies from Khurāsān proper, Muḥammad b. Ṭāhir had invested him with the governorates of Sīstān, Kābul, Kirmān and Fārs, and in 255/869 he began to make these claims a reality by taking Kirmān. Then in 255–262/869–875, he was engaged in a three-cornered fight in Ahwāz and Fārs with a local adventurer, Muḥammad b. Wāṣil al-Tamīmī, and the caliph's brother al-Muwaffaq. The 'Abbasids were particularly concerned lest the Saffarids should join forces with the Zanj rebels of the Baṣra area, but although they both benefited from each other's activities, the Saffarids refused the formal cooperation offered by the Zanj leader, 'Alī b. Muḥammad. In 262/876, there was a final trial of strength; Ya'qūb advanced on Baghdad. The 'Abbasids were prepared to offer him all the offices held by the Tahirids, not only the governorate of Khurāsān and the east but the command of the police in Baghdad as well. Ya'qūb, however, continued his advance only to be defeated by al-Muwaffaq and Mūsā b. Bughā at Dayr ʿĀqūl, near Baghdad in 262/876.

This setback and Yaʿqūb's subsequent death near Ahwāz in 265/879 freed Iraq from the Saffarid menace. Yaʿqūb's role was taken over by his brother ʿAmr. His position was less secure and he faced prolonged opposition to his rule in Khurāsān, which meant that he greatly valued the legitimacy which the ʿAbbasids alone could confer on his government, and he was given title to Khurāsān, Fārs, Iṣfahān, Sīstān, Kirmān and Sind. Relations between al-Muwaffaq and ʿAmr were not always cordial, although the Saffarid was prepared to pay irregular but substantial sums of tribute in return for caliphal approval. He made no further attempts on Iraq, but Fārs – despite a determined campaign by al-Muwaffaq and his son Abu'l-ʿAbbās, the future Caliph al-Muʿtaḍid, in 271–274/884–887 – remained in Saffarid hands. In Iṣfahān, the situation was complicated by a struggle between Saffarids and a local dynasty of Arab origin, the Dulafids, the ʿAbbasids supporting the cause first of one party and then the other. While never becoming as close to the ʿAbbasids as the Tahirids had been, the Saffarids under ʿAmr had ceased to be a threat to the existence of the dynasty and, if it had not been for the dispute over Fārs, might have become firm partners.

The Saffarids were outsiders who had become powerful and then received recognition from the caliphs. The main challenge to the ʿAbbasids in the west came from a member of the Sāmarrā ruling group who profited from the anarchy to break away. Aḥmad b. Ṭūlūn was the governor of Egypt from 254/868 until his death in 270/884 (see pp. 265). During these years, he used the wealth of the country to build up a substantial army which he employed to gain control over Syria and to mount expeditions against the Byzantines from the Syrian frontier lands which usually acknowledged his authority. Ibn Ṭūlūn never ceased to acknowledge the ʿAbbasids as caliphs and he probably continued to make some payments to their treasury. Al-Muʿtamid welcomed him and his financial contributions, as it seemed to lessen his dependence on his brother, and in 269/882 he made an attempt to transfer to Tulunid territory. Ibn Ṭūlūn's relations with al-Muwaffaq were less friendly, and the two men clearly saw each other as rivals. There were territorial clashes as well; the Tulunids occupied not just Syria but the Jazīra as far as Raqqa, uncomfortably close to the centres of ʿAbbasid power. But Ibn Ṭūlūn too had his problems, with dissident generals in his own army and the rivalry of Isḥāq b. Kundājīq, a Turkish general of much the same background as himself, who supported the ʿAbbasid cause in Mosul and the northern Jazīra. In these circumstances, he never sought to take over Iraq as well. After Ibn Ṭūlūn's death in 270/884, al-Muwaffaq attempted to retake Egypt and sent his son al-Muʿtaḍid to challenge Khumārawayh b. Aḥmad b. Ṭulūn, but the attempt ended in failure and in a compromise under which the Tulunids were to pay 300,000 *dīnārs* in tribute every year in exchange for recognition.

In contrast to the Tulunids or 'Amr b. Layth, with whom cooperation was possible, the Zanj of southern Iraq were the most radical and formidable of the challenges which faced the caliphate after the anarchy. They were a threat not just because of their military prowess, or because they operated in the 'Abbasid heartland of Iraq, but because they presented a challenge to the whole order of society and established religion. They threatened the very survival of the caliphate, and the struggle against them was a war to the death.

The Zanj was the name given to the slave population of southern Iraq, most of them of East African origin. It seems that at least since early Islamic times, large numbers of slaves had been used by landowners in the marsh areas of southern Iraq to reclaim land. Under Islamic law, reclaimed land brought under cultivation belonged to the man who made it productive and so it was worth investing large sums in this work. This seems to have been the only area in the Islamic world where this sort of large-scale agricultural slavery was practised; elsewhere, farming was conducted by free peasants, while slaves were used for domestic, administrative or military purposes. There is no doubt that many of these slaves lived in very bad conditions, and there had been at least two minor rebellions before in Umayyad times. The revolt in this period, however, was made much more formidable by the weakness of the government and the participation of other, non-slave elements.

The rebellion was not a spontaneous explosion but was the work of one rather unusual man. 'Alī b. Muḥammad had been born of Arab parents in a village near Rayy in central Iran. He had first tried to make his career as a poet in Sāmarrā but it would seem that his talents were not as great as his ambition and, seeing the chaos in the government, he decided to enter politics. He first went to Yamāma in eastern Arabia, where Musaylima had raised the Banū Hanīfa during the *Ridda* wars and which was later to be a stronghold of the Qarmaṭīs. It seems that he too claimed to be a Prophet and attracted some following among the tribes of the area, but his supporters were soon routed and with a small number of loyal companions he went to Baṣra in 254/868. There, he made a few more converts to his cause but soon came to realize the potential of the slaves as a source of support. What his religious position was is not quite clear; he seems to have abandoned the idea of prophethood for himself and contented himself with claiming to be a member of the 'Alid family, or rather, according to his detractors, different members of the 'Alid family on different occasions. What is more clear is the strong social content of his message; the slaves were going to be rich and free and their masters were going to suffer.

The rebellion broke out in Ramaḍān 255/September 869, just under a year before the accession of al-Mu'tamid and al-Muwaffaq. It spread very quickly and for ten years enjoyed an almost unchallenged success. The first attempts to subdue the ex-slaves were made by the Basrans, their former masters, but these were beaten off with ease, and the bitterness of the rebels was demonstrated by their policy of executing all prisoners without distinction. The enfeebled and preoccupied government was able to offer little support to the people. The rebels were aided by the difficult marshy terrain, ideal for guerrilla warfare conducted by men who knew the area well but almost impenetrable to a strange, largely cavalry army like the Turks. Aided by nomads of northeastern Arabia, notably from the Banū Tamīm and Banū Asad, they succeeded in 257/871 in taking Baṣra itself. The city, a great commercial centre and one of the cultural capitals of early Islam, was destroyed by the rebels, the mosques were burned, the inhabitants massacred; once more, the ferocity of the war is conspicuous. Their control spread to Wāsiṭ and beyond, and over much of the province of Ahwāz. 'Alī b. Muḥammad ruled from a new capital he founded, Mukhtāra, on a canal to the east of Baṣra; he minted his own coins and took the title of *mahdī*. How much power the Zanj themselves enjoyed is not entirely clear. All the known leaders seem to have been Arabs, mostly men who had joined 'Alī in Yamāma or in Baṣra before the rebellion started, and it may be that the slaves, now slaveowners themselves, had little say in the direction of policy.

When the 'Abbasid response did come, it was methodical, systematic and effective. From 266/879, al-Muwaffaq and his son Abu'l-'Abbās began a slow advance, concentrating on destroying the ships which gave the Zanj such mobility in the marshes. The army was large, perhaps 50,000, but the terrain meant that progress was slow. 'Alī ordered the evacuation of threatened areas and a retreat to the stronghold at Mukhtāra. There, the rebels were eventually besieged before 'Abbasid forces entered the city, which had to be taken street by street in Ṣafar 270/August 883. 'Alī b. Muḥammad was killed in the fighting. The rebellion was finally crushed, but the damage caused had been enormous. Slave farming and large-scale reclamation of land were never begun again, and it seems unlikely that the city of Baṣra ever fully recovered. Trade routes had been disrupted for too long, merchants had found other ways of communicating with the east – via Sīrāf in southern Iran, for example – and Baṣra and southern Iraq in general entered a long period of decline. Once again, the social antagonisms in the area led to large-scale popular movements which threatened the order and prosperity of society.

With the Caliph al-Mu'tamid increasingly a puppet after 269/882 and the effective ruler being al-Muwaffaq, the system of joint rule continued until al-Muwaffaq's death in 278/891. This did not, however, lead to a renewal of the caliph's power, since al-Muwaffaq was immediately succeeded by his son Abu'l-'Abbās, who took the title of al-Mu'taḍid, and when the caliph himself died the next year, his son was easily brushed aside, and al-Mu'taḍid, unlike his father, became caliph in his own right (279/892). The new caliph was very much a man in his father's mould, a strong personality who took good care to remain on close terms with the military and took part in campaigns himself. He inherited the largely Turkish army which had been built up by his father and Mūsā b. Bughā, with which he himself had done his apprenticeship.

The army remained loyal to him throughout his reign and became the chief instrument of his policy.

The main objectives of the new caliph were to increase the territory under the effective control of the government and, in order to accomplish this, to establish a viable financial administration. To do this, he collected a remarkably able and compatible government team. His *wazīr*, 'Ubayd Allāh b. Sulaymān b. Wahb, was the son of one of al-Muwaffaq's most influential secretaries. Like his father, he was given wide-ranging powers, not just over the civil administration but over military affairs as well, participating actively in campaigns. This close connection between civil and military leaders had been a major feature of al-Muwaffaq's success and it was continued by his son. The main army commander, Badr, was the son of a freedman of al-Mutawakkil and had served al-Muwaffaq. Under al-Mu'taḍid, he was the most prominent general, and the caliph's son married his daughter. He was also a firm friend of the *wazīr*, 'Ubayd Allāh, thus eliminating most of the friction which might have arisen.

The *wazīr* was in no position to supervise the day-to-day financial administration, partly because he does not seem to have had the technical knowledge and partly because military campaigns often meant that he was away from the capital. Financial administration was therefore left to the Banu'l-Furāt brothers, Aḥmad and 'Alī, who had served under Ismā'īl b. Bulbul. Despite this connection, their abilities secured them a position in the new government and they soon made themselves indispensable, reforming the revenue gathering, a process which involved the widespread use of tax farming, a procedure which was to prove very damaging in the future but was probably inevitable in the circumstances. They also allowed the caliph to build up a separate, private purse, again a development which may have had advantages with a strong and effective ruler like al-Mu'taḍid but was to lead to problems later. In 286/899, the Banu'l-Furāt were replaced by the other important family of *kuttāb*, the Banu'l-Jarrāḥ, and control of the finances was entrusted to Muḥammad b. Dāwūd and his nephew, 'Alī b. 'Īsā. When the *wazīr* 'Ubayd Allāh died in 288/901, the caliph ensured continuity by appointing his son al-Qāsim to succeed him. The new team was an able one, but there was dissension among them. There grew up a fierce rivalry between the Banu'l-Furāt and the Banu'l-Jarrāh. for control of the administration, each side being supported by groups of lesser secretaries who attached themselves to one party or another. This seems to have been a simple power struggle, but there is some evidence that the Jarrahids favoured a policy of closer cooperation with the military while the Banu'l-Furāt were determined to maintain the supremacy and separateness of the civil administration. Both the caliph and his *wazīr*, however, were strong, and these rivalries were not allowed, at this stage, to cause any serious problems.

The reign of al-Mu'taḍid saw the definitive return of the capital to Baghdad. Until the last months of his reign, al-Mu'tamid had continued to live in Sāmarrā, but al-Muwaffaq and his army had used Baghdad as their base against the Zanj and remained there even after the rebellion was crushed. It was natural then that al-Muʿtaḍid would continue his father's policy in this as in other matters. The city saw a considerable building activity at this time. Al-Manṣūr's Baghdad had been established on the west bank of the Tigris, but during the disturbances of the third/ninth century, much of this area had fallen into ruin. Al-Muʿtaḍid moved to the east bank, slightly farther downstream than the original city, and the site he chose has remained the centre of Baghdad to the present day. Both he and his son and successor, al-Muktafī, devoted large sums of money for the reconstruction of this part of the city and the building of new palaces and mosques. The caliph's concern for civil administration did not end there; we are told that he arranged for the digging-out of the bed of the Dujayl canal and collected contributions to the expense from those who held estates which would benefit from the irrigation work. He also arranged that the tax year should be changed so that the *kharāj* was demanded after the harvest rather than earlier in the year when farmers would find it more difficult to pay.

But it was a military activity which absorbed most of the caliph's energies. No 'Abbasid caliph, not even al-Muʿtaṣim, spent as much time on campaign as did al-Muʿtaḍid. He was also a skilful diplomat, always prepared to make compromises with those who were too powerful to defeat. He was prepared to leave eastern and northern Iran, Syria and Egypt to their own rulers as long as these acknowledged 'Abbasid sovereignty, but he was determined to assert real control over Iraq, the Jazīra, the Byzantine frontier area and western Iran, including Iṣfahān and Fārs.

With the Tulunids, the caliph was friendly but firm. On his accession, Khumārawayh sent presents for the new caliph and contracted a marriage alliance. After the death of Khumārawayh in 282/896, the Tulunid state began to disintegrate. A large number of soldiers defected to the 'Abbasids and were welcomed by the army minister Muḥammad b. Sulaymān. Within a year, the new sovereign, Jaysh b. Khumārawayh, had been murdered, in turn, and replaced by his brother Hārūn. In 284/897, there were riots between pro-Tulunid and pro-'Abbasid parties in Tarsus, the main base for raids against the Byzantines. The 'Abbasid faction triumphed, the caliph's authority was acknowledged and the leadership of the *ṣā'ifa*, the summer expedition against the Byzantines, was once again an 'Abbasid privilege. The new Tulunid ruler was obliged to make other concessions to gain recognition from the 'Abbasids and agreed to surrender Qinnasrīn and the province of al-'Awāṣim, that is, all of Syria north of Homs, to the 'Abbasids and to increase the tribute to 450,000 *dīnārs* per year. By the end of his reign, without striking a blow, 'Abbasid authority had been restored over an important area.

In the Jazīra, the situation was complicated by the rivalries of different leaders who had established themselves during and after the anarchy, often playing off the Tulunids against the 'Abbasids to preserve their independence. The Turkish strongman of the Mosul area, Isḥāq b. Kundājīq, had died the year before al-Mu'taḍid's accession, and his son Muḥammad was driven out by a rival adventurer, Aḥmad b. 'Īsā b. Shaykh. Aḥmad's father had been a Shaybānī bedouin leader who established himself first in Palestine and later in the northern Jazīra with his capital at Āmid. He was now the unofficial ruler of the area and was trying to expand his authority northwards into Armenia. A further threat in the area was posed by the Taghlibī leader Ḥamdān b. Ḥamdūn, who had numerous contacts among the Khawārij and the Kurds. The caliph began his campaigns with characteristic energy in 280/893 when he travelled north, chastising the Banū Shaybān and restoring 'Abbasid rule in Mosul. The next year, he was in Mosul again (after a stay in Baghdad and a campaign in Iran in the interim) seeking out the elusive Ḥamdān b. Ḥamdūn. During this campaign, he made contact with ḥamdān's son al-ḥusayn, who later secured his father's release and a position for himself and his followers in the caliph's army, in return for capturing a Khārijī leader. This marks the beginning of the rise of the Hamdanids, and al-Ḥusayn, with his highly mobile Arab following, was to provide the most effective troops the 'Abbasids could find against the Qarmaṭī menace.

Aḥmad b. 'Īsā died in his capital at Āmid in 285/898 and although he was succeeded by his son Muḥammad, al-Mu'taḍid saw this as the opportunity for a fundamental reorganization in the area. The next year, he launched a major expedition which forced the surrender of Muḥammad after a siege. He then left his son 'Alī al-Muktafī to arrange for the administration of the frontier areas and northern Syria and the Jazīra while he returned to Raqqa. By a mixture of force and diplomacy, the caliph had brought the whole area back under the control of the 'Abbasids. In Armenia and Āzarbayjān to the north and east, however, the caliph was unable to exercise any real authority at all; the local military commander, Muḥammad b. Abi'l-Sāj, remained effectively independent and the caliph was wise enough not to attempt a campaign in these distant regions. Even the death of Muḥammad in 288/901 and the subsequent dispute between his son Dīvdād and his brother Yūsuf allowed the 'Abbasids no opportunity for intervention.

In Iran, al-Mu'taḍid's policy was based on friendship with the Saffarid leader 'Amr b. Layth, with whom he exchanged gifts and courtesies. He was even content to allow the Saffarids to retain Fārs, while he struggled to assert 'Abbasid sovereignty in the Jibāl and Iṣfahān. The leading power in this area was the Dulafids and once again it was the death of an established member of the family (in this case Aḥmad b. 'Abd al-'Azīz b. Abī Dulaf in 280/893) which enabled the caliph to take action. He refused to allow Aḥmad's son 'Umar to succeed, and the next year, 281/894, he went to the province in person. Here, he divided the Dulafid domains, appointing his son 'Alī al-Muktafī to govern Rayy, Qazvīn, Qumm and Hamadhān, while 'Umar was restricted to the Dulafids' ancestral lands around Karaj and Iṣfahān. Even here, he was subjected to harassment, and in 283/896 he was obliged to surrender to the *wazīr* 'Ubayd Allāh b. Sulaymān and the army commander Badr. A member of the Baghdad army, 'Īsā al-Nawsharī, was appointed the governor of Iṣfahān and, despite some guerrilla campaigns by 'Umar's brothers, Dulafid rule was ended. 'Abbasid control in Rayy proved ephemeral; pressure from the 'Alids of Ṭabaristān and others made the city untenable and in 284/897 it was handed over to 'Amr b. Layth, then at the height of his power, while the young prince 'Alī made his way west to take up new responsibilities in the Jazīra. Despite this setback, 'Abbasid power had notably increased in the Jibāl area and 'Īsā al-Nawsharī remained the governor of Iṣfahān for the rest of the reign.

The end of the reign saw a major change in 'Abbasid policy in Iran. In 285/898, al-Mu'taḍid appointed 'Amr b. Layth to Transoxania, the region then held by Ismā'īl b. Aḥmad the Samanid. In view of subsequent events, this has been seen as a piece of 'Abbasid duplicity, but in fact it accords well with al-Mu'taḍid's previous policy of support for 'Amr. The Saffarid's attempt to assert his power in the area led to disaster; he was totally defeated, captured and sent to Baghdad, where, in 289/902 just after the caliph's death, he was killed. Ismā'īl b. Aḥmad was now acknowledged as the ruler of Khurāsān. In some ways, this revolution benefited the 'Abbasids, since the Samanids had no ambitions in western Iran or Iraq, but relations were never as close as they had been with 'Amr, and there is no evidence that the Samanids ever sent significant tribute to the caliphs; unlike the Tahirids and the Saffarids, they can be described as truly independent. The fall of 'Amr encouraged the 'Abbasids to make another attempt to retain Fārs, but despite campaigns by 'Īsā al-Nawsharī and Badr, the Saffarids, under 'Amr's grandson Ṭāhir b. Muḥammad, proved unexpectedly resilient and Fārs was not retaken by the 'Abbasids until the reign of al-Muqtadir.

This picture of gradual and systematic reestablishment of 'Abbasid power was threatened by the rising tide of discontent among the bedouin Arabs. The first campaign of al-Mu'taḍid after he became caliph had been to discipline the Shaybān of the Jazīra. When, from 286/899, their activities were coordinated by the leaders of the Qarāmiṭa or Carmathians (sing. Qarmaṭī), the tribes began to pose a more serious threat to the state. As long as al-Mu'taḍid and his military commander Badr lived, the menace was kept under control, but under al-Muktafī and his successors, they were to prove the most dangerous enemies the 'Abbasids had faced since the time of the Zanj.

Al-Mu'taḍid died in 289/902 and his son al-Muktafī, who was in the Jazīra at the time, was proclaimed caliph by the *wazīr* al-Qāsim b. 'Ubayd Allāh. Like his father, the new caliph had had extensive experience of government, in Rayy and the Jazīra, before he became caliph. In general, he followed in his father's footsteps but showed none of al-Mu'taḍid's amazing energy and does not seem to have exercised the same degree of control or to have led his army in person. It is very similar to the reign of al-Wāthiq after that of al-Mu'taṣim – a peaceful continuation of the same policies by a less forceful personality.

The reign was marked from the beginning by the determination of the *wazīr*, al-Qāsim b. 'Ubayd Allāh, to secure an effective monopoly of power.

As soon as the new caliph was installed, the *wazīr* secured the recall of Badr from the campaign in Fārs and his execution. The death of al-Muʿtaḍid's most important military leader meant that al-Qāsim was free to extend his control over the military. He did this through the agency of the clerk of the *dīwān al-jaysh* (the government office in charge of paying the troops), Muḥammad b. Sulaymān, who had been in charge of paying the army for some years and had welcomed the Egyptian military leaders who defected to Baghdad after the death of Khumārawayh. He was obviously liked and trusted by the military and now, despite his background as a *kātib*, he effectively became the commander of the army.

The most critical threat faced by the new regime was the Qarāmiṭa of the Syrian Desert. Faced by this menace, the 'Abbasids made peace in Iran, acknowledging Samanid control in Rayy and Saffarid control in Fārs. The first attempts to fight the Qarāmiṭa were heavily defeated, and the rebels threatened both Aleppo and Damascus. At the end of 290/903, Muḥammad b. Sulaymān was put in charge of a major expedition to the west to deal with the menace. Early next year, the 'Abbasid army won a major victory against the rebels near Ḥamāh, and the Qarmaṭī leaders were sent captive to the caliph at Raqqa. Muḥammad and his commanders were given a triumphal reception in Baghdad. The danger from the Qarāmiṭa was by no means over, and they continued to raid and pillage in the cities of Syria and Iraq which bordered on the desert, but the most serious threat had now passed.

Having achieved this triumph, Muḥammad b. Sulaymān then set out to retake Egypt from the Tulunids. The Tulunids had been weakened by internal strife since the death of Khumārawayh, and many of the officers in Muḥammad b. Sulaymān's army had previously served the Tulunids, especially Turks, dissatisfied with the favour Hārūn b. Khumārawayh showed to the Berbers and others. Tulunid rule had been further weakened by the Qarāmiṭa. Despite the successful defence of Damascus by Ṭughj b. Juff (the father of Muḥammad b. Ṭughj al-Ikhshīd, the future ruler of Egypt), the Tulunids had proved totally unable to defend the settled people of Syria against the threat from the desert. Muḥammad planned the expedition carefully; his army of 10,000 was very large by the standards of the time and he was aided by naval support from the fleet of Tarsus and further desertions from the Tulunid army. The campaign was something of a triumphal progress, and in 292/905, after only a little fighting, the Tulunid dynasty was brought to an end and 'Abbasid control restored. The triumph was not complete, however, and a revolt flared up under Ibrāhīm al-Khalījī. It was not until another year's fighting, in 293/906, that the province was finally subdued.

This triumph was succeeded the next year by a series of decisive victories over the Qarāmiṭa in the Syrian Desert, and although they continued to threaten Iraq from their base in Baḥrayn, their Syrian supporters were dispersed and subdued. Once again, the forces of the Hamdanid leader al-ḥusayn b. ḥamdān played a vital role in this.

The death of al-Muktafī in 295/908 marks the high point of the 'Abbasid revival. Not only were Syria and Egypt subdued but the treasury was full and the caliph left 15 million *dīnārs*. The army seems to have been effective and firmly under the control of the caliph and his civilian administrators. When al-Qāsim died in 291/904, he was in a position to nominate his successor. He suggested either the Jarrahid 'Alī b. 'Īsā or al-'Abbās b. al-Ḥasan al-Jarjarā'ī, another bureaucrat from the Sawād of Iraq, being determined to the last to exclude Ibn al-Furāt. 'Alī declined the offer and al-'Abbās assumed the powers his predecessor had built up. When the caliph died in 295/908, it fell to him to order the succession.

The disastrous reigns of al-Muqtadir and his successors: 295–334/908–946

Al-Muktafī had been ill for some time before his death, probably in fact for much of his short reign, and this may account for his failure to give clear guidance on the question of the succession. The choosing of the new caliph reveals clearly where power now lay. When al-Wāthiq had died in 232/847, the choice of the new caliph had been made by a group which consisted of the *wazīr*, two *kuttāb*, the chief *qāḍī* and two important representatives of the military, Ītākh and Waṣīf. In 295/908, however, only the bureaucrats were involved in the decision making. The *wazīr*, al-'Abbās b. Ḥasan, asked for advice from various quarters. Muḥammad b. Dāwūd the Jarrahid pronounced in favour of the talented and experienced 'Abd Allāh, son of the Caliph al-Mu'tazz, while the other leading Jarrahid, 'Alī b. 'Īsā, would not be drawn. 'Alī b. al-Furāt, however, persuaded the *wazīr* to appoint a weak candidate, al-Muktafī's brother Ja'far. It was a sinister development, since Ibn al-Furāt was clearly suggesting a candidate whom it would be possible to manipulate and control. In the end, the *wazīr* was persuaded and Ja'far was installed with the title of al-Muqtadir. It was an inauspicious beginning to what was to prove one of the most disastrous reigns in the whole of 'Abbasid history. For a quarter of a century, the place of al-Manṣūr and Hārūn was occupied by a youth who was constantly manipulated, exploited and deceived by his advisers, and it was a quarter of a century when all the work of his predecessors was undone.

The accession of the new ruler was a triumph for the civilian aristocracy. By their close relations with the military, al-Muwaffaq, al-Mu'taḍid and al-Muktafī had prevented army mutinies and rebellions, but under the new ruler, this link was lost. In addition, the bureaucrats were far from united and the bitter feuds which had divided them in the previous reign were allowed to flourish unchecked. We know a lot about these men and their manoeuvre, since their histories were recorded in detail by later administrators, notably Hilāl al-Ṣābī and Abū 'Alī Miskawayh, half in admiration, half as an awful warning of the consequences of bad government. There were still two main, and many minor, factions among the *kuttāb*. The Banu'l-Furāt were led by Abu'l-Ḥasan 'Alī. In many ways, he was a great man, an extremely able financier committed to the reform of abuse and the raising of state revenues without oppression. He was also highly cultured and extremely wealthy, with all the extravagant and conspicuous generosity which could be expected of such a man. But his character was not without flaws; he was to an extent ruthless and unscrupulous when it came to furthering his own interests, and he failed to restrain the rapacious cruelty of his son al-Muḥassin, whose excesses alienated many. The leader of the Banu'l-Jarrāḥ, 'Alī b. 'Īsā, is portrayed as a perfect foil to this *grand seigneur* personality. He too was a skilled administrator, devoted to the eradication of corruption, but he was austere, pious and even mean. He did not have an affable public manner and made enemies easily. Nonetheless, later generations praised his carefulness and probity, and he became known as the "good vizier". He also enjoyed the confidence of the military. The leading figure in the Baghdad forces, said to have numbered 9,000, was now Mu'nis, known as al-Muẓaffar, "the Victorious", after a successful campaign against the Byzantines. He was the most powerful military officer throughout the reign and remained an ally of 'Alī and a supporter of his methods. He also acquired vast landed estates, notably in Fārs after its reconquest by 'Abbasid forces. Around these figures, there grouped numerous lesser men – relatives and hangers-on. Each change of government meant not just a change of *wazīr* but changes in many other areas as well. The court was alive with intrigue and competition for favour.

This competition was made much more dangerous by the continuous financial crisis of the reign. The government was always short of money to discharge its immediate obligations and *wazīrs* were often forced to borrow to pay the next month's salaries. It is not entirely clear why this crisis had become so pressing. It is clear that revenues from the Sawād of Iraq had been declining for at least a century. In early Islamic times, the Sawād is said to have produced over 100 million *dirhams* in tax revenue each year, and this remained true until the reign of al-Ma'mūn. By the reign of al-Muqtadir, in a survey of 306/918–919, it seems to have yielded only 31 million *dirhams*, a dramatic decline, and it is clear that much of this was never collected or was embezzled before it reached the capital. The decline in revenue from the Sawād was all the more damaging because many other areas, like Egypt and Fārs, contributed little or no taxes during the second half of the third/ninth century.

War and maladministration probably account for much of this. The agricultural economy of the area was potentially very rich, but it was also very fragile; it required constant investment in canals and irrigation if prosperity was to be maintained. The series of long drawn out campaigns of the third/ninth century must have caused immense damage. In Umayyad and early 'Abbasid times, we hear of large-scale agricultural development in the area. From the third/ninth and fourth/tenth centuries, we hear of occasional attempts to restore damaged systems, but it would seem that no one was prepared to make long-term investments. The problem was aggravated when the government was obliged to grant lands to military officers whose tenure was insecure and whose only concern was to extract as much as possible before moving on. As von Kremer remarked:

> One fact appears to emerge with certainty from the list of the tax-payments of Sawād province; it is the decline of the agricultural economy, while simultaneously the grandees of the state, the members of the ruling families, established for themselves widespread latifundia.

The problem the 'Abbasids faced at this time cannot be understood unless the economic and financial problems are given due attention.

Despite the long-term decline in the prosperity of the Sawād, however, al-Mu'taḍid and al-Muktafī were both able to save about 1 million *dīnārs* per year out of current revenue, and both left substantial sums in the treasury. Furthermore, the revenues available to al-Muqtadir actually increased in some ways; the reconquest of Fārs was said to have brought in an extra 18 million *dirhams* per year, more than enough to pay the salary bill of the troops Mu'nis commanded in Baghdad, and the revenues of Egypt under the administration of the Mādharā'ī brothers were much greater than al-Muqtadir's predecessors had enjoyed. The caliph also resorted to widespread confiscations of the goods of deposed *wazīrs*, amounting to 2.3 million *dīnārs* on the one occasion from Ibn al-Furāt and his family. Writing at the time of the Buyid 'Aḍud al-Dawla half a century later, Miskawayh blamed the caliph for squandering and wasting this money. Some contemporaries shared this point of view; 'Alī b. 'Isā as *wazīr* made sustained attempts to reduce court salaries and cut out extravagant expenditure and in this he was supported by Mu'nis, who considered that the palace was responsible for most of the problems. It was here that the private purse of the caliph became such a problem, as the *wazīr* was unable to supervise it, while al-Muqtadir (and even more so his mother, who controlled many of his activities) insisted that all the everyday expenses of court and government be met out of public funds. The army was certainly costly. The 9,000 troops Mu'nis commanded in Baghdad are said as of 315/927 to have been paid 600,000 *dīnārs* (about 9 million *dirhams*) per year: monthly and in cash. The root of the problem was that both of the great consumers of public wealth – the palace and the military – were in a very strong position; the palace because the courtiers effectively controlled the caliph and could secure the dismissal of *wazīrs* like 'Alī b. 'Īsā, who reduced their allowances, and the military because they could threaten mutiny and were the only people who could hope to defend Iraq from the Qarāmiṭa, although their military abilities and enthusiasm seem to have been very limited. When Ibn Rā'iq finally broke up this army, he found that it contained many merchants, women and others who collected salaries but performed no military duties at all. Most attempts to solve immediate problems tended to reduce revenue in the long term, and in the end it was financial disaster which destroyed the great

'Abbasid caliphate. The overall picture suggests that Iraq was burdened with a military and court establishment out of all proportion to its real wealth.

To deal with these problems, *wazīrs* tried a variety of expedients. The first and most obvious was to extract money from previous holders of the office, and the high turnover of top administrative officials is in marked contrast to the stability of the previous two reigns, when 'Ubayd Allāh b. Sulaymān and his son al-Qāsim had both held office until their deaths. The procedure, frequently repeated, went like this: there was a financial crisis and some ambitious bureaucrat or businessman would approach the caliph saying that he was in a position to increase the revenue and extract a vast sum from the present *wazīr*. The caliph would agree that the hapless *wazīr* was dismissed and he and his assistants interrogated, often under torture, and would promise to pay huge fines. The new holder of the office would then discover that the fines were mostly unpaid, since the victims did not have the money, and he was wholly unable to raise the promised sums, whereupon the whole dismal cycle began all over again.

The government was supposed to extract the revenue from the Sawād and the provinces. There were three ways in which this could be done. The first was by direct taxation on land, the *kharāj*, which was assessed according to area and collected annually. This was an ideal system, and *wazīrs* like Ibn al-Furāt and 'Alī b. 'Īsā strove to uphold it, realizing that it was the best method of paying the expenses while maintaining the prosperity of the country, but it was increasingly difficult to sustain. It needed a number of skilled, honest, salaried tax gatherers who were themselves a strain on the public purse – but more importantly under the circumstances, it was very inelastic. A sudden demand for money could not be met, and deficit financing, borrowing against next year's anticipated income, was very difficult. Equally, a bad harvest one year or a provincial rebellion could reduce tax yields dramatically and cause a major political crisis. In the circumstances of the time, *wazīrs*, often against their better judgement, were compelled to resort to the second alternative: tax farming. The collection of revenues was often granted to individuals in return for a guaranteed sum for the exchequer. The entrepreneur was then entitled to collect what he could from the unfortunate local people. Such tax farmers appear frequently in the chronicles, among them the fabulously rich farmer of Wāsiṭ, Ḥāmid b. al-'Abbās. He was at one time made *wazīr* himself, although it soon became apparent that the abilities needed for tax farming and for being *wazīr* were quite different, and he was obliged to leave everyday affairs to 'Alī b. 'Īsā. After their reconquest, Syria and Egypt were farmed out to two Iraqi businessmen, the Mādharā'ī brothers, who agreed to pay 1 million *dīnārs* a year to the public purse while paying the Syrian and Egyptian armies themselves. The system solved some problems but led to others – the peasants were often exploited for short-term profits, and tax farmers were often unable to meet their obligations. The Mādharā'īs, for example, made the bargain for Syria and Egypt in 306/918 and paid up the first year, but thereafter the threat of

Fatimid invasion diverted the revenues. In 320/932, Syria and Egypt were said to have contributed no revenues to Baghdad for the previous four years.

The third option was the granting of an *iqīā*'. Basically, this meant that the revenues of a given area would be assigned to an individual who would undertake to provide the government with a number of troops or a sum of money. It differed from tax farming in that the person concerned was effectively the governor and military leader as well as the tax officer of the area. Ḥāmid b. al-'Abbās as a tax farmer collected the revenues of the Wāsiṭ area and forwarded the agreed sum to Baghdad, where the *wazīr* used it to pay salaries to troops and courtiers. Security and civil government in the area of the tax farm were the responsibility of separate officials. By contrast, an *iqīā*' holder like Yūsuf b. Abi'l-Sāj in Armenia and Āzarbayjān would collect the revenues, pay the army of the area himself and exercise all the powers of government while sending an agreed sum to Baghdad. This *iqṭā*' system first seems to have been used in Āzarbayjān in the time of al-Ma'mūn when the caliph, faced with a prolonged local rebellion, was prepared to offer the revenues and the governorship of the province to anyone who was able to crush the dissidents. Such bargains continued to be made in outlying areas. Soon after the accession of al-Muqtadir and his own appointment as *wazīr*, Ibn al-Furāt persuaded Yūsuf b. Abi'l-Sāj to accept the authority of Baghdad, which he had not previously done, and pay the fairly modest sum of 120,000 *dīnars* per annum in exchange for the recognition of his titles, thereby attaching the area, at least in some measure, to the caliphate. At the same time, Ibn al-Furāt was attempting to regain control of Fārs, a valuable province which had been taken over by a supporter of the Saffarids called Subkarā. The *wazīr* was prepared to offer Subkarā a bargain, but the terms were steep. Subkarā could not offer more than 10 million *dirhams* per annum, after paying for the army and administration in the province, and the *wazīr* would not accept less than 13 million *dirhams*, with the result that a military expedition was sent, the area was brought under direct government control and a tax farmer was appointed. The idea of the *iqīā*' originated as a way of settling the problems of outlying areas, but as time went on, it was used nearer to home. In 317/929, after an attempted coup against al-Muqtadir, the *wazīr* Ibn Muqla was obliged to sell off state lands to the military at very reduced prices. In addition, these new landholders were obliged to pay only the tithe (*'ushr*) not the full *kharāj* to the government, keeping the difference between the two rates of tax for themselves, with the result that those lands had the same fiscal status as the *iqīā'*. In this way, financial expediency caused the spread of these concessions into the heartland of the caliphate.

The political history of al-Muqtadir's reign is full of incidents but not very easy to follow. Two attempts were made to depose the useless caliph. In 296/908, very shortly after his accession, the Jarrahids and elements of the military, including the Hamdanid leader al-Ḥusayn b. Ḥamdān, attempted a coup in favour of Ibn al-Mu'tazz. The young caliph was saved by the loyalty of the military, recruited by his father the caliph al-Mu'taḍid and now led by Mu'nis, who were determined that the caliphate should remain in their old master's family. More by good luck and the panic of their opponents than by their own abilities, al-Muqtadir's supporters were able to defeat the rebels, and the Jarrahid leaders were imprisoned and executed, except for 'Alī b. 'Īsā, who had been careful to distance himself from the whole operation. In 317/929, there was a military coup launched by Mu'nis after his trusted 'Alī b. 'Īsā had been removed from the wazirate. For a few days, the caliph's brother Muḥammad al-Qāhir was accepted as caliph before another army mutiny resulted in the restoration of al-Muqtadir. The third attempt was decisive. In 320/932, Mu'nis, again exasperated by the failure to curb court expenditure and repeated attempts to remove him from the centre of power, marched south from Mosul, where he had been sent in semi-exile. He was opposed by rival military leaders, but once again shortage of money and the caliph's own lack of courage meant that his army dispersed. Mu'nis entered the capital in triumph and installed al-Qāhir as caliph; once again, the military were deciding the course of government.

As far as external opposition was concerned, the early years of al-Muqtadir's caliphate were comparatively successful, and the gains made by al-Mu'taḍid and al-Muktafī were retained. Fārs was retaken, Āzarbayjān acknowledged the sovereignty of the caliph, the Byzantine frontier was defended, raids were launched against the Greeks and the Fatimids were prevented from taking Egypt. From 311/923, however, the position began to change. The Qarāmiṭa had been quiescent since the defeats they had suffered during al-Muktafī's reign, but although they did not recover their power in the Syrian Desert, the Qarāmiṭa of Baḥrayn began to raid Iraq. This may have been connected with the fall of 'Alī b. 'Īsā as *wazīr* and his replacement by Ibn al-Furāt at this time, because 'Alī believed in paying subsidies to the rebels, while his rival favoured military action. Under their new leader, Abū Ṭāhir al-Jannābī, with 1,700 men they entered and sacked the once great city of Baṣra, and although Ibn al-Furāt sent troops, they had already disappeared into the desert. Early next year, the *ḥajj* caravan was attacked on the return from Mecca. This disaster led to a crisis in the government. Ibn al-Furāt, now *wazīr* for the third time, was an old man and seems to have forgotten much of his earlier moderation. In the quest for money, he had allowed his son al-Muḥassin to torture government officials with a brutality never seen before, while to maintain his power against the military, he had secured the semi-exile of Mu'nis to Raqqa. The sack of Baṣra and destruction of the *ḥajj* led to riots in the streets and a military takeover. Ibn al-Furāt was arrested, Mu'nis recalled, and the old *wazīr* and his son executed in prison. This coup really marked the end of the civil domination of government. Ibn al-Furāt lost the support of the army because he could not pay the salaries regularly and lost popular support because of his failure against the Qarmaṭīs. He had even alienated most of the *kuttāb*, by his tortures and exactions. From now on, the military came to play an ever-increasing role in the nomination first of *wazīrs* and then of caliphs; it was only a matter of time before a general felt it necessary to take over the government himself.

The raids of the Qarāmiṭa continued, and despite an escort 6,000-men strong, the *ḥajj* was attacked again the next year, and the *wazīrs* who followed Ibn al-Furāt were deposed for being unable to meet their financial commitments. In 314/926, the *wazīr* al-Khaṣībī invited the ruler of Āzarbayjān, Yūsuf b. Abi'l-Sāj, to come to Iraq with his men to fight the rebels who were threatening the Sawād itself. There was no question of paying them salaries, since there was no money, but instead all the revenues of the Jibāl and northwestern Iran were to be paid directly to Ibn Abi'l-Sāj "for his table" during the campaign. In effect, all the Iranian provinces except Fārs were to be given to him as a vast *iqṭā'* in addition to Āzarbayjān and Armenia, which he held already. In the event, the Qarāmiṭa proved too much for him, perhaps because his followers from the mountainous areas of northwestern Iran were unused to fighting in the desert terrain. He was captured and killed by the rebels, and Sajid rule in Āzarbayjān, which had lasted since the days of al-Mu'tamid, was brought to an end with his death. The next year, Mu'nis succeeded, against the advice of the courtiers, in securing the appointment of 'Alī b. 'Īsā to the wazirate just before the rebels pressed home their attack towards Baghdad in 315/927. For a while, it seemed as if the capital must fall, but the attack was held off by Mu'nis, with help from the Hamdanids, and the danger passed. In 317/930, the Qarāmiṭa sacked Mecca and removed the Black Stone from the Ka'ba, a serious blow to the prestige of the caliph, but after that the rebels were divided by internal disputes and ceased to be a threat to the 'Abbasids for some decades.

The disasters of the campaign against the Qarāmiṭa and the loss of revenue from the devastated Sawād caused tensions within Baghdad to reach a climax. In 316/928, the court party secured the dismissal of 'Alī b. 'Īsā, and Mu'nis now felt that he had to take control of the civil administration. For three years, there were coups and countercoups as Mu'nis and his enemies disputed for control of the caliphate, until in 320/932 Mu'nis defeated and killed al-Muqtadir.

As before, the murder of a caliph was the signal for a period of continuing anarchy, but this time, after the death of al-Muqtadir, there was to be no recovery. The military takeover of government which had begun with the removal and execution of Ibn al-Furāt gained momentum with the death of al-Muqtadir, the first caliph to die a violent death since al-Muhtadī, sixty years before. The military leaders did not attempt to change the dynasty at this time, but from the death of al-Muqtadir onwards, the choice of caliphs was decided not by the 'Abbasids, as it had been during the great days of the caliphate, or even by the *kuttāb*, as it had been when al-Muqtadir himself was appointed, but rather by the leading military figures in Baghdad at the time. The political history of this new anarchy was dominated by the struggles of military men to control the caliphate and, perhaps more importantly, the revenues of the Sawād, which would enable them to satisfy the demands of their followers. In the aftermath of the coup against al-Muqtadir, as has been mentioned, the victorious party put on the throne his brother Muḥammad, who had briefly been caliph three years before after a somewhat similar coup, and as before he took the title of al-Qāhir. The new caliph was a man of some determination and energy but was given to violence and brutality. He put on a show of puritanism to dispel the reputation of extravagant court immorality, which had been a major factor in the undoing of al-Muqtadir, but he himself, like many of his contemporaries, was frequently drunk and incapable. The first concern of the new regime was to destroy the power of their rivals who had supported al-Muqtadir in his last fight and had now established themselves in the area of southern Iraq and Ahwāz. They were dispersed by diplomacy and violence, but the area became subject to the rising power of the Barīdī family. For some years now, this family had farmed extensive taxes in southern Iraq, around Basra and in Ahwāz, but they now aspired to political power. They began by backing different groups in the army but soon developed a military power base of their own. Although they had little military experience, they seem to have been able to raise considerable funds when the need arose, both because of their own financial expertise and because the lands they farmed had been less ravaged by recent wars than other parts of Iraq. In a political situation where everyone else was short of cash, this put them in a strong position, and their power in the south was a constant factor up to the consolidation of the Buyid regime.

Mu'nis and his fellow officers hoped that they had secured a monopoly of military power and control over the revenue, but they were soon alarmed to find that the caliph they had installed was negotiating with Muḥammad b. Yāqūt and other members of the faction they had so recently defeated. Feeling their position threatened, they decided to depose the caliph, but he was too quick for them and they were arrested and killed; even the veteran Mu'nis (a leading figure in the army since the time of al-Mu'taḍid), his throat cut "like a sheep" (321/933). Needless to say, these measures merely exacerbated the problems of the caliphate, and al-Qāhir was unable to find officers who were as capable and influential among the troops to replace Mu'nis. The violent and brutal nature of the caliph and the distrust now felt against him by many in the army allowed discontent to spread. Inevitably, there was a conspiracy, coordinated in this case by Ibn Muqla, who had been *wazīr* up to the failure of Mu'nis' conspiracy. Al-Qāhir was seized while drunk, deposed and blinded (322/934) by the rank and file of the army, who now produced one of al-Muqtadir's sons, Muḥammad, who took the title of al-Rāḍī as caliph. They then sent for the ex-*wazīr*, 'Alī b. 'Īsā, to explain the proper protocol for proclaiming caliphs. Compared with his predecessor, al-Rāḍī was quiet and affable and given to the company of scholars, but he had little chance to display any political talents he may have had.

The intrigues and conspiracies which surrounded the caliph in Baghdad were becoming increasingly irrelevant to most of the Muslim world. In

305/918–919, during his third and last term as *wazīr*, ʻAlī b. ʻĪsā had caused a list of the revenues of the caliphate to be drawn up. Neither north Africa nor Khurāsān were included, since they made no contributions – but Egypt, Syria, the Jazīra, western Iran (including Rayy) and Fārs were all listed, the Sawād, Ahwāz, Fārs and Egypt being the most profitable areas. No doubt even when it was drawn up, the list was optimistic; seven years later, during al-Rāḍī's caliphate, it was no more than a historical curiosity. Not just the distant provinces but even the Sawād of Iraq itself had been seized from ʻAbbasid control. Egypt and Syria were in the hands of Muḥammad b. Ṭughj the *ikhshīd*, Mosul and the Jazīra in the hands of the Hamdanids. Western Iran had been taken over by groups of Daylamite soldiers of fortune and Fārs had passed into the hands of the first of the Buyid rulers. None of these areas now made any contribution to the revenues of the caliph. More critical still was the position in Iraq. In the south, the Barīdīs frequently withheld revenues from their area and began to negotiate with Aḥmad b. Būya with a view to taking over the whole country. In Wāsiṭ, the military governor, Muḥammad b. Rā'iq, refused to pay any of the revenues to Baghdad, saying that he needed them for his own purposes. The *wazīr*, Ibn Muqla, made an attempt in 323/935 to remedy the situation by leading an expedition to Mosul to try to assert his authority, but intrigues forced him to return. The next year, he persuaded the caliph to undertake an expedition against the nearest of the usurpers, Muḥammad b. Rā'iq in Wāsiṭ, but it failed to materialize and the *wazīr* was himself arrested. Not for the next 200 years was an ʻAbbasid caliph to launch a military campaign on his own initiative.

It was bankruptcy, not military defeat, which finally brought ʻAbbasid power to an end. The previous year, Ibn Rā'iq had suggested that he himself should take over both the civil and military administrations of the caliphate. Al-Rāḍī had refused, but now he saw no alternative. He wrote to Ibn Rā'iq, who in 324/936 came to Baghdad to take over the entire administration. It was a momentous change. From this time onwards, real power remained with Ibn Rā'iq – who was given the title of *amīr al-umarā'* (commander of commanders) – and his secretary. The caliph had neither soldiers nor administrators to command. It was a revolution in another way as well. Ibn Rā'iq's military power was based on a group of Turks newly arrived from Iran, where they had served with the Daylamite Mardāvīj b. Ziyār until his assassination the year before. The leading figures in this group were Bajkam and Tūzūn, each of whom later became *amīr al-umarā'* in his own right. When Ibn Rā'iq took over the administration, he entirely disbanded and cashiered the old army of Baghdad, and its members were dispersed. It was the military force which al-Muwaffaq and Mūsā b. Bughā had built up and which had sustained the ʻAbbasid revival. Now that this army was no more, there was no body of troops to whom the dynasty could look. The arrival of Ibn Rā'iq also meant the end of the old wazirate. Ibn Muqla was the last of a tradition that stretched back to the Barmakids and before, the great ʻAbbasid *wazīrs*. On the orders of the vengeful *amīr al-umarā'*, Ibn Muqla's tongue was torn out, and his hand, which had produced the most beautiful calligraphy of the age, was cut off "like a thief's". He died of dysentery, alone in a squalid dungeon, denied even a drink of water. From then onwards, it was the secretary of the *amīr al-umarāʾ* who conducted such administration as was needed. The old *dīwāns*, with their specialized methods and procedures, were abandoned, and only the most basic functions of government remained.

The success of the new *amīr al-umarāʾ* was short-lived. The Barīdīs, who had supported his move, began to negotiate with the Buyids again, while he himself faced discontent among his own military led by Bajkam. A short but destructive campaign saw him removed from power by his former protégé in 326/September 938. Thereafter, there followed a very confusing period of struggle for control of the caliphate in Baghdad. The main participants were the Turkish military of the capital, who produced two *amīr al-umarāʾ*s: Bajkam (326–9/938–941) and Tūzūn (331–334/943–945); the Hamdanids, one of whom became *amīr al-umarāʾ* briefly with the title of Nāṣir al-Dawla (-330–331/942–943); and the Barīdīs, who, being civilians by training, did not aspire to the title of *amīr al-umarāʾ* but attempted briefly to run the government as *wazīrs*. The constant changes reveal both the bankruptcy and the unimportance of the caliphate during this period. Al-Rāḍī himself died peacefully in 329/940, and his brother Ibrāhīm took the title of al-Muttaqī, nominated by the then *amīr al-umarāʾ*, Bajkam. Al-Muttaqī seems to have been more forceful than al-Rāḍī in his attempts to restore the caliph's power, and after Bajkam was murdered by some Kurds while out hunting in 329/941, he attempted to restore the wazirate in the old way and dispense with the office of *amīr al-umarāʾ* entirely, but the attempt failed and the military soon regained control. Three years later, in 333/944, the caliph had a last chance when Muḥammad b. Ṭughj, the ruler of Egypt, came to see him in Raqqa and encouraged him to join him in Egypt. Unwisely, he refused and returned to Baghdad, where Tūzūn blinded and deposed him.

A new ʿAbbasid caliph, who took the name of al-Mustakfī, was appointed by Tūzūn, but affairs in Baghdad were increasingly overshadowed by the activities of Aḥmad b. Būya, sometimes supported by the Barīdīs in southern Iraq. While Tūzūn lived, he and his Turkish followers were able to maintain the independence of the city, but when he died, peacefully in his palace in 334/945, it was only a matter of time before the Buyids advanced. A last attempt was made by his secretary Ibn Shīrzād to arrange an alliance with the Hamdanid Nāṣir al-Dawla of Mosul but it came to nothing, and on 11 Jumādā II 334/17 January 946 Aḥmad camped outside Baghdad and was received by al-Mustakfī and acknowledged as *amīr al-umarāʾ*. The Buyid era in Baghdad had begun.

After the anarchy which followed the death of al-Mutawakkil, the ʿAbbasid caliphate was able to mount a sustained revival of power, but in the crisis of the first half of the fourth/tenth century, no such revival was possible. We can suggest a number of reasons for this. The first was perhaps the caliphs themselves. The earlier revival had been possible because of the close relationship that al-Muwaffaq had developed with the military commanders in Baghdad – but none of the 'Abbasids of al-Muqtadir's time seem to have done this; they remained secluded in the palaces of the dynasty until fortune thrust them, for good or ill, into the limelight. When made caliphs, they had neither experience nor contacts on which to build political power.

The nature of the army had changed as well. At the end of the Sāmarrā anarchy, most of the military leaders, men like Ṣālih. b. Waṣīf and Mūsā b. Bughā, were second-generation supporters of the 'Abbasids who had been brought up in the service of the dynasty. Mu'nis was the last commander with such a background; Bajkam and Tūzūn were newly arrived from the east, where they had been serving with Mardāvīj, who rejected the caliphate entirely and felt no tradition of loyalty. The same was true of their followers. The fate of the dynasty was sealed when Muḥammad b. Rā'iq disbanded the old Baghdad army. In the Sāmarrā anarchy, the Turks had attempted to dominate the caliph so that they could guarantee salaries and rewards for their followers. They were not in fact hostile to caliphal power; they simply wanted to control it in their own interest. The soldiers of the fourth/tenth century, by contrast, were not dependent on salaries, and the winning of lands became their priority. Men like Ibn Rā'iq were intent on building up their own landed holdings, and any revival of central government could only be detrimental to their ambitions.

Over and over again, the problems of the 'Abbasids at this time boiled down to shortage of money. The constant civil strife and the depredations of the Qarāmiṭa meant that the war-torn countryside of the Sawād of Iraq was exhausted, unable to yield the revenues which alone could make a revival possible. Ahwāz, Fārs and even Mosul seem to have remained comparatively prosperous but none of these was in 'Abbasid hands, and the Baghdad countryside remained devastated. The military adventurers of the time totally disregarded the interests of the people and the economy of the area. In 326/937, Ibn Rā'iq, striving to impede the armies of his rival Bajkam by flooding, cut the great Nahrawān canal which watered much of the Sawād. The manoeuvre failed, but the consequences remained. Within four years, both Ibn Rā'iq and Bajkam were dead and the causes for which they fought forgotten. Yet, in the struggle they had destroyed for short-term military advantage the labour of generations. Never again would the countryside around Baghdad be able to support the flourishing civilization it had in early 'Abbasid times and before. The breach of the Nahrawān canal was simply the most dramatic example of a widespread phenomenon of the time; and it was symbolic of the end of 'Abbasid power, just as the breach of the Mārib dam was of the end of the prosperity of pre-Islamic south Arabia.

7 The early Islamic economy

The early Islamic caliphate from the first Muslim conquests in the Middle East until the mid-tenth century was the richest and most populous state in the whole of Western Eurasia. Globally, only the almost contemporary Tang Empire in China could rival it for the size of its cities, wealth of its people, the scale of its trade and manufacturing and its cultural output. In this chapter, I shall try to suggest some of the reasons for this prosperity in the first three centuries of Muslim rule and the seismic changes which occurred during the tenth and early eleventh centuries. There is a large and growing literature on this subject, combining archaeological and written evidence and at least one large volume could be written on the subject. This chapter can only attempt to sketch the general arguments and point to some of the most important studies and it cannot be a comprehensive survey.

Estimating the comparative size of the early Islamic economy in the absence of comprehensive statistical data can only be conjectural. Perhaps the clearest evidence comes from the cities. Estimates suggest that Baghdad in the ninth century probably had a population of between 250,000 and half a million at a time when it is unlikely that Paris or London could boast a population of 10,000. Coined money, gold dinars, silver dirhams and copper *fulūs*, millions of them, were used to collect taxes, pay soldiers and buy and sell food and consumer goods. It has been estimated that there are some half a million silver dirhams surviving from the ninth, tenth and eleventh centuries, three quarters of them found in deposits in northern Europe (Kovalev, 2007). These can only have been a small percentage of the total coins in circulation at this time and the writings of the period are full of references to money, collected, spent, given away, stolen or hoarded. The markets of the big cities stimulated agricultural and manufacturing in the wider countryside and merchants grew rich by importing exotic, status-enhancing luxuries.

Of course we do not have the sorts of evidence which drive economic history in the modern period, there are no accurate figures of population, no systemic collection of income data, no possible measurements of gross domestic product. Instead, we have to rely on comments and anecdotes in historical writings by authors for whom economic history, as we might

DOI: 10.4324/9780429348129-7

understand it, is not the centre of their interests. More revealing are the writings of the Arab geographers of the late ninth and tenth centuries with their descriptions of roads and countries, products and peoples. The *Ṣūrat al-ard* of Ibn Ḥawqal is perhaps the most aware of the working of economic factors in the lands he visited.

Equally if not more important is the material evidence. Numismatics clearly have a central role. The number of coins, gold dinars, silver dirhams and copper *fulūs* which survive from this period is enormous but they alone can only be one part of the story: very fine coinage does not by itself indicate an economic activity on a wider scale. More revealing is the archaeological evidence. City surveys of Samarra, Marw, Rayy, Paykent and numerous others tell their story of expansion or decay. Surveys of rural areas can show us the extent of cultivation and settlement and surveys from the hinterland of Baghdad, the Middle Euphrates valley and the Syrian steppe lands are all crucial to our understanding.

By using textual, numismatic and archaeological evidence together, we can piece together something of the structure and extent of this remarkable economic efflorescence, and, on a more sombre note, some of the reasons for its apparent retreat after two centuries.

Fundamental to our understanding of the comparative size and complexity of this economy is the fact that the early Islamic state was the only post-late antique polity which preserved a structure of public taxation, collected in coined money and distributed by the state and its agents to certain select groups, most obviously the military and the bureaucrats who ran the system, in the form of regular salaries. This, in turn, created the demand for goods and services in the economy which formed the driver of economic development and diversification.

As described elsewhere in this volume, the initial Arab military conquests were followed by waves of immigration from the Arabian Peninsula, those from western Arabia and Yemen tended to head for Palestine, Syria and Egypt, those from Central Arabia and the lands bordering the Gulf, to Iraq. In areas like Iraq and Syria, these new arrivals may have amounted to 10 or 15% of the total population.

Within a few years of the first conquests, it became important to decide how these new arrivals were to integrate into the local society and economy. Although there were village people from highland Yemen and Oman, most of these incomers came from pastoral bedouin backgrounds. They were unused to ploughing the land and cultivating palm-trees and they probably did not want to undertake this hard menial work either. Nevertheless, some of the conquering Arabs demanded that the lands be divided up between them so that they could settle and live off the labour of the existing local inhabitants.

This option was rejected. It was pointed out that each of the conquerors would enjoy the labour of just three local peasants, hardly a luxurious lifestyle. Inevitably, they would mingle with the local people, losing their identity, their elite status and even their Islamic religion. Instead, the controlling ruling group in the capital Medina, the city of the Prophet, led, are told, by the second caliph ʿUmar, made a radical alternative plan, one which was to affect the history of the Middle East for centuries to come and which meant that the Arab settlement of the Middle East was to be very different from the Germanic conquests of Western Europe in the fifth century where the invaders were soon absorbed into the local population.

The rulers of the new empire decided that the Arabs were to be settled in garrison cities (*miṣr,* pl. *amṣār*) where they could be kept, ready for war and further conquests. They were to live off revenues collected from the subject population in the form of taxation. At first, some of this taxation was to be collected in kind, wheat, oil and so on, but quite soon, certainly before the end of the Umayyad period, it was arranged that tax should collected in coined money. At the same time, the Arabs in the cities were to be paid in this same money. The scheme was first rolled out among the settlers in central and southern Iraq where the two garrison cities of Kufa and Basra were established, but it was later adopted in other provinces where there was substantial Arab settlement. Other garrison cities followed, Mosul in northern Iraq, Fustat (Old Cairo) in Egypt, Qayrawan in Tunisia, while in the east garrison cities were established, in Shiraz in southern Iran and Marw (Turkmenistan) on the northeast frontier. In all cases, the model was similar. Tax revenues were brought to the cities and dispensed to the conquerors as cash wages.

The system had important consequences far beyond the mechanics of paying the army, especially because of the large numbers of the beneficiaries, 60,000 we are told in Kufa, 80,000 in Basra during the early Umayyad period, and that was just the adult males. Soon, they were joined by converts to Islam among the subject population. Three things were needed to make this system work, the measurement of land to assess tax, the production of large quantities of cash to pay it and literate and numerate administrators to run it. This, in turn, led to the establishment of a class of salaried soldiers and bureaucrats, people with more than enough money for basic subsistence, people with money to spend on luxury foods, clothes to show their status, perfumes to adorn themselves with and ultimately education and books. This fiscal structure was fundamental to the growth of the wider economy and the rich and varied cultures it sustained.

Paying the army was by far the most important function of the administration. In the first three centuries of Islam, soldiering became increasingly professionalized. New technologies of warfare, like mounted archery in the third/ninth century, meant that the military were increasingly professional and they demanded to be paid on a regular basis and woe betide any ruler who could not find the money. Bureaucrats grew wealthy managing the payment and merchants came from all over the Muslim world to offer their goods in the great markets of Baghdad and other expanding cities.

The military may have been the most conspicuous sector of the population with money to spend but they were by no means the only ones. In an important article, Pamuk and Shatzmiller (2014) have argued from Iraqi and Egyptian evidence that wages for labourers were consistently above the costs of a "bare bones" basket of food stuffs in the period from c.700 to c.1000 CE. They suggest that this was a result of demographic decline following the Justinianic plague of 540 and its recurring outbreaks. Adapting the comparative data from the Black Death of 1347–49, they argue that workers benefitted from a labour shortage to increase or at least maintain wages. It also encouraged female participation in the work force which again increased family incomes and specialization in the labour market. Along with this, there was essentially free movement of labour in most areas with the possible exception of Egypt. Many workers were not tied to their jobs and could move when new opportunities of work, great building projects like the Round City of Baghdad or new farming openings in the Jazira, appeared. This, in turn, expanded the markets for goods and services. Building labourers did not grow their own food; they bought it in urban market. The Pamuk-Shatzmiller argument is based on evidence in chronicles and other texts, supplemented in the case of Egypt by papyri and the Cairo Geniza, but such evidence, while mostly reliable, is not comprehensive. However, if the argument is broadly correct, it explains the development of demand in the economy which extended far beyond a privileged elite.

Supplying food for the new and expanding cities of the early Islamic world was one of the major driving forces in the economic development of the period. While the food supply of ancient Rome has attracted considerable scholarly interest and the food supply of Constantinople has also been investigated, there has been virtually no research on the provisioning of the great early Islamic cities. If a city like Baghdad had half a million inhabitants, a plausible estimate, each of whom could aspire to have at least one meal a day, the food supply must have been a huge and complex operation. We can however be reasonably certain of two things, first that it must have led to the construction of complex and widespread networks and second that these networks were fairly efficient in that we rarely have mention of serious food shortages before the fourth/tenth century. The food supply was not, unlike that of ancient Rome with its government-run system of *annona*, organized by the *sulṭān*. It seems to have been essentially a private enterprise system. There was no general-free handout of food: people paid for what they ate and, fortunately for them, the supply was generally cheap and reliable.

In the account of the foundation of Baghdad in al-Ṭabarī's *Ta'rīkh*, al-Manṣūr is shown to be well aware of the importance of food supply. He describes how his new city will have access to the grain supplies of the Jazīra which can reach the capital by the Tigris and Euphrates rivers and the dates which can be brought up along the southern river systems from Basra and southern Iraq. He also talks about routes for goods from India and China, coming up the Gulf. These economic networks led to the creation of a Greater Mesopotamian economic area. It was above all in this area between c.700 and c.900 that agriculture expanded into areas in which there had been little or no farming. I use the term Greater Mesopotamia to include the valleys of the Euphrates and Tigris rivers between the great bend of the Euphrates in northern Syria and the head of the Gulf. It also includes the lands of Khuzistan, now in southwest Iran. This area was the breadbasket of the caliphate and the generator of a large part of its tax revenues. It was marked by a core of easily irrigated lands along the great watercourses and a more extensive periphery which could be brought under cultivation by investment in favourable circumstances and when the market encouraged it, but left to pastoralists and herdsmen when a precarious economic situation or political insecurity was discouraging.

The archaeological evidence for the expansion of settled agriculture in this area from the middle Umayyad into the early ʿAbbasid period is consistent and convincing. The results of this can be seen in the traces on the landscape recovered by archaeological survey. In 1965, Robert Adams published *The Land behind Baghdad* in which he used the distribution of pottery sherds to reconstruct the history of human occupation in the Diyala river valley to the northeast of Baghdad. Although some of his dating has been questioned, it is clear that the greatest expansion of settled agriculture occurred during the late Sasanian and earliest Islamic periods. Surveys from the Middle Euphrates, the Khabur and Balikh valleys and the plains watered by the Dujayl (Little Tigris) in Khuzistan all point in the same direction; new canal systems led to the foundation of new villages and individual farms. This expansion is confirmed in the written sources, especially al-Balāḏhurī's *Futūḥ al-Buldān*, in which the author describes how the elite of the Umayyad state invested in digging new canals and encouraging settlers to farm the lands along them. This was perhaps a two-stage process. In the Umayyad period, the initiative was taken by the elite; in the early ʿAbbasid period, it looks as if smaller scale entrepreneurs were taking the lead. We can see this in the case of the settlement at Hiṣn Maslama in the Balīkh river valley, now in northern Syria. As the name suggests, this was an elite fortified settlement established by the Umayyad princes Maslama b. ʿAbd al-Malik. It was a classic Umayyad *qaṣr*, a square enclosure within well-built fortified walls. In the early ʿAbbasid period, the walls were breached and unplanned settlement spread out beyond the old fortifications into the surrounding plain.

The Islamic conquests made a fundamental change to the economic gravity of the Middle East. The unification of the Roman and Sasanian sectors of Greater Mesopotamia led to an economic integration of the area which had not been possible before. The grain-growing lands of the northern Jazira had access to the rapidly expanding urban markets of Central and Southern Iraq. With grain came the products of the northern uplands, fruits and honey from the Anatolian mountains, animal products from Azerbayjan and Armenia.

The rise of Greater Mesopotamia contrasted with contraction and abandonment of other areas. The areas which benefitted were those which had access to the river systems and markets of Greater Mesopotamia but those which were cut off failed to thrive. The most obvious of such areas were the inland parts of Syria and Palestine. There are unmistakable signs of economic distress in inland Syria and Palestine from the beginning of the third/ninth century. The archaeological evidence shows many examples of settlements large and small, which had survived the Muslim conquests, flourished in the Umayyad period but withered and died after the year 800. From the abandoned villages of the limestone hills of Syria in the north to the Negev Desert in the south, the evidence is plain and the silent witness of ruined houses and churches fills the landscape. No new towns were developed in greater Syria after Ramla in the second/eighth century. The urban centres which survived were coastal towns, subsidized by the *sulṭān* to defend against Byzantine attacks and centres of government, like Tiberias, capital of the province of Jordan which seems to have thrived until the fifth/eleventh century.

The reasons for this are probably twofold. The first was transport. Moving large quantities of goods from inland Syria and Palestine overland to the growing towns of Greater Mesopotamia was difficult and uncompetitive. The second is that the new ʿAbbasid *sulṭān* no longer recruited and paid men from the great Syrian tribes like Kalb who had sustained Umayyad rule. They must have been the customers who bought in the Umayyad period *sūqs* attested by archaeology in towns like Palmyra-Tadmur and Scythopolis-Baysān. It was the smaller towns along the desert margins in the Hawran, the Jordanian steppe and the Negev which suffered worst and urban life in these areas almost completely disappeared.

New areas were certainly being brought under cultivation but this was not the only new development. In 1983, Andrew Watson published a book called *Agricultural Innovation in the Early Islamic World.* In this, he challenged an established assumption that the coming of these nomad conquerors led to a decline, even devastation of rural agricultural communities as more and more villages and small towns were abandoned and the flocks and herds of the pastoralists roamed where they would. The abandoned sites of these rural settlements could be seen throughout the steppe lands Syria and Palestine, their gracious but melancholy ruins testifying to a lost era of quiet prosperity. Watson argued that there was another, different story to tell. The coming of Islamic rule stimulated the development of new crops as old barriers to diffusion were broken down. Rice and the hard durum wheat used to make pasta spread through the Muslim world and then across the Mediterranean to southern Europe. It was a tale of innovation and enterprise.

This hypothesis proved controversial and historians have been keen to point out that things were not quite so simple. Many of the crops which Watson saw as new were in fact already to be found though not widely distributed. The debate rumbles on but the basic conclusion is that the coming of Muslim rule enabled and encouraged the much wider diffusion of new crops. More recent research has begun looking at agricultural techniques, especially technologies of irrigation like underground qanats. Did these technologies spread along with new crops?

The growing demand led to increased specialization and the development of cash crops. Richard Bulliet in his *Cotton, Climate and Camels in Early Islamic Iran* (2005) has shown how a "cotton boom" developed in central Iran when entrepreneurs established new villages and brought water to barren lands. The cultivation of sugar cane brought not only a new cash crop but also a new industrial process.

The economic and intellectual flourishing was dependent on freedom of movement. Merchants travelled with goods to sell, artisans and labourers moved to find jobs in new construction projects, students and scholars travelled to sit at the feet of great masters. Following another pioneering work by Bulliet, *The Camel and the Wheel* (1975), it is now clear that wheeled vehicles disappeared from the roads of the Islamic Middle East. Instead, it was caravans of pack-animals, horses, mules and, above all, camels which did the heavy lifting. Wheeled vehicles in the twentieth century world have had a profound effect on the shape and design of roads both within and between cities. The disappearance of such vehicles in Late Antiquity and had an equally profound effect. The carefully constructed roads of the Roman period with their stone surfaces and masonry bridges fell into disuse because pack-animals did not need them. City streets and lanes in markets could become narrower, where people and animals pushed past each other.

Although the camel caravan was universally used, water transport was also important. The Nile was the transport as well as the irrigation backbone of Egypt. In Greater Mesopotamia, the Euphrates and Tigris rivers were essential for the transport of goods. The Euphrates was navigable downstream from Bālis, described as the *furda* (entrepot) of Syria where goods could be imported from Aleppo and the Mediterranean coast. The Tigris was navigable from Jazīrat Ibn ʿUmar (now Cizre in Turkey, close to the Syrian border). More surprisingly, we are told of navigation on the Khabur, a northern tributary of the Euphrates, which can only have transported small, shallow draft vessels. We have very few practical details about the water transport but evidence from the nineteenth and early twentieth centuries suggests that this traffic was mostly one way: goods were loaded on boats or rafts and floated down to the markets of Baghdad and southern Iraq where they would be broken up and the wood sold. We can see the emergence of towns along the river banks to handle this trade. Most important of these was Raqqa, normally thought of as a military political centre, but which probably also handled the grain trade of the Jazīra. The history of two smaller towns shows how this river traffic generated urban settlement. Jazīrat Ibn ʿUmar was developed by a local tribal chief, al-Ḥasan b. ʿUmar al-Taghlibī at the point where the Tigris cuts through the Anti-Taurus Mountains and enters the flat plains of northern Iraq and the river becomes navigable. From here, the products of the forests, timber, honey and wax could be exported south. Al-Raḥba, sometimes called Raḥbat

Mālik b. Tawq (d. 260/873–874) after the Taghlibī chief who developed it, was also called simply al-Furda, the river port. The town lay on the right bank of the river and flourished from the trade. Probably in the eleventh century, however, the riverbank site was abandoned and a new fortress was built on the escarpment at the edge of the desert. Defence had become more important than trade as the decisive factor in siting the settlement.

In Central Asia, the mighty river Oxus provided the easiest way to traverse the Black Sand and Red Sand deserts. The river was navigable from Termez to Khwarazm but we have little information about how it was used. Faḍlān in his account of his travels mentions that he took a boat from the river crossing at Amul near Bukhara to Khwarazm of his way north.

If the provision of basic food supplies was fundamental to the economy, it was consumer goods, the little luxuries of life, which provided the icing on this cake. The goods were important not only for the pleasure they gave but for the status they generated. Conspicuous consumption was the order of the day. Fine textiles were the most important goods for personal display but also the least visible in the historical record. We have virtually no material examples, just descriptions in texts. As well as the fabric themselves, there were dyestuffs. Bright, clear colours demanded trade in the natural products which provided them, indigo from the Jordan Valley for the blues, beetles from Armenia for crimsons and so on. There were exotic ceramics, including Chinese imports as found in the famous Belitung shipwreck, imports which stimulated local artisans to imitate them and develop the almost metallic hues of classical Muslim lustre ware. Then, there were raw materials from distant lands like rock crystal from far-off Madagascar to be carved into exquisite vases.

Exotic foods were very much part of this demand. We have descriptions of feasts but also contemporary recipe books with ingredients like cloves from Spice Islands of Indonesia. The complexity of this market is shown by the demand for dried fruit, especially dried melons, from Central Asia. It is possible to grow melons around Baghdad and plenty of sunshine to dry them in, but the melons of Marw were more sought after to the extent that it was worth transporting them more than a thousand miles to Baghdad where they would command the best prices. And then there were perfumes, both incenses to burn and unguents to adorn the body. Most of these told a story of long-distance trade from exotic and scarcely known countries where Muslims scarcely ventured.

The early Islamic was a period of urban expansion. Cities grew as centres of economic activity and political power, often at the expense of smaller towns in their areas. As Fanny Bessard has shown in her *Caliphs and Merchants* (2020) great merchants became the social and political as well as the economic leaders of the caliphate. This mass of comparatively affluent and comparatively educated people were also the consumers of culture, above all of writing and books. The new technology of paper making was embraced with enthusiasm, enabling the democratization of literature, the commercialization of book production. Baghdad in the ninth century was probably the first society on planet earth in which an author could make a living, if only a precarious one, by writing books and selling them to public in the hundred bookshops that are noted in a single quarter of the great city. As Beatrice Gruendler has shown in her recent work *The Rise of the Arabic Book* (2020) has explored the publishing industry of the time. None of this would have happened without a thriving economy which put money into men's sleeves and purses.

There is little evidence that the government directly encouraged trade by making trade agreements with neighbouring powers or maintaining the infrastructure of travel. There were other areas in which the *sulṭān* played a less active but still vital role. The most obvious of these was the keeping of routes safe from brigands and robbers. It also kept travelling merchants safe from tax collectors. There is little or no evidence of internal taxes on the movement of goods before the fourth/tenth century; the caliphate was a single market. Nor is there any evidence for the taxation of transactions in the market. The *sulṭān* made money from markets by charging ground rents on shops. This benign, light touch, fiscal regime allowed trade to flourish.

The second was that the *sulṭān* itself, whether in Abbasid Baghdad or Fatimid Cairo, formed the most important market for goods and services. Rich textiles and other objects of desire were sourced from all over the caliphate to show prestige and reward service. Where the caliphs led, their elite supporters followed. But perhaps most important was the role of the *sulṭān* in pumping money into the economy by paying salaries to soldiers and others. It was this that created a reliable continuing market to encourage investment.

The third way in which the *sulṭān* supported trade was by the provision of coinage.

Coins are one of the commonest and most visible signs of the economic vitality of this period. The Muslims inherited a tri-metallic system of coinage, gold denarii/dinars and copper folles/fulus in the ex-Byzantine lands and silver drahms/dirhams in the Sasanian territories. After the currency reforms of ʿAbd al-Malik at the end of the first/seventh century, these two zones were more or less integrated, dirhams were regularly used in the West, while dinars were certainly an accepted, if less widely used, currency in the East. The effect of this must have been to facilitate long-distance trade between different areas of the caliphate, a process encouraged by the development of simple financial instruments like the *suftaja* and the *ṣakk* which allowed the movement of wealth without the actual transport of large quantities of coin. Of course, the system was not entirely stable. The dirham/dinar exchange rate fluctuated from about 12:1 in the earliest Islamic period to about 20:1 by the fourth/tenth century. Furthermore, the developing silver "famine" meant that dirhams were increasingly and openly adulterated with lead and other metals leading to "Black dirhams" especially in Khurasan. Despite these problems, however, Islamic currency facilitated exchange over wide areas and, despite the emergence of new dynastic polities from the four/tenth century with rulers inscribing their own regional titles on their coins, money seems to have moved freely throughout, measured by purity and weight more than face value.

The proper functioning of the *sulṭān* was the necessary framework for the development of the economy but growth was generated by individual and private initiatives.

The coming of Muslim rule had a profound effect on patterns of trade throughout early medieval Eurasia. There were major ruptures. The decline of trans-Mediterranean trade which had flourished in classical antiquity had begun before the Muslim conquests but they certainly accelerated it. The Sea itself became a conflict zone and large-scale regular trade became impossible, though it is clear that trade in slaves from Western Europe continued to be the backbone of a smaller but continuing commerce, while the fact that cloves and spices from Indonesia were still to be found on the tables of Emperors and Popes points to the survival of some luxury trade at an elite level. The olive-oil of Tunisia was no longer shipped to Constantinople and points east in the distinctive African red-slip pottery which is so commonly found in archaeological sites of the period. Not only did the trade in oil stop but so did the manufacture of the ceramics which contained it. The surplus grain from Egypt, which had sustained the populations first of the city of Rome and then Constantinople, and provided the backbone of Mediterranean trade, was cut off. Instead, the surplus was shipped via the re-opened Trajan's canal from Cairo to the Red Sea to the burgeoning Holy Cities of Mecca and Medina.

In the east too, trade routes were changed though the process was slightly later. The economic importance of the fabled "Silk Road" from Chine to Persia and Rome has probably been exaggerated but it was nonetheless significant and it supported a vibrant commercial and cultural network. Those great middlemen of the early Middle Ages, the Soghdian merchants of Central Asia, became rich and prosperous. Just as pilgrims from Western Europe continued to travel to the Holy Places in Palestine after the fall of the Western Empire so Buddhist pilgrims from China made the long and arduous journey through the central Asian deserts and the mighty Hindu Kush mountains of Afghanistan to visit the sites of the Buddha's life in India. By the year 800, all this had changed and the overland silk route had become impractical, partly it would seem, because of the prolonged An Lushan rebellion on western China.

While some of the old patterns declined, new trade routes were developed in response to the growing size of Middle Eastern markets. Trade with the China and the Far East continued but in a very different form. There were trade links between the Mediterranean world and India which were well established in Roman times and Persians conducted some trade in the Sasanian period, though the details are hard to recover. From the second/eighth century however, Indian Ocean trade began to expand. More and more

Muslim merchants, based in the Gulf at ports like Basra and Sīrāf, began to sail as far as China where there was a large Muslim commercial colony in Canton by the mid-third/ninth century. It was not just the routes which changed, from overland to maritime, but the nature of the goods. It would seem that silks ceased to be the dominant trade goods, not least because the inherent dampness of travel by sea made them unsuitable. Instead, the main goods were spices, the ingredients for perfume (musk, ambergris) and ceramics. The evidence for the trade in Chinese ceramics has been spectacularly confirmed by the Belitug shipwreck with its 60,000 pieces, apparently destined for the Middle East market. This, in turn, spurred potters in the Islamic world to rise to the challenge and develop new glazed wares of their own.

Another area of new trade was the Russian and Scandinavian north. From the third/ninth century, an important new trade route developed though the river systems of what is now Russia. This led from the Baltic and Scandinavia to the markets of Central Asia in the lands ruled by the Samanid dynasty. The goods traded were furs and above all slaves, especially females, trafficked from the Slav lands. In return, the Muslim merchants paid in silver Samanid dirhams, hundreds of thousands of them. They do not seem to have been spent but rather stored in hoards where they lay untouched. These hoards are found as far away as the Isle of Skye of the west coast of Scotland. Apart from the famous, vivid travel account of Ibn Faḍlān's voyage to the Volga basin, we hear little about these from written sources but the coins reveal the size and extent of this trade. And it had long-term consequences: it brought Scandinavian merchants, who seem to be referred to as Rūs, into what is now Ukraine where, by the year 1000, they had established the principality of Kiev and converted to Greek Orthodox Christianity. On the other side, it seems to have drained northeastern Iran of silver contributing to the silver famine. By the early fifth/eleventh century, this trade had essentially dried up. The routes from north-west Europe to the Middle East now led through the Mediterranean.

The economic crisis of Iraq in the fourth/tenth century led to a major shift in the patterns of global trade. By the year 1000, the cities of Greater Mesopotamia had ceased to be the most important market for imported goods and in the first half of the fifth/eleventh century, the balance of economic power had shifted to Egypt and, to an extent, the cities of the Iranian plateau like Isfahan and Rayy. The rise of the Egyptian market meant that the maritime trade of the Indian Ocean basin, including the East African coast, shifted from the Gulf to the Red Sea. It was also the background to the appearance of western merchants, Franks, in the ports of the eastern Mediterranean. They mostly came from Italy, Amalfi in the south and, a bit later, Venice, Pisa and Genoa in the north. They came in search of consumer goods, fine textiles and, above all, pepper and spices, transhipped through Cairo and Alexandria from the Indian Ocean areas. The driving force of this expansion was the growing economy of north-west Europe, the opening up of new silver mines. This means that, for the first time since antiquity, Western Europe was a market with sufficient surpluses to generate a regular market. The great expansion of trade at the time of the Crusades in the twelfth and thirteenth centuries was the acceleration of a pattern which had begun in the eleventh.

If the Red Sea and the Mediterranean were increasingly the scene of a lively commerce in the late tenth and early eleventh centuries, the position was very different in Greater Mesopotamia. In a real way, this system here had depended on a sort of virtuous circle. Government expenditure encourages spending and investing and the economy expanded. But it was also vulnerable. In a sense, it was very highly leveraged. A risk assessment would show small number of bad years of political disturbance or warfare could do unsustainable damage and in the first half of the tenth century, bad years came thick and fast. Civil wars and social rebellion destabilized the tax system and the military, concerned above all to secure their pay, showed no compunction in deposing and murdering both caliphs and bureaucrats.

In economic terms, these changes led to important changes in the patterns of settlement and economic activity. One of these was the contraction of agriculture in the lands of Greater Mesopotamia. Baghdad, and to a lesser extent other cities, no longer offered the open and dynamic markets of the time of the military/bureaucratic state. They still existed as medium-sized local centres but as rulers and their entourages moved from one castle to another, and fought each other for control of a decreasing resource base, the market which had encouraged the investment of the earlier period withered. This is noticeable in the changed pattern of investment of surplus wealth. In the late Umayyad and early ʿAbbasid periods, the elite invested the profits of office and warfare in landed property, buying up and developing estates. From the mid-tenth century, however, we see anecdotal evidence of elite figures hiding their wealth in the form of cash and treasure or simply burying it in the ground. Land was no longer considered a safe repository for wealth. Throughout the area, irrigation canals were abandoned, settlements moved from the riverain plains to defendable high ground. For the first time, we see internal customs posts set up by local rulers to extract tolls from merchants travelling from one part of the Muslim world to another. Finally, it was during this period that ʿAbbasid Greater Mesopotamia lost its position as the economic and later cultural power house of the Islamic world to Fatimid Cairo. To take just one example, the production of fine lustre work ceramics moved from Iraq to Egypt as the craftsmen migrated, taking their expertise with them, in search of the new elite markets.

The flowering of early Islamic society and culture was based on a thriving and varied economy. Without this widespread prosperity, the arts and sciences would not have flourished and Islamic civilization might have looked very different. But if it was the beginning of one story, it was the end of another. The Abbasid caliphate was the last of that great series of ancient empires which stretched from the Kings of Sumer and Akkad in the third millennium BC, through the Assyrians, Babylonians and Persians. In the tenth century, this came to an end. Never again would a power based on the wealth of greater Mesopotamia power lead the world in richness and culture.

8 The structure of politics in the Muslim commonwealth

The fourth/tenth century saw a profound change in the political society of the Islamic world. The superficial characteristics of this are well documented and easy to recognize – the caliphate disintegrated into a bewildering variety of successor states. The Muslim sources present these states as being ruled by dynasties, the 'Uqaylids of Mosul, the Marwanids of Mayyāfāriqīn and so on, each of which tended to last for about a century, and many of which seemed to go through a similar cycle of emergence, expansion under a strong ruler and decay under his weaker successors. Modern scholarship has tended to take over this traditional perspective, and it often seems to the casual enquirer that these states were sort of political mushrooms, pop-up states whose appearance is unexplained and whose collapse was the result of personal feebleness on the part of decadent rulers. In reality, however, the successor states varied greatly in their organization and outlook, and reflected closely the economic and social structures of the society which produced them; it is only by concentrating on at least some of them in detail that we can see how the changes of this time affected the Muslim world.

The breakup of the 'Abbasid caliphate in the first half of the third/tenth century is generally seen as a sad, lamentable decline, with the loss of the political unity of the Muslim *umma*. But there are a number of sides to this story. Certainly, the dissolution of the 'Abbasid caliphate was accompanied by economic decline and social disruption in some areas, notably in Baghdad and central Iraq, but also in agricultural areas bordering the Syrian and Jaziran deserts. The clearest examples of this can be seen in the archaeological record from the middle Euphrates valley and its tributaries, the Khabur and Balikh rivers. Recent surveys by Sophie Berthier, Karen Bartl and others have shown a common pattern, with expanding agricultural settlement in the late Umayyad period which reached a peak under the early 'Abbasids as demand for food and supplies from the huge city of Baghdad made farming secure and prosperous. The same surveys show a steep decline and abandonment of these settlements through the tenth century as political chaos and economic uncertainty made people reluctant to invest in agricultural infrastructure. The inhabitants of these communities may simply have perished, but it is more likely that many of them adopted a pastoral lifestyle

DOI: 10.4324/9780429348129-8

and attached themselves to the bedouin tribes whose growing power in the Fertile Crescent is one of the most conspicuous features of the late tenth and early eleventh centuries. In other areas, however, the arrival of political independence led to economic growth and social development. At the most basic level, it meant a new and vastly improved water supply for the citizens of Mayyāfāriqīn in the southeast of the Anatolian plateau; on a larger scale, it led to a sort of golden age in Fārs, a potentially rich area of Iran which had been exploited by outsiders since the Muslim conquests but which now became independent and prosperous under the Buyid dynasty; the picture of urban decline in Kūfa and Baṣra has to be balanced by the picture of growth in Shīrāz and Sīrāf.

On the cultural level as well, the period of the dissolution of the caliphate was one of great activities and achievements, what Adam Mez described in a famous book as the "Renaissance of Islam". Some of this cultural activity was concerned with the collection and codification of the treasures of the classical Arabic past. Ibn al-Nadīm's (d. 385/995) *Fihrist* was an index of all the works of Arabic literature then available, while Abū'l-Faraj al-Iṣfahānī (d. 356/967) sought to produce a comprehensive collection of the lives and works of the great Arabic poets in his *Kitāb al-Aghānī*, or *Book of Songs*. In this respect, these authors were perhaps analogous to those sixth-century figures in the West like Cassiodorus and Isidore of Seville, who attempted to keep alive classical learning in a hostile environment. But the culture of the age went far beyond the preservation of the past. In all fields, the fourth/tenth and early fifth/eleventh centuries were periods of great achievement. Al-Mutanabbī (d. 354/965) and Abū'l 'Alā' al-Ma'arrī (d. 449/1058) in poetry, Ibn Sīnā (Avicenna) (d. 428/1037) in medicine and philosophy, al-Mas'ūdī (d. 345/956) in historiography and al-Muqaddasī (d. after 375/985) in travel writing are only a few of the great figures of the time. This cultural efflorescence was in some ways a product of the political fragmentation of the time, which provided new sources of patronage for authors. The doctrinal disputes of the age, especially the growing division between Sunnī and Shī'ī Islam, also gave rise to important theological writing and debate. While Baghdad remained important, it no longer played the dominant role as a cultural centre it had under the earlier 'Abbasid caliphate, and the patronage of the caliphal court was replaced by support from many different sources, which allowed a great variety of writing to emerge and writers like al-Mutanabbī and Avicenna, for example, to move around freely from one area to another if they thought it would be advantageous.

Two major changes underlay these developments: the conversion of the majority of the population to Islam and the economic decline of Iraq. The question of conversion to Islam is very problematic, since, clearly, there were no census records or reliable statistics available. We know that there were no Muslims in the Near East before the time of the Prophet, and we can be reasonably certain that by the sixth/twelfth century, the non-Muslims formed a minority of the population in most areas: between these two poles, there is much room for speculation. The problem has been reexamined by R. Bulliet in his book *Conversion to Islam in the Medieval Period*, using Iranian genealogies to establish the dates when families became Muslim. His method was to look at the ancestors of men of learning as recorded in biographical dictionaries. He found that a significant proportion of these genealogies went back to a non-Muslim ancestor (in this, he was helped by the fact that non-Muslim names in Iran were totally different from Muslim ones). By calculating back from the date of the subject of the biography and reckoning each generation as twenty-five years, Bulliet could get some idea of the period at which the family had been converted. The method is obviously not foolproof and there are bound to be special circumstances in each family, but Bulliet worked from a sample of almost 500 genealogies, enough to give a representative picture. According to his research, Iran was only about 8 per cent Muslim at the time of the 'Abbasid revolution in 132/750, but this changed rapidly in the years which followed; by the early third/ninth century, the proportion of Muslims was probably about 40 per cent, and this increased to between 70 and 80 per cent in the fourth/tenth century. It is more difficult to extrapolate from the Iranian data to other areas of the Muslim world, but we should probably be correct in assuming that the rate of conversion was faster in Iraq than in Iran but slower in Egypt, where the Muslims remained a small ruling group among a largely Coptic population until Fatimid times. Bulliet admits that his hypotheses are speculative and unprovable, but they do seem realistic and provide a useful basis for discussion.

The Islamization of the Near East had profound effects on political history. Under the Umayyads and early 'Abbasids, the Muslims had been a fairly small ruling élite, whose links were with their fellow Muslims rather than with the non-Muslim populations of the areas in which they lived. There was a high degree of mobility among the ruling groups and, for example, a man of Syrian origin could govern Yemen for a period and then be transferred to Egypt or Armenia. Just as most of the British civil servants who administered India felt that their links were with their fellow Britons and with their British "home" rather than with the Indians who lived around them, the early Muslims preserved a sense of common identity, usually coupled with the common language of Arabic. Conversion, however, weakened this *esprit de corps*, and the élite lost its cohesion. As they became converted, people in the various provinces demanded to be admitted to the political process as full members of the Muslim community. In this way, the provinces came to be dominated by men whose roots and families were entirely local. They were good Muslims, but their loyalty to a caliph and centralized Muslim government hundreds, even thousands, of miles away in a land they had never seen was naturally limited. The progress of conversion meant that anti-Muslim revolts in the Near East almost completely died out even in areas like Egypt and Iran, where resistance had persisted in the Umayyad and early 'Abbasid times. The only attempt in the fourth/tenth century to set up a non-Muslim state in the area, the move by Mardāvīj b. Ziyār (d. 323/935) to restore Zoroastrianism, was a conspicuous failure. The breakup of the caliphate was in no way a reaction against Muslim conquest, it was rather a natural product of its success and the evolution from a Muslim empire ruled by a small Muslim élite to a Muslim commonwealth where most of the population were Muslims was as natural, and in many cases as peaceful, as the emergence of the independent commonwealth countries of Australia, New Zealand and Canada from the British Empire.

The spread of Islam also led to the formalization of differences within the community. Of course, even in the days when the Muslims were a small minority of the population, there were vigorous debates and violent struggles to decide the nature of Muslim government. In the fourth/tenth century, however, these differences tended to become more rigid, and the sects tended to develop separate memberships and structures of leadership. There were many reasons for this process, but at least in part it was a product of the increasing numbers of Muslims from different geographical and social backgrounds. When Christianity became the dominant religion in the Roman Empire in the fourth century, heresy became a major political and social issue; when Islam became the dominant religion in the Near East in the fourth/tenth century, sectarian division came to the fore.

The second major cause of change, the economic collapse of Iraq must always be borne in mind as a fundamental, underlying factor in the collapse of the ʿAbbasids and the difficulties of the Buyids of Baghdad. It also meant that the Muslim world developed something of a hollow centre. The old heartlands became impoverished and suffered a constant haemorrhage of their more able and dynamic citizens to more recently converted areas like Iran and Egypt. The old ruling élite based in Mesopotamia was replaced by outsiders, men from such marginal groups as the Kurds of the Zagros Mountains, the Daylamites from the southern Caspian area and the Berbers of the hinterland of Ifrīqiya. The Muslim world no longer had a centre, a metropolis to look to, but rather a whole galaxy of regional centres, each developing its own political society and culture.

The successor states of the ʿAbbasid caliphate were, in political terms, entirely independent, but they were bound together by many ties of language and culture. The most obvious of these was the use, throughout the Muslim Near East, of Arabic as the main administrative language. As Latin was used by bureaucrats in medieval Europe in areas where the vernacular was quite different, Arabic was used in Islamic chanceries even in areas where the population spoke Kurdish, Persian, Armenian or Aramaic. The only important exceptions were in the courts of the Samanids and Ghaznevids in eastern Iran where New Persian emerged as a literary language but even there bureaucrats were expected to be literate in Arabic too. As in the medieval West as well, the common language led to the creation of bonds among bureaucrats in different states and a common bureaucratic culture. Administrative expertise acquired in one area could be used to carve out a career in another. The *wazīr* al-Ḥusayn b. al-Maghribī (d. 418/1027), for example, could begin his career with the Hamdanids of Aleppo, pursue it in Fatimid Egypt and ʿUqaylid Mosul and end up a distinguished elder statesman in Marwanid Mayyāfāriqīn. This common Arabic-language bureaucratic culture was a major source of unity.

This unity was expressed at a formal level by the recognition of the theory of the caliphate. The ideal of the of the caliphate lived on after the demise of its political authority. One dynasty in the area, the Fatimids, set up a rival caliphate, but like the ʿAbbasids, they claimed the leadership of the entire Muslim world and inherited the pan-Islamic ideas of their ʿAbbasid rivals. Among the other dynasties, there were few who did not acknowledge the rights of a caliph in the *khuṭba*, the Friday sermon in which political allegiances were made public, although some rulers, like Qirwāsh b. al-Muqallad the ʿUqaylid, might change their allegiances to suit their political needs. For some years after the Buyid takeover in Baghdad, the Samanids of eastern Iran continued to pledge allegiance to a now dead ʿAbbasid rather than the Buyid nominees. But whatever the practical reservations, no dynasty dispensed entirely with the idea of the caliphate or proclaimed an absolute independence. The grant of a title by the caliph remained a sign of political legitimacy and a sign that the recipient was now an accepted ruler. In the Fertile Crescent and much of Iran, the title of, for example, "Rukn al-Dawla" (Pillar of the [ʿAbbasid] State) was sought after by all who tried to establish their rule, and it brought with it the assumption of caliphal authority, however powerless that might be in practice. Again, the medieval West provides an illuminating comparison: in eleventh- and early twelfth-century France, the actual power of the king in the more distant parts of his realm was nonexistent, but the barons of those areas, the dukes of Normandy and Aquitaine, the counts of Champagne and Toulouse acknowledged the monarchy and its role and did not call themselves kings even if they were independent in every practical way.

There were other signs of the nonpolitical unity of the commonwealth. As far as we know, no Muslim state erected trade barriers against any other. Travellers in this period like Ibn Ḥawqal, al-Muqaddasī and Nāṣir-i Khusrau seem to have been able to move about without government interference. Robbers and thirst may have posed problems for the travellers; visas and frontier posts did not. Politically, the Muslim world may have been divided; economically and socially, it remained a unity.

This contrast between the division of government and the unity of culture and society was a product of the changing nature of government. The ʿAbbasids and their rivals the ʿAlids attempted to create a truly Islamic state. It was a very ambitious programme of moral reform and rule by the Qurʾān and Sunna, a bold attempt to restructure society according to the vision of the Prophet, an ideal which has parallels in our own day. The dynasts of the Muslim commonwealth had no such aspirations. The functions of government were restricted to collecting taxes and providing a minimum of security to enable these dues to be gathered in peace. There were rulers who went further in developing their territories economically – ʿAḍud al-Dawla, Badr b. Ḥasanūya and the Marwanids of Mayyāfāriqīn stand out in this respect. Others, like the Hamdanids and the ʿUqaylids of Mosul, seem to have made no such effort, but none of them attempted to restructure society according to Islamic principles. For many people, the functions of government were marginal to their daily lives. In most cities, it was the urban élite of merchant and property-owning families who exercised everyday control over mosque and market. For the people of the villages, it was increasingly the *iqṭa'* holder, claiming rights of *ḥimāya*, or protection, who represented government on a day-to-day basis. Even the Fatimid dynasty, with its Ismāʿīlī doctrine and its universal ambitions, made only intermittent attempts to spread its propaganda outside the governing class. It was as if Muslims had come to accept that government would not create a perfect Muslim society – at best, it could only provide the framework in which men could strive to become good Muslims.

Just as the functions of government became restricted, the profession of arms became confined to certain, mostly marginal, groups within the Muslim community. In early Islamic armies and, indeed, the armies of the ʿAbbasid revolution, the soldiers were simply the male Muslims prepared for battle, and the principle which lay behind the *muqātila* organization was that all Muslims should be able to do military service if called upon, and it was this which entitled them to their *ʿaṭā'*, or salary. Even the Khurāsāniyya of the early ʿAbbasid caliphate were in many ways part-time soldiers, owning property and conducting business in Baghdad, marrying, having families and eventually losing their military identity entirely. These armies were often very large: 40,000 soldiers from Baghdad followed ʿAlī b. ʿĪsā when he set out to march against Khurāsān in 195/811, and numbers of around 100,000 are quoted for the Caliph Hārūn al-Rashīd's armies against the Byzantines. Almost always, these armies contained a majority of foot soldiers, often outnumbering the cavalry two to one, and on occasion even those who were mounted fought on foot. But ʿAlī b. ʿĪsā's great army was defeated by Ṭāhir's much smaller force, and this may have been the death knell of the huge armies of the early Islamic era. From the third/ninth century, and particularly after the military reforms of al-Muʿtaṣim, armies became smaller and more strictly professional. This seems to have accompanied a changeover to cavalry warfare, and particularly mounted archery, which required greater specialization and more equipment; the day of the part-time soldier was over. Increasingly, these specialist troops were Turks imported as slaves or otherwise recruited in eastern Iran or the areas to the north of the Caucasus Mountains. They were distinguished from the Muslim civilians not only by their function, notably their abilities in the highly specialized skill of mounted archery, but also by their race and language. In the third/ninth century, many of these Turks seem to have produced children who were fully Arabized Muslims like Mūsā b. Bughā and Aḥmad b. Ṭūlūn, ruler of Egypt (254–270/868–884), who began the integration of the families into Muslim society and the loss of their identity as a separate group.

The late fourth/tenth and early fifth/eleventh centuries saw the heyday of the *ghulām* system, which was so important in the history of the Muslim commonwealth. The *ghilmān* formed the core of the new army formed by al-Muwaffaq and al-Mu'taḍid after the return of the caliphate to Baghdad. And after the breakup of the caliphate and the destruction of the old 'Abbasid army on the orders of the *amīr al-umarā'* Ibn Rā'iq in 325/936, their role became fundamental to many of the new emerging polities. There had been Turkish troops in the armies of the caliphs before, but what seems to have distinguished the *ghilmān* of this period was their social organization. They fought in bands, often only a few hundred strong, recruited by a leader. The leader, usually himself a Turk, was responsible for securing their pay and employment. The young *ghilmān* looked to their leader as a sort of father-figure and often took his name as a sign of gratitude; the great Anūshtakīn (d. 432/1041) was always known as al-Dizbarī after an obscure Daylamite commander called Dizbar who had favoured him in his youth.

It was to their leader, rather than to the sovereign who employed them, that they owed their loyalty. Their leaders became like the *condottieri* of fourteenth- and fifteenth-century Italy, powerful men, experienced professional soldiers, always seeking reliable paymasters to satisfy the needs of their followers. On the whole, they were efficient, expecting and needing to be highly paid for their services; if they were not, they could not maintain their horses and equipment. If one paymaster failed, then they were obliged to take service with another in order to survive as a fighting unit, and much of the apparent disloyalty and treachery can be explained in terms of financial necessity. Many of the lesser dynasts of the Near East could not afford to maintain *ghilmān* at all. Sayf al-Dawla, the Hamdanid ruler of Aleppo (d. 356/967), had recruited considerable numbers of *ghilmān*, but his son Sa'd al-Dawla (d. 381/991), living in greatly reduced circumstances, could not afford to pay them, let alone recruit any more. Faced with this situation, they had two choices: some left to take service with the Fatimid rulers of Egypt, while others stayed in Aleppo and took over the government of the city for themselves, while continuing to acknowledge the exiled Hamdanid as a theoretical ruler. When, in 364/975, Alptakīn, the leader of the *ghilmān* in Baghdad, could no longer maintain himself against the Daylamite forces of 'Aḍud al-Dawla, he led his followers, about 300 of them, to new pastures in Damascus, which they took over for a while, and then to the Fatimid court in Cairo, where some of them reached high positions. His first responsibility was to his followers rather than his paymasters.

The *ghilmān* seem to have lived celibate lives. We know little of how they were recruited in this period and only in the case of Anūshtakīn al-Dizbarī, whose early life was chronicled by the Damascus historian Ibn al-Qalānisī, do we know anything of their origins. Anūshtakīn came from eastern Iran and seems to have become a *ghulām* of his own volition, seeing it as a way of advancement in the world. He came west and ended up in Fatimid Cairo. By the early fifth/eleventh century, there seems to have been an established system of education for *ghilmān* at the Fatimid court, and Anūshtakīn distinguished himself in his class and made contacts which enabled him to further his career. Among the *ghilmān* of Baghdad, however, there is no trace of any such school and it is likely that senior *ghilmān* simply recruited likely looking lads for their service and trained them themselves. Anūshtakīn was also an exception in that he married and produced children. There is no evidence to suggest that most *ghilmān* were eunuchs, but it is clear that very few of them left heirs; neither of the two famous leaders of the Baghdad *ghilmān*, Sabuktakīn (d. 364/974) or his successor Alptakīn, left sons whom we know of, and they were succeeded by *ghilmān* who had been brought up in their service but were not, apparently, blood relations.

Instead, the *ghilmān* seem to have produced a strongly homosexual subculture. This has left literary traces, especially in Persian poetry, but it was disapproved of by outsiders, and chroniclers give us examples of the disastrous effects of such involvements; the *ghulām* Fātik, who briefly governed Aleppo for the Fatimids, was murdered by his *ghulām* lover while he slept, and the Buyid prince Bakhtiyār's infatuation with a *ghulām* is given as one of the reasons he lost his throne and his life. The absence of family life and offspring was one of the reasons that *ghilmān*, despite their power, were never able to start dynasties or proclaim their independence (the only exception being the Ghaznavid dynasty of distant Afghanistan, which originated among the *ghilmān* of the Samanid dynasty), and even the most powerful of them, like Sabuktakīn of Baghdad and Anūshtakīn al-Dizbarī, never became rulers in their own right.

The *ghulām* system was characteristic of the century and a half of the Muslim commonwealth. It was employed by Buyids, Fatimids and many lesser dynasties. The system was not necessarily a bad one. In the main, *ghilmān* were loyal and effective troops and their small numbers meant that warfare between *ghulām* armies was not, on the whole, very destructive. The people of Damascus certainly seem to have preferred the rule of the *ghulām* Alptakīn to the lawless Berber troops of the Fatimid army. However, the payment of the *ghilmān* often imposed a crippling financial burden on governments, and bands of roaming *ghilmān*, seeking employment, could be a scourge.

While the *ghilmān* were the most distinctive feature of the military organization of the period, they were not the only soldiers. The other main military groups were marginal peoples from the fringes of Islamic society, the bedouin of the Syrian Desert, the transhumant Kurds of the Zagros Mountains, the Daylamites of the southwestern shores of the Caspian Sea and the Berbers of the mountains of Ifrīqiya. Some dynasties like the bedouin ʿUqaylids and the Marwanid Kurds could rely on their tribal followings to the extent that they had no need to employ *ghilmān*, but they were the exceptions; even dynasties like the Buyids and the Fatimids, which had strong ethnic followings among the Daylamites and the Berbers, were obliged to employ *ghilmān* to supplement their other followers.

In short, the military were recruited not from the main bulk of the Muslim population but from certain specialized groups. Furthermore, there was an almost complete separation between military and civilian élites. *Ghilmān* did not become *wazīrs*, financial officials or religious dignitaries. Nor did they become merchants. Equally, members of the civilian élite did not become soldiers; one of the reasons the Barīdī tax farmers of southern Iraq failed in their bid to take over Baghdad in the confusion which preceded the coming of the Buyids was that they did not have the military experience to lead their armies. Members of the civilian élite, like the Fatimid *wazīr* Ya'qūb b. Killis in Egypt, might recruit *ghilmān* as their private military following, but they did not themselves take up arms. There were, of course, some exceptions, notably among the *wazīrs* of the Buyids in Fārs and al-Jibāl, but on the whole, the gulf between civil and military leaders was a constant feature of the age.

It may seem that too much attention has been paid to the question of military organization, but in fact it is crucial to the understanding of the political structures of the time. The dynasties which emerged after the dissolution of 'Abbasid power can be divided into those which were dependent on *ghilmān* for their military support and those which were dependent on tribal followings. Among those dependent, to a greater or lesser extent, on *ghilmān* were the Buyids of Baghdad, the Fatimids of Egypt and the Hamdanids of Aleppo and Mosul, while those which depended on tribal support were the Mazyadids of Ḥilla, the 'Uqaylids of Mosul and the Mirdasids of Aleppo, all dependent on bedouin tribes, and the Hasanuyids, the 'Annazids, the Rawwadids and the Marwanids, all dependent on Kurdish groups.

These different sorts of military support generated different sorts of political ecology. In polities which depended on *ghilmān*, the paying of the troops was the major preoccupation of government. This could be done in two ways, either by collecting taxes directly and paying salaries, usually monthly, to the troops or by giving out grants of *iqṭā'*, which were essentially areas of land and villages from which the soldiers could collect the revenues directly. In either case, the object of the ruling dynasty was to acquire and keep settled lands which would yield cash revenues. Such a system could allow the individual ruler great power, since he controlled the revenues and a bureaucracy to collect them – and in the hands of a man like the Buyid 'Aḍud al-Dawla (d. 372/983), the system was very effective. There were, however, many pitfalls; inefficient or corrupt revenue collecting and short-term liquidity crises meant that governments frequently relied on expedient grants of unsupervised *iqṭā'*, and in some areas, like Baghdad and central Iraq, this led to prolonged periods of disturbance and anarchy.

In states based on a tribal following, however, the priorities of government were entirely different. The ruler's most important obligation was to his followers, and their main concern was to secure adequate grazing for the animals on which they depended for their livelihood, and the policies of the ruling dynasty were dictated by pastoral considerations rather than the need to round off a compact state based on settled lands. Thus, the pastoral states tended to have uncertain boundaries and were often based on certain routes rather than on cities and villages. This is not to say that cash revenues were irrelevant. The leaders of the tribes needed revenues to reward their followers and to make up for the limitations of the pastoral economy and to this extent they needed to rule settled areas. The model of such rule was not, however, direct government, using paid agents and tax collectors, but rather indirect tribute gathering, in exchange for protection, an arrangement known as a *ḥimāya*. This meant that the leading citizens of the town agreed to pay certain sums to the ruler but were themselves responsible for the raising of the tax. In states where the government was dependent on the *ghilmān*, the ruler and his bureaucracy were usually based in the main city – Baghdad, Cairo, Shīrāz – whereas in tribal states, the ruler was more likely to spend his time away from the main cities, in the nomad camp or the mountain castle.

This pattern of indirect control was the main reason for the development at this time of an unprecedented degree of civic autonomy. In the towns we know most about, Aleppo under the Mirdasids and Āmid (now Diyarbakir) under the Marwanids, this took the form of local citizens exercising power through the office of *ra'īs al-balad* or of *qāḍī*, which came to mean more than simply "judge" and came to embrace administrative functions as well. In order to secure peace, the towns also produced their own militia, often known as the *aḥdāth*, who were part-time volunteers who usually fought on foot. Such signs of city self-government manifested themselves in areas controlled by tribal dynasties, not in cities like Fusṭāṭ, Baghdad, Baṣra or Shīrāz, which were ruled by settled dynasties dependent on *ghilmān* and other professional soldiers. The intermediary between the tribal leader and the citizens was often the *wazīr*, and in tribal states (and in the Buyid kingdom of al-Jibāl, which was structurally much more akin to the tribal states than the other Buyid kingdoms), the *wazīrs* acquired great importance as the essential intermediaries between the two lifestyles.

Another significant difference between the two types of state was in the structure of the ruling families. In tribal states, the ruling family tended to act as a kin group, dividing effective power among themselves. This could be a centrifugal force – we see in both the 'Uqaylids of Mosul and the Hasanuyid Kurds how different members of the ruling house sought to acquire *ḥimāyas* over different areas and hence to establish a form of independence. In the Marwanid family of Mayyāfāriqīn, by contrast, the ruling kin were much more united, and it was this family solidarity which preserved their rule. In more bureaucratic states, the ruling kin played a smaller part. The clearest example of this comes from Fatimid Egypt, where only the ruler and his heir apparent seem to have had any political role at all. What happened to the brothers and cousins of the caliph we simply do not know. In the Buyid states, there was a constant tension between the necessity to establish a single dominant ruler and the traditional demands of kin solidarity, which decreed that each member of the ruling clan should enjoy a share of the power and wealth of the group.

These two different types of state were able to flourish together for a century and a half of the Muslim commonwealth. It was a system which, though apparently chaotic, in practice allowed the diverse groups which now formed the Muslim community to reach their own political solutions, the ones most appropriate to their needs. The combination of political diversity with cultural unity forms the background to the great intellectual and cultural achievements of the period. From the mid-fifth/eleventh century, the coming of the Ghuzz Turks and their Seljuk leaders suppressed much of this variety in favour of uniformity of government and religion, and with the coming of this order and uniformity much of the vitality of the previous era was lost forever. The Muslim commonwealth deserves more attention from historians than it usually receives.

9 The Buyid confederation

Origins

The failure of the 'Abbasid caliphate to recruit and pay a reliable army during the first half of the fourth/tenth century meant that there was a political vacuum. This vacuum was filled by the warlike peoples of the mountainous areas, mostly newly converted to Islam, notably the Kurds of the Zagros Mountains and the people of the northern Iranian provinces of Gīlān and Daylam, usually grouped together under the name of Daylamites. The latter group produced the most famous ruling family of the period, the Buyids (also sometimes known as the Buwayhids). Gīlān was the name given to the area on the southwestern shores of the Caspian Sea; Daylam was the mountainous hinterland. The hills and valleys of this district were inhabited by warlike peasant people, cut off by mountains from the Iranian plateau and even from their immediate neighbours. In pre-Islamic times, they had served as mercenaries for the Iranian kings but had probably maintained their independence from the Sasanian monarchy. The area had been little affected by the coming of Islam and, like the mountain peoples of nearby Āzarbayjān and the remoter parts of Khurāsān, its inhabitants had never been effectively conquered by the Arabs, and there was no Arab settlement there. They remained isolated, ruled by kings who took pride in the preservation of old Iranian styles and beliefs. Indeed, the coming of the Arabs may have increased Persian influence in the area by causing an influx of refugees from the plains, like the rulers of the mountain provinces of northern Spain adopting Visigothic styles only after the fall of the Visigothic kingdom of Toledo to the Arabs.

Two characteristics in particular seem to have distinguished the Daylamites and determined the role they were later to play in the Islamic world. The first was their ability as foot soldiers, as hardy and formidable as the mounted Turks but with quite a different fighting technique. This meant that they were a strong military force but that a purely Daylamite army was not really effective, since they had to find allies, usually Turks, sometimes Kurds, who could provide the cavalry to make a balanced fighting unit. The second feature was the importance of family ties. Unlike the contemporary

DOI: 10.4324/9780429348129-9

Turks, with their strange *ghulām* system, the Daylamites showed strong family loyalties; true, there were often disputes among the kin, but their leaders tended to think in terms of family rather than in terms of more abstract ideas of state or the Muslim community. Like the feudal families of western Europe in the eleventh and twelfth centuries, they divided their lands among their sons and sought to conquer new lands to provide inheritances for their kinsmen. Marriage links were an important way of consolidating alliances, and links through the female line were more important than in much of Islamic society. This was especially true in the Buyid kingdom of Rayy, where traditional Daylamite customs seem to have been less affected by Islamic norms than in Fārs or Iraq.

Throughout the mountainous regions to the south of the Caspian Sea, power was in the hands of kings of minor dynasties of native Iranian origin, some of which traced their origins back to pre-Islamic times. Until their conversion to Islam, however, these rulers could play little part in politics outside their own localities. As early as the reign of Hārūn al-Rashīd, members of the 'Alid family had sought sanctuary among these independent people, and in the second half of the third/ninth century, 'Alid missionaries mostly from the Zaydī branch of the family converted many of the people to Islam. In Daylam and Gīlān, this process was hastened by the work of al-Ḥasan b. 'Alī al-Utrūsh, an 'Alid who worked in the area from 289/902 until his death in 304/917. Al-Ḥasan, allied with local rulers, attempted to conquer the whole southern Caspian area, with intermittent success – but despite their military activities, the 'Alids were never able to establish independent states, and their efforts were increasingly undermined by family rivalries. The local chiefs, notably the Ziyarid kings of Gīlān and the Justanids of Daylam based in the Alamūt area in the mountains, held the real power, and it was they, not the 'Alids, who were able to take advantage of 'Abbasid weakness.

The immediate cause of the Daylamite expansion was the withdrawal of Ibn Abi'l-Sāj, the formidable governor of Āzarbayjān, to Iraq with his army in 314/926 to fight the Qarāmiṭa. Among the first to take advantage of the opportunities offered was Mardāvīj b. Ziyār, a scion of the ruling house of Gīlān, who had established himself by 315/927 in the area of Rayy and Iṣfahān, the no man's land which lay between the Samanid zone of influence in Khurāsān and the 'Abbasids in Iraq and Fārs. Among those he recruited was the son of a fisherman from the Caspian coast, 'Alī b. Būya, who, in turn, invited his two younger brothers, al-Ḥasan and Aḥmad, to join him. 'Alī was soon rewarded with an appointment to Karaj, near Iṣfahān, a position which enabled him to recruit followers and become a military leader in his own right. His independent nature soon brought him into conflict with his authoritarian and overbearing master Mardāvīj and in 320/932 he set off south to Fārs with 400 Daylamite followers. This fertile province in the mountains of southwestern Iran had been the centre of the two greatest Persian empires of pre-Islamic times, the Achaemenids and the Sasanians, and the magnificent ruins of Persepolis still testify to its ancient greatness. The Arab armies had had to fight hard to conquer the area, and there was sporadic resistance to Muslim rule well into the Umayyad period. Under the early 'Abbasids, the province had played little part in the political life of the caliphate and its history is obscure. At the beginning of the fourth/tenth century, however, this position began to change. One reason for this was that Fārs seems to have maintained its prosperity at a time when the economy of Iraq was in prolonged crisis, making it relatively more wealthy and important. A second factor was the progress of conversion, which resulted in the emergence of a powerful class of Muslim landowner-bureaucrats who were to play a vital role in the success of the Buyids. The memory of Sasanian greatness seems to have lingered on, for we find Fārsīs with such evocative names as Sābūr (Shāpūr) b. Ardashīr (the names of Sasanian kings), but the province produced no great military or political leaders of its own, the leading families being more concerned with administrative skills and cultural patronage.

Until 315/927, this prosperous and peaceful area had been an important source of revenue for the struggling regime of the Caliph al-Muqtadir, but in this year it was taken over by a Turkish general from Baghdad called Yāqūt, who used, or rather misused, his position to deny the 'Abbasids any share of the revenue and build up a substantial private army. Despite his large forces, he seems to have been an uncertain and vacillating leader, unclear whether he should remain in Fārs or support the schemes of his more dynamic son in Baghdad politics. Meanwhile, the maintenance of this large and ill-disciplined force resulted in oppressive taxation and the alienation of most of the prominent figures in the area.

It was in these circumstances that 'Alī b. Būya, anxious to establish his independence from Mardāvīj, was contacted by an important landowner, of 'Alid descent, from the Arrajān region of Fārs, Zayd b. 'Alī al-Nawbandajānī. Nawbandajān and its area are praised by writers of the fourth and fifth centuries for their prosperity and it seems that much of this was due to Zayd himself, who withheld the revenues of the *ḍiyā'*, the caliph's estates, in the area and used the money to develop the district, constructing a magnificent bridge across the local river as well as a castle for himself. Zayd, anxious to protect his prosperity against the depredations of Yāqūt's undisciplined soldiery, agreed to finance and supply 'Alī b. Būya and his men at a cost of 200,000 *dīnārs* so that they could acquire a foothold in the area before taking on Yāqūt. Thus began the alliance of Buyid princes and Fārsī landowners which was to be the foundation of the Buyid state. 'Alī arrived with about 900 Daylamite supporters in 321/933 and soon began to establish himself, sending his brother al-Ḥasan to collect dues from nearby Kāzirūn and other areas of Fārs. Despite this promising start, it seems that 'Alī lost his nerve when faced with Yāqūt's army and tried to escape east to Kirmān but found his enemy blocking the road with an army said to have numbered 17,000, a large force by the standards of the time. Battle was joined in Jumādā II

322/June 934 and despite the great disparity in numbers, the discipline of the Daylamites and 'Alī's bold leadership won the day. Yāqūt's men fled in disorder and the road to the capital, Shīrāz, lay open.

Once in possession, 'Alī set about consolidating his power. Like all the military leaders of his time, the most intractable problem he faced was raising sufficient money to pay his men. In this, he is said to have been aided by the chance discovery of hidden treasure – but he also received more lasting support from the local magnates who farmed the taxes for him and supplied him with ready cash. Among these were his first sponsor, Zayd b. 'Alī al-Nawbandajānī, and al-'Abbās b. Fasānjas, the first known member of a family which was to provide *wazīrs* and advisers for the ruling family for the next century. 'Alī also began to recruit more troops for his army, many of them, inevitably, Turkish cavalry to complement the Daylamite infantry, a move which soon led to tensions between the two groups.

After establishing his power within Fārs, 'Alī could turn to regulating his position in the wider Islamic world. The first priority was to secure the consent of the 'Abbasid caliph for his actions, and he succeeded in doing this by promising the 'Abbasid envoy tribute, which was never in fact paid. Another area of concern was the vast, sparsely populated province of Kirmān, on the eastern frontiers of Fārs, which was the scene of a confused conflict between the Samanids of Khurāsān and a locally based adventurer, Muḥammad b. Ilyās. 'Alī decided that his brother Aḥmad should try to establish himself there and sent him with a small force of Daylamites and Turks. The problems proved more difficult than had been anticipated and Aḥmad had serious difficulties with the Qufṣ and Balūch hill peoples in the southeast of the province. In the end, Aḥmad's elder brother had to send men to extricate him from his difficulties. Ibn Ilyās returned to take over the province, and it was to be another fourteen years before the Buyids were able to hold the area.

A more pressing problem faced 'Alī in central Iran, where Mardāvīj was still the leading power and the most prominent of the Daylamite leaders. He was one of the most remarkable personalities of his age. Brutal and aggressive as he was, he nonetheless had a vision of a restored Iranian monarchy, ordering that the old Sasanian palaces at Ctesiphon (al-Madā'in, near Baghdad) should be restored to await his arrival. He rejected the authority of the 'Abbasid caliphate entirely and sought to displace Islam as the dominant religion and restore the old Zoroastrian faith, ostentatiously reviving the old ceremonies of fire worship. It is therefore with some satisfaction that Muslim writers record his death at the hands of some disillusioned Turkish troops in 323/935, the year after 'Alī b. Būya took over in Fārs. He is significant as being the last man to try to stem the tide of Islam in Iran. But despite his personal power, his efforts to revive the old faith seem to have met with little popular support and were, at least indirectly, responsible for his death. All subsequent rulers of Iran, including the Buyids, were careful to show their attachment to Islam, even when they tried to revive ancient political glories.

Mardāvīj's death could not have come at a better time for 'Alī. It removed the only serious outside threat to his position in Fārs and left him as the most powerful and successful Daylamite chief. He was also able to recruit a considerable number of Mardāvīj's soldiers into his own army. Mardāvīj was succeeded by his brother, Vushmgīr, who seems to have lacked Mardāvīj's personal authority and was unable to sustain his position in central Iran against attacks from the Samanids from the east and the Buyids from the south. In the end, he was obliged to withdraw to the mountains at the south-eastern corner of the Caspian, where his successors, known as the Ziyarid dynasty, survived until the time of the Seljuks, hereditary foes of their more successful fellow-countrymen, the Buyids. The vacuum caused by the death of Mardāvīj was filled by 'Alī b. Būya's brother, al-Ḥasan, who, after some setbacks, was able to establish himself as the ruler of central Iran, from Rayy to Iṣfahān, in 335/947. Aḥmad, the third brother, turned to Iraq after his failure in Kirmān. The political collapse of the 'Abbasids and the rivalries between military adventurers for the title of *amīr al-umarā'* meant that there was no united opposition, and Aḥmad's attempts were supported and encouraged by the Barīdīs, powerful and grasping tax farmers in southern Iraq, who were trying to secure independence from the caliphate. In 332/944, Aḥmad attempted to take Baghdad for the first time but was beaten off by the Turkish *amīr al-umarā'*, Tūzūn. A year and a half later, however, Tūzūn was dead and his secretary Ibn Shīrzād was struggling to enforce his authority as *wazīr*. Aḥmad easily occupied the city with his forces and was accepted by the Caliph al-Mustakfī as *amīr al-umarā'* in 334/945.

By 335/946, the three sons of Būya had established themselves in effective control of Fārs, Iraq and Rayy, and their descendants were able to maintain themselves in most of those areas until the coming of the Seljuks, a century later. The history of the Buyid period is very confused and full of marches, battles and succession disputes which seem both ephemeral and pointless. The historian's task is complicated by the fact that there were at least three (and sometimes more) centres of activity which were at the same time closely interconnected. This means that the narrative thread is thoroughly tangled and the position is made more difficult by the fact that the sources are very uneven. It is clear that Fārs was the most important province of the Buyid confederation but the narratives on which we depend are largely based on Baghdad material and show almost no concern for events in Fārs at all, while, however, we are very well informed about Iraqi affairs, which were in some ways marginal to Buyid history. Nonetheless, events in Baghdad are of great interest for social and cultural reasons, since it was in Baghdad at this time that the doctrinal positions of *imāmī* Shi'ism and Sunnī Islam were worked out. Baghdad, then, attracts more attention than its purely political importance would warrant.

Buyid history can be chronologically divided, roughly, into two divisions. The first half-century, up to the death of 'Aḍud al-Dawla, greatest of the Buyid rulers, in 372/983, is one of growth and consolidation, when the political initiative was firmly in the hands of the princes of the ruling dynasty. From that point, however, the Buyids were on the defensive, especially in Iraq and central Iran, and political initiative passed to the hands of groups of soldiers and administrators who strove to manipulate their nominal rulers in their own interests.

Expansion and conflict

The initial success of the Buyids was due partly to the absence of any important rivals in the area after the death of Mardāvīj, and partly to their own power, firmly rooted in the support of their Daylamite troops. Although they were not themselves kings of Daylam, their success and ability to give attractive rewards meant that they became the natural focus for the loyalty of ambitious Daylamites, and a stream of recruits seems to have left the mountains to take service with them. Their success was first and foremost a military one; as Mottahedeh says of ʿAlī b. Būya, "He understood the soldiers' game of the mid-tenth century as few other leaders did and ended as its most successful player".[1] They also worked in cooperation with local landowning and bureaucratic aristocracies, who provided political advisers and administrators. This is especially noticeable in the cases of the Buyid kingdoms on the Iranian plateau, where this alliance with the local civilian élite was a major source of strength for the dynasty. Only in Baghdad, with its powerful Turkish soldiers and its growing religious tensions, was there serious local resistance to their rule.

In theory, the Buyid brothers exercised authority as governors for the ʿAbbasid caliphs. Given their modest social origins and their position as outsiders in the Islamic world, it was vital for them to secure the approval and authority of the caliphs for their actions. When Aḥmad entered Baghdad, there was already a role awaiting him, the position of *amīr al-umarā'*, created for Ibn Rā'iq ten years previously, and he was offered this by the caliph. Similarly, his brothers were "appointed" to provincial governorates, and the forms of both the ʿAbbasid government and the old provincial boundaries remained unchanged. The Buyids are said to have been Shīʿīs, and it may seem curious that they did not replace the ʿAbbasid caliph with a member of the ʿAlid family. However, the religious allegiances of the first generation of Buyid rulers are far from clear and there were problems faced by any ruler at this time who wished to establish an ʿAlid caliphate. If they belonged to the Twelver group among the supporters of the house of ʿAlī, then they acknowledged that the last *imām* had gone into occultation seventy years before; while if they were Zaydīs, the only *imām* they could accept was a descendant of Alī who had secured power for himself by his own efforts. It is clear that the appointment of an ʿAlid caliph would have been a major revolution in the state and aroused massive opposition which the Buyids were not strong enough to suppress. They were not out to overthrow the established order but to find a place in it, and like many of the Germanic leaders who assumed power in the Roman Empire in the fifth century, they were more concerned to maintain the status quo and derive legitimacy from it than to destroy it.

While the caliphate was respected, the individual caliph was not. Al-Mustakfī was deposed soon after the Buyid takeover in Baghdad and replaced by the more pliable al-Muṭīʿ, but not before he had granted the Buyids honorific titles which expressed their devotion to the ʿAbbasid *dawla* (state); ʿAlī was to become ʿImād al-Dawla (Support of the State); al-Ḥasan, Rukn al-Dawla (Pillar of the State); and Aḥmad, Muʿizz al-Dawla (Glorifier of the State). This form of title was not new; al-Ḥasan the Hamdanid was titled Nāṣir al-Dawla when he had become *amīr al-umarāʾ* a few years previously, but it became general among the Buyids, and the princes of the dynasty are usually known by these honorifics rather than by their personal names.

At the same time as they acquired this status among their Muslim subjects, the Buyids also revived some of the traditions of Persian monarchy. They did not, unlike their compatriot Mardāvīj, think of undoing the Muslim conquest, but leading members of the family revived the old Sasanian title of *shāhanshāh* (king of kings). By this, they intended to establish their legitimacy with their Iranian subjects and, above all, with their fellow Daylamites. They came from an area where the ancient traditions of Iranian monarchy had never died and where rulers like the Ispahbādhs of Ṭabaristān had preserved the forms and titles of royal rule long after they had disappeared from the rest of Iran. None of these petty kings, however, had claimed the title of *shāhanshāh*, and it was only the Buyids, with their extensive domains and control over the Sasanian homeland of Fārs, who were able to do so. It also enabled them to claim superiority over the kings of Daylam without the latter losing their royal status. The Buyids themselves never ruled the Daylamite homelands. They needed to remain on good terms with the local dynasties to allow the recruitment of more troops, and they made marriage alliances with such old-established lineages as the Justanids of Alamūt. Some of the most serious challenges the Buyids faced in establishing their power, like the rebellion of Rūzbahān and his brothers in 345/956–957, came from their fellow Daylamites, and it was by the adoption of this grandiose title, redolent with memories of imperial greatness, that the sons of the fisherman Būya sought to establish their legitimacy and prestige in a world which might well despise them as adventurers and upstarts.

The Buyid lands formed a federation, rather than an empire. The major political units were the principalities centred in Fārs, with its capital at Shīrāz; al-Jibāl, based in Rayy; and Iraq, including Baghdad, Baṣra and, very briefly, Mosul. After the death of the last of the original Buyid brothers, Rukn al-Dawla al-Ḥasan, in 366/977, the western half of the principality of al-Jibāl was detached to form a new unit based on Hamadhān and Iṣfahān, while from time to time Kirmān in the east enjoyed independence from Fārs, an independence which became permanent after the death of Bahāʾ al-Dawla in 403/1012. There were in addition Buyid princes of other towns like Baṣra from time to time, but their existence was always ephemeral. Of these principalities, Fārs was by far the most important, maintaining its power and prosperity well into the fifth/eleventh century. Baghdad enjoyed prestige as the centre of the caliphate and it remained a cultural and intellectual centre of great importance. Politically and economically, however, it was very weak, and after the death of its first Buyid ruler, Mu'izz al-Dawla, in 356/967, it became apparent that the only Buyid rulers who could exercise power effectively in Baghdad were those like 'Aḍud al-Dawla and Bahā' al-Dawla, who also ruled Fārs. The fortunes of the rulers of Shīrāz and Baghdad were therefore closely linked. The principality of Rayy, however, remained somewhat separate, never being ruled by the same prince as Fārs and facing different problems, notably the danger of attack from the east, by the Samanids or Ghaznavids.

One of the main sources of the intermittent conflicts which mark the history of the period was the question of succession to the various principalities. The possessions of the family were always considered the property of the whole group, rather than of individual branches, and relatives felt that they had the right, even the duty, to interfere in times of trouble, as when 'Izz al-Dawla Bakhtiyār seemed unable to administer Iraq effectively in 367/978 and his cousin 'Aḍud al-Dawla stepped in to restore family rule in the area. Despite this family solidarity, the Buyids never developed an ordered system of inheritance; as in eleventh- and twelfth-century Europe, each powerful ruler sought to provide a suitable inheritance for all his sons, even if it had to be done at the expense of his cousins. Correspondingly, all Buyid princes could feel entitled to a share of the patrimony, and this right was even claimed by some, like Ibn Kākūya, who secured the independence of Iṣfahān in the early fifth/eleventh century, who were only related to the Buyid family by marriage.

The complex nature of family ties and obligations provided enough scope for conflict within the dynasty but there were other points of friction as well. One such was the question of succession to the title of *shāhanshāh*, effectively the presidency of the confederation. The powers this title conferred were not extensive; it was more a recognition of seniority within the family than an office with authority, rather like the title of grand prince of Kiev in twelfth-century Russia. From the beginning, there was no idea that the title was hereditary, or that it was attached to any particular principality. Thus, 'Alī b. Būya, the founder of the family fortune, was the undisputed leader in his lifetime but on his death in 338/949 the title passed, not to his successor in Fārs, 'Aḍud al-Dawla, but to his brother Rukn al-Dawla in Rayy. After Rukn's death in 366/977, the leadership of the family passed back to Shīrāz, to his son 'Aḍud al-Dawla. 'Aḍud al-Dawla was a member of a new generation of Buyids and his political education had been in Fārs, heartland of the old Sasanian Empire of which he had become the ruler when only thirteen. He seems to have broken away to some extent from the ideal of the family confederation and attempted to create something more akin to an absolute monarchy over the Buyid realms. He used the excuse of Bakhtiyār's incompetence to take over Baghdad in 367/978, and worked in alliance with his brother Mu'ayyid al-Dawla to drive the third brother Fakhr al-Dawla into exile. By his death in 372/983, 'Aḍud al-Dawla was the effective ruler of the entire confederation with his brother Mu'ayyid al-Dawla as a junior partner, but when he died, the title passed not to any of his sons but to his exiled brother, Fakhr al-Dawla, the only surviving son of Rukn al-Dawla, who then returned to take over Rayy. Daylamite traditions of seniority within the family reasserted themselves over ideas of centralized monarchy. When Fakhr al-Dawla, in turn, died, the primacy went to the most powerful of 'Aḍud al-Dawla's sons, Bahā' al-Dawla, who, until his death in 403/1012, was the last ruler of the family to call himself *shāhanshāh* with any conviction.

The tensions between the traditional Daylamite clannishness and the needs of settled government were not the only causes of conflict. In many cases, especially in the second half of the Buyid century, princes were persuaded or obliged to take the offensive by different groups of their followers. After 'Aḍud al-Dawla's death, a group of wealthy Iraqis, whom 'Aḍud had sent into exile in Fārs, persuaded his son Sharaf al-Dawla, against the advice of his Fārsī counsellors and his own better judgement, to attack Iraq so that they could be restored to their possessions. It was his *wazīr*, the Ṣāḥib Ibn 'Abbād, who induced Fakhr al-Dawla to attack Iraq in 379/989. The most serious and lasting source of such quarrels was the rich lands of southern Iraq and Khūzistān, whose lush *iqṭā's* were the envy of troops from less favoured areas. With the ravished lands around Baghdad almost useless as a source of revenue, the lands of Khūzistān and Wāsiṭ were vital for the support of the largely Turkish garrison of Baghdad, while they were also converted by the Daylamite troops from Fārs. No Buyid prince could afford to ignore demands from his soldiers that he seize these areas, and they were a continuing source of conflict between the princes of Baghdad and Shīrāz until Bahā' al-Dawla's administrators worked out a careful division of the territories around the turn of the fifth/eleventh century.

There were also prolonged conflicts in and around the Buyid principality of Iraq, in contrast to Fārs, which remained largely peaceful under 'Imād and 'Aḍud al-Dawla. The first problem which faced Mu'izz al-Dawla after he took over Baghdad in 334/945 was that of relations with the Hamdanids, who were now firmly in control of Mosul and northern Iraq. Nāṣir al-Dawla had been *amīr al-umarā* before and sought to regain his position by launching an attack on Baghdad which was beaten off only with difficulty. From then on, the relations of Mu'izz al-Dawla with the Hamdanids were based on an uneasy balance of forces, tested from time to time when the Buyids tried to take the Hamdanid base at Mosul. Nāṣir al-Dawla was able to maintain his independence by withdrawing to his mountain fortresses when attacked but was obliged to promise tribute, only intermittently paid. The failure to subdue al-Jazīra had important consequences in Baghdad, since the area had been a major source of grain for the city, and its loss was one of the reasons for the repeated famines which caused so much misery in Buyid times.

'Imād al-Dawla had taken Fārs by destroying and driving out the army of Yāqūt, from which point he was able to build up a new army of his own. Mu'izz al-Dawla, however, had taken Baghdad by peaceful agreement and had had to reach an accommodation with existing forces in the city. He brought with him his own Daylamite followers but was obliged to employ the troops, most of them Turks, who were already settled in the city. He also brought with him a number of Fārsī bureaucrats, notably members of the Fasānjas family. These arrangements meant that he had a military establishment which was much larger and more expensive than the country could support and he was faced with a major economic crisis as soon as he arrived, resulting in famine and appalling hardship for the civilian population. It also became clear that the revenues were totally inadequate to pay regular salaries to the inflated numbers of soldiers and he was forced to grant out much of Iraq as *iqṭā's* to his Daylamite and Turkish soldiers. This merely postponed the problem, however, since the troops soon complained that their revenues were inadequate, while it was very difficult for the government to recover its financial and political power in the future because the tax base was now so small. The collapse of the old fiscal system which had been so marked under the caliphate of al-Muqtadir, now reached its logical conclusion, and the traditional financial administration based on the collection of *kharāj* and the payment of salaries which had originated with the *dīwān* of 'Umar effectively disappeared.

The granting of *iqṭā's* did not solve the problems of military discontent. This was in part because the *iqṭā'* holders were often robbed or deceived by the agents they employed to collect their revenues, or because the lands they relied on had been ruined by war. The problem was exacerbated by the fact that different groups of soldiers were treated differently. It has been estimated that in the early fourth/tenth century, foot soldiers were being paid about six *dīnārs* a month, while the cavalry received forty. This meant that the cavalry became a privileged class, anxious to preserve their position, and the conflict was made worse by the fact that the cavalry were Turks, while the infantry were almost entirely Daylamites. In times of need, Mu'izz al-Dawla tended to favour the Turks at the expense of his compatriots, and the historian Miskawayh describes the Turks being goaded by greed, while the Daylamites were driven by want and poverty. Whatever the underlying causes, it is clear that the feud between these two groups of soldiers was the most important cause of the problems which beset the Buyid rulers of Baghdad.

Discontent in the army of Iraq came to a head in 345/956–957, when there was a major rebellion of the Daylamite troops led by Rūzbahān b. Vindādh-Khūrshīd. This expressed the frustration of the Daylamites at being neglected by Mu'izz al-Dawla and being sent, for the third time, on a difficult and unrewarding campaign against rebels in the marshes of southern Iraq.

Rūzbahān was himself a Daylamite, probably of aristocratic stock, who felt that he had as good a right as the Buyids to lead his people. The rebellion was only defeated because of Mu'izz al-Dawla's personal bravery and the loyalty of the Turks, and the result was to depress the status of the Daylamites still further, since they were dispersed on small *iqṭā's* throughout southern Iraq, becoming small-scale landholders and merchants, oppressing the local people but providing no useful support for the dynasty.

Mu'izz al-Dawla died in 356/967. He had not been an entirely unsuccessful ruler. He had secured Buyid control over most of southern Iraq and Khūzistān and received homage and on occasion tribute from both Mosul and Aleppo. He himself was a simple and uncouth soldier, much given to drink. He spoke little Arabic and left the civil administration to his highly competent *wazīr*, al- Ḥasan b. Muḥammad al-Muhallabī, descendant of the famous Muhallabī family of early Islamic times. He was the first of the great Buyid *wazīrs*, a group which includes celebrated names such as the two Ibn al-'Amīds, father and son, and the Ṣāḥib Ibn 'Abbād, and he fulfilled a role rather similar to the first British prime minister, Sir Robert Walpole, acting as an intermediary between a foreign ruler (George I) and his subjects.

Despite Miskawayh's laments about the decline of administrative skills as a result of the prevalence of *iqṭā's*, the *wazīrs* of the Daylamite rulers were men of great importance in the state. Their background and role had changed since the days of the great 'Abbasid *wazīrs* like the Banu'l-Furāt and the Banu'l-Jarrāḥ. These earlier *wazīrs* had been above all experts in the financial administration of the Sawād of Iraq, and they had largely been recruited from local landowning families, descendants of the *dihqāns* of late Sasanian times. The decline of agricultural prosperity and of direct taxation meant that this expertise was no longer required, and we find members of these families emigrating to Egypt, where their skills would be appreciated. The *wazīrs* of the Buyids owed their importance to their position as intermediaries between the unsophisticated Daylamī soldier-princes and their subjects. The first generation of Buyid rulers seem to have known little Arabic, which was still the standard administrative language throughout the area. A knowledge of Persian language and customs was also important, and the *wazīrs* of the Buyids were drawn mostly from the Iranian families of Fārs or Rayy. When Mu'izz al-Dawla established himself in Baghdad, he recruited his administrators from Shīrāz, not from the local bureaucratic families of Baghdad. The Buyid *wazīrs* did not confine themselves to purely administrative functions. They advised on, and sometimes decided, policy and in some cases commanded armies in their own right. The distinction between the civil and military administrations which was apparent in the later phases of 'Abbasid government had largely disappeared.

Neither the abilities of the *wazīrs* nor the intermittent enthusiasm of the Buyid *amīrs* were enough to remedy the long-term structural problems of the economy and administration of Iraq. Mu'izz al-Dawla himself made some effort to repair the agricultural economy, setting a personal example by carrying loads of earth to repair irrigation ditches, but he was unable or unwilling to tackle the fundamental problems of the area by reducing the military establishment or making the army more efficient. There was no serious attempt to pay the army out of revenue or to revive the old system of direct taxation, and the use of *iqṭāʿs* remained chaotic and corrupt.

Muʿizz al-Dawla was succeeded by his son Bakhtiyār, who was given the title of ʿIzz al-Dawla and who attempted to rule Buyid Iraq for eleven years, between 356 and 367 (967–978). Our main source, Miskawayh, gives a partisan and highly critical view of his character but even allowing for this bias, it is clear that he lacked the military grasp of his father or the political and administrative acumen of his cousin, ʿAḍud al-Dawla. It is also clear, however, that many of the problems which plagued his reign were not of his making but were inherited from his father, and subsequent experience was to suggest that Buyid Iraq, on its own, was virtually ungovernable.

The main reasons for this situation are clear: i.e. the demands of the military, strong enough to force their will on the government but too inefficient to conquer areas like Mosul, which might have yielded increased revenue, and the steady decline of the resources of central Iraq. None of these features were new but they were made worse by the ruler's ineptitude and the failure to organize the existing resources effectively. Bakhtiyār allowed a vicious rivalry to develop between various groups in the bureaucracy and no commanding figure emerged to replace al-Muhallabī in overall charge of the administration. From 362/973, his chief adviser was a man called Ibn Baqiyya, who had risen to power not through the financial offices of the state but through the kitchens. The failure to produce a competent *wazīr* was symptomatic of the general crisis of the administration.

Bakhtiyār also failed to secure the loyalty of the military, alienating both Turks and Daylamites. He was unfortunate in that the Turks in Baghdad were led by Sabuktakīn (not to be confused with his contemporary Sabuktakīn of Ghazna in Afghanistan, founder of the Ghaznavid dynasty), a general of considerable political ability whose authority they accepted. By 361/972, relations between Bakhtiyār and his military commander were so bad that he tried to replace him with a fellow Turk, but Sabuktakīn proved too powerful and was allowed to retain his position.

The crisis took a new turn the next year (362/973) when news arrived of Byzantine incursions deep into Muslim territory. In the previous decade, the important cities of Tarsus and Antioch had fallen to the ancient enemy and the Byzantine expansion gave no signs of coming to an end. The small frontier principality of Aleppo lacked the resources to deal with this threat. Popular opinion in the Muslim world, especially in Baghdad and Khurāsān, was stirred up by the arrival of refugees from the conquered areas, and the people demanded that their rulers take action to defend their fellow Muslims. Bakhtiyār gave orders that Sabuktakīn should prepare an army for the *jihād*, but this, rather than drawing the rival factions together in a common cause, simply made things worse. Sabuktakīn recruited and armed a large number of volunteers but these were mobilized not against the Byzantines, but in support of the Turks in Baghdad and they remained in the city, strengthening the anti-Buyid party. In the meantime, Bakhtiyār's new adviser Ibn Baqiyya persuaded his master that the best chance of raising money was a new expedition to Mosul, where the Hamdanid ruler, Abū Taghlib, who was being hard pressed by the Byzantines, might be easy to subdue. Accordingly in 363/974, Sabuktakīn and Bakhtiyār, though hardly on speaking terms, set off north. The attempt was a fiasco; Abū Taghlib, taking advantage of his superior mobility, caused a diversion in Baghdad and forced Sabuktakīn to return there. Bakhtiyār, still in Mosul but now isolated from the main body of his army, was forced to make terms. Like so many of his schemes, his own incompetence and the rivalry with the Turks had brought the expedition to nothing.

After this failure, Ibn Baqiyya and his master felt that an all-out breach with Sabuktakīn was inevitable. They left Baghdad, where the Turkish leader had mobilized popular support, for Wāsit. and Ahwāz, which they intended to make their base. Here, they cultivated the cause of the Daylamites, whose interests they wanted to make their own, and took over the *iqṭā'*s of the Turks in the area, including those held by Sabuktakīn himself. Open warfare between the two parties began in Dhū'l-Qa'da in 363/July 974 and Sabuktakīn was able to take over Baghdad entirely. The Buyid palaces were captured and members of the family expelled, while the victorious Turkish general replaced the ailing Caliph al-Muṭī' with his son al-Ṭā'i'. The remaining Daylamites were expelled from the city and their houses were taken over by the Turks. By the end of 363/autumn 974, there was virtually a Turkish amirate in the capital and the Turks were attacking Bakhtiyār in Wāsiṭ itself.

There can be little doubt that Buyid rule in Baghdad would have come to an end at this point if Bakhtiyār had not appealed to the rest of his family for support. Rukn al-Dawla of Rayy, the senior member of the clan, entrusted the task to his son 'Aḍud al-Dawla, ruler of Fārs, who began to mobilize his resources. The arrival of 'Aḍud al-Dawla changed the balance of power, and the Buyid cause was further aided by the death of Sabuktakīn, from natural causes. He was succeeded as the leader of the Turks by his deputy Alptakīn, who seems to have lacked something of his predecessor's sureness of touch. Bakhtiyāār and his cousin began to advance on Baghdad from Wāsiṭ, and Bakhtiyār called in other allies as well, notably Abū Taghlib the Hamdanid from Mosul, who came south to pillage the city. The Buyids were also joined by two bedouin tribes, the Asad from the west and the Shaybān from the east of the city. In Jumādā I 364/ January 975, Alptakīn and the Turks were decisively defeated on the Diyālā river and the Buyid cousins entered the city in state. Alptakīn with many of his men fled west to Damascus and many of them were later to enter Fatimid service.

In the short term, Buyid authority was restored. But the crisis of 361–364 (972–975) had important long-term effects and represents something of a turning point in the history of the area. The first effect was the physical devastation of the city. It is true that Baghdad had been besieged and sacked before, but this time, despite the efforts of ʿAḍud al-Dawla, it does not seem to have recovered its vitality. The Buyid period was one of continuous urban crises in Baghdad. This showed itself in frequent popular disturbances and brigandage, as well as the struggles among different bands of unpaid soldiers. In late Buyid times, even the rulers of the city were reduced to abject poverty, Jalāl al-Dawla being forced to dismiss his servants and set loose his horses because he could no longer afford to feed them. Part of the explanation for this seems to lie in the decline in trade. In Buyid times, the richest people in the city were not merchants but government servants. Tax collecting, military service and *iqṭāʿs* rather than commerce were the main sources of wealth. Those who did make money invested it in land rather than trade. There also seems to have been a continuous emigration of wealthy families – the Banu'l-Furāt, for example, to Egypt, where prospects were much brighter.

Government action or inaction was partly responsible for this. The sacking and pillaging of markets had become too frequent to make commercial investment viable, and even in times of "peace" the markets were subject to extortion by bankrupt *wazīrs* or unpaid soldiers. The absence of basic security effectively prevented economic recovery.

Another major contributory factor was the emergence of Shīʿī and Sunnī as armed political groupings and the division of the city into strictly Sunnī and Shī quarters. The memory of ʿAlī and his family had always been venerated in Iraq. In the previous century, Muʿtazilism had been the issue which divided the Muslims, and while veneration for the memory of ʿAlī was part of the Muʿtazilī position, it was around the issue of the createdness of the Qur'ān that the debate had crystallized. Al-Mutawakkil had caused great offence by destroying the tombs of the ʿAlids when he broke with the Muʿtazilī position, but this had not led to popular uprisings in Baghdad. After the anarchy at Sāmarrā, Muʿtazilism largely ceased to be a political issue, although there were still Muʿtazilī thinkers and teachers. In the early fourth/tenth century, the status of ʿAlī was becoming a major source of controversy among the Muslims of Baghdad. It is important to recognize that veneration of the name of ʿAlī by itself does not imply commitment to Shiʿism; most, but not all, Sunnīs respected his memory as an early Muslim and one of the closest companions of the Prophet.

It was in Buyid Baghdad that "Twelver" Shiʿism (so-called from the fact that its adherents acknowledge twelve *imāms*, the first of whom was ʿAlī) developed both as a system of belief and as a religious community. On the theoretical level, the most important development was the idea of the hidden *imām*. At least from the time of Jaʿfar al-Ṣādiq (d. 148/765), many supporters of the house of ʿAlī had accepted that the leadership of the family was vested in al-Ḥusayn b. ʿAlī and his direct descendants. In 260/874, the last of these publicly acknowledged *imāms*, al-Ḥasan al-ʿAskarī, died in Sāmarrā, where he had lived quietly among supporters of the Family, and al-Nawbakhtī, an

'Alid sympathizer writing at the end of the third/ninth century, lists no less than fourteen different opinions as to the rightful successor to al-'Askarī. During the course of the fourth/tenth century, however, it became widely accepted among the Shī'a that the last *imām* had left a son who had remained hidden and never died but would come again to establish the rule of true Islam. Meanwhile, he had left representatives in the world who would guide the Faithful in his absence. Acceptance of the *imām* was, however, fundamental to true belief, since he was the *ḥujja*, the proof of God without whom there could be no Islam. This theory of the imamate was developed in Baghdad by scholars such as al-Kulaynī (d. 329/940–941) and above all al-Shaykh al-Mufīd (d. 413/1022), who produced the view of the imamate generally held by Twelvers down to the present day. Despite the violence and the economic problems of the city, this intellectual activity was centred in Baghdad, especially in the old commercial quarter of al-Karkh, which became the main stronghold of the Shī'a, and scholars from all over the Muslim world, like the famous Muḥammad b. al-Ḥasan al-Ṭūsī (d. 460/1067) from Khurāsān, were attracted to the city. These scholars were not patronized directly by the Buyid rulers but were helped by figures closely connected with the court, like Bahā' al-Dawla's *wazīr*, Sābūr b. Ardashīr, a bureaucrat of Fārsī origin, who established a major Shī'ī library in al-Karkh in 381/-991–992. The scholars were also patronized by rich local families of 'Alid descent who were in many cases, like the Sharīfs al-Rāḍī (d. 406/1015) and al-Murtaḍā (d. 436/1044), close to the Buyid court. While some Buyid rulers, notably 'Aḍud al-Dawla, seem to have discouraged speculation which might divide the Muslim community, others at least tolerated it and allowed their courtiers to provide patronage for the needy intellectuals involved.

While the development of Shi'ism had an intellectual aspect, it also had a more practical and, in the end, political one; for it was in Buyid Baghdad that Twelver Shi'ism became a distinct and separate sect. The new elements which distinguished this Shi'ite party were the public denigration of the first two caliphs (Abū Bakr and 'Umar, who were held to have usurped the rights of 'Alī); the development of certain exclusively Shī'ī public festivals, notably the mourning for al-Ḥusayn on the 10 Muḥarram and the celebration of the Ghadīr Khumm on 18 Dhū'l-Ḥijja (when the Prophet was said to have acknowledged 'Alī as his successor during the Farewell pilgrimage in 10/632); and the development of the tombs of members of the 'Alid family as centres of pilgrimage. These three elements mark off the development of the true Shi'ism of the fourth/tenth century from the reverence for 'Alī or support of 'Alid pretenders to the caliphate which had been common in previous centuries. It was no part of the programme of this new mature Shī'a to use force to install an 'Alid caliph immediately.

The three distinguishing features of the new Shi'ism described above were all essentially public acts and at least two were exclusive; while any Muslim could accept the veneration of the tomb of 'Alī, if not those of all his descendants, no one could accept the celebration of the Ghadīr Khumm or the cursing of the first two caliphs without cutting himself off from a large number of other Muslims. Thus, the mature Shi'ism of the Buyid period defined itself as a distinct group or party. One either followed it or rejected it – no compromises were possible. In this way, the Muslims of Iraq in the fourth/tenth century divided into two, increasingly hostile, camps.

We can follow the chronology of these developments in some detail. During the reign of al-Muqtadir, there is no evidence of Sunnī–Shī'ī strife in Baghdad. In 313/925, the mosque at Barāthā in the Karkh quarter of Baghdad was demolished on the orders of the caliph. It was held that 'Alī himself had prayed at Barāthā and the mosque had become a centre of pro-'Alid elements, but there is no mention of the cursing of the first caliphs or the other distinguishing feature of the Shī'ī party. It is striking that in the confused violence of al-Muqtadir's reign, no one attempted to raise the Sunnīs against the Shī'īs or vice versa, a clear indication that the two parties were not a serious force in politics. Soon after this, we begin to get signs of communal tension and its origins lay with the Ḥanbalīs (it is still too early to talk of the Sunnīs), who had rejected the Mu'tazila and continued to insist on the importance of Tradition and respect for the Companions as the basis of true Islam. In 323/935, the caliph was obliged to issue a decree to prevent the Ḥanbalīs from attacking the Shī'a, the first sign of popular violence.

Communal tension had been increasing in Baghdad before the coming of the Buyids, but the policies of Mu'izz al-Dawla and Bakhtiyār were to prove a decisive factor. From the time of their arrival in Baghdad, the Daylamites had become associated with the Shī'a point of view, and allowed and encouraged the development of a Shī'ī party in the capital, partly to secure the support of at least one element among the Baghdad populace. As early as 341/952, Mu'izz al-Dawla is said to have ordered the release of preachers who expounded the doctrine of transmigration of souls, a belief common to the more extreme pro-'Alid elements. In 351/962, Mu'izz al-Dawla took the more blatant step of having curses on the first two caliphs painted on walls in Baghdad. In the end, his *wazīr*, the astute al-Muhallabī, persuaded him that only Mu'āwiya should be mentioned, a course safe enough in Iraq (but not in Syria, where at about this time a man was trampled to death in the mosque for giving 'Alī precedence over Mu'āwiya). In 353/964, Mu'izz al-Dawla encouraged the public celebration of the important Shī'ī festivals of the 10 Muḥarram and the Ghadīr Khumm, to the intense annoyance of many others in Baghdad. At the same period, we see signs of increased reverence for the Shī'ī shrines of Iraq and Iran, which came to replace the more perilous Mecca and Medina as the goal of pilgrimage for many Shī'īs. In 342/953, we hear for the first time of an officer from Baṣra requesting to be buried by al-Ḥusayn at Karbalā', and the practice soon grew in popularity. On his death in 399/1009, Aḥmad b. Ibrāhīm al-ḍabbī, the Buyid *wazīr* at Rayy, instructed that his body be taken to Karbalā' for burial, as did al-Ḥusayn b. al-Maghribī (d. 418/1027), *wazīr* of the Marwanid ruler of Mayyāfāriqīn. This is in marked contrast to the early Islamic practice of burying great men where they died and shows the increasing importance attached to Shīʿī shrines. Under Buyid patronage, most of the famous Shīʿī shrines were embellished, not only the tombs of ʿAlī and al-Ḥusayn, but that of Fāṭima in Qumm and of ʿAlī al-Riḍa near Ṭūs (now known as Mashhad). The patterns of Shīʿī devotion which emerged at this time have remained characteristic of the sect ever since.

The most important stage in the separation of the Sunnī and Shīʿī parties came in the crisis of Bakhtiyār's reign from 361/972 onwards. The Turkish leader Sabuktakīn diverted the enthusiasm of the Baghdadis for the *jihād* against the Byzantines into attacking the Buyids and their Daylamite and Baghdadi supporters as heretics. The Shiʿites were fewer in number, and their centre, the Karkh area, was burned down twice during this period. Miskawayh, a contemporary observer, is quite specific about the nature of the change that resulted: "the dispute between the two factions (Sunnī and Shīʿī), which had formerly been on religious questions, now became political as well, as the Shīʿa adopted the watchword of Bakhtiyār and the Daylamites while the Sunna adopted that of Sabuktakīn and the Turks".[2] The fighting resulted in the arming of both factions and the increasing division of the city into fortified quarters, each with its own sectarian character. These divisions persisted after the immediate political quarrel had finished and in the end became permanent, and it is to the events of these years that we can ascribe the definitive break between Sunnism and Twelver Shiʿism. It was also at this time that the Turks became identified with the anti-Shīʿa party. There is no evidence that the Turks of Sāmarrā in the third/ninth century had shown any hostility at all to the house of ʿAlī, and many of them had supported the Muʿtazilī movement. From Bakhtiyār's reign, however, they became associated with the Sunnī cause, a development which became firmly established in the next century when Turkish rulers like Maḥmūd of Ghazna and the Seljuks emphasized their role as champions of Sunnism.

Throughout the second half of the Buyid period, processions on sectarian feast days and the writing of inflammatory slogans, particularly the cursing of the Companions of the Prophet and the first three caliphs, were to provide flash-points for continuing violence. Despite the efforts of determined rulers of Baghdad like ʿAḍud al-Dawla and Ibn Ustādh-hurmuz to put an end to the growth of sectarian tension, the divide between the Shīʿa and their opponents continued to harden. In the years after the death of ʿAḍud al-Dawla in 372/983, those who can now confidently be described as Sunnīs who opposed the claims of the Shīʿā were developing their own festivals, notably the feast of the Cave, just eight days after the Ghadīr Khumm, when the Sunnīs remembered how the Prophet and Abū Bakr had taken refuge together in a cave during the *Hijra* from Mecca to Medina, emphasizing the unique closeness of the first caliph to Muḥammad. Again, the processions and public festivities were an occasion for violence. This movement was given added impetus by the Caliph al-Qādir (381–422/991–1031), who made moves to codify a Sunnī doctrinal and ritual position to counter that of the Shī'a and to strengthen his position against the absent Buyid ruler Bahā' al-Dawla. The 'Abbasid caliphs became firmly attached to the Sunnī cause, and they were encouraged in this by the rising power of Maḥmūd of Ghazna, who linked himself firmly to the Sunnī, anti-Buyid position.

By this time, the damage had been done. Baghdad was firmly divided between the adherents of the two rival sects, each armed and defending its own areas. The divisions soon spread to other Iraqi towns like Wāsit. and to other parts of the Islamic world. It is probable that the divisions between Sunnī and Shī'ī would have hardened in this period in any case, partly because of the establishment of the Fatimid caliphate, but there can be no doubt that the political rivalries in Baghdad accelerated and defined the process, not just because sectarian differences were encouraged for local political reasons but because Baghdad remained such an important intellectual centre for Sunnī and Shī'ī alike.

Another change which becomes noticeable during the crisis of Bakhtiyār's reign is the decline of the countryside around the capital. In its heyday, Baghdad had been the centre of a flourishing agricultural area, but it had also needed to import grain by river from the Jazīra area. By the fifth/eleventh century, this had changed. The Jazīra was controlled by the Hamdanids and their 'Uqaylid successors, usually hostile to Buyid rule. The agricultural land was despoiled and much of it had become nomad pasture. The bedouin Asad, Khafāja and 'Uqayl tribes approached the city from the north and west, while the Kurdish 'Annazids took over fertile lands in the Diyālā basin to the east. Against this background, the economic problems of the city and intermittent famine and social unrest were inevitable.

The death of Sabuktakīn and the reconquest of Baghdad by Bakhtiyār and 'Aḍud al-Dawla in 364/975 had restored Buyid rule to the city, but it had not solved the problem of the unfortunate Bakhtiyār. 'Aḍud al-Dawla made no secret of the fact that he thought that Bakhtiyār ought to abdicate, and in the circumstances there was little he could do. Respite came from an unexpected quarter. 'Aḍud al-Dawla's father, Rukn al-Dawla, was furious that his son should dispossess his cousin and ordered him to withdraw from Iraq. Reluctantly, 'Aḍud al-Dawla obeyed the old man's wishes. The withdrawal encouraged Bakhtiyār to make another attempt to restore his position and he cast around wildly for allies, looking not just to other Buyids like 'Aḍud al-Dawla's brother Fakhr al-Dawla of Rayy but also to the Kurdish leader Ḥasanūya (or Ḥasanwayh), his old enemy Abū Taghlib the Hamdanid and bedouin tribal chiefs, who used this opportunity to inflict further damage on the settled countryside around Baghdad. His position was too weak to be able to make use of this support, and when Rukn al-Dawla died in 366/977, 'Aḍud al-Dawla lost no time in mounting a new invasion, which culminated in a battle near Sāmarrā in Shawwāl 367/May 978 in which Bakhtiyār was defeated, captured and finally beheaded on the orders of his cousin.

Iraq thus passed into the hands of the most famous of the Buyid rulers, Fanā-khusrau, titled 'Aḍud al-Dawla. He had been the ruler of Fārs for almost thirty years and it is to this province we must look if we want to understand the sources of his power. At the same time, the history of Fārs is shrouded in mystery and we know much more about his five-year rule in Baghdad than the much longer period which preceded it. He had succeeded to the position of his uncle 'Imād al-Dawla, the founder of Buyid power in Fārs, in 338/949. He was only thirteen at the time and his political education was left in the hands of experienced bureaucrats like the elder Ibn al-'Amīd, his father's *wazīr*. He thus acquired a very different view of government from the soldier adventurers who formed the first generation of Buyid rulers. Of all the members of his family, he was the one most admired by posterity, and even the Seljuk *wazīr*, Niẓām al-Mulk, servant of the dynasty which overthrew the Buyids, used his methods as an example for his own sovereign.

His rule in Fārs was something of a golden age for the province as 'Aḍud al-Dawla made it the basis for his imperial schemes and, realizing that the prosperity of the area was fundamental to his plans, took active steps to encourage both agriculture and trade. In the agricultural sector, he invested heavily in irrigation projects, one of which, a great dam known as the Band-i Amīr, remains to this day as a testimony to his activities. He continued the close relations his predecessor 'Imād al-Dawla had built up with the local landowning bureaucratic class and they implemented the policy from which they too benefited. The long years of peace saw agriculture booming. It is true that he distributed *iqṭā's* to the military, but in Fārs this process was kept under strict control and it does not seem to have led to the abuses prevalent in parts of Iraq. Unlike other members of his family, he did not employ an all-powerful *wazīr*, probably because he supervised so much of the administration in person, but the Fārsīs found new opportunities after the conquest of Iraq, where 'Aḍud al-Dawla used many of them as administrators in preference to the local people.

Agricultural prosperity was matched by commercial and urban development. The fullest evidence for this comes from the port of Sīrāf on the south coast, where both literary sources and archaeological evidence suggest great trading activity and wealth. The disturbances in southern Iraq, the sacking of Baṣra by the Qarāmiṭa and the growing impoverishment of the whole country meant that centres for Indian trade shifted farther down the Gulf coast. Sīrāf was not a naturally inviting site, being very hot and barren, but under the Buyids it had safe and secure access to Shīrāz and thence to other areas of Iran. Great fortunes were made by Sīrāfī merchants, and for the century of Buyid rule, this out-of-the-way harbour became one of the great maritime centres of the Islamic world. There could be no clearer sign of the benefits of Buyid government. The capital, Shīrāz, itself expanded. 'Aḍud al-Dawla built a new suburb to house the Daylamites, with its own markets, and derived a substantial income from this urban development. The city itself remained unwalled until the disturbances at the end of the Buyid period in the mid-fifth/eleventh century, another indication of the prosperity and security of the area. He also developed markets at Rāmhurmuz and Kāzirūn on the routes from southern Iraq to Fārs.

The success of the local economy is commented on by travellers (notably al-Muqaddasī at the time and Ibn al-Balkhī during the Seljuk period) but is also demonstrated by the wealth that 'Aḍud al-Dawla could invest in projects such as the invasion of Iraq. He was consistently better equipped than his opponents and could dispose of large amounts of cash to satisfy his troops' demands. The changed relationship between Fārs and Iraq could be symbolized by Miskawayh's story of how 'Aḍud al-Dawla caused plants to be taken from Fārs to restock the ruined gardens of Baghdad. His successes rested on sound administration and economic policy, not on military skill or brilliant generalship.

On the domestic front, Fārs enjoyed almost uninterrupted peace, except in 345/956–957 when the rebellion of the Daylamite chief Rūzbahān in Iraq led to a similar rising by his brother in Fārs, but the movement was soon crushed by 'Aḍud al-Dawla's old mentor, the *wazīr* Ibn al-'Amīd, and does not seem to have caused prolonged disturbances. This peace allowed 'Aḍud al-Dawla to develop an expansionist foreign policy. In 357/968, he was able to take over Kirmān because of disputes among the sons of Ibn Ilyās. He took firm measures against the Qufṣ and Balūch hill people and appointed his son Shīrdil as the governor. Henceforward, Kirmān was attached to the Buyid domains until the coming of the Seljuks eighty years later. A second area of concern to 'Aḍud al-Dawla was 'Umān. This was of strategic importance because of its position at the entrance to the Gulf and the effect this could have on the trade of Baṣra and Sīrāf. In 354/965, the governor, who seems to have maintained friendly relations with the Buyids, was driven out by the local people, who invited in the Qarāmiṭa of eastern Arabia. Both Mu'izz al-Dawla in Iraq and his nephew 'Aḍud al-Dawla considered this a threat to the prosperity of their dominions, and a major maritime expedition was launched under the command of a leading Fārsī bureaucrat, now working in Baghdad, Muḥammad b. al-'Abbās b. Fasānjas. The army sailed from Baṣra, picked up reinforcements in Sīrāf and conquered the province. Thereafter, it seems to have been a dependency of Fārs, at least until the end of the century.

The third and most important area of 'Aḍud al-Dawla's foreign policy was in the invasion of Iraq. As long as his uncle Mu'izz al-Dawla was alive, Iraq remained outside his sphere of influence. But almost as soon as Bakhtiyār succeeded in 356/967, 'Aḍud al-Dawla began to take advantage of his weakness, though it was not until the death of his father in 366/977 that he finally had a free hand, and he marched on Baghdad. He was partly concerned to expand his power and establish a direct link with the caliph but he may have felt that all the Buyid lands were threatened by the misfortunes of Bakhtiyār's rule and he could not afford to tolerate an area of instability on his frontiers where disaffected Turks and Daylamites could work against him. He could count on the resources of Fārs and the loyalty of its administrators and soldiers and this was to prove decisive. After the fall of Baghdad and later Mosul, Fārsīs were given important offices, including that of chief *qāḍī* in Baghdad and military commander in Mosul, while dissident Iraqis were despatched to exile in Fārs. Although he was to spend the rest of his reign attempting to solve the problems of Iraq, he still regarded the province he had ruled for so long as his base, and his household remained there until his death.

After his victory over Bakhtiyār, 'Aḍud al-Dawla's immediate concern was to consolidate the frontiers of his new realm. To the north of Buyid Iraq lay the Hamdanid kingdom of Mosul, still independent despite the repeated attempts of both Mu'izz al-Dawla and Bakhtiyār to subdue it. Abū Taghlib, the Hamdanid ruler, had aided Bakhtiyār in his last fight, fearing above all a strong ruler in Baghdad. In the past, the Hamdanids had always been able to abandon their capital and the plains of al-Jazīra and retire to their mountain strongholds, taking with them the administrators who collected the taxes. Although the Buyids were able to take Mosul, they never had sufficient resources to besiege the mountain fortresses or the experienced personnel to tax al-Jazīra. Sooner or later, they were forced to come to terms. It was typical of 'Aḍud al-Dawla's determined and systematic approach that he was prepared for this. With ample resources, he recruited exiled Mosulis in Baghdad to run the administration of their hometown. Within a month of his victory over Bakhtiyār, he had taken Mosul and went on to reduce the mountain castles. Abū Taghlib fled across the desert to Syria, and Hamdanid power in the area was destroyed forever. 'Aḍud al-Dawla had achieved the triumph which had so often eluded his predecessors.

He also turned his attention against the pastoral people who had come to Bakhtiyār's aid. The Shaybānī and Asadī bedouin who had threatened the countryside around Baghdad were ruthlessly controlled, and even the unruly 'Uqaylīs of al-Jazīra were disciplined by holding the chiefs responsible for any misdemeanours their followers might commit. He also took action against the powerful Barzikānī Kurds who dominated the route from Baghdad to Hamadhān and the Iranian plateau, a vital link with the Buyid kingdom of Rayy. Here, he was aided by the death of the veteran Ḥasanūya, which allowed 'Aḍud al-Dawla to lend support to one of his sons, Badr, and secure his protégé's triumph. Only in the marshes of southern Iraq was he unable, by either force or diplomacy, to assert his authority.

In 370/980–981, he moved on to organize the affairs of the other Buyid kingdom, in al-Jibāl and central Iran. The death of his father, Rukn al-Dawla, four years before left two of his sons in contention. One, Fakhr al-Dawla, whose power was based in Rayy, was determined to maintain his independence, even if it meant allying with the hereditary enemy of his family, Qābūs b. Vushmgīr of Ṭabaristān, whose uncle Mardāvīj had opposed the early independence of the Buyids. The other brother, Mu'ayyid al-Dawla, was prepared to work with 'Aḍud al-Dawla, and they combined to oppose Fakhr and his eastern allies; Fakhr al-Dawla was driven into exile and Mu'ayyid al-Dawla ruled as his brother's junior partner.

The last two years of his reign 'Aḍud al-Dawla spent in Baghdad, embarking on a programme of restoration and rebuilding. He spent large sums on palaces and on fundamental works like the restoration of the canal network which had been so vital for the city's prosperity. He was determined, far-sighted and ruthless with corrupt and inefficient subordinates, but his stay in Baghdad was very short and many of his cherished projects must have been unfinished at his death. He also succeeded in calming the endemic dissension between the Turks and Daylamites in the army. This was largely due to successful financial administration, and 'Aḍud al-Dawla could call on the revenues of Khūzistān, Wāsiṭ, Mosul and Fārs, none of which had been available to his predecessor. He also ensured that the troops were paid regularly. The army had waged successful foreign wars under his leadership and these may have brought in booty. He was equally methodical in his treatment of sectarian disturbances. He made a great show of his good relations with the 'Abbasid caliph but beyond that took care to show favour neither to Sunnī nor to Shī'ī. In particular, he forbade inflammatory preaching, including attacks on the Companions of the Prophet and the celebration of provocative, sectarian festivals. Muslims, he held, should spend their time reading the Qur'ān rather than arguing over contentious points of doctrine. Sunnī–Shī'ī tensions do not seem to have been a problem in Fārs, and 'Aḍud al-Dawla was powerful enough not to need the support of either group in Baghdad.

To some extent, his reputation has been exaggerated by chroniclers, always eager to seize on examples of strong and just rule to make moral points. Nonetheless, the record presents a convincing picture of a conscientious, self-educated man, solving problems by careful organization, planning and attention to detail. The dynasty was not to produce another figure of his stature.

The years of decline: 372–440/983–1048

'Aḍud al-Dawla's death in 372/983 was the occasion for further divisions among the Buyids. In this case, it is quite apparent that different princes were adopted by different pressure groups, military or civilian, in different areas to advance their own interests. 'Aḍud al-Dawla had used his ample resources to keep the balance between these groups, but none of his successors was in a strong enough position to follow his example. Two sons appeared as rivals for power. The first of these was Ṣamṣām al-Dawla, who was established by his supporters in Baghdad even before his father's death had been made public. A mild and easygoing man, he seems to have lacked his father's brutal determination, and his political life was to be full of misfortunes brought upon him by others. From the very beginning, he was plagued by military rebellion in Baghdad and the loss of the valuable provinces of

Ahwāz and Baṣra in the south, and he was soon forced to abandon Mosul and al-Jazīra to the Kurds and 'Uqaylī Arabs.

The other son was Shīrdil ('Lionheart' in Persian), who had been in control in Kirmān at the time of his father's death but soon established himself in Shīrāz, the capital of Fārs, with the title of Sharaf al-Dawla. 'Aḍud al-Dawla had used Fārs as a place of exile for obstreperous Baghdadi notables, among whom were the ex-*qāḍī* Ibn Ma'rūf and a vastly rich descendant of 'Alī, Muḥammad b. 'Umar. These were now released, along with other political prisoners, and began to urge Sharaf al-Dawla to take over Iraq so that they could regain their positions. Another group, led by the *wazīr* al-'Alā' b. al-Ḥasan and 'Aḍud al-Dawla's former agent in Mosul, Abū Naṣr Khwāshāda, opposed this. Like Sharaf al-Dawla himself, they were natives of Fārs and felt, with some justification, that involvement in Iraq would only lead to problems. At first, Sharaf al-Dawla followed the advice of his Fārsī counsellors, making a treaty with Ṣamṣām al-Dawla in 376/986–987, but his mind was changed by Muḥammad b. 'Umar. Sharaf al-Dawla advanced from Ahwāz towards Baghdad and was soon joined by leaders of all groups, Turks and Daylamites alike. Once again, the wealth of the ruler of Fārs provided a striking contrast to the poverty of the Baghdad government. The Daylamī troops in the city mutinied and went over to Sharaf al-Dawla, hoping, no doubt, that he would prove to be a more reliable paymaster. Sharaf al-Dawla's change of policy seemed to have been vindicated, his Iraqi supporters were restored to their estates and honours and the unfortunate Ṣamṣām al-Dawla deported to Fārs, where, in a remote prison near Sīrāf, he was blinded. But Sharaf al-Dawla's success in reuniting his father's domains was short-lived; after just two years and eight months in Baghdad, he died in 380/990 aged only twenty-eight, and the whole question of the leadership became open again.

Before his death, Sharaf al-Dawla had sent his young son Abū 'Alī to Fārs as the governor, but the latter was rejected by the notables of the province, led by the *wazīr* al-'Alā b. al-Ḥasan, who were determined to have a prince who was responsive to their own local concerns. They turned, perhaps surprisingly, to the blind prisoner of Sīrāf, Ṣamṣām al-Dawla, who was released and restored as prince, only in Fārs this time, not Baghdad. Meanwhile in Baghdad, a third son of 'Aḍud al-Dawla, Fīrūz, was proclaimed as Bahā' al-Dawla. Inevitably, the supporters of the two princes began the struggle for control of the rich border areas of Ahwāz and Khūzistān. The fighting was made more bitter by increasing polarization between Turks and Daylamites. Al-'Alā b. al-Ḥasan had secured the accession of Ṣamṣām al-Dawla in Fārs by relying almost exclusively on Daylamite support, obliging many Turks to go into exile in Baghdad. At first, a settlement was patched up which allowed Ṣamṣām al-Dawla to keep Fārs and Arrajān, while Ahwāz was to pass to Bahā' al-Dawla, but Ṣamṣām al-Dawla's Daylamite followers could not allow so rich a prize to slip from their grasp, and three years later, in 383/993, the army of Fārs took possession of the province. The Turks of

Baghdad counterattacked and the Daylamites were driven out with great slaughter. This produced a further reaction in Fārs, where the remaining Turks were driven out or massacred. Thus by 385/995, the army in Fārs was almost entirely composed of Daylamites, commanded by their new and forceful leader, Abū 'Alī b. Ustādh-hurmuz, while in Iraq and Baghdad the Daylamites had lost all influence, and Bahā' al-Dawla was totally dependent on the Turks. The struggle continued with Ibn Ustādh-hurmuz taking Ahwāz for the Daylamites in 387/997, but the next year, 388/998, the whole situation was changed again when Ṣamṣām al-Dawla died, aged only thirty-five, leaving Bahā' al-Dawla as the only survivor of 'Aḍud al-Dawla's sons.

In Fārs, there was confusion, but in Ahwāz, Ibn Ustādh-hurmuz took the decisive step of bringing his Daylamites over to the cause of Bahā' al-Dawla, despite their anxieties about the intentions of Bahā' al-Dawla's Turkish followers. A detailed settlement was worked out by Bahā' al-Dawla's *wazīr*, Abū 'Alī b. Ismā'īl, called al-Muwaffaq, between the leaders of the Turks and Daylamites to divide and distribute the valuable *iqṭā's* of the disputed area, and the major cause of conflict was thus resolved. The adherence of Ibn Ustādh-hurmuz to Bahā' al-Dawla had changed the military balance decisively, and al-Muwaffaq was able to enter Shīrāz without any real opposition. Here, he undertook a radical review of the *iqṭā's* in the province, redistributing them among the Daylamites. The next year, he went on to Kirmān, where again he reformed the *iqṭā'* system, cancelling all existing grants and replacing them with salaries. So Bahā' al-Dawla succeeded to the inheritance of his father in Shīrāz as well as Baghdad. As a result of the work of al-Muwaffaq and Ibn Ustādh-hurmuz, rather than his own efforts, he could now count on a reformed army, a reformed system of payment which put more emphasis on salaries and at least comparative harmony between Turks and Daylamites. Bahā' al-Dawla was able to settle in Fārs in 388/998; he never left the province again and died in 403/1012, but thanks to the work of his ministers, he was able to exercise almost unchallenged control over Fārs, Kirmān and parts, at least, of Iraq.

In the northern and central areas of Iraq, the Buyid government came under increasing pressure from the bedouin. Since its conquest by 'Aḍud al-Dawla in 369/979, Mosul had always been on the fringes of the Buyid domains, and in the confusion which followed his death, the position deteriorated rapidly. Control over the Mosul countryside was effectively lost by 379/990 when the governor was forced to grant extensive *iqṭā's* to the 'Uqaylī tribe, while the city itself was finally abandoned in 386/996 when it was taken over by the ambitious 'Uqaylī chief al-Muqallad b. al-Musayyib. Thereafter, 'Uqaylī power spread well to the south, and the towns of the Baghdad countryside like Kūfa and Anbār were often under their control. Al-Muqallad, shortly before his death in 391/1001, even attempted to take Baghdad itself. The only effective opposition to the 'Uqaylī advance came not from the Buyid authorities in Baghdad, but from the rival Asadī tribe of the Ḥilla area under the leadership of the Mazyadid family. Things were no better to the east of Baghdad, where the country and the road to the Iranian plateau were now dominated by the Shādhinjānī Kurds under the leadership of the ʿAnnazid family.

This meant that from about 386/996 onwards, Baghdad was very much an island of Buyid control in a countryside dominated by powerful bedouin tribes. If only for reasons of prestige, however, Bahāʾ al-Dawla was anxious to hold on to it, and in this aim he was aided by two remarkable and efficient governors, both brought up in the administrative traditions of ʿAḍud al-Dawla, who made a real effort to restore peace and sound government to the troubled city. The first of these was Abū ʿAlī b. Ustādh-hurmuz, the Daylamite leader who had come over to Bahāʾ al-Dawla after Ṣamṣām al-Dawla's death. In 392/1002, he entered Baghdad and immediately set about restoring order to the city. He laid special stress on the abolition of provocative religious activities and the crushing of bandits and robbers, who had been the scourge of the town. His prestige and experience as the leader of the Daylamites ensured that he had the military support to do this. His attitude was summed up in the drowning of leading brigands of the ʿAbbasid and ʿAlid factions, tied together in death. After his death in 401/1010, he was succeeded by his *wazīr*, Fakhr al-Mulk, who continued in his tradition. A notable patron of culture, he secured a measure of peace in the city until after the death of Bahāʾ al-Dawla in 403/1012.

The death of Bahāʾ al-Dawla in Shīrāz undermined the position of Fakhr al-Mulk in Baghdad, and in 407/1016 his son and successor Sulṭān al-Dawla was prevailed on to have him executed. This marked the end of the comparative peace which the city had enjoyed since the arrival of Ibn Ustādh-hurmuz fifteen years before and the beginning of a long and destructive period of civil strife. Once again, the root causes of the trouble were the tensions between the Turks and the Daylamites and the financial problems of Baghdad. Sulṭān al-Dawla in Fārs was dependent on Daylamite support, and he sent, as the governor of Baghdad, a Daylamite commander, Ibn Ṣāliḥān, with a large number of troops. The Turks in the city resented this and appealed to Sulṭān al-Dawla to come from Shīrāz in person, which he did, but the experiment was not a success, as he was too closely tied to the Daylamite interest. In 412/1021, it was agreed that Baghdad should be ruled by his younger brother, Musharrif al-Dawla, while he returned to Shīrāz. There followed a period of sporadic warfare until Sulṭān al-Dawla died in 412/1021 of drink at the age of thirty-two, to be followed six months later by his brother Musharrif al-Dawla.

The war between Sulṭān al-Dawla and Musharrif al-Dawla marked another stage in the decline of the Baghdad amirate as the city was now deprived of any financial aid from Fārs and Ahwāz, and Musharrif al-Dawla was dependent on the half-ruined cities of Baghdad and Wāsit. and the ravaged countryside immediately surrounding them. After his death, the Turks of Baghdad were faced with a choice. They could accept the sovereignty of Abū Kālījār Marzbān, the new Buyid ruler in Shīrāz; this would have the advantage that he would probably be able to pay their salaries but the disadvantage that he would exercise his authority through the Daylamite troops who served him in Fārs; and he made it clear, on the advice of his Fārsī *wazīr*, that he would not repeat his predecessor's mistake and come and settle in Baghdad. The other possibility open to the Turks was that they should appoint a Buyid *amīr* of their own. Such an *amīr* would be obliged to look after their interests as far as possible, but his financial resources would be extremely limited. Morale among the Turks seems to have been very low and discipline virtually nonexistent. They produced no leader of the calibre of Sabuktakīn and even when they wanted to, they seem to have been unable to maintain order. From 421/1030 to 425/1034, the city was terrorized by a bandit known as al-Burjumī and neither the Turks nor their chosen *amīr*, Jalāl al-Dawla, was able to put an end to his depredations. In the end, it was the 'Uqaylī bedouin leader, Qirwāsh, who captured and drowned him; there could hardly be a clearer indication of the shift in the centre of power from the city to the nomad camp.

After Musharrif al-Dawla's death, the Turks had begun by accepting the authority of Abū Kālījār of Fārs, but when he refused to come to Baghdad, they turned instead to his uncle, Jalāl al-Dawla, who arrived in the city in 416/1025 and remained *amīr*, with interruptions, until his death in 435/1044. It was not a happy time, either for the city or for the *amīr*. The continued economic decline of the city led to the further growth of organized crime, often conducted by groups of *'ayyārūn* claiming to represent the Sunnī or Shī'ī party, while government policing effectively ceased to exist. Physically, the city was divided into different quarters, each fortified and separated from the others by stretches of uninhabited ruins. The poverty of the city was reflected in the penury of its unhappy *amīr*, unable to pay even his personal servants and forced in 422/1031 to dismiss his attendants and set his horses loose, since he could no longer afford salaries for the former or fodder for the latter. He was treated by the Turks with open contempt, but they made no effort to produce an *amīr* from their own ranks.

The last decades of Buyid rule in Baghdad, despite the political chaos, witnessed a religious development which was to affect the whole subsequent history of Islam: the so-called Sunnī revival. This was not, in fact, so much of a revival as the formulation and definition of Sunnism in response to the contemporary emergence of *imāmī* (Twelver) Shi'ism. While Shi'ism was intermittently patronized by the Buyids and their representatives in Baghdad, the lead in the elaboration of Sunnism was taken by the 'Abbasid caliph.

Since Mu'izz al-Dawla had deposed al-Mustakfī in 334/946, the 'Abbasid caliphs had had a negligible effect on public life. Pampered but powerless, al-Muṣī' (334–363/946–974) and al-Ṭā'i' (363–381/974–991) had been almost entirely confined to their vast palace complex on the east bank of the Tigris in Baghdad, providing legitimacy for the regime by rubber-stamping its appointments. In 381/991, Bahā' al-Dawla, then resident in Baghdad, deposed al-Ṭā'i', who he felt was becoming obstreperous, and appointed instead his cousin, who took the title of al-Qādir. At first, he was content to do Bahā' al-Dawla's bidding, but when the Buyid *amīr* moved to Shīrāz, al-Qādir was able to take a more positive part in public affairs. As has already been explained, popular feelings between Shī'īs and their opponents had been growing in Baghdad, despite the efforts of Ibn Ustādh-hurmuz and others to suppress them. In 394/1003, Bahā' al-Dawla was rash enough to propose a leading 'Alid, Abū Aḥmad al-Mūsawī, as chief *qāḍī* in Baghdad. For the first time, the 'Abbasid caliph put himself at the head of the popular protest and, successfully, refused to accept the nomination. Thereafter, he began to defend the cause of the Traditionists against the claims of Twelver Shi'ism. He did, however, find common ground with the Buyids in his opposition to the claims of the Fatimids, and when Qirwāsh b. al-Muqallad, the 'Uqaylī chief, proclaimed his allegiance to the Fatimids in 401/1010, he responded by putting pressure on Bahā' al-Dawla, who obliged the bedouin chief to accept the 'Abbasids once again. Interestingly for the future, al-Qādir took the opportunity to issue a decree, attacking both Fatimid ideology and the genealogy by which the Fatimids claimed descent from 'Alī. In this way, he established himself as a spokesman for both Sunnīs and Twelver Shī'īs.

The death of Bahā' al-Dawla allowed him more scope. In 409/1018, he took a major step, issuing a decree which condemned Mu'tazilism and Shi'-ism and asserted that the Companions of the Prophet and all of the first four caliphs should be venerated by true Muslims. These doctrines were repeated and elaborated in 420/1029 when the doctrine of the createdness of the Qur'ān was explicitly condemned. This creed, the so-called *Risālā al-Qāādiriyya*, marks a fundamental development for two reasons, first because Sunnism was defined explicitly and positively. Hitherto, the supporters of the Sunna had largely been defined by their opposition to the claims of the Twelver Shī'īs; now there was a body of positive belief which had to be accepted by anyone claiming to be a Sunnī. Like the Twelver doctrines developed during the previous century, it was exclusive; the acceptance of the veneration of the first four caliphs meant rejecting the claims of the Twelvers that 'Alī had been unjustly deprived of the caliphate. It was no longer possible to be simply a Muslim; one was either a Sunnī or a Shīī.

The second important development was that the 'Abbasid caliph had emerged as a spokesman for the Sunnīs. It is fair to say that the early 'Abbasid caliphs were not, in the modern sense, Sunnīs; indeed, the whole 'Abbasid claim to the caliphate was dependent on a recognition that the Family of the Prophet had a unique claim to leadership. They usually opposed the claims of the 'Alids to political power, but that did not make them Sunnīs. From the time of al-Ma'mūn, with the notable exception of al-Mutawakkil, they had espoused or sympathized with the Mu'tazilī doctrines which al-Qādir explicitly condemned. By his action, al-Qādir had become the champion of the Sunnīs and Traditionists against the claims of Twelver Shī'īs and Fatimids alike. He had also created a new and lasting role for the 'Abbasid caliphate. As Ja'far al-Ṣādiq had shown in the second/eighth century that it was possible to be an *imām* from the house of ʿAlī without taking an active role in politics or making claims to the caliphate, al-Qādir showed that there was a religious role for the ʿAbbasid caliphs, a role which they could fulfil even if their temporal power was nonexistent.

Al-Qādir was able to take this position because he had more political independence. To begin with, the Buyid amirate of Baghdad had become so weak that it could not afford to take action against the caliph. He could also count on a large body of support in Baghdad itself. The people might not fight to restore the political power of the ʿAbbasid caliph but many of them would support the Sunnī cause against the pretensions of the Shīʿa. In addition, he received powerful moral support from the eastern Islamic world. From 388/998 until his death in 421/1030, the leading power in Iran was Maḥmūd of Ghazna. He was a fierce opponent of the Buyids on a political level, but he also gave a religious dimension to the conflict by accusing them of being heretics and claiming that he was the champion of Sunnī Islam. He established himself as the protector of the *ḥajj*, a role traditionally played by the leaders of the Muslim community. This moral support from the east enabled al-Qādir to distance himself from the Buyids. But this did not lead to direct political power. By the time of his death, al-Qādir had established his moral and religious authority, but the ʿAbbasid caliph had no troops to command and no land to call his own beyond the gates of his palace. His final act, however, was to appoint his own successor without reference to the Buyids – perhaps the first time since the death of al-Muktafī in 289/902 that the ʿAbbasid caliph had been able to do this.

Al-Qādir's son, who took the title of al-Qā'im, survived the last, melancholy days of the Buyid amirate of Baghdad and remained in office until his death in 467/1075, long after the Seljuk conquest. He seems to have continued the lines of policy laid down by his father, reiterating his religious decrees. It is noticeable, however, that he was the first ʿAbbasid since before the Buyid period to have a *wazīr* of his own, another sign that the caliph's influence was slowly expanding.

Jalāl al-Dawla continued as *amīr* until his death in 435/1044 at the age of fifty-one, comparatively old for a Buyid prince, many of whom died in their twenties and thirties. After this, control was briefly assumed by Abū Kālījār of Shīrāz and for the last time the resources of Fārs sustained Buyid government in Baghdad. But when he died in 440/1048, the last vestiges of effective rule disappeared and the last traces of the Buyids were soon to be swept away by the Seljuk onslaught.

The last decades of Buyid rule in Fārs are shrouded in obscurity and it is very difficult to gauge the state of the country. However, lack of evidence may not necessarily be a sign of decline. Buyid rule in Fārs survived after Buyid rule in al-Jibāl had vanished, and Buyid government in Baghdad had been reduced to a shambles. In 403/1012, Bahā' al-Dawla died in Arrajān at the age of forty-two. He had appointed as his successor his son, who took the title of Sulṭān al-Dawla and established himself in Shīrāz. Of his reign in

Fārs (403–412/1012–1021), little is known and it seems to have passed peacefully. Kirmān was the only part of the Buyid possessions in southern Iran not under his direct control, and it was entrusted to his uncle Abu'l-Fawāris Qiwām al-Dawla. This separation led to the only serious disturbance of the reign when in 407/1016–1017 Abu'l-Fawāris was supported by the rising power of Maḥmūd of Ghazna in the east. Maḥmūd was now strong enough to intervene in Buyid succession disputes, a warning of things to come, for it was Maḥmūd who put an end to the Buyid kingdom of Rayy in 420/1029. This time, however, he was unsuccessful and Sulṭān al-Dawla was able to reestablish his position in Shīrāz without great difficulty.

Sulṭān al-Dawla's death produced another of the family conflicts which dominated Buyid political life. The Daylamite soldiery of Shīrāz expressed their preference for Abu'l-Fawāris over Sulṭān al-Dawla's son, Abū Kālījār, then ruling in Baṣra. At first, Abu'l-Fawāris was successful, but Abū Kālījār counterattacked and drove his uncle out. The most significant feature of the episode is the way in which the Buyid contenders were cynically manipulated by the Daylamites, anxious to squeeze as much money as possible out of them; when the Daylamites decided that there should be peace, the rival princes were obliged to agree and Abū Kālījār was left in possession of Fārs while his uncle retired to Kirmān. In a final effort to restore his position, Abu'l-Fawāris turned to the Kurds and recruited an army of 10,000 of them. Up to this point, the Kurdish population of Fārs, in contrast to those farther north in the Zagros, had played little part in politics, but from this time onwards, they became more active, and it was they who, in the end, were responsible for ending Buyid control of the area.

Despite this inauspicious beginning, Abū Kālījār's long reign in Fārs (415–440/1024–1048) was on the whole a period of peace. Like his predecessors, he ruled in partnership with the local bureaucratic élite, notably al-'Adil Bahrām b. al-Māfinnā from Kāzirūn. Bahrām was the last of the great Buyid *wazīrs*. Like some of his predecessors, he was not just a skilled administrator but also a patron of culture. He founded a large library at Fīrūzābād and was the patron of the historian Hilāl b. al-Muḥassin al-Ṣābī, to whose work, now mostly lost, we owe much of our knowledge of the later Buyid period. On his death in 433/1041–1042, he was replaced by a member of the Fasānjas family who had supported the Buyids since 'Alī b. Būya had arrived in Fārs more than a century before.

In external affairs, the power of Buyid Fārs remained impressive. In 419/1028, Abu'l-Fawāris died and Abū Kālījār was able to take over that province. In 422/1031, Kirmān was attacked by the formidable Maḥmūd of Ghazna but the Daylamite garrison, aided by the *wazīr* Bahrām, were able to drive him off. 'Umān, too, remained a Fārsī protectorate under the control of a Fārsī bureaucratic family. In Iraq, Abū Kālījār extended his authority over Baṣra and Wāsit. and even, in the end, Baghdad from 435/1044 onwards, although he made little attempt to solve the almost impossible problems of governing the city.

The last years of the reign were marked by growing threats, both internal and external. The power of Maḥmūd of Ghazna was replaced by the more insidious and continuous pressure of Ghuzz Turks, and this migration was more difficult to resist than the more conventional forces of the Ghaznavids. These pressures led to a resurgence of Kurdish activity. Kurdish tribes displaced from the Iṣfahān area by the advancing Turks were driven down to Fārs, and the authorities were unable to prevent them settling. The local Kurds, too, began to take over towns and villages, and one of them, Faḍlūya b. 'Alī of the Shabānkāra, became a virtual ruler of the province after the death of Abū Kālījār. These changes, and the apparent inability of the Daylamī troops of the Buyids to counter them, were probably the reason why Abū Kālījār found it necessary to fortify Shīrāz from 436/1044 onwards. When he died in 440/1048 on an expedition to subdue a rebel Daylamī commander in Kirmān, he was succeeded in theory by his young son, but in reality the forces which he had succeeded in keeping at bay swept over Fārs and destroyed not only his heirs but the whole Daylamī–Fārsī establishment and much of the prosperity of the country. When Ibn al-Balkhī came to describe Fārs in the next century, his account was full of cities which had existed under the Buyids but were now laid waste, relics of a golden age when Fārs had been the wealthy centre of an empire.

The Buyid kingdom of Rayy

The Buyid kingdom of Rayy and al-Jibāl was in many ways separate from the kingdoms of Fārs and Iraq. While the affairs of the latter provinces were closely intertwined, the political history of Rayy was determined by other considerations. 'Aḍud al-Dawla, Bahā' al-Dawla and Abū Kālījār all ruled both Fārs and Iraq but none of them ruled Rayy, Hamadhān and Iṣfahān, which always had their own sovereigns. The political history of the third kingdom is dominated by external threats to its existence. Until the accession of Fakhr al-Dawla in 366/977, the most serious threat had come from the Samanids of Khurāsān to the east, who considered, with some historical justification, that Rayy was a rightful part of their domains. On at least three occasions, the last one being in 357/967, Samanid armies attempted to take Rayy, but each time they were defeated. The Samanid threat was especially dangerous since they allied with the hereditary enemies of the Buyid family, the Ziyarid rulers of Ṭabaristān and Jurjān. The Ziyarids were the family of Mardāvīj b. Ziyār, the Daylamite ruler of central Iran who had been murdered in 323/935, opening the way for the Buyid takeover. His family were driven to take refuge in the mountainous areas to the southeast of the Caspian Sea but they never gave up their claim to authority in Rayy. Mardāvīj's brother Vushmgīr (d. 356/967) and his successors Bīsutūn (d. 367/978) and Qābūs (d. 402/1012) pursued their ambitions with the aid of the Samanids and other enemies of the Buyids. While never strong enough by themselves to challenge Buyid control, allied with others they were a major threat, especially dangerous because they represented a rival focus for the loyalty of the Daylamites. The decline of the Samanids in the later fourth/tenth century did not free the Buyids from threats from the east. The rising power of the Ghaznavids and the immigration of the Ghuzz Turkmen were to undermine the power of the Daylamites and in 420/1029 Rayy itself fell to Maḥmūd.

In the face of these external threats, the Buyids of Rayy and al-Jibāl looked for sources of strength nearer home. Their army, of which we know very little, seems to have been composed almost entirely of Daylamites, and there is no indication that they recruited large numbers of Turks, as did Buyid rulers in other areas. To supply these troops, they were dependent on the cooperation of the traditional Daylamite ruling families, with whom they made marriage alliances, and the allies they acquired in this way were to be crucial in the success of their government. The first of these was ʿAlī b. Kāma (the son of Rukn al-Dawla's sister), who was the right-hand military man of both Rukn al-Dawla and Mu'ayyid al-Dawla and seems to have enjoyed great prestige among the Daylamites. He was put to death by Fakhr al-Dawla on his accession in 366/977, but Fakhr made his own network of Daylamī alliances. His mother came from a family of Daylamī princes and he married the daughter of the *Ispahbad* (prince) Sharvīn of Ṭabaristān. After his death, she became a virtual ruler of Rayy in the name of their young son, Majd al-Dawla. Her brother, Dushmanziyār, held office for the Buyids, while his son Muḥammad, known as Ibn Kākūya (or son of the maternal uncle) took over Iṣfahān in 398/1008 and became the independent ruler of the Iṣfahān–Hamadhān part of the kingdom. He was the founder of a dynasty which survived under Seljuk patronage until the sixth/twelfth century. These close relations with the Daylamite princes and the role played by marriage alliances were important factors in the resilience of the Buyids of Rayy in the face of threats from the east.

The Buyids were also on good terms with the Hasanuyid Kurds. Rukn al-Dawla scandalized his *wazīr* Ibn al-ʿAmīd the Elder by the lenient view he took of their depredations. Badr b. Ḥasanūya provided and led Kurdish troops in the armies of both Mu'ayyid al-Dawla and Fakhr al-Dawla, amounting in the latter case to 4,000 men, probably cavalry to complement the Daylamī infantry. After the death of Fakhr al-Dawla in 387/997, Badr came to Rayy to try to organize the affairs of the infant Majd al-Dawla, but his advice was rejected and he increasingly distanced himself from the affairs at Rayy. When the last Buyid ruler was threatened by Maḥmūd of Ghazna, he could no longer count on the Kurdish alliance which had sustained his father, uncle and grandfather.

Rukn al-Dawla relied from the beginning of his reign on the services of Ibn al-ʿAmīd, an administrator whose father had served Mardāvīj and Vushmgīr in Rayy. He served Rukn al-Dawla loyally until his death in 360/970, when he was succeeded by his son, also known as Ibn al-ʿAmīd. According to the hostile testimony of Miskawayh, the son lacked his father's circumspection and loyalty, made the mistake of trying to double-cross both Rukn al-Dawla and ʿAḍud al-Dawla to acquire a position with the ill-fated Bakhtiyār in Baghdad and was disgraced in 366/976–977. The most famous of all Buyid *wazīrs* was Ismāʿīl b. ʿAbbād, known as al-Ṣāḥīb (the master or boss) who served the Buyids of Rayy for a quarter of a century, from 360/-970–971 to 385/995.

The *wazīrs* of this period were general administrators rather than financial experts. They certainly arranged, or tried to arrange, the payment of armies but they also organized and participated in campaigns. They acted, too, as intermediaries between members of the Buyid family. In 365/976, Ibn al-ʿAmīd the Younger was responsible for arranging a reconciliation between his master Rukn al-Dawla and his son ʿAḍud al-Dawla in Fārs. When Mu'ayyid al-Dawla of Rayy died in 373/983, it was Ibn ʿAbbād who arranged that his brother Fakhr al-Dawla be invited from his refuge in Jurjān to take power. In more normal times, the *wazīrs* arranged government appointments and gave advice on the making of alliances and all sorts of administrative decisions, but it is as patrons of Arabic culture that they are chiefly remembered. The elder Ibn al-ʿAmīd was renowned for his knowledge of classical Arabic poetry, while Ibn ʿAbbād was the patron of Abū'l-Faraj al-Iṣfahānī – whose *Kitāb al-aghānī* (Book of Songs) is the most important record we have of early Arabic poetry and poets – besides being an accomplished Arabic stylist himself. The most important Muslim intellectual of his generation, Abū ʿAlī b. Sīnā (d. 428/1037), known in the West as Avicenna, served for the last nine years of his life as a *wazīr* to a member of the Buyid clan, the Kakuyid ruler of Iṣfahān and Hamadhān. Apart from ʿAḍud al-Dawla, the Buyid sovereigns were not themselves known as patrons of culture – it was their *wazīrs* who encouraged the great efflorescence of Arabic writing at this time.

For the purposes of political history, it is conventional to think of the Buyid *amīrs*, their *wazīrs* and their armies as the government, but this is in some ways a distorted picture. In many areas, the *amīrs*, with their very limited military forces, worked in partnership with local élites who owed their power to local circumstances rather than to appointment by the *amīr*. The local administration of one important provincial town in the Buyid kingdom of al-Jibāl, Qazvīn, has been studied in some detail.[3] Situated west of Rayy and at the southern edge of the Daylamī mountains, it was in early Islamic times an important fortress protecting the plains against the depredations of the still unconverted Daylamites. It may have been this role as a garrison city which accounts for the comparatively large number of people of Arab origin to be found there. After the Daylamite expansion, the city continued to be a centre of some importance without ever becoming an independent amirate. The Buyids, and the other dynasties who took over the town for short intervals, ruled in close cooperation with the local oligarchy. In the early Buyid period, the undisputed leaders of this oligarchy were from the ʿIjlīs, an Arab tribe which had colonized the Jibāl area extensively since the first century after the conquest. Under the ʿAbbasids, they had frequently been local governors, but under the Buyids they had the honorific unofficial title of *ra'īs*. Their supremacy was not unchallenged, and during the fifth/eleventh century, they were effectively supplanted by the leaders of a family connected with the ʿAlids, the Jaʿfarīs, whose power may have been built up by the Buyids. Along with the *ra'īs*, the other major local figure was the *qāḍī*, always chosen from one of the leading local families, and while his appointment was endorsed by the administration in Rayy, the real power of selection must have lain with the local community leaders.

It appears that sometimes there was a Daylamī military officer posted in the town. We have the diploma of appointment written for one of these by al-Ṣāḥib Ibn ʿAbbād, the *wazīr* of Mu'ayyid al-Dawla in Rayy. He was given widespread powers over the civil administration and the maintenance of law and order, but it is not clear that these extensive powers were normally invested in the *amīr*. Indeed, it is significant that he is the only *amīr* of Qazvīn in the period whose name has come down to us. Neither this patent, nor the various measures taken to suppress riots and civil disturbance in the city suggests that there was a regular Daylamī garrison of any importance, and the maintenance of law and order seems to have been the responsibility of a militia (*aḥdāth*) probably recruited locally. There does not seem to be any mention of a government-appointed tax collector, and we must assume that the collection of the sums demanded by Rayy was the responsibility of local leaders. This suggests decentralized government, heavily dependent on the cooperation of local élites. For the man in Qazvīn bazaar, the real and effective government must have been vested in local officials, the *ra'īs* and the *qāḍī*, while the comings and goings of *amīrs* and their retinues were probably marginal to the day-to-day administration. The government required taxes and a basic minimum of law and order. As long as these were maintained, it had little further interest in the area.

The Buyid period is often considered a confusing and largely negative period in Islamic history. This is not really fair. It is true that the dynasty did not supply the strong centralized government historians tend to admire, but the way local urban élites and tribes worked out a measure of autonomy within the general framework of Buyid rule may actually have benefited most people much more than strong government and the fierce taxation which inevitably went with it. It is true that there were many wars, but it must be remembered that armies were small, much smaller than those of the early ʿAbbasid period or of the Seljuk Turks, and the wars do not seem to have been very destructive. There are few mentions of sieges – rather, encounters between princes and their bands of followers in open country, and the warfare was probably more similar to the baronial wars of eleventh- and twelfth-century France than to the great campaigns of previous centuries. The great failure of the dynasty was the failure to secure the prosperity and stability of Iraq, but this was a problem whose origins went back before Buyid times and whose solution was probably beyond the powers of any contemporary government. In central Iran, and above all in Fārs, Buyid rule seems to have been an era of prosperity and development, an era brought to a premature close by the influx of the Ghuzz Turkmen in the middle of the fifth/eleventh century.

Notes

1 R. Mottahedeh, *Loyalty and leadership in an early Islamic society* (Princeton 1980), p. 81.
2 *Tajārib al-Umam*, ed. H. Amedroz, II, Oxford 1920–, p. 328.
3 R. Mottahedeh, "Administration in Būyid Qazwīn", in D. S. Richards (ed.), *Islamic civilisation 950–1150* (Oxford 1975), pp. 33–45.

10 The Kurds

The Daylamīs were the most conspicuous of the indigenous peoples of eastern and central Iran to take advantage of the weakening of ʿAbbasid government, but they were not the only ones. The Kurds, a people with their own language and culture distinct from Arabs and Persians, had inhabited much of the area of the Zagros Mountains and the uplands to the north of Mosul for many centuries before the coming of Islam. Like the Daylamīs, however, they had played only a marginal part in the politics of the Islamic state until the fourth/tenth century, being mentioned as rebels or mercenaries in the chronicles. The failure of central government, coinciding with the spread of Islam among the Kurdish tribes, however, allowed the emergence of a number of independent Kurdish principalities alongside of, and sometimes in competition with, the Daylamite ones. This Kurdish efflorescence survived until the coming of the Ghuzz Turkmen in the 430s/1040s, who sought to take over their pastures and effectively squeezed them out of many of their traditional areas.

In the mid-fourth/tenth century, the Kurds were distributed all along the Zagros chain from Fārs in the south to Āzarbayjān and the Araxes river in the north. They were also influential in southeastern Anatolia as far west as Āmid, and we even hear of Kurdish leaders in the mountains of northern Syria at the time of the Hamdanids. The geographer Ibn Ḥawqal describes the Kurds as the bedouin of Iran, and it would appear that they were largely sheep-rearing transhumants who exploited the pastures of the high Zagros in the summer and the lowland plains of eastern Iraq in the winter. They must have lived very much like their Turkish successors in the southern Zagros, the Qashqāʾī and the Bakhtiyārī, do today, each group occupying a summer pasturage and a winter area and the route through the mountains connecting them. The Hadhbānī Kurds, one of the most powerful tribes in the period, are described as spending the summer in Āzarbayjān around the area of Salmās, northeast of Lake Urmiyya, and the winter on the plains along the Greater and Lesser Zāb rivers east of Mosul. Interestingly, the winter pastures of the Hadhbānī Kurds were the same as the summer pastures of the Shaybānī Arabs, who would move in from the desert to be near the permanent water supply provided by the rivers, a clear example of the

DOI: 10.4324/9780429348129-10

complementary role of these two pastoral peoples. Not all Kurds, however, were transhumant shepherds, and their leaders often seem to have maintained fortresses along the migration routes where their valuables were kept and where they could take refuge at the time of danger. There were Kurdish populations in many of the small towns of the mountain area like Shahrazūr and Salmās, and there were also Kurds who lived in villages. The Marwanid rulers of Mayyāfāriqīn came from a family who were headmen of a village near Sī'ird (modern Siirt).

The Kurdish dynasties which emerged in the second half of the fourth/tenth century, the Hasanuyids and 'Annazids of the central Zagros, the Rawwadids and Shaddadids of Āzarbayjān and the Marwanids of south-eastern Anatolia, based their power on the military prowess of the Kurdish tribesmen. They never needed to employ Turkish *ghilmān*, as the Buyids did, because they provided mounted soldiers from their own ranks. They also changed the political geography of the area: the 'Abbasid, Buyid and Hamdanid regimes were all based in cities and their surrounding agricultural land. By contrast, the power of the Kurdish rulers, with the exception of the Shaddadids, was based on their control of the transhumance routes, and it was the valleys of the Zagros and anti-Taurus which formed the nucleus of these states, not because they were rich and fertile and produced high tax yields, but because it was there that the tribesmen passed on their biannual migrations. In the Zagros, the power of the chiefs was based in fortresses which commanded the routes and in which they kept their treasure, not in the major towns. The relationship of the Hasanuyids with the town of Hamadhān, like the relationship of the Marwanids with Āmid or the Shaddadids with Dwin and Ganja, was based on indirect influence rather than direct control; the Shaddadids and the Marwanids especially established close links with local, non-Kurdish urban élites. The administration of the Kurdish states tended to be very basic; the Marwanids employed *wazīrs* but there is no indication that the other groups employed any bureaucrats at all: the cities paid an agreed tribute and for the rest, the traditional mechanisms of tribal authority were sufficient. The *Ḥimāya* (protection agreement) was the underlying basis of government.

There were large numbers of Kurds in the province of Fārs, but, perhaps because Fārs was such an important Buyid base, they seem to have played little part in politics before the breakdown of government at the end of Abū Kālījār's reign. Further north, however, Kurdish principalities came to dominate the most important of all the routes through the Zagros, the road from Hamadhān to Ḥulwān, the great road between Khurāsān and Baghdad which had been so important in 'Abbasid history. The first of these states to achieve independence was based in the area around Qarmīsīn (Kirmānshāh). From 350/961, the chief of the Barzikānī Kurds of this area was Ḥasanūya b. al-Ḥusayn. He consolidated his position by maintaining close relations with the Buyids of Rayy, helping them against the Samanid threat from the east. Soon, he began to use his position to encroach on the settled areas around

Hamadhān and demand protection money from the people of the area, and when the governor tried to prevent him, Ḥasanūya used force to intimidate him. Rukn al-Dawla's veteran *wazīr* Ibn al-ʿAmīd led an army to crush him, but in 360/970 during the course of the campaign, the *wazīr* died and his son was prepared to make peace, allowing Ḥasanūya virtual independence in return for a tribute of 50,000 *dīnārs* a year. Rukn al-Dawla seems to have been reluctant to take strong measures against his ally, and Ḥasanūya's power in the area was effectively unchallenged until his death in 369/979 in a fortress at Sarmāj, near the celebrated "Gates of Asia" at Bīsitūn on the road from Iraq to Iran as it passed through the mountains.

Ḥasanūya's numerous sons began to dispute his inheritance, some looking for support from Fakhr al-Dawla in Rayy, others from ʿAḍud al-Dawla, now firmly in control in Baghdad. ʿAḍud al-Dawla, pursuing his centralizing policies here as elsewhere, sought to use the dispute to assert his control in the area. He besieged and took the castle at Sarmāj and established his protégé, Badr b. Ḥasanūya, in the inheritance at the expense of his brothers, most of whom were killed. The death of his patron in 372/983 left Badr in authority in the district, and he reigned virtually unchallenged until his death in 405/1014. Like ʿAḍud al-Dawla, he is held up by the chroniclers as a model ruler, particularly in his defence of the settled cultivators against his own nomad supporters, while he sought to increase the prosperity of his followers by opening a market in Hamadhān, the main regional centre, whose profits, estimated at 1.2 million *dirhams* per year, would pass to him. Badr was even in a position to finance the *Ḥajj* from Iraq and pay for its protection on the pilgrimage road, a role which brought him considerable prestige and which was taken over after his death by the great Maḥmūd of Ghazna. In political terms, this power enabled him to play an important part in the politics of the Buyid kingdom of Rayy, especially after the death of Fakhr al-Dawla in 387/997 (see above, p. 244). His power remained firmly based on his tribal following and his mountain castles. He was influential in Hamadhān, where he kept an agent but never ruled the city directly. At Rayy, he could provide valuable support for any of the factions struggling to control the young Buyid prince, Majd al-Dawla, and was able to send 3,000 horsemen to support Ibrāhīm al-Ḍabbī when he sought reinstatement as *wazīr* in 392/1002, but typically, he exercised his power at a distance, not going to Rayy or playing any part in court life himself. His career illustrates both the opportunities open to an able and astute tribal leader and the limitations on his power. Badr was so successful because he never lost the support of his Kurdish followers or distanced himself from them to live in some urban centre.

The end of his life was marred by family strife and the emergence of a rival Kurdish power in the area, the ʿAnnazids. The ʿAnnazids were the leading clan of the Shādhinjān Kurds. They occupied lands farther down the road to Baghdad than the Barzikānīs who supported Badr, having their territories around Ḥulwān and Shahrazūr. The ʿAnnazids were bitter rivals of the Barzikānīs, probably because of disputed grazing rights in the

Zagros Mountains. As early as 343/954, we hear of one Abū'l-Shawk and his Shādhinjānī followers kidnapping Buyid government envoys from their base at Ḥulwān. At this time, they were suppressed by Mu'izz al-Dawla's general Sabuktakīn but they clearly remained powerful in the Ḥulwān area. Later, weaker Buyid governments were obliged to look to the Kurds for allies, and Bahā' al-Dawla (in Baghdad from 379/989) favoured the 'Annazid chief Abū'l-Fath. Muḥammad b. 'Annāz, who emerged as the ruler of Ḥulwān, which he was given as an *iqṭā'* with government support from 381/991. While Badr and his Barzikānī followers looked to Rayy and Hamadhān, the 'Annazids and their Shādhinjānī tribesmen were patronized by the Buyid authorities in Baghdad. As so often, local rulers were closely involved, for better or for worse, in rivalries between the various centres of Buyid power. When Bahā' al-Dawla took up residence in Shīrāz, Abu'l-Fath. remained on good terms with the governor he'd left behind in Baghdad, Abū Ja'far al-Ḥajjāj, joining him in campaigns against the 'Uqaylids. On the appointment of Ibn Ustādh-hurmuz to Baghdad in 392/1002, al-Ḥajjāj attempted to rally his friends to resist his successor, and Abū'l-Fath. joined him with both Kurdish and Shaybānī Arab followers. In the battle which ensued against the Mazyadid supporters of Ibn Ustādh-hurmuz, Abū'l-Fath. was deserted by the Shaybān and many Kurds but stood firm with 200 Shādhinjānī horsemen. After this reverse, he was soon won over by the new governor and the traditionally close relations between the 'Annazids and the Baghdad authorities were resumed. This alliance was to prove especially useful in 397/1006 when Badr dislodged Abū'l-Fath. from Ḥulwān and he was given both shelter and support in Baghdad.

Abū'l-Fath. died in 401/1010 and was succeeded by his son Abū'l-Shawk, under whom the power of the family reached its apogee. The success of the 'Annazids was largely due to the disasters which affected their main rival, Badr b. Ḥasanūya. Badr had quarrelled with his eldest son Hilāl and was only able to defeat him by calling on the support of the Buyid authorities in Hamadhān. He himself died in 405/1014, but his grandson Ṭāhir b. Hilāl, again with the support of the Hamadhān Buyids, attempted to regain his grandfather's position against the 'Annazids, who had taken advantage of the confusion to take the Barzikānī centre at Qarmīsīn. In the end, it was only the treacherous murder of Ṭāhir that saved the 'Annazid. Shortly afterwards, Shams al-Dawla, the Buyid ruler of Hamadhān, was defeated in person by Abū'l-Shawk. The result of the murder of Ṭāhir and the defeat of Shams al-Dawla was that the 'Annazids were now supreme in the central Zagros area, members of the ruling clan controlling not only Ḥulwān and Shahrazūr on the edge of the Iraqi plain but upland areas such as Dīnawar and, sometimes, Qarmīsīn. The Buyids of Baghdad were much too feeble to offer any serious challenge, while the Kakuyids who established themselves in Hamadhān were content to remain as neighbours.

As family feuds had been the undoing of Badr b. Ḥasanūya, so they were to be of the 'Annazids. The expansion of their territories meant that members of the family had acquired their own fortresses and interests. In 431/1040, a bitter dispute broke out between Abū'l-Shawk's son, called Abū'l-Fath. like his grandfather, and the chief's brother, Muhalhil. Once again, internal divisions led to outside intervention, Muhalhil turning to the Kakuyid 'Alā' al-Dawla, who took Dīnawar and Qarmīsīn, while Abū'l-Shawk appealed without much success to the feeble Jalāl al-Dawla of Baghdad. Some members of the family developed ties with other Kurdish groups, further dividing the clan. The 'Annazids developed no system of government or central control – no *wazīrs* are mentioned – and the expansion of the area under their control led inevitably to disintegration. It was thus a divided and weakened Kurdish tribe which faced the onslaught of the Turkmen from 437/1045 onwards, Abū'l-Shawk taking refuge in his fortresses while they ravaged his lands. Some members of the family, like Muhalhil, looked to the Seljuks as allies. The catastrophe of the mid-fifth/eleventh century was more than the fall of a dynasty; the Turkmen soon usurped the position of the Kurds, and never again was there to be an important Kurdish dynasty in the central Zagros area. None of the 'Annazids had proved as great a ruler as Badr b. ḥasanūya, but they had defended the position of their family and tribe in an uncertain and difficult time.

Farther north, the Kurds played an important part in the history of the rich and variegated province of Āzarbayjān. The geography of the area is confused, with towns and fertile plains being separated by areas of high mountains and steppe lands, of great importance since they offer reliable and extensive summer grazing, much sought after in the Middle East. The Islamic conquest seems to have made little impact on the area besides the establishment of a few garrison towns, notably the provincial capital at Ardabīl. In early 'Abbasid times, there was some Arab immigration and settlement in towns such as Tabrīz and Marand, but the settlers' numbers seem to have been limited and they were probably absorbed by the local population. By the fourth/tenth century, there is no record of any significant Arab presence. Until the time of the rebellion of Bābak (see above, p. 164), essentially a protest against outsiders coming into the province, most of the area seems to have been inhabited by indigenous cultivators speaking a variety of different languages. The systematic and drawn-out campaigns of al-Afshīn (220–222/835–837) crushed the local resistance. The defeat of Bābak does not seem to have resulted in any large-scale settlement of outsiders, but al-Afshīn probably left some forces in the area, since during the anarchy at Sāmarrā a leader from his home country of Ushrūsana, called Abū'l-Sāj Dīwdād, took over the province. On his death in 279/892, he was succeeded by two of his sons, in turn: Muḥammad, who was appointed by the 'Abbasid Caliph al-Mu'tamid to rule Āzarbayjān and took the title of al-Afshīn (the hereditary title of the princes of Ushrūsanā'), and then, from 288/901 Yūsuf. At the beginning of al-Muqtadir's reign (295/908), the *wazīr*, Ibn al-Furāt, attempted to regularize the position, offering Yūsuf b. Abī'l-Sāj complete control in Āzarbayjān and Armenia in exchange for a fairly modest tribute of 120,000 *dīnārs* per year.

Ibn Abī'l-Sāj was, however, an ambitious man, anxious to play a part in the politics of the caliphate. He was a warlord, pure and simple. His polity had no ethnic or ideological foundations. His project was based on securing enough resources to pay a mercenary army to defend it and when Ibn Abī'l-Sāj perished, his enterprise perished with him. The Christian princes of Armenia to the west were the victims of his aggression, and he cast covetous eyes on the province of Rayy to the east as well, claiming (falsely, it would appear) that the *wazīr* 'Alī b. 'Īsā had assigned it to him. He even offered to pay 700,000 *dīnārs* a year for this expanded dominion, but the caliph refused to accept this and a military expedition was sent under Mu'nis, which led eventually in 307/919 to his capture and removal to Baghdad. There, his followers seem to have been given jobs, since from that time onwards, we find his nephew acting to maintain law and order in Baghdad and a new regiment of Sājī troops being stationed in the capital, while in Āzarbayjān a follower of his called Sabuk took over the administration. At the court of the caliph, pro- and anti-Sajid groups emerged in the administration among those who felt that the service of so powerful a figure should be used to serve the government and those who felt he should be crushed. After three years of detention, he was allowed to return to Āzarbayjān, while the Sajid troops became an integral part of the Baghdad army. Four years later in 314/926, the caliphate was faced by a crisis in the shape of the attacks of the Qarāmiṭa on Iraq, attacks which the existing army seemed quite unable to deal with. In this extremity, the *wazīr* al-Khaṣībī persuaded Ibn Abī'l-Sāj to come to Iraq, not this time as a prisoner but as a much needed ally. Furthermore, he was given very extensive financial privileges, including the revenues of all the eastern provinces except Iṣfahān and Fārs, which were to be assigned to him to pay his army, a degree of financial control which even the most prominent of the Baghdad generals, Mu'nis, had never been allowed.

In the event, the Sajid troops, used to fighting in the mountainous terrain of their native Āzarbayjān, were unable to face the Qarāmiṭa along the fringes of the desert. Ibn Abī'l-Sāj was captured and, after a short captivity which he endured with calmness and dignity, was executed. His career illustrates a stage in the disintegration of the caliphate. While his power was based on the revenues of Āzarbayjān and the soldiers he could raise there, he was, like the Tahirids, Ibn Ṭūlūn and Nāṣir al-Dawla the Hamdanid, closely involved in the politics of the caliphate. To think of him as an independent ruler is misleading; like many of his contemporaries, he was very much a product of 'Abbasid administration, rather than a local man with local roots. In the next generation, the people who tried to rule Āzarbayjān were all native to the province and few of them made any effort to play a role beyond its confines.

The death of Ibn Abi'l-Sāj left something of a power vacuum in the province, especially as so many of his supporters had gone to join the Sajid army in Iraq. In these circumstances, two different groups attempted to dominate the province – the Kurds and the Daylamites. The Kurds seem to have predominated in the west of the province, where the Hadhbānī tribe had their summer pastures, while the Daylamites' strongholds were in the east in the mountains which bordered the southwestern corner of the Caspian Sea. However, there does not seem to have been any hard and fast frontier between the two – it was probably that each group occupied a different environment, the Daylamites farming land and the Kurds (like the transhumant Shahsevan nomads of present-day Āzarbayjān) occupying pastoral lands. There were substantial cities in the province, notably Ardabīl, the capital, and Marāgha, but we know little of their inhabitants, beyond the fact that they usually seem to have preferred Kurdish to Daylamite rule.

To the west of Āzarbayjān lay Armenia. Here, the bulk of the local chiefs were Christian, notably the Bagratids in the north around Ani and the Ardzrouni rulers of Vaspurakan around Lake Van to the south. The Armenians were a settled agricultural people determined to maintain their independence. There were also Muslims in Armenia; these mostly seem to have been of Arab origin, notably from members of the Sulaym tribe, whose members had settled soon after the Islamic conquest and whose leaders had supplied numerous governors for the area. By the fourth/tenth century, they were confined to the amirate of Manzikert, ruled by a Sulamī dynasty, and the districts along the northern shores of Lake Van, an area with a temperate winter climate. Farther north, again in a temperate zone, the Araxes valley, lay the capital of Muslim Armenia, Dabīl or Dwin. This was a town of mostly Christian population but ruled over by Muslim *amīrs* of Arab or Kurdish extraction.

This ethnic and linguistic diversity made it very difficult for the leader of any one group to establish control over the whole area and the confused politics of the period reflect this problem. The period which followed the death of Ibn Abi'l-Sāj saw a prolonged struggle between the Kurdish leader Daysam and the Daylamite Marzbān b. Musāfir. Daysam had been a follower of Ibn Abi'l-Sāj and had played an active part in the last Khārijī revolts in northern Iraq. These Iraqi connections suggest that he enjoyed the support of the Hadhbānī tribe, which wintered in Iraq. He was also supported by the Hamdanids of Mosul and had contacts in Vaspurakan, where Kurds and Armenians coexisted, providing a place of refuge.

Despite Daylamite challenges, Daysam managed to retain control of the province until he made a common but fatal error: he sought to establish his supremacy over other Kurdish leaders by recruiting Daylamites to his army and favouring them above his own people. The Kurds resented this, while many Daylamites remained unhappy under Kurdish rule. Leadership of the Daylamites' cause was assumed by Marzbān b. Muḥammad b. Musāfir. He came from the family of the Daylamite princes of Ṭārum, who held castles on the borders between Daylam and Āzarbayjān. The family was unconnected with their more successful fellow-countrymen, the Buyid family, with whom their relations were usually bad. Marzbān was a man of ambition, daring and energy and led a Daylamite army against Daysam. In the crucial battle (330/941), ethnic solidarity prevailed and Daysam's Daylamite troops suddenly switched sides, forcing him to flee despite the support of the townspeople of Ardabīl and Tabrīz. He went first to the Armenian ruler of Vaspurakan and then to Mosul, where he attempted to find support from the Hamdanids. After this defeat, however, Daysam was effectively finished as a leader of the Kurds. For the next generation, Āzarbayjān was dominated by the Daylamites, and when the Kurds did recover the leadership, it was under a new chief.

Marzbān now consolidated his rule; while the élite of his army were Daylamites, he recruited large numbers of Kurds as well. His newly won position was threatened by outsiders. In 333/945, Russian raiders sailed up the Kūr river from the Caspian and sacked the Muslim city of Bardha'a, where Marzbān's representative and the garrison of 3,000 Daylamites were killed. As if this were not enough, he was also threatened by the Hadhbānī Kurds, who, with Hamdanid support, attacked the province from the southwest. Despite this war on two fronts, both enemies were driven out, the Russians by dysentery, the Kurds by thick snow, and Marzbān's authority was restored and enhanced. Even after a temporary reverse following an unsuccessful attack on Rayy in 337/948, Marzbān was stronger than any ruler of Āzarbayjān since Yūsuf b. Abī'l-Sāj and was receiving tribute from numerous princes of the area, both Muslim (like Muḥammad b. Aḥmad, the ruler of Shīrvān and Abū'l-Hayjā' al-Rawwādī of Āhar) and Christian (like the Bagratids of Armenia and the rulers of Vaspurakan).

Marzbān's death in 346/957 opened the door to the family disputes which were typical of Daylamite rule. After much confused fighting, the dead ruler's brother, Vahsūdhān, kept the ancestral lands of the family around Ṭārum in eastern Āzarbayjān, while Marzbān's son, Ibrāhīm, supported by the Buyid Rukn al-Dawla of Rayy, ruled the rest of the province. He never enjoyed the ascendancy his father had had over the local princes, although he had agreements with the rulers of Shīrvān and Ganja, and his men raided as far as Bāb al-Abwāb. His authority was further weakened after the death of his patron Rukn al-Dawla of Rayy in 366/976. On his death in 373/983, power in Āzarbayjān passed out of Daylamite hands altogether, although Vahsūdhān and his family continued to hold Ṭārum until well into the next century.

Kurdish dominance in the area was reestablished under the leadership of the Rawwādī family. The origins of this clan are something of a mystery and the period of their rise to power, the later fourth/tenth century in Āzarbayjān, is extremely badly recorded. In the early 'Abbasid period, an Azdī Arab family called the Banū Rawwād is found among the colonists who settled the towns of Āzarbayjān, but it is not clear that there was any connection between them and the later Kurdish dynasty of the same name. It has been plausibly suggested that the Rawwadids were in fact the leading family of the Hadhbānī Kurds and that they are to be identified with the Rawwādīs after whom was named the town of Rawanduz (fortress of the Rawand), which dominates the route between upland Āzarbayjān and the plains of northern Iraq, where the Hadhbānīs wintered. Like the Hasanuyids farther south, their power was based on the leadership of a Kurdish tribal group and the control of the transhumance routes. The Rawwādīs are first heard of in the Tabrīz–Marāgha area, where the Hadhbānīs had their summer pastures, but by the time of Marzbān's death in 346/957, we find Abu'l-Hayjā' al-Rawwādī among his vassals in the area of Āhar to the west of the provincial capital at Ardabīl. Taking advantage of the weakening of Ibrāhīm b. Marzbān's power and his death in 373/983, the Rawwādīs took over central Āzarbayjān. The heyday of the dynasty seems to have been in the fifth/eleventh century under the rule of Vahsūdhān b. Mamlān (416–451/1025–1059), but the source material is very scanty and we know little of the details.

This Kurdish ascendancy was soon threatened, as elsewhere in the Zagros and southern Anatolia, by the arrival of the Ghuzz Turkmen tribes. As early as 420/1029, these pasture-hungry nomads had reached Marāgha and killed a number of Kurds. Thereafter, the pressure from Turkish tribes was almost continuous. The Turks were much more of a threat to the Kurds than were the Kurds' traditional rivals, the Daylamites and Armenians, who, being settled farmers, could coexist with transhumant pastoralists like the Kurds; clearly, there were sometimes clashes of interests, but these could be settled. The Turks, however, were sheep-rearing nomads, in direct competition for the rich summer grazing of upland Āzarbayjān, and the days of Kurdish dominance in the Zagros were numbered.

Just as the Kurds were threatened by the Turks, so the Christian Armenian principalities were threatened in the first half of the eleventh century by the expansionist policies of the Byzantine emperors. Gradually, the little principalities which had formed a buffer between Christian and Muslim empires since the eighth century were absorbed, and in some cases, the population was moved farther west in Anatolia. In 1021, Vaspurakan had lost its independence, and in 1045, Ani, ancient seat of the great Bagratid family, was also taken over. In the fourth/tenth century, Āzarbayjān and Armenia were divided into a mosaic of small dominions, each ruled by groups of local origin, Armenian, Daylamite or Kurdish. The fifth/eleventh century saw the end of this period of local autonomy and the whole area became a battleground between two outside powers, the Turks and the Byzantines, with the unfortunate local inhabitants, caught in the middle, being the main sufferers.

To the north of Āzarbayjān proper, across the Kūr river, there was a group of small principalities which maintained their independence. In the low-lying areas along the Caspian coasts, like Shīrvān and Bāb al-Abwāb, these were ruled by Muslim dynasties but farther into the mountains the people were either Christian, like the Georgians, or pagan, like the rulers of a number of small states in the northern Caucasus, whose mythical wealth the

Arab geographers liked to describe. Sometimes faced with strong rulers of Āzarbayjān like Yūsuf b. Abī'l-Sāj and Marzbān, they were obliged to pay tribute, but these powers always proved ephemeral, and the principalities soon recovered their autonomy. Among these principalities was the town of Ganja, ruled for many years by a Kurdish dynasty called the Shaddadids. Thanks to the lucky survival of sources and the work of Minorsky, we know more about this state than most others, and it is worth discussing its history in some detail, for it is a microcosm of the history of the whole area and provides insight into the political society of the time, the competing claims and interests of nomad, peasant and city dweller, Christian and Muslim, Kurd and Armenian.

Muḥammad b. Shaddād emerged as a tribal leader of consequence in c. 340/951, during a disturbed period of Marzbān's reign. He, his family and his clan were welcomed by the people of the city of Dwin to protect them – in the absence of any central authority – from the depredations of the Daylamite soldiery and the Armenians of the highlands, who almost surrounded the town; once again, the city people seem to have preferred Kurdish protectors to any others. In the absence of his father, Ibrāhīm b. Marzbān tried to subdue the town, first by encouraging the Armenians and others to attack it and then by coming from the capital at Ardabīl in person. But all this was to no avail and Muḥammad established himself in the role not so much of ruler, but of guardian of the city. He built quarters for himself and his tribesmen outside the city walls. In 343/954, this period of prosperity came to an end when Marzbān himself was able to turn his attention to Dwin. Muḥammad was now betrayed by the Daylamī garrison of the citadel, who went over to the attacker, and then by the townspeople anxious for peace. He and his family retired to the Armenian principality of Vaspurakan around Lake Van, where Kurds and Armenians seem to have coexisted quite happily. From here, he tried to gain support from the Byzantine authorities but without effect, and he died shortly afterwards in 344/955.

Muḥammad's sons, 'Alī Lashkarī and Marzbān (not to be confused with the Daylamī leader of the same name), were content to remain as leaders of their small tribe in Vaspurakan, but the third son, al-Faḍl, set off with a small band of followers to fight the infidels on the Caucasus frontier. On his way, he passed by the city of Ganja, then ruled by the Daylamīs; here, he was invited to stay, as his father had been at Dwin, to protect the city from brigands in return for a share of the revenues (359/969). From here, he wrote to his elder brother, encouraging him to come and share in the good fortune. 'Alī was reluctant, remembering how the townspeople of Dwin had betrayed his father, but al-Faḍl was insistent, saying that 'Alī should not spend all his life serving people (the Armenian rulers of Vaspurakan) who were not only Christian unbelievers but, even worse, settled farmers, an interesting insight into the nomad scale of values. Eventually, 'Alī, Marzbān and the rest of the tribe were induced to come to Ganja. Here in 360/970, they made a formal agreement with the *ra'īs* of the town, Yūsuf al-Qazzāz, a silk merchant judging from his name. This agreement established the terms under which the Shaddadid Kurds would become guardians of the city. ʿAlī and his family fulfilled their side of the bargain, resisting the attempts of Ibrāhīm b. Marzbān to reconquer the city and driving the hated Daylamīs out of the area for good. From then onwards, the family was well established in the city, especially during the long and peaceful reign of al-Faḍl b. Muḥammad, who succeeded his brother in 375/985 and ruled until his death in 422/1031. He defended Ganja against the Georgians and other attackers and agreed to submit peacefully to the Seljuks when they arrived in the area.

What emerges from the story of the Shaddadids is a clear picture of the interaction of urban and nomad groups that must have characterized other areas we know less about. In the absence of a respected central power, the townspeople did not attempt to set up their own militias, as happened, for example, in northern Italy in the eleventh and twelfth centuries, but turned to the local nomads who were employed as a standing defence force, their leaders being essentially *condottieri*. Perhaps the nearest equivalent is the relationship in medieval Russia between the urban leaders of Novgorod and the princes whom they employed to guard the city. The system suited both parties; the townspeople were protected and enjoyed a wide measure of urban autonomy without having to do military duties, for which they were both untrained and unwilling, while the nomads were given a secure income and status without abandoning their military traditions. It was a political arrangement which could work very well, as it seems to have done at Ganja, where for a century, townspeople and nomads worked together in harmony.

Farther west, in southern Anatolia, the Kurds were also increasingly politically active. After the breakdown of the Hamdanid regime in the later fourth/tenth century, the Kurds of this area too began to establish their own principalities. The founder of the main dynasty (known rather confusingly as the Marwanids, having nothing to do with the branch of the Umayyad family of the same name) was a chieftain called Bādh, who is described as a huge, ugly brigand and chief of the Ḥumaydī Kurds. Under Hamdanid rule, the Kurds of the mountains to the north of the Jazīra had been fairly peaceful, but the attempts of ʿAḍud al-Dawla to establish firm central authority meant that they were bound to resist, probably because the government tried to control their access to winter pastures in the northern Jazīra; the Hamdanids had had a working relationship with the Kurds of this area, the Buyids had not. Bādh and his tribesmen began to defy the Buyids from 372/982 onwards. Like the Hamdanids before them, the Kurds were always able to retreat to their mountain fastnesses if the Turkish cavalry threatened to overwhelm them on the plains. In 374/984, the government of Ṣamṣām al-Dawla agreed that Bādh should control Diyār Bakr and the western part of the Ṭūr ʿAbdīn. His ambitions did not stop there, however, and in 379/990 he gathered an army of 5,000 Kurds to march on Mosul itself. This time, he was opposed by two surviving members of the Hamdanid family, Ibrāhīm and al-Ḥusayn, and they proceeded to recruit soldiers from one group whose livelihood was directly threatened by the activities of Bādh, the 'Uqaylī and Numayrī Arab tribesmen of the Jazīra, whose pastures might be taken over by the Kurds. They were fewer in number than the Kurds but their horsemen were said to have been more mobile than their opponents and they were able to drive them from the open plains of the northern Jazīra. Bādh was killed during the flight but his sister's son, al-Ḥasan b. Marwān, escaped to the mountains with 500 horsemen, where he was able to establish himself in the small city of Mayyāfāriqīn (modern Silvan).

Al-Ḥasan b. Marwān ruled from Mayyāfāriqīn for seven years, from 380 to 387 (990–997) and consolidated the hold of the dynasty over a considerable area of southeastern Anatolia. He took measures in 382/992–993 to defend Akhlāṭ and Manzikert from Byzantine attacks and thus extended his influence in the area to the north of Lake Van. He made a twenty-year truce with the Byzantines which effectively safeguarded the northern frontier of the state. But the centre of the principality remained Mayyāfāriqīn and Āmid, together with Arzan, a sort of family shrine where al-Ḥasan's blind father Marwān lived on in retirement. He also had to come to terms with the people of the main town. The *amīr* suspected the inhabitants of Mayyāfāriqīn of favouring the Hamdanids and he took brutal measures against some of the leading citizens. The people of Āmid, however, were a more difficult proposition and they had an ally in Sharwa b. Mamma, the son of al-Ḥasan's *wazīr*. When the *amīr* attempted to assert his authority in Āmid as he had done at the capital, a conspiracy of the leading citizens, headed by the *qāḍī*, succeeded in murdering him. Sharwa then secured the succession of al-Ḥasan's brother Sa'īd, who was granted the honorific tide of Mumahhid al-Dawla by the 'Abbasid caliphate, the first member of the family to be so honoured. His authority was generally accepted except in Āmid. Here, the *qāḍī* Yūsuf b. Damna held out with the support of the leading citizens, and the *amīr* was forced to come to terms; Ibn Damna would rule the town in return for a payment of 200,000 *dirhams* to the *amīr* and the mention of his name in the *khuṭba* and on the coinage. As at Ganja, the power of the urban patriciate to negotiate on equal terms with would-be *amīrs* and organize their own affairs becomes apparent. Ibn Damna carried on independent correspondence with the Buyids, the Fatimids and even the Byzantine emperor, Basil II. The town also had its own '*askar*, or military force. Ibn Damna ruled Āmid for twenty-eight years, effectively independent from the Marwanid *amīr* in Mayyāfāriqīn, and it was remembered as a period of great prosperity in the history of the city.

In 401/1011, Sharwa was persuaded by a *ghulām* of his to arrange the assassination of the *amīr* and to assume power in his own name. This time, he was not as successful as before. Mayyāfāriqīn was taken over, but the governor of Arzan, where old, blind Marwān still lived, resisted. The leaders of the Kurdish tribes refused to accept the usurpation and turned to the dead ruler's brother, Abū Naṣr, living in semi-exile in Sī'ird in the extreme east of the Marwanid domains. Sharwa fortified himself in Mayyāfāriqīn, supported by the Georgian *ghilmān* he had recruited but opposed by many of the townspeople, who suspected him of wanting to turn the city over to the Byzantines. It was the shaykhs of the city who obliged him to surrender to Abū Naṣr, who had him executed.

The fall of Sharwa marked the beginning of the reign of the greatest ruler of the dynasty. For half a century (401–453/1011–1061), Abū Naṣr, who took the title of Naṣr al-Dawla, remained *amīr*. It was a golden age for Mayyāfāriqīn and the surrounding area. The Marwanid state extended as far as Akhlāt. and the Muslim areas to the north of Lake Van in the northeast, but the centre of their power lay on the routes from the Anatolian plateau to the plains of the Jazīra, at Mayyāfāriqīn in the centre, Arzan and Sī'ird (which commanded the route to the Van area via Badlīs) to the east and the semi-independent city of Āmid to the west. Until the coming of the Ghuzz Turks in 433/1041–1042, there were no serious external threats to the state. The Byzantines were cautious and seem to have accepted the Marwanids, like the Hamdanids and the Mirdasids of Aleppo, as a buffer state between them and the wider Muslim world. Neither the Mirdasids nor the 'Uqaylids of Mosul, both dynasties based on the bedouin Arab tribes of northern Syria and al-Jazīra, had any reason to invade the mountains to the north. The Marwanids usually acknowledged the sovereignty of the 'Abbasid caliphate but maintained correspondence with the Fatimids as well, and neither of the rival caliphates sought to exert pressure on them.

The failure of Sharwa's attempted coup and the accession of Naṣr al-Dawla had shown that the real power of the dynasty still lay with the Kurdish tribesmen, and apart from the Georgians recruited by Sharwa, there seems to have been no significant body of *ghilmān*. As usual in tribal states, the ruling kin remained very important, and Naṣr al-Dawla, like his brothers before him, took care to provide for members of his own family. The administration of the Marwanid domains was more developed than that of some other Kurdish principalities. As in the Buyid amirates, relations between the ruler and the local people were conducted by the *wazīr*. After the death of Sharwa, Naṣr al-Dawla attempted to do without a *wazīr* for two years, but his affairs became so disorganized that he had to recruit a new one. He turned not to one of his own subjects, but to an outsider from a family of professional bureaucrats, al-Ḥusayn b. 'Alī al-Maghribī. His grandfather and father had been *wazīrs* to Sayf al-Dawla the Hamdanid, but his father 'Alī abandoned Sa'd al-Dawla, Sayf's successor, for the lusher pastures of the Fatimid court. Here, his son, al-Ḥusayn, was educated in the bureaucratic tradition and rose high in the administration of the Caliph al-Ḥākim. Unlike so many of that monarch's servants, he escaped from Cairo with his life and took service with the Buyids of Iraq, then with Qirwāsh, the 'Uqaylid ruler of Mosul, before he was recruited in 415/1024–1025 by Naṣr al-Dawla, whose *wazīr* he remained until his death in 418/1027. After this, Naṣr was again forced to scout around and picked another professional, Ibn Jahīr, then at Mosul but unemployed and out of favour with the ruling

'Uqaylids. Ibn Jahīr became *wazīr* for the rest of the reign. The history of the wazirate is interesting, since it shows how important such freelance administrators had become. Talented and experienced men could leave the service of one dynasty and find employment with another, their education and abilities always being sought after. Both as authors and as patrons, this class of freelance bureaucrats was important for the literary culture of the day. We also know that the Marwanids had an official called the *'ārid al-jaysh* to administer the army, but we know little of the military organization; most unusually for the period, the chronicler of the Marwanids, Ibn al-Fāriqī, has more to say of peaceful developments than of military campaigns.

The main centres of Marwanid power lay on the transhumance routes from the Anatolian plateau to the plains, and there is no doubt that the Marwanids used this position to maintain contact and influence with the Kurdish tribes. Unlike the 'Uqaylids, however, the rulers did not, on the whole, live in tribal encampments but exercised power from their palaces in Mayyāfāriqīn. They were heavily dependent on the townspeople, and nothing contributed more to Naṣr al-Dawla's success than the partnership between the dynasty and the urban élites. Āmid remained more or less autonomous.

In 415/1024–1025, Ibn Damna was killed in a domestic intrigue and Naṣr al-Dawla took over the town. The city was obliged to share a *qāḍī* with Mayyāfāriqīn, but the *amīr* appointed his own son as his deputy and allowed him his own *wazīr*, suggesting some administrative independence. Later in 429/1037–1038, a new *qāḍī*, Ibn Baghl, was appointed from among the leading citizens and became an effective ruler of the town under the *amīr*'s son. In the capital, Mayyāfāriqīn, civic autonomy never developed as it did in Āmid, although the leading merchants were influential and wealthy. Naṣr al-Dawla lived something of a transhumant life himself. In the spring, the court would abandon the capital and migrate up the valley of the Batman Su. In an almost lyrical passage, Ibn al-Fāriqī explains how they would enjoy the meadows and the flowers of the spring until they returned to Mayyāfāriqīn in the summer.

The result of this peace and the large measure of civic autonomy was a period of great urban prosperity. Public works were undertaken, notably the building of city walls, bridges (important for the transhumant Kurds) and the city water supplies. Until the time of the Hamdanids, the people of Mayyāfāriqīn had been dependent on wells for their drinking water. Sayf al-Dawla had brought a canal of fresh water to the Hamdanid palace on the city walls, but under the Marwanids, two more canals were brought, not by the ruler, but by leading citizens of the town. The position of the towns on the north–south routes clearly encouraged trade, and the leading citizens of both Āmid and Mayyāfāriqīn had their wealth and influence firmly based on the *sūqs*. However, this wealth does not seem to have been entirely confined to the Muslim urban élite; in the 1030s, the Jacobite patriarch of Antioch, Dionysius IV, came to live in Marwanid territory at Āmid to escape Byzantine persecution.

The history of the Marwanid state is only a small fragment of the mosaic of the Muslim commonwealth, but it is an extremely interesting one. Because of the excellence of the main source, we know much more about the nature of government and society than in other parallel states, like 'Uqaylid Mosul or Kakuyid Iṣfahān. The picture that emerges is essentially a favourable one of a society where tribal and urban elements coexist to their mutual benefit. Far from being a disaster for Āmid and Mayyāfāriqīn, the break-up of the 'Abbasid caliphate brought prosperity and local autonomy there. In Mayyāfāriqīn, it even brought a vastly improved water supply. The broad annals of the Muslim world seem to show a pattern of violence and chaos and it is only through vignettes like this that we can arrive at a corrective picture. The later years of Naṣr al-Dawla's rule were darkened by the increasing threat of the Ghuzz Turkmen, although it was not until after his death that they seriously threatened the state. The vast transformation they effected in the population of the area meant that a new balance had to be worked out between the pastoral and settled communities.

Minorsky has written of the Iranian intermezzo in Persian history between the coming of the Arabs in the first/seventh century and the Turks in the fifth/eleventh. In the Near East as a whole, we can also talk of a Kurdish interlude. In the century 950–1050, a number of different Kurdish states were set up in different areas, but they had much in common. All were set up in mountainous regions, the natural pasture grounds of the Kurdish tribes, and many were based on the great transhumance routes between summer and winter pastures. On the whole, their administrations were primitive. Some, like the 'Annazids, seem to have lacked any bureaucracy at all, and the ruling kin remained influential as a group in a way they did not in more centralized and bureaucratic states. But the picture is not one of chaos and anarchy, as might at first appear. Some of the Kurdish rulers, notably Badr b. Ḥasanūya and Naṣr al-Dawla the Marwanid, left reputations for good government which few of their contemporaries could match. Equally telling are the good relations Kurdish leaders frequently developed with leading citizens with whom they frequently worked in partnership. The collapse of 'Abbasid rule allowed local élites to emerge, and it is fascinating to see how the people of each area developed their own political solutions, a pattern of variety and local autonomy soon to be extinguished by the coming of the Turks.

11 The Hamdanids

Of all the dynasties which succeeded the 'Abbasid caliphate, the Hamdanids have perhaps the highest reputation with posterity. This is partly due to the personality of the *amīr*, Sayf al-Dawla, who is seen as a representative of all the Arab virtues of generosity and courage, fighting against overwhelming odds on the Byzantine frontier. This romantic image has been much enhanced by Hamdanids' interest in poetry, notably Sayf al-Dawla's patronage of al-Mutanabbī, arguably the greatest of the classical Arabic poets, and of Sayf al-Dawla's cousin, Abū'l-Firās. Contemporaries were not so favourably impressed, however; the geographer Ibn Ḥawqal, who travelled through the Hamdanid domains, was deeply critical of their oppressive policies, painting a grim picture of overtaxation and exploitation. Even the capital of Aleppo seems to have been more prosperous under the following Mirdasid dynasty than under the Hamdanids. After the first generation of Nāṣir al-Dawla in Mosul (d. 358/969) and Sayf al-Dawla in Aleppo (d. 356/967), they produced few leaders of great ability, and while Mosul soon fell to the Buyids, Hamdanid Aleppo was ruled more by their *ghilmān* than by members of the dynasty. Nor should we imagine that the Hamdanids were bedouin chiefs of the traditional sort. They rose to power originally because of the support they could command among their Taghlibī fellow-tribesmen, but as soon as they established a territorial base, they dispensed with this support, preferring to base their power on taxation and an army of salaried *ghilmān*. In this way, the Hamdanid state was more similar to Buyid Iraq or Ikhshidid Egypt than to bedouin states like the Mirdasids and 'Uqaylids which succeeded it.

The Hamdanids of Mosul

The Hamdanids were drawn from the Banū Taghlib, a tribe which had grazed the Jazīra area since pre-Islamic times. During the anarchy in Sāmarrā, if not before, they had come to dominate the city of Mosul, and various Taghlibī chiefs succeeded each other as governors, defending the city against the Khārijī brigands of the steppe lands who had threatened the area since later Umayyad times. Around 266/879, the Taghlibī chiefs were replaced by

DOI: 10.4324/9780429348129-11

a Turkish soldier, ʿĪsā b. Kundājīq, in an effort to restore the power of the Baghdad government in the area, with the natural result that the Taghlibī chiefs, among them Ḥamdān b. Ḥamdūn, went over to the Khārijīs in an effort to recover their position, and disorder spread throughout the Jazīra. In 279/892, the new Caliph al-Muʿtaḍid determined to reestablish order in the area, and in a series of campaigns he reduced most of the dissidents to obedience. Ḥamdān was one of the most stubborn in resistance and he was strengthened by his hold over various strong points in the mountains to the north of the Jaziran plain. In the period before al-Muʿtaḍid's advance, he had acquired a series of strong points, notably Mārdīn to the west and Ardamusht near Jazīrat Ibn ʿUmar (now Cizre) in the east, and he seems to have reached a working alliance with the Kurdish tribes of the foothills. This meant that Ḥamdān was more than simply a bedouin chief. The refuge offered by the mountain fortresses and the relationship with the Kurds were important factors in the survival of the Hamdanids in the years to come.

Ḥamdān's career ended in failure when, in 282/895, after an epic chase, he was forced to give himself up to al-Muʿtaḍid in Mosul. This surrender might have seemed the end of the family fortunes, as it was for other local leaders in the area, had not Ḥamdān's son, al-Ḥusayn, made himself useful to the government. In 283/896, al-Ḥusayn was released from prison and allowed to recruit a small army of his followers to fight against the remaining Khārijīs in the Jazīra. The campaign was a success and in return for his services, al-Ḥusayn was able to request, not only that his father be released, but that the taxes on the Banū Taghlib be remitted and that he himself be allowed to recruit a body of 500 Taghlibīs to form a group in the armies of the caliphate and be paid by the government. This secured his position, not only with the caliph but also among the Taghlib. To the caliph, he offered a group of experienced warriors under his own skilled and loyal leadership; to the Taghlib, and other people in the Jazīra, he offered the prospect of salaries and booty; and to his own family, military command and the opportunity of acquiring wealth in government service. It was in fact not as an independent tribal leader, but rather as an intermediary between government and the Arabs and Kurds of the Jazīra that al-Ḥusayn made the family fortune. His troops were conspicuous in ʿAbbasid campaigns, especially against the Qarāmiṭa, the bedouin heretics who were such an intractable problem for the ʿAbbasid government of the time, where their experience made them particularly valuable, but also in campaigns in the Jibāl and during the ʿAbbasid reconquest of Egypt in 292/904–905.

By the end of al-Muktafī's reign in 295/908, al-Ḥusayn had established his position as one of the leading generals in the armies of the caliphs, while other members of his family were rewarded with office elsewhere, the most important of these being in the old Taghlibī preserve of Mosul, where al-Ḥusayn's brother, Abū'l-Hayjā', was appointed the governor in 293/905. These two centres of power, in Mosul and in the army of the caliph, enabled the family to survive storms which destroyed less well-established families.

Al-Ḥusayn was naturally drawn into Baghdad politics; in 296/908, he was one of the leaders of the abortive coup against al-Muqtadir launched in the name of Ibn al-Mu'tazz, but he seems to have lost his nerve and fled to Mosul when he saw that the putsch was encountering resistance. Other leading participants were executed, but Abū'l-Hayjā' negotiated a reprieve for his brother, who saw government service again in the Jibāl and finally as the governor of the area of Diyār Rabī'a to the west of Mosul. In 302–303/914–915, he became involved in another rebellion. This time it seems to have been in protest against the attempts of 'Alī b. 'Īsā to reduce government spending and his own exclusion from power in Baghdad. It is a measure of his continuing influence in the area that he was able to raise a force of 30,000 Arabs and Kurds, but the rebellion failed when he was captured by the forces of the leading 'Abbasid general Mu'nis and taken to Baghdad, where, in 306/918, he was executed.

Once again, the influence of the family appeared to have been destroyed, but as before, the Hamdanids proved too useful and well entrenched to be excluded from power for long, and Abū'l-Hayjā' was soon back in government service. Like his brother, he distinguished himself against the Qarāmiṭa. In 312/924, he had been captured by the rebels while escorting the *Ḥajj* but was able to negotiate not only his own release but that of the other captives as well. This apparently close relationship with the Qarāmiṭa, who usually put their prisoners to death, has been seen by Canard, the great historian of the dynasty, as a sign of sympathy between the Ismā'īlī Qarāmiṭa and the Shī'ī Hamdanids. Despite the early involvement of the family with the Khārijīs, the Hamdanids are usually said to have been a Shī'ī dynasty. In practice, this seems to have affected their policies very little; they were, in fact, prepared to acknowledge the sovereignty of 'Abbasids, Buyids or Fatimids, depending on political circumstances. The Hamdanids flourished before the division between Sunnīs and Shī'īs had become as clear-cut as it was to be later. Soon after this, we find the Qarāmiṭa actually being recruited into the 'Abbasid armies, and the occasional signs we find of cordiality between them and the Hamdanids are probably the result of common political interests of the moment rather than of lasting religious sympathy. During the crisis of 315/927, Abū'l-Hayjā' played a key role in defending Iraq from Qarmaṭī attack.

Abu'l-Hayjā' left the affairs of Mosul in the hands of his son al-Ḥasan, while he himself became increasingly entangled in the complexities of Baghdad politics. Unlike his dead brother al-Ḥusayn, however, he was on consistently good terms with Mu'nis, with whom he worked on numerous occasions, and it was his alliance with Mu'nis and the policies of 'Alī b. 'Īsā which was to cause his downfall; in 317/929, he was a leading supporter of al-Qāhir in his unsuccessful coup and was killed fighting bravely to defend his candidate for the throne.

The ups and downs of Baghdad politics did not destroy the position of the family in the Jazīra and from this time onwards, Mosul and its surroundings are the centre of family activities. After the death of Abū'l-Hayjā', leadership in the family was divided among his surviving brothers and his son, al-Ḥasan, who gradually established his supremacy. The Hamdanids refused to be drawn into further rebellions against al-Muqtadir and supported him in his final struggle against Mu'nis, who even occupied Mosul for a time. By 324/935, the authorities in Baghdad had been obliged to accept al-Ḥasan as the ruler of Mosul and the Jazīra as far as the Byzantine frontier in exchange for a payment of 70,000 *dīnārs* a year and supplies of flour for Baghdad and Sāmarrā. From this time onwards, the power of the family was established. It had also changed its nature. Ḥusayn b. Ḥamdān had come to power by raising Taghlibī troops for the caliph, but relations between the Ḥamdānīs and their fellow-tribesmen gradually became more distant and we no longer hear of Taghlibī troops under their command. A key stage in this process seems to have occurred in 323/935 when a rival Taghlibī chief, al-'Alā' b. al-Mu'ammar from the Ḥābib clan in the area of Niṣībīn, took 10,000 of his followers and crossed the frontier to Byzantium to escape Hamdanid control and, above all, Hamdanid taxation. There were several factors involved in this unprecedented move. The Taghlib had been a Christian tribe for many years after the Muslim conquest, and it is possible that many of its members still held to their old faith and this would have made Byzantine authority much more acceptable than it would have been to a Muslim group. It also seems likely that the Taghlib were coming under increasing pressure in their native grazing areas from aggressive tribes like the 'Uqayl and Numayr, moving into the area from the south, and that the removal to Byzantine territory was forced on them. The movement of such a large number across the frontier is said by contemporaries to have been an important factor in Byzantine successes in the area, and it is certainly ironic that in the very year that al-Ḥasan's authority was recognized over the whole area, the Taghlib tribe should have disappeared as a political force. The Hamdanids did not, then, base their power on their tribal following. Certainly, Arabs were mentioned in their forces but they came from tribes like the 'Uqayl and the Numayr, not the Taghlib, and usually figure as irregulars and temporary allies rather than as regular supporters.

In the main, the Hamdanids, like most of their contemporaries, seem to have relied on *ghilmān* of Turkish extraction for their armed forces, often recruiting those who were dissatisfied with the government in Baghdad. The Kurdish element was probably important as well. The early Hamdanids seem to have established close relations with the Kurds who wintered on the plains of the Jazīra, notably the Hadhbānīs around the Zāb and the Jalālī Kurds farther south around Shahrazūr. The mountain fortresses especially, which played so important a part in Hamdanid survival, were often in Kurdish territory. Members of the dynasty intermarried with Kurds as well; both Abū'l-Hayjā' and his grandson Abū Taghlib had Kurdish mothers, and these connections may well have brought military support. Certainly when the dynasty's last stronghold in the Mosul area, Ardamusht, was surrendered to ʿAḍud al-Dawla, the Hamdanid commanders in the fortress were a Kurd and a Turkish *ghulām*.

The Hamdanids then, in both Syria and Mosul, asserted their authority by means of a professional army recruited from different sources. Like all their rivals, they were faced with the problem of paying them, and both al-Ḥasan and his son and successor Abū Taghlib were faced by mutinies of their Turkish soldiers. The revenues to pay this force were drawn from the towns and countryside of the Jazīra, and the geographer Ibn Ḥawqal gives a breakdown of the sources of revenue from the Niṣībīn area. The main source of revenue, as everywhere in the Muslim world, was the land tax collected in kind: 10,000 *kurr* (a dry measure of approximately 2,500 kg) of grain valued at 5 million *dirhams* (about 300,000 *dīnārs*). The *jizya* from the Christians, by contrast, raised only 5,000 *dīnārs*, a tax on wine brought in 5,000 *dīnārs* and on food markets the same amount. Urban rents, including inns (*khāns*), baths, mills, shops and private houses brought in 16,000 *dīnārs*. This would seem to suggest that the land tax brought in about ten times as much as urban taxation, but this may be misleading. The land tax was collected in kind and valued, whereas urban taxes seem to have been collected in coin. Whether the theoretical value of the grain was ever realized in fact is not clear, and it is probable that urban dues paid in *dīnārs* were essential for paying troops and other government expenses which had to be settled in cash. Ibn Ḥawqal describes how he was at Mosul in 358/969 when the accounts were presented to Abū Taghlib and criticizes what he considered to be overtaxation. All the Hamdanids had secretaries, but it is not clear that there was any elaborate administration at Mosul, and the ease with which the court could take refuge in the mountains if necessary suggests that it may have been fairly basic.

Among the outgoings of the Hamdanids of Mosul, the payment of tribute to the Buyids was a major factor. In the later years of al-Ḥasan Nāṣir al-Dawla, this tribute seems to have been assessed at between 2 and 4 million *dirhams* per year, when it was paid at all. Abū Taghlib, in a much weaker position, was obliged to find 6 million *dirhams*. It is probable that payments of that size made it very difficult for him to recruit and pay enough *ghilmān* to maintain his position. As always, political and financial weakness went together; rulers were anxious to be independent because it was almost impossible to pay a large tribute and maintain a regular *ghulām* army.

The establishment of al-Ḥasan as the ruler of the Jazīra by the agreement of 324/935 did not mark the end of the ambitions of the family in Baghdad. The intrigues which surrounded the office of *amīr al-umarāʾ* tempted al-Ḥasan to play a part, and when in 330/942, the caliph, al-Muttaqī, and the leading Turkish officer, Tūzūn, both urged him to try to drive the Barīdīs from Baghdad, he allowed himself to be persuaded. He marched south and was installed as *amīr al-umarāʾ* in the capital with the title of Nāṣir al-Dawla, but despite his good intentions, the attempt was not a success. The problems were, as always, financial, especially as the Barīdīs were still in control of the rich lands of southern Iraq. Nāṣir al-Dawla sent his brother, ʿAlī, with an army to conduct the war in the south, as a reward for which he was given his famous honorific Sayf al-Dawla (Sword of the State). Sayf al-Dawla's army was composed of Turks, Daylamites and Qarmaṭīs with irregular support from Kurds and Numayrī, Kilābī and Asadī Arab tribesmen. The campaign had only been under way a short time when Tūzūn led a mutiny in the army. Coupled with disturbances in Baghdad, this forced the Ḥamdānīs to withdraw. Nāṣir al-Dawla, however, never forgot that he had once ruled in Baghdad and it made him very unwilling to accept the suzerainty of the Buyids who came to occupy the office.

Nāṣir al-Dawla retired to Mosul where he reached an agreement with the new *amīr al-umarāʾ*, Tūzūn, allowing him the Jazīra and northern Syria (which he did not in fact possess) in exchange for an enlarged tribute of 3.6 million *dirhams*. From this time onwards, Nāṣir al-Dawla had a tributary relationship with the rulers of Baghdad. It was, however, a constantly changing relationship depending on the varying fortunes of each side. Nāṣir al-Dawla paid the tribute when he was forced to but took every opportunity to avoid it. On several occasions, in 334/946, for example, and at the time of Rūzbahān's rebellion against the Buyids in 345/956–957 (see above, p. 221), the Hamdanids attempted to retake Baghdad, capitalizing on rivalries among the Daylamites and between Daylamites and Turks, but they were never able to maintain themselves in the city. Muʿizz al-Dawla, in retaliation, tried to take over the Hamdanid lands and on several occasions actually captured Mosul itself. Hamdanid tactics on these occasions were simple but effective; unable to withstand Buyid armies in the open field, they abandoned Mosul and retired to the foothills of the mountains and the fortresses like Mārdīn and Ardamusht, where they kept their treasure, being careful to take with them all records of government properties and taxation. The invading forces found themselves unable to find supplies and harassed by the guerrilla tactics of the Hamdanid supporters and the hostility of the people of the cities to the Daylamite forces. After a short occupation, the Buyids would be forced to make terms again and the Hamdanids could return to Mosul. The most serious of these attacks was in 347–348/958–959, when Nāṣir al-Dawla was forced to flee to his brother Sayf al-Dawla in Aleppo, who received him with honour. It was Sayf al-Dawla who negotiated a new agreement with Muʿizz al-Dawla and from this time onwards, the Aleppo branch of the family seems to have been more powerful than the Mosul branch, extending its influence over Diyār Muḍar on the east bank of the Euphrates.

In the end, family conflicts damaged the Hamdanid cause more than Buyid attacks. In 353/964, Muʿizz al-Dawla launched another attack; once more, Nāṣir al-Dawla was driven out of Mosul and fled to the hills, but this time the counterattack was led by his son, Abū Taghlib, who eventually came to a new arrangement, a sign that the old man had ceased to be an effective leader. In 356/967, his brother, Sayf al-Dawla, with whom he had maintained good relations, died. Not only was this a personal loss for Nāṣir al-Dawla, but it also meant that the Hamdanids of Aleppo were unable to offer the Mosul branch any further support against Buyid aggression. Nāṣir al-Dawla's increasing feebleness was shown by his failure to take advantage of the death of his old rival Mu'izz al-Dawla in the same year, and he was confined by his sons to the fortress at Ardamusht, where he died two years later.

Nāṣir al-Dawla was succeeded as the head of the family by his son Abū Taghlib, whose leadership was accepted by most of his brothers. Family unity had been a major source of strength for the Hamdanids in earlier generations but this advantage was now dissipated. It seems that Nāṣir al-Dawla had considered passing the succession not to Abū Taghlib, but to another son by a different mother, Ḥamdān, and in his last years he had established him in an apanage around Niṣībīn, Mārdīn and Raḥba. Ḥamdān now refused to accept his brother's authority, and open warfare developed between the two. This rivalry was complicated by relations with the Buyids. While Nāṣir al-Dawla had been a deadly rival of Mu'izz al-Dawla, Abū Taghlib generally remained on good terms with his son and successor, Bakhtiyār. Unlike his father, Abū Taghlib had no claims to authority in Baghdad, while Bakhtiyār had too many problems maintaining himself in Iraq to spare much time for aggressive moves against Mosul. These good relations did not, however, prevent Bakhtiyār from giving Ḥamdān and other dissident members of the family a place of refuge when necessary, and Ḥamdān was able to maintain himself as a constant threat to his brother's authority. In 362/973, Bakhtiyār actually took Mosul, and one of the conditions of the subsequent peace was that Ḥamdān be reestablished in all his old properties. In 367/977, it was Bakhtiyār's turn to seek help against his aggressive cousin 'Aḍud al-Dawla, who had driven him out of Baghdad, and Abū Taghlib promised to support him in exchange for Ḥamdān, who was handed over and executed. But the family unity which resulted had come too late. 'Aḍud al-Dawla did not overlook the support Abū Taghlib had given his defeated rival and he soon began to advance on Mosul. This time the Buyids were much more organized, 'Aḍud al-Dawla brought with him men who were familiar with the administration of Mosul, and the old Ḥamdānī tactics failed. Mayyāfāriqīn, Āmid and even the fortress at Ardamusht were taken by siege. Abū Taghlib was forced eventually to flee across the Syrian Desert to Palestine, where he tried to persuade the Fatimid authorities to grant him the governorate of Damascus. In doing so, he made powerful enemies, notably the Ṭayy chief Daghfal b. Mufarrij, and was finally killed at Ramla (369/979).

Abū Taghlib's surviving brothers, al-Ḥusayn and Ibrāhīm, took service with 'Aḍud al-Dawla, who was thus assured of peaceful possession of the Jazīra. Hamdanid rule in the area had effectively come to an end, but there was to be a postscript. Under 'Aḍud al-Dawla's weaker successors, Buyid control in the area was challenged by the Kurds under Bādh, the effective founder of the Marwanid dynasty, and the then Buyid leader, Bahā' al-Dawla, hoped to use al-Ḥusayn and Ibrāhīm to form a coalition against the invaders. In 379/989, the brothers reestablished Hamdanid rule in Mosul, basing their power largely on the 'Uqaylī tribesmen, who were now influential in the area. But while the 'Uqaylis succeeded in restricting the Kurds to the mountainous areas to the north, they were not prepared to accept Hamdanid leadership for old time's sake. The 'Uqaylī leaders established themselves in Mosul and killed al-Ḥusayn, while Ibrāhīm was released by the Kurds and took service with the Fatimids in Egypt and Syria. Though there seems to have been some pro-Hamdanid feeling in cities like Mosul and Mayyāfāriqīn, based on hostility to the Daylamites, the last Hamdanids of the Mosul branch lacked the support of either a powerful tribal backing or a strong central government, and their attempt was doomed to failure.

The Hamdanids of Aleppo

The establishment of the Hamdanids in Aleppo and northern Syria came later than at Mosul. While the Banū Taghlib had long been influential in the Jazīra, they had no traditional interest in the lands to the west of the Euphrates, and the Hamdanids had not shown any concern with the area until after Nāṣir al-Dawla's failure to maintain himself in Iraq as *amīr al-umarā'* in 330/942. Nāṣir al-Dawla himself retired to Mosul, but his ambitious younger brother, 'Alī Sayf al-Dawla, who had been his chief military commander in the unsuccessful Iraqi campaign, sought a new area in which to establish himself. Aleppo was at this time more or less under the authority of the *ikhshīd*, the ruler of Egypt who governed mostly through Turkish officers who had left Baghdad to seek their fortunes elsewhere. As far as the *ikhshīd* was concerned, Aleppo itself does not seem to have been of paramount concern; he was able to accept a stable buffer state against both Byzantines to the north and Iraqi generals from the east, but he was determined to keep Damascus and Palestine under his control. In 333/944, Sayf al-Dawla was able to take over Aleppo with the support of the leading bedouin tribe of the area, the Banū Kilāb who inhabited the steppe lands to the east and southeast of the city.

For the first decade of his reign, Sayf al-Dawla was preoccupied with reaching agreements to establish his position with the *ikhshīd* and his successors and with the Arab tribes. After his success in Aleppo, Sayf al-Dawla made an attempt to take Damascus as well, but the *ikhshīd* himself came to put a stop to this and a peace was arranged the next year (334/945) which allowed Sayf al-Dawla control over Aleppo, Antioch and Homs but not over Tripoli and Damascus. Despite a renewed attempt on Damascus by Sayf al-Dawla after the *ikhshīd*'s death, these areas were to be the continuing centres of the Hamdanid state in Syria. The political division between Aleppo and the frontier areas on the one hand and Damascus and Palestine on the other was to persist into the fifth/eleventh century, when the Mirdasids to the north and the Fatimids in the south divided the area between them.

Sayf al-Dawla's other major problem in the early years of his reign was his relations with the bedouin tribes. The key to his policy in this area was his alliance with the Kilāb, who had played an important part in establishing him in Aleppo in the first place. This was not always an easy alliance, but the strategic position of the tribal lands near Aleppo and the ability to cut communications with the east made it essential to handle their leaders with care. Farther south, the Kalb of the Homs region, who had played so important a part in Umayyad politics, were more hostile; many of them had been connected with the Qarmaṭī revolts in the area and probably resented the Hamdanid alliance with their Kilābī rivals. In 344/955, Sayf al-Dawla was faced with a major rebellion of all the tribal groups, including the Kilāb in the north, and the Kalb, ʿUqayl and Numayr in the Salamiyya region to the east of Homs. He crushed it by dividing his opponents. The Kilāb were allowed to make peace on easy terms; the others were ruthlessly chastised, many being driven out to the desert to die of thirst. This campaign altered the nomad geography of the Syrian steppe considerably. The Numayrīs were encouraged to move across the Euphrates to the Jazīra, while the Kalb were forced to move away from their traditional centres around Homs to the Jawlān (Golan) further in the south. The Kilāb, however, were allowed to expand south into the old Kalb lands, and it seems that this increased territory led other members of the tribe to migrate to the area from Iraq, thus confirming their preponderance in northern Syria.

The crushing of the bedouin revolt probably marks the high point of Sayf al-Dawla's success and power. His state was based on the area of central Syria from Homs to Aleppo and on the eastern part of the Jazīra where Mayyāfāriqīn became a sort of second capital, increasingly important in later years when Byzantine pressure from the west increased. The coastal areas of Syria as far south as Ṭarṭūs but excluding Tripoli were also in Hamdanid hands. It would also seem that Sayf al-Dawla exercised some suzerainty over Antioch and even Maṣṣīṣa and Tarsus in the Cilician plain, although these seem to have been independent for practical purposes. Canard remarks that the state was Mesopotamian rather than Syrian in character; certainly, none of the Hamdanids seem to have made any effort to develop a fleet and conduct a Mediterranean policy as the Fatimids were to do. Sayf al-Dawla's power rested on the members of his family, his alliance with the Kilāb and other bedouin tribes and the force of *ghilmān* he recruited. The Hamdanid family were important in the establishment of Hamdanid power and were employed in governing key centres like Homs and Manbij, where Sayf al-Dawla's cousin and "court poet" Abū'l-Firās was the governor. In addition, his nephew Muḥammad, son of Nāṣir al-Dawla of Mosul, often acted as his deputy in Aleppo. Bedouin leaders are also found in his entourage and as governors, but as the reign progressed, the *ghilmān* became more and more influential. In 338/950, he had 2,000 of them, led by a Turkish officer, when he consolidated his power in the Jazīra, and later in the reign they came to hold many key posts. After Sayf al-Dawla's death, his *ghilmān* were an important factor in the politics of the area, some of them trying to become independent or accepting Fatimid overlordship. Hamdanid Syria, like Hamdanid Mosul, was not basically an Arab tribal state; it was rather based on the principles of late ʿAbbasid government, with its extensive use of *ghilmān*, and it is useful to remember how closely Sayf al-Dawla had been involved in Baghdad politics before he ever came to Syria.

Much of Sayf al-Dawla's reputation, both with his contemporaries and with posterity, rested on his role as a champion of Islam against the military might of the Byzantine Empire, and before discussing his contribution, it is appropriate to consider the history of the frontier throughout the early Islamic period.

After the initial success of the Arab conquests, the Byzantines retained control of the highlands of Anatolia as far as the passes through the Taurus Mountains. At first, the Muslims seem to have preferred to keep the land to the south of this as a no man's land, a sort of *cordon sanitaire*, between them and the enemy. Muslim forces tended to concentrate on bases to the rear like Antioch and Dābiq. The Cilician plain, which had been rich and prosperous in classical antiquity, was left almost uninhabited. In the early second/eighth century, however, this position began to change. After the reign of the Umayyad Caliph Sulaymān b. ʿAbd al-Malik (96–99/715–717), there were no more major attacks on Constantinople, and it became clear that the Byzantine Empire and the Muslim caliphate were going to coexist for some time. This change was confirmed at the time of the ʿAbbasid revolution when Byzantine forces led by Constantine V (741–775) began to take the initiative and Muslim cities like Malaṭiya, which had been in Arab hands since the conquests, were threatened by the enemy. Under the later Umayyads and early ʿAbbasids, the frontier provinces began to be settled and fortified in depth. In the Cilician plain, Adana, Maṣṣīṣa (Misis) and above all Tarsus became great Muslim cities, while farther to the east, Marʿash, Ḥadath and Malaṭiya became centres of population and military activity. These Muslim outposts were mostly urban in character, and all were situated in the plains or river valleys, while the Byzantines were restricted to the highlands and the cities of the plateau to the north. The Muslims continued to raid Byzantine territory, and sometimes, as in the later years of Hārūn's reign (187–193/803–809) and the reign of al-Muʿtaṣim (218–227/833–842), there were full-scale military campaigns, but the objectives were booty and prisoners and the demonstration of the caliph's role as the defender of Islam, rather than the acquisition of new territory.

For 200 years, the Muslim cities of the frontier provinces enjoyed security and growing prosperity. It has been suggested that they were major centres of Arab–Byzantine trade, but there is no evidence for large-scale cross-border commerce, and we hear mostly of exchanges of prisoners and ransoms. The wealth of the area was derived from local commerce and industry, especially the textile workshops of Tarsus. They also enjoyed a very favourable fiscal status, since rates of taxation were kept low on the frontiers in order to encourage settlement and because the frontier cities received continuous subsidies from other parts of the Muslim world on account of their role in the *jihād* (Holy War). Ibn Ḥawqal, writing in the mid-fourth/tenth century, describes how there were hostels in Tarsus for *ghāzīs*, warriors for the Faith from every corner of the Muslim world, where these volunteers could come and take part in the struggle against the infidel; these hostels were supported by pious donations from the provinces whose *ghāzīs* were lodged there. The prosperity and security of the frontier areas then were largely based on continuing support, both financial and in men, from the rest of the Muslim world.

In the fourth/tenth century, this happy state of affairs began to change. The Byzantine emperors, encouraged by the great military landowning families of eastern Anatolia, began systematic campaigns of conquest. At the same time, the political fragmentation of the Muslim world meant that the traditional support from the rest of the Islamic world was greatly reduced. The Byzantine advance began in earnest in 322/934 when the general John Curcuas took Malaṭiya, the first large Muslim city to fall into Greek hands, the Baghdad government of al-Muqtadir and al-Qāhir being quite unable to send support to the threatened outpost, despite repeated appeals for help. It is against this sombre background that Sayf al-Dawla's role in the *jihād* must be considered.

Even before he became the ruler of Aleppo, Sayf al-Dawla had shown his commitment to the *jihād*. In 328/940, he led a foray to the Van area and on to the Byzantine territory to loosen the enemy's grip on the town of Qālīqalā (Erzerum). After he took over Aleppo in 333/945, he could not avoid facing the Byzantines almost every year. Until 345/956, he was moderately successful, holding his own in a long series of raids, ambushes and brief treaties. Sometimes, his expeditions were on quite a large scale: in 339/950, he led 30,000 of his own men and 4,000 men of Tarsus into the mountains on a raid which proved disastrous. He also took care to restore frontier fortresses like Mar'ash and Ḥadath in 341/952. From 345/956, however, he faced increasing Byzantine pressure, which he was quite unable to resist effectively. The main reason for this change seems to have been the arrival on the eastern frontiers of the Byzantine Empire of a new commander, Nicephorus Phocas, later to be the emperor, and his brother Leo, and a new army, composed largely of Armenians, like the young officer John Tzimisces, who was to be Nicephorus' successor on the imperial throne. The policy of raids was replaced by one of territorial expansion: in 346/957, the rebuilt Ḥadath was sacked, in 347/958 Sumaysāṭ. (Samosata) fell and in 349/960 Sayf al-Dawla suffered a major defeat when his army was attacked in the mountains by the troops of Leo Phocas. He himself escaped, but his capacity to resist the Byzantines on anything like equal terms was lost. In 351/962, the Byzantine army attacked Aleppo itself. Sayf al-Dawla had been unable to offer any serious opposition, retired beyond the Euphrates and abandoned the city to its fate. While a small garrison in the citadel continued to resist, the rest of the town and the Hamdanid palace outside the walls were devastated. After this blow, nothing could stop the inexorable advance of Byzantine armies: in the same year, Mar'ash fell and in 354/965 Maṣṣīṣa and Tarsus were taken and Byzantines established control over all the rich Cilician plain.

One reason for the success of Byzantine arms at this time was the massive superiority in numbers which they enjoyed. Although the figures are no doubt exaggerated, it is said that Byzantine armies numbered up to 200,000, whereas Sayf al-Dawla could never call on more than 30,000 and usually very much fewer. Furthermore, he was unable to call on resources from without his own limited domains. When the Byzantines had attempted offensives in the early 'Abbasid period, Hārūn al-Rashīd or al-Mu'taṣim had been able to call on the resources of the whole Muslim world and raise up to 100,000 men. But since the fragmentation of the caliphate, this was impossible. Even his own brother, Nāṣir al-Dawla of Mosul, was unable or unwilling to offer Sayf al-Dawla effective support – still less would the Buyids of Iraq or the *ikhshīd* of Egypt. It was not a question of the Byzantine Empire against the Muslim world but rather the Byzantine Empire against Sayf al-Dawla's small, northern Syrian principality. Furthermore, the disputes of the rest of the Muslim world were often reflected on the frontiers. In the years before the Byzantine conquest, Cilicia had seen bitter strife among supporters of the Ikhshidids, the Hamdanids and local leaders. Faced with the final crisis, the governor of Tarsus, Rashīq al-Nāsimī, received no outside support at all in his struggle.

This was not because there was no popular enthusiasm for the *jihād*. Byzantine successes, the deportation of Muslim populations and the conversion of mosques into stables provoked popular indignation in the Muslim world. In 353/964, a group of 5,000 *ghāzīs* from Khurāsān arrived to help defend Maṣṣīṣa against the Byzantines, but they were thwarted by famine conditions and retired to Antioch, where they formed another party in the already divided city. In 355/966, a large number of Khurāsānīs, 20,000, arrived at Rayy on their way to the Byzantine frontier and demanded vast sums from the Buyid ruler, Rukn al-Dawla, to support them in this enterprise. When this was not forthcoming, they attacked the city, pillaged the palace of the *wazīr* Ibn al-'Amīd and almost killed Rukn al-Dawla himself before being dispersed by his Daylamite soldiers; none of them seems to have reached the frontier. In 361/972, refugees brought news of further Byzantine successes to Baghdad and the populace demanded that the caliph and the Buyid ruler, Bakhtiyār, take action to defend the Muslims, but the politicians diverted the enthusiasm for their own purposes – much of Baghdad was pillaged, but the army never set out. Compared with the inaction or indifference of other Muslim rulers, it is not surprising that Sayf al-Dawla's popular reputation remained high; he was the one man who attempted to defend the Faith, the essential hero of the time.

The Byzantine successes had important long-term consequences for the history of the area. Towns like Tarsus and Malaṭiya had for two centuries been Muslim Arabic-speaking centres. The Byzantine conquest changed that forever. When the Greeks took these cities, they did not simply replace one government with another; they drove out or enslaved all the existing inhabitants, and mass deportations to central Anatolia and expulsions to other areas of the Muslim world effectively depopulated the cities. These empty areas required inhabitants, and in order to people them, Nicephorus Phocas encouraged Christians living under Muslim rule to come and settle. The historian Yaḥyā b. Sa'īd, who left Egypt to escape the uncertainties of the Fatimid Caliph al-Ḥākim's rule and settled in Byzantine Antioch, was one such. The most extensive settlement was around Malaṭiya. Nicephorus invited the Monophysite (Jacobite) patriarch of Antioch, who normally lived around Raqqa or Ḥarrān, to come north with his followers. The settlement of Christians is reflected in the expansion of the ecclesiastical administration. In the century between 950 and 1050, ten new bishoprics appeared around Malaṭiya, four around Mar'ash and five in the area of Sumaysāṭ, and the Chronicle of Michael the Syrian mentions fifty-six new monasteries in the area between 936 and 1047. This influx of Jacobite Christians, who were regarded as heretics by many in the Constantinople establishment, was to cause problems in the next century, and in the 1030s the Patriarch Dionysius IV preferred to live under Muslim rule in Āmid than under Byzantine authority in Malaṭiya. On the coast, the cities of Antioch and Laodicea seem to have been settled by Greek Orthodox Christians, and as well as refugees from Egypt like himself, Yaḥyā b. Sa'īd records in 404/1013 that large numbers of Christians from Palestine fled the depredations of the Banū Ṭayy to settle in the area. In Cilicia, the most important settlement was the fifth/eleventh-century migration of Armenians from eastern Anatolia. By the year 1050 then, the Muslims had been eliminated from a large swathe of territory along the frontiers and in northern Syria, and Arab civilization had been almost entirely uprooted. When these lands again passed into Muslim hands, they were settled not by Arabs but by Turkish-speaking tribesmen.

It was not only on the Byzantine front that Sayf al-Dawla's last years were beset by problems. The last six years of Sayf al-Dawla's life (350–356/961–967) were marked by an almost complete collapse of his government. This was to some extent because he was afflicted by partial paralysis, which made it difficult for him to play an active role. The conquest of Aleppo by the Byzantines in 351/962 was a terrible blow to his prestige and power. When the enemy approached the city, he was unable to put up any serious resistance and abandoned the people to their fate. It was the citizens who manned the city walls to resist the attackers and the shaykhs of the city who finally negotiated a treaty with the enemy. It is said that 10,000 prisoners were taken to Byzantine territory, most of them young people, and Aleppo must have been something of a ghost town. Sayf al-Dawla abandoned his capital almost completely and retired across the Euphrates to Mayyāfāriqīn, leaving Aleppo in the care of his *Ḥājib* (chamberlain) Qarqūya.

These misfortunes and Sayf al-Dawla's manifest inability to deal with the problems which was faced by him led to a number of rebellions. In 354/965, Marwān al-ʿUqaylī, an ex-Qarmaṭī leader long in his service, led a rebellion in the Homs area and was able to enter Aleppo itself before he died of wounds received in the battle for the city. Later the same year, there was a major disturbance in Antioch, now directly threatened by Greek advances in the Cilician plain, and led originally by the exiled governor of Tarsus, Rashīq al-Nasīmī. Once again, the issue must have been Sayf al-Dawla's failure to protect the area. A force of 5,000 men, led by a Daylamī commander, Dizbar, attacked Aleppo, and Sayf al-Dawla himself came west to confront them. His prestige was not entirely dead; the Kilābī tribesmen who had joined the rebel cause returned to him and he was finally victorious. Severe reprisals were taken against the people of Antioch, only four years before it fell to the Byzantines.

In Safar 356/February 967, Sayf al-Dawla died aged fifty-one. He had ruled Aleppo for twenty-three years and died in the city, but his body was embalmed and taken to Mayyāfāriqīn for burial. He was succeeded without opposition by his only surviving son, Sharīf Saʿd al-Dawla, but the disasters of the last year of his father's life meant that the inheritance was not an easy one. Sayf al-Dawla's chief minister in Aleppo, Qarqūya, accepted Saʿd al-Dawla as the ruler but advised him to stay away from the city. Many of his father's companions went to join his cousin, Abū Taghlib, in Mosul, while he himself with only 300 followers was refused entry to Ḥarrān and was turned away from Mayyāfāriqīn by his own mother. For the next ten years (357–367/968–977), he had neither state nor capital. Aleppo was ruled by Qarqūya, supported by Sayf al-Dawla's *ghilmān*, who were determined to preserve their position now that their old master was dead.

The main problem Qarqūya faced was in relation to the Byzantines. In 358/969, they took Antioch and began setting up the Byzantine province of Syria, which was to include the coastal hills as far south as Ṭarṭūs. Faced by this formidable power, Qarqūya had to make terms. In 359/969, the Byzantines temporarily occupied Aleppo, and Qarqūya made a treaty which effectively made Aleppo a Byzantine tributary state. It also made provision for the free passage of commercial caravans between Aleppo and Antioch. This truce laid the foundations of Byzantine policy towards Aleppo for the next half-century. The Byzantines seem to have had no wish to annex the city to the empire. Instead, they sought to keep it as an independent, tribute-paying buffer state. Normally, they do not seem to have interfered in internal affairs, but they were prepared to take military action if any outside Muslim power threatened to take over the city. In the same year, the position was further altered by the Fatimid conquest of Egypt. This meant that the feeble government of the Ikhshidids to the south of the Hamdanid state was replaced by a determined and energetic administration, prepared to make serious efforts to gain control. From 358/969 onwards, the weakened and truncated principality of Aleppo was to be the scene of constant rivalry between the two superpowers. These years saw the high point of Byzantine power in Syria during the reign of John Tzimisces (969–976), who in 361/972 led a great expedition which reached as far south as Caesarea and Tiberias in Palestine, although the southern boundary of Byzantine Syria remained approximately on the modern Lebanese–Syrian border.

Sa'd al-Dawla's position improved in 367/977 when two of his father's *ghilmān*, who had established themselves in the country to the south of Aleppo, invited him to join them in a bid to take over the city. By this time, power in Aleppo had passed from Qarqūya into the hands of a Circassian *mamlūk* (military slave) of his called Bakjūr. (It seems that the Hamdanids were the first dynasty to recruit *ghilmān/mamlūks* from Circassia at the Black Sea end of the Caucasus Mountains. Circassian *mamlūks* were later to be extremely important in the Middle East, notably in Egypt, where they provided most of the sultans from 784/1382 to the Ottoman conquest in 922/1517.) Despite some setbacks, Sa'd al-Dawla was able to set up a siege of Aleppo and, with the aid of the Banū Kilāb who had served his father so well, to take the city. Bakjūr had to be placated with the governorate of Homs, which he used as a base for intrigue with the Fatimids.

Once established in Aleppo, Sa'd al-Dawla released Qarqūya to serve him until his death three years later (380/990–991). After this, Sa'd al-Dawla continued his policy of dependence on the Byzantines, who supported him with up to 6,000 Greek and Armenian troops against the attacks of Bakjūr and his Fatimid supporters.

Sa'd al-Dawla died in Ramaḍān 381/December 991. Towards the end of his reign, he seems to have regained something of his father's position, but he was heavily dependent on the Byzantines and his father's *ghilmān*, while his principality was confined to Aleppo and its environs. He was never wealthy enough to build up his own corps of *ghilmān*. All the coastal area was now in Byzantine hands – the Jazīra, including the second capital of Mayyāfāriqīn, had been lost to the Kurdish Marwanid dynasty, while the southern towns around Homs were usually in the hands of the Fatimids or their supporters. His death caused another rash of defections. His young son Sa'īd al-Dawla was dominated by his military adviser Lu'lu', who continued the policy of alliance with the Byzantines. Other *ghilmān* resented him and went over to the Fatimids, who launched a series of attacks on Aleppo between 382 and 384 (993–995), and in 995 the city was only saved by the arrival of the Byzantine Emperor Basil II in person. In 392/1002, Sa'īd al-Dawla died, and Lu'lu' soon exiled the rest of the family to Egypt and took over power in his own name. He tried to break away from overly close dependence on the Byzantines and acknowledged the authority of the Fatimids. After his death in 399/1008, his son, Manṣūr, took over, but he was now little more than a Fatimid governor. The city state of Aleppo was unable to sustain itself against the pressure of the bedouin tribes, notably the Banū Kilāb. Manṣūr tried to solve the problem by one of those macabre dinner parties which were a feature of Middle Eastern political life. He invited the leaders of

Kilāb to a feast in the citadel of Aleppo and had them murdered. One leader, Ṣālih. b. Mirdās, escaped and it was he who roused the tribe to vengeance. Manṣūr was forced into exile in Byzantine territory, where he was given some castles in the mountains near Antioch whence he could survey the affairs of the city he had once ruled. With his departure in 406/1016, the last traces of the Hamdanid state perished. Only the desire of the Hamdanid *ghilmān* and the Banū Kilāb to remain independent of the Fatimids and the support of the Byzantines had kept it alive so long.

12 Bedouin political movements and dynasties

Origins

Despite their Arab origins, the Hamdanids were products of the middle ʿAbbasid political system, relying on *ghilmān* for their military power and professional bureaucrats to collect their taxes. After the early stages, their role as tribal leaders played no part in their government, and the tribe from which they sprang disappeared into obscurity. In both Mosul and Aleppo, they were succeeded by leaders, the ʿUqaylids and Mirdasids, whose power was directly dependent on their tribal followings, who employed no *ghilmān* and remained first and foremost bedouin shaykhs even when they acquired the rights to collect taxes from settled areas and cities. Nor was this process confined to Mosul and Aleppo; all around the Fertile Crescent from southern Iraq to Palestine, we find bedouin tribes and their leaders establishing or attempting to establish small independent states. The Banū Asad (Mazyadids) in the Kūfa area, the Numayrīs in Ḥarrān, the Banū Kalb in the Damascus area and the Banū Ṭayy in southern Palestine are all examples. Some of the tribes which became prominent at this time, notably the Banū Kalb and Banū Asad, had been important in their areas since Umayyad times, but many others, including the ʿUqayl, Numayr, Kilāb and Ṭayy, seem to have been mostly newcomers to the districts they came to dominate. Equally tribes which had been important in the Umayyad and early ʿAbbasid periods are heard of no more. The example of the Taghlib has already been cited, but other important groupings – the Tamīm and Shaybān in Iraq, the Tanūkh, Lakhm and Judhām in Syria – seem to have declined during the ʿAbbasid period. The rise of the bedouin dynasties of the fourth/tenth century was the result of both an upheaval among the bedouins of the Syrian and north Arabian Deserts and the changing relationships between the settled and pastoral peoples of the area. To understand this process, we must investigate the history of the bedouin in the previous century.

The bedouin tribes of the Arabian and Syrian Deserts had formed a large part of the armies of the Islamic conquests. In Umayyad times, they had continued to be influential, as supporters of the dynasty or of factions

DOI: 10.4324/9780429348129-12

within the ruling house or as Kharijite rebels opposing Umayyad authority. After the 'Abbasid revolution, however, their importance began to decline. The Khurāsāniyya who formed the most important group in the armies of the new dynasty lived not as bedouin but as townsmen settled in cities like Raqqa and Baghdad. Tribal leaders like Yazīd b. Mazyad of Shaybān and Kharijite rebels like al-Walīd b. Ṭarīf (killed in the Jazīra, 179/795) continued to play a reduced part in the politics of the caliphate but the defeat of al-Amīn (198/813) and the rise to power of the military and bureaucratic élite under al-Mu'taṣim (218–227/833–842) meant an end to this role. From this time, the bedouin were effectively refused access to government and to government patronage and they no longer received any subsidies. From being a dominant Arab race, they became, once again, as they had been before the coming of Islam: the ignorant, uncouth, despised outsiders.

As has already been pointed out, the bedouin life is not economically self-sufficient. The bedouin are dependent on settled people for additional income and, by paying them *'aṭā'* (salaries), entertaining them at court and allowing them to participate in the military expeditions against the Byzantines, the early Islamic state had subsidized them. The cutting off of these subsidies by al-Mu'taṣim led to a revival of nomad pressure on the settled people of the area, which was to be the major feature of the fourth/-tenth- and fifth/eleventh-century history of the Fertile Crescent. Disturbances among the bedouin were not unknown in the third/ninth century. In 230/845, there were widespread disturbances in the Ḥijāz caused by the Banū Sulaym, who were taxing markets and stopping caravans. The Caliph al-Wāthiq sent one of his Turkish generals, Bughā the Elder, with an army of Turks and Berbers to suppress them and took the opportunity to intimidate other tribes, notably the Banū Kilāb, then found in central Arabia farther to the east. The discontent remained. In 251/865, the Banū 'Uqayl, complaining about their poverty, blocked the road between Mecca and the port of Jedda, a vital route for supplies for the Holy City. A generation later in 285/898, the Banū Ṭayy were responsible for pillaging the *Ḥajj* (pilgrimage) caravan as it passed through their territory. Not only was the safeguarding of the *Ḥajj* a matter of concern to the government for religious reasons but it was also the main commercial activity in Arabia, and the bedouin were signalling that they wanted a share of the profits. The Ṭayy acquired great wealth from this attack, and it is a sign of changing circumstances that they do not seem to have been effectively punished.

These discontents were given a unity and an ideological purpose in the rebellions of the Qarmaṭīs (or Qarāmiṭa, often referred to as Carmathians in Western writings). The Qarmaṭī movement led to fundamental changes in the distribution and relative strengths of the bedouin tribes in the Syrian and Arabian Deserts and this probably marks the most important such movement between the Islamic conquests and the Wahhābī wars of the eighteenth and early nineteenth centuries which largely shaped the modern tribal map of the Syrian and north Arabian Deserts.

The Qarāmiṭa

The Qarāmiṭa were a branch of the Ismāʿīlī movement. It seems that the sect was named after one Ḥamdān Qarmaṭ, who, before 260/873–874, had begun to spread Ismāʿīlī ideas among the agricultural peasantry on the Sawād of Kūfa, preaching and collecting contributions from the faithful. At first, the movement was not particularly militant, but it inevitably came into conflict with the ʿAbbasid authorities and there were a series of small-scale rebellions from 284/897 onwards, all of them crushed by the government of the able and ruthless Caliph al-Muʿtaḍid. The Ismāʿīlī movement also began to suffer from internal divisions. The exact nature of these disagreements is shrouded in mystery, but their consequences were to be far-reaching. It seems that the movement was directed from a base at Salamiyya, on the western edge of the Syrian Desert, probably by ʿUbayd Allāh, who was to become the first Fatimid ruler in north Africa ten years later.

The original doctrine of the Ismāʿīlīs concerned the identity of the true *imām* and a division of opinion as to who was the rightful successor of Jaʿfar al-Ṣādiq (d. 148/765). His son, Ismāʿīl, who was originally held to be his successor, had died before his father. By the mid-fourth/tenth century, the majority of the Shīʿa of Iraq believed that Mūsā al-Kāẓim, another son, was Jaʿfar's successor and that the line of rightful *imāms* descended from him. As their name implies, however, the Ismāʿīlīs held that Ismāʿīl, or his son Muḥammad, was the last true *imām*, that he would come in glory as the *mahdī* and that until that time there was no visible and acknowledged *imām* on earth. ʿUbayd Allāh the Fatimid, however, broke with this, claiming that he was himself a descendant of Muḥammad b. Ismāʿīl and that the Ismāʿīlīs should pay him homage as the true *imām*. This move provoked strong opposition in the sect and many, among them Ḥamdān Qarmaṭ, refused to accept the new doctrine. A split developed between those who accepted that ʿUbayd Allāh was indeed the *mahdī* and those who believed that the Ismāʿīlīs should continue to await the return of Muḥammad b. Ismāʿīl.

The immediate effect of the schism was to weaken the movement in Iraq, and Ḥamdān himself disappears from the record. Other missionaries, however, continued to spread the word in different areas, keeping to the old Ismāʿīlī faith. They and their followers are conventionally known as Qarmaṭīs or Qarāmiṭa to distinguish them from the supporters of the Fatimids. They no longer derived their main support from the Sawād of Kūfa but began to proselytize in other parts of the Muslim world.

The first of these was the desert to the west of Kūfa on the road to Tadmur (Palmyra) and Damascus. This area was dominated by the powerful Kalb tribe, who it would seem had already been attacking traffic on this route. A Qarmaṭī missionary from the Sawād called Zikrawayh sent his son al-Ḥusayn to make contact with these bedouin, and he made enough conversions to be able to mobilize a considerable military force. He was joined by Yaḥyā, who was probably his brother. They took code names to conceal their identities – Yaḥyā being Ṣāḥib al-Nāqa (Master of the She-camel), while al-Ḥusayn was Ṣāḥib al-Shāma (the Man with the Mole). In 290/903, they besieged Damascus, but the city was stoutly defended by Ṭughj, father of Muḥammad b. Ṭughj the *ikhshīd* (ruler of Egypt, 323–334/935–946), the attack was repulsed and the Ṣāḥib al-Nāqa killed. This was not the end of the affair, however. The Ṣāḥib al-Shāma took over leadership and the Qarmaṭī army pillaged much of northern Syria, including the towns of Homs, Ḥamāh, Maʻarrat al-Nuʻmān and Baʻalbak. A contemporary source describes the army as "most of the people of the desert" and there could be no clearer illustration of the resurgent power of the bedouin. It was at this time too that the Qarāmiṭa took Salamiyya and destroyed the residence of ʻUbayd Allāh the Fatimid, who had prudently left for north Africa shortly before.

This full-scale rebellion produced a major ʻAbbasid reaction. A large army under the command of Muḥammad b. Sulaymān was sent to Syria, and in 291/904 the Qarāmiṭa were severely defeated east of Ḥamāh and the Ṣāḥib al-Shāma killed. Despite this setback, the movement continued to attract support. In 293/906, the Kalb and other Qarmaṭī tribes sacked the Ḥawrān area and Tiberias as well as making another unsuccessful attempt on Damascus. In the same year, Zikrawayh himself left his hiding place near Kūfa and took the field in person for the first time. The next year (294/907), he was killed leading an attack on the *Ḥajj* caravan, and with his death the Qarmaṭī movement among the tribesmen of the Syrian Desert effectively came to an end. It is noteworthy that the leadership of the movement came from the settled people of the Sawād. The bedouin were obviously restive before the arrival of the Qarmaṭī missionaries, but it was the preaching of the sect which acted as a catalyst and gave purpose to their raids. The leaders of the armies were the two sons of Zikrawayh, both of whom claimed religious authority as descendants of Muḥammad b. Ismāʻīl, not shaykhs of the Kalb or any other tribe. The aims of the military activity, however, reflected the priorities of the bedouin: to secure tribute or booty from the settled communities. No effort was made to occupy conquered cities or establish an administration to control them. The effect of the rebellion was to weaken the settled communities to the advantage of the bedouin, a process which was to continue throughout the next century and a half.

Another area where Qarmaṭī missionaries met with success was in Baḥrayn. (In the early Islamic period, this term applied to the mainland areas of the Ḥasā' province of Saudi Arabia as well as the island nowadays called Baḥrayn, which was then known as Uwāl.) This area was inhabited by a heterogeneous population of farmers in the oases, merchants travelling the Gulf to such ports as Baṣra and Sīrāf, and the bedouin of the desert areas. It was among this varied population that an Ismāʻīlī missionary of Persian origin, Abū Saʻīd al-Jannābī, managed to recruit a large number of followers.

By 286/899, the year of the split in the Ismāʿīlī movement, he had converted much of the population and married into one of the leading commercial and landowning families, that of al-Ḥasan b. Sanbar. He also looked for allies among the bedouin of the desert and found them in the Banū Kilāb and the Banū ʿUqayl, who now came to occupy the leading position among the tribes of central and eastern Arabia, as the Tamīm and ʿAbd al-Qays had done in early Islamic times. This partnership between the Qarmaṭī leadership, their followers among the settled population, and the bedouin was to prove extremely formidable. Hajar, the capital of the province and seat of the ʿAbbasid governor, was taken, and in 287/900, an ʿAbbasid army was decisively defeated. Then, the Qarāmiṭa began to threaten the city of Baṣra itself. This first militant stage was brought to an end in 300/913 when Abū Saʿīd was assassinated in his new capital at Ḥasāʾ near Hajar. He was succeeded by his son Saʿīd, who entered into negotiations with the Baghdad authorities. He stressed the poverty of his followers and seems to have sought a subsidy from the government and trading opportunities, an interesting insight into the motivations of these early Qarāmiṭa.

While ʿAlī b. ʿĪsā was influential in Baghdad, this policy proved effective, and in 303/915–916 the *wazīr* sent presents and granted the right of free trade in Sīrāf, on the eastern shore of the Gulf. In 310/922–923, however, the position changed when Saʿīd was replaced by his much more militant younger brother Abū Ṭāhir, while the next year ʿAlī b. ʿĪsā lost power to Ibn al-Furāt, who was less inclined to take a conciliatory attitude. From this point onwards, it was war. In 311/923, Baṣra was taken and sacked by the rebels, with great destruction of life and property. Since 303/916, the *Ḥajj* had been allowed to go in peace, but in 311/924, it was attacked by a force of Qarāmiṭa, 800 horse and 1,000 foot, who pillaged it. The same happened again the next year, while the *Ḥajj* of 313/926 was allowed to go in peace only after the payment of a heavy subsidy. By 315/927–928, Baghdad itself was threatened, and the *wazīr*, al-Khaṣībī, sent for Ibn Abīʾl-Sāj of Āzarbayjān for more troops. The effectiveness of the Qarāmiṭa contrasted markedly with the uselessness of the Baghdad army, a fact commented on by contemporaries. Interestingly, ʿAlī b. ʿĪsā, observing, rightly, that Ibn Abīʾl-Sāj would not be successful, suggested that it would be better to employ the bedouin Banū Asad to guard the *Ḥajj* and the Banū Shaybān to attack the Qarāmiṭa; neither of these tribes were involved in the rebel movement and both could be expected to oppose the Kilābīs and ʿUqaylīs who fought for the Qarāmiṭa. His advice was not accepted and the Baghdad forces were again defeated.

In 317/930, not only was the *Ḥajj* attacked by the Qarāmiṭa and most of the pilgrims killed, but the Black Stone of the Kaʿba was stolen and taken to Baḥrayn.. This act caused great outrage, but the Baghdad government was powerless and the stone remained in Qarmaṭī hands in Ḥasāʾ until 339/951. The reasons for the removal of the stone are not entirely clear. There is no reason to suppose that it was a protest against idolatry; the Ismāʿīlī Fatimids were to be notable patrons of the *Ḥajj* in later years and the Qarāmiṭa do not seem to have destroyed other shrines. They appear to have had no objection to the *Ḥajj* as long as they, and especially their bedouin supporters, were properly rewarded for allowing its safe passage. They must certainly have hoped for concessions from the government in exchange for its return and may even have hoped to divert the *Ḥajj*, with the trading opportunities it presented, to their own capital at Ḥasā'.

The seemingly unstoppable advance of the movement was brought to an end by internal feuds. In 319/931, Abū Ṭāhir was persuaded that a Persian adventurer of obscure origin was indeed the promised *mahdī*, and yielded authority to him. The adventurer's behaviour soon made it clear that the Qarāmiṭa had been duped. He was deposed and killed, but the event seems to have damaged the morale of the sect. Aggressive activities did not cease, but the Qarāmiṭa seem to have been anxious for peace. As early as 320/932, we find Qarmaṭīs serving as soldiers in the army of the 'Abbasid general Mu'nis. In 327/939, Abū Ṭāhir made his peace with the Baghdad authorities, promising to protect the *Ḥajj* in exchange for an annual subsidy and a payment by the pilgrims. The death of Abū Ṭāhir in 332/944 and the return of the Black Stone to Mecca in 339/951 mark the assimilation of the Qarmaṭī state into the Muslim political order. Ibn Ḥawqal gives an interesting account of the community as it existed in the 350s/960s. The ruler was advised by a council, called the 'Iqdāniyya, whose opinions he was obliged to take into account. The administration included al-Ḥasan b. Sanbar's son, himself called Sanbar, whose family were effective partners in government with the descendants of Abū Saīd al-Jannābī. There was a *ṣāḥib al-shurṭa* (chief of police), a *kātib* (secretary), an army commander (who was a member of the Kilābī bedouin tribe) and a *ṣāḥib al-barīd* (chief of the post, who was also a Kilābī). The bedouin seem to have played an important part in military affairs. The revenues of the state were drawn from the land tax, tolls on the Baṣra and Mecca roads, taxation of the pilgrimage and tolls from shipping in the Gulf; commerce was vital to the financial well-being of the Qarmaṭī state. They maintained representatives in Kūfa, near Baṣra and eventually in Baghdad itself to organize their affairs. There was a marked contrast between the peace and prosperity of the Qarmaṭī state and the tyranny and chaos which prevailed elsewhere in the Fertile Crescent.

The last outbreak of Qarāmiṭa militancy was connected with the Fatimid conquest of Egypt. In the main, they kept on good terms with rulers of the Fertile Crescent, the Ikhshidids and the Hamdanids who sent them gifts, but relations with the Fatimids were complicated by the fact that the Qarāmiṭa did not acknowledge the Fatimid claims to be the true *imāms*. From 353/964, the Qarāmiṭa began to take an aggressive line under the leadership of al-Ḥasan al-A'ṣam. An expedition was launched against Syria, perhaps to help the Fatimids in their plans to take Egypt but possibly to secure increased tribute from the Ikhshidid government. Tiberias was sacked. In 357/968, the adventure was repeated and both Damascus and Ramla were taken by the Qarmaṭī armies, and again in 358/969 after the Fatimid takeover of Egypt, when al-Ḥasan b. 'Ubayd Allāh the Ikhshidid agreed to pay tribute for Ramla and Damascus. The Qarāmiṭa seem to have felt that Syria was now their protectorate, and this led to a dramatic breakdown in relations with the Fatimids. Open warfare soon flared. The Qarmaṭī effort was hampered by internal strife at Ḥasā' but in 360/971 Damascus and Ramla were taken and Egypt invaded. To demonstrate their disenchantment with the Fatimid regime, the Qarāmiṭa proclaimed 'Abbasid authority in the areas they captured. Thereafter, Qarmaṭī attacks on Egypt and Syria continued until they were defeated by the Caliph al-'Azīz in 368/978. They retreated to Ḥasā' in exchange for the promise of a subsidy. Apart from a brief late occupation of Kūfa, this marked the end of the Qarmaṭī threat to the neighbouring lands.

The movement was now confined to Baḥrayn. In accepting this, it lost the allegiance of the bedouin tribesmen who had supported the sect when there was the opportunity for booty and tribute. In the end, it was a tribal leader from the Muntafiq branch of the 'Uqayl who turned against them, capturing and pillaging Ḥasā' in 378/988. After this, the Qarāmiṭa could no longer tax the commercial routes of the north Arabian and Syrian Deserts, and it was nomad tribal leaders who took over this role.

The bedouin dynasties

The rise and decline of the Qarāmiṭa were the prelude to the establishment of the bedouin dynasties of the late fourth/tenth and fifth/eleventh centuries. The Qarāmiṭa had profoundly affected the balance of power among the tribes in the north Arabian and Syrian Deserts, and in the main it was tribes which had been involved in the movement which came to dominate the area – not, however, in the name of a religious ideal but for their own tribal interests; and they were now led not by missionaries from the settled peoples but by their own tribal shaykhs. Kilāb and 'Uqayl had been the leading supporters of the Qarāmiṭa of Baḥrayn and it seems that in the second half of the fourth/tenth century, many of them, disillusioned with the decline of the power of the movement, drifted north to join fellow-tribesmen already established in the hinterlands of Mosul and Aleppo. The influence of the Kalb in central Syria had probably been consolidated by their leading role in the rebellions of the Syrian Qarāmiṭa, while the Ṭayy seem to have moved from north Arabia to Palestine during the last waves of Qarmaṭī attacks on the area. Of the tribes which founded bedouin states at this period, only the Asadīs in the Kūfa area had played no part in the movement.

The establishment of the bedouin states was, however, more than just the result of a new wave of Arab immigrants from Arabia. The founders of these bedouin states all owed something to the patronage of rulers of settled states. The Kilābīs owed much of their predominance in northern Syria to the support given them by Sayf al-Dawla the Hamdanid. The primacy of the ruling clan of the 'Uqayl was greatly aided by 'Aḍud al-Dawla the Buyid, who made them responsible for the disciplining of their fellow-tribesmen, thus giving their authority the support of his government. It was the attempts of the last Hamdanids to counter the influence of the Kurd Bādh in the Mosul area by granting lands to the ʿUqaylids which ensured their control of northern Iraq. Equally, the Mazyadid leaders of the Asad tribe owed much to the patronage of Bakhtiyār and later contenders for power in Buyid Baghdad who sought their support, while Ibn Ustādh-hurmuz (Buyid governor of Baghdad, 392–401/1002–1010) was to rely on them to discipline the bedouin of the area. None of the dynasties would have achieved power without the patronage of settled rulers.

The dynasties which prospered were only able to do so because they controlled the revenues of towns and settled areas. The power of ʿUqaylid rulers lay in their tribal following, but it was control of Mosul which brought them the wealth these followers needed. Ṣāliḥ. b. Mirdās was simply one of a number of Kilābī chiefs until he took possession of Aleppo, a position which assured his primacy in the tribe. In the desert, a nomad state was impossible since no chief could command absolute authority. Contact with settled powers and peoples enabled some ruling clans to establish themselves as effective dynasts, even while retaining a nomad lifestyle. The possession of the revenues of settled lands also helped the chiefs to increase their tribal following. At first, the dominant position of the ʿUqayl in northern Iraq looks to be the product of a vast influx of tribesmen from Arabia, but this may be something of an illusion. There certainly were new immigrants from northern Arabia at this time, but it may also be that many of the members of these newly dominant tribes in fact came from other groups, had attached themselves to the successful tribe and were henceforward counted among the ʿUqayl or Kilāb. Such a process would account in part for the greatly expanded numbers of these tribes and for the disappearance from historical sources of other bedouin tribes in the area.

In economic terms, the changing relationships between the nomads and the settled population can be seen in the laments of numerous sources about the decline of settled agriculture and the occupation by the bedouin of farmland. The areas worst affected were probably Trans-Jordan, where almost all urban and much village life seems to have come to an end at this time, the Ḥawrān south of Damascus, and the northern Jazīra, where Ibn Ḥawqal describes the process most clearly. But there is evidence from the immediate neighbourhood of Damascus, Homs and in central Iraq (in the once fertile Sawād) which all points in the same direction. There can be no doubt that the century 950–1050 saw a vast increase in the area used for nomad pasture and the collapse of the agricultural economy in districts which had once been the granaries of the ʿAbbasid caliphate. It would be wrong to present a purely negative view of these changes. There were cities which benefited from the bedouin ascendancy. Aleppo seems to have been more prosperous under the Kilābī Mirdasids than it had been under the Hamdanids. It may have been that tax levels were lower under bedouin rule than under the domination of regimes like the Buyids or Hamdanids with expensive *ghilmān* to pay. Certainly, the city which suffered the best-documented urban crisis in this period, Baghdad, was never under bedouin control, while in nearby Ḥilla the camp of the Mazyadid clan of the Banū Asad developed into a flourishing city.

The Mazyadids

The Banū Asad owed their rise to power in the Kūfa area to Buyid weaknesses and the endemic tensions between Turks and Daylamites in Iraq. From their modest beginnings as bedouin shaykhs, the Mazyadid clan used the power of the tribe to found an enduring and powerful state whose influence was to last for a century and a half in the lands that bordered the Euphrates to the south of Baghdad and whose most lasting achievement was the foundation of the city of Ḥilla, which replaced Kūfa as the leading town of the area and is today the local provincial capital. The shaykhs of Asad first began to play an important role in politics in 364/974–975, when the Buyid Bakhtiyār was attempting to dislodge the Turkish commander Alptakīn from Baghdad and invited one Ḍabba b. Muḥammad al-Asadī to raid the area around the city; it was a sinister portent for the future as, for the first time, nomad depredations were given government approval. Two years later, in 366/977, when Bakhtiyār was facing the army of his cousin ʻAḍud al-Dawla, he called on the support of another Asadī leader, Dubays b. ʻAfīf. Like so many of the things Bakhtiyār did, this turned out to be an ill-judged move; not only did the Asadīs desert him in the conflict, precipitating the breakup of his army, but they also pillaged his baggage.

ʻAḍud al-Dawla was strong enough to take firm measures against the bedouin, and in 369/979–980 he sent an army to the desert stronghold of the Banū Asad at ʻAyn al-Tamr. The tribe was scattered and their leaders only just escaped. The death of ʻAḍud al-Dawla in 372/983 and the rivalry between his sons shifted the balance once more in favour of the bedouin. As soon as ʻAḍud was dead, Dubays b. ʻAfīf was employed by a Buyid rival to challenge the power of ʻAḍud successor, Sharaf al-Dawla. In 387/997–998, ʻAlī b. Mazyad, now apparently the chief of the Asadīs, refused to pay tribute to Bahāʼ al-Dawla in Baghdad and declared instead for Ṣamṣām al-Dawla, then ruling in distant Shīrāz. Bahāʼ al-Dawla's forces marched against ʻAyn al-Tamr, but unable to secure their supplies in the desert, they were forced to make peace. This treaty confirmed ʻAlī's power and status, and from this time onwards, the Mazyadids enjoyed virtual independence. The failure of the Buyids to prevent this was largely a product of their own internal rivalries. The nomads were able to provide a force of cavalry which made them sought-after allies in times of conflict, while on those occasions when the government did try to reassert its power, they could take advantage of desert retreats where only ʻAḍud al-Dawla was able to reach them.

The Asadīs became increasingly bold in their raids into settled areas, sometimes in alliance with the Banū ʻUqayl. In 389/999, they pillaged Dayr

'Āqūl on the Tigris, and in 392/1002 Asadīs and 'Uqaylids joined forces to prevent the Buyid commander in Baghdad from retaking al-Madā'in, then under 'Uqaylid "protection". The Buyid ruler, Bahā' al-Dawla, was by now permanently resident in Shīrāz, and his commander in Baghdad, Abū Ja'far al-Ḥajjāj, found himself almost entirely surrounded by bedouin or Kurdish nomad forces, the city an island of Buyid control in a countryside dominated by pastoral peoples. For a time it seemed as if Baghdad too would be lost, but in 392/1002, a decisive battle was fought near Ḥilla between a joint army of 'Uqaylid and Asadī bedouin on the one side and al-Ḥajjāj, aided by the bedouin Banū Khafāja and the Kurdish 'Annazids, on the other. Baghdad was saved for the Buyids but the incident shows how powerful the Arab tribes had become and how they could roam at will through the Sawād; Asadīs from west of the Euphrates could sack Dayr 'Āqūl on the east bank of the Tigris. Not since the time of the Arab conquest had nomad bands had such freedom, and their activities must have been both a cause and a consequence of the impoverishment and depopulation of rural, agricultural communities.

The replacement of al-Ḥajjāj by Ibn Ustādh-hurmuz in Dhu'l-Ḥijja 392/October 1002 gave the Mazyadids further opportunities for meddling, and for the next five years, they supported their old enemy al-Ḥajjāj in opposition to his successor. In 397/1007, an agreement was reached whereby 'Alī b. Mazyad was given the honorific title Sanad al-Dawla (Support of the State) as a recognition of his status as an independent ruler under Buyid overlordship. Thereafter, Ibn Ustādh-hurmuz and his successor in Baghdad, Fakhr al-Mulk (401–407/1011–1016), usually kept on good terms with 'Alī and even used him as a sort of policeman to maintain some Buyid influence in their area. In 404/1011, for example, when the lawless Banū Khafāja pillaged the *Ḥajj* caravan, the authorities in Baghdad turned to 'Alī, who was able to recover much of the booty and bring the marauders under some sort of control.

When 'Alī b. Mazyad died in 408/1018, he left his tribe as the leading group in the areas to the south and southwest of Baghdad and his own family as the leading clan and the most reliable allies of the Baghdad authorities. Both tribe and family, however, still had rivals. The Banū Asad were opposed by the 'Uqaylids from the north. In 401/1010, the 'Uqaylid leader, Qirwāsh, made his ill-fated attempt to transfer his allegiance from the 'Abbasid caliphs to the Fatimids and the collapse of his bid for total independence severely weakened 'Uqaylid power in the Baghdad area. Their place was taken to some extent by the Banū Khafāja, who now became the Asadīs' main bedouin rivals in the lands to the west of the Euphrates. Within the tribe, 'Alī had also faced opposition, and the Buyid governors of Baghdad had, on occasion, sided with his opponents to prevent him from becoming too powerful. On his death, his son and successor, Dubays, who had already been invested with the title Nūr al-Dawla by the Buyids, was opposed by his brother al-Muqallad, who sought the alliance of the Turkish soldiers of

Baghdad who pillaged his brother's camp. But Dubays, too, found allies in the city, and al-Muqallad was eventually driven out and forced to find refuge with the 'Uqaylids in northern Iraq.

Dubays was to remain a leader of the Mazyadid clan for the next sixty-three years, until 474/1081, a period which allowed the consolidation of their power in the area. It is worth remarking on the great longevity of many of the nomad chiefs of this period. Dubays reigned longer than any other ruler in the medieval Islamic world. Some of his contemporaries were equally fortunate; the Kurd Naṣr al-Dawla the Marwanid ruled for fifty-two years and Qirwāsh b. al-Muqallad the 'Uqaylid chief for forty-nine. Among sovereigns of more established, urban dynasties, only al-Mustanṣir the Fatimid at fifty-eight years could rival the nomad dynasts and that only because he, unlike them, succeeded as a small child. By contrast, the Buyids tended to die young after short reigns. Sharaf al-Dawla, to name only one, had taken possession of the lands of his father, 'Aḍud al-Dawla, and had ruled in Fars and Iraq. He might well have been able to restore the fortunes of the dynasty, but he died in 380/990 after just two years in charge, aged only twenty-eight. This longevity had a political importance, since it enabled these dynasties to establish themselves without the ceaseless succession disputes and minorities which damaged other regimes. After the deposition of Fakhr al-Mulk in 407/1016, no Buyid ruler or governor in Baghdad was powerful enough to threaten his independence, while the 'Uqaylids were increasingly preoccupied by affairs in the north. In 435/1044, Dubays allied with his old rival, the 'Uqaylid Qirwāsh, against their new common enemy, the Ghuzz Turkmen invaders, and defeated them. With the establishment of Seljuk power in Baghdad, Dubays was faced with a new and much more formidable government in the city, but the Mazyadids were able to maintain, and even increase, their power.

The rise of the Mazyadids illustrates the complex and changing relations between the Buyid government and the bedouin. The Mazyadids needed and exploited the Buyids for the granting of titles and subsidies, while the Buyids, in turn, needed them, intermittently, for military support against their rivals and as policemen on the fringes of the desert. The rivalries between the Buyids and the tensions between Daylamites and Turks on the one hand, and the rivalries within the Banū Asad, and between the Asad and other bedouin tribes on the other, meant that the position was constantly changing, and the political history of this period is often tortuous.

In many ways, the early Mazyadids ruled as bedouin shaykhs. At first, their priorities were pillage and tribute. As they became more powerful in the later years of 'Alī's leadership and in the time of Dubays, they began to make permanent *Ḥimāya* agreements with settled communities. At least until the second half of the fifth/eleventh century, the Mazyadids lived a bedouin, nomad life rather than settling in cities. They employed no expensive *ghilmān*, relying instead on their tribal following of up to 2,000 horsemen, a substantial force by the standards of the time. And since they had no *ghilmān* to pay they needed only the most basic administration and seem to have felt no need for *wazīrs* and bureaucrats. This did not mean that they were hostile to urban life; it is fascinating to observe how the *Ḥilla* (encampment) of the Mazyadids was transformed during their rule, into Ḥilla, the walled permanent city which became their capital.

The 'Uqaylids

In the Jazīra and northern Iraq, power passed into the hands of the leaders of the Banū 'Uqayl tribe. Of all the dynasties which appeared at this time, the shaykhs of the Banū 'Uqayl were perhaps the most truly bedouin in character, never settling in towns and remaining entirely dependent on their tribal followers for military support. Leadership among the members of the ruling clan was decided on traditional bedouin lines, the whole kin sharing in the exercise of authority, and no one man achieved the absolute status typical of more settled dynasties.

The 'Uqaylīs are found in the Jazīra in Umayyad times and consolidated their hold on the pastoral lands of the area in the Hamdanid period, when they were the chief beneficiaries of the decline and emigration of the Banū Taghlib. Along with the Numayrīs, they are found as irregular troops in the armies of the Hamdanids. This period also shows the increasing incursions of the nomad tribes on settled areas, and the geographer Ibn Ḥawqal presents a vivid impression of the decline of agriculture around such Jaziran towns as Ra's al-'Ayn and Ḥarrān. As with the Asadīs in the Sawād, the rise of the bedouin dynasties was both a cause and a consequence of the decline of agriculture in favour of pastoral economy. The takeover of the Jazīra and Mosul by 'Aḍud al-Dawla in 369/979 led to a firm government policy with regard to the tribes, and 'Aḍud al-Dawla insisted that 'Uqaylid chiefs, among them al-Musayyib b. Rāfi', be responsible for the actions of their followers – a policy which caused some of them to take refuge across the Euphrates out of his reach. After 'Aḍud al-Dawla's death in 372/983, the situation became disturbed again and the 'Uqaylīs and Numayrīs were obliged to defend their lands from the Kurds under Bādh to the north. When, in 379/989, Bahā' al-Dawla sent the Ḥamdānī brothers Ibrāhīm and al-Ḥusayn to Mosul to rally support against Bādh, they turned to the 'Uqaylīs for support, offering in exchange control of the old Taghlibī centres of Jazīrat Ibn 'Umar, Balad and Niṣībīn. The Kurdish threat was contained, but the 'Uqaylī chief Muḥammad b. al-Musayyib b. Rāfi' took advantage of the confusion to execute the last Hamdanid in the area and the rival chief of the Numayrīs and make himself master of Mosul itself, the first member of the tribe to acquire an interest in the city.

Muḥammad pledged his allegiance to Bahā' al-Dawla and was obliged to accept a Buyid presence in Mosul, while enjoying a share of the revenue. Shortly after his death in 386/996, however, the last Buyid governor was forced to withdraw. Mosul came under 'Uqaylid rule and was to remain so for the next century. After Muḥammad's death, a power struggle developed between his brothers. It was 'Uqaylid custom that leadership pass to the eldest, 'Alī, who was supported by the majority of the tribe but opposed by another brother, al-Muqallad, who had acquired interests in revenue collecting in a number of districts on the Euphrates between Anbār and Kūfa, and had developed contacts with the Buyids and the Baghdad military. He therefore offered to take over the revenue farming of Mosul and began recruiting Turks and Daylamites to his cause. At first, 'Alī was prepared to allow his brother Mosul while he himself continued to live a bedouin existence as the chief of the tribe, but his secretary persuaded him that this was impossible and that if al-Muqallad was the master of Mosul, he would certainly use his position and wealth to subvert 'Alī's authority. In 386–387/996–997, there was much confused fighting, which resulted in a compromise and the division of the revenues between 'Alī and al-Muqallad. The failure of al-Muqallad's bid determined the whole nature of the 'Uqaylid state. 'Alī stood for traditional bedouin leadership and relied on the military power of the tribe, al-Muqallad, for a government based on Turkish *ghilmān* and Daylamite troops, very much in the Hamdanid mould. Both brothers were given honorifics by the Buyids, Janāh. al-Dawla for 'Alī and Ḥusām al-Dawla for al-Muqallad, so marking their effective independence. Despite lavish gifts, al-Muqallad was unable to win the support of more than 2,000 of the 'Uqaylis, while 'Alī could count on 10,000. There were strong pressures exerted by the tribe on the two brothers to avoid war, and al-Muqallad was obliged to agree to a compromise after his sister, in a very traditional gesture, had threatened to shame herself in front of the whole tribe if he did not. Al-Muqallad, we are told, was "like wax in her hand". 'Alī's victory meant that the 'Uqaylid shaykhs would not follow in the footsteps of the Hamdanids and replace their tribal following with salaried *ghilmān* but would continue to rely on the Banū 'Uqayl for military support. The dynasty based its power on the bedouin, and its policies reflected their needs.

The division of authority continued after 'Alī's death when his brother, al-Ḥasan, took over his position with the tribe, while al-Muqallad devoted most of his energy to his interests in central Iraq. He even tried to make himself the master of Baghdad and was negotiating with army leaders there when he was murdered by his Turkish retainers in 391/1001. His position was inherited, not without difficulty, by his son, Qirwāsh, the greatest of the early 'Uqaylid chiefs, who united the tribe under his leadership. It was he who led 7,000 'Uqayl, in alliance with the Banū Asad, when they fought the Baghdad commander Abū Ja'far al-Ḥajjāj and his allies from the Banū Khafāja near Ḥilla in 392/1002. The battle was a humiliating defeat for the 'Uqaylid leader and the women of Khafāja raided and pillaged the 'Uqaylid camp: it was like the *jāhiliyya* all over again.

This defeat and the reassertion of Buyid control under Ibn Ustādh-hurmuz soured relations between Qirwāsh and the Buyids. In an effort to regain control in the areas around Baghdad which his father had dominated – not only Anbār to the west and the Euphrates lands but also al-Madā'in to the southeast – Qirwāsh resorted to raiding and kidnapping. His priorities also changed after the death of the last of his uncles, Muṣ'ab b. al-Musayyib in 397/1006–1007, left him the most senior of the 'Uqaylid shaykhs and gave him further responsibilities in the Jazīra. Here, the position of the tribe was threatened by the Fatimids and their protégés, the marauding Khafāja.

It was against this background of worsening relations with the Buyids and Fatimid advances from the west into the Euphrates valley that Qirwāsh, in 401/1010, transferred his allegiance to the Fatimid caliphs and had the *khuṭba* pronounced in the name of al-Ḥākim in the mosques of all the towns under his control, including Mosul, Anbār, Kūfa and al-Madā'in. This was a challenge which could not be ignored and Bahā' al-Dawla the Buyid ordered his governor in Baghdad, Ibn Ustādh-hurmuz, to take action, sending him 100,000 *dīnārs* for the purpose. Qirwāsh recognized that he had overstepped the mark and, in default of any support from the Fatimids, he returned to formal allegiance to the 'Abbasid caliphate. Like the Hamdanids and the Mazyadids, the 'Uqaylids are usually said to have been a Shi'ite dynasty, but there is little evidence to support this. That Qirwāsh had no great regard for the 'Alid family is suggested by the fact that he kidnapped one of its leading members in Kūfa in 395/1004–1005 and held him to ransom for 100,000 *dīnārs*. Apart from his brief flirtation with the Fatimids, Qirwāsh was content that the name of the 'Abbasid caliph should be mentioned in the *khuṭba* in his domains. The truth is probably that he was committed to neither Sunnī nor Shī'ī party and that he was comparatively indifferent to the claims of formal religion.

The failure of the bid for independence in 401/1010 marks the beginning of the decline of 'Uqaylid influence in the lands al-Muqallad had acquired in the Sawād. The 'Uqaylids were faced with the alliance of the Buyid governors in Baghdad and the Mazyadids, while their position was attacked by the rival Khafāja 'Uqaylids in the desert west of Anbār and Kūfa. The main reason for the continuing conflict was the need for pasture. It would seem that the 'Uqaylīs used the same grazing lands occupied by the eastern Shammar in the nineteenth century. Their summer pastures were in the northern Jazīra, while their winter pastures were in the Anbār–Kūfa area. If Qirwāsh were to be acceptable as the leader of the 'Uqayl, he had to ensure that his followers had access to these grazing areas. The priorities of the 'Uqaylī leaders remained the priorities of a pastoral society. They had no difficulty in maintaining amicable relations with the Marwanid Kurds, for example, because there was no such competition, but they were deadly enemies of the Khafāja, who threatened their grazing. Qirwāsh's own mother was a Hadhbānī Kurd and relations with them seem to have been friendly. In 411/-1020–1021, Qirwāsh was defeated near Sāmarrā by a coalition of Mazyadids, Baghdad troops and dissident members of his own clan, a defeat which led to the establishment of a branch of the family in Takrīt. In 417/1026, the 'Uqaylids, allied with the Mazyadids, suffered a humiliating defeat when

10,000 men in their army were defeated by a much smaller force of 1,000 Khafāja. After this, they continued to hold Anbār but seem to have been driven out of the more southerly areas around Kūfa.

In 417/1026, Qirwāsh's leadership was challenged in the north at exactly the same moment that the Sawād possessions were being lost to the Mazyadids and the Khafāja. The opposition was led by his brother, Badrān, who seems to have wanted his own emirate in Niṣībīn. Both sides prepared for battle, Qirwāsh raising 13,000 men with help from the Marwanids of Mayyāfāriqīn. But in the end, peace was arranged and Badrān was allowed to keep Niṣībīn. Thereafter, Qirwāsh's position seems to have been unchallenged until the whole tribe was threatened by the arrival of the Ghuzz Turkmen. The Ghuzz were an existential threat to the 'Uqayl, since they too were pastoral nomads and sought to take the same area and role as the Arabs. There was no room for compromise. When they first attacked in 433/1041–1042, Qirwāsh and his Kurdish allies were defeated, and he was forced to take refuge in Mosul for fear of them. Here, both bedouin and townsmen tried to defend the city against the common enemy but to no avail. The city was taken and Qirwāsh fled by ship, leaving his treasure in the hands of the enemy. A popular rebellion in the city against the Turks in 435/1043–1044 was brutally suppressed. Meanwhile, Qirwāsh was seeking allies against the intruders. He had written to Jalāl al-Dawla, the useless Buyid ruler of Baghdad, who was in no position to help, as well as to the Mazyadid leader Dubays and several Kurdish chiefs, notably Abū'l-Shawk the 'Annazid. Faced with the common peril, Arabs and Kurds joined under Qirwāsh's leadership to defend their pastures and their territories. In Ramaḍān 435/April 1044, the two armies met to the northwest of Mosul. At first, the Turkmen were victorious and drove the Arabs right back to their tents. Then, the fortunes of battle changed and the Arabs defeated their enemies with great loss of life. It was Qirwāsh's greatest moment, and his victory was celebrated by poets in the traditional manner. He had certainly saved not just the 'Uqayl but other pastoral peoples in the area from being overwhelmed by the newcomers. Qirwāsh must have been an old man by this stage and it may have been his increasing feebleness which led to his being put under house arrest by his brother, Baraka, in 441/1049 after yet another conflict within the ruling clan. For the last three years of his life, he was deprived of all power and died a captive in Rajab 444/October 1052.

Qirwāsh dominated the politics of the Jazīra for half a century. All his life he remained very much a bedouin shaykh, glorying in a genealogy which went back to the fathers of the Arab race. In his poetry, he despises inherited wealth and boasts of the swiftness of his horse, the sharpness of his sword and the generosity with which he gives. As far as we can tell, he usually lived in the *Ḥilla*, the nomad encampment, only visiting the towns under his control when they were threatened, like Anbār in 417/1026 or Mosul in 435/-1043–1044. His recorded utterances suggest that he had a very low opinion of townsmen but that does not mean that 'Uqaylid rule was particularly oppressive; certainly, the people of Mosul were prepared to take up arms alongside their 'Uqaylī masters against the Ghuzz Turkmen. The centre of power had shifted from the city to the camp, and 'Uqaylid "government" was remote from the affairs of the town. Unfortunately, we are very badly informed about the history of Mosul or the other 'Uqaylid towns in this period. In 411/1020–1021, Qirwāsh had a dispute with his representatives in Mosul, who were his *wazīr*, Ibn al-Maghribī (later to move to the service of Naṣr al-Dawla the Marwanid), and a local landowner called Sulaymān b. Fahd, which suggests that he employed non-bedouin agents in the cities; and we should probably be right to assume that in Mosul, as in other towns of the period, local urban élites played an important part in day-to-day administration. The pattern of rule was not that of direct government of the cities and taxation of the countryside, as practised under the 'Abbasids, but rather the *Ḥimāya* or protection agreement where, as in the modern *khuwa* agreement, the settled people pay the bedouin for their protection but otherwise manage their own affairs.

Qirwāsh's obligations were to the Banū 'Uqayl who followed him; his major concern was to provide them pasture and the fruits of taxation. Within his own clan, he was obliged to allow the formation of sub-amirates centred on towns such as Takrīt and Niṣībīn to satisfy the demands of his kin for their own *Ḥimāyas*. The appearance of these secondary states should not be seen as a sign of disintegration but rather as a sign that traditional patterns of clan rule were being followed.

The Mirdasids

In Aleppo, the position of the Hamdanids was taken over by the shaykhs of another bedouin tribe, the Banū Kilāb. Like the 'Uqaylīs, the Kilāb had appeared in northern Syria in the aftermath of the Islamic conquest but, again like their neighbours to the east, they seem to have been strengthened by a new wave of immigration at the beginning of the fourth/tenth centuries and taken over lands along the fringes of the desert previously inhabited by tribes such as the Tanūkh. They had helped Sayf al-Dawla, the first of the Hamdanids, to power in the city and under Hamdanid rule their power had prospered at the expense of their neighbours to the south, the Kalbīs. Byzantine attacks on Aleppo are said to have diverted trade farther east through the Kilābī dominated town of Khunāṣira. By the end of the fourth/tenth century, the tribe controlled most of the area to the east and south of Aleppo itself, along with the Euphrates towns of Bālis and sometimes Raḥba. After the failure of the Hamdanid dynasty, Aleppo was the scene of a struggle between the last of the Hamdanid *ghilmān*, led by Lu'lu' and his son Manṣūr, with Byzantine support, the Fatimids and the Kilābīs, in which the Kilābī leader, Ṣālih. b. Mirdās, finally emerged victorious.

Aleppo was different from Mosul in a number of ways. While the 'Uqaylids in Mosul could feel comparatively secure from attempts by the later Buyids to assert their power, Aleppo lay on the frontier between the Byzantine and Fatimid spheres of influence. The area controlled by the tribe was comparatively small, certainly smaller than the Hamdanid state of Sayf al-Dawla. Antioch to the west was in Byzantine hands, while Homs and Ḥamāh to the south were usually under Fatimid domination. This meant that successful rulers of Aleppo had to be diplomats to manoeuvre among the great powers as well as being able to secure the support of their followers. The sources for Aleppo in this period are much fuller than those for Mosul and the ʻUqaylid areas, and this allows us to see more clearly the interaction of nomad and settled elements in the state. The Kilābī tribesmen remained the backbone of the army, and without their support no member of the Mirdasid family could exercise effective control. While the bedouin were a fairly effective military force, even defeating a large Byzantine army on one occasion, they demanded a say in the running of the state in return. The Mirdasid family were not old-established leaders of the tribe. It was the fact that Ṣāliḥ. seized Aleppo which gave him paramountcy among the shaykhs of the tribe. There were other clans who felt that the Mirdasid family had no more rights than their own, and some of them were prepared to make alliances with the Fatimid general Anūshtakīn al-Dizbarī when he drove the Mirdasids from the city in 429/1038. The Kilābīs did not settle down but maintained their nomad life, often camping close to Aleppo so that they could exert political pressure if necessary.

The other important element was the people of Aleppo, who, led by the *ra'īs al-balad* or *shaykh al-dawla* chosen from a leading local family, often played an important role in politics. The city had its own militia, the *aḥdāth*, which was not dependent on the Mirdasids but usually cooperated with them. This uneasy partnership was the natural result of bedouin rule, and both sides needed each other. It would be a mistake to imagine that this bedouin rule was resented by the townsmen. Such evidence as we have suggests that the city was more prosperous under the Mirdasids than it had been under the Hamdanids. Among the citizens themselves, there were divisions between rich and poor, and this often prevented them from maintaining a common front against an external foe. Nonetheless, the people of Aleppo, mostly fighting as infantry, were a force to be reckoned with. An additional complication was provided by the citadel, then as now standing high above the centre of the city, which could often maintain itself as a separate political unit and withstand blockades of up to a year. This sometimes led to a divided governorate, one authority for the town and another for the castle, and it was control of the citadel which enabled the Fatimids at various times to maintain a presence in Aleppo when they had been ejected from the city.

The rule of the Mirdasid family in Aleppo, which lasted, with interruptions, from 414 to 472 (1023–1079), was always precarious and dependent on balancing the interests of the ruling family, the Kilābī tribesmen, the citizens of the town and the surrounding great powers. Ṣāliḥ. b. Mirdās himself gained possession of the city from the Fatimid garrison in 414/1023, with the aid of some of the citizens, including Sālim b. Mustafād, who became *ra'īs al-balad*, but he himself never seems to have lived there. No sooner had he appointed deputies to manage the city in his absence than he left for Palestine to join the great coalition of bedouin tribes, the Kilāb, Kalb and ṭayy, against the Fatimids and the general Anūshtakīn al-Dizbarī. He does not appear to have returned to the city before his death in 420/1029 and the battle of Uqḥuwāna near Lake Tiberias, where the bedouin were decisively defeated by the Fatimids. After his death, his inheritance was divided – one son, Thimāl, getting the citadel, while another, Naṣr, took the town. But the arrangement broke down the next year when Naṣr, with Byzantine support, took over the citadel as well, while Thimāl retired to the east to Bālis and Raḥba, where he enjoyed the support of the kilābī tribesmen. Naṣr also had to face the opposition of Sālim b. Mustafād and the *aḥdāth*, but they were crushed when they rebelled. On the international side, Naṣr attempted to maintain good relations with Byzantines and Fatimids alike; in 422/1031, he joined the Byzantines to suppress a Druze disturbance in the Jabal Summāq which threatened both their interests, while the Fatimids accepted him as their representative in Aleppo.

This dual control, Naṣr in the city, Thimāl with the tribe, lasted until 429/1038 when the aggressive Fatimid commander in Syria, Anūshtakīn al-Dizbarī, launched a major expedition against the city, supported not just by the Turkish and Berber troops of the Fatimid army but by the bedouin Ṭayy, Kalb and even some Kilāb. Naṣr gathered his army and his clan, including his brother Thimāl, to face the enemy but he was no match for superior forces and was killed fighting bravely. Thimāl took refuge in Aleppo. Here, the shaykhs of the city promised to support him against the enemy but his own advisers urged him to flee, saying that the townspeople would hamper his efforts and that if he remained in the city, the Kilābī tribesmen would desert him. It was the classic dilemma of the nomad ruler: did the town or the tribe have priority? Thimāl decided for the tribe and, leaving his nephew al-Muqallad b. Kāmil in the city, fled east across the Euphrates to take refuge in the Jazīra. Al-Muqallad was soon forced to surrender, Anūshtakīn's men entered the city and *mamlūks* (slave soldiers) were appointed to run it. It seemed as if Mirdasid rule had come to a premature end.

The Mirdasids were saved by rivalries within the Fatimid administration between the *wazīr* al-Jarjarā'ī and the military commander, Anūshtakīn. Anūshtakīn was deprived of office and al-Jarjarā'ī was happy to have Thimāl and his nephew al-Muqallad appointed as Fatimid governors in Aleppo, and Kilābī forces succeeded in ejecting the Fatimid garrison. Thimāl's reign from 433 to 449 (1041–1057) was the high point of Mirdasid fortunes. Until the last years, he succeeded in balancing all the different elements superbly. Fatimids and Byzantines, Kilābīs and citizens were all prepared, or forced, to accept his authority. With the Byzantines, who had no aggressive designs on Aleppo and whose main interest lay in keeping the city free from direct Fatimid rule, relations were uniformly good. The Mirdasids paid tribute but received gifts and Byzantine titles in exchange. Thimāl himself was made *magistros* in 433/1041–1042, and other members of his family, including his wife 'Alawiyya, received the titles of *strategos* or *patrikios*. Even his agreements with the Fatimids did not interrupt these friendly relations.

The Fatimids made three determined attempts to destroy the independence of Aleppo. In 439/1047–1048, Thimāl had a dispute with Cairo about some money the Fatimid forces had left in the citadel when they left the city at the beginning of his reign. The Caliph al-Mustanṣir sent a member of the Hamdanid family, al-Ḥasan b. al-Ḥusayn, against the city, a reminder that although the Hamdanids had disappeared from Mosul and Aleppo, they still remained influential in the Fatimid Empire. The people of Aleppo, however, showed no enthusiasm for this scion of the old dynasty and went out to fight him but were defeated and Aleppo was only saved by a flood which destroyed the enemy's camp and equipment. The next year, the assault was renewed by the Berber governor of Homs, Abū Shujā' b. Kulayd, but he was defeated at Kafarṭāb well to the south of the city itself, by an army of Kilābī bedouin citizens of Aleppo and the local *fallāḥīn* (peasants: a very rare example of the use of peasants in military activity at this time) under the command of al-Muqallad b. Kāmil al-Kilābī, Thimāl's nephew and second-in-command. The third attack was led by a *ghulām* of the Fatimids called Rifq. He had a large army and actually entered the city in 441/1050, but dissensions within his army led to the breakup of the expedition, while he himself died of wounds.

After this third attempt, Thimāl sent a peace mission to Cairo which included his wife, the redoubtable 'Alawiyya, known as al-Sayyida (the Lady) and the *shaykh al-dawla*, the leader of the citizens. They secured a treaty which confirmed Thimāl in his possessions and which remained in force for the rest of his rule. Despite some stresses, his relations with the people of Aleppo seem to have been friendly. His rule was remembered in the city as a period of prosperity, and the citizens seem to have preferred Mirdasid to Fatimid rule. There is no mention of any very developed administrative system, although each ruler had a secretary with the rather grand title of *wazīr*. Under Naṣr, two of these were Christians, but Thimāl seems to have only employed Muslims. The only one who achieved more than local fame was Muḥammad b. Jahīr, an experienced administrator who took service with Thimāl in 446/1054–1055. He doubled the revenues and reorganized the finances, but in doing so made himself unpopular and he was eventually forced to leave.

Ironically, Thimāl's reign was brought to an end not by outside invasion, but by the opposition of his fellow Kilābī tribesmen. He was very aware of the dangers of alienating these men, who provided the military backing for his regime. He recruited no *ghilmān* to rival them in the exercise of power and he was careful to distribute money and favours among them. Despite this, however, their leaders remained resentful, feeling that they had as much right as he to wealth and power. Once again, we see the conflict between the ideas of shared leadership in a nomad society and the rule of a single man demanded by an urban state. In the end, in 449/1057, pressure from the Kilāb became intolerable and he resigned his post to the Fatimids in exchange for Beirut, Acre and Jubayl, not because they were richer or carried more prestige but simply because they were farther away from the Banū Kilāb.

Although Mirdasid rule was restored three years later, and Thimāl himself made a short-lived return, the dynasty never again enjoyed the same power. The international scene had changed. Byzantine power, which had been essential for the continuing independence of Aleppo, was greatly weakened. The rising power of the Seljuk Turks was a serious threat. The Byzantines had been pleased to have Aleppo as a buffer state, but the Seljuks sought to deal the Fatimids a mortal blow and needed to use northern Syria as a base. In addition, their Turkmen followers coveted the pastures of the Banū Kilāb. The days of the bedouin dynasts were numbered.

Other bedouin tribes

The Mazyadids, ‘Uqaylids and Mirdasids were the most successful of the bedouin leaders who attempted to establish their autonomy in the Fertile Crescent, and it is their names and genealogies which appear in the handbooks of Islamic history, but they were by no means the only ones. Sandwiched between the Banū ‘Uqayl to the east and the Banū Kilāb to the west, the shaykhs of Banū Numayr were able to establish a transitory authority over Ḥarrān and Edessa until its conquest by the Byzantines in 422/1031. Farther south in Syria and Palestine, the nomads were unable to secure control over the settled lands for a long enough period to establish states. Although they were numerous and wide-ranging, the Banū Kalb never established themselves in Damascus; while the Jarrahids, the leading family of the Banū Ṭayy, occupied Ramla on several occasions and did great damage to the town and the surrounding countryside, they never held on to it for long enough to set up any sort of state. Equally in Iraq, the Banū Khafāja, despite some sporadic successes, were never able to dominate any settled area permanently.

The reasons for these failures lay not so much in the weakness of the tribes as in the strength of the forces opposed to them. While the Mazyadids and the ‘Uqaylids were faced with the enfeebled Buyid regime of Baghdad, anxious to acquire bedouin support and prepared to make concessions to get it, the tribes of southern Syria and Palestine were opposed by a government which could field large armies of Berber troops and Turkish *ghilmān*. Under the capable leadership of Anūshtakīn al-Dizbarī in the early fifth/eleventh century, the Fatimid cause prospered and, in a great trial of strength, the combined forces of the bedouin tribes were defeated at the battle of Uqḥuwāna. While the Fatimids were prepared to tolerate an independent state in distant Aleppo, at least at certain times, they could not afford to do so in Damascus or on their own doorstep in Ramla and they used all the resources of Egypt to prevent this happening. The case of the Khafāja was somewhat different – here, it was more powerful bedouin rivals, the Banū Asad and the Banū ʿUqayl, who prevented them acquiring rights over settled communities, and their attempts to ally with the Buyids or Fatimids against their rivals achieved nothing.

The possession of revenues from settled areas affected not just the wealth of the tribe as a whole but its internal structure. Groups like the Kalb which lacked this sort of revenue seem to have had a weak decentralized structure of the sort that is typical of pastoral tribes. When revenue rights were acquired, however, the money was channelled through the chief to the tribesmen; just as the payment of *ʿaṭāʾ* through tribal chiefs in the early Islamic period had strengthened their position against the rank and file of the tribe, so in the fifth and sixth (tenth and eleventh) centuries, the acquisition of revenues put the ruling clans in a much stronger position. They were then in a position to found dynasties with real authority, rather than be permanently dependent on the consent of the tribe.

The prosperity of the bedouin regimes began to decline after the middle of the fifth/eleventh century. While the Mazyadids were able to survive for another century, the ʿUqaylids and Mirdasids were undermined by the advance of the Turkmen tribes. The Kilāb soon disappeared entirely as a bedouin tribe, while the mighty ʿUqayl dwindled to a small remnant in the Ḥarrān area, losing their tribal identity and name in the process. The century 340–440 (approximately 950–1050) was the high-water mark of Arab nomad influence in the Fertile Crescent. In the long term, the century can perhaps be seen as the culmination of half a millennium of penetration by Arabic-speaking pastoral peoples of the settled areas, a process which began in late Byzantine and Sasanian times and continued through the Islamic conquests and the advances of the Qarāmiṭa until it reached its furthest extent in this period.

13 The Eastern Iranian world in the tenth and early eleventh centuries

The Samanids

After the reestablishment of the unity of the ʿAbbasid caliphate under the rule of al-Ma'mūn, the management of Greater Khurasan, that is, the provinces of Khurasan and Transoxania, was handed over to the Tahirid family. The Tahirids were an integral component of the Abbasid system with their bases in the East and Baghdad and they fell together, the collapse of Tahirid power coinciding with the crisis of the caliphate of Samarra from 861 to 870. Tahirid rule was replaced by the more unstable regime of the Saffarids who expanded their control from their native province of Sistan to Khurasan in the north and Kirman and Fars to the south and west. Yaʿqūb b. Layth, however, still seems to have thought in terms of controlling the caliphate and the still prosperous lands of southern Iraq, rather than establishing any sort of independent state in the Iranian East. It was his ambitions in Iraq which led to his defeat and the collapse of his imperial aspirations. His successor, his brother, ʿAmr was more conciliatory, attempting to win caliphal approval for his rule in Fars and Kirman as well as Khurasan. Like his brother, however, he was undone by his own ambitions. In 278/900, he attempted, with the apparent backing of the caliph al-Muʿtaḍid, to extend his authority over Transoxania and here he met his match in the leader of the Samanid family, Ismāʿīl b. Aḥmad.

The encounter became famous as an example of the vicissitudes of fortune: ʿAmr's much larger army failed to fight effectively and their leader was captured by the Samanid forces. At the beginning of the day, he lamented, his kitchen was carried on four hundred camels; that evening, a dog ran off with his meagre meal in a single frying pan.

The origins of the Samanids are not entirely clear. They claimed descent from the great hero of the Sasanian period, Bahram Chubīn, stressing an aristocratic Persian past, in contrast to the Tahirids who confected a descent from a noble Arab tribe. In fact, they seem to have originally been a family of landowners from Samān, probably a small town in the neighbourhood of Samarqand, and bore the title of Saman-khudā. The first reliable historical accounts say that they accept Islam at the hands of the Umayyad governor,

DOI: 10.4324/9780429348129-13

Asad b. ʿAbd Allah al-Qasrī, around 117/735 around the same time as the Barmakids. Unlike their contemporaries, however, the Samanid family did not join the armies of the ʿAbbasid revolution and apparently continued to live on their estates in obscurity. There is no record of them attending the court of al-Ma'mūn in Marw. After the caliph had left for Baghdad, the governor he appointed in Khurasan, one Ghassān b.ʿAbbād, advanced four sons of Asad to important offices in the provinces, Nūh as the governor of Samarqand, Aḥmad of Farghana, Yaḥyā of Shāsh and Ilyās of Herat. In time, they became the most important supporters of the Tahirids in the lands beyond the Oxus. When Tahirid rule collapsed with the loss of Nishapur in 259/873, Naṣr b. Aḥmad found himself an effectively independent ruler of Samarqand and in 261/875 the caliph al-Muʿtamid directly appointed him as the governor of Transoxania.

On Nasr's death in 279/892, his son Ismāʿīl inherited the leadership of the family. With the defeat of ʿAmr the Saffarid in 287/900, Ismāʿīl's triumph was complete and the caliph al-Muʿtaḍid appointed him the governor not just of Transoxania but Khurasan as well, so beginning a period of Samanid hegemony which was to last for almost a century.

The history of the Samanids embodies many contradictions and their reputation among later historians contributes to the confusion. For Niẓām al-Mulk, writing his book of political advice, the *Siyāsat-Nāmeh*, a century after the collapse of the dynasty, they offered the example of a state with an ordered and developed administrative system with a whole system of diwans dealing with different areas of correspondence and finance. He also describes the system of education and promotion among the Turkish military slaves who formed the backbone of the Samanid army. This impression of order and stability is supported by the testimony of the contemporary geographers, Ibn Ḥawqal in his *Kitāb ṣurat al-arḍ* and al-Muqaddasī in his *Aḥsan al-taqāsim*, both of whom comment on the sound and honest administration and the prosperity of the people. Ibn Ḥawqal's work makes an implicit contrast with the maladministration and disorder he found in the Fertile Crescent at the same time.

This ideal picture is not reflected in the most important narrative sources. Despite their reputation as patrons of literature, the Samanids were not well served by the chroniclers of the day. There was no equivalent of the works of Miskawayh on the Buyids or Bayhaqī on the Ghaznavids to bring life and character to the events and personalities of the Samanid era. Nonetheless, the rather dry annals of Gardīzī's *Zayn al-akhbār* and Ibn al-Athīr's *Kāmil fī'l-ta'rikh* present a very different picture from the calm and order of the *Siyāsat-nāmeh*. In their accounts, Samanid rule was a period of almost continuous rebellion, insurrection and civil war as numerous different actors, members of the ruling family, local dynasts and Turkish military commanders fought each other, either to become rulers themselves or to take control of the Samanid amirs, whose personal power declined dramatically in the course of the century. Of the rulers of the dynasty, only Ismāʿīl emerges as a great figure and the doings of the amirs of the second half of the Samanid century are almost completely eclipsed by accounts of their military commanders and viziers.

The resolution of this apparent paradox may lie in the nature of warfare at the time. This seems to have consisted of battles between fairly small armies of professional soldiers, each attaching themselves to leaders who they hoped would be able to pay them and provide a modicum of prosperity. There are few examples to major sieges or the destruction of cities and irrigation systems. For Narshakhī writing his *History of Bukhāra* in 332/-943–944, in the middle of the Samanid period, the greatest disaster which occurred in the city in time was not the result of siege or warfare but a fire accidentally started by a baker in a *harīsa* shop in 325/937 which destroyed the bazaars and much of the rest of the city centre. Perhaps like eleventh-century France, a condition of almost non-stop warfare could coincide with a period of economic prosperity and cultural achievement.

Another paradox in the reputation of the Samanids was their Persian identity. As already noted, they seemed to have emerged from the calls of *dehqan* landowners in Transoxania and they certainly sought to emphasize their Iranian identity by tracing their lineage to the Sasanian house. Later historians have emphasized their cultural achievements and the development of New Persian as a court and literary language, a legacy which survived the rule of Turkish dynasts for centuries after the passing of the dynasty. There is certainly some truth in this. Some of the earliest New Persian poets, Rudakī and Daqīqī, benefitted from Sasanian patronage and the first great New Persian prose work to have survived, the "translation" (actually more of a paraphrase) of the great *Ta'rīkh* of al-Ṭabarī was written at the Samanid court by Balʿamī, a bureaucrat who served the dynasty. Most importantly in the eyes of later generations, it was under Samanid patronage that the first steps were taken in the translation into New Persian and the versification of the ancient legends and Sasanian history which culminated in Firdawsī's *Shahnāmeh* in the early Ghaznevid age. It was also towards the end of the Samanid period that the ancient Soghdian language (an Iranian language cognate with Persian) disappeared and was replaced by New Persian.

The Samanid century may have seen the establishment of New Persian as a major language of culture but it was also a period when the influence of Turkish speakers in politics and the military became more and more important, leading to the establishment of Turkish rulers like the Ghaznevids and the Karakhanids in the next century. The key to this was the gradual conversion of the steppe Turks and their leaders to Islam during the course of the Samanid century. Before this, these Turkish chiefs could never have entered the Muslim commonwealth and the rulers of Transoxania could gather their supporters in a *jihād* against these infidels. With their conversion to Islam, however, the religious motives for opposing Turkish rule evaporated and the citizens of the ancient towns and villages of Transoxania court accepted Turkish rule without any pious qualms.

The Samanid realm was not a unified political entity, more a patchwork of provinces, united, more or less, by the power of the Samanid dynasty. Local tensions were seldom far below the surface and when the dynasty faltered, they sometimes broke out into open rebellion. When Ismāʿīl was granted his right to rule by the caliph, it included all the lands from the Pass of Hulwan, that is where the plains of Iraq joined the western slopes of the Zagros Mountains, to the edge of the Muslim world in the East. In fact, much of this territory in Western Iran was never under Samanid rule and the furthest west that their rule ever extended was Rayy and that was soon lost to the Buyids. The Caspian provinces too were only controlled by the dynasty for very short periods. The core lands were around the capital Bukhara and Samarqand in ancient Soghdia, areas normally ruled by members of the Sasanian family, and Farghana to the northeast was often under the members of the dynasty rule as well. This family domination did not always lead to peace and harmony and different members of the family often used their appanages as bases for trying to take power over capital at Bukhara and with it the apparatus of the state. Along the northern banks of the Oxus, there were a number of small principalities whose origins can be traced back to before the first Muslim conquest. Ruled by long-established families like the Muhtājids of Chaghāniyān and the Farīghunids of Juzjān, they generally accepted Samanid overlordship and often played important roles in the Samanid government. The Muḥtajids, for example, served in the key role of governors of Khurasan for in the first half of the fourth/tenth century. The most important province, and the most restless, was Khurasan with its capital at Marw or Nishapur. Khurāsān was never governed by members of the local elite but by princes like the Muḥtājids or Turkish soldiers like the Simjurids. Samanid rule was often challenged and neighbouring powers like the Ziyārid princes of Ṭabaristan provinces and the Buyids of Rayy were often eager to support rebellions among the restless subjects in Khurasan.

The Samanids took the title of Amīr and projected themselves as governors for the ʿAbbasid caliphs. When Ibn Faḍlān passed through the Samanid capital of Bukhara in 309/921, he found the young Amīr Naṣr, in a court that looked very much like a smaller version of the Caliph's court in Baghdad. No doubt tutored by his famous vizier al-Jayhānī, he enquired politely after the health of his master the caliph al-Muqtadir. While this was no doubt sincere, it was little more than a diplomatic politeness. No Samanid ruler ever visited the ʿAbbasid court, no taxation or other revenues were requested and none were sent. After the assumption of power in Iraq by the Buyids in 945, the independence of the Samanids was complete.

This led to an effective division of Iran between West and East, the boundary being great expanses of the Dashti Kavir and other salt deserts. Only at the pivotal city of Rayy and, less crucially, in Kirman to the south, did the two halves share a frontier zone. Marked differences emerged between West and East. In Western Iran, often, and rather confusingly referred to by contemporaries as Iraqi ʿAjam, or Persian Iraq, the ruling powers were the various branches of the Buyid family. The leaders were adherents of Shiʿa Islam and the language of administration was Arabic. Even though Iraq was in economic and political crisis for much of this period, Baghdad was still the centre of political culture and aspirations. In the East, things were very different. Baghdad was both remote and irrelevant. Increasingly, the language of culture administration and, perhaps most important, poetry was New Persian. Only the Islamic religious sciences continued to use Arabic as the language of common discourse.

Apart from struggles over Rayy and parts of Tabaristan, the focus of the Samanids lay to the north and east. It was a period of opening to the vast steppes of Central Asia and the Turkic nomad peoples who inhabited them. This opening up took two main forms. The first was the employment of ever larger numbers of Turkish soldiers in the Samanid armies. Of course, this was nothing new. The ʿAbbasid armies of the third/ninth centuries had after all had large numbers of Turks in their ranks. Under the Samanids, however, the Turks became by far the most important element in the armies and their leaders the key supporters of the regime. In the Samanid state, there emerged the classic division between the Persian bureaucrats (Men of the Pen) and the Turkish soldiers (Men of the Sword) which was to characterize the history of Iran for centuries to come.

The other way in which the Samanids interacted with the Turkic people of the steppe was through trade and missionary activity. In the first half-century of Samanid rule, a flourishing trade developed in the lands of the Volga basin north of the Caspian Sea, a trade whose tentacles reached as far as Scandinavia and the Western Isles of Scotland. This trade was enabled and fuelled by a vast production of silver dirhams. This was made possible by the opening up of new silver mines in the neighbourhood of Shāsh (Tashkent) and the use of this silver to strike coins in the local mint. While the Buyids of Iraq and Baghdad struggled to produce enough of their grubby and misshapen dirhams, mostly made of lead and other base metals, the Samanids mints, at least in the first half-century of their rule, turned out regular and elegant coins containing a high proportion of real silver.

We know about this trade through the remarkable travelogue of Ibn Faḍlān. Coming from Baghdad as an emissary of the caliph, he travelled north from the Samanid realm with a caravan of merchants trading with the Rus who met them on the Upper Volga River and exchanged the slaves and furs they had brought from the Slav lands of eastern Europe for Samanid dirhams. Along with commerce went missionary activity. The Rus, of course, eventually converted to Greek Orthodox Christianity by 1000 AD but Islam made more progress among the Turkish people like the Eastern Bulgars (Eastern to distinguish them from the Western Bulgars who settled the lands of modern Bulgaria and, like the Rus, converted to Christianity). Accounts of the process of conversion are very rare but Ibn Faḍlān's narrative makes a number of important points. The initiative for the mission came not from the Caliph but from the king of the Bulghars (called here *ṣaqāliba)* who sent a message "people to instruct him in law and acquaint him with the rules of Islam according to the *sharīʿa*, and to construct a mosque and build a minbar from which he could proclaim al-Muqtadir's name throughout his kingdom. He also beseeched him to build a fortification to protect him against the kings who opposed him (notably the Khazars who had converted to Judaism)". The king wanted to convert to join the Muslim community. He was prepared to accept the overlordship of the distant caliph and adopt his name. He also wanted the new technology of masonry building. Conversion seems to have been top-down; the king became a Muslim and his subjects followed. All did not go well, however, because the king had also been promised a substantial sum of money to pay for the building and when this did not appear, he was furious though this does not seem to have led him to reject Islam and he accepted Ibn Faḍlān's instructions about the call to prayer and the Muslim rules of inheritance. The details of this process of conversion may be hard to recover but it is clear that by the end of Samanid rule in 395/1005, many of the Turkish tribes of the steppe had converted to Islam, a development which laid the foundations for the Karakhanids and Seljuk Turks to take power in Eastern Iran in the first half of the fifth/eleventh century. Importantly, under Samanid influence, the Turkic tribes were converted to Sunni, rather than Shi'ite Islam, despite the fact that Ismāʿīlī missionaries were active in Iran and even for a time at the Samanid court. The identification of Turkic peoples with Sunnism persisted in Central Asia and in the Ottoman Empire and gave aspiring rulers of the Ghaznevid and Seljuq lines the opportunity to position themselves as leaders of the "orthodox" Muslims against the Shi'ite "heretics".

The first half of the fifth/eleventh century saw Samanid power at its apogee. Despite the origins of the family in the Samarqand area, they established their capital in Bukhara and their rule saw the city becoming a major commercial and cultural centre. A powerful government collected plentiful taxes to pay an efficient army. In 280/893, the Amir Ismāʿīl led an expedition to distant Talas and returned with a vast booty of slaves. At the same time, the Amirs exerted their authority over the local princes of Transoxania and venerable lines like the Bukhārakhudās and the Afshīns of Ushrūsana, who had held power in their areas since before the coming of Islam, now disappeared. In the West, however, Samanid attempts to establish firm authority over the Zaydi rulers of the Caspian provinces area were only intermittently successful and the city of Rayy passed into Buyid hands in the second half of the fourth/tenth century.

On Ismāʿīl's death in 301/907, he was succeeded by his son Aḥmad who attempted to assert Samanid power in the Caspian provinces to the west and Sistan to the south but his reign was cut short when he was murdered by his Turkish slaves, allegedly because he allowed himself to be dominated by the religious *ʿulamā* at their expense. He was succeeded by his young son Naṣr. Despite challenges from other members of the Samanid family who attempted to seize power, he was not deposed. Under the tutelege of his able vizier Abū ʿAbd Allah al-Jayhānī, he survived these attempts and his long reign 301–331/914–943 was the high point of Samanid power. It was during his reign that the Samanids were able to control Rayy in 314/925–926 when the caliph al-Muqtadir confirmed the Samanids as rulers of the city. It was also in his reign that Ismāʿīlī influence became important at the Samanid court. This was the time when the Ismāʿīlī Qarāmiṭa threatened Baghdad and the very existence of the ʿAbbasid caliphate and the Ismāʿīlī Fatimids were establishing their caliphate in North Africa. In the Samanid realms, there was, however, a vigorous reaction and the supporters of the Ismāʿīlīs were purged by the orthodox Sunnis. Ismāʿīlism survived in remote areas like Badakhshan but apart from that, Transoxania remained firmly part of the Sunni world, a position confirmed with the increasing conversion of the steppe Turks to Sunni Islam.

The Samanids emulated the ʿAbbasid in the development of a bureaucratic state in which ten diwans supervised the chancery the collection of taxes and the payment of the army. Both the contemporary historian of Bukhara, Narshakhī, and the eleventh-century statesman Nizām al-Mulk writing for the Saljuk rulers stress the orderly and complex administration maintained by the Samanids. The Samanid administration developed two main branches, the *darqāh* or military court, commanded by the chief *ḥājib* and the civilian bureaucracy headed by the *wazīr.* The impression of order sound government may well have been idealized by both contemporary and later commentators. Niẓām al-Mulk, for example, describes with admiration the system of promotion by which Turkish *ghilmān* could rise from humble servile origins to the great offices of state and even, as the example of the Ghaznevids in the next century was to demonstrate, to the throne itself. Revenue was collected from the rich agricultural lands of Transoxania and Khurasan, as well as dues collected from the import of Turkish slaves.

The state was not dependent on loyalties of clan or tribe. The Turkish soldiers, who became increasingly powerful and influential as the Samanid century progressed, served as individuals and the group loyalties were to commanders who took them into their households and raised and promoted them. The court itself seems to have been largely static, based in the capital of Bukhara. Apart from the governor of the other great city, Samarqand, who was usually a member of the ruling family, the Samanids could count on the loyalty of a number of local dynasties in Transoxania, mostly claiming ancient Iranian origins. The government of Khurasan, the lands to the west of the Oxus with its capital at Nishapur, was more problematic.

The chief problem that he, and later Samanids, faced was the government of Khurasan. While Transoxania remained the heartland of their power, the rich cities of Khurasan, especially Nishapur, now more populous and wealthy than the old capital at Marw, were also vital. The province was the focus of a three-way struggle between the Buyids, who sought, successfully in the end, to rule in Rayy, the Ziyārid rulers of Jurjān and Tabaristan and the Samanids. The Amirs themselves do not seem to have been active in Khurasan, preferring to rule from their capital in Bukhara, and they appointed military commanders to govern on their behalf. The difficulty was that successive commanders used their power to establish their own semi-independence.

The problem was finding someone who had sufficient power and influence to govern the province but who would not use his position to challenge the authority of the Amir in Bukhara. Two families came to dominate and alternate the government of the province between them, the Iranian Amirs of Chaghāniyān and the Turkish Simjurids. The Muḥtājid Muḥammad b. al-Muẓaffar was the governor of Khurasan from 321/933 until his death in 329/941 when he was succeeded by his son Abī ʿAlī Aḥmad. In 333/945, he was dismissed, apparently because he was not prepared to accept Nūḥ's authority over his army and replaced by Ibrāhīm b. Sīmjur. Abū ʿAlī mounted a full-scale rebellion and at one point deposed Naṣr but in the end peace was made, perhaps because he was the only man who could command the allegiance of the army of Khurasan and he returned to office in 335/946. After little more than a year, he was dismissed again but made a comeback in 340–343/952–954 and governed until his death from plague in 343/954. He was the last Muḥtajid to govern Khurasan but his family seem to have continued to rule their ancestral province of Chaghāniyān.

Ibrāhim b. Sīmjūr had governed Khurāsan on two occasions before his death in 336/948 in 336/948. In 345/956, his son Abū'l-Ḥasan Muḥammad was appointed the governor and, with a brief interruption held office until 371/989, some thirty three years later, by far the longest tenure of any Samanid Amir or governor. Gardīzī gives us a rare character sketch:

> Abū'l-Ḥasan took up his post and treated the subjects very benevolently, spreading his justice widely....He always used to cultivate the learned classes and turned completely away from those evil ways which he had previously followed and from which the subjects had suffered much; he now conciliated people, put aside that evil behaviour and abandoned reprehensible behaviour.

It would be nice to imagine that his conduct contributed to his long and peaceful tenure of office. Until the last decade of Samanid rule, the Sīmjūrīs, increasingly partners rather than subjects of the dynasty, represented the best solution the Samanids found to the Khurasan problem.

At the end of Naṣr's reign, he seems to have come under the increasing influence of the Ismāʿilīs at court. This, in turn, led to a plot to have him assassinated which was forestalled when his son Nūḥ was able to persuade him to retire and occupy himself with religious devotions. On his death in 331/943, he was succeeded by his son Nūḥ. Nūḥ's reign was marked by the beginning of financial problems. The treasury was empty and in 334/945–946 there were mutinies among the troops of the army in Khurasan which led to the brutal executions of the army commander and the vizier as Nūh tried to pacify the discontent. The other big problem of the reign was relations with Abū ʿAlī the Muḥtajid, deposed from his position as the governor of Khurasan but powerful in his native Chaghāniyān. He was put in charge of the capture and execution of a self-styled prophet (*mutanabbi*) who had appeared in the mountains to the East of Chaghānyān. Abū ʿAlī attempted a reconciliation with the Amīr, sending a delegation of shaykhs and leading citizens from Nishapur to Bukhārā but before they reached the capital, the Amir was dead.

The Samanid dynasty continued to rule in theory for another half-century after Nūḥ's but the chroniclers tell us a very letter about their personalities or activities as they were increasingly side-lined by old-established military leaders like the Sīmjurids in Khuasan and from the 340s/950s a new generation of Turkish *ghilmān.* Nūḥ was succeeded by one of his sons, ʿAbd al-Malik, who reigned for six years, 343–350/954–961. His reign saw the eclipse of the power of the Muḥtajids with the death of Abū ʿAlī, his body being taken to his native Chaghāniyān. At the same time, it saw the rise of a new Turkish *ghulām*, Alptegin, who is first mentioned in 345/956–957 as Ḥājib (senior military commander in the Samanid hierarchy) when he organized the murder of the vizier Bakr b. Mālik in public at the gate of the *Dār al-sulṭān* in Bukhara. He disdainfully refused the governorate of Balkh as beneath his dignity and in 349/961 he had himself appointed the governor of Khurasan and went to Nishapur. Here, he worked in tandem with the vizier Abū ʿAlī Balʿamī, father of the celebrated historian, as effective rulers of the Samanid state.

This arrangement came to an end when the Amīr ʿAbd al-Malik died, apparently being thrown of his horse, playing polo while drunk. The vizier Balʿamī asked Alptegin's advice about the member of the family who should succeed him. Alptegin made his choice but unfortunately for him the members of the Samanid family and the military leaders in Bukhārā had already chosen the dead Amīr's brother Manṣūr. Alptegin was dismissed and forced to flee with his most loyal *ghilmān,* after burning his camp and equipment. They fled through the Oxus valley to remote Ghazni, then an unimportant town in what is now eastern Afghanistan, on the route to the plains of India. Here, he established himself, ostensibly as a loyal, if distant, vassal of the Samanids. Among the *ghilmān* who followed him was one Sebüktagin, the founder of the Ghaznevid dynasty.

The annals tell us little about the reign of the new Amīr (350–365/961–976) and such details as we do have are mostly concerned with the activities of Abū'l- Ḥasan Sīmjurī in Khurasan and the establishment of a peaceful arrangement with the Buyids, now firmly in control of Rayy. On his death, he was succeeded by his son Nūḥ who was still a child at the time. His reign of over twenty years was the second longest in the history of the dynasty but during this period, power slipped away from the Samanids into the hands of their Turkish military officers, while the Karakhanid threat loomed larger on the eastern frontiers.

He began his reign by strengthening the position of Abū'l-Ḥasan Simjūri in Khurasan, writing him a fulsome letter and bestowing a title, Nāṣir al-Dawla, the sort of honour which had previously only been bestowed by caliphs on independent rulers like the Buyids and Hamdanids. During the course of the reign, Abū'l-Ḥasan's son Abū ʿAlī began to take over from his father, able but more ruthless than his parent, he was to be a major player in the final collapse of Samanid rule. At this time too, a new generation of Turkish officers appear on the Samanid political scene. They seem to have been slave-soldier *ghulāms* without any clear family or geographical origins. Fā'iq and Tāsh are found constantly manoeuvring at court and in provincial appointments, sometimes allies, more often rivals.

In 387/989, Abū'l-Ḥasan died, having sex with a slave girl with whom he was much enamoured in the garden of his palace. With his death, the dynasty lost one of its most loyal supporters. His son inherited much of his power; he did not have the same commitment to the ruling family. He had numerous troops and an ample treasury. He used these resources to take over the whole of Khurasan, collecting all the taxes for himself and "inflicted every humiliation on Nūḥ", proclaiming himself Amīr al-Umara, though he still kept Nūḥ's name in the *khutba.* The breach became open and irreparable when the Karakhanid Ilek Khan took over Bukhara, apparently without meeting any serious resistance, in 381/991–992. Nūḥ's commanders were quick to offer their services to the invader, Fā'iq, entering his entourage and Tāsh being awarded the governorship of Balkh. Abū ʿAlī himself wrote to the Khan offering his support. Nūh who seems to have withdrawn to the Oxus crossing at Amūl wrote increasingly desperate letters to him asking for troops and money but Abū ʿAlī sent no reply.

The Samanid only survived because the Khan got sick in Bukhara and left the city to return to the healthier air of the steppe but died on the way. Nūḥ now turned to the only man who would offer him any effective support, Sebüktagin of Ghazna. He with his ambitious and able son Maḥmūd now came to take over the leadership of the Samanid forces in Khurasan. In 384/994, there was a decisive encounter between the Samanid army and the forces gathered by Abū ʿAlī Simjūrī outside Herat. Gardīzi paints a picture of the battle scene:

> Contingents of *ghilmān* and banners came into view from every side and there were so many rampant elephants, cavalrymen and infantrymen that the actual earth's surface could not be seen....Then there arose the sound of drums, barrel shaped drums and kettledrums trumpets with tapered tubes, cymbals. jangling ornaments and bells of elephants, deep toned trumpets and conches, together with the shouting of warriors and the noise of horses to such a pitch that the world grew dark. The wind arose, with dust and stones swirling in it (75–6).

As later Persian miniatures show, every important battle had to have an orchestral accompaniment.

It was at this point that Abū ʿAlī lost his nerve. Fearing treachery among the ranks of his supporters, he and his *ghilmān* abruptly fled from the field, leaving his camp with its valuables and equipment to be pillaged by Sebüktagin and his men. It was not quite the end for Abū ʿAlī. He was given shelter by the Buyid ruler of Rayy but left his place of safety "because of a love affair with a woman" in Nishapur. In the end, he was captured, and handed over to Sebüktegin who ordered that he be imprisoned in distant Gardīz in the mountains to the east of Ghazni where he was killed soon after. Only shortly after this in 387/997, both Sebüktagin and the luckless Amir Nūh died.

He was succeeded by his son Manṣūr who was still a boy. His disturbed reign only lasted two years (387–389/997–999) and he never had a chance to establish himself and he was deposed and blinded after trying to assert himself against the leaders of the Turkish military. Meanwhile, powerful neighbours were poised to move into the political vacuum. From the south, Sebüktagin's son Mahmūd moved to take over Khurasan, while from the east, the Karakhanid Khan moved his followers into Bukhārā. In Dhū'l-Qaʿda 389/October 999, the Khan established himself in the seat of government and the last Samanid Amir, ʿAbd al-Malik, and his family were taken to Uzgend at the eastern end of the Farghāna valley where they soon perished.

The dynasty destroyed and no-one attempted to recreate Samanid power but their memory lingered on. Later generations remembered their system of government, the great and wise viziers from the Jayḥānī, Balʿamī and ʿUtbī families, and the flourishing of Persian poetry at their court. They were the most important figures in what the historian Minorsky called the "Iranian intermezzo", the century or so between the collapse of the Arab rule of the caliphate and the rise of Turkish powers like the Karakhanids and the Ghaznavids. And they left one of the first and most exquisite Islamic buildings in the Persian world, the family mausoleum in Bukhara. Deep in an ancient cemetery, half buried among the tombs, it survived undisturbed before being resurrected by twentieth-century restorers for us to enjoy today.

The Ghaznavids

Ghaznavids emerged from the collapse of the Samanid state. The first leader of the group of *ghilmān*, who formed the nucleus of Ghaznavid power, was Alptigīn who had fled the Samanid court for semi-exile in Ghazna, a then remote small town on the route from Kabul to the plains of northern India. Here, he maintained himself in semi-independence as the Samanid regime in Transoxania and Khurasan disintegrated. On his death, leadership of the group passed to Sebüktagīn who assumed control in 366/977. He had been a slave captured in what is now Kyrgyzstan who had been promoted by Alptigīn. As we have already seen, he answered the pleas of the Samanid amir Nūḥ b. Naṣr for military support and defeated Abū ʿAlī Simjūrī.

This ex-slave was now rewarded with the overlordship of most of modern Afghanistan and the prestigious title of Nāṣir al-Dīn wa'l-Dawla, while his able and ambitious son Maḥmūd, now a leader of the forces in Khurasan, was called Sayf al-Dawla. For the first time, a *ghulām* had been clearly and publicly one of the leading powers in the Muslim world. When Sebüktagīn died in 987/997, he was, after a short struggle for power among his sons, succeeded by Maḥmūd. Again, it was the first time a *ghulām* family had established a hereditary succession.

The final collapse of the Samanids left Maḥmūd and his *ghilmān* in effective control of all the Samanid lands west and south of the Oxus river. He also made an agreement with the Karakhanids that they would rule Transoxania, including Bukhārā and Samarqand and by and large both sides respected this arrangement. In the west, Maḥmūd accepted Buyid control over Rayy and the increasingly feeble Buyids posed no real threat. Sistan, however, was another problem. The vast distances and scattered populations of the Helmand river basin meant that Ghaznavid control was both precarious and unprofitable.

To sustain his new position, Maḥmūd required military power and legitimacy as a Muslim ruler. The power of the Ghaznavids rested on their army. The core of this army was a comparatively small force of some 4,000 *ghilmān* though much larger numbers were sometimes assembled for campaigns to the plains of India as recruits joined the expeditions hoping for the rewards of *jihād*. In 414/1023, Maḥmūd is said to have reviewed 54,000 men and 1,500 elephants with complete outfits or armour at Ghazna but this must have been an exceptional occasion. Unlike the neighbouring Karakhanids, the Ghaznavids had no tribal following or support on which they could rely. The problem, as the contemporary Buyids and Hamdanids were finding out, was that *ghilmān*, even though their numbers might be quite small, were very expensive and if they were not paid, their loyalty would soon evaporate. In order to sustain this expenditure, the Ghaznavids had to tax their territories heavily and unremittingly. Whether in the great towns of Khurasan or the scattered villages of Sistan, tax collectors were, or attempted to be, ruthless. This, in turn, alienated many of their subjects. Except in Sistan, violent resistance was uncommon but the rapacity of the tax system meant that their subjects offered little or no resistance when the Ghuzz Turkomen and the Saljuq leaders appeared to offer an alternative from the 1030s onwards.

The question of legitimacy within the Muslim commonwealth was of crucial importance to the Ghaznavids. Despite their slave *ghulām* origins, they had to find a discourse which explained why they should rule over the community of Muslims in their area. They tried to achieve this in three ways. The first was securing the support of the ʿAbbasid caliphs in Baghdad. During the second half of the fourth/tenth century, the caliphs were powerless figureheads under the control of the Shi'ite Buyids. With the accession of the caliph al-Qādir (381–422/991–1031), this began to change as Buyid power in Baghdad and Iraq declined, so the caliph was able to assert some independence and develop his claim to be the leader of a Sunni community. Assailed by the Fatimids and their Ismāʿīlī followers from Egypt and the West, al-Qādir was able to look to the Ghaznavids whose adherence to Sunni Islam was without doubt. Maḥmūd wrote to the caliph stressing his allegiance and arguing that he had only replaced the Samanids because of their disloyalty. In return, the caliph invested him with the governorship of Khurasan, a robe of honour, a crown and the titles of Yamīn al-Dawla and Amīn al-Milla (right hand of the dynasty and trustworthy supporter of the faith). He enthroned himself in the ancient city of Balkh, wearing robe and crown and holding public audience for high and low. Maḥmūd and his successor Masʿūd never claimed the title of caliph as the Fatimids and Umayyads of al-Andalus had done. Instead, they ruled with the title of Amīr (prince or governor) and the informal designation of *sulṭān*, a word which changes at this time from meaning authority or the state to being the title of an independent ruler.

His second role was as a champion of the emerging Sunni orthodoxy against the Ismāʿīlī heretics. Since the failure of their attempt to convert the Samanid court, the scattered groups of Ismāʿīlīs can hardly have represented a major threat but their secrecy meant that conspiracies could easily be imagined. The attachment to Sunni orthodoxy was also useful as an ideological weapon against the Shi'ite Buyids of Rayy. Maḥmūd was not only the appointed representative of caliphal power; he was also the defender of orthodox Islam.

The third pillar of Ghaznavid authority was their role in leading a *jihād* in the plains of northern India. There had been previous Muslim raids on Sind from Umayyad times but they had always come by sea or the long and arduous march through Baluchistan and Makran. Maḥmūd's expeditions were the first to use the northern route to the heart of the Punjab. These raids served a dual purpose. They provided a role for Maḥmūd as the great *ghāzī*, the leader of the Muslims against the infidels. The Hindus of the area were certainly not People of the Book and their towns and even more their temples were legitimate targets. The caliph himself wrote to congratulate Maḥmūd's triumphs for the faith. It was not just religious prestige which spurred Maḥmūd; it was also a question of money, the rich booty which was taken from the conquered. These helped to give Maḥmūd the resources to sustain his expensive court and military establishment.

Under the firm, even brutal, leadership of Maḥmūd, the system worked. The Ghaznavids maintained what was almost certainly the largest standing army in the eastern Islamic world at the time. It was a world of rich feasts and opulent palaces. Maḥmūd and his administration attracted the admiration of the most influential political commentators, Niẓām Al-Mulk, writing for the Seljuqs who by 442/1050 had taken over almost all the Ghaznavid lands apart from small principality based on Ghazna itself. It was also a fragile system. It could not sustain long and unprofitable wars against fellow Muslims in Khurasan and Khwarazm and the plains of India were no longer providing easy pickings in the way they had done before. Under the rule of Maḥmūd's son Masʿūd, the strains became more apparent until they led to the catastrophic defeat by the Ghuzz Turks at Dandānqān in 1040.

Maḥmūd was a man of enormous and ferocious energy, travelling long distances on campaigns almost every year. He was also a master of tactics, whether of amphibious warfare on the rivers of India or employing miners and siege engines to destroy the walls of cities and fortresses. After the establishment of his power in Khurasan in 389/999 and the death of the last Samanid pretender, al-Muntaṣir in 395/1005, Maḥmūd fought on two main fronts, Khurasan and India.

In Khurasan, his campaigns were focussed on retaining control of what he had against and asserting his power over Khwarazm. At first the main threat came from the Qarakhanids who had taken over the Transoxanian part of the Samanid domains but as time went on, they became less of a problem and the peace negotiations of 415/1024 seem to have achieved a lasting non-aggression arrangement with the Oxus as the frontier. Much more difficult to contain were the increasing depredations of the Ghuzz Turkmen of the steppes around the Jaxartes (Syr Darya) river. In 418/1028, people from small towns on the edge of the Qarakum desert came to Maḥmūd's court to complain about the attacks of the nomads. He sent his right-hand man in Khurasan, Arslān Jādhib, the amir of Tus, renowned for his ferocity and his devotion to his sovereign, to repel them but he was unable to make much progress against these swift and mobile predators. The next year, Maḥmūd himself came to Tus and he and Arslān were able to disperse the Turkmen, slaughtering many of them, while the rest fled to the mountains. The threat was ended for the moment but it was to be the undoing of his son and successor, Masʿūd.

Another area of concern to Maḥmūd was the ancient kingdom of Khwarazm. At the beginning of his reign, it was ruled by an old-established dynasty of Iranian origin who held the hereditary title of Khwarazmshāh. They had converted to Islam in the aftermath of the Arab Muslim conquests of the early second/eighth century but Khwarazm seems to have retained a very separate identity. Ibn Faḍlān found them speaking their own very distinctive language, "like the chattering of starlings" and the Khwarazmshāh holding court as a semi-independent vassal of the Samanids. The Ghaznavids began to put pressure on the rulers and in 406/1015–1016, the then Shāh Abū'l-ʿAbbās-al-Ma'mūn wrote to Maḥmūd asking for the hand of his daughter in marriage. Not everyone in Khwarazm was pleased about this and a faction whom Gardīzī dismisses as "intriguers and dregs of the population" but who were probably just people who did not want to see their native land dragged into the Ghaznavid orbit rose in rebellion and assassinated the Shāh. This of course gave Maḥmūd the excuse for military intervention and he himself came to take command. Despite stiff resistance, the Ghaznavid army prevailed in a battle in 408/1017 and the leaders of the opposition were taken prisoners and punished. Maḥmūd did not abolish the ancient title of Khwarazmshāh but instead appointed one of his chief military commanders, Ḥājib Altuntash, to the office. He remained a faithful servant of Maḥmūd but his son Masʿūd was to find Altuntash less obedient.

It is India, however, which absorbed most of Maḥmūd's military energies. Much of Sind as far north as Multan had been conquered by Muslim armies in the Umayyad period. Since then, however, the Muslims had not made major advances and the Hindu kingdoms of the northern Punjab and the Ganges basin had been untroubled by Muslim raids. The southern part of Sind was under nominal control of the ʿAbbasid caliphate, while Multan was ruled by a local dynasty which had adopted Ismāʿīlī beliefs.

Almost as soon as he became the ruler, Maḥmūd launched his first attack on the plains of the Punjab. Ghazna was in the mountains but with quick if not easy access to the plains. No previous Muslim rulers of Ghazna or other parts Afghanistan had done this but the advantages in terms of both financial gain and religious prestige were obvious. The first target was the kingdom of the Hindūshahids based on the old city of Wayhind. In 393/-1002–1003, he took Wayhind and the king Jaypāl and many from his family were taken prisoners and sold as slaves in Khurasan. As was often to be his custom in the years to come, Maḥmūd wintered in the plains before returning to Ghazna laden with treasurers and captives in the spring. In 393/1004 he led a more ambitious campaign which peneyrated deep into the plains of the Punjab where he took Bhatinda. Again, his armies were victorious, much treasure was taken, many captives slaughtered, while the king Bājī Rāy committed suicide with his own dagger.

The pattern of raids continued for most years of his reign. In 401/1010–1011, he took Multan on the pretext that most of the people were heretics and all the "Qarāmiṭa" were executed. Attempts to penetrate the mountains of Kashmir were less successful. He led campaigns in 404/1013 and 406/1015–1016 but the fortresses were too strong and the winters too cold to allow him to make much progress. New campaigns in the Ganges basin followed to Qanawj in 409/winter 1018–1019 and further south to Gwalior in 413/1022–1023. The most spectacular and best remembered of his campaigns was the raid on the great temple of Somnath on the shore of the Arabian Sea in what is now the Gujarat province of India. Apparently, he had heard stories about the immense wealth of the temple and city and was determined to loot and destroy it even though it was far away in hostile territory. In 417/1026, his army ransacked the temple, destroyed the statues and took away a vast treasure. The way back was not so easy. He chose a roundabout route through the Indus valley but his troops were mauled by the indigenous Jhat people and many of them lost their lives and many of the beasts of burden they were using to carry their loot died. In 418/1027, he launched his twelfth and last expedition to India to punish the Jhats, fighting an amphibious campaign among the islands in the Indus. He may have taken his revenge but the fighting was hard and the booty was meagre.

Maḥmūd's campaigns were a new chapter in the history of Muslim penetration into the sub-continent. The victories and the loot, proudly displayed to his admiring subjects at the palace in Ghazna, were impressive but there was no permanent settlement or annexation of territory.

Maḥmūd died in 421/April 1030 after a prolonged illness. His death set off a vicious power struggle between two of his sons Muḥammad and Masʿūḍ and when Masʿūd finally triumphed in 421/October 1030, he inaugurated a purge not only of those who had supported his defeated brother but also of those military and civilian leaders who had been closest to his father. It set a pattern of suspicion and treachery which drove away many potential supporters.

Masʿūd's reign marked the end of the Ghaznavids as a major power in the eastern Islamic world. This decline is the focus of the surviving parts of Bayhaqī's *Ta'rīkhī Masʿūdī*, perhaps the most impressive of Persian chronicles and one of the greatest works writing anywhere in the Medieval world. It has the added advantage that we now have a superb English translation with notes and commentary by C. E. Bosworth which means that it is widely accessible. He chronicles in fascinating detail the court intrigues, and the jealousies and the fearsome cruelty which characterized Masūd's court along with details of the display and performance of monarchy which can be found nowhere else. As a dissection of autocratic power, it bears comparison with the *Memoirs* of the Duc de Saint-Simon which tells us so much about the court of Louis XIV of France.

From the beginning, Masʿūd's exercise of power was dogged by the increasingly bold raids of the Turkmen from the steppes, now led by the Seljuk family. Ghaznevid taxation lay heavily on the populations of towns and villages and the army which was paid from this revenue was large but slow and ineffective against these nomads. The elephants which were the pride of the army were virtually useless in the steppes and mountains where the Turkmen hung out. Even more of a problem was that the populations of the towns often preferred to make agreements with the Turkmen rather than fortify themselves and await the Ghaznavid army to repel the attackers. Masʿūd continued his father's policy of raiding India. Twice, he led winter raids in 424/1033–1034 and 427/1036–1037 but the fighting was hard and the wealth acquired seems to have been meagre compared with the loot his father had collected. Worse still he faced rebellions among his troops in India and had to use Indian troops to suppress them.

It was, however, the Turkmen who proved his downfall. Led by the Seljuk Dāwūd Chaghri Beg, they penetrated further into Ghaznavid territory, even threatening the winter capital at Balkh. Exasperated by his inability to counter them, he launched a major campaign which he himself led, into the steppes of the Qarakum desert. In Bayhaqī's account, he slows that almost everyone in the Ghaznavid court knew that this was a mistake, but none dared contradict the Amir. As the army march out towards the little caravan town of Dandānqān on the road to Marw, he describes soldiers sitting beside the road weeping because they knew they were doomed. And so it proved to be. In Ramadan 431/May 1040, the Ghaznavid army was decisively defeated. The Amir himself is said to have fought bravely but many of his troops abandoned the field or even went over to the enemy. In the end, he withdrew ignominiously to Ghazna. Here, he set about punishing commanders who he believed had been treacherous or cowardly. This was not enough to restore the position so he loaded his treasures onto pack animals and withdrew to the plains of India. Misfortune followed him. Seeing his weakness, sections of his army pillaged his caravan and he himself was captured by a group of his own soldiers in Jamādā 432/ January 1041 and executed.

The defeat at Dandānqān was one of the most decisive battles of the age. It destroyed the Ghaznavids and left the way open for the Seljuqs and their Ghuzz followers to invade and dominate first Iran and then the wider Middle East.

The Karakhanids or Ilek Khans

The Karakhanids (the name does not appear in the older sources but is used by modern scholars to denote the dynasty because of the prevalence of the word "Kara", meaning black but also strong or magnificent in their titulature) were a dynasty and extended which ruled, more or less effectively, over Transoxania and Central Asia as far East as Kashgar and Khotan in the eleventh and twelfth centuries and survived as vassals of the Kara-Khitay until the coming of the Mongols. Most of their history lies beyond the scope of this volume, but their appearance as a major power on the far northeast of the Muslim world in the half-century 1000 to 1050 is nonetheless interesting.

The reconstruction of the history of the dynasty is made problematic because of the almost complete lack of sources. There are no surviving historical narratives from within the Karakhanid realms and outsiders like Gardīzī and Ibn al-Athīr who we rely on for Samanid history, and provide patchy and sometimes confusing details. Numismatic evidence attests the names and sometimes the chronology of the rulers but little more and archaeological evidence is very patchy.

Turkish tribes had been constant neighbours and often enemies of the Muslims in Transoxania since the first Muslim conquests. They lived nomad lives in the steppes which stretched from the edges of the fertile lands as far as China. They are always represented in the Muslim sources, whether Arabic or Persian, as the other, seldom given either names or speaking parts in the historical narrative. ʿAbbasid governors and Samanids alike could project themselves as defenders of Islam and use the rhetoric of Holy War to unite their subjects against the hostile alien forces. In around 344/955, however, this paradigm began to change when the then leader of the Qarakhanid family, Satoq Bughrā Khān, converted to Islam and seems to have brought with him the vast majority of his followers. This fundamentally changed the dynamics of the Turkish involvement in Central Asia. They were now fellow Muslims and could be accepted as rulers by Muslim populations. When the last Samanids attempted to rouse the people of Bukhārā to resist a Karakhanid takeover of the city, the *ʿulamā* rejected their calls because the newcomers were as good Muslims as the existing dynasty.

The details of this conversion process are very obscure. There is no indication that any violence was involved. It is likely that Muslims from Transoxania, like Ibn Faḍlān and his party, acted as both merchants and missionaries but they were preaching to people who were interested in anticipating in the wider world which conversion would open up for them. From Iceland and Scandinavia in the West to Central Asia in the East, the fourth/tenth century was a time when pagan peoples adopted the monotheism of their southern neighbours. In almost all cases, the new religion brought with it written texts and masonry architecture. The conversion and acculturation of the Karakhanids can be seen as part of a global process.

The new converts did not just become Muslims but they became Sunni Muslims and adhered to the Ḥanafī School of Islamic, as did almost all the Turkish dynasties which followed, right down to the Ottomans. In fourth- and fifth/tenth- and eleventh-century terms, this meant that they became a powerful counterweight to the Ismāʿīli Fatimids and other Shi'ite groups to the West.

The conversion of the Karakhanids was the largest expansion of Muslim-ruled territory since the mid-eighth century. The new territories included most of the southern parts of modern Kazakhstan, Kyrgyzstan and the ancient trading cities of Kashgar and Khotan in the western parts of the Chinese province of Xinjiang. The limits of Muslim religion and culture established by the Karakhanids in these areas have, essentially, remained its limits down to the present day.

The emergence of Karakanids also brought the Turks into the wider mosaic of Muslim-ruled lands as full participants in the *umma*. They and their realms were Turkish in the sense that the rulers and probably most of their subjects spoke Turkic dialects as their main language. Many of them also shared the Turkish nomadic traditions of dwelling in round felt yurts and raising horses and camels. It was under Karakhanid patronage that the first grammar-encyclopaedia of Turkish culture, the *Diwān Lughāt al-Turk*, was composed by Maḥmūd Kāshgharī in the second half of the fifth/eleventh century, championing, for the first time, Turkish as a literary language. Having said that, Arabic was used for religious discourse and Persian for many court purposes. At least two of the later Khans wrote Persian poetry but written poetry in Turkish had to wait for another two centuries.

The dynasty also began the first large-scale building patronized by Turkish speakers. Although they came from nomad backgrounds, the Karakhanid period saw the foundation and development of the first cities in these areas, notably the old settlement at Kashgar and the new city of Balāsāghun whose ruins now lie in Kyrgyzstan. The minarets they commissioned to demonstrate their commitment to Islam still survive in Bukhara and Balāsāghun, while the recently discovered remnants of a painted hall in their palace in the citadel of old Samarqand point to a developed secular architecture.

The Karakhanids had first intervened in Transoxania in 382/992 when they temporarily occupied Bukhara and permanent occupation followed in 398/999 at the same time as the Ghaznavid Maḥmūd b. Sebükatigīn took over Khurasan, the lands to the west and south of the Oxus, thus carving up the old Samanid realm. For the next forty years, the Oxus remained the frontier between the Karakanids and the Ghaznavids. Shortly afterwards, in the year 396–397/1006, the eastern Karakhanids finally established their control over Khotan.

The Karakhanid territory was divided, at least from c. 1040 into an Eastern and Western khanate. The Eastern, with two capitals at Balāsāghun and Kashghār, was the senior and its ruler bore the prestigious title of Arslān (Lion), while the Western Khan, ruling from Samarqand, was called Bughrā or male camel. In practice, the empire was considered the common patrimony of the ruling dynasty. Under the overall leadership of the Khāqān, there were lesser princes bearing princely titles like *tigīn* below them. These princes frequently changed their titles and their territories as they moved up or down the pecking order, making the dynastic politics very difficult to understand.

The Qarakhanid rulers continued a semi-nomadic life style. It seems that they spent the winter in towns like Bukhārā and Samarqand where they built palaces but in the spring and summer, they would roam the steppe with their nomad followers. In this way, they maintained contact with the Turkish tribes on whom the military support depended. They never seem to have recruited an army of *ghilmān* slave soldiers. This was in marked contrast to the Ghaznavids on the other side of the Oxus whose *ghilmān* were the mainstay of their power. An important consequence of this was that they did not demand the heavy taxes which were required to pay for this professional army and there is some evidence that the cities and villages they controlled were ruled with a lighter touch. Certainly, old-established Persian-speaking civilian elites and religious scholars continued to flourish and urban patriciates seem to have co-existed with semi-nomadic rulers. This style of government also meant that there was no need for an elaborate bureaucracy, which, in turn, may account for the dearth of written records and narratives compared with their Ghaznavid neighbours.

The normally dry narrative of Gardīzī takes a break from names and dates to describe a meeting of these two new Central Asian powers. In 415/1024, news reached the Khaqan of the Karakhanids, Yūsuf Qadīr Khan (r. 417–424/1026–1032) in Kashghar that Maḥmūd of Ghazna had crossed the Oxus in an apparent challenge to the agreement between the two powers. His pretext was that the people of Transoxania were complaining about the oppression of their masters. Maḥmūd constructed a bridge of boats which is elaborately described. It is the fullest description of the construction of such a bridge from this period and suggests that the author may have been an eye-witness. The Khaqan hastened to Samarqand and then on to meet Maḥmūd. Neither party seems to have wanted a conflict but both were keen to show their power and prestige and outdo the other in generosity and gift-giving. They camped a few kilometres apart and arranged a meeting place.

Here, we see two great princes, both of Turkish extraction, meeting together to decide the future of the eastern Islamic world. Their festival of food and music, set in a garden surrounded by fragrant plants, is a forerunner of all those princely parties portrayed so vividly in Persian-illuminated manuscripts from the fourteenth century onwards. Maḥmūd brings the riches of the Islamic world from as far away as the Maghrib, Qadīr Khan the furs of Siberia and the fine silks of China. Competitive display and gift-giving are seen as central to the princely culture.

"When Qadir Khan arrived, Maḥmūd ordered trays of food to be set as splendidly as possible and the two monarchs sat down and ate at the same table. When they had finished the feast, they moved on to the place where music and other festive entertainments had been prepared. This had been magnificently decorated with rare and unusual sweet-smelling plants, luscious fruits and precious jewels. The hall had goblets of gold and crystal, remarkable mirrors and various rare objects so Qadir Khan remained in the midst of all this dazzled. They remained seated for a good length of time. Qadir Khan did not drink wine for it was not customary for the monarchs of Transoxania, and especially the Turkish ones, to drink wine. They listened to music and singing for a while and then they arose.

Amir Maḥmūd then ordered a display of presents on a scale worthy of the occasion to be brought in: gold and silver drinking vessels, costly jewels, unusual specialities imported from Baghdad, fine clothes, expensive arms, valuable horses with gold accoutrement with goads studded with jewels, ten female elephants with gold trappings and goads set with jewels, mules from Bardha'a (a town in Azerbayjan) with golden bells, litters with mules with girths, moon-like ornaments of gold and silver with bells for their necks, litters covered with embroidered brocade and woven patterns, valuable carpets including those from Armenia with raised patters and particoloured rugs, pieces of woven and embroidered cloth. Lengths of rose coloured cloth from Ṭabaristan with designs on the, Indian swords, aloes wood from Khmer, yellow tinged sandalwood, grey-flecked amber. There were she asses, skins of Barbary panthers, hunting dogs, eagles trained to a high pitch for hunting down cranes, gazelles and other game animals. He sent Qadir Khan back homewards with great honour and magnificence, heaping favours on him.

When Qadir Khan got back to his encampment and the saw the immense amount of precious objects, furnishings and carpets, weapons and wealth. He was filled with astonishment and did not know how he could requite Maḥmūd for them. He ordered the treasurer to open up the treasury door. He took out of it a great amount of wealth and sent it to Amīr Maḥmūd, together with various items which were specialities of Turkistan, including fine horses with precious trappings and accoutrements of gold, Turkish slave boys with golden belts and quivers, falcons and hawks, pelts of sable, grey squirrel, ermine and fox, vessels made from leather skins, narwhal or walrus horn, delicate cloth and Chinese brocade, Chinese *dārkhāshāk* and such like. The two monarchs parted from each other completely satisfied and in peace and benevolence".

14 Early Islamic Egypt and the Fatimid empire

Early Islamic Egypt was a rich country. The taxes that could be gathered from the peasants of the Nile valley meant that, after the Sawād of Iraq, it was the largest contributor to the budget of the ʿAbbasid caliphs. The wealth of the area was not, however, translated into political importance and power. Under the Umayyads, the province was usually the apanage of a branch of the Umayyad family, while under the early ʿAbbasids the governors were often men of local importance only. Although richer, it was politically much less important than Syria or Khurāsān. The reason for this lay largely in the makeup of the population. As far as we can tell, there had been no significant Arab settlement in Egypt before the coming of Islam; and even after the Arab conquest, immigration was very limited. The small number of Arabs who did come lived almost entirely in the two main towns, Fusṭāṭ and Alexandria, apart from some bedouin in the Ḥawf region along the eastern borders of the delta. Conversion seems to have been slow, and the tightly knit Coptic community retained its loyalty to the church under Islamic rule as it had under the equally unsympathetic Byzantine government. Much of the local administration remained in the hands of local people, and the Arab impact on everyday life was probably very slight. This meant that there was no large body of Muslims who would provide a power base for an ambitious governor or would-be dynast. It was not until military forces from outside the country were established there in the third/ninth century that Egypt first became a political power within the Islamic world.

Early Islamic Egypt had been largely controlled by a group of Arab families in Fusṭāt. mostly of south Arabian origin and descended in the main from men who had arrived at or soon after the initial conquest. They provided the *qāḍī* and the *Ṣāḥib al-shurṭa*, the chief of police, who controlled the local militia and functioned as a chief adviser to the governor. The civil wars after Hārūn's death destroyed the power of this élite, and when ʿAbd Allāh b. Ṭāhir brought the area back under the control of the Baghdad government during the reign of al-Ma'mūn, the administration was entrusted to outsiders, Turkish and Armenian soldiers. It was only a matter of time before one of these decided to use the resources of the area to improve his own position rather than to benefit the caliph.

DOI: 10.4324/9780429348129-14

The anarchy at Sāmarrā which followed the death of al-Mutawakkil in 247/861 meant that provincial governors throughout the Muslim world were forced to rely on their own resources, and many moved towards independence. In order to try to solve the problem of paying the Turkish troops, caliphs of the period took to granting the Turkish leaders revenues from provinces, which they could then distribute to their followers. And so in 254/868, al-Mu'tazz granted Egypt to Bāyikbāk. He, in turn, appointed his stepson Aḥmad b. Ṭūlūn to govern the province in his name and so ensure that the revenues were collected and delivered. Aḥmad was himself of Turkish origin, his father having been sent from Bukhārā to serve in al-Ma'mūn's entourage during the civil war which followed Hārūn's death; Aḥmad was born in 220/835. He was given a military training in Sāmarrā and, more surprisingly, a theological education in Tarsus, and thus emerged as an Arabic-speaking Muslim rather than a first-generation Turkish immigrant from the central Asian steppes, a factor which was probably crucial in his success.

Such was the importance of the tax revenues of Egypt to the 'Abbasid government that it was the custom that the financial administrator of the province should be independent of the governor and responsible directly to Baghdad or Sāmarrā. When Aḥmad arrived in the province, the financial administrator was the shrewd and often brutal Ibn al-Mudabbir, who had no intention of allowing the young governor to take over his role. For four years, the two were rivals for power, but in the end developments in Palestine and Syria swung the balance in Ibn Ṭūlūn's favour. These provinces were disturbed by a series of local rebellions which the caliphs were unable to crush. They therefore turned to Ibn Ṭūlūn, who alone seemed capable of restoring order in the area. He used the opportunity to seize control of the financial administration from Ibn al-Mudabbir and to use the revenues of the province to recruit a large new army, some of them slaves, mostly Negroes and Greeks, and some of them professionals, mostly Greeks. This meant that for the first time, the revenues of Egypt were spent on raising and paying an army in the province under the control of the governor. Egypt began to acquire a political importance commensurate with its financial one, and Ibn Ṭūlūn became powerful in a way no previous governor of the province had been.

His financial and political independence was increased by the system of joint rule established in the caliphate between the Caliph al-Mu'tamid and his brother, and effective military commander, al-Muwaffaq in the years after 256/870, for the caliph relied on Ibn Ṭūlūn as a counterweight to the vast power exercised by his brother and depended on him for contributions to his own treasury. Al-Muwaffaq clearly resented his situation but his energies were occupied in the long drawn-out campaigns against the Zanj rebels, and so he was unable to take any action against Ibn Ṭūlūn.

It would be a mistake, however, to regard Ibn Ṭūlūn as an independent breakaway ruler. His constitutional position remained that of deputy governor of Egypt. His methods of government were based on the model of the ʿAbbasid court in which he grew up, and his new suburb to the north of the old city of Fusṭāṭ, al-Qaṭāʾiʿ was very much Sāmarrā on the Nile, even down to the style of the Great Mosque which was closely based on Sāmarrā patterns.

While Egypt seems to have enjoyed a period of peace and prosperity under Ibn Ṭūlūn's rule, he was concerned, like all rulers of Egypt, with the stability of Syria and Palestine, and much of his diplomatic and military activities was concerned with ensuring his influence there. In 263/877, al-Muwaffaq attempted to regain control of Egypt, needing the resources of the province for his campaigns against the Zanj, and sent one of his leading Turkish generals, Mūsā b. Bughā, to displace Ibn Ṭūlūn. The attempt failed because Mūsā's army disintegrated and Ibn Ṭūlūn now felt that he had to take the initiative and occupy Syria, participation in the *jihād* against the Byzantines providing the perfect justification. His relations with al-Muwaffaq remained cool and in 269/882 he tried to persuade the Caliph al-Muʿtamid to come to Fusṭāt. and establish himself in Egypt away from the influence of his brother, but the scheme failed and led to a breakdown in relations. Al-Muwaffaq realized, however, that he had to come to terms with his Egyptian rival, and negotiations were in progress when Ibn Ṭūlūn died the next year (270/884). Ibn Ṭūlūn never repudiated the authority of the caliphate and seems to have continued to make some contribution to the ʿAbbasid treasury. The circumstances of the period, the anarchy in Sāmarrā followed by the period of dual control under al-Muʿtamid and his brother al-Muwaffaq, coupled with the long and very costly war against the Zanj, meant that he was a provincial governor of great importance and independence; it did not mean that he was attempting to be an independent ruler in Egypt. In his policies, as in his upbringing, he remained very much a product of the ʿAbbasid establishment.

Before his death, Ibn Ṭūlūn had secured the acknowledgement of his son Khumārawayh as heir, replacing another son, al-ʿAbbās, who had rebelled against his father. Khumārawayh now succeeded without opposition in Egypt, but al-Muwaffaq was determined to exploit his youth and inexperience to regain authority, and there followed three years of undistinguished campaigning before an agreement was reached in 273/886. This treaty stipulated that Khumārawayh would acknowledge the caliph and pay a substantial tribute (perhaps 300,000 *dīnārs* a year) in exchange for the governorate of Egypt, Syria and part of the western Jazīra for thirty years, the provisions being hereditary. In 279/892, the accession to the caliphate of al-Muʿtaḍid, son of Ibn Ṭūlūn's old enemy, al-Muwaffaq, led to the confirmation of the treaty with minor changes, including the Tulunids' loss of their Jaziran possessions.

Khumārawayh inherited the army his father had built up, and it was upon this that his power was based. He himself recruited a private guard from the Ḥawfī Arabs of Egypt to supplement the existing forces. His reign is usually considered one of luxury and decay, but it seems unlikely that the growing financial problems were purely a product of the ruler's extravagance. The Tulunid court was based on the Sāmarrā model and it seemed that the system had some of the same weaknesses as were found in the 'Abbasid system, notably the inability of the state to fund a large, mostly inactive army on a permanent basis. The solution to these financial problems was entrusted to a bureaucrat of Iraqi origins, 'Alī b. Aḥmad al-Mādharā'ī, whose efforts were only partially successful, since when Khumārawayh was murdered in 282/896 by his own slaves, the treasury was empty. Despite this, however, the twelve years of his rule were largely peaceful and saw a measure of calm not only in Egypt but, more unusually, in Syria.

After his death, the decline of the power of the family followed with startling rapidity. He was succeeded by his youthful son Jaysh, who was soon deposed, and then by another son, Hārūn – but neither of these two boys was able to keep the state intact. In 292/905, Muḥammad b. Sulaymān and the 'Abbasid army entered Fusṭāt. and brought an end to the Tulunid dynasty. The end of family rule may have been ignominious, but the memory of the Tulunids lingered on and showed that Egypt, under wise and energetic leadership and administration, could be the centre of a major regional power. Many later rulers were to develop the themes first worked out under their rule: careful financial administration, the recruitment of soldiers from outside the province and the concern to control Palestine and Syria.

The restoration of direct 'Abbasid rule did not result in peace and prosperity. Once again, the resources of Egypt were exploited for the benefit of outsiders, or at least that was the theory. An element of continuity was provided by the fact that the Mādharā'ī family retained control over the financial administration. The governorship during this period was in the hands of Turkish generals, of whom Takīn b. 'Abd Allāh was the only one to enjoy power for any significant length of time. It seems likely that the Baghdad government was reluctant to allow these any more power than was necessary for fear that they would try to emulate the career of Ibn Ṭūlūn. That this was indeed so is suggested by the fact that Takīn's son, Muḥammad, attempted to secure his father's position after his death in 321/933. Apart from the instability of governors, the most serious threat facing Egypt at this period came from the Fatimids, established in Tunisia since 297/909, who made two major attempts to conquer Egypt in 301–302/913–915 and 307–309/919–921. In order to counter these, Mu'nis, the military strongman of al-Muqtadir's reign, was obliged to come west to undertake the campaign in person, suggesting again that the local governors were not allowed sufficient resources to do it.

'Abbasid control over the area was at best precarious, and it effectively came to an end during the disturbances of the later years of al-Muqtadir's reign. The beneficiary of this uncertainty was another military man of eastern Iranian extraction, Muḥammad b. Ṭughj. His grandfather had come from the Farghānā area of Khurāsān to the court at Sāmarrā where he was a contemporary of Ibn Ṭūlūn's father. His son Ṭughj served the Tulunids as a governor in Aleppo and Damascus and it seems that his son, Muḥammad, who had been born in Baghdad in 268/882, was able to make use later of contacts established at this stage. Ṭughj himself joined Muḥammad b. Sulaymān and the ʿAbbasid forces against the last of the Tulunids but was arrested after the fall of Ibn Sulaymān and died in prison in 294/906. His son, Muḥammad, escaped and soon found himself a post under Takīn, the governor of Egypt, who appointed him to the ʿAmmān area. In 306/918, Mu'nis came to Egypt to defend it against the second Fatimid attack, and Ibn Ṭughj used the opportunity to gain the friendship of this powerful figure whose patronage was to be of key importance. In 316/928, he broke with Takīn, and it was probably Mu'nis' influence which led to his appointment to Damascus three years later. After the death of Takīn in 321/933, he was briefly appointed the governor of Egypt itself, but the move came to nothing when Mu'nis fell from power. Only the fact that Takīn's successor Aḥmad b. Kayghalagh was totally unable to keep order in the province allowed Ibn Ṭughj a second chance. In 323/935, he was again appointed the governor, probably with the intervention at court of al-Faḍl b. Jaʿfar b. al-Furāt, who, like him, had been a supporter of Mu'nis.

Once appointed, he lost no time in restoring his control over Egypt. Ibn Kayghalagh, his predecessor, fled to the Fatimids, but he was able to win over both Takīn's son, Muḥammad, and the Mādharā'ī financial administrators to his cause. In some ways, the Fatimid threat actually helped Ibn Ṭughj. He loyally supported ʿAbbasid claims, and the caliphs were prepared to give their approval to his rule in return. In 324/936, he defeated a third Fatimid attack and was rewarded with the title of *ikhshīd*. This had been the title held by the king of the Farghānā area from which his grandfather had come. There is no evidence that he was of royal descent, but the choice of the honorific shows how attached he remained to the memory of his family's homeland. Like Ibn Ṭūlūn before him, the *ikhshīd* took care to build up a strong military force in Egypt, recruiting many blacks and Turks. In many ways, however, he was less ambitious than Ibn Ṭūlūn. In Syria, he was prepared to reach an accommodation with Sayf al-Dawla the Hamdanid in 334/945, which left the Hamdanids in control of Aleppo, Antioch and Homs, all areas which the Tulunids had ruled, while Ibn Ṭughj controlled Damascus and Palestine (see above, pp. 273–274). His only attempt to influence events in the rest of the Muslim world seems to have been in 333/944 when he met the Caliph al-Muttaqī at Raqqa. He tried to persuade the caliph, as Ibn Ṭūlūn had tried to persuade al-Muʿtamid, to come with him to Egypt. The luckless ʿAbbasid allowed himself to be persuaded by the *amīr al-umarā'*, Tūzūn, to remain in Iraq, where he was blinded and deposed shortly afterwards.

Ibn Ṭughj died in 334/946. Although he lacked the flamboyance of the Tulunids and does not seem to have been a patron of the arts in any way, he followed them in making Egypt and its army the basis of his power and in concerning himself with the administration and agriculture of the province.

In 333/944, he had made an agreement with the caliph whereby he was to have the governorate of Egypt for thirty years, and this was to be hereditable by his children. It is interesting to note that the terms were the same as Khumārawayh had made with the caliph in 273/886. When the *ikhshīd* did die shortly afterwards, his son, Ūnūjūr, succeeded him without any real opposition. The smooth transfer of power was arranged by the black eunuch Kāfūr. He had been recruited into Ibn Ṭughj's service along with many of his compatriots, and he had come to the ruler's attention because of his obvious talents. He was used on diplomatic and military missions and became a tutor to the young Ūnūjūr. On his father's death, ūnūjūr succeeded to the throne, but the administration remained firmly in the hands of Kāfūr, who was to be the virtual ruler of Egypt for the next twenty-two years. The Ikhshidid princes (ūnūjūr, 334–349/946–961 and 'Alī, 349–355/961–966) were little more than puppets in the hands of this gifted administrator, who preserved the substance of the state founded by the *ikhshīd* against outside attack from Hamdanids and Fatimids as well as internal disturbances and economic problems. With the death of 'Alī in 355/966, Kāfūr took over power in his own right and remained the ruler of Egypt until his death two years later, an event which left the way open for the long-threatened Fatimid takeover.

The Tulunids and the Ikhshidids shared important characteristics. Both states were marked by an adherence to 'Abbasid legality and the working out of treaty arrangements with the caliphs, and they were characterized by the development of powerful slave and mercenary armies recruited almost entirely from outside Egypt. They were also concerned with the economy of the country, and rulers of both dynasties tried to ensure that the prosperity on which their power was ultimately based remained intact. Indeed, it is the financial administrators who provide a major element of continuity through this period, the Mādharā'īs linking the Tulunids with the Ikhshidids, while the Fatimids employed Kāfūr's financial official, Ya'qūb b. Killis. The Fatimids, of course, rejected any allegiance to the 'Abbasid caliphs, but in other ways they built on the foundations laid by their predecessors, and the Fatimid state can only be understood in relation to them.

The Fatimid caliphate emerged from the Ismā'īlī movement of the third/ninth century. Towards the end of the century, the movement was divided by the claims of 'Ubayd Allāh, then living in Salamiyya in Syria, that he was a descendant of Ismā'īl and the true living *imām*. Many Ismā'īlīs, notably those who were to form the Qarmaṭī movement, rejected these claims but others accepted them. Among the latter was the *dā'ī* (missionary) known as Abū 'Abd Allāh al-Shī'ī, who spread the Ismā'īlī message first in Yemen and then from 280/893 in the province of Ifrīqiya in north Africa (roughly modern Tunisia). Here, he avoided the plains around the city of Qayrawān, the stronghold of the Aghlabid dynasty, which had controlled the area since the time of Hārūn al-Rashīd, and travelled instead among the Kutāma Berbers of the Kabyle Mountains to the west. The Berber population of north

Africa had always resented the rule of the Arabized élite of Qayrawān and expressed their disaffection by adopting heterodox approaches to Islam. In the Umayyad and early ʿAbbasid periods, Kharijism had attracted a wide following among these people, and it is not surprising that the wandering teacher and holy man Abū ʿAbd Allāh should be welcomed by them. Despite inevitable tensions, the Kutāma Berbers were to form the main support of the Fatimid dynasty for over a century to come. When the Qarāmiṭa threatened ʿUbayd Allāh the Fatimid and forced him to leave Salamiyya, he made his way to join Abū ʿAbd Allāh among the Berbers. From their base in the mountains, they made a series of attacks on the Aghlabids which culminated in victory in 297/909 when they expelled the last Aghlabids and the Fatimid dynasty was established in Qayrawān.

The moment when a revolutionary movement achieves power is always of crucial importance. Fatimid propaganda seems to have promised the Berbers a divinely inspired *imām*, possibly capable of doing miracles, certainly providing charismatic leadership. ʿUbayd Allāh, however, seems to have found these claims something of an embarrassment when power was eventually his. While the Berbers were dismayed to find their leader a mere mortal after all, ʿUbayd Allāh was determined to establish his authority and he succeeded in executing Abū ʿAbd Allāh, his *dāʿī*, and suppressing dissident movements among both the Kutāma and the settled peoples.

Having surmounted the original crisis, ʿUbayd Allāh set about creating a state apparatus which was surprisingly conventional. Later, Ismāʿīlī groups, like the Assassins of northern Iran, tried to break away from the pattern of military government which had become usual in the Islamic east, but the Fatimids made no such attempt. ʿUbayd Allāh was proclaimed the caliph with the messianic title of al-Mahdī and the claim to be the true leader of the Family of the Prophet. As such, he claimed authority not just over Ifrīqiya as the Aghlabids had done, but also over the entire Islamic world. Ifrīqiya was to play the role that Khurāsān had done in the ʿAbbasid revolution, while the Kutāma were to fulfil the role of the Khurāsāniyya. In order to do this, the Kutāma were formed into a regular, paid militia, while slaves were recruited from sub-Saharan Africans, Greeks and *Ṣaqāliba*, i.e. Slav and other European *ghilmān* employed by Spanish Muslim rulers. A navy was also formed, a development which was to be very important in the history of the caliphate. The first objective was to be the conquest of Egypt, and in 301–302/913–915, a Kutāma chief, Ḥabāsa, led the first expedition there. Although the Berber forces managed to maintain themselves in the country for some time, the expedition ended in failure when the local Turkish commander, Takīn, was reinforced by the general Mu'nis from Iraq. A second attempt five years later, led this time by the caliph's son, Abū'l-Qāsim, ended in failure again, although this time the Fatimid army stayed two years in Egypt: the turning point was once again the arrival of Mu'nis from the east and the destruction of the Fatimid fleet by the fleet of Tarsus.

After these two failures, the caliphate developed more or less peacefully in north Africa. In 308/920, a new capital was built at Mahdiyya on the coast, a natural port and stronghold, away from the potentially hostile people of Qayrawān. The reconciliation of Ismā'īlī ideals with the government of largely Sunnī people was gradually worked out. At one level, there was very little attempt at conversion and certainly no mass coercion. Ismā'īlī beliefs remained the faith of the Kutāma and of other members of the governing élite. Among these was the *qāḍī* al-Nu'mān b. Muḥammad, who worked out the theoretical nature of the Fatimid claims, attempting to clarify the genealogy and showing how the *imāms* were the natural, foreordained leaders of the entire Muslim community. This did not mean that all subjects had to become active Ismā'īlīs; for those not involved in government, passive acceptance was enough.

After the two initial attempts to take Egypt, Fatimid expansion in the east came to a temporary halt. There were a number of reasons for this, notably the establishment of a fairly strong government in Egypt under Muḥammad b. Ṭughj and problems nearer home. From 331/943 to 335/947, Ifrīqiya itself was disturbed by the rebellion of a different Berber group, the Hawwāra of the Aurès Mountains under a charismatic Kharijite leader called Abū Yazīd, known as "the man on the donkey". This rebellion nearly destroyed the Fatimids entirely, and after its defeat they were forced to pay more attention to affairs in the west. Here, they began a long drawn-out struggle for influence over the Maghrib (the areas of modern Morocco and Algeria) with the rival Umayyad caliphs of Cordova. It was not until 347–349/958–960, when Jawhar, now the leading Fatimid general, conquered Sijilmāsa and Fez, that the position was secured.

The Fatimids had not, however, lost interest in the east entirely. In particular, they seem to have renewed contact with their fellow Ismā'īlīs, the Qarāmiṭa, now at a safe distance. In 339/951, they persuaded the Qarāmiṭa to return the Black Stone of the Ka'ba, a sign of both their influence and their renewed determination to play a part in the affairs of the eastern caliphate. In 341/953, al-Mu'izz succeeded to the Fatimid throne and seems to have been determined to pursue the eastern ambitions of the dynasty. The Fatimids had always had contacts in Egypt. At the time of the accession of Muḥammad b. Ṭughj, there had been a party of *Maghāriba* (westerners, i.e. north Africans) in the country who supported the claims of Aḥmad b. Kayghalagh against Ibn Ṭughj and his *Mashāriqa* (easterners or Turks), and after Ibn Ṭughj's triumph, his defeated rival took refuge with the Fatimids. In the later days of Kāfūr's reign, problems began to reassert themselves in Egypt and it became possible once again for the Fatimids to fish in troubled waters. A series of inadequate Nile floods resulted in discontent, famine and reduced revenue for the government. The governing class was increasingly divided between the civil administration, the *kuttāb*, led by Ja'far b. al-Faḍl b. al-Furāt,[1] and the army built up by the Ikhshidids. The Fatimids developed contacts with many groups in Egyptian society, among them were members of leading ʿAlid families and the financial administrator, Yaʿqūb b. Killis, who fled to the Fatimid court because of his hostility to Ibn al-Furāt. Fatimid propaganda in Fusṭāt. was organized by a rich merchant, Aḥmad b. Naṣr, whose activities became increasingly open in the last years of Kāfūr's rule. He took care to assure all elements in Egypt that the Fatimid Caliph al-Muʿizz really had their interests at heart. On the fringes of the Nile valley, Fatimid agents stirred up trouble among the bedouin of the Egyptian deserts, notably the Banū Qurra, now the leading group among the Arabs of the Ḥawf on the east of the delta, and the Banū Hilāl and Berber nomads of the western oases. In Syria, their allies, the Qarāmiṭa, attacked Ikhshidid possessions.

Despite these favourable signs, the expedition was planned with great care to ensure that there would be no repetition of previous problems. In 357/968, Kāfūr died and power passed to the hands of the infant Ikhshidid, Aḥmad b. ʿAlī. Ibn al-Furāt, in charge of the bureaucracy, was confronted by the opposition of al-Ḥasan b. ʿUbayd Allāh, who came from a branch of the Ikhshidid family established in Damascus, and Shamūl, leader of the army. The leader of the Fatimid expedition was Jawhar, an ex-slave probably of Greek origin who had risen by his abilities to a leading position in the Fatimid army and enjoyed the confidence of the caliph. In Rabīʿ I 358/February 969, he left Ifrīqiya with an army, said to have been 100,000 strong, mostly Berber horsemen. As he approached Egypt, he began negotiations with different groups. These were complex and resulted in a series of agreements, the basic outlines of which were that the *kuttāb* and the leading members of the civilian élite, including the *qāḍī* of Fusṭāṭ, were guaranteed their property and position. Agreement with the Ikhshidid military was more difficult and there were some violent confrontations, but the opposition was divided and leaderless, and in Shaʿbān 358/July 969, Jawhar entered the capital, and the prayers in the old mosque of ʿAmr, still the centre of religious devotion, were said in the name of the Fatimid caliph.

Jawhar remained an effective ruler of Egypt for the next four years until the arrival of his master al-Muʿizz, and he was responsible for the main features of the post-conquest settlement. Jawhar inherited the Ikhshidid state apparatus. Ibn al-Furāt served the new administration as he had served Kāfūr and the Ikhshidids. More remarkable was the fact that the *qāḍī* of Fusṭāṭ, Abū Ṭāhir, an old man in his eighties, and the *khaṭīb* (preacher) of the mosque of ʿAmr, a member of the ʿAbbasid family, were both kept in office. There was continued opposition from some members of the Ikhshidid army, but most people seem to have welcomed the arrival of stable government, and Jawhar made no attempt to force Ismāʿīlī practices on an unwilling populace.

Jawhar's most important act was the foundation of a new capital, al-Qāhira (Cairo), i.e. the Victorious, about 3 miles to the north of the old city of Fusṭāt. The foundation of a new settlement was not new in the history of Islamic Egypt; Fusṭāt. itself had been founded by the conquering

Muslims outside the walls of the Roman fortress at Babylon, and Ibn Ṭūlūn had founded a new centre, complete with mosque, at al-Qaṭā'i', to house his newly recruited army. The Fatimid city was, however, the most ambitious and the most carefully planned of all these enterprises. The primary purpose of the new city was to house the government and the Berber army, many of whom remained to settle in Egypt. Here, they could be safe from popular disturbances, and the newly arrived troops would not clash with local inhabitants. From a religious point of view, it was important to have a mosque where the Ismā'īlī rite could be celebrated without opposition, and Jawhar immediately began the building of the Azhar mosque, soon to become an important centre of Ismā'īlī education and propaganda. Economic benefits accrued because of the state ownership of land in the city. When al-Manṣūr had founded Baghdad, he had left the development of the markets to his subjects, to whom the land was granted. In Cairo, however, the markets were state property, bringing in substantial revenue. Most of the new city was occupied by mosques and two vast palaces where the opulent, formal and hierarchic Fatimid court operated away from the public gaze. Throughout the Fatimid period, Cairo remained very much the government enclave. Fusṭāṭ, from which it was separated by a belt of gardens, remained the centre of population and economic activity. The three great mosques retained their separate identities: the mosque of 'Amr was the centre of popular devotion and the place where the *qāḍī* of Fusṭāt. held court; the mosque of Ibn Ṭūlūn with the adjacent *Dār al-Imāra* (government house) was the site of the *maẓālim* court, where fiscal and political cases were dealt with; while the Azhar, soon to be supplemented by the mosque of al-Ḥākim, was the court mosque.

While the establishment of the Fatimids in Egypt was comparatively peaceful and successful, the question of Syria and Palestine was, and remained throughout the period, the government's major preoccupation. This was partly for security reasons. As events were soon to show, Fatimid Egypt could not be held unless Palestine and Damascus at least were under the control of Cairo. There was also an economic aspect; Syria was an important alternative source of supplies in years when the Nile did not rise sufficiently to provide for the needs of Egypt. One of the reasons for the collapse of the Ikhshidids had been that the raids of the Qarāmiṭa had meant that grain could not be imported from Syria to relieve distress in Egypt. The Fatimid regime could not afford to allow the populace to go hungry.

There were two possible solutions to the Syrian problem. The less ambitious was the Ikhshidid approach. This consisted of basing power in Damascus and allowing northern Syria to remain independent under the Hamdanid dynasty. The second option was the Tulunid solution, which meant that all Palestine and Syria as far as the Byzantine frontier should be brought under Egyptian rule. The Tulunid option was tempting in that it brought more land under Fatimid rule and meant that the caliphs would have the prestige of defending Islam against Byzantine attacks. But it also led to problems. The Arab tribes of Syria were difficult to control – the people of Aleppo had strong separatist tendencies and were quite prepared to seek Byzantine support to preserve their independence from their Muslim neighbours. Direct confrontation with the Byzantines would demand all the military resources of the state, and there were practical problems in supplying and controlling a large army far from the centre of power. In the aftermath of the conquest, Jawhar sent a leading Kutāmī Berber general, Ja'far b. Fallāḥ, to take over the remaining Ikhshidid possessions. The last Ikhshidid governor, al-Ḥasan b. 'Ubayd Allāh, was captured at Ramla and sent to north Africa, and Damascus was occupied.

This was only the beginning of the problem, however, for the Fatimids now came into direct conflict with their sometime allies, the Qarāmiṭa. The Ikhshidids had been paying the Qarāmiṭa very large subsidies – 300,000 *dīnārs* a year – to keep them peaceful, but Ja'far decided that these should be cut off. The response was swift. The Qarāmiṭa of Syria called on their fellows in Baḥrayn and secured arms and subsidies from the Buyid Bakhtiyār in Baghdad. Thus prepared, they killed Ja'far and drove his Berber troops out of the city and back to Egypt. Nor did they stop there, but, recruiting disaffected supporters of the Ikhshidids en route, they marched on Cairo itself. Jawhar constructed a line of fortifications outside the city at 'Ayn Shams. In Rabī' I 361/December 971, a fierce battle was fought around this line, and the Qarāmiṭa were defeated. It had been a near-run thing and the caliphate almost perished. After the battle, Berber reinforcements, led by al-Ḥasan b. 'Alī, called Ibn al-'Ammār, arrived from Ifrīqiya. Egypt was safe, although there was still opposition in some parts of the delta, but the problem of Syria was far from being solved. In the aftermath of victory, many Ikhshīdī supporters who had, or were thought to have, allied with the Qarāmiṭa were rounded up and imprisoned, but an attempt to regain Palestine was prevented by the Qarāmiṭa who occupied Ramla.

Early in 362/late 972, al-Mu'izz left Ifrīqiya to come east. He brought with him his entire court, his possessions and the coffins of his ancestors; he did not intend to return. By Sha'bān (May 973), he was at Alexandria where he held court at the foot of the Pharos, which had been restored by Ibn Ṭūlūn and was still largely intact. Here, he received the leaders of the bedouin tribes and the civil élite of Fusṭāṭ, accepting their professions of loyalty and explaining that he had only come to pursue the war against the infidels and to open the route to Mecca for pilgrims, the traditional public duties of the caliph. In Ramaḍān 362/June 973, he finally entered Cairo. Jawhar was retired with wealth and honour, although he remained a trusted counsellor, and al-Mu'izz began his personal rule.

He brought with him two men who were to have an important influence on the making of early Fatimid policy: the *wazīr* Ya'qūb b. Killis and the *qāḍī*, al-Nu'mān b. Muḥammad. Ya'qūb, a converted Jew, of Iraqi origin like so many of the Egyptian governing class, had been trained in administration under Kāfūr. Ideologically, he was a firm supporter of the Ismā'īlī doctrine, produced a book of law based on the pronouncements of the Caliphs al-Mu'izz and al-'Azīz, which he caused to be used in the mosque of 'Amr, and played a major part in the establishment of the Azhar as an Ismā'īlī educational institution. In practical affairs, however, he tended to run financial and foreign policy as it had been under Kāfūr, thus ensuring a strong element of continuity in Egyptian government.

Soon afterwards, he and his colleague, the Berber 'Uslūj b. al-Ḥasan al-Kutāmī, established themselves in the old *Dār al-Imāra* by the mosque of Ibn Ṭūlūn and began a searching investigation into the revenues of the government. They increased the tax farms and revised upwards the taxes they demanded at all levels, most noticeably from the textile towns of the delta, Tinnīs and Damietta. These taxes were to be assessed in the new, very fine gold *dīnārs* al-Mu'izz now had minted. These measures put government finances on a secure footing and enabled the Fatimids to survive crises which would have destroyed a less prosperous dynasty.

The other figure, *qāḍī* al-Nu'mān, who had long served the Fatimids in Ifrīqiya, died shortly after the Fatimids settled in Cairo, but his son, 'Alī, inherited his position and took over from the ageing *qāḍī* of Fusṭāṭ, Abū Ṭāhir. In 365/975, 'Alī began the teaching of Ismā'īlī doctrine in the Azhar and remained until his death in 374/984 chief *qāḍī* of the caliphate and a leading adviser of the caliphs. He founded a dynasty of *qāḍīs* who were pillars of the regime for the next half-century.

Al-Mu'izz, perhaps under the influence of these new arrivals, moved away from Jawhar's tolerant policy on religious issues. There were four areas of change in public religious observance. The first was naturally the acceptance of the Fatimids as the rightful caliphs, which seems to have caused few problems, even in non-Ismā'īlī circles. The second was the use of Shī'ī law, particularly the pronouncements of Ja'far al-Ṣādiq (d. 148/765), the sixth *imām* and the last to be accepted by all Shī'īs. The third aspect was the distinctive Shī'ī call to prayer (which includes the words "Come to the best of works" not used by the Sunnīs) and the fourth, that most contentious of issues, the particularly Shī'ī festivals of Ghadīr Khumm (18 Dhū'l-Ḥijja) and the mourning for al-Ḥusayn (10 Muḥarram). The introduction of Shī'ī law produced some resentment, notably in the case of inheritance law, where Shī'ī *fiqh* gives women a larger share, but there was no widespread opposition. 'Alī b. al-Nu'mān was prepared to employ a Sunnī *faqīh* (expert in religious law) as a *qāḍī* on the understanding that he would judge according to Shī'ī law. Jawhar had refrained from introducing the controversial Shī'ī festivals, but al-Mu'izz did, a move which led to open opposition on 10 Muḥarram 363/11 October 973 when Sunnī merchants in Fusṭāt. insisted on keeping the *sūqs* open in defiance of official pressure for them to shut as a sign of mourning, but again the disturbances seem to have been short-lived.

In general, the Ismā'īlī rite was the faith of the ruling élite and the Berbers but it was not forced on others. The separation of the two communities helped as well, the Ismā'īlīs being dominant in Cairo, while Fusṭāt.

remained largely Sunnī. A man is said to have been expelled from Cairo for keeping in his house a Sunnī law book, the *Muwaṭṭa'* of Mālik b. Anas. There was much less sectarian violence in Egypt than there was in Baghdad and Iraq during this period, and a contemporary observer, the geographer al-Muqaddasī, who visited Egypt at this time, stresses that there were few differences between the two branches of the faith. When popular disturbances did break out, as happened during the reign of al-'Azīz, they took the form of anti-Christian riots rather than sectarian strife among the Muslims. At first sight, the imposition of an Ismā'īlī ruling class on an essentially Sunnī, traditionist population would appear to have been a recipe for civil conflict – but in the event, realism and an element of give and take on both sides, coupled with stable government and economic prosperity, meant that religious differences never got out of hand.

In contrast to the comparative stability in Egypt, the Fatimid government continued to face serious problems in Syria and Palestine. In 363/974, the Qarāmiṭa again invaded Egypt but were defeated, and 1,500 prisoners were taken to Cairo, where they were executed. Syria was still disturbed when al-Mu'izz died in Rabī' II 365/December 975. Of the promises he had made to the Egyptian leaders at Alexandria, one was fulfilled: in 364/975, the *Ḥajj* was able to travel overland from Egypt, and the Fatimid caliph was acknowledged at Mecca. Circumstances in Syria, however, meant that he was unable to pursue a campaign against the Byzantines, who had taken Antioch in the same year that Jawhar had entered Cairo. Furthermore, to the disgust of refugees from the recently conquered territories, Byzantine ambassadors were received in Cairo. The problems in Syria also meant that it was out of the question to launch any attempt to subdue Iraq and the eastern Islamic world, despite the claims of the dynasty to the leadership of the entire Muslim community.

Al-Mu'izz was succeeded by his son, Nizār, who took the title of al-'Azīz, and he and his *wazīr*, Ya'qūb b. Killis, immediately addressed themselves to the problem of Syria. Ya'qūb, in this as in other respects, followed the Ikhshidid tradition. He believed that the Fatimids should concentrate on controlling Palestine and southern Syria while leaving the north of the Hamdanids and their successors to form a buffer state against the Byzantines, with whom the caliph should try to keep on good terms. This modest strategy formed the basis of Fatimid policy throughout the early years of al-'Azīz.

The government of Damascus remained the principal problem. The city had been occupied by the Berber troops of the Fatimids during al-Mu'izz's reign, but they had been ill-disciplined, and tensions with the citizens resulted in disturbances and a major fire. The Berbers were so unpopular that the people of the city turned to the Turkish leader Alptakīn, who, with 300 mounted followers, took the town just before the old caliph's death. These Turks had come from Baghdad, whence they had been expelled by 'Aḍud al-Dawla when he took over the city, and they now hoped to live off the revenues of the area while entering into negotiations with the Fatimids to see if they could take service with them. Alptakīn fulfilled the hopes of the people by restoring peace and driving the bedouin away from the Ghūṭa (the oasis of Damascus). He also secured an alliance with the Qarāmiṭa and took over many of the coastal cities, including Sidon, Beirut and Jubayl. The new caliph, al-ʿAzīz, was determined to crush this emerging Syrian state and despatched a large force led by the veteran Jawhar, the original conqueror of Egypt, but Alptakīn and his Qarmaṭī allies were able to drive him back to Ascalon, where he endured a seventeen-month siege. Under pressure from his Kutāma followers, he finally entered into negotiations, agreeing that all of Palestine from Ascalon north should be under the control of the Turks, while the Fatimid presence was to be confined to Gaza in the extreme south. To sweeten the pill, Alptakīn agreed that al-ʿAzīz should be formally acknowledged as caliph in the areas under his control. Jawhar and his men were allowed to return to Egypt.

Yaʿqūb b. Killis realized that this could not be the basis of a permanent settlement. Fatimid prestige had been severely damaged, and the presence of a potentially hostile power in Ascalon and Ramla left Egypt dangerously vulnerable. In addition, he himself, and no doubt other members of the Fatimid establishment, had valuable properties in the Damascus area which they were reluctant to relinquish. He persuaded the caliph to undertake a major campaign in person, and in Muḥarram 368/August 978, a massive Fatimid army defeated Alptakīn and the Qarāmiṭa in southern Palestine. The victory reestablished Fatimid prestige, but the victors realized that compromises would have to be made. The Qarāmiṭa were guaranteed a subsidy in return for their leaving for Baḥrayn, and the settlement marks the end of the Qarmaṭī threat to Syria. Ibn Killis also realized that Syria could not be held without the cooperation of the Turks; the disastrous attempt to govern Damascus through a Berber garrison had made this clear. He therefore arranged that the defeated Alptakīn should be reconciled with al-ʿAzīz and taken into Fatimid service. He returned to Cairo with the caliph and was treated with great honour. The integration of Alptakīn and his Turkish followers into the Fatimid state marked a major change. Hitherto the Fatimid army had been composed almost entirely of Kutāma Berbers and black and Slav slaves, the Berbers forming the cavalry. Although Alptakīn himself died a few years after his arrival in Egypt, the Turks remained as a major influence in the Fatimid state. There developed a *ghulām* system very similar to that found in eastern Islamic lands, and it is interesting to note that the *wazīr* Ibn Killis acquired his own *ghilmān*, distinct from those of the caliph. The Turks were prominent in Cairo, often as rivals to the Berbers, but they were especially important in Fatimid Syria. The government of Damascus was often in Turkish hands, and continuing efforts were made to attract the services of successful Turkish *condottieri* in Syria.

The victory of 368/978 had not solved the problem of Damascus. With Alptakīn's surrender, power in the city was taken over by local people, anxious no doubt to prevent another Berber occupation. The city was effectively controlled by a citizen called Qassām, supported by the local *aḥdath* (militia), a notable example of urban self-government of the period. The situation was complicated by the arrival of Abū Taghlib, the last Hamdanid ruler of Mosul, who, expelled from his own domains, now sought a position with the Fatimids, offering to take Damascus for them if they sent troops. There then followed a confused pattern of intrigue. Ibn Killis sent a *ghulām* of his, another converted Jew called al-Faḍl b. Ṣāliḥ, with a large army of Berbers. On the way, they entered into an agreement with the leader of the most powerful bedouin tribe in southern Palestine, Daghfal b. Mufarrij b. al-Jarrāh. al-Ṭayyī, guaranteeing him possession of Ramla, which he alleged was threatened by Abū Taghlib, a threat which was made more real by the fact that Abū Taghlib had with him a body of ʻUqaylī bedouin who might have coveted the Ṭayy pastures. No serious attempt was made to take Damascus by force, although al-Faḍl did make a show of force in the coastal cities. On the way back, Ibn al-Jarrāh. and the Ṭayy, in alliance with al-Faḍl and his Berber troops, attacked and routed Abū Taghlib and his ʻUqaylī followers, killing their leader, before al-Faḍl returned home. The whole confusing episode is of some importance. It showed that the Berber army was not strong enough to take Damascus. It marked, too, the establishment of Ibn al-Jarrāh Ramla and as a major figure to be reckoned with in the area. He recognized Fatimid sovereignty in theory but in practice was an independent agent. The victory of the Ṭayy over the ʻUqayl meant that they were to be the major bedouin power in the area and a continuing problem for the Fatimid authorities. As in so many other areas at this time, we see the bedouin extending their authority over settled communities, in this case Ramla, while not abandoning their tribal lifestyle. The episode also shows the strength of Ibn Killis, operating through his *ghilmān* and making all the decisions of importance in the campaign.

The problem of Damascus remained. A further expedition in 369/979–980 under the Kutāmī chief Sulaymān b. Jaʻfar b. Fallāh. (son of that Jaʻfar b. Fallāh. who had been killed in 361/971) with 4,000 Berbers failed to achieve anything, while the problem of Ibn al-Jarrāh. became more pressing. Al-Faḍl b. Ṣālih. attempted to control him in alliance with the ʻUqayl. Most serious, however, were the depredations of the bedouin in settled areas; Ramla was reduced to a ghost town by the activities of the Ṭayy, while the bedouin virtually destroyed the agriculture of the Ghūṭa of Damascus and the Ḥawran, causing great hardship in the city. The people were saved not by the Fatimid government, but by the Turk who governed Homs for the Hamdanids, Bakjūr, who produced supplies for the areas under his control. The failure of Ibn Fallāḥ's Berber army to restore order or maintain its own discipline meant that the next Fatimid expedition to Syria was led by a Turk, Baltakīn, who had been one of Alptakīn's associates. This was the first time a Turk had led a Fatimid army. The campaign was a conspicuous success. The bedouin Ibn al-Jarrāh. was forced to flee north to Byzantine territory and Qassām surrendered Damascus on terms which allowed him to remain the effective ruler under the nominal control of a Berber governor.

Fatimid policies were helped by the decline and impoverishment of the Hamdanid state of Aleppo under Saʻd al-Dawla, which meant that many erstwhile supporters of the dynasty in Syria now entered Fatimid service. One such was Rajā' al-Ṣiqlabī, who came over with 300 followers and was rewarded with the governorate of Acre and Caesarea – but the most important recruit was the governor of Homs, Bakjūr, who now offered to govern Damascus for the Fatimids. The offer produced a major rift in the Fatimid administration between the caliph and Ya'qūb b. Killis. Baltakīn had become a protégé of the *wazīr* and Yaʻqūb was anxious to ensure that his man remained in control. Bakjūr, however, had made contact directly with the caliph. He offered al-ʻAzīz the prospect of governing not just Damascus and Homs but Aleppo as well. Ibn Killis was opposed to such a forward policy. For the first time, however, al-ʻAzīz overrode his mentor and Baltakīn was forced to hand it over to Bakjūr.

The disagreement over the appointment of Bakjūr was one of the causes of the brief estrangement between al-ʻAzīz and Ibn Killis. At the same time, an inadequate Nile flood resulted in poor harvest, high prices and famine in Fusṭāt.. There were riots and Ibn Killis and his assistant al-Faḍl b. Ṣāliḥ. were arrested. The confinement lasted only two months. On his release and reinstatement, the *wazīr* continued to work for the removal of Bakjūr, and in 377/989 he was able to persuade the caliph to appoint one of his (Yaʻqūb's) *ghilmān*, Yaʻqūb al-Ṣiqlabī, to the post. The *wazīr*'s cause was aided by the fact that Bakjūr had made himself unpopular in Damascus by his cruelty, and when the Fatimid forces approached, he fled to Raqqa, which he used as a base to attack the Hamdanids, but he played no further part in Fatimid politics. Damascus was not the only military problem the caliphate faced. In the Ḥijāz, the bedouin were making the *Ḥajj* almost impossible and once again it was a Turk, Baltakīn, who was sent to rectify the position and a Fatimid garrison was established at Wādi'l-Qurra.

In 380/991, the *wazīr* Yaʻqūb b. Killis died. More than anyone else he had guided the Fatimid caliphate through the difficult early years. Drawing on his experience under the Ikhshidids, he organized the administration of Egypt and pursued a cautious policy in Syria which, if it was not entirely successful, at least kept Egypt secure from invasion. He had also played a decisive part in reducing the monopoly of military power held by the Berbers. He had used his position to recruit and promote Turkish *ghilmān*, and the refugees who arrived with Alptakīn and their successors became a major force in the state.

The death of the old *wazīr* allowed the caliph a free hand to pursue a more aggressive and expansionist policy in Syria. Yaʻqūb's nominee was immediately dismissed from the governorship of Damascus and replaced by one of al-ʻAzīz's own *ghilmān*, the Turk Manjūtakīn, who was to be the instrument of his new forward policy. In Manjūtakīn, al-ʻAzīz found a capable and loyal commander. The prospects were further improved by the death of Sa'd al-Dawla the Hamdanid in 381/991 and the takeover of power by Lu'lu'. In 381, 382, 383 and 384 (991–994), Manjūtakīn launched campaigns against the territory of Aleppo. He took Homs and the little towns of Apamea and Shayzar from their Arab rulers, but his attempts on Aleppo itself aroused the opposition of the citizens and brought the Fatimids for the first time into direct conflict with the Byzantines, who regarded the city as being under their protection. Manjūtakīn was powerful enough to defy the *dux* (governor) of Antioch, but in 385/995 the Emperor Basil II arrived in person and conducted a major show of force throughout northern Syria, forcing the Fatimid general to retreat to Damascus. Faced with this threat, the caliph himself decided to take the field in person as the champion of Islam against the aggressive Greeks, but he died before he could put the plan into effect. The land campaigns were accompanied by an increase in naval activity. A fleet prepared in the port of Cairo was destroyed by fire, apparently by accident, but the incident gave rise to serious anti-Christian riots. Another fleet was constructed and set sail to join Manjūtakīn in the siege of the small coastal town of Ṭarṭūs. Seaborne campaigns were always hazardous, and while Manjūtakīn waited for vital reinforcements, the ships were destroyed by a storm. The approach of the Greek army forced the Fatimid forces to retreat again. As Ibn Killis had foreseen, interference in the affairs of Aleppo, however tempting the prospects seemed to be, resulted in a conflict with Byzantium, a conflict both expensive and unproductive.

The situation in Syria remained unstable. The Fatimids controlled the coastal cities from Tripoli south and some inland areas like Tiberias. Ramla and southern Palestine under Ibn al-Jarrāh. and the Banū Ṭayy were frequently disturbed, and the activities of the bedouin in the area were to prove a continuing problem to the Fatimid authorities. Damascus, however, seems to have been brought firmly under control by Manjūtakīn, who used it as his base. It is interesting to note how Fatimid rule had changed the political and economic geography of Syria. In particular, naval activity had increased. Manjūtakīn's army was largely supplied by sea through the port of Tripoli, which became a major commercial centre for the first time since the classical period. The governorships of coastal cities like Tyre, Sidon, Ascalon and Gaza became important offices. The Fatimid use of naval power to control Syria, in fact, seems to have led to the beginnings of a revival in the fortunes of the coastal towns which was to be continued in the eleventh and twelfth centuries. The eastern Mediterranean was becoming the scene of peaceful navigation once again, not just a zone of conflict.

In other areas, too, the reign of al-'Azīz had seen the increase of Fatimid influence and authority. The Fatimids took over the protection of the *Ḥajj*, at least of those pilgrims who came from the western Islamic world. This was an expensive operation – in 383/994, for example, the *Ḥajj* required an escort of 3,500 men, and the expenditure, including the cost of the new *kiswa* (the cover of the Ka'ba), of 300,000 *dīnārs*. The prestige gained no doubt offset the cost. The eastern *Ḥajj* was also patronized and financed by local rulers, Badr b. Ḥasanūya in the late fourth/tenth century and Maḥmūd of Ghazna in the early fifth/eleventh, but it was the Fatimids who provided the *kiswa* and were acknowledged by the *amīr* of Mecca. Relations with the ruler of Mecca were polite rather than close. The *amīr* acknowledged the Fatimid as caliph while maintaining his independence. In 384/994, ʻĪsā b. Jaʻfar al-Ḥasanī, then *amīr*, came to Egypt and was given substantial gifts. Relations with Mecca were commercial as well as political, and al-Maqrīzī quotes an account of al-Muʻizz buying ebony from Aden through a middleman in Mecca. In 382/992, the influence of the Fatimids spread farther and they were acknowledged as caliphs in Yemen, though without enjoying any real power there. Since the retreat of the Qarāmiṭa to Baḥrayn, they too recognized the Fatimid claims. The increased interest in the *jihād* and the care for the *Ḥajj* suggest that after the death of Ibn Killis, al-ʻAzīz began to pursue a much more caliphal policy, that is to say that he demonstrated his ability and willingness to undertake the two major public responsibilities of a caliph, to safeguard the *Ḥajj* and to lead the Muslims against the infidel Byzantines. The acknowledgement of Fatimid claims in areas over which they had no direct political control bears witness to the success of this policy.

Fatimid policy towards north Africa, the cradle of the dynasty, is a conundrum. Nothing is more striking than the speed with which they were prepared to allow north Africa to go its own way. In the time of al-Muʻizz and the early years of al-ʻAzīz's reign, there had been some continued emigration from Ifrīqiya to Egypt, but by the end of al-ʻAzīz's reign, this seems to have come to a halt. While the claims of the Fatimids to the caliphate were acknowledged in Ifrīqiya, practical power lay with the Zirid viceroys from the Ṣanhāja group of Berbers. In 382/992, al-ʻAzīz appointed Bādīs b. al-Manṣūr b. Zīrī to be his father's heir apparent, thus effectively making the dynasty hereditary. Relations were maintained by the exchange of sumptuous presents, but any claims to real political power were neglected. Ṣandal, the governor of Barqa, brought presents but again there is no sign of direct control.

In internal affairs, the departure of Ibn Killis led to some confusion and division of responsibility within the administration. The Berber military leader al-Ḥasan b. ʻAmmār refused to take over financial responsibilities, and these devolved at first on Ibn Killis' old protégé al-Faḍl b. Ṣāliḥ. and his rival, the *qāḍī* Muḥammad b. al-Nuʻmān. An attempt to persuade the veteran Ibn al-Furāt to take up office failed when he resigned after only a few months. Thereafter, administrative responsibility was increasingly taken over by the Christian Īsā b. Nasṭūris, who was given charge of all the *dīwāns* in 384/994. But this period does not seem to have been one of decline and confusion – indeed, a major reform of weights was undertaken.

In the last year of his life, al-ʻAzīz was preparing to take up arms in person against the Byzantines and he ordered a massive mobilization of men and resources. Before he set out, however, he died on 28 Ramaḍān 386/14 October 996. He was only forty-two when he died but his long reign had shown him a firm but prudent ruler. The sources comment at length on his clemency, and his reign seems to have been remembered as a period of peace and prosperity. While he owed much to his *wazīrs*, notably Ibn Killis and Ibn Nasṭūris, his later years showed that he was no mere cypher and had determined views on the nature of the caliphate. Despite his predilection for hunting, he rarely left Cairo and its immediate surroundings. After his visit to Ramla at the instigation of Ibn Killis in 368/978, he never again left Egypt. This tradition of static monarchy was typical of the Fatimid caliphate, in contrast to the restlessness of the Buyids and Hamdanids. There was no problem about the succession; no sooner had he breathed his last than the eunuch Barjuwān sought out the caliph's young son Manṣūr, placed on his head the jewelled turban and kissed the ground before him. So came to the throne the most famous of all the Fatimid caliphs, al-Ḥākim bi-Amr Allāh.

The new caliph was only eleven at the time of his accession. He was, of course, unable to exercise the autocratic control for which he later became famous. The accession of a minor gave the signal for various groups to try to redress their grievances. The last years of al-'Azīz's reign had seen the increased influence of the Turks, notably the general Manjūtakīn in Damascus, and of the Christian *wazīr*, Ibn Nasṭūris, in many ways the successor of Ibn Killis. This had caused great discontent among the leaders of the Kutāma Berbers, who felt that they had been deprived of their position in the state. Immediately after the death of the caliph, the Kutāma shaykhs made it clear that their allegiance to his son was dependent on their being given control of the government. Accordingly, al-Ḥasan b. 'Ammār was made *wāsiṭa* (intermediary between caliph and people, in effect prime minister) and the Kutāma were rewarded with the choicest contents of the treasury. Ibn Nasṭūris, the leading survivor of the old regime, was executed. In Syria, this coup provoked an immediate response. The Turk Manjūtakīn decided to march on Egypt to redress the situation. The attempt was not a success. Ibn 'Ammār mobilized the Berbers under the leadership of Sulaymān b. Ja'far b. Fallāḥ, and Manjūtakīn was defeated by Ibn Fallāh. and taken to Cairo in captivity. Here, he lived in quiet retirement until his death ten years later in 397/1007. Sulaymān continued to Damascus to take over as the governor.

Ibn 'Ammār's government in Cairo soon began to get into trouble. The Kutāma Berbers who had brought him to power used the opportunity to pillage the state. Not only did they deprive the Turks and other military groups of their positions but they cut off the salaries of the *kuttāb*, the secretaries. The chaos could not continue for long, and after a year, fighting broke out between the Turks and Berbers. Ibn 'Ammār was arrested and eventually killed, and the role of *wāsiṭa* was taken over by the young caliph's tutor, Barjuwān; the excesses of the Berbers were halted and the position of the *kuttāb* restored. It was not a complete defeat for the Berbers, however. Sulaymān

b. Ja'far b. Fallāh. was replaced in Damascus by another Berber, Jaysh b. al-Ṣamṣāma, and both Sulaymān and his brother, 'Alī, were to continue to play an important role in Fatimid government. It was rather an attempt to restore the balance as it had existed under al-'Azīz, and Barjuwān chose a new Christian *kātib*, Fahd b. Ibrāhīm, to replace the dead Ibn Nasṭūris.

As had happened before, the attempt to rule the towns of Syria through Berber garrisons ran into difficulties. As usual, they were unpopular in Damascus, which was then entrusted to an old Ikhshīdī officer, Bishāra, but the fiercest resistance came from the coastal city of Tyre. It is indicative of the increasing importance of these coastal cities that one of them should have begun an open rebellion against the Kutāma garrison under the leadership of a sailor called al-'Alāqa. The threat was increased when the rebels appealed to Byzantine support, but in the end they were obliged to surrender and the city was sacked by the army. Meanwhile in the north of the country, Jaysh b. al-Ṣamṣāma continued the war Manjūtakīn had conducted against the Byzantines and the remnants of the Hamdanid state, retaking Apamea and Shayzar. In reply to this, the Emperor Basil II launched a new and devastating campaign in northern Syria, and although he failed to take Tripoli, he pillaged Homs and the coast around Jubayl and Beirut in 390/999. It was after this that the Fatimids succeeded, through the intermediary of the patriarch of Jerusalem, in negotiating a ten-year truce. This was to be of the greatest importance in al-Ḥākim's reign. The caliph and the emperor both had concerns elsewhere and were content to accept the status quo. Aleppo remained independent under Byzantine protection, while the cities of Antioch and Lattakia and their hinterland as far south as the Homs–Tripoli gap remained part of the Byzantine Empire. Tripoli itself remained in Muslim hands, usually acknowledging the Fatimids but effectively independent under its own governors and *qāḍīs*. Despite the strains caused in later years by the destruction of the Church of the Holy Sepulchre and persecution of the Christians, the Byzantines responded by trade sanctions rather than warfare, and the peace in northern Syria remained almost uninterrupted. This long peace meant that military expenditure was reduced and may be one of the reasons why al-Ḥakim's government survived despite the ruler's eccentricities.

In Rabī' II 390/April 1000, the young caliph decided to show his independence. With the aid of a servant, he in person murdered his tutor and guardian Barjuwān. Aged only fifteen, he was now an absolute master of the state. His personality has been the subject of much controversy. The main sources we rely on, which are not on the whole anti-Fatimid in tone, present a picture of an unstable psychopath, ruling by whim and terror. His disordered personality showed itself in his attacks on Christians, Jews and his closest servants. All but a very few of those who served al-Ḥakim in senior offices were done to death, usually suddenly without trial or explanation. At times, whole classes of troops and palace servants and even common people were threatened by his vengeful cruelty, but more often it was leaders of the military and the *kuttāb* who suffered from his murderous proclivities. His eccentricity was not confined to murder, however. He introduced dietary regulations, including the banning of alcoholic drinks, and the prohibition of watercress and fish without scales and such general social matters as the forbidding of chess and the killing of dogs. At the beginning of his reign, he demanded that the *sūqs* be kept open all night for his amusement. The most striking feature of his decrees is, however, their inconsistency. Regulations would be introduced and abandoned without warning. At one time, the appearance of the cross in the streets was forbidden as an anti-Christian measure; yet shortly afterwards, all Christians were obliged to wear large crosses, thus making nonsense of the previous decree. His attitude to Islam was varied. At some times, he encouraged the spread of Ismāʿīlī customs, while at others, he seems to have permitted Sunnī practices which had been banned by his father. Towards the end of his reign, he is alleged to have neglected the conventional demands of religious law entirely, to have become increasingly ascetic and considered himself divine.

Various attempts have been made in recent years to make sense of this picture. Vatikiotis has suggested that he was the only Fatimid to take the idea of the divinely appointed monarch seriously and that his behaviour was necessary to sustain Ismāʿīlī morale and protect the state against its enemies.[2] Shaban has argued that his apparently bizarre dietary regulations are in fact sound measures to protect the rural economy.[3] But it is hard to see how the prohibition of chess fits into these explanations. In the most thoughtful recent appraisal of the problem, Forsyth, while stressing the strong irrational element in his behaviour, has drawn attention to the populist nature of some of his policies.[4] Certainly, his measures against the Christian and Jewish communities, and even his attacks on senior Muslim army officers and financial officials, may have gained some popularity, but the sources make it clear that the terror was by no means confined to the upper classes, and the burning of Fusṭāt. at the end of the reign was a culmination of previous acts of random brutality. While it would be wrong to see al-Ḥākim as a populist ruler, appealing over the heads of the administrative and military classes to the common people, it is striking that there was no concerted rebellion against his rule in either the cities or the countryside. The only serious challenge came from nomad groups who had many reasons for opposing settled authority, and it seems to have been almost unconnected with the caliph's bizarre conduct.

It seems most likely that, as was suggested by the chronicler Yaḥyā b. Saʿīd, who knew him personally, al-Ḥakim was mentally unbalanced. It is not difficult to see why. Perhaps already psychologically disturbed, he came to the throne in early adolescence and was surrounded by people who at one and the same time assured him that he had absolute authority over a vast empire and attempted to manipulate him for their own purposes. The delight in his own power, the ability he discovered at the time of Barjuwān's death to quite literally get away with murder, completed his development.

Chroniclers note that he was not without virtues. He could be generous, and rigorous in enforcing justice. He often refrained from confiscating the goods of men he had murdered and allowed their families to inherit to demonstrate his incorruptibility. He also founded an institute of learning, the *Dār al-ʿIlm*, but it must be said that he later murdered many of the teachers he had appointed. In his personal behaviour too, he showed some qualities. Especially towards the end, he seems to have tried to escape the pomp of his position, wearing ragged clothes and forbidding visitors to kiss the ground. But none of this was consistent or reliable. Even his most intimate assistants might suddenly be murdered, and the terror he inspired gave rise to moments of general panic when all classes petitioned the caliph for guarantees of their personal safety.

In the immediate aftermath of Barjuwān's death, the caliph set about creating a new government. Ruling in person without a *wāsiṭa*, he kept on the Christian, Fahd b. Ibrāhīm, as the secretary, who was given the title of *ra'īs* (chief). Military power was entrusted to al-Ḥusayn, the son of Jawhar, who had led the original Fatimid conquest of Egypt and a man who was acceptable to the Berbers as well as having his own following among the *Ṣaqāliba ghilmān*. The caliph was also careful to conciliate both Berbers and Turks; throughout his reign, he does not seem to have favoured either group at the expense of the other but to have kept a balance. He also employed other experienced officers at court, notably al-Faḍl b. Ṣāliḥ, and the family of ʿAlī b. al-Ḥusayn b. al-Maghribī, *kuttāb* who had been in the service of the Hamdanids and now, like many others from the Hamdanid court, sought employment with the Fatimids. Syria, in the meantime, was ruled by Berber chiefs in Damascus; Jaysh b. al-Ṣamṣāma, who died in 390/1000, was soon succeeded by the Kutāma leader, ʿAlī b. Jaʿfar b. Fallāḥ, who had succeeded his brother, Sulaymān, as the head of his family. ʿAlī was to prove the great political survivor of the reign, dying only shortly before the caliph after a riding accident.

Few of his fellows were so lucky. In 393/1003, al-Ḥākim began the first of his series of purges of political leaders. Fahd b. Ibrāhīm was executed, but his death was to be only the first in a long and grisly series. At the same time, the persecution of Christians and the destruction of churches began, and by the next year (394/1004) the situation was so threatening that the Kutāma en masse petitioned the caliph for a guarantee of safety, which was granted. The caliph next turned on the chief *qāḍī*, al-Ḥusayn b. al-Nuʿmān, who had succeeded his father ʿAlī and his uncle, Muḥammad, in office. Al-Maqrīzī records that he was the first *qāḍī* whose body was burned after he was killed. He was not to be the last.

The year 395/1004–1005 saw an intensification of the terror. It was at this stage that al-Ḥākim began to introduce the public cursing of the first caliphs, a Shīʿī measure which always produced violent resentment among Sunnīs and one which his father had avoided. This was combined with further measures against the Christians, including, in 400/1009, the demolition of the Church of the Holy Sepulchre in Jerusalem, and the dietary prohibitions. More groups followed the Kutāma example and asked for guarantees of safety from their unpredictable ruler. The *kuttāb* begged his forgiveness for their no doubt imaginary crimes, while different elements in the army – Turks, *ghilmān* and followers of the Hamdanids – all sought to avail themselves of this protection.

There was no effective internal opposition to the caliph, and when trouble came it seems to have originated outside Egypt and to have had little or nothing to do with his tyrannical behaviour. In 395/1005, an adventurer of Umayyad descent arrived from Spain to Barqa in Cyrenaica and began to stir up trouble among the Sunnī Berber tribesmen. Although his real name was al-Walīd b. Hishām, he was generally known as Abū Rakwa in Egypt. He was joined by the Banū Qurra, the leaders of the bedouin Arabs of the Ḥawf district, who had caused trouble in Egypt since Umayyad times. Having taken Barqa and defeated the first military expedition sent by al-Ḥākim, Abū Rakwa and his followers, with their families and flocks, set out for Egypt. The arrival of this large force faced al-Ḥākim with a major crisis. He responded by summoning Arab tribes from Syria to his aid, notably the shaykhs of the Ṭayy tribe, the Banu'l-Jarrāh.. These were given money and arms to oppose the rebels. In his anxiety, the caliph also relaxed many of his dietary and anti-Sunnī measures to placate the people. He need not have worried; the people of the towns may have been in terror of al-Ḥākim but they showed no wish to welcome a horde of wild Arab and Berber tribesmen. Abū Rakwa scored one significant victory against 'Alī b. Ja'far b. Fallāḥ, now returned from Damascus, at Giza, and there was panic in Cairo. But he allowed himself to be diverted to the Fayyūm, where he was defeated in Dhū'l-Ḥijja 396/August 1006 by al-Faḍl b. Ṣālih.. The Banū Qurra were persuaded to desert his cause and he fled to Nubia, where he was captured, brought to Cairo and executed. The whole episode had been dangerous for al-Ḥākim, but there was no sign of rebellion against his cruelty or of an alliance between the Sunnī population of Fusṭāt. and the Sunnī invaders. As long as they had no support from the people of Egypt, the nomad invaders were unable to achieve any permanent gains.

The removal of the external threat allowed al-Ḥākim to pursue his policies with greater severity. The next few years were a time of increasing hardship, and a series of bad Niles led to high prices and food shortages. They were also a period of growing terror. Christian churches were destroyed, and the *kuttāb* and *Ṣaqāliba* were killed in mass nighttime executions. In 399/1009, al-Faḍl b. Ṣāliḥ, the man who had saved al-Ḥākim from Abū Rakwa's forces, was summarily executed. The next year, two other leading figures, al-Ḥusayn b. Jawhar and the *qāḍī* 'Abd al-Azīz b. al-Nu'mān, fled for their lives but were persuaded to return by offers of safe conduct. Their trust was entirely misplaced; in 401/1010, they shared the fate of so many of their colleagues among the ruling class.

More wary than either of his colleagues was the *kātib* al-Ḥusayn b. al-Maghribī. Himself a refugee from the Hamdanid court, he may have been more adaptable than his fellows raised in the Fatimid ambience. He, too, fled Cairo but took refuge with Ibn al-Jarrāḥ, the Ṭayy leader of southern Palestine, a man always ready to defy the powers of central government, in 402/1011–1012. Ibn al-Maghribī refused al-Ḥākim's blandishments and persuaded the bedouin chief to break with the Fatimids altogether. Instead, he invited the 'Alid *amīr* of Mecca, al-Ḥasan b. Ja'far, nominally a vassal of the Fatimids, to come to Palestine as the caliph in 403/1012. It was the high point in the fortunes of the Jarrahid leaders. All Palestine from the borders of Egypt to Tiberias was in their hands except for the coastal cities. In an effort to win further support, al-Ḥasan encouraged the restoration of the Church of the Holy Sepulchre in Jerusalem and the appointment of a patriarch. But the nomad domination had a negative aspect as well; it was marked by the destruction and desolation of many of the settled communities and, as elsewhere in the Fertile Crescent at this period, the extension of nomad-controlled areas at the expense of the urban and agricultural areas. The 'Alid was established at the Jarrahid capital at Ramla, but his moment of glory was to be short-lived. Not for the first time, the Jarrahids allowed themselves to be bought by the Fatimid government, and the discomfited 'Alid pretender was soon obliged to return to the Ḥijāz. Ibn al-Maghribī left for Iraq, where he was to enjoy a distinguished career with Qirwāsh, the 'Uqaylid ruler in Mosul, and then with the Marwanids of Mayyāfāriqīn. The bid for independence turned sour for the Jarrahids. Al-Ḥākim sent 'Alī b. Ja'far b. Fallāh. and his Kutāma army against them. They were heavily defeated and the bedouin were forced to abandon their hold on Ramla.

In domestic policy, the reign of terror continued. Al-Ḥākim himself began to assume an ascetic lifestyle, cutting down on the pomp and circumstance of court life and beginning those wanderings which were to lead to his eventual disappearance. At this time, too, Christians were permitted to leave Egypt for Byzantine territory to escape persecution, and many of them, including the chronicler Yaḥyā b. Sa'īd of Antioch, took advantage of this. While he took measures to placate the army and distributed *iqṭā's* generously to them, his own servants and ministers, all by now men whom he himself had raised to favour, were still the victims of his murderous caprice; his only regret when the *kātib* Zur'a b. Nasṭūris died of natural causes was that he had not been able to execute him himself. Among the Muslims, it seems that he increasingly abandoned orthodox Ismā'īlī or Shī'ī practice. While he now forbade the cursing of the first two caliphs and became the first Fatimid to take prayers in the old mosque at Fusṭāṭ, a stronghold of Sunnism, much of his policy was simply antinomian, abandoning all the practices of ordinary Islam. As he renounced the conventional splendours of Fatimid rule, he lost interest in the *Ḥajj* and the celebrations of the Islamic calendar.

This may have been connected with the strangest events of his final years, the beginning of the Druze religion. Ismā'īlī doctrine had always stressed the authority of the divinely appointed *imām*, but since the time of the *qāḍī* al-Nuʿmān, writers and caliphs alike had stressed that the caliph/*imām* was not himself divine. But just as the Rāwandiyya had ascribed divine powers to the ʿAbbasid Caliph al-Manṣūr, some Ismāʿīlīs sought to proclaim the divinity of their own ruler. This was not a break with the Ismāʿīlī tradition so much as a development of one aspect of it. Al-Manṣūr had rejected all attempts to ascribe divine status to himself, but al-Ḥākim was more susceptible to the idea. It seems to have been in 408/1017–1018 that Muḥammad b. Ismāʿīl al-Darazī, probably of Persian origin, began to spread the doctrine that al-Ḥākim was in fact God. Al-Ḥākim does not seem to have dissuaded him, but for others this was simply too much and al-Darazī was set upon by some Turkish soldiers and murdered. This was not, however, the end of the affair, for his work was continued by one Ḥamza b. Aḥmad, who is alleged to have proclaimed not only the divinity of the caliph but the abolition of the *Sharīʿa*. The role of the caliph in this is not clear; his behaviour became more eccentric and he is said to have made a point of eating in the mosque during Ramaḍān. It is also alleged that the burning of Fusṭāt. at the end of his reign was intended to punish the fiercely Sunnī inhabitants for rejecting his divinity. But al-Ḥākim's madness was always guided by a kind of shrewdness, and he was careful not to become too closely involved. It is quite possible that he advised Ḥamza to leave Egypt and preach his message in Syria, where the Druze religion was to take root, and where it exists to this day.

Al-Ḥākim's death in 411/1021 was as mysterious and bizarre as his life. The most prosaic version is that he was murdered during one of his solitary rambles in the Muqaṭṭam hills on the outskirts of Cairo on the orders of his sister, Sitt al-Mulk, who had become alarmed that he was turning against her. But his body was never found and, in the opinion of the Druzes, he simply disappeared and will come again at the end of the world.

The reign of al-Ḥākim is dominated by his bizarre personality. Few Muslim rulers can have exercised so absolute an authority over their subjects, both great and small. There are features which remain a puzzle: why was there no organized attempt to remove this dangerous lunatic from power? Furthermore, the period showed no real diminution of Fatimid authority in the international sphere. It is true that Ifrīqiya became increasingly independent, but this was simply a culmination of earlier developments and does not seem to have caused any real concern in Cairo. In Palestine, the power of the Jarrahids was kept at bay, while Damascus was always under Fatimid authority. The temporary allegiance of Mosul to the caliphate in 401/1010 had more to do with the politics of Qirwāsh b. al-Muqallad al-ʿUqaylī than al-Ḥākim, but the fact remains that the Fatimid caliphate was a credible alternative to the ʿAbbasids. Much of the secret of al-Ḥākim's success must have lain in his personality. He picked off his enemies one by one, including virtually all the old guard of the Fatimid state, and there seems to have been no shortage of men willing to serve him, although increasingly they were slaves or ex-slaves. He also inspired great awe and fear among his entourage.

He was careful to placate the army, not just slave soldiers but the Kutāma Berbers who followed his most trusted military commander, ʻAlī b. Jaʻfar b. Fallāḥ, and the power of the Berbers within the Fatimid state was probably greater under al-Ḥakim than it had been under his father. The paradox remains that after a quarter of a century of al-Ḥākim's mad rule, the Fatimid state seems to have been as powerful as ever.

The disappearance of al-Ḥākim left power firmly in the hands of his sister, Sitt al-Mulk, known as al-Sayyida, the Lady. She was determined to control the succession to her own advantage. Her instrument in this was a Kutāmī Berber leader, al-Ḥusayn b. ʻAlī b. Dawwās, and together they were responsible for the elevation to the throne of al-Ḥākim's sixteen-year-old son ʻAlī, who took the title of al-ẓāhir li-I'zāz Dīn Allāh. There was little opposition, only one Turkish *ghulām* protesting that he would not swear allegiance until he knew his old master was dead, a protest which rapidly led to his own death. The beginning of the new reign was almost as bloodthirsty as the end of the old. Sitt al-Mulk, according to the chronicler al-Maqrīzī, was determined to hide her participation in her brother's death, and soon all who had been involved in the conspiracy, if such there was, were killed, including her right-hand man, Ibn Dawwās. His two successors as *wazīr* enjoyed very short tenures of office, but thereafter the administration became more stable. For the first five years of the reign, until her death in 415/1024, Sitt al-Mulk had effectively ruled the country, appointing the ministers and keeping the treasury full. Three years after her death, effective power was taken by the man who was to be *wazīr* for the next eighteen years: Aḥmad b. ʻAlī al-Jarjarā'ī. He came from a bureaucratic dynasty of Iraqi origin and had rashly taken service with al-Ḥākim, during which time he had had his hands cut off. Despite this handicap, he was able to assume the wazirate and became the most successful incumbent of the office since Ibn Killis. Much of the comparative peace of al-ẓāhir's reign must be ascribed to his talents.

For the rest of al-Ẓāhir's reign, the Egyptian annals are very scanty. It would seem that the caliph devoted most of his time to pleasure. The only major disturbance was an outbreak of trouble between the Berbers and the Turks in Cairo in 420/1029. Significantly, the Berbers seem to have enjoyed popular support, and a large number of Turks were killed in the fighting. In the end, peace was restored, but most of the Turks left Egypt, and this may have been a contributory factor in the subsequent weakness of the state. The balance between Berber and Turk which al-ʻAzīz had created and al-Ḥākim had been careful to maintain was now upset.

Against the comparatively peaceful state of Egypt in these years, the very disturbed state of Syria must be set. The last years of al-Ḥākim's reign had seen the extension of Fatimid power farther than ever before, especially to Aleppo which, more by diplomacy than military conquest, came under Fatimid rule from 404/1015 to 414/1023. This picture was, however, threatened by the growing power of the bedouin tribes. The Banū'l-Jarrāh. of Palestine had threatened Ramla and Fatimid control in that area for many years but had usually been kept in check. More ominous was the growing power of the Banū Kalb in the Damascus area and the Banū Kilāb around Aleppo. In 415/1024–1025, the main bedouin leaders, Ṣālih. b. Mirdās of the Kilāb, Sinān b. 'Ulyān of the Kalb and Ḥassān b. al-Jarrāh. of the Ṭayy, met and agreed to work together against the Fatimid and to effect a complete takeover of Syria. The reign of al-ẓāhir saw the crisis of nomad expansion in the area of Syria and Palestine, its check and the beginning of decline.

The man responsible for stemming the nomad advance was the Fatimid commander in Syria and Palestine, Anūshtakīn al-Dizbarī, one of the most successful soldiers and administrators of his day. He was a Turk born in the little mountain principality of Khuttal in Transoxania whence he was captured and taken to Kashgār. He escaped from there to Bukhārā, from where he was brought, as a slave, to Baghdad and then to Damascus, which he reached in the middle of al-Ḥākim's reign in 400/1009–1010. Here, he was bought by a Daylamī *condottiere*, Dizbar, who had worked for the Hamdanids and from whom he was to take his name. Three years later, he was sent with a group of *ghilmān* to Cairo for training at the Fatimid court. He proved himself extremely able and when the training finished in 405/1014–1015, he secured himself a position at court. The next year, he was sent back to Damascus, where he took care to look up his old master, Dizbar, and make himself generally appreciated, and soon after he was given his first independent appointment, as the governor of Ba'albak. Here, he acquired a good reputation with the local people and a patron in Fātik, the Armenian *ghulām* who governed Aleppo for the Fatimids. His reputation led to promotion, first to Caesarea as the governor and then in 414/1023 to the whole of Palestine. Here, he began to take severe measures against the depredations of the Arabs and came up against the opposition of the Ṭayy leader, Ḥassān b. al-Jarrāh.. The conflict was fought out in the field in Palestine and at the court in Cairo. In 417/1026, Ḥassān persuaded the *wazīr*, al-Ḥasan b. Ṣālih. al-Rudhbārī, to recall Anūshtakīn to the capital. The bedouin chief's triumph was short-lived. Anūshtakīn continued to keep himself well informed about affairs in the area by special messengers. When the new *wazīr*, al-Jarjarā'ī, was looking for a commander to lead an expedition to take action against the bedouin, he naturally turned to Anūshtakīn. He was duly despatched with 7,000 new troops to Ramla and then to Jerusalem, collecting more reinforcements on the way. Meanwhile, the bedouin confederation gathered their forces, Ṣālih. b. Mirdās coming south from Aleppo. In 420/1029, the two armies met at al-Uqḥuwāna near the Sea of Galilee. The outcome was a decisive victory for the Fatimid forces. Ṣalih. b. Mirdās was killed and the bedouin coalition dispersed.

Anūshtakīn became the governor of Damascus and Syria, a post he held until his death in 432/1041. During the later years of al-Ḥākim's and the early part of al-ẓāhir's reign, Damascus, ruled by Turkish soldiers and members of the Hamdanid family, had suffered greatly from the depredations of the bedouin who invaded the Ghūṭa and destroyed agriculture. The victory at al-Uqḥuwāna seems to have changed the position, and the period of Anūshtakīn's rule was remembered in the city as one of peace and prosperity. His career demonstrates how the *ghulām* system allowed men of humble origins but proved ability to rise to the highest ranks. In other ways, he was exceptional among the *ghilmān* of the age. He was a successful administrator as well as a soldier, and he was a family man, having a son, who died young, and four daughters. He used his marriages, and those of his daughters, to develop contacts with important figures in Syria and the Fatimid court. In Palestine, he broke the power of the Jarrahids; there were still nomads in the area but never again was a nomad chief able to threaten the settled cities of Palestine as Ḥassān b. al-Jarrāh. had done. In a real sense, al-Uqḥuwāna represented the high-water mark of nomad activity.

In 427/1036, the Caliph al-Ẓāhir died. He does not seem to have been a very forceful politician, and authority was exercised by the capable *wazīr* al-Jarjarā'ī in Cairo and the military commander Anūshtakīn al-Dizbarī in Syria. While these two did not always see eye to eye and there were disagreements, especially about policy towards Aleppo, their partnership had assured stability and peace in the later part of the reign. al-Ẓāhir was succeeded by his son Ma'add, who took the title of al-Mustanṣir. The new caliph was only seven years old, but his accession was not contested. In striking contrast to the Umayyad and early 'Abbasid caliphs, succession disputes did not play an important part in the political life of the Fatimid caliphate. Al-Ḥākim, al-Ẓāhir and al-Mustanṣir all succeeded to the throne as boys, but no attempt was made to challenge their right to rule, and not until the death of al-Mustanṣir himself in 487/1094 was the succession disputed. One reason for this was the emphasis that Ismā'īlī thought put on the inherited nature of authority. The Fatimid claim to legitimacy was based on the notion of direct descent from 'Alī. The Fatimids therefore had a theory of hereditary succession which the Umayyads and 'Abbasids never fully developed. To challenge the right of the heir to succeed challenged not just his right but the whole justification for Fatimid sovereignty. There were other reasons, connected with the power structure of the state. The members of the Fatimid family played very little part in politics. The leading men were *wazīrs* and *qāḍīs* from the civilian élite, and Berber and Turkish military men. On the whole, members of the Fatimid family neither governed provinces nor led armies, not even appeared as advisers at court. This meant that none of them built up independent power bases or attracted groups of supporters. Rather than succession disputes of the sort that were common in contemporary Buyid politics, debate and dispute in the Fatimid caliphate were concentrated on controlling the office of *wazīr* and governorates in Syria and, above all, on policy towards Aleppo. This was the main point of difference between al-Jarjarā'ī and Anūshtakīn. Like many of the Turkish troops based in Syria, Anūshtakīn sought the outright conquest and occupation of the city, while al-Jarjarā'ī, following the tradition of Ya'qūb b. Killis, preferred friendly relations with a Mirdasid buffer state.

The early years of al-Mustanṣir's reign were in all respects a continuation of his father's rule. In 429/1038, Anūshtakīn achieved his ambition and captured Aleppo, driving out the Mirdasids and appointing two of his *ghilmān* to govern before returning to Damascus. But inevitably the conquest was threatened by the Byzantines, who wanted the city to remain independent, and by the Mirdasids, who never lost the support of the Kilābī bedouin to the east of the city. In 432/1041, Anūshtakīn was able to defeat a Byzantine counterattack, which was supported by the Mirdasids, but his triumph was short-lived because he died, of natural causes, later in the year (432/1041). The Fatimid Empire was soon to suffer from the loss of his strong authority. The immediate result was the return of the Mirdasids to Aleppo. Thimāl b. Ṣālih. was able to retake the city with little difficulty, and the caliph, presumably guided by al-Jarjarā'ī, acknowledged his authority without hesitation. Anūshtakīn's position in Syria was taken over by al-Ḥasan b. al-Ḥusayn, a member of the Hamdanid family, the son of that al-Ḥusayn b. al-Ḥasan who had made the final attempt to restore Hamdanid authority in Mosul in 379/981 and grandson of the *amīr* Nāṣir al-Dawla. He took the honorific title of Nāṣir al-Dawla, once held by his grandfather.

In 436/1044–1045, al-Mustanṣir seems to have taken the initiative in a renewed propaganda offensive in the Muslim world, sending *dā'īs* (missionaries) to Iran and Transoxania. While some of these were executed, their preaching seems to have had some effect. We have the diary of an Iranian convert, Nāṣir-i Khusrau, who came from his homeland in Khurāsān to visit the Fatimid capital at this time. His book, while it is undoubtedly a propagandist work, makes a clear contrast between the impoverished state of much of Iran and the prosperity of coastal Syria and above all of Egypt. His account of the capital shows the Fatimid caliphate at the height of its power and prosperity; the caliph rich and awesome, surrounded by a ceremonial more elaborate than any other Muslim dynasty had attempted. He also witnessed a display of military power, a review of the vast cosmopolitan Fatimid army, which showed a military strength vastly superior to the puny armies of the Buyids or the bedouin hordes of the 'Uqaylids.

In 436/1045, the *wazīr* 'Alī b. Aḥmad al-Jarjarā'ī died. He had run the Fatimid state for the previous eighteen years, and his passing marked the end of an era of peace and prosperity. No one was able to inherit his authority. The anarchy of the Fatimid state in the next generation lies beyond the scope of this volume, but the outlines of the problem began to emerge as soon as the old *wazīr* was dead: the rivalry between his protégés for control of the administration; the attempts by ambitious *wazīrs* to favour the Berbers in the army at the expense of the Turks and so attract their support; the role of the ambitious Hamdanid Nāṣir al-Dawla in stirring up and leading the Turks; and the growing unrest among the bedouin Banū Qurra. Underlying all these was a fundamental problem which had existed from before the Fatimid conquest of Egypt. At the beginning of this chapter, it was stressed that the Muslim community in early Islamic Egypt was comparatively small, and this meant that there was not a numerous and powerful local ruling and military class. Instead, from the third/ninth century onwards, Egypt became the centre of a struggle between the *Mashāriqa* (easterners), represented by the Turks and the Iraqi immigrants who ran much of the bureaucracy and the commercial life of the country, and the *Maghāriba* (westerners), mostly Berbers but including some Arabs from north Africa and Spain. The Ikhshidid government had been based on the *Mashāriqa*, and at first the Fatimid conquest had represented a victory for the *Maghāriba*, at least in military affairs. Almost the only people of local Egyptian origin who played an important part in the Fatimid caliphate were the Christians who were so often employed in the bureaucracy right up to the highest levels. When Ya'qūb b. Killis, himself an easterner, began introducing Turkish troops into the army, the *Maghāriba* were obliged, often unwillingly, to share power. Under strong rulers, a rough balance could be kept between these two factions, but without that it could develop into civil war. This is what happened in the mid-fifth/eleventh century, and when order was eventually restored, this was only achieved by another outsider from a different background, the Armenian Badr al-Jamālī.

The success of the Fatimid caliphate from the time of al-Mu'izz's arrival in Cairo to the crisis of the reign of al-Mustanṣir, in spite of these divisions, was in great measure a product of the financial health of the state, what it is fair to describe as the Fatimid economic miracle. The evidence is for the prosperity not just of the state but of many of its citizens. Contemporary accounts are full of references to the splendour of court ceremonial, the jewels and the fabrics, and the contrast is made with the poverty of the 'Abbasid caliph during the time of al-Qādir (381–422/991–1031). It was this money which enabled the caliphs to pay their troops and avoid, at least for a time, the military mutinies and disorders which were typical of the Buyid state. The wealth of Egypt also led to a major emigration of talented and skilled men from Iraq to Egypt. Many of the great Fatimid *wazīrs*, Ibn al-Furāt, Ya'qūb b. Killis, Aḥmad b. 'Alī al-Jarjarā'ī and, during the reign of al-Mustanṣir, al-Ḥasan b. 'Alī al-Anbārī and Hārūn b. Sahl al-Tustarī, had Iraqi backgrounds. Nor was this migration confined to the bureaucratic élite. The Geniza documents reveal that many of the merchants whose activities are described had migrated from the east to make their fortunes in Egypt. This migration was both a cause and a sign of the prosperity of the area.

The reasons for this wealth are complex. As always with the economic history of this period, our sources document trade much better than agriculture, but there can be no doubt that agriculture was the main source of wealth. Despite periodic failures of the Nile, and the resultant famines, it would seem that Egyptian agriculture was prosperous at this time. Certainly, the expanding urban community of Cairo must have created a market for surpluses, and the evidence suggests that the Egyptian farmers could, in most years, produce enough to support immigrants from east and west who settled in the city. The role of the state in agriculture was limited. Perhaps the most important contribution was the peace and stability of the early Fatimid years. Apart from the revolt of Abū Rakwa and occasional bedouin incursions, there were no major civil wars to damage the rural economy. Nor were the military given a free hand, as in contemporary Iraq, to exploit the country as they wished. Apart from the bizarre enactments of al-Ḥākim, there is no evidence of government decrees to help farmers, but the fact that the opening of the canals which marked the beginning of the Nile flood was one of the great state occasions of the Fatimid court is an indication of government concern at the highest level. In addition, the Fatimid government patronized the textile industry, which, in turn, boosted demand for flax and other agricultural products necessary for textile manufacture. Finally, and fundamental for the understanding of the wealth of Egypt at this time, was the fact that revenues collected in the country were largely spent there; apart from the endless Syrian wars, and the more productive expenditure on the *Ḥajj*, the taxes raised in Egypt remained there. The Fatimid court and administration were fixed in Cairo, and the wealth they collected, they spent in Egypt.

But it is the commercial prosperity of the state which has left most trace in the records. Fatimid Egypt was a centre of manufacturing and of international trade. One reason for this was the gold trade of the Nile valley from Nubia. Nubia, along with Ghāna,[5] was the main source of gold for the Mediterranean and Islamic worlds, and Egypt benefited greatly from the influx of precious metal. The *dīnārs* of the Fatimid caliphs were of an unrivalled fineness, and sound coinage certainly helped assure the loyalty of soldiers and bureaucrats alike. In Fatimid times, Egypt also became the main transit market between the Indian Ocean and Mediterranean worlds. Essentially, Cairo took over the role of Baṣra, reduced by the instability of Iraq and sacked by the Qarāmiṭa. The evidence suggests that the Red Sea route, via the port of ʿAydhāb and Qūṣ on the middle Nile, came to replace the Gulf/southern Iraq route from the Indian Ocean to the central Islamic lands. Equally significant, however, was the changing nature of trade in the Mediterranean. Much of Egypt's trade in the early Fatimid period was with Muslim north Africa, by sea and by overland caravan, but trade with Christian Europe was also becoming significant. This was essentially a result of the growing prosperity of western Europe. For the first time since antiquity, western Europe became a significant market for the luxury products of the East, the fine textiles and above all the pepper and spices of the Indian Ocean area. From the reign of al-ʿAzīz, shortly after the establishment of the Fatimids in Egypt, there are references to merchants from Amalfi in southern Italy in Cairo and by the mid-eleventh century they had their own hospice and church in Jerusalem. The Geniza documents are full of references to the arrival of the Franks at Alexandria and the effect this had on prices and local prosperity. Nor was this prosperity confined to Egypt – Nāṣir-i Khusrau observed that ships sailed from Tripoli, in Syria, to western Europe. Fatimid policy itself helped to revive the Syrian coastal ports, used to transport men and supplies to Fatimid armies in the area. Government policies towards trade seem to have been very much *laissez-faire*, and apart from the patronage of the Egyptian textile industry to supply the needs of the court, there was little active encouragement. What the Fatimids did was to assure a measure of security and a sound coinage, but much of Fatimid greatness and prosperity was founded on changing economic patterns which they did little to cause. If the 'Abbasid caliphate was destroyed by economic collapse in Iraq, the Fatimid caliphate was in a sense created by economic prosperity in Egypt.

Notes

1 Ja'far b. al-Faḍl b. al-Furāt was a scion of the Banu'l-Furāt (who had played such an important role in 'Abbasid politics during the reign of al-Muqtadir) and, like many leading figures in Egypt, an immigrant from Iraq.
2 P. Vatikiotis, "Al-Hakim bi Amrillah: the god-king idea realised", *Islamic Culture*, xxix, 1955, 1–8.
3 M. A. Shaban, *Islamic history: a new interpretation*, II, Cambridge, 1976, 206–10.
4 J. H. Forsyth, "The Byzantine chronicle of Yahyā b. Sa'īd al-Antakī", unpublished Ph.D thesis, Michigan, 202–96.
5 Medieval Ghāna lay on the southern fringes of the Sahara Desert between the headwaters of the Niger and Senegal rivers.

Postscript

The coming of the Seljuks[1]

"Turks" was the collective name given by Arab authors to the members of the nomad tribes who roamed the great steppes and wastes between the northeastern frontiers of the Muslim world and the borders of China. From these areas, they occasionally expanded and threatened the peace of their neighbours. The Huns, whose attacks did so much to destroy the Western Roman Empire in the fifth century, came from this group, as did the Mongols who were later to cause such havoc in the Near East. The Turks were almost entirely nomad in lifestyle, dependent on their horses, flocks and their hardy Bactrian camels. Only in a few areas along the fringes of the Muslim world, in towns like Jand on the lower reaches of the Syr Darya (Jaxartes) river had any of them settled down; most of them, however, remained as nomads, jealous of their traditional ways and suspicious of the culture of the urban and settled folk they came into contact with. The nomad Turks were essentially pagan, although those who encountered settled peoples tended to convert to Islam. Like all nomad peoples, they had a very decentralized "political" system; prestige and some power lay in the hands of families who established themselves as ruling clans and sometimes took the title of *jabghū* or *khāqān*, but their power remained dependent on their acceptability to their followers; only when Turks came to rule settled communities were the rulers able to acquire any effective authority over their tribesmen, and even then it was often bitterly resented.

The Arabs had come into contact with the Turks from the earliest days of the conquest of Khurāsān, and the Muslims of the area always had to struggle to contain them and defend the settled territories. But, despite setbacks, they had always been successful, until the beginning of the fifth/eleventh century. That is not to say, of course, that there were no Turks within the Muslim world. We have seen how large a part Turks played in the armies of both 'Abbasid caliphs and the *amīrs* of the successor states. These were almost all working as professional soldiers; there do not seem to have been any Turks living as nomads or transhumants in the Near East. Nor were there any Turks living a tribal life; they owed their loyalties and their social organization to the military framework in which they operated and their allegiance to the commander of the group of *ghilmān* in which they served, rather than to a clan or kinship group. The Turks who swept through the eastern Islamic world in the fifth/eleventh century were, by contrast, whole people on the move; they came with their animals and their tents, groups of poor, often desperate pastoralists, seeking booty if they could find it but more important, grazing for the precious beasts on which they depended for their survival. These were the people the Muslim sources came to call Türkmen, to distinguish them from other Turks, already established in the Near East or serving in the retinue of the Seljuk sultans. The Seljuk family did not lead this movement but rather followed in its wake and attempted, with some success, to forge a traditional Muslim state out of this unpromising material.

The Türkmen who flooded into the Near East came from a group known as the Ghuzz or Oghuz. They were supposedly divided into nine tribes, so were known in Turkish as the Dokuz (nine) Oghuz, or, as the Muslim sources chose to write it, Taghuzzghuzz. It seems that they had moved into the area of the lower Syr Darya, to the southeast of the Aral Sea, at the beginning of the fifth/eleventh century when one of their leading families, the Seljuks, became Muslim. In this position, they became involved as allies and mercenaries in the complex struggles for control of Muslim Transoxania between the last representatives of the Iranian Samanid dynasty, the Turkish Karakhanids and the great Maḥmūd of Ghazna, Turkish by origin but thoroughly assimilated into the Muslim world. The eponymous Seljuk seems to have died before his family began their march west. One of his sons Arslan (Lion) Isrā'īl entered Transoxania with his followers, but in about 418/1027, he was arrested by Maḥmūd – and his followers, under the leadership of his son Qutlumush, were driven out of Maḥmūd's domains, not eastwards whence they had come, but towards the west. Destitute and without any territory to call their own, they fled along the southern flanks of the mountains of Ṭabaristān and Daylam, the congenial upland pastures of Āzarbayjān, which thus became the first area of central Islamic lands to suffer their onslaught. Here, they plundered and attempted to establish themselves without great success, since they were consistently opposed by the local Kurdish population. Many of them were forced to flee to the wild mountains of the Hakkāri Kurds to the southeast of Lake Van, while others went to Iraq, where they briefly occupied Mosul before being defeated by Qirwāsh b. al-Muqallad al-'Uqaylī with his Arab and Kurdish army in 475/1044. It was only when more Turks joined them from the east that these Türkmen were able to establish themselves as a dominant population and transform the ethnic map of the Near East.

Arslan Isrā'īl had two nephews, cousins of Qutlumush, called Tughrïl Beg and Chagrï Beg, who remained in the traditional lands of the tribe on the Syr Darya. But during the 420s/1030s, they were driven out by their local rivals and were obliged to attack the Ghaznavid towns in Transoxania. Here, they were received with caution but not complete hostility by the local notables. The rule of the Ghaznavids was oppressive, in that taxes were heavy and, by this time, not very efficient. The Ghaznavid Sultan Mas'ūd naturally marched to defend his lands, but in 431/1040, he met the Seljuk army at Dandānqān near Marv and was decisively and totally defeated. It is interesting to note that the Seljuks are said to have had 16,000 horsemen in this battle, as well as another 2,000 they had left to guard the camp. While this was smaller than the Ghaznavid army, it was probably very much greater than the armies normally employed by the Buyids and their rivals in Iraq and western Iran.

After Dandānqān, the Ghuzz Turks of Tughrïl's army followed in the traces of their predecessors, with whom they soon joined up while Chaghrï remained in Khurāsān. The lead was taken by the Türkmen, under the nominal leadership of Ibrāhīm Ïnal, a member of the Seljuk family; by 433/-1041–1042, he had established himself in Rayy before moving on the next year to Hamadhān. Tughrïl himself followed more slowly, trying to establish a rudimentary administration as he did. By 442/1050–1051, he was in Iṣfahān, where he seems to have paused. He diverted the restless Türkmen, under Ibrāhīm Ïnāl and Qutlumush, towards the eastern territories of the Byzantine Empire, while he himself made a treaty with Abū Kālījār, the Buyid ruler of Fārs, and entered into negotiations with the Caliph al-Qā'im in Baghdad. In Baghdad, all was chaos. The Buyid sovereign al-Malik al-Raḥīm was quite unable to establish any sort of government. An ambitious Turkish *ghulām* commander, al-Basāsīrī, was scheming to bring Iraq over to the Fatimid cause. In these circumstances, it was natural that the caliph's *wazīr*, Ibn al-Muslima, looked for support to the new power in the east, especially as Tughrïl made clear his devotion to the Sunnī cause and his hatred for the "heretic" Buyids. Tughrïl's position grew stronger as each year passed. In 440/1048, Abū Kālījār died and Fārs was open to Türkmen raids; Shīrāz was raided in 444/1052–1053, and even Ahwāz, in torrid Khūzistān, was attacked. In 447/1055, Tughrïl announced his intention of making the *Ḥajj* and of attacking the Fatimids. He assembled his followers in the Zagros Mountains, and in Ramaḍān 447/December 1055, he entered Baghdad. Al-Basāsīrī fled; al-Malik al-Raḥīm was deposed. The era of the Great Seljuks had begun.

Note

1 This is not a book about the Seljuks and I have not provided a detailed bibliography but it is fair to say that our understanding of Seljuk conquest and rule has been transformed in the last ten years by a new wave of scholarship and those who are interested should be aware of this, especially the works of Andrew Peacock and David Durand-Guedy.

Principal sources for the history of the Near East, 600–1050

Our understanding of the history of the Near East between 600 and 1050 is derived essentially from chronicles and other literary works and archaeological and numismatic sources, but with rare exceptions the latter have not been integrated into the treatment of the general history which is still almost exclusively based on narrative sources. Recently, historians have begun to explore the documentary evidence, mostly from Egypt, which is much more prolific than was previously realized but there is still much work to be done in this area. This point is important because the nature of the evidence determines the type of history we can write.

In the last two decades, there has been an increasing interest among scholars in the materiality of the book, that is how books were physically produced, marketed and how they survived the vicissitudes of time. Although there had been research in this area before, the recent discussion was essentially begun by Jonathan Bloom in his *Paper before Print: The History and Impact of Paper in the Islamic World* (New Haven, Yale U.P., 2001) in which he argued that paper, as a cheaper and more efficient writing support than either parchment or papyrus, had a transformative effect on books production. Shawkat Toorawa's, *Ibn Abī Ṭāhir Ṭayfur and Arabic Writerly Culture: And Ninth-Century Book-man in Baghdad* (London, Routledge, 2005) discussed the reality behind the production, copying and selling of books, themes further developed by Beatrice Gruendler in her *The Rise of the Arabic Book* (Harvard, Harvard University Press, 2020) in which she examines the role of stationer and the whole business of creating and publishing books in Abbasid Baghdad. Marina Rustow, meantime, published her *The Lost Archive: Traces of a Caliphate in a Cairo Synagogue* (Princeton, Princeton UP, 2020), a wide-ranging and scholarly survey of documentary and archiving practices in the early Islamic and Fatimid periods. These, and other works, have transformed the way we look at the huge volume and variety of Arabic literary production in the first four centuries of Islam.

We are extremely fortunate in the vast range of literary evidence available, from brief annals which may do little more than contribute a missing name or date to great compilations like al-Ṭabarī's *Ta'rīkh al-rusul wa'l-mulūk* (History of the Prophets and Kings) or al-Balādhurī's *Ansāb al-ashāf*

(Genealogies of the Nobles) which contain a vast amount of anecdotal and circumstantial details to fill in the bare facts and give life and substance to the names. By no means, all the literary sources are chronicles; there are also administrative geographies and travel books, collections of poems (which for the early period are an important if somewhat intractable form of historical evidence), collections of letters and other sorts of *adab* (an Arabic term which means, roughly, essays on literary, social, historical or ethical themes). Most of the chronicles are in Arabic, but there are also Greek writings and a substantial corpus of Syriac literature which sheds light on some obscure aspects of the subject. There is also a body of writing in the New Persian language which appeared from the third/ninth century onwards but which sometimes, as with the translation of al-Ṭabarī by the Persian Bal'amī and the anonymous *Ta'rīkh-i Sīstān* (History of Sīstān), contains much older material not to be found in any of the Arabic sources.

The literary material is so good, lively and interesting, often written by men of great intelligence and discernment that it can blind us to the fact that it tends to limit the sort of historical approaches which can be used, and there are whole areas of Islamic history which will forever remain obscure. Take the issue of landownership, for example. We know from literary sources that many high officials, generals and even successful poets had *ḍiyā'*, that is to say landed estates which they were given or into which they invested the salaries or gifts they had received. In some cases, we are even given overall figures for the revenues they received from these estates, which were considerable. But if we try to go further than that, to ask questions like: How were the estates administered? Who collected the owner's share of the crops? What proportion of the revenues were taken by the owner? Was there a village headman and if so, what was his role? – we are met by an almost impenetrable wall of silence. Even in the case of the *Ṣawāfī*, the estates owned by the Umayyad and 'Abbasid caliphs, we have only the vaguest ideas about their extent or the proportion of government revenue which was raised from them. Only in Egypt, as shown in much recent scholarship, most importantly Petra Sijpesteijn's *Shaping a Muslim State: The World of a Mid-Eighth Century Muslim Official* (Oxford, Oxford UP, 2013), can we see how these issues were worked out at a local level.

The strength of the Arabic material lies in its grasp of narrative and its portrayal of character: individuals loom large in the account. They are also fully in control of their behaviour. Divine intervention works in a more distant fashion than in much Western medieval, or indeed, Syriac and Byzantine literatures. Rarely is the hand of God directly and immediately involved in punishment of sinners; there is rather a strong sense of human responsibility, coupled with the idea that man is ultimately subject to God's will. The crimes which bring men low are foolish incompetence or, above all, arrogance and overconfidence. Fate strikes at those who feel that they have reached a position of eminence and security, but it is rarely a reward for moral failings or wickedness. The judgements of the Muslim historians are based on the premise that man is a free agent who determines his own actions and, despite the deep religious faith of many of the authors, their writing is much more "humanist" than much of the historical tradition of the medieval West.

Sources for the history of the Prophet, the Rāshidūn and the Umayyad caliphs: the classic period of Islamic historiography

The historiography of the early Islamic period is immensely full and rich. In many ways, we have more information about it than any subsequent period before the appearance of documentary sources in late Mamluk Egypt and the Ottoman Empire. But this historiography also presents a unique and baffling problem, or series of problems which have been the subject of a wide-ranging scholarly debate. The substance of the debate is that while the accounts we have are very full and detailed, frequently including verbatim eyewitness reports, there is a significant time lag between the events they describe and the dates by which we know that they were written down, that is, in the decades after the ʿAbbasid revolution of 132/750. Thus in the case of events surrounding the life of the Prophet and his immediate successors, over a century had elapsed between the events and the first written record we have. Questions naturally arise as to the means by which these accounts were passed down in the interval and thence to the question of whether they are in fact genuine at all or invented later to justify a position or establish a usage. Were those who purported to record them simply those who made them up?

The problem would exist even if the events concerned were of no more than antiquarian interest, but there is an additional complicating factor. The events of the Prophet's life and, to a lesser but still important extent, those of his immediate successors were, and still are, normative for the behaviour of the Muslim community. Thus what Muḥammad did on a certain occasion, his last "farewell" pilgrimage to Mecca, for example, has determined the correct way of performing the pilgrimage ever since and hence it is of vital importance for the Muslims that the accounts of the farewell pilgrimage be accurate. The historicity of some incidents is extremely controversial. The question as to whether Muḥammad designated ʿAlī b. Abī Ṭālib as his successor, for example, is one such issue; Shīʿīs argue strongly that he did so, and that the accounts were deliberately suppressed by supporters of Abū Bakr, ʿUmar and the Sunnīs. Sunnī tradition, by contrast, insists that no such designation was ever made.

Early Muslim authors were themselves very conscious of the problem of authenticity and aware that false traditions, especially about the life of the Prophet, were liable to creep into, or be inserted in, the corpus. In an effort to solve this problem, they took to citing their sources in the form of *isnāds*. The *isnād*, which introduced each section of the narrative, consisted of the name of the narrator from whom the author had taken it followed by those from whom he had taken it and so back to the original eye- or ear-witness in the form "I was told by *x* who was told by *y* who was told by *z* that he heard the Prophet saying…". In this way, the authors attempted to establish the reliability of their information. To do this, they worked to establish the dates and general character of the narrators. If the narrators in each stage of the *isnād* overlapped chronologically and if they were known to be of good character and not given to lying, then the account could be considered trustworthy. It is not hard to see the limitations of this approach as a method of historical criticism, but it did mean that Muslim authors, even after the formal *isnād* system had been largely abandoned in later centuries, tended to be much more careful to acknowledge their sources than were their contemporaries in the medieval West.

In the last three decades of the twentieth century, the reliability and historicity of the Arabic sources for the first century of Islam were the subject of a lively and sustained polemic. The debate was effectively opened with the publication of Albrecht Noth's *Quellenkritische Studien zu Themen, Formen und Tendenzen frühislamicher geschichtsüberlieferung* (Bonn; this should now be used in the revised English edition by Lawrence Conrad, *The Early Arabic Historical Tradition* [Princeton, 1994]) in 1973. Noth argued that many of the apparently detailed accounts of the events of the early Islamic period were essentially topoi, anecdotes and themes which appeared in different contexts as the author saw fit, and his conclusions call into question many of the apparently realistic details of the history of the early Muslim conquests.

A much more radical critique of the early Muslim sources was advanced by J. Wansbrough with the publication of *Qur'ānic Studies*, Oxford, 1977 and *The Sectarian Milieu*, Oxford, 1978. His ideas were developed and popularized by P. Crone and M. Cook in their *Hagarism: The Making of the Islamic World*, Cambridge, 1977. The argument advanced by Cook and Crone rests on the fact that the sources on which we rely for our knowledge of early Islam are in their present form all much later than the events they purport to describe. Instead of being historical narratives, they are accounts generated in the 'Abbasid period to give validity and identity to the emerging religion of Islam and, especially, to differentiate it from Judaism and Christianity. From this premise, it is possible to argue that the whole story of Muḥammad's life is a fiction, elaborated to provide the religion with a convincing historical origin. The authors argued that we should disregard the Muslim testimony concerning the life of Muḥammad, since this could be fabricated and is in any case full of internal contradictions, and look at non-Muslim accounts of the origins of Islam, particularly those given by contemporary Christian authors. Here, we find no mention of a new religion or to events referred to in the *sīra* but rather a collection of accounts, usually very short, often confused, which clearly give no impression that Islam was, at that stage, a separate entity. There may be genuine historical information in the early Muslim accounts but it is impossible to separate from later polemic accretions.

The publication of Cook and Crone's work gave rise to a storm of controversy. Both Muslim scholars and some non-Muslims were affronted that the whole basis of our understanding of early Islam could be challenged in this way, and for a time the academic community was polarized into two opposing camps. Gradually, however, scholars have attempted to move forward and to reach a new synthesis, or at least to develop new approaches. F. M. Donner's *Narratives of Islamic Origins* (1998) opens with a useful account of the whole debate and goes on to argue that the Muslim tradition should be used bearing in mind the purposes for which it was compiled: "the underlying purpose of the narratives of Islamic origins was to articulate the validity of the Muslims' communal identity" and that "[n]ot by rejecting the whole Islamic tradition as 'opaque', but rather by patiently unravelling the strands and layers of the complex traditional material, will the Islamic origins story finally come, at least partially to light".

A different perspective is offered in Robert Hoyland's *Seeing Islam as Others Saw It* (1997). As the title suggests, this is an examination of the non-Muslim sources for the earliest Islamic period. He argues that non-Muslim sources are more supportive of the Islamic narratives than the sceptics have suggested and that

> the testimony of Christian, Jewish and Zoroastrian writers can be used alongside that of Muslim authors to furnish us with an enriched and expanded vision of the history of the Middle East in early Islamic times, to offer us new perspectives on its character and to suggest to us new directions for study.

Chase Robinson's survey *Islamic Historiography* (Cambridge, Cambridge UP, 2003) argues that a work like Ibn Hishām's *Sira* may tell us more about the attitudes and concerns of the early 'Abbasid period than about the facts of the Prophet's life, but he does not reject the historicity of the entire corpus.

The debate is certainly not over, but certain issues seem to have been clarified. Few would now support the extreme sceptic position which says that we do not and cannot know anything about the early history of Islam. However, the old certainties have disappeared, and it is clear that early Islamic sources have to be read with a much keener awareness of when, why and for whom they were composed.

The formation of the Muslim accounts of the life of the Prophet (the *Sīrat al-Nabī*, hereafter referred to simply as the *sīra*) and the account of the conquests and the early caliphate was essentially a two-stage process. The first stage was represented by the development of short narratives, either oral or written, of incidents each with its own *isnād*. These were referred to as *khabar* (pl. *akhbār*) or, especially, if they referred to words or deeds of the Prophet as *Ḥadīth* (tradition). These soon began to be collected, sometimes by the emerging class of religious scholars in Medina or Iraq, sometimes among tribes or families wishing to preserve the memory of the great deeds of their ancestors, or at the Umayyad court where caliphs from Muʿāwiya onwards encouraged the retelling and collection of *akhbār* both about the Prophet and about secular subjects and poetry. The second stage was the attempt to fit such *akhbār* into an orderly chronological framework. This seems to have been begun in the Umayyad period; the form of the *sīra* may have been fixed as early as the time of ʿUrwa b. al-Zubayr (d. 94/712) and his pupil Muḥammad b. Muslim al-Zuhrī (d. 124/741). The earliest account of the *sīra* to have survived in its original form, however, is that of Muḥammad b. Isḥāq (d. 151/761), by which time we can be sure that the main outlines of the Prophet's life were established. The basic chronology of the Islamic conquests was established a generation or two later, possibly at the time of Muḥammad b. ʿUmar al-Wāqidī (d. 207/823), although we know that there were earlier accounts, like those of Ibn Isḥāq and Abū Mikhnaf (d. 157/774), which may have attempted to determine the sequence of events. These second/eighth-century compilers were faced with the formidable task of attempting to put the numerous, often very detailed *akhbār* at their disposal into a chronological framework. It is hardly surprising if different compilers sometimes came to different conclusions about the ordering of events which had happened a full century before their time.

The question as to how far the early *akhbār* were written down and how much they were simply passed on by oral tradition is a complex one, still unresolved. The Muslim sources often use verbs of speech like *dhakara* (he mentioned) or *qāla* (he said) to describe the early accounts, but this does not necessarily mean that they were not written down; Arabic, like English, uses the metaphor "he says in his book…" when no suggestion of speech is intended. In addition, there was a halfway stage between oral and written transmissions which was common in Islamic intellectual life whereby a scholar would expound or dictate his work to his pupils, who would copy it down from his spoken words. The work of Gregor Schoeler in *The Oral and the Written in Early Islam* (London, Routledge, 2006) has shown how the process is not a simple story of oral narratives being recorded in writing but a more complex one in which written texts are expounded orally and then rewritten in a slightly different form and context. The complex nature of this reiterative process probably accounts for much of the apparent confusion to be found in these narratives. The evidence of surviving Arabic papyri shows that the keeping of Arabic written records was commonplace in the first century of Islam, and we should probably be right to think that many *akhbār* were written down at this time in collections which were then used by the collators of the second century to produce their chronological narratives. The loss of this first generation of Muslim historical literature need not surprise us, since when it had been incorporated in later compilations, the original was essentially redundant, just as the compilation of a cartulary meant that the monks of a medieval Western religious house could dispense with the bulky and inconvenient original charters. It should be remembered that the rate of loss among later Islamic historical writing has been depressingly high, and many of the surviving classics, the *Ta'rīkh* (History) of Khalīfa b. Khayyāṭ for example, are only represented by a single manuscript, so the disappearance of the original texts is no indication that they did not exist.

The Life of the Prophet Muḥammad poses further and unique historical problems. Our understanding of the Life is essentially based on the written work of four compilers:

1. The *Sīrat al-Nabī* of Ibn Isḥāq (d. 151/761) in the later recension of Ibn Hishām (d. 218/813), ed. F. Wüstenfeld, 2 vols, Göttingen 1858–60; also ed. M. al-Saqqa et al., Cairo, 1955 (English translation by A. Guillaume, Karachi, 1955).
2. The *Kitāb al-maghāzī* of al-Wāqidī (d. 207/823), ed. J.B.M. Jones, 3 vols, Oxford, 1966 (English translation by R. Faizar, London, 2011).
3. Muḥammad b. Sa'd (d. 230/844), *Kitāb al-ṭabaqāt al-kabīr*, 9 vols, ed. E. Sachau, Leiden, 1904–40.
4. Muḥammad b. Jarīr al-Ṭabarī (d. 310/923), *Ta'rīkh al-rusul wa'l-mulūk*, ed. M. J. de Goeje, Leiden, 1879–1901; the biography of Muḥammad is treated in Section 1, 1073–1816.

The material of the *sīra* is extremely impressive, as regards both its bulk and the detailed information it provides. The account of Ibn Isḥāq runs to something over 300,000 words in the English translation (compared, for example, with the Gospel according to St Matthew, which recounts the life of Jesus in less than 30,000). We are given a vast amount of information, especially about the last part of Muḥammad's life from the *Hijra* (AD 622) onwards when he was leading the Muslim community in Medina and the names of numerous people who met him. We are also given a great deal of circumstantial anecdote to enliven the story and give context to events; for all its great length, the *sīra* makes very interesting reading.

As already noted, the reliability of the *sīra* as a historical source has been challenged by some modern scholarship. A particular problem stems from the complex relationship between the *sīra* and the Qur'ān. From the earliest time, there has been a debate as to the interpretation of some passages in the Qur'ān and the historical events to which they refer. At least some of the *sīra* material seems to be exegetical, that is to say that the narrative was developed to explain the context of a part of the Revelation rather than as a straightforward historical account, and it should not be treated as such. In some cases, this may be true, although it is impossible to say which passages are historical, and simply because a passage explains the context of part of the Qur'ān, this does not mean that it is not at the same time a record of a historical event.

As with the life of Muḥammad, so the story of the first four caliphs of Islam is largely derived from a limited number of chronicles, although the problems concerned with using them change somewhat. Of the four major sources for the *sīra* discussed above, two are no longer of any use: the works of Ibn Isḥāq and al-Wāqidī effectively come to an end with the Prophet's death. Ibn Sa'd gives biographies of numerous early Muslims, but of the four, only al-Ṭabarī systematically continues his work beyond this period. This does not mean, however, that there is any dearth of records, for other writers appear who had either not treated the *sīra* at all, or who had given an abbreviated account which added little new material. In the main, these writers lived in the third/ninth century and continued their narratives up to their own times, so it is perhaps acceptable to discuss their entire works at this point.

For the period of the Rāshidūn, the Umayyads and the coming of the 'Abbasids, all these authors seem to have drawn, directly or indirectly, on a generation of historians whose original works are lost but whose writings survive in the books of later scholars. Among the most important of these were Abū Mikhnaf (d. 157/774), 'Awāna b. al-Ḥakam (d. 147/764), Sayf b. 'Umar (d. 180/796), al-Haytham b. 'Adī (d. 206/821) and al-Madā'inī (d. 225/839). Of these works, only fragments of Sayf b. 'Umar's *Kitāb al-Ridda wa'l-Futūḥ* (ed. Qasim al-Samarrai, 2 vols, Leiden, 1995) survive in their original form. All these sources essentially use the *isnād* technique for establishing the genuineness of the material and their work takes the form of vivid but disjointed narrative accounts of incidents. Their works were composed in a number of different forms: collections of stories (*akhbār*) about individual incidents, studies of broader themes like the conquests or the *Ridda* wars, studies of the history of one area or city and even books about a whole era, like the Umayyad period. In later years, annalistic historiography (that is to say the arrangement of events under the years in which they took place) was to be the most important single form in Arabic historical narrative. How far that was the case among these earlier historians is not entirely clear; it has been suggested that the annalistic frame was developed by the end of the second/eighth century. It is possible, too, that this was a legacy of the Greek and Syrian historical tradition, where, as in medieval Western historiography, the annalistic form had been developed in late antiquity.

Apart from the problems of transmission and apparent contradiction in the sources, a further problem is raised by the issue of deliberate bias and distortion. Factions and political groups soon emerged in early Islam and later authors certainly looked back to the formative years of the Islamic world for justification of their attitudes. In the first/seventh century, there are perhaps two major issues on which Muslim opinion was divided: the battle of Ṣiffīn and the subsequent arbitration agreement, and the death of al-Ḥusayn b. 'Alī. The historiography of Ṣiffīn has been discussed by E. L. Petersen (*'Alī and Mu'āwiya in Early Arabic Tradition*, Copenhagen, 1964), who disentangled the various versions and layers of narrative. The main points of difference concern basic and clearly stated moral issues such as whether 'Alī was betrayed at the arbitration which followed Ṣiffīn, or indeed whether the arbitration was held at all, and the historiography has certainly been deeply influenced by later debates about the claims of the Umayyads, 'Alids and 'Abbasids to be considered as rightful caliphs. In the case of the death of al-Ḥusayn b. 'Alī, there is little dispute about the main facts. No one denied that al-Ḥusayn had been killed on the orders of the Umayyad governor of Iraq, that the Umayyad forces were vastly superior to his and that the people of Kūfa, on whom he had relied for help, took no action to save him. Authors allow their opinions to show in the way in which they embellish the story: pro-'Alid or Shī'ī authors will recount anecdotes to show the blameless nature of al-Ḥusayn's death, the sufferings he and his family underwent and the cruelty of the Umayyad soldiers. For the searcher after religious inspiration and moral example, these passages are of great importance; for the historian, they are marginal except insofar as they illustrate the thinking of later commentators. In both these key incidents of early Islamic history, the main outlines of the events are not really in dispute. When it comes to circumstantial details and opinions, the author's feelings are usually apparent. If we understand the sources, how and why they were compiled, the question of deliberate bias becomes much less of a problem: of course, the authors have opinions about the past – that is what makes them so interesting.

The issue of reliability has another dimension. It is easy to assume that eyewitnesses or participants in events must necessarily be accurate guides to what took place, but a moment's reflection will show clearly that that is not so. Many of the reports we have of the incidents at Ṣiffīn must have been based on rumour, second-hand information and partly understood manoeuvres. The importance of this to the historians is that, obviously, we should not place uncritical trust in the narratives, however good the *isnād* may be, but it also points to another moral: we should not imagine that contradictions and confusions are the results of deliberate bias or of a conscious scheme to distort the truth. They are rather part of the very nature of oral testimony. They require a very different approach therefore from the careful sifting of deliberate chronicle evidence, an approach more similar to that of the police officer trying to reconstruct the exact details of a fast-moving crime from those who only witnessed a portion of the action.

Of course, the editors of these accounts, from Abū Mikhnaf onwards, exercised their judgement in deciding which accounts they would include and which they would omit and this sort of censorship allowed them to attach weight to traditions which reflected well on 'Alī or vice versa if they so wished, but it would seem that they did so within the limits of the material available, rather than simply inventing a more favourable version of events. In early 'Abbasid Iraq, it would have been effectively impossible for any one man to produce a "cover-up"; there were clearly too many others who would be aware that traditions had been falsified or important arguments omitted. Propaganda, if there is such, is developed by a selective choice of traditions, allowing them to speak for themselves; there are few, if any, of the passionate denunciations and attacks which are met with so frequently in Christian historiography, both Eastern and Western. The question of reliability in the Arabic sources is then very complex and this rich and tightly interwoven texture of narrative rarely allows one to say "Fulān's chronicle is pro-'Alī or pro-Mu'āwiya". Similarly, attempts to differentiate different "schools" of historical writing, notably a Medina school and an Iraqi school, have not been entirely convincing. We must conclude that most of the early Islamic historiographical material is not tendentious propaganda, aimed to push a particular point of view, but is rather the work of serious historians attempting to recover the truth, as they saw it, from a mass of different traditions, some written, some still in oral form, and to arrange them into a convincing narrative and chronological structure.

Not all early Islamic historiography is made up of *akhbār* introduced by *isnāds* – indeed, the first work on Islamic history to survive in its entirety, the *Ta'rīkh* (History) of Khalīfa b. Khayyāṭ (d. 240/854–855), ed. Akram Ḍiyā' al-'Umarī, Najaf 1967, is brief and selective, often using abbreviated *isnāds*. His work is entirely annalistic, events being recorded under the year in which they took place, marking the coming of age of this genre of historical literature in Arabic. Slightly more discursive is the *Ta'rīkh* of Aḥmad b. Wāḍih. al-Ya'qūbī (d. 284/895), ed. M. Houtsma, 2 vols, Leiden, 1883 and 2 vols, Beirut, 1960, which is arranged not annalistically but according to reigns of caliphs, and is almost entirely without *isnāds*. He is often described as pro-Shī'ī, but what this really amounts to is that he gives considerable space to the sayings and deeds of some of the descendants of 'Alī. Al-Ya'qūbī's work is useful in that it provides a check on the fuller chronicle of al-Ṭabarī, and sometimes, when establishing the names of governors of distant provinces like Armenia or Sind, for example, he supplies information unobtainable from al-Ṭabarī's much longer work. Contemporary with al-Ya'qūbī was the Iranian author Aḥmad b. Dāwūd al-Dīnawarī (d. 282/895). His *Akhbār al-ṭiwāl*, ed. V. Guirgass and I. I. Krachkovskii, Leiden, 1912; ed. 'Abd al-Mun'im 'āmir and Jamāl al-Dīn al-Shayyāl, Cairo, 1960, is a general history to the early 'Abbasid period in which the early Islamic sections are dealt with under the reigns of the caliphs and which has a pronounced interest in Iranian affairs. The text is confused and full of strange omissions, which suggest that what has come down to us is a *mukhtaṣar* (abridgement) of the original.

Apart from al-Ṭabarī himself, the greatest figure in early Islamic historiography was Aḥmad b. Yaḥyā al-Balādhurī (d. 279/892). He wrote two major works, both of which appear to have survived in their entirety. The *Futūh. al-buldān*, ed. M. J. de Goeje, Leiden, 1866; ed. Ṣalāh al-Dīn Munajjid, Cairo, 1957; English trans. Hugh Kennedy, A History of the Arab Invasions London, 2022 is the shorter and more accessible work, having been edited in its entirety. It is an account of the Islamic conquest of the different areas of the Muslim world, paying special attention to whether they were taken by force or by treaty, since this affected their fiscal status. Most of the material relates to the period of the Rāshidūn caliphs, but he also includes events in the later Umayyad and early 'Abbasid periods which concern areas like the Byzantine frontier, where there were still conquests to be made. He is also important in that he was one of the few authors to discuss the possession and history of landed estates, and much that we know of the estates of the Umayyad family, for example, comes from his work. A full and complete edition of his other work, the vast *Ansāb al-ashrāf*, has been published in ten volumes under the auspices of the Deutsche Morgenlandische Gesellschaft in the series Bibliotheca Islamica in Beirut from 1979 to 2008. None of it is available in English translation. The *Ansāb* is arranged according to genealogies, but the biographies of the caliphs are expanded to include lengthy discussions of events in their reigns. The wealth and importance of this vast work can hardly be exaggerated, and it is a major source for early history of the Islamic community.

The history of the Rāshidūn and the Umayyad caliphs is dominated by the *Ta'rīkh al-rusul wa'l-mulūk* (History of the Prophets and Kings) by al-Ṭabarī. His account is based on the work of earlier traditionists and compilers like Abū Mikhnaf and Sayf b. 'Umar already mentioned. The presentation is that of a vast collection of *akhbār*, each introduced by its appropriate *isnād*. Al-Ṭabarī often gives different, sometimes conflicting, accounts of the same incidents; only rarely does he make a judgement between them. In some ways, his history of the Umayyad period is simply a compendium of sources, a sort of *Rolls Series* or *Monumenta Germanicae Historica* of the Islamic world, only compiled by a tenth-century Muslim rather than a team of nineteenth-century scholars. The question of how far al-Ṭabarī edited his material remains an open one; the issue is whether he selected the *akhbār* he used in order to develop and illustrate major themes about the history of the Islamic state or incorporated into his text the available material, and his presentation simply reflects the weight of the sources at his disposal. The picture is further complicated because there is no ancient copy of the whole of the *Ta'rikh*. Sometime after the thirteenth century, the complete text was lost and only some sections survived and the text was reconstructed from a number of partial manuscripts by the team of editors led by M. J. de Goeje in Leiden in the late nineteenth century, in itself one of the great achievements of orientalist scholarship. However, we do have some early witnesses of the text, notably the sections edited into his *Tajārib al-umam* by Abū 'Alī Miskawayh around the year 1000 (ed. Sayyid Kisrwai Hasan, Beirut, Dar Kutub al-Ilmiya, 2002) and the edition incorporated in his *Kāmil fi'l-ta'rīkh* by the great Mosuli historian Ibn al-Athīr (ed. C. J. Tornberg, Leiden, Brill, 1867) in the early thirteenth century. These texts suggest that the version we use today is very close to al-Ṭabarī's original. His work remains absolutely central to any discussion of early Islamic history, and its full potential has hardly yet been investigated.

The Rāshidūn and Umayyad caliphs also receive extensive coverage in the *Kitāb al-futūḥ* (Book of Conquests) of Aḥmad b. A'tham al-Kūfī (d. 314/926), ed. Muḥammad 'Abd al-Mu'īd Khan et al. (8 vols, Hyderabad, Osmania Oriental Publications Bureau, 1968–75). Despite the similarity of title between Ibn A'tham's work and the *Futūh. al-buldān* of al-Balādhurī, the form of the work is different. While al-Balādhurī arranges his material by regions, Ibn A'tham's approach is broadly chronological. He also devotes very considerable attention to internal military affairs, like the revolt of al-Mukhtār against the Umayyads, as well as external conquests. He belongs to the classical school of Islamic history writing, basing himself firmly on *akhbār* introduced by their *isnāds*. He uses many of the same sources as al-Ṭabarī but seems to edit and abridge them with more freedom to emphasize religious and pietistic themes and motivations.

While these are the principal historical sources for the period of the Rāshidūn and the Umayyads, there are other works of a more literary kind which are nonetheless important for the general history. Perhaps the most important of these is the *Murūj al-dhahab* (Meadows of Gold) of the polymath 'Alī b. al- Ḥusayn al-Mas'ūdī (d. 345/956), ed. with French trans. C. Barbier de Meynard and A. Pavet de Courteille, 9 vols, Paris, 1861–77, ed. C. Pellat, 4 vols, Beirut, 1973, which is an anecdotal history of the early caliphate. Al-Mas'ūdī was one of the most wide-ranging of the intellectuals of the fourth/tenth century, and his work reflects a cultured mind and a broad range of interests.

Of great value is the magnificent *Kitāb al-aghānī* of Abū'l-Faraj 'Alī b. al- Ḥusayn al-Iṣfahānī (d. 365/975), ed. I–XX, Būlāq, 1867, XXI, ed. Brünnow, Leiden, 1888 with index tables by I. Guidi, Leiden, 1895–1900; ed. in 24 vols, Beirut, 1955. The *Kitāb al-aghānī* (Book of Songs) is essentially a book about poets and singers of the pre-Islamic, Umayyad and 'Abbasid periods. For the historian, however, its value is much greater than the title would suggest, since the biographies are full of interesting and lively details and allow us a rare glimpse into the underworld of early Islamic society. Many of the poets were men of obscure origin and disreputable behaviour, the sort of people who make little impression on the general narrative of political events, and the *Aghānī* provides a useful corrective to the general histories. By the same author is another important work, also very much *sui generis*, the *Maqātil al-ṭālibiyīn*, ed. Aḥmad Ṣaqr, Cairo, 1949. This is a more sombre work, giving an account of the circumstances of the killing of members of the 'Alid family who met violent deaths in Umayyad and early 'Abbasid times. It is full of direct and vivid narrative and a source of major importance for the history of the pro-'Alid movements of the time.

Another work which reflects a pro-'Alī viewpoint is the *Waq'at ṣiffīn* of Naṣr b. Muzāḥim al-Minqarī (d. 212/827), ed. 'Abd al-Salām Hārūn, Cairo, 1962. Naṣr was himself active in the 'Alid cause and he selected traditions concerning the conflict between 'Alī and Mu'āwiya which reflected that point of view. He is also a traditional historian who was careful to quote traditions in full with their appropriate *isnāds*, and his work is an important source for the limited period it covers.

Sources for the 'Abbasid period: 132–329/750–940

In many ways, the coming of the 'Abbasids marks the end of what might be called the classic phase of Arab historiography, the period when historical writing is dominated by compilation of ancient *akhbār*, introduced by their own *isnāds*. Some authors who had been extremely important sources for Umayyad and earlier history now ceased to be important if only because, like Abū Mikhnaf, for example, they do not seem to have concerned themselves with the events of their own lifetime. Of the compilers, some of whose records were very important up to this point fade out. Most importantly, al-Balādhurī soon ceases to be a major source, although his *Ansāb* has a good deal to say about al-Saffāh. and al-Manṣūr, and the *Futūḥ* is important for the history of frontier regions. Likewise, Ibn A'tham's account of the 'Abbasids, although it includes events as late as Bābak's rebellion in the early third/ninth century, is much thinner than the comparable section on the Umayyads. Neither al-Dīnawarī nor Khalīfa b. Khayyāt. devoted as much time to the 'Abbasids as they did to the Umayyads and their works become increasingly brief and factual. The two works of al-Iṣfahānī, the *Aghānī* and the *Maqāātil al-ṭālibiyīn*, continue to be of great importance in the early 'Abbasid period.

The change in the nature of historiography is most clearly apparent in the case of al-Ṭabarī. Unlike the other authorities on early Islamic history, al-Ṭabarī did not abandon interest when he came to the affairs of the 'Abbasid caliphs, but his methods and approach are significantly different, the change becoming apparent not at the moment of the 'Abbasid revolution in 132/750, but rather at the death of the Caliph al-Saffāh. in 136/754. From this point, al-Ṭabarī begins to abandon the classic technique of giving different *akhbār* about each event, but concentrates on giving a single narrative, sometimes from a named source, sometimes simply introduced by the phrase "Abū Ja'far (al-Ṭabarī) said", or no introduction at all. This does not mean that there was a total change; as before, he sometimes includes the works of earlier historians verbatim; the use of 'Umar b. Shabba's account of the rebellion of the 'Alid Muḥammad the Pure Soul in 145/762 is a case in point. On controversial issues like the events which surrounded the death of the Caliph al-Hādī in 170/786, he continues to give different versions. But the practice is no longer general and a linear narrative comes to replace the mosaic of individual *akhbār*.

There is also something of a change in the background of al-Ṭabarī's informants. The early collectors of *akhbār*, Ibn Isḥāq and Abū Mikhnaf, for example, seem to have been men with a background in religious scholarship and essentially of independent means, not directly connected with the caliphal court or dependent on official patronage. Such men continued to exist; al-Ṭabarī himself seems to have been one such independent author. Increasingly, however, his sources were men connected with government and with the bureaucracy, the *kuttāb* class. While the heroes of early Islamic history are warriors and men of action, the heroes of ʿAbbasid history tend to be the great administrators, the most famous of them being the Barmakids. And just as the memory of the great tribal warriors of early Arabia and the Islamic conquests was kept alive by their tribesmen, anxious to bask in their reflected glory, so the memory of the Barmakids and their successors were kept alive among the *kuttāb* of Iraq and it was on such sources that al-Ṭabarī, who was writing in Baghdad during the period when such *wazīrs* as Ibn al-Furāt and ʿAlī b. ʿĪsā enjoyed great power and prestige, drew. In the third/ninth century, he seems to have had access to government-sponsored accounts of military expeditions, especially the campaigns of al-Muʿtaṣim's reign and the war against the Zanj, which take the form of straightforward linear accounts of the achievements of the ʿAbbasid armies. To say that al-Ṭabarī is biased in favour of the ʿAbbasids is misleading. He certainly did not want to deny the legitimacy of the ʿAbbasids or to incur the wrath of the ruling dynasty, but the Baghdad in which he wrote permitted a great variety of intellectual activity to take place and he did not rely on government funds or gifts from the caliph to ensure the author's livelihood. On the contrary, he made sure of his economic independence by working as a scribe, copying forty pages of manuscript a day and living on the revenues of the family estates in his native Ṭabaristān. It was rather that his information for the early ʿAbbasid period reflected a certain point of view, bureaucratic, metropolitan and keenly interested in the affairs of Iraq. Some of his history too seems to have been based on official government records of the appointment of governors and other detailed administrative matters. The compilers on whom he relied for the Umayyad sections of the *Ta'rīkh* were more varied in occupation, geographical distribution and the range of their contacts than his ʿAbbasid sources. This perhaps accounts for a certain myopia in al-Ṭabarī's vision which allows little time for events away from Iraq and the capital. Nonetheless, his achievement remains astonishing and it is impossible to read even the later stages of his chronicle without being full of admiration for his care and understanding.

While the old sources dry up or change their character, the coming of the ʿAbbasids also witnessed the development of new types of history. In one case, this was a direct product of the ʿAbbasid movement itself. The anonymous *Akhbār al-ʿAbbās*, ed. ʿAbd al-ʿAzīz al-Dūrī, Beirut, 1972, was written to commemorate the various stages by which the ʿAbbasid *da'wa* had emerged from obscurity to take over the Muslim world and to record the names of those who had served it. The material in it is detailed and allows us some insight into the processes by which the ʿAbbasids came to power. Other new writing developed out of the bureaucratic tradition; the most famous of these is the *Kitāb al-wuzarā'* (*Book of Viziers*) of Muḥammad

b. ʿAbdūs al-Jahshiyārī (d. 331/942), ed. Muṣṭafā al-Sayqa et al., Cairo, 1938. Written at a time when the position of the *kuttāb* was being undermined by the decay of the Iraqi economy and the growing threat of military takeover of the ʿAbbasid state, al-Jahshiyārī's work is a monument to the bureaucratic tradition. It is not clear how long the original was or was intended to be; the surviving sections deal with the ʿAbbasid *wazīrs* up until the time of al-Ma'mūn (d. 218/833). The tradition of writing biographies of the *kuttāb* was continued by Hilāl al-ṣābī (d. 448/1056), but only a fragment of his *Ta'rīkh al-wuzarā'*, covering the early years of the reign of the Caliph al-Muqtadir, has survived, ed. H. Amedroz, London, 1904; ed. ʿAbd al-Sattār Farrāj, Cairo, 1958. Besides biographical information, this work also contains the text of documents, especially valuable for the financial history of the caliphate. Court ceremonial is dealt with in another work of Hilāl's, the *Rusūm dār al-khilāfa* (Customs of the Caliph's Palace), ed. Mīkhā'īl ʿAwwād, Baghdad, 1964; trans. Elie A. Salem, Beirut, 1977.

The bureaucratic milieu is reflected in the development of a tradition of administrative geography which detailed the various provinces, the routes between different centres and, frequently, the amount of tax revenue (*kharāj*) which could be expected from each one. The earliest of these to survive is *Kitāb al-masālik wa'l-mamālik* of ʿUbayd Allāh b. Khurdādhbih, ed. M. J. de Goeje, Leiden, 1889, of which the first edition was probably produced in 232/846, although it was subsequently revised by the author. This was followed in about 276/889–890 by the *Kitāb al-buldān* of al-Yaʿqūbī, ed. M. J. de Goeje, Leiden, 1892, already mentioned for his history. Yaʿqūbī's *Buldān* is especially important as the main primary source for the design and population of the great ʿAbbasid capitals of Baghdad and Sāmarrā. The bare bones of administrative geography were increasingly used as a framework for items of curious or entertaining information which can often be of great use to the historian; the most notable of the early geographers in this respect was Ibn al-Faqīh al-Hamadhānī whose *Kitāb al-buldān* was completed around 290/903. It survives in a slightly abbreviated form, ed. M. J. de Goeje, Leiden, 1885, which still, however, contains useful historical information on subjects such as the history of Ṭabaristān and the origins of the Barmakids. Another important geographical source is the *Kitāb al-aʿlāq al-nafīsa* (The Book of Precious Objects) of Aḥmad b. Rusta, part of a general encyclopaedia, the rest of which has been lost, which dates from around 290/903, ed. M. J. de Goeje, Leiden, 1892. Ibn Rusta's account of the Jibal province survives and is notable for the information he gives about the countryside he passed through. Perhaps the most useful of all the geographical works of the period is the *Kitāb al-kharāj* (Book of Taxes) of Qudāma b. Jaʿfar (d. 337/948), partial ed. M. J. de Goeje, Leiden, 1889, full ed. Muḥammad ḥusayn al-Zubaydī, Baghdad, 1981, which is the most important single source for the taxation of various areas of the caliphate.

Part of Qudāma's work along with the *Kitāb al-kharāj* of Yaḥya b. ādam (d. 203/818) and the *Kitāb al-kharāj* of the *qāḍī* Abū Yūsuf Yaʿqūb b. Ibrāhīm al-Anṣārī (d. 182/798) have been translated into English with introductions and notes by A. Ben Shemesh, 3 vols, Leiden, 1967–69. All three authors are concerned with the legal basis of taxation and incorporate many traditions of the Prophet and the early caliphs. Abū Yūsuf, and to a lesser extent Qudāma, also deals with more practical aspects of tax gathering. Also important for the law of taxation and the history of coinage is the *Kitāb al-amwāl* of Abū ʻUbayd b. Sallām (d. 224/838) ed. Muḥammad Khalīl Harrās, Beirut, 1988 with an English translation, *The Book of Revenue* by I.A.K Nyazee (Reading, 2003).

Both the histories of the *wazīrs* and the economic geographies show how much the development of Arabic culture owed to the bureaucratic élite which was attached to the ʻAbbasid court. The disintegration of the court in the fourth/tenth century meant the loss of this sort of cultural along with political unity but, by way of compensation, it did allow the development of regional centres which produced their own historiographical tradition. Despite its misfortunes, however, Baghdad continued to be surprisingly vital as a centre of intellectual activity and this is reflected as much in the writing of history as in any other sphere.

The successors of al-Ṭabarī, and the Reichschronographie

The last entry in al-Ṭabarī's *Ta'rīkh* concerns an attack on the *Ḥajj* by the supporters of the Qarāmiṭa in 302/915. The finish of this great work left a major gap in Islamic historiography, but the annalistic tradition continued to flourish, and a variety of authors emerged to fill the gap which the ending of the great man's work had caused. Some of these were avowedly continuations of al-Ṭabarī, notably the *Ṣilat ta'rīkh al-ṭabarī* of the Spanish Muslim ʻArīb b. Saʻd al-Qurṭubī (d. c. 365/975), ed. M. J. de Goeje, Leiden, 1897, which in fact starts some years earlier in 291/903 and continues until 320/932. Despite his distance from the scene of events, ʻArīb was astonishingly well informed about the affairs of the ʻAbbasids and his work is a major contribution to the understanding of the very well-documented crisis-ridden reign of the Caliph al-Muqtadir (295–320/908–932).

The most lasting continuation of al-Ṭabarī, however, is contained in the work of five authors whose chronicles seem to have been among the most impressive in the entire corpus of Arabic historical writing. This chronicle tradition was described by C. H. Becker as the *Reichschronographie*, because the centre of its interest lay in the caliphal capital of Baghdad. Four of these authors came from a family of Sabians, that is to say pagans from Ḥarrān in the northern Jazīra, who served successive caliphs as physicians. They were therefore in an excellent position to observe events without themselves being involved. The first member of the family to write history was Thābit b. Qurra (d. 288/901) who was asked by the Caliph al-Muʻtaḍid (-279–289/892–902) to write an official history of his reign. This was a new and original departure in Islamic historiography. Hitherto historians had worked in religious or bureaucratic circles but they do not seem to have enjoyed direct government patronage for their work. This work (now lost) seems to have begun the tradition of historical writing in the family.

Thābit's grandson, Thābit b. Sinān, continued the work of al-Ṭabarī until his death (probably 363/974), when it was continued in great detail by his relative Hilāl b. al-Muḥassin al-Ṣābī until his own death in 448/1056 when the chronicle, by now something of a family business, was continued by his son, Ghars al-Niʿma Muḥammad. Of this great work, only a fragment of Hilāl's writing covering the years 389–393/999–1003 survives in its original form, ed. with English trans. H. Amedroz and D. S. Margoliouth, *The Eclipse of the Abbasid Caliphate*, Oxford, 1921, III, 334–460; trans. VI, 359–489, translation reprinted *The Eclipse of the Abbasid Caliphate* London, I. B. Tauris, 2015, III, 359–489, and this shows it to have been an extremely rich source, virtually an annotated diary of the political and social events in Baghdad. In this, it differs greatly from earlier Islamic writing since it seems to be a meticulous record of contemporary events rather than a reconstruction of the past by means of traditions and *akhbār*. The loss of this chronicle is not entirely surprising; its vast length must have made copying it extremely expensive and time-consuming, and it is possible that it was among the works destroyed when the Mongols sacked Baghdad in 656/1258.

The chronicle survived for long enough to be, either directly or at second hand, the foundation of later accounts of the fourth/tenth and fifth/eleventh centuries. Notable among these are the *Kāmil fi' l-ta'rīkh* of Ibn al-Athīr, ed. C. J. Tornberg, 14 vols, Leiden, 1851–76, and the *Mir'at al-zamān* of Sibt. Ibn al-Jawzī (d. 654/1256), of which the section dealing with the years 345–447 (956–1055) was edited by Jalāl Jamīl al-Hamawundi (Baghdad, 1990). Ibn al-Qalānisī, the great twelfth-century chronicler of Damascus, also used Hilāl's work, and his own writing is modestly entitled "Continuation (*dhayl*) of the History of Hilāl al-Ṣābī". In this way, the shadow of the Sabian chronicle is visible in most later accounts of the period; it is extremely frustrating not to have more of the substance.

The closest we can come to the work of Thābit b. Sinān is through the *Tajārib al-umam* of Abū 'Alī Miskawayh (d. 421/1030), ed. H. Amedroz and D. S. Margoliouth, *Eclipse*, I–II, trans. III–IV. There is now a reprint of the English version of this chronicle with a new introduction by H. Kennedy, London, 2015. Miskawayh's work is a history of Islam down to 369/980 when he was a young man in the service of the Buyid bureaucracy. As already mentioned, the early sections are an edition of al-Ṭabarī with many of the *isnāds* and alternative versions omitted, and it is only after the end of al-Ṭabarī's chronicle that his work becomes an original source of great importance. His account of the fourth/tenth century seems to be based on Thābit b. Sinān's chronicle with the addition of other information and accounts which seemed relevant. As such, it is by far the most important source for the history of the 'Abbasids and Buyids in this period as well as for the bedouin dynasties like the 'Uqaylids and Mazyadids. But there is more to

Miskawayh's work than useful historical facts. He imposes on his material a strong ethical and philosophical point of view. It is very much a secular, bureaucratic view of history, and the author, cautious, humane, tolerant and sympathetic, represents the best of the ideals of the *kuttāb* class. His heroes are the great administrators, 'Alī ī b. 'Īsā, "the good *wazīr*", Mu'izz al-Dawla's *wazīr* al-Muhallabī, Rukn al-Dawla's *wazīr* Ibn al-'Amīd the Elder and above all the Buyid prince 'Aḍud al-Dawla, the ideal bureaucrat-king. The villains are those who he felt had betrayed the traditions of the *kuttāb*, Bakhtiyār's *wazīr* Ibn Baqiyya and the younger Ibn al-'Amīd. His vision goes beyond personalities, however, and his work is as much a treatise on good government as it is a historical record. He constantly laments the passing of the old bureaucratic traditions, and Ibn Muqla, the 'Abbasid *wazīr* and calligrapher, brutally tortured to death in 328/940, becomes a tragic figure in his account. He is also very critical of administrative abuse, the unrestricted granting of *iqṭā's*, for example. With his vision of good government and high ideals of the responsibility of rulers, Miskawayh's work rises above the level of simple annals and distinguishes him, along with Ibn Khaldūn, as a real philosopher of history.

The work of Miskawayh was continued by Abū Shūjā' al-Rūdhrawārī, a *wazīr* of the Seljuks, but his work, ed. H. Amedroz and D. S. Margoliouth, *Eclipse*, III; trans. VI, although extremely useful, has little of the depth of his great predecessor and it is considerably briefer and more limited in scope. This continuation, in turn, ends in 393/1003 where the manuscript breaks off. Thereafter, we are dependent on later compilers like Ibn al-Athīr and Sibt. Ibn al-Jawzī working from Hilāl b. al-Muḥassin's lost chronicle and other sources. We are fairly well informed about the main outlines of the history of Iraq and Baghdad in the first half of the fifth/eleventh century, but our information lacks the depth and interest of the fourth/tenth-century material.

In addition to the great chronicles, there are a number of other historical works which emanate from Baghdad circles during this period. Among these is the *Kitāb al-awrāq* of the courtier Abū Bakr al-Ṣūlī (d. 335/946), partially published. The section on the caliphs from al-Wāthiq to al-Muhtadī (227–256/842–870) has been edited by A. B. Khalidov, St Petersburg, 1998 and the account of al-Rāḍī and al-Muttaqī (322–333/934–944), as *Akhbār al-Rāḍī wa'l-Muttaqī*, ed. J. Heyworth-Dunne, Cairo, 1935; French trans. M. Canard, 2 vols, Algiers, 1946, 1950. A complete edition remains a major desideratum. It is essentially a picture of life at the caliphs' court during the reigns of al-Rāḍī and al-Muttaqī. It is entertaining, gossipy and much concerned with poetry and other literary themes. At the same time, it is entirely devoid of the political understanding we find in Miskawayh. A typical example of this concerns the appointment of Ibn Rā'iq as *amīr al-umarā'* in 324/936; as Miskawayh (and probably Thābit b. Sinān before him) saw, this represented the real end of the political power of the 'Abbasid family. For al-Ṣūlī, however, it is simply another incident in court life, the same as the appointment of any other official. If the ʿAbbasid caliphs were surrounded by courtiers with al-Ṣūlī's narrowness of vision and essentially frivolous attitudes, it is not, perhaps, surprising that they lost their political power.

From a rather different milieu come the anecdotes of the *qāḍī* Abū ʿAlī al-Tanūkhī (d. 384/995). He belonged to the court circle of ʿAḍud al-Dawla and may easily have met Miskawayh there but the perspectives of the two men were very different. Al-Tanūkhī composed two collections of anecdotes, the *Nishwār al-muḥāḍara*, ed. with English trans. D. S. Margoliouth, 2 vols, London, 1922, and the *Faraj ba'd al-shidda*, ed. ʿAbbūd al-Shālijī, 5 vols, Beirut, 1971–73, the first part of which has been translated by Julia Bray, *Stories of Piety and Prayer* in Library of Arabic Literature (New York University Press, 2019). These are essentially anecdotes of social life mostly based on the theme of escapes from difficult situations and impending disasters. They are important for social history as well as giving some insight into the personalities of prominent political figures. While Miskawayh's contacts and outlook are those of a secular administrator, al-Tanūkhī's are those of a religious scholar and *qāḍī*; the distinction even applies to their literary style: al-Tanūkhī is careful to provide his information with *isnāds* in the classical style, while Miskawayh only names his sources when it seems relevant.

"Official" historiography of the Buyids seems to be represented by the *Kitāb al-tājī* of yet another member of the Ṣābī family, Ibrāhīm b. Hilāl, grandfather of the chronicler Hilāl b. al-Muḥassin. This work only survives in an epitome made in Yemen in the seventh/thirteenth century, ed. with English trans. M. S. Khan, Karachi, 1995. Ibrāhīm was a *kātib* in the service of the unfortunate Buyid Bakhtiyār, and when his master was dispossessed and killed by ʿAḍud al-Dawla in 367/978, he was in disgrace, and the writing of the *Kitāb al-tājī* may have been the price for being restored to favour. It seems to have been a sustained attempt at propaganda on behalf of the Buyid family with a determination to show that they could claim descent from the Sasanid prince and legendary hero, Bahrām Gūr. The material which survives in the epitome mostly concerns the activities of the ʿAlids in Ṭabaristān at the time of the rise of the Buyid dynasty, since it was this, rather than details of the military and political history of the Buyids themselves, which interested the Yemeni editor.

The Buyid period also saw the flourishing of the art of official letter writing, and three important collections survive, those of the *Ṣāḥib* Ibn ʿAbbād (d. 385/995), ed. ʿAbd al-Wahhāb ʿAzzam and Shawqī Ḍayf, Cairo, 1947, Ibrāhīm b. Hilāl al-Ṣābī, partial ed. Shakīb Arslān, Baʿabda, 1898, mentioned above, and ʿAbd al-Azīz b. Yūsuf al-Shīrāzī (d. 388/998), which has not been edited. The *Ṣāḥib* was *wazīr* to the Buyid rulers of al-Jibāl and central Iran Mu'ayyid al-Dawla and Fakhr al-Dawla; Ibrāhīm served Bakhtiyār and then ʿAḍud al-Dawla and al-Shīrāzī succeeded Ibrāhīm in charge of the chancery of ʿAḍud al-Dawla. These three figures then were contemporaries and sometimes corresponded with each other. Their letter collections concern all sorts of diplomatic and political events and give considerable insight into the politics of the time as well as throw light on subjects not mentioned by the chronicles; the correspondence of Ibn 'Abbād, for example, contains the patent for the appointment of the local governor of Qazvīn, which gives us information available nowhere else about the government of this small but important city. In the main, however, this correspondence has not been sufficiently utilized by historians.

The period which followed the disintegration of the caliphate produced a new generation of geographers. While in some cases they still retained the framework of the administrative geographies of the previous generation, they tend to be much fuller and in many cases to include firsthand personal observations which make them extremely useful for the general historian. The most useful authors are Ibn Ḥawqal (along with the closely related text of al-Iṣṭakhrī) and al-Muqaddasī. Ibn Ḥawqal, whose *Kitāb ṣūrat al-ard.*, ed. M. J. de Goeje, Leiden, 1873; ed. J. Kramers, Leiden, 1938–39; French trans. J. Kramers and G. Wiet, 2 vols, Paris, 1964, was finished in about 378/988. He gives vivid and useful accounts of the areas through which he passed and is especially useful in his comments on trade and taxation. He gives us a full, and none too optimistic, picture of the Jazīra under Hamdanid rule, including details of the otherwise entirely obscure taxation system, and he gives us a full account of the government system of the Qarāmiṭa in Baḥrayn, which is a useful corrective to the generally negative reports we receive about these people from other sources. His contemporary al-Muqaddasī, whose *Aḥsan al-taqāsim*, ed. M. J. de Goeje, Leiden, 1906, English trans. B. Collins, Reading, 2001, was composed around 380/990, came from Jerusalem and was a notable local patriot, but he provides fresh and interesting information based on personal observation of many areas of the Muslim world. He came from a family of architects and his descriptions of buildings are of especial interest. With their enquiring minds, their originality and the simple elegance of their Arabic prose, both these authors are typical of the best of the writing of this period.

In the next century, travel writing is represented by the *Safar nāma* of Nāṣir-i Khusrau (394–c. 465/1003–4/1072), ed. with English trans. by W. M. Thackston. His work is a travel diary rather than a work of geography. He himself came from eastern Iran and wrote in Persian but he was a convert to Isma'ilism and came west to visit the Fatimid court. He gives a glowing description of the wealth and magnificence of Cairo but also gives more general information about the condition and economy of the country he passed through. Perhaps the most striking feature of this is the contrasts he draws between the prosperity of the towns of Egypt and coastal Syria and the poverty of much of the eastern Islamic world. He is an important source for the increased commercial activity of the Syrian ports at the time.

Before leaving the field of general history, attention should be drawn to two late compilations which are essential research tools for anyone seeking to understand the early Islamic period. The first is the great geographical dictionary, the *Mu'jam al-buldān* of Ya'qūb b. 'Abd Allāh al-Yāqūt al-Ḥamawī

(d. 626/1229), ed. F. Wüstenfeld, 6 vols, Leipzig, 1866–73. This work is a mine of information, partly because it identifies most places whose names appear in the classical Arab sources and partly because it incorporates extracts from geographers whose original work is lost. The second compilation is the *Wafayāt al-a'yān*, a biographical dictionary by Ibn Khallikān (d. 681/1282), ed. F. Wüstenfeld, 4 vols, Göttingen, 1835–50; ed. M. M. Abd al-Hamid, 6 vols, Cairo, 1948; English trans. Wm. McGuckin de Slane, 4 vols, Paris and London, 1842–71. Like al-Yāqūt's work, Ibn Khallikān's dictionary contains material from sources now lost. While it is not of great importance for the Umayyad and early 'Abbasid period, it is extremely useful for the fourth/tenth and fifth/eleventh centuries.

Local histories

The sources described so far belong to what might be called the metropolitan, in effect Iraqi, school of writing, connected either with the caliphal court and bureaucracy or with religious circles in Iraq. With the growing rate of conversion, and the increasing literacy in Arabic which resulted from it, there developed local schools of historical writing, moved by the desire to establish their hometowns as centres of political importance and religious learning. Among the oldest of these is the *Ta'rīkh al-Mawṣil* (History of Mosul) of Abū Zakariyyā al-Azdī (d. 334/945), the surviving section of which has been edited by 'Alī Ḥabība, Cairo, 1968, and covers the years 101–224/719–839. It is an extremely full and mature piece of historical writing, skilfully interweaving local history with events from the wider context of the Islamic world. It is lively, full of firsthand accounts quoted verbatim and contains many precious details about life in Mosul and its countryside. After al-Azdī, the Mosul tradition seems to have been maintained by 'Alī b. Muḥammad al-Shimshāṭī. Al-Shimshāṭī was a courtier and poet at the court of Abū Taghlib, the last Hamdanid ruler of Mosul, and he seems to have continued in the service of their successors the 'Uqaylids, for he composed a history of Mosul which he dedicated to Qirwāsh b. al-Muqallad al-'Uqaylī (391–442/1001–50). Unfortunately, his work only survives in fragments incorporated by later writers – a sad loss because we are very badly informed about Mosul in this period.

From the little town of Mayyāfāriqīn, on the southern fringes of the Anatolian uplands, we have the *Ta'rīkh Mayyāfāriqīn* of the local historian, Ibn al-Fāriqī (d. 572/1176). The early sections of his work *Ta'rīkh al-Fāriqī*, ed. B. A. 'Awaḍ, Cairo, 1959, are the fullest source for the Marwanid dynasty and, like the best local histories, it contains much incidental topographical and social history, which makes it a precious source not only for the doings of the dynasts but also for urban life and culture.

Damascus produced a vast biographical dictionary, the *Ta'rikh madīnat Dimashq* by Ibn 'Asākir who died in 571/1175, ed. 'Umar al-Amrawī, 80 vols, Beirut, 1995–98. This contains an enormous range of historical traditions about people from the Prophet down to the author's own time who had some connection with Damascus. It incorporates material from earlier, now lost sources which makes it especially valuable. Only recently published in full, it is a source which has yet to be fully exploited by historians. For a useful discussion of the importance of this text for early Islamic history, see J. E. Lindsay (ed.), *Ibn 'Asakir and Early Islamic History*, Princeton: Darwin Press, 2002.

Aleppo also produced a continuing school of local history which reached its climax in the works of Kamāl al-Dīn Ibn al-'Adīm (d. 660/1262), who incorporated earlier sources now lost. Ibn al-'Adīm left two works; the larger of these is a biographical dictionary, the *Bughyat al-Ṣalab fī ta'rīkh ḥalab*, ed. Suhayl Zakkār, 12 vols, Damascus, 1988, which begins with a geographical introduction and then continues with the biographies of famous and worthy people connected with Aleppo and northern Syria. Much shorter is his chronological history of Aleppo, the *Zubdat al-ḥalab*, which gives an outline history of the city from the coming of Islam to 641/1243. Like the other great compilers of the seventh/thirteenth century, Ibn al-Athīr and Sibt. Ibn al-Jawzī, Ibn al-'Adīm had access to a wealth of records which are now lost. His chronology of Aleppo under the Umayyads and 'Abbasids, although brief, is still valuable, and the author fills out his text as it gets nearer his own time. His discussion of the Mirdasids and the troubled fifth/eleventh century in Aleppo is an essential source.

The historians of Egypt

From early Islamic times, Egypt developed a parallel but separate historical tradition from the metropolitan Iraqi one. So far, the distinctively Egyptian historiography of the early Islamic period has received little scholarly attention but see now Ed. Zychowsky-Coghhill, "How the West Was Won: Unearthing an Umayyad History of the Conquest of the Maghrib", in Andrew Marsham (ed.), *The Umayyad World* (Routledge: London, 2020).

The surviving tradition begins with the *Futūh. Miṣr* (Conquest of Egypt) by Ibn 'Abd al-Ḥakam (d. 257/871) ed. C. Torrey, New Haven, 1922, part narrative history and part legal text; it reflects the viewpoint of a member of an old Islamic élite family at a time when he and his class were losing their position to the newly arrived Turkish military. The next main sources for the history of Egypt are the two parallel works of Muḥammad b. Yūsuf al-Kindī (d. 350/961), *Kitāb al-wulāt* (Book of Governors) and *Kitāb al-quḍāt* (Book of Judges). These survive in the same British Museum manuscript and have been edited in the same volume by R. Guest, Gibb Memorial Series (GMS), XIX, London, 1912, repr. 1964. Al-Kindī came from an old-established Arab family in Egypt and seems to have access to a wealth of local tradition and government records in the country; his work is not in any way dependent on the Iraqi historians like al-Ṭabarī, and he provides a useful check on them. He does not provide much in the way of social history or of topographical detail, but he is very strong on basic chronology and the outline of political events, and his work is a worthy beginning to the great tradition of historical writing in Egypt. The Book of Governors goes up to 334/946, while the Book of Judges stops earlier in 246/861.

The period from the end of al-Kindī's chronicle to the death of the first Fatimid caliph of Egypt al-Mu'izz in 365/975 was covered in the now entirely lost chronicle of al-Ḥasan b. Zūlāq al-Laythī (d. 385/997). He wrote a history which included full biographies of both the Ikhshidid Muḥammad b. Ṭughj and the Fatimid Caliph al-Mu'izz. This work forms the basis of the accounts of this period in later annals, like the work of al-Maqrīzī (on which see below, p. 370) and the *Nujūm al-zahira* of Ibn Taghrī Bardī, ed. Cairo, 1963–72, 16 vols, which explicitly acknowledges Ibn Zūlāq and quotes from him directly. Thereafter, the history of Fatimid Egypt is based on more complex sources. As with contemporary Iraq, the historiography of this period is dominated by the ghost of a lost chronicle, in this case the work of Muḥammad b. 'Ubayd Allāh al-Musabbiḥī (d. 420/1029), which recounted the history of the Fatimids to 415/1025. Like his younger contemporary Hilāl al-Ṣābī in Iraq, al-Musabbiḥī was close to the centre of events at the Fatimid court, being the director of the *Dīwān al-tartīb* (payments office), and wrote a very detailed account of events which is as much an official diary as a work of history. It was a vast work, running apparently to 40 volumes of 26,000 pages. Like Hilāl's also, two years of his work, 414 and 415 (1023–1025) have been preserved in the original, thus giving us a glimpse of the fullness and richness of the material it contained. The surviving portion has been edited from the unique Escorial Manuscript by Ayman Fu'ād Sayyid and T. Bianquis, as vol. XIII in the series *Textes Arabes et études Islamiques* of the Institut Français d'Archéologie Orientale du Caire, Cairo, 1978.

Most of our knowledge of the work of al-Musabbiḥī, however, is gained from the later abbreviation of it made by the ninth/fifteenth-century Egyptian historian Aḥmad b. 'Alī al-Maqrīzī in his history of the Fatimids entitled *Itti'āz. al-Ḥunafā'*, ed. Muḥammad Ḥilmī and Jamāl al-Dīn al-Shayyāl, 3 vols, Cairo, 1967–73. Al-Maqrīzī, a famous historian in his own right, produced a condensation of the work of al-Musabbiḥī which is greatly superior to epitomes of the work of Hilāl al-Ṣābī which were produced in Iraq and Syria; while we must regret the loss of the original, we can only be grateful to al-Maqrīzī for having preserved so much. His account of the early Fatimids in north Africa and Egypt, as well as digressions on the Qarāmiṭa, is well written and full of interesting information. From the end of al-Musabbiḥī's work in 415/1025, al-Maqrīzī seems to have depended on the chronicle of Muḥammad b. Yūsuf b. Muyassar (d. 677/1258), which was, in turn, probably based on al-Musabbiḥī and from 415/1025 on a now entirely lost work of the fifth/eleventh century. Ibn Muyassar's work, ed. Ayman Fu'ād Sayyid, *Textes Arabes et études Islamiques*, XVII, Cairo, 1981, was necessarily not as full as al-Musabbiḥī's, but in the surviving sections, which cover some of the reign of al-Mu'izz and the period of the later Fatimid caliphate

439–553/1047–1158, it is revealed as a full and comprehensive chronicle. Interestingly, we know that al-Maqrīzī knew the work of Ibn Muyassar partly by comparison of his text with the surviving portions of Ibn Muyassar's work and partly because the unique manuscript of it is based on a copy made by al-Maqrīzī himself. This complex annalistic tradition means that we are very well informed about Fatimid politics despite the loss of most of the firsthand sources. Al-Musabbiḥī was probably an Ismāʿīlī sympathizer, but neither Ibn Muyassar nor al-Maqrīzī was. Nonetheless, both of them respected the Fatimids as rulers who had brought great prosperity to their country, and the accounts they give are not significantly biased against the rulers they must have regarded as heretics. The limitations of this tradition are more geographical than ideological. Attention is concentrated on the activities of the Fatimid court and therefore mostly on Egypt. To get a fuller perspective on Fatimid policy in Palestine and Syria, it is necessary to turn to local sources like Ibn al-Qalānisī of Damascus and Ibn al-ʿAdīm of Aleppo.

New Persian historiography

By the end of the fourth/tenth century, there had developed in Iran the beginnings of a Persian-language Muslim historiography, one of whose first achievements was the translation of al-Ṭabarī by Muḥammad al-Balʿamī, which exists in a number of manuscripts, ed. Muḥammad Taqī Bahār, Tehran, 1974, French trans. H. Zotenberg, 4 vols, Paris, 1867–74. Balʿamī edited al-Ṭabarī's work into a continuous narrative by removing most of the critical apparatus. He also added new material from Iranian sources, notably on the ʿAbbasid revolution and the story of Abū Muslim. For the history covered in this book, however, the Persian sources are not of very great value compared with those in Arabic. The reason for this is largely that the new Persian literature was developed farther east at the courts of the Samanids and Ghaznavids, while Arabic remained the language of administration and literature in the Buyid-controlled areas of western Iran. Miskawayh, for example, a bureaucrat of Iranian origin, might easily have followed the example of his young contemporary Bayhaqī (d. 470/1077), who wrote his history of the Ghaznavids in Persian (Muḥammad Bayhaqī, *Ta'rīkh-i Bayhaqī*, ed. ʿAlī Fayyād, Mashhad, 1971 and now brilliantly translated into English by C. E. Bosworth, *History of Beyhaqi* 3 vols., Cambridge, Mass., 2011). Miskawayh, however, being firmly within the Buyid sphere, wrote in Arabic. The Persian historical tradition is mostly of use in giving details of areas of Iran which tend to be neglected by the more general historians. Among such works are the anonymous *Ta'rīkh-i Sīstān*, ed. Malik al-Shu'arā Bahār, Tehran, 1935, the *Ta'rīkh-i ṭabaristān* of Ibn Isfandiyār (d. after 613/1217), ed. ʿAbbās Iqbāl, Tehran, 1944; abridged English trans. E. G. Browne, London, 1905, which fills in gaps in our knowledge of events in the mountainous areas at the south end of the Caspian Sea, and the *Fārs-nāma* of Ibn al-Balkhī, ed. G.

Le Strange and R. Nicholson, GMS, London, 1927, which, although written in Seljuk times, is an important source for Fārs under the Buyids. Persian material can also be useful when it preserves, in part, lost Arabic chronicles. Among these are Muḥammad b. Ja'far al-Narshakhī's *History of Bukhara*, English trans. R. Frye, Cambridge, Mass. 1954, which is useful for Transoxania in 'Abbasid times, and the *Ta'rīkh Qumm* of al-Ḥasan b. Muḥammad al-Qummī, which is interesting on taxation and the settlement of members of the 'Alid family in the Qumm area (where they are still prominent) in the third/ninth century.

Christian historiography and the early Islamic period

Most of the sources mentioned so far, whether in Arabic or Persian, were written by Muslims. There was, however, a strong indigenous Christian historical tradition which, although by no means as elegant or as full as the Muslim one, is nonetheless of value. In one sense, it is somewhat artificial to class these non-Muslim sources together, since they vary greatly in language, scope and content – from Syriac monastic chronicles written by monks whose acquaintance with the outside world hardly extended beyond the walls of their monasteries to sophisticated Arabic products of courtiers like Yaḥyā b. Sa'īd of Antioch. In the main, the Syriac-language works tend to be more concerned with religious affairs and the internal affairs of the Christian community, while the Arabic ones are more secular in tone and pay more attention to political history. There was no tradition of historical writing in Greek in Muslim lands, but some Byzantine authors are of importance.

There are a number of Christian sources which date from the period of the Islamic conquests and throw some light on them. Many of the Syriac sources have been collected and translated in A. Palmer, *The Seventh Century in the West-Syrian Chronicles*. From Egypt, we have the *Chronicle* of the Copt John of Nikiou, which survives only in an Ethiopic version, ed. Zotenberg, Jean de Nikiou, *Chronique*, in *Notices et extraits des MSS. de la Bibliothèque Nationale*, Paris, 1883; English trans. R. H. Charles, 1916, an important source for the Arab conquest of Egypt. Another contemporary source, *The Armenian History Attributed to Sebeos*, has been translated by R. W. Thomson, Liverpool, 1999. The only Greek account, that of Theophanes, ed. De Boor, Berlin, 1883–85; English trans. *The Chronicle of Theophanes* by C. Mango and R. Scott, was written almost two centuries after the event and certainly depends not on independent Greek traditions but on Arabic or Syriac ones.

For the early 'Abbasid period, there is an important Syriac Monophysite history which used to be known as the Chronicle of the Pseudo-Dionysius of Tell-Mahré, but is now known as the Chronicle of Zuqnīn after the monastery in which it was composed. This can now be consulted in the translation by A. Harrak, Toronto, 1999. It gives a vivid and sometimes harrowing picture of rural life in the Jazīra and campaigns on the Byzantine frontier up to 157/774. It is of considerable interest for the information it gives on the practical effects of ʻAbbasid taxation on a rural community; the picture painted is not an optimistic one. Thereafter, the Syriac tradition has a large gap which is only filled by the Chronicle of Michael the Syrian (who died in 595/1199), ed. with French trans. by J.-B. Chabot, 3 vols, Paris, 1899–1910. While much of this is concerned with theological controversy and church affairs, the section dealing with the civil wars after the death of Hārūn al-Rashīd (193/809) seems to be based on the real chronicle of Dionysius of Tell-Mahré (d. 850) and is a historical source of considerable importance for the period. After the mid-third/ninth century, Michael's account becomes very thin, mostly concerned with church affairs, and not until the coming of the Seljuks does he again provide useful evidence.

Christian writing in Syria and the Jazīra is also represented by the Arabic *Kitāb al-ʻunwān* of Agapius (Maḥbūb) of Manbij, ed. with French trans. by A. Vasiliev in *Patrologia orientalis*, VIII, Paris, 1911, 399–550, which covers Islamic history to around 158/775 and is especially good on the early ʻAbbasid period, describing the ʻAbbasid revolution and the subsequent disturbances from a non-Muslim viewpoint.

While the Christian historical tradition in Syria was intermittent, historical writing among the Christians of Egypt continued. In Egypt, the ancient liturgical language of Coptic ceased to be used for historical work, unlike the Syriac of the Jacobite Christians, which continued to be an important literary language for that community down to the time of Bar Hebraeus at the end of the seventh/thirteenth century. In Egypt, Christians, both Monophysite (Coptic) and Diophysite (Melkite or Greek Orthodox), wrote in Arabic. Indeed, it is an indication of the spread of the language, even in the Christian communities, that the two leading Christian writers of the fourth/tenth century, Saʻīd b. Biṭrīq and Severus b. al-Muqaffa', should have chosen to express themselves in Arabic.

The Coptic tradition was represented by the *History of the Patriarchs of Alexandria*, ed. and trans. B. Evetts in *Patrologia Orientalis* I, 99–215; V, 1–216; X, 357–553, and ed. C. F. Seybold, *CSCO Scriptores Arabici* vols 8–9, Leiden, 1962, a series of lives which may have traditionally been ascribed to the theologian Severus b. al-Muqaffaʻ (fl. 955–987) bit which have been shown to be the work of an eleventh-century layman, Mawhūb Ibn Manṣūr Ibn Mufarrij. He treats the history of the patriarchs by reigns and is essentially concerned with ecclesiastical history, touching on secular affairs only when they impinged on the well-being of the church but shedding an interesting light on the lives of non-élite members of society.

The Greek Orthodox tradition begins with the *Ta'rīkh* (also known as the *Naẓm al-Jawhar*) of Saʻīd b. Biṭrīq, ed. L. Cheikho, Leipzig, 1906–09. He was a doctor who took the name of Eutychius when he entered the church, where he became a patriarch of Alexandria from 933 to 940. Like his Melchite (Orthodox) contemporary, Agapius of Manbij, Eutychius was more concerned with secular history than the Monophysites of Syria or Egypt. His chronicle deals with history from the creation of the world until his own time. The information on Muslim politics is abbreviated from Muslim accounts and presents little original material, but the work was of importance in being one of the first accounts of the Muslim world available in the West, being translated into Latin during the seventeenth century by Edward Pococke, the first professor of Arabic at Oxford, as *Contextio Gemmarum, sive Eutychii Patriarchae Alexandrini Annales*, 2 vols, Oxford, 1658–59, and it was used by, among others, Edward Gibbon in his account of the early Muslim state.

Sa'īd's work was continued by the most accomplished of the Christian Arabic historians, Yaḥyā b. Sa'īd, who may have been a relative of his. Like Thābit b. Sinān in Iraq and Sa'īd himself, Yaḥyā was a physician of some importance at the Fatimid court, but unlike Sa'īd, he never entered the church. He was probably born around 370/980 and was thus a fairly young man when, in 405/1014–1015, he, like many other Christians, was obliged to leave Egypt because of the increasingly hostile behaviour of the Caliph al-Ḥākim. He went to settle in Antioch, which the Byzantines had captured from the Muslims just over thirty years previously and where his Melkite faith would cause no problems. Antioch at this time must have been a very cosmopolitan city, where Greeks and Arabs rubbed shoulders, and it was here that he lived until his death in about 458/1066. His *Ta'rīkh*, ed. 'Umar 'Abd al-Salām Tadmurī, Tripoli (Lebanon) 1990, takes over where Eutychius left off, and the surviving portions go up to 425/1034, but originally it seems to have continued beyond that date. Yaḥyā is an important primary source for the reign of al-Ḥākim, for events in Syria in Hamdanid times and later and for Arab–Byzantine relations. He breaks away from the strictly annalistic formula used by most of his Muslim contemporaries, and his approach is more thematic and discursive. Much of what he wrote was based on personal experience, especially the account of al-Ḥākim, but he also had access to a number of other Arabic sources, notably the *Reichschronographie* tradition in the work of Thābit b. Sinān and the work of al-Musabbiḥī, whom he must have known personally. Yaḥyā's career and writing illustrate the best of the historiographical culture of the period, with his access to a wide variety of written sources and his skill at integrating them with his own experience.

Documentary sources

One of the most important changes in our perception of the source material for early Islamic history in recent years comes from the study of documentary sources. Until recently, it was an accepted and largely unchallenged view that the early Islamic world provided very few documentary sources compared with the wealth of charters, account books, bills and letters we find for western European Medieval history. In her recent book, *The Lost Archive: Traces of a Caliphate in a Cairo Synagogue*, Marina Rustow challenges this perception straight on: "For the period before 1100, the Near East has in fact far *more* original documents than Europe, whether they've been stored in limbo or recovered archaeologically" and she goes on the argue, "The medieval Middle East possessed a robust culture of written documentation. State officials produced records, including decrees, memoranda, order, accounts, registers, and receipts and they form a corpus so coherent in their graphic presentation that anyone with a modicum of exposure to them can recognize them at first sight, Courts of law and government offices produced written acts and maintained constant procedures for authenticating them; their personnel had an interest in ensuring that rights claims depended on more than personal whim – the ruler's or anyone else's. Scribes developed diverse technical specialisations in the art of record keeping. And along with those came division of labour among administrative and legal personnel. And along with those, in turn, came systems of document organization and retrieval".[1] The evidence is partial but compelling and these are important perspectives to born in mind when we read of court intrigues and violent clashes: it was all going on in the background. Having said that, the evidence is very patchy geographically. The vast bulk of the evidence comes from Egypt. There are much smaller but very important collections in Bactrian, Pahlavi (Middle Persian) and Arabic from central and eastern Iran, but apart from a few tiny fragments, nothing survives from Iraq and the documentation of the Abbasid caliphate, which must have been vast, is completely lost to us.

Until the fourth/tenth century, when it was largely supplanted by paper, papyrus was the medium for most administrative correspondence of Egypt, as it had been in classical times. Papyrus has a much better rate of preservation than paper, and a considerable volume of Arabic papyri, and papyri written in Greek after the Islamic conquest, has been preserved. The most important of these from the point of view of administrative history date from the Umayyad period and, despite their fragmentary condition, give a real insight into the day-to-day administration of the province. They can also be useful for establishing dates of governors and official titles of caliphs and others, points about which chroniclers writing in a later period may make mistakes. A. Grohmann, *From the World of Arabic Papyri*, Cairo, 1952, remains a good introduction. The papyri – Greek, Coptic and Arabic – relevant to early Islamic history are detailed by P. M. Fraser in his edition of A. J. Butler, *The Arab Conquest of Egypt*, Oxford, 1978, lxxvi–lxxxiii. See also Y. Raghib, *Marchands d'étoffe du Fayyoum*, 4 vols, Cairo, 1982–96, for the use of papyri in the economic history of early Islamic Egypt. For a small but important collection from southern Palestine in the early Umayyad period, C. J. Kraemer, *Excavations at Nessana*, vol. 3, Non-Literary Papyri, Princeton, 1958. P. Sijpesteijn's *Shaping a Muslim State: The World of a Mid-Eighth-Century Egyptian Official* Oxford, 2013) shows how this material can be used to illuminate the functions of government at a local level.

Papyri also preserve the oldest texts of Arabic historical writing, albeit in very fragmentary form. They are nonetheless useful for our understanding of the growth of the historiographical tradition; texts have been published, with translation and a very important introduction in N. Abbott, *Studies in Arabic Literary Papyri I: Historical Texts*, University of Chicago Oriental Institute Publications, LXXV, Chicago, 1957.

The other source of documentary material is the Cairo Geniza. The Geniza documents are the correspondence, contracts and legal decisions of the Jewish community of Fusṭāt. during the Fatimid times. Although paper documents, they were preserved because it was felt that any writings containing the name of God could not be thrown away but rather put in a storeroom above the synagogue. In this way, a mass of material was preserved, much of it of an ephemeral nature, not the sort of thing that archivists normally preserve but fascinating for the historian. The Geniza material concerns all aspects of the life of the community, including extensive commercial and personal correspondence. It is also extremely difficult to use; this is only partly because of the language, which is mostly Arabic written in Hebrew characters, but because it was stored in a chaotic condition, as a dump, not a reference collection. Furthermore, it has passed in fragments to a large number of different libraries in Europe, including Russia, and America, distributed at random without any regard for the subject matter. The best introduction to the geniza and its importance for the study of Islamic history see Marina Rustow, *The Lost Archive* Princeton, 2020. The classic account of the society revealed in the Geniza documents is S. D. Goitein, *A Mediterranean Society*, 6 vols, Berkeley and Los Angeles, 1967–93. Goitein's magisterial work is almost an original source in itself, a gold mine for anyone interested in the history of the Islamic world in the Fatimid period. For examples of the documents themselves, G. Khan, ed. and trans., *Arabic Legal and Administrative Documents from the Cambridge Genizah Collection*, Cambridge, 1993.

Recently, a new collection of documents has emerged from northern Afghanistan. From the point of view of Islamic history, the most important of these come from what seems to be a family archive of the Ru'b-khān, the local ruler of Ru'b and Samangan. These Arabic documents, written on parchment, date from the period from 138/775 to 160/777 and are mostly concerned with tax receipts and other contracts. They show clearly how the 'Abbasid government's administrative systems were broadly the same in this far eastern corner of the caliphate as they were in contemporary Egypt as revealed by the papyri. The documents are published with English translation and commentary in G. Khan, *Arabic Documents from Early Islamic Khurasan*, London, The Nour Foundation, Studies in the Khalili Collection V, 2007.

Recently too, a series of Pahlavi language documents, apparently from the Qumm area and probably dating from the early Islamic period, have been published. More cryptic and difficult to interpret than the Arabic documents from Khurasan, they give some insight into local administration. Some of the texts have been published with German translation and commentary as well as photographs of the originals in D. Weber, *Berliner Pahlavi-Dokumente: Zeugnisse spatsassanidischer Brief-und Rechskultur aus fruhislamischer Zeit*, Wiesbaden, Harrossowitz Verlag, 2008.

Numismatic and epigraphic evidence

Islamic coinage from the period covered by this book is abundant and much of it has been catalogued in many different places. There is as yet no handbook or synthesis to which the historian can turn for an overview of the material. After the time of the Umayyad Caliph ʿAbd al-Malik, Islamic coinage is almost entirely epigraphic in design, with inscriptions rather than pictures on its surfaces. It is useful, as the papyri and inscriptions on stone and textiles (*ṭirāz*) are useful, for establishing names, dates and titles not only of rulers but of governors and indeed of rebels who were powerful enough to issue their own coins. The right to mint coins (*sikka*) was a government monopoly in early Islamic society and there was no equivalent to the private coinage of western Europe; the mention of a caliph or other ruler's name on the coinage was, along with the mention in the sermon or *khuṭba* at Friday prayers, one of the ways in which sovereignty was acknowledged. Apart from its epigraphic uses, coinage can also shed light on general economic trends, although the evidence must be used with care; coinage of low intrinsic value does not necessarily point to economic decline. Nonetheless, we can be reasonably sure that, for example, the extreme fineness of Fatimid *dīnārs* reflects the wealth and stability of the state. The bibliography of Muslim coinage is very scattered. The classic account of the earliest Islamic coinage remains J. Walker, *A Catalogue of Muḥammadan Coins in the British Museum*, vol. i, *The Arab-Sassanian Coins*, London, 1941; vol. ii, *The Arab-Byzantine and Post-reform Umaiyad Coins*, London, 1956, but this should now be supplemented by the critique of M. Bates, "History, geography and numismatics in the first century of Islamic coinage", *Revue Suisse de Numismatique*, 65, 1986, 231–65. See also S. Heidemann, "The merger of two currency zones in early Islam", *Iran*, 36, 1998, 95–112. For the early coinage of Palestine, see I. Ilisch, *Sylloge Numorum Arabicorum Tübingen Palastina IV*, Tübingen, 1993. ʿAbbasid coinage has been much less fully studied; for an introduction, see T. S. Noonan, "Early ʿAbbasid mint output", *Journal of the Economic and Social History of the Orient*, xxix, 1986, 113–75. See also L. Treadwell, "Notes on the mint at Samarra", in C. F. Robinson (ed.), *A Mediaeval Islamic City Reconsidered* and T. El-Hibri, "Coinage reform under the ʿAbbāsid caliph al-Ma'mūn", *Journal of the Economic and Social History of the Orient*, xxxvi, 1993, 58–83. G. C. Miles's *Numismatic history of Rayy*, New York, 1938 is an important regional study and the article "Numismatics" by the same author in R. N. Frye (ed.), *Cambridge history of Iran*, IV, 1975, 364–77 contains useful references. On the coinage of Egypt, see W. C. Schultz, "The monetary history of Egypt, 642–1517", in C. Petry (ed.), *Cambridge History of Egypt*, i, 318–38. Also dealing with Egyptian coinage is J. Bacharach, *Islamic History through Coins: An Analysis and Catalogue of Tenth Century Ikhshidid Coinage*, Cairo, American University in Cairo, 2009 which also includes an interesting general discussion about the use of coins as historical evidence. There is a useful discussion of the literature on Sasanian and early Islamic coins in M. Morony, *Iraq After the Muslim Conquest*, Princeton, 1984, 548–53 and a bibliography of material on later coins in H. Busse, *Chalif und Grosskönig*, Beirut, 1969, 543–6. The fifth/eleventh-century coinage of the Jazīra is discussed in S. Heidemann, *Die Renaissance der Stadte in Nordsyrien und Nordmesopotamien*, Leiden, 2002. For monumental and other non-numismatic inscriptions, see the *Thesaurus d'Epigraphie Islamique* curated by the Fondation Max van Berchem.

Note

1 Rustow, *Lost Archive*, 3,5. Archaeological Evidence rather than providing a partial list of the growing body of material on early Islamic archaeology, I would refer readers to the excellent Oxford Handbook of Islamic Archaeology eds. Bethay Walker, Timothy Insoll and Corisande Fenwick, Oxford, OUP, 2012 which provides full bibliographies.

Suggested further reading

This is not in any sense a comprehensive bibliography, rather some suggestions for those who would like to read more about the topics covered in this book.

Abbreviations

BSOAS	Bulletin of the School of Oriental and African Studies
GMS	Gibb Memorial Series
IC	Islamic Culture
IJMES	International Journal of Middle East Studies
IQ	Islamic Quarterly
Islam	Der Islam
JAOS	Journal of the American Oriental Society
JESHO	Journal of the Economic and Social History of the Orient
JNES	Journal of Near Eastern Studies
JRAS	Journal of the Royal Asiatic Society
JSS	Journal of Semitic Studies
REI	Revue d'Etudes Islamiques
RSO	Rivista degli Studi Orientali
SI	Studia Islamica

General

Antrim, Z., *Routes and realms: the power of place in the early Islamic world*, Oxford, Oxford University Press, 2012

Berkey, J., *The formation of Islam*, Cambridge, MA, Harvard University Press, 2003.

Bloom, J. M., *Paper before print: the history and impact of paper in the Islamic World*, New Haven, CT and London, Yale University Press, 2001.

Bosworth, C. E., *The new Islamic dynasties*, Edinburgh, Edinburgh University Press, 1996.

Bulliet, R., *Conversion to Islam in the medieval period*, Cambridge, MA, Harvard University Press, 1979.

Bulliet, R., *Islam: the view from the edge*, New York, Columbia University Press, 1994.
Cambridge history of Egypt, vol. *1* ed. C. Petry, Cambridge, Cambridge University Press, 1998.
Cambridge history of Iran, vol. *4* ed. R. Frye, Cambridge, Cambridge University Press, 1975.
Cornu, G., *Atlas du monde arabo-islamique à l'Epoque Classique IX–X siècles*, Leiden, Brill, 1985.
Crone, P. and Cook, M., *Hagarism, the making of the Muslim world*, Cambridge, Cambridge University Press, 1977.
Dennett, D., *Conversion and poll-tax in early Islam*, Cambridge, MA, Harvard University Press, 1950.
Eickelman, D., *The Middle East: an anthropological approach*, London, Prentice-Hall, 1981.
Gil, M., *A history of Palestine, 643–1099*, trans. E. Broido, Cambridge, Cambridge University Press, 1992.
Goldziher, I., *Muslim studies*, ed. and trans. C. R. Barber and S. M. Stern, 2 vols, London, George Allen and Unwin, 1967, 1971.
Hodgson, M. G. S., *The venture of Islam*, vol. 1, Chicago, University of Chicago Press, 1973.
Humphreys, R. S., *Islamic history: a framework for inquiry*, Princeton, NJ, Princeton University Press, 1991.
Kennedy, H., *The Armies of the Caliphs*, London, Longman, 2001.
Kennedy, H. ed., *An historical atlas of Islam*, Leiden, Brill, 2002.
Kennedy, H., *Caliphate: the history of an idea,* London, Pelican, 2016.
Le Strange, G., *Palestine under the Moslems*, London, Alexander Watt, 1890, reprint London, I. B. Tauris, 2014.
Le Strange, G., *Lands of the eastern caliphate*, Cambridge, Cambridge University Press, 1905; reprint London, I. B. Tauris, 2014.
New Cambridge history of Islam, vol. *1* ed. C. F. Robinson and vol. *4* ed. R. Irwin, Cambridge, Cambridge University Press, 2010.
Shaban, M. A., *Islamic history: a new interpretation*, *2* vols, Cambridge, Cambridge University Press, 1971, 1976.
Verkinderen, P., *Waterways of Iraq and Iran in the early Islamic period: changing rivers and landscapes of the Mesopotamian plain*, London, I. B. Tauris, 2015.

In addition, the reader should refer to the three editions of *The Encyclopaedia of Islam*. The first edition, 4 vols and supplement, Leiden, Brill, 1913–42, is still useful, but many of the articles are dated. The second edition, Leiden, Brill, 1954, is fuller and also accessible on CD-ROM. The third edition is in the course of publication, Leiden, Brill 2007–. Many of the articles are of great scholarly value and the *Encyclopaedia* should always be used to supplement other reading. Another important reference tool is the *Encyclopaedia Iranica*, ed. E. Yarshater (London and New York 1985–), which contains more discursive articles and is still incomplete. For bibliography, readers should use *Index Islamicus: a bibliography of books, articles and reviews of Islam and the Muslim world from 1906* (published 1958 onwards and available on CD-ROM).

Historiography

Conrad, L. I., "The conquest of Arwād: a source-critical study in the historiography of the early medieval Near East", in A. Cameron and L. I. Conrad (eds.), *The Byzantine and early Islamic Near East I: problems in the literary source material*, Princeton, NJ, Darwin Press, 1992, 317–401.

Cooperson, M., *Classical Arabic biography*, Cambridge, Cambridge University Press, 2000.

Donner, F. M., *Narratives of Islamic origins: the beginnings of Islamic historical writing*, Princeton, NJ, Darwin Press, 1998.

Duri, A. A., *The rise of historical writing among the Arabs*, ed. and trans. L. I. Conrad, Princeton, NJ, Princeton University Press, 1983.

El-Hibri, T., *Reinterpreting Islamic historiography: Hārūn al-Rashīd and the narrative of the ʿAbbāsid caliphate*, Cambridge, Cambridge University Press, 1999.

Howard-Johnston, J., *Witnesses to a world crisis: historians and histories of the Middle East in the seventh century*, Oxford, Oxford University Press, 2010.

Hoyland, R., *Seeing Islam as others saw it: a survey and evaluation of Christian, Jewish and Zoroastrian writings on early Islam*, Princeton, NJ, Darwin Press, 1997.

Kennedy, H. ed., *Al-Tabari: a medieval historian and his work*, Princeton, NJ, Darwin Press, 2008.

Meisami, J. S., *Persian historiography to the end of the twelfth century*, Edinburgh, Edinburgh University Press, 1999.

Robinson, C. F., *Islamic historiography*, Cambridge, Cambridge University Press, 2003.

Shoshan, B., *Poetics of Islamic historiography: deconstructing Tabari's history*, Leiden, Brill, 2004.

Historical and geographical sources in English translation

Arabic and Persian

Abū Yūsuf Yaʿqūb b. Ibrāhīm, *Kitāb al-Kharāj: taxation in Islam, III*, trans. A. Ben Shemesh, Leiden, Brill, 1969.

al-Balādhurī, Aḥmad b. Yaḥyā, *Futūh al-Buldān* trans. H. Kennedy as *The Arab Invasions,* London, Bloomsbury, 2022

al-Masʿūdī, *Murūj al-dhabab: the meadows of gold: the Abbasids*, partial trans. P. Lunde and C. Stone, London and New York, Kegan Paul, 1989.

al-Māwardī, *Aḥkām al-Sulṭāniyya: the ordinances of government*, trans. W. H. Wahba, Reading, Garnet, 1996.

al-Muqaddasī, *Aḥsan al-Taqāsim: the best divisions for knowledge of the regions*, trans. B. Collins, Reading, Garnet, 2001.

al-Sīrāfī, AbūZayd, *Accounts of China and India*, ed. and trans. T. Macintosh-Smith, New York, New York University Press, 2014.

al-Ṭabarī, *Ta'rīkh: the history of al-Ṭabarī*, ed. Y. Yarshater, 38 vols, Albany, State University of New York Press, 1985–2000.

Ibn al-Ḥaytham, *Kitāb al-Munāẓarāt: the advent of the Fatimids*, trans. W. Madelung and P. E. Walker, London, I. B. Tauris, 2000.

Ibn Ḥabīb, Muhammad, *Prominent murder victims of the pre- and early Islamic periods*, ed. and trans. G. J. van Gelder, Leiden, Brill, 2020

Ibn Isḥāq, *Sīrat Rasūl Allāh: the life of Muhammad*, trans. A Guillaume, Karachi, 1955, repr. 1967.

Ibn Khallikān, *Wafayāt al-a'yān: Ibn Khallikān's biographical dictionary*, trans. M. de Slane, *4* vols, Paris, 1842–71.

Idrīs 'Imād al-Dīn, *'Uyūn al-akhbar*, trans S. Jiwa, "The Founder of Cairo", London, I. B. Tauris, 2013.

Khalīfa ibn Khayyāṭ, *History of the Umayyad Dynasty*, trans. C. Wurtzel and R. Hoyland, Liverpool, Liverpool University Press, 2015.

Miskawayh, *Tajārib al-Umam: the eclipse of the 'Abbasid caliphate*, trans. S. D. Margoliouth, *3* vols, London, I. B. Tauris, 2015.

Nāṣir-i Khusraw, *Safarnāma: book of travels*, trans. W. M. Thackston, Costa Mesa, Mazda, 2001.

Qudāma b. Ja'far, *Kitāb al-Kharaj: taxation in Islam, II*, trans. A. Ben Shemesh, Leiden, Brill, 1965.

Yaḥyā b. Ādam, *Kitāb al-Kharāj: taxation in Islam, I*, trans. A. Ben Shemesh, Leiden, Brill, 1967.

Eastern Christian sources

Anon., *The chronicle of Zuqnin Parts III and IV AD 488–773*, trans. A. Harrak, Toronto, 1999.

Anon., *The Life of St Simeon of the Olives: an Entrepreneurial Saint in Islamic North Mesopotamia*, ed. and trans. R. Hoyland, S. Brock, K. Brunner, and J. Tannous, Piscataway, NJ, Gorgias Press, 2021.

Den Heijer, *Mawhūb Ibn Manṣūr Ibn Mufarriğ et l'historiographie copto-arabe*, Louvain, 1989.

Sebeos, *The Armenian history*, trans. R. W. Thomson with notes by J. Howard-Johnston, *2* vols, Liverpool, Liverpool University Press, 1999.

Theophanes, *The chronicle of Theophanes the Confessor: Byzantium and Near Eastern history AD 284–813*, trans. C. Mango and R. Scott, Oxford, Oxford University Press, 1997.

Various, *The seventh century in Western Syrian chronicles*, trans. A. Palmer, Liverpool, Liverpool University Press, 1993.

Wood, P., *The Chronicle of Seert: the Christian Historical Imagination in Late Antique Iraq*, Oxford, Oxford University Press, 2013.

Wood, P., *The Imam of the Christians: the World of Dionysius of Tel-Mahre c.750–850*, Princeton, Princeton University Press, 2021.

The matrix of the Muslim world

Bowersock, G. W., *Roman Arabia*, Cambridge, MA, Harvard University Press, 1982.

Bowersock, G. W., Brown, P. and Grabar, O., eds., *Interpreting late antiquity: essays on the postclassical world*, Cambridge, MA, Harvard University Press, 2001.

Cambridge history of Iran, III "The Seleucid, Parthian and Sasanian periods", ed. E. Yar-Shater, Cambridge, Cambridge University Press, 1983.

Daryaee, T., *Sasanian Persia: the rise and fall of an empire*, London, I. B. Tauris, 2009.

De la Vassiere, E., *Soghdian traders. A history*, Leiden, Brill, 2005.

El Cheikh, N. M., *Byzantium viewed by the Arabs*, Cambridge, MA, Harvard University Press, 2004.

Foss, C., "The Near Eastern countryside in late antiquity: a review article", *Journal of Roman Archaeology, Supplementary Series, 14*, 1995, 213–34.

Foss, C., "Syria in transition, AD 550–750", *Dumbarton Oaks Papers, li*, 1997, 189–270.

Fowden, G., *Empire to commonwealth: consequences of monotheism in late antiquity*, Princeton, Princeton University Press, 1993.

Frye, R., *The heritage of Persia*, London, Weidenfeld and Nicolson, 1964.

Haldon, J., *Byzantium in the seventh century*, Cambridge, Cambridge University Press, 1990.

Horden, P. and Purcell, N., *The corrupting sea: a study of Mediterranean history*, Oxford, Blackwell, 2000.

Hoyland, R., *Arabia and the Arabs: from the bronze age to the coming of Islam*, London, Routledge, 2001.

Kennedy, H., "From polis to medina: urban change in late antique and early Islamic Syria", *Past and Present, 106*, 1985, 3–27.

Kennedy, H., "Syria, Palestine and Mesopotamia", in A. Cameron, B. Ward-Perkins and M. Whitby (eds.), *Cambridge Ancient History, XIV*, Cambridge, Cambridge University Press, 2000, 588–611.

Kennedy, H., "From Shahristan to Medina", *Studia Islamica 102/3*, 2006, 5–34.

Morony, M., *Iraq after the Muslim conquest*, Princeton, Princeton University Press, 1984.

Pourshariati, P., *The decline and fall of the Sasanian Empire*, London, I. B. Tauris, 2008.

Retso, J., *The Arabs in antiquity: their history from the Assyrians to the Umayyads*, London, Routledge, 2003.

Rubin Z., "The Sasanian monarchy", in A. Cameron, B. Ward-Perkins and M. Whitby (eds.), *Cambridge ancient history, XIV*, Cambridge, Cambridge University Press, 2000, 638–61.

Tannous, J., *The making of the Medieval Middle East: religion, society and simple believers*, Princeton, Princeton University Press, 2018

Wickham, C., *Framing the early Middle Ages: Europe and the Mediterranean, 400–800*, Oxford, Oxford University Press, 2005.

Wiesehofer, J., *Ancient Persia*, London, I. B. Tauris, 1996.

Bedouin society and the birth of the Islamic stateCole, D. P., *Nomads of the nomads: the Āl Murrah bedouin of the Empty Quarter*, Chicago, Aldine, 1975.

Conrad, L. L., *The Arabs*, in A. Cameron, B. Ward-Perkins and M. Whitby (eds.), *Cambridge Ancient History, XIV*, Cambridge, Cambridge University Press, 2000, 678–700.

Cook, M., *Muhammad*, Oxford, Oxford University Press, 1983.

Crone, P., *Meccan trade and the rise of Islam*, Oxford, Oxford University Press, 1987.

Donner, F. M., *Muhammad and the believers: at the origins of Islam*, Cambridge, MA, Harvard University Press, 2010.

Hawting, G. R., *The idea of idolatry and the emergence of Islam: from polemic to history*, Cambridge, Cambridge University Press, 1999.

Heck, G. W., "Gold mining in Arabia and the rise of the Islamic State", *JESHO, 42*, 1999, 364–95.

Kister, M. J., *Studies in Jahiliyya and early Islam*, London, Variorum, 1980.

Lancaster, W., *The Rwala bedouin revisited*, Cambridge, Cambridge University Press, 1981.

Lings, M., *Muhammad: his life based on the earliest sources*, Cambridge, Islamic Texts Society, 1991.

Munt, H., *The Holy City of Medina: sacred space in early Islamic Arabia*, Cambridge, Cambridge University Press, 2014.

Peters, F. E., *Muhammad and the origins of Islam*, Albany, State University of New York Press, 1994.

Rubin, U., *The eye of the beholder: the life of Muhammad as viewed by early Muslims – a textual analysis*, Princeton, Darwin Press, 1995.

Watt, W. M., *Muhammad at Mecca*, Oxford, Oxford University Press, 1953.

Watt, W. M., *Muhammad at Medina*, Oxford, Oxford University Press, 1956.

Watt, W. M., *Muhammad, prophet and statesman*, Oxford, Oxford University Press, 1961.

Conquest and division in the time of the Rāshidūn caliphs

Afsaruddin, A., *Striving in the path of God: jihad and martyrdom in Islamic thought*, Oxford, Oxford University Press, 2013.

Butler, A. J., *The Arab conquest of Egypt*, ed. P. M. Fraser, Oxford, Oxford University Press, 1978.

Donner, F. M., *The early Islamic conquests*, Princeton, Princeton University Press, 1981.

Firestone, R., *Jihad: the origin of holy war in Islam*, Oxford, Oxford University Press, 1999.

Hill, D. R., *The termination of hostilities in the early Arab conquests*, London, Luzac, 1971.

Hinds, G. M., *Studies in early Islamic history*, Princeton, Darwin Press, 1996.

Hoyland, R., *In God's path: the Arab conquests and the creation of an Islamic empire*, Oxford, Oxford University Press, 2015.

Jafri, S. M., *The origins and early development of Shi'a Islam*, London, Longman, 1979.

Kaegi, W. E., *Byzantium and the early Islamic conquests*, Cambridge, Cambridge University Press, 1992.

Kennedy, H., *The great Arab conquests*, London, Weidenfeld and Nicolson, 2007.

Madelung, W., *The succession to Muḥammad: a study of the early caliphate*, Cambridge, Cambridge University Press, 1997.

Petersen, E. L., *'Alī and Mu'āwiya in early Arabic tradition*, Copenhagen, Scandinavian University Books, 1964.

Shoufani, E., *Al-Riddah and the Muslim conquest of Arabia*, Toronto, University of Toronto Press, 1972.

Wellhausen, J., *The politico-religious factions in early Islam*, trans. R. C. Ostle, Amsterdam, New-Holland, 1975.

The Umayyad caliphate

Borrut, A. and Cobb, P. eds., *Umayyad legacies. Medieval memories from Syria to Spain*, Leiden, Brill, 2010

Borrut, A. and Donner, F. eds., *Christians and others in the Early Islamic state*, Chicago, Oriental Institute, 2016

Crone, P., *Slaves on horses*, Cambridge, Cambridge University Press, 1980.

Crone, P. and Hinds, G. M., *God's caliph: religious authority in the first centuries of Islam*, Cambridge, Cambridge University Press, 1986.

Fowden, G., *Quṣayr 'Amra: Art and the Umayyad elite in late antique Syria*, Berkeley and Los Angeles, University of California Press, 2004.

Hamilton, R., *Walīd and his friends: an Umayyad tragedy*, Oxford, Oxford Studies in Islamic Art, *VI*, 1988.

Hawting, G. R., *The first dynasty of Islam: the Umayyad caliphate A.D. 661–750*, London, Routledge, 2000.

Khalek, N., *Damascus after the Muslim Conquest: text and image in early Islam*, Oxford, Oxford University Press, 2011.

Marsham, A., *Rituals of Islamic Monarchy: accession and succession in the first Muslim Empire*, Edinburgh, Edinburgh University Press, 2008

Marsham, A. ed., *The Umayyad World*, London, Routledge, 2021

McMillan, M. E., *The meaning of Mecca: the politics of pilgrimage in early Islam*, London, Saqi Books, 2011.

Robinson, C., *Empire and élites after the Muslim conquest: the transformation of northern Mesopotamia*, Cambridge, Cambridge University Press, 2000.

Robinson, C., *'Abd al-Malik*, Oxford, Oneworld, 2005.

Savant, S. M., *The new Muslims of post-conquest Iran: tradition, memory, and conversion*, New York, Cambridge University Press, 2012.

Sijpesteijn, P. M., *Shaping a Muslim state: the world of a mid-eighth-century Egyptian official*, Oxford, Oxford University Press, 2013.

Walmsley, A., "Production, exchange and regional trade in the Islamic East Mediterranean: old structures, new system?" in L. I. Hansen and C. J. Wickham (eds.), *The long eighth century*, Leiden, Brill, 2000.

Wellhausen, J., *The Arab kingdom and its fall*, trans. M. G. Weir, Calcutta, Calcutta University Press, 1927.

The early 'Abbasid caliphate

Agha, S., *The revolution which toppled the Umayyads. Neither Arab nor 'Abbāsid*, Leiden, Brill, 2003.

Bennsion, A., *The great caliphs: the golden age of the Abbasid empire*, London, I. B. Tauris, 2009.

Bernheimer, T., *The 'Alids: the first family of Islam, 750–1200*, Edinburgh, Edinburgh University Press, 2013.

Bonner, M., *Aristocratic violence and holy war. Studies in the jihad and the Arab-Byzantine frontier*, New Haven, Yale University Press, 1996.

Cobb, P. M., *White banners: contention in 'Abbasid Syria, 750–880*, Albany, State University of New York Press, 2001.

Cooperson, M., *Al-Ma'mun*, Oxford, Oneworld, 2005.

Crone, P., *The nativist prophets of early Islamic Iran: rural revolt and local Zoroastrianism*, Cambridge, Cambridge University Press, 2012.

Daniel, E. L., *The political and social history of Khurasan under Abbasid rule*, Minneapolis and Chicago, Bibliotheca Islamica, 1979.

El Cheikh, Nadia, *Women, Islam and Abbasid identity*, Cambridge, MA, Harvard University Press, 2015

El-Hibri, T., *Reinterpreting Islamic historiography: Hārūn al-Rashīd and the narrative of the 'Abbāsid caliphate*, Cambridge, Cambridge University Press, 1999.

El-Hibri, T., *The Abbasid Caliphate; A history*, Cambridge, Cambridge University Press, 2021

Kennedy, H., "Central government and provincial élites in the early 'Abbāsid caliphate", *BSOAS*, *44*, 1981, 26–38.

Kennedy, H., *The early Abbasid caliphate: a political history*, London, Croom Helm, 1981.

Kennedy, H., *The court of the caliphs: the rise and fall of Islam's greatest dynasty*, London, Weidenfeld and Nicolson, 2005 (published in the US as *When Baghdad ruled the Muslim world*, Cambridge, MA, Da Capo, 2004).

Lassner, J., *The topography of Baghdad in the early Middle Ages: text and studies*, Detroit, Wayne State University Press, 1970.

Lassner, J., *The shaping of 'Abbāsid rule*, Princeton, Princeton University Press, 1980.

Lassner, J., *Islamic revolution and historical memory: an inquiry into the art of 'Abbāsid apologetics*, New Haven, Yale University Press, 1986.

Le Strange, G., *Baghdad during the Abbasid caliphate*, London, Cambridge University Press, 1909, reprint, London, I. B. Tauris, 2014.

Shaban, M. A., *The Abbasid revolution*, Cambridge, Cambridge University Press, 1970.

Sharon, M., *Black banners from the East*, Leiden, Brill, 1983.

Sharon, M., *Revolt: the social and military aspects of the 'Abbasid revolution*, Jerusalem, Hebrew University Press, 1990.

Sourdel, D., *Le vizirat abbaside, 2* vols, Damascus, Institut Francais de Damas 1959–60.

Yücesoy, H., *Messianic beliefs and imperial politics in Medieval Islam: The Abbasid Caliphate in the early ninth century*, Columbia, SC, University of South Carolina Press, 2009.

Zaman, M. Q., *Religion and Politics under the Early Abbasids Leiden*, Leiden Brill, 1997.

The middle 'Abbasid caliphate

Ayalon, D., "The military reforms of Caliph al-Mu'taṣim: their background and consequences", in D. Ayalon (ed.), *Islam and the abode of war*, Aldershot, Variorum, 1994, 1–39.

Bowen, H., *The life and times of 'Alī b. 'Īsā, the good vizier*, Cambridge, Cambridge University Press, 1928.

Gordon, M. S., *The breaking of a thousand swords: a history of the Turkish military of Samarra (AH 200–275/815–889 CE)*, Albany, State University of New York Press, 2001.

Gutas, D., *Greek thought, Arabic literature: the Graeco-Arabic translation movement in Baghdad and early 'Abbāsid society*, London, Routledge, 1998.

Kennedy, H., "Caliphs and their chroniclers in the middle Abbasid period (third/ninth century)", in C. F. Robinson, (ed.), *Texts, documents and artefacts: Islamic studies in honour of D. S. Richards*, Leiden, Brill, 2003, 17–35.

Melchert, C., "Religious policies of the caliphs from al-Mutawwakil to al-Muqtadir, AH 232–295/AD 847–908", *Islamic Law and Society*, *iii*, 1996, 316–42.

Popovic, A., *The revolt of the African slaves in Iraq in the 3rd/9th century*, Princeton, Markus Wiener, 1999.

Robinson, C. ed., *A medieval Islamic city reconsidered: an interdisciplinary approach to Samarra*, Oxford, Oxford Studies in Islamic Art XIV, 2001.

Stetkevych, S. P., *Abū Tammām and the poetics of the 'Abbāsid age*, Leiden, Brill, 1991.

Turner, J. P., *Inquisition in early Islam: the competition for political and religious authority in the Abbasid empire*, London, I. B. Tauris, 2013.

van Berkel, M., El-Cheikh, N., Kennedy, H. and Osti, L., *Crisis and continuity at the Abbasid court: formal and informal politics in the caliphate of al-Muqtadir (295–320/908–32)*, Leiden, Brill, 2013.

Waines, D., "The third century internal crisis of the 'Abbasids", *JESHO*, *xx*, 1977, 282–306.

Zaman, M. Q., *Religion and politics under the early 'Abbāsids: the emergences of the proto-Sunni élite*, Leiden, Brill, 1997.

The economic foundations of early Islamic history

Ashtor, E., *Social and economic history of the Near East*, London, Collins, 1976.

Bates, M., "History, geography and numismatics in the first century of Islamic coinage", *Revue Suisse de Numismatique*, *65*, 1986, 231–65.

Bessard, F., *Caliphs and merchants: cities and economies of power in the Near East (700–950)*, Oxford, Oxford University Press, 2020.

Bulliet, R., *Cotton, climate and camels in early Islamic Iran*, New York, Columbia University Press 2005

Cooper, J., *The Medieval Nile: route, navigation and landscape in Islamic Egypt*, Cairo, American University Press, 2015.

Gruszczynski, J., Jankowiak, M. and Shepard, J., *Viking Age trade: silver, slaves and Gotland*, London, Routledge, 2020.

Heidemann, S., "The merger of two currency zones in early Islam", *Iran*, *36*, 1998, 95–112.

Kennedy, H., "Military pay and the economy of the early Islamic state", *Historical Research*, *75*, 2002, 155–69.

Kennedy, H. and Bessard, F., *Land and trade in early Islam*, Oxford, Oxford University Press, 2022.

Kovalev, R., and Kaelin, A., "Circulation of Arab silver in Medieval Afro-Eurasia," *History Compass*, *5*/1, 2007, 1–21.

Lombard, M., *The Golden Age of Islam*, new ed., Princeton, Markus Wiener, 2004.

Noonan, T. S., "Early 'Abbasid mint output", *Journal of the Economic and Social History of the Orient*, *xxix*, 1986, 113–75.

Shatzmiller, M., *Labour in the medieval Islamic World*, Leiden, Brill, 1993

Shatzmiller, M., "Plague, wages and economic change in the early Islamic Middle East 700–1500", *Journal of Economic History*, *74*, 2014, 196

Shatzmiller, M. and I. Pamuk, "Economic performance and economic growth in the early Islamic world", *JESHO 54*, 2011, 132–184

Watson, A., *Agricultural innovation in the early Islamic world: the diffusion of crops and farming techniques, 700–1100*, Cambridge, Cambridge University Press, 1983.

The Buyid confederation

Bosworth, C. E., "Military organization under the Buyids of Persia and Iraq", *Oriens, xviii–xix*, 1965–6, 143–67.
Bowen, H., "The last Buwayhids", *JRAS*, 1929, 225–45.
Cahen, C., "L'évolution de l'*iqṭā*' du IXe au XIIIe siècle", *Annales, viii*, 1953, 25–52.
Donohue, J., *The Buwayhid dynasty in Iraq 334H./945 to 403H./1012. Shaping Institutions for the Future*, Leiden, Brill, 2003.
Frye, R., *The golden age of Persia*, London, Weidenfeld and Nicolson, 1975.
Madelung, W., "The assumption of the title shāhanshāh by the Būyids", *JNES, xxviii*, 1969, 84–105, 168–83.
Makdisi, G., *Ibn 'Āqīl: religion and culture in classical Islam*, Edinburgh, Edinburgh Press, 1997.
Mez, A., *The renaissance of Islam*, trans. Khuda Bakhsh, New Delhi, Kitab Dhavan, 1937.
Minorsky, V., *La domination des Dailamites*, Paris, Leroux, 1932.
Mottahedeh, R., *Loyalty and leadership in an early Islamic society*, Princeton, Princeton University Press, 2nd edn, 2001.
Richards, D. S. ed., *Islamic civilisation, 950–1150*, Oxford, Cassirer, 1973.

The Kurds and Azarbayjān

Amedroz, H. F., "The Marwanid dynasty of Mayyāfāriqīn", *JRAS*, 1903, 123–54.
Madelung, W., "Abū Isḥāq al-Ṣābī on the Alids of Ṭabaristān and Gīlān", *JNES, xxvi*, 1967, 27–57.
Minorsky, V., *A history of Sharvan and Darband in the 10th–11th centuries*, Cambridge, Cambridge University Press, 1958.
Vanly, I. C., "Le déplacement du pays Kurde vers l'ouest", *RSO, 1*, 1976, 353–63.

The Hamdanids and the Byzantine frontier

Bosworth, C. E., "The city of Tarsus and the Arab–Byzantine frontiers in early and middle 'Abbasid times", *Oriens, xxxiii*, 268–86.
Canard, M., *Histoire de la dynastie des H'amdanides de Jazîra et de Syrie*, Paris, 1953.
Dagron, G., "Minorités ethniques et religieuses dans l'Orient byzantin à la fin du Xe et au XIe siècles: l'immigration syrienne", *Travaux et Memoirs, vi*, 1976, 177–216.
Eger, A., *The Islamic-Byzantine frontier: interaction and exchange among Muslim and Christian communities*, London, I. B. Tauris, 2014.
Haldon, J. F. and Kennedy, H., "The Arab–Byzantine frontier in the eighth and ninth centuries", *Recueil des travaux de l'Institut d'Etudes byzantines (Belgrade)*, Presses Universitaires de France, *xix*, 1980, 79–116.
Honigmann, E., *Die Ostgrenze des byzantinischen Reiches*, Brussels, Institut de philologie et d'histoire orientales, 1961.
Von Sievers, P., "Merchants and nomads: the social evolution of the Syrian cities and countryside, 780–969/164–358", *Islam, lvi*, 1979, 212–44.
Von Sievers, P., "Taxation and trade in the 'Abbasid Thughur", *JESHO, xxv*, 1982, 71–99.

Bedouin political movements and dynasties

Cahen, Cl., "Mouvements populaires et autonomisme urbain dans l'Asie musulmane du moyenage", *Arabica*, *v*, 1958, 225–50, *vi*, 1959, 25–56, 223–65.

Heidemann, S., *Die Renaissance der Stadte in Nordsyrien und Nordmesopotamien: Stadtische Entwicklung und wirtschaftliche Bedingungen in ar-Raqqa und ḥarrān von der Zeit der beduinischen Vorherrschaft bis zu den Seldschuken*, Leiden, Brill, 2002.

Makdisi, G., "Notes on Ḥilla and the Mazyadids in medieval Islam", *JAOS*, *lxxiv*, 1954, 249–62.

Zakkar, S., *The emirate of Aleppo 1004–1094*, Beirut, Dar al-Amanah, 1971.

Eastern Iran

Barthold, V., *Turkestan down to the Mongol invasions*, London, Gibb Memorial Series, 1968.

Biran, M., "Qarakhanid studies: a view from the Qara Khitai edge", *Cahiers d'Asia Centrale*, *9*, 2001, 73–85.

Bosworth, C. E., *The Ghaznavids: their empire in Afghanistan and Eastern Iran 994–1040*, Edinburgh, Edinburgh University Press, 1963

Bosworth, C. E., "The rulers of Chaghāniyān in early Islamic times', *Iran*, *19*, 1981, 1–20

Folz, R., *A history of the Tajiks: Iranians of the East*, London, Bloomsbury, 2019.

Frye, R., *Bukhara: the medieval achievement*, Oklahoma, University of Oklahoma Press, 1965

Frye, R., *The golden age of Persia: the Arabs in the East*, London, Weidenfeld and Nicolson, 1988

Peacock, A, *Medieval Islamic historiography and political legitimacy; Bal'ami's Tarikhnāma*, London, Routledge, 2007

Soucek, S., *A history of inner Asia*, Cambridge, Cambridge University Press, 2000.

Treadwell, L., "The Samanids: the first Islamic Dynasty of Central Asia", in E. Herzig and S. Stewart (eds.), *Early Islamic Iran. The idea of Iran*. London and New York, I.B. Tauris, 2011, 3–15

Early Islamic Egypt and the Fatimid empire

AbūIzzeddin, N. M., *The Druzes. A new study of their history, faith and society*, Leiden, Brill, 1984.

Bacharach, J. L., "The career of Muḥammad ibn Ṭughj al-Ikhshīd", *Speculum*, *50*, 1975, 586–612.

Bareket, E., *Fustat on the Nile: the Jewish élite in medieval Egypt*, Leiden, Brill, 1999.

Barrucand, M. ed., *Egypte fatimide: son art et son histoire*, Paris, Presses d'universite Paris-Sorbonne, 2000.

Bianquis, T., "La prise de pouvoir par les Fatimides en Egypte", *JESHO*, *23*, 1980, 67–101.

Bianquis, T., *Damas et la Syrie sous la domination Fatimide (359–468/969–1076)*, *2* vols, Damascus, Institut Francais de Damas, 1986–89.

Cortese, D., *Women and the Fatimids in the world of Islam*, Edinburgh, Edinburgh University Press, 2006.

Daftary, F., *The Ismāʿīlīs: their history and doctrines*, Cambridge, Cambridge University Press, 1990.
Goitein, S., *A Mediterranean society*, *4* vols, Berkeley, University of California Press, 1967–83.
Halm, H., *The empire of the Mahdi: the rise of the Fatimids*, Leiden, Brill, 1996.
Halm, H., *The Fatimids and their traditions of learning*, London, I. B. Tauris, 1997.
Lev, Y., *State and society in Fatimid Egypt*, Leiden, Brill, 1991.
Petry, C., *The Cambridge history of Egypt, I, Islamic Egypt, 640–1517*, Cambridge, Cambridge University Press, 1998.
Rustow, M., *Heresy and the politics of community: the Jews of the Fatimid caliphate*, Ithaca, Cornell University Press, 2008.
Saunders, P., *Ritual, politics and the city in Fatimid Cairo*, Albany, State University of New York Press, 1994.
Staffa, S., *Conquest and fusion: the social evolution of Cairo*, Leiden, Brill, 1977.
Walker, P. E., *Exploring an Islamic empire: Fatimid history and its sources*, London, I. B. Tauris, 2002.

Glossary

abnā' Literally "sons" Used (a) of the descendants of Persian settlers in Yemen at the time of Muḥammad, and (b) of the descendants of the Khurāsānīs who came west with the 'Abbasid armies and settled in Baghdad.

aḥdāth An urban militia.

amīr Army commander, provincial governor or ruler of a small independent state.

***amīr al-umarā'* Literally "commander of commanders"** Title given to those who took over secular authority in Baghdad from the 'Abbasid caliphs after 324/936.

***Anṣār* Literally "helpers"** The inhabitants of Medina who supported Muḥammad.

ashrāf See *sharīf*.

'aṭā' Salary paid to soldiers.

'ayyār Originally a derogatory term meaning "vagabond" but later used for irregular troops and vigilante groups.

bay'a Oath of allegiance to the caliph or other ruler.

dā'ī Missionary, usually of clandestine religio-political movements.

dā'wa Missionary movement (cf. ***dā'ī***).

dawla Dynasty or state, e.g. the 'Abbasid *dawla* or the Fatimid *dawla*.

dehqan Persian term for landowners in Iran and Iraq, usually gentry rather than members of the higher aristocracy.

dihqān Arabic form of *dehqan*.

dīnār Standard gold coin.

dirham Standard silver coin.

dīwān Originally list of those entitled to state salaries. Also office or department of government.

ḍiyā' Plural of ***ḍay' a*** meaning landed estate, usually applied to the lands owned by the 'Abbasid caliphs (cf. ***ṣawāfī***).

fitna Civil war or dispute within the Muslim community.

ghāzī A Muslim volunteer who fights in the ***jihād***.

ghazw Bedouin tribal raid.

ghulām*, pl. *ghilmān Literally "young men" or "pages"; term used for Turkish soldiers especially in fourth/tenth century (cf. ***mamlūk***).

ḥājib Doorkeeper, chamberlain.

ḥajj The annual pilgrimage to Mecca.

ḥaram Sanctuary area, esp. around the Ka'ba in Mecca.

hijra The emigration of Muḥammad from Mecca to Medina in 622, which marks the beginning of the Muslim era.

ḥimāya Protection; once a form of lordship in which an important figure exercises fiscal rights over an area or community.

imām Spiritual leader of the Muslim community.

iqṭā' Assignment to an individual of right to collect taxes from an area or community, usually in exchange for military service. In common use from the fourth/tenth century.

jāhiliyya Period of ignorance or savagery in Arabia before the coming of Islam.

jizya Poll tax levied on non-Muslims.

jund Army; one of the administrative districts of Syria and Palestine.

kātib Secretary.

kharāj Land tax.

khuṭba Address in mosque at Friday prayer which included mention of the ruler's name, a sign of sovereignty.

kuttāb Pl. of ***kātib***.

Maghāriba Troops recruited in north Africa.

mamlūk A slave soldier; this term, occasionally used in early Islamic history, came to replace the term ***ghulām*** from the fifth/eleventh century onwards.

mawlā, pl. ***mawālī*** Originally "client", often non-Arab client of an Arab tribe, hence the use of ***mawālī*** to describe non-Arab Muslims in the first century of Islam. Later more commonly "freedmen" in the 'Abbasid period, the term passes out of general use in the fourth/tenth century.

Muhājir, pl. ***Muhājirūn*** Those who participated in the ***Hijra***, that is, the Meccans who accompanied Muḥammad to settle in Medina.

naqīb Representative; used (a) of those in Medina appointed by Muḥammad to look after his interests before the ***Hijra***, and (b) of those who led the 'Abbasid movement in Khurāsān during Umayyad times.

qāḍī Muslim judge.

qaṭī'a Form of landholding common in the Umayyad and early 'Abbasid period. Land was alienable, heritable and subject to a lower rate of tax than ***kharāj*** land. Not to be confused with ***iqṭā***'.

qurrā A term of disputed etymology, probably meaning (Qur'ān) readers; used for the early Muslim settlers in Iraq, some of whom later joined the Khawārij.

ra'īs al-balad Unofficial leader of the native civilian population of a town.

ridda Apostasy from Islam; hence, the wars in Arabia which followed Muḥammad's death are known as the ***Ridda*** wars.

sābiqa Precedence, especially precedence in conversion to Islam, i.e. the earlier a person was converted, the greater his ***sābiqa***.

ṣadaqa The payment of alms enjoined by Muslim law.

Saqāliba Slaves of Slav or western European origin.

ṣawāfī Lands belonging to the Muslim community or to the caliph, especially in Iraq in early Islamic times (cf. ***ḍiyā'***).

Sharī'ā Muslim religious law.

sharīf, pl.ashrāf In Umayyad times, tribal leader, chief; by the fourth/tenth century, the title is usually confined to descendants of 'Alī.

shūra A council formed to choose a caliph.

shurṭa Police force or military escort.

Sunna The sayings and actions of Muḥammad used as legal precedents.

sūq Market.

umma The Muslim community.

wāsiṭa Literally intermediary; hence in Fatimid Egypt the intermediary between the caliph and his subjects, chief minister.

wazīr Chief minister in the 'Abbasid and Buyid governments.

Index

Note: Page numbers followed by "n" denote endnotes.